BANKING ON THE FUTURE OF ASIA AND THE PACIFIC

50 YEARS OF THE ASIAN DEVELOPMENT BANK

Peter McCawley

© 2017 Asian Development Bank
6 ADB Avenue, Mandaluyong City, 1550 Metro Manila, Philippines
Tel +63 2 632 4444; Fax +63 2 636 2444
www.adb.org

All rights reserved. Published in 2017.

ISBN 978-92-9257-791-9 (Print), 978-92-9257-792-6 (e-ISBN)
Publication Stock No. TCS178707
DOI: http://dx.doi.org/10.22617/TCS178707

The views expressed in this publication are those of the authors and do not necessarily reflect the views and policies of the Asian Development Bank (ADB) or its Board of Governors or the governments they represent.

ADB does not guarantee the accuracy of the data included in this publication and accepts no responsibility for any consequence of their use. The mention of specific companies or products of manufacturers does not imply that they are endorsed or recommended by ADB in preference to others of a similar nature that are not mentioned.

By making any designation of or reference to a particular territory or geographic area, or by using the term "country" in this document, ADB does not intend to make any judgments as to the legal or other status of any territory or area.

ADB encourages printing or copying information exclusively for personal, educational, and noncommercial use with proper acknowledgment of ADB. Users are restricted from reselling, redistributing, or creating derivative works for commercial purposes without the express, written consent of ADB. Please contact pubsmarketing@adb.org if you have questions or comments with respect to content, or if you wish to obtain copyright permission.

Notes:
In this publication, "$" refers to US dollars.
Corrigenda to ADB publications may be found at http://www.adb.org/publications/corrigenda

ADB recognizes its members by their official designations as indicated in https://www.adb.org/about/members. However, some variations to these designations may be found in this publication for reasons of historical accuracy.

On the front cover:
Early morning at the Central Thailand Solar Farm in Nakhon Pathom, Thailand; with 148,608 solar modules generating a total capacity of 28.5 megawatt-hours of electricity. Completed in December 2013, the project is consistent with ADB's country partnership strategy for Thailand (2007–2011) with its three core strategic areas: infrastructure, environmental sustainability, and capital markets.
Photo by Gerhard Joren

Printed on recycled paper

ABOUT THE AUTHOR

Peter McCawley is an economist from the Arndt-Corden Department of Economics at the Australian National University (ANU) in Canberra, who has worked on development issues in Asia and the Pacific for many years.

He has a PhD in economics (1972) from the ANU. He later taught at Gadjah Mada University in Yogyakarta in the early 1970s before becoming head, Indonesia Project, at the ANU. In 1986, he joined Australian Aid as a Deputy Director General.

Much of his work in Asia has been with the Asian Development Bank (ADB). Between 1992 and 1996, he was a member of the ADB Board of Directors. Later, in 2003–2007, he became Dean of the ADB Institute in Tokyo.

He was also Co-chair and Chair of Asian Development Fund negotiations between 1999 and 2008.

He has numerous publications about development issues in Asia and the Pacific.

CONTENTS

About the Author	iii
Foreword	xii
Preface	xvi
Contributors	xxi
Abbreviations	xxii
ADB Regional and Nonregional Members	xxiv
ADB Time Line	xxv

Chapter 1—Introduction — 1
- A Multilateral Agency — 2
- A Development Organization — 3
- A Financing Institution — 6
- The Leadership Succession — 11
- The Challenge of Development — 15

BEGINNINGS (UNTIL 1966)

Chapter 2—Asia in the 1960s: Ferment and Transformation — 17
- Japan and the Flying Geese — 18
- The Four Tigers — 18
- Instability in Southeast Asia — 21
- Stagnation in South Asia — 22
- Isolation of the People's Republic of China — 23
- Delayed Independence in the Pacific — 24
- Other Economic Challenges — 24
- Regional Cooperation — 26
- International Trends — 28

Chapter 3—Establishing the Bank — 31
- Earlier Proposals — 31
- Takeshi Watanabe and the Tokyo Study Group — 33
- Help from the United Nations Economic Commission for Asia and the Far East — 35
- Two Streams Merge — 39
- The Scope of Membership — 40
- Japan and the United States — 41
- Serious Preparations — 42
- Drafting the Charter — 44
- Headquarters of the Bank — 48
- The First President — 51

FIRST DECADE (1967–1976)

Chapter 4—Asia: Building Momentum and Facing Shocks   53
    Strengthening Agriculture   54
    The Drive for Industrialization   56
    Coping with Economic Shocks   60

Chapter 5—ADB: The Character of the Bank   69
    A Vision for the Bank   70
    A Careful Start   73
    Research Activities   74
    Other Main Studies   77
    The First Technical Assistance and Loans   78
    Early Priorities   79
    Trends in Lending   81
    Sources of Finance   83
    Increases in Capital   84
    ADB Bonds   85
    Special Funds   87
    Transition of the Leadership   89
    Shiro Inoue   91
    Crisis-Related Programs   93
    Second General Capital Increase and Establishment of ADF   95
    Borrowing in Capital Markets, Cofinancing,
        and Recycling of Oil Money   99
    Operational Summary   100
    Ten Years Old   102

SECOND DECADE (1977–1986)

Chapter 6—Asia: Transformation in the Region   107
    Consequences of Stagflation   108
    Basic Human Needs and Structural Adjustment   109
    Geese Become Tigers   110
    Southeast Asia: Swings of Fortune   112
    South Asia   115
    Pacific Island Countries   116
    People's Republic of China   116
    Growth Continues   119

Chapter 7—ADB: Toward a Broader Development Bank — 121
- Taroichi Yoshida — 121
- Widening Agenda for ADB — 123
- Creating New Loans — 126
- Surveys and Reviews — 130
- Pressures for Fundraising — 131
- Masao Fujioka — 132
- Priorities in the 1980s — 134
- Increasing Lending and First Private Sector Operations — 136
- Staff and First Resident Mission — 139
- Agreeing on Country Strategies and Flexible Lending Arrangements — 140
- Raising Funds in Hard Times — 141
- A Regional Development Institution — 142
- The People's Republic of China Joins the Bank — 144
- India as a Borrower — 146
- Operational Summary — 147
- Into a Third Decade — 149

THIRD DECADE (1987–1996)

Chapter 8—Asia: Reemergence of the Region — 157
- Changes in Capital Flows — 158
- New Trade Arrangements — 159
- A Broadened International Development Agenda — 160
- States and Markets — 162
- The Influence of Globalization — 163
- The Newly Industrialized Economies — 165
- People's Republic of China — 166
- Southeast Asia — 167
- South Asia — 169
- Central Asian Republics — 170
- Pacific Island Countries — 171
- Increasing Strength in Asia — 171

Chapter 9—ADB: New Members and New Regions — 173
- Managing Member Priorities — 174
- Kimimasa Tarumizu — 180

New Resources	182
Strategic Planning	184
Reverberations from Europe	185
Transition Economies	185
Asia's Giant Economies	187
Mitsuo Sato	189
Running Out of Headroom	190
Resource Mobilization	192
New Ways of Working	192
New Lending Instruments and Scholarships	196
New Offices Abroad and the ADB Institute	197
Operational Summary	199
Calm before the Storm	204

FOURTH DECADE (1997–2006)

Chapter 10—The Asian Financial Crisis — **207**
- Thailand: The Crisis Erupts — 208
- Republic of Korea: A Rapid Response — 209
- Indonesia: Political Upheaval — 211
- Other Asian Neighbors — 212
- The ADB Response — 213
- Programs in Thailand — 215
- Programs in the Republic of Korea — 216
- Programs in Indonesia — 217
- Impact on ADB — 219
- Graduation of Newly Industrialized Economies — 222
- Policy Reforms, Research, and Advocacy — 223
- Turmoil in Asia: What Went Wrong? — 225
- Weak Fundamentals or Investor Panic — 227
- Criticism of International Rescue Operations — 228
- Regional Initiatives — 229
- Asia and ADB after the Crisis — 232

Chapter 11—Asia: A New Century Dawns — **235**
- Recovery and Ascent in Asia — 236
- Growing Intraregional Trade and Capital Flows — 238
- Making Globalization Work — 239

    Broader View of Development and Millennium
        Development Goals   242
    Changing Finance Architecture   244
    The Fourth ADB Decade   247

Chapter 12—ADB: The Widening Development Agenda   **253**
    Tadao Chino   253
    A Corporate Strategy   256
    Organizational Changes   258
    Assisting Fragile States   260
    Concerns for Sustainable Development and Governance   262
    More Accountable and Effective Assistance   264
    Three Asian Development Fund Replenishments   267
    Ordinary Capital Resources Operations and Funding   270
    Haruhiko Kuroda   272
    Building on Past Measures   274
    Revitalizing Regional Cooperation   277
    New Corporate Directions   280
    Operational Summary   283
    A Challenging and Transformative Decade   285

FIFTH DECADE (2007–2016)

Chapter 13—Asia: Growth in Uncertain Times   **289**
    Progress with Variations, but Growth Gathering Momentum   289
    Global Financial Crisis and Asian Resilience   291
    Rebalancing Growth to Sustain Development   293
    Rising Inequality and Pressure on Environment   296
    Actions Needed for Climate Change   298
    Sustainable Development Goals   301
    New Sources of Development Finance   301
    Issues Surrounding Globalization   303
    Solid Growth of Asia   304
    The Fifth ADB Decade   306

Chapter 14—ADB: Stronger, Better, Faster   **307**
    New Long-Term Strategic Framework   307
    Global Financial Crisis and Response   312
    The General Capital Increase   314

Ninth and Tenth Asian Development Fund Replenishments	318
ASEAN Infrastructure Fund and Credit Guarantee and Investment Facility	319
Improving Performance and Accountability	319
Human Resources	321
Takehiko Nakao	322
Midterm Review of Strategy 2020	324
Toward a "Stronger, Better, Faster" ADB	325
Financial Innovation: Combination of Asian Development Fund Lending Operations and Ordinary Capital Resources	332
Eleventh Asian Development Fund Replenishment	336
Cofinancing and Trust Funds through the Decades	339
Cooperation with New Multilateral Development Banks	343
Operational Summary	344
Looking Ahead	347

Chapter 15—Epilogue: Looking beyond 50 Years	**357**
Bibliography	**361**
Appendixes	**379**
1. Asia: Regional Overview Tables	381
2. ADB: Institutional, Operational, and Financial Highlights Tables	418
3. ADB: Impact of the ADF–OCR Merger and ADB's Financial Statements	467
4. ADB: Time Line of Key ADB Milestones, 1950s to 2016	473
Index	**495**

FIGURES, TABLES, AND BOXES

Figures

1.1	Per Capita Gross Domestic Product in the People's Republic of China, India, Indonesia, and Japan, 1900–2010	4
1.2	Share of ADB's Operations to Total Gross Domestic Product of Developing Asia (excluding the People's Republic of China), 1968–2015	9
5.1	Operational Approvals by Fund Type, 1968–1976	94
5.2	Operational Approvals by Sector, 1968–1976	101
5.3	Operational Approvals by Region, 1968–1976	102
7.1	Operational Approvals by Fund Type, 1977–1986	137
7.2	Operational Approvals by Sector, 1977–1986	148
7.3	Operational Approvals by Region, 1977–1986	149
9.1	Establishment of Field Offices	198
9.2	Operational Approvals by Fund Type, 1987–1996	200
9.3	Operational Approvals by Region, 1987–1996	201
9.4	Operational Approvals by Sector, 1987–1996	202
10.1	Selected Indicators in the Republic of Korea, Indonesia, Malaysia, the Philippines, and Thailand, 1992–2002	226
12.1	Operational Approvals by Fund Type, 1997–2006	281
12.2	Operational Approvals by Region, 1997–2006	284
12.3	Operational Approvals by Sector, 1997–2006	285
13.1	Comparing the Millennium Development Goals and the Sustainable Development Goals	302
14.1	Operational Approvals by Fund Type, 2007–2016	336
14.2	Operational Approvals by Region, 2007–2016	345
14.3	Operational Approvals by Sector, 2007–2016	346

Tables

2.1	Gross Domestic Product and Export Growth of the "Four Tigers" and Japan, 1953–1980	20
2.2	Post-World War II Food Supplies in Selected Countries	25
2.3	Studies of the United Nations Economic and Social Survey of Asia and the Pacific	26
3.1	Establishment of ADB—Chronology of Official Meetings	36
3.2	First Signatories of the Articles of Agreement	50
3.3	Board of Directors and Voting Groups, 1966	52
4.1	Structure of Production in Selected Economies, 1960–1985	57
5.1	Selected Operational, Institutional, and Financial Information, 1966–1976	104

6.1	Major Reform Steps in the People's Republic of China, 1978–1986	117
7.1	Selected Operational, Institutional, and Financial Information, 1967–1986	150
9.1	Selected Operational, Institutional, and Financial Information, 1977–1996	205
10.1	Currency Stabilization Support Programs during the Asian Financial Crisis	210
10.2	Main Crisis-Related Loans and Technical Assistance, 1997–1999	214
11.1	Key International Steps toward Development Effectiveness	245
12.1	Selected Operational, Institutional, and Financial Information, 1987-2006	286
14.1	General Capital Increases and Capital Composition	316
14.2	Cofinancing in 1967–2016	340
14.3	Selected Operational, Institutional, and Financial Information, 1997–2016	348

Boxes

3.1	Agreement Establishing the Asian Development Bank	46
5.1	ADB as a Family Doctor to Developing Countries in Asia	72
5.2	ADB's First Loans	79
5.3	Establishment of the Asian Development Fund	96
7.1	ADB's Health Sector Projects	127
7.2	Project, Program, Multiproject, and Sector Loans	128
7.3	First Program Loan	129
7.4	First Loans without Government Guarantee	138
9.1	Two Bridges in Shanghai	176
9.2	ADB's Education Sector Projects	179
9.3	Selected Policy Papers, 1987–1996	193
12.1	Working with Stakeholders: Example of the Nam Theun 2 Project	266
12.2	Important Instruments under the Innovation and Efficiency Initiative	275
12.3	ADB Subregional Cooperation Programs	278
14.1	ADB Support to the Turkmenistan–Afghanistan–Pakistan–India Natural Gas Pipeline	311
14.2	ADB's Urban Sector Projects	326
14.3	ADB Response to Typhoon Haiyan, 2013	328
14.4	ADB's Reengagement with Myanmar	337

FOREWORD

When the Asian Development Bank (ADB) was established in 1966, the Asia and Pacific region was defined by poverty. It was the poorest region in the world with an annual per capita income of about $100 (less than one-fourth that of Latin America and below Sub-Saharan Africa). One of the most important challenges in the region was how to feed the large and growing population by increasing agricultural productivity, which ADB supported in its operations in initial years.

Half a century later, Asia has emerged as a center of global dynamism. Today, it accounts for one-third of global GDP and contributes to more than half the world's economic growth. Asia's stunning development over the past several decades has raised living standards. More than a billion people have been lifted out of extreme poverty since 1990.

ADB has played an important role in the transformation of Asia. Fifty years ago, ADB was created through the collective wishes and collaborative efforts of countries within and outside the region. From this 50-year ADB history book, we can tell that ADB is a child of genuine aspiration by people across the region, and that the establishment of ADB represents the spirit of regional cooperation.

I would like to introduce some interesting episodes from the early days of ADB that are covered in this book written by Peter McCawley.

Beginning in March 1963, there were many preparatory meetings for the establishment of ADB in Bangkok, Manila, Wellington, and other Asian cities. Many people made great contributions to the creation of the Bank. ECAFE (UN Economic Commission for Asia and the Far East) Executive Secretary U Nyun, from Myanmar, led initial discussions. Florentino Feliciano, a Filipino lawyer helped write the ADB Charter. He drafted and redrafted the Charter provisions by incorporating diverse country opinions and learning from the experiences of other multilateral development banks. Eugene Black, a former World Bank president and an investment banker, encouraged ADB to mobilize resources from capital markets. Young officials from Japan Masao Fujioka and Tadao Chino, who would become the fourth and seventh Presidents of ADB, were also among them.

And, of course, Takeshi Watanabe, a former senior official from the Ministry of Finance in Tokyo with rich international experience, played a central role in preparing the establishment of ADB before he became the first ADB President. He was closely supported by C. S. Krishna Moorthi from India and Douglas Gunesekera of Ceylon, who later served as ADB's first

Vice-President and Secretary, respectively. President Watanabe's motto of ADB as a "family doctor" for Asian countries and an institution that "learns before teaching" remains an integral part of ADB's tradition.

Manila, Tehran, Tokyo, and several other cities competed to host ADB. At a meeting held in late 1965 in Manila, 18 Asian prospective members voted to decide the location of the headquarters. In the first round of balloting, Tokyo took 8 votes, Tehran 4, and Manila 3. In the third and final round, Manila edged out Tokyo 9 votes to 8 (with one abstention). Despite Tehran's candidacy, Iran later decided not to apply for ADB membership. Manila turned out to be a good decision. Manila has brought ADB closer to its developing member countries. ADB has benefited from the warm hospitality of the Filipino people and a strong pool of English-speaking professionals.

When ADB had its opening ceremony in Manila on 19 December 1966, we began in a modest way. ADB's original members totaled 31 (19 regional and 12 nonregional), compared to today's 67 members (48 regional and 19 nonregional). At that time, ADB had 20 Board members (10 directors and 10 alternate directors), and yet only 40 staff. We started with small office space in Makati, spread across several buildings. Today, ADB has offices in 31 countries including in Manila.

This book aims to review how ADB over 50 years has responded to Asia's challenges given its unique regional perspective. The book contains three historical narratives: on Asia's economic development; on the evolution of the international development agenda; and on the story of ADB itself. It is very useful to know how ADB has evolved in terms of its membership, operations, knowledge work, funding, organization, staff, strategies, and succession of leaders. At the same time, the unique character of this book is to look back at Asian economic history in a fair and balanced manner, from the perspective of development and based on the rich experience of ADB's interactions with countries.

I was recently asked by a writer from the *Economist* magazine what we have achieved in these 50 years. In my view, ADB's achievements are summarized in its three broad functions. First is support for developing members in combining finance and knowledge, through sovereign and nonsovereign projects in both infrastructure and social sectors. Second is the promotion of good policies through high-level dialogue, technical assistance and capacity building, and policy-based lending (budget support for reforms). ADB has also provided emergency budget support when members were hit by crises. Third is catalyzing regional cooperation and friendship. We support initiatives for subregions in Central Asia, South Asia, Southeast Asia, the Pacific, and the Greater Mekong.

Today, there is much discussion on mobilizing private resources to finance the large development needs of Asia. But it should be noted that ADB itself was created as a financial intermediary to channel private funds from global capital markets by issuing bonds and leveraging taxpayers' money of shareholders. ADB is as much a bank as a development institution.

Asia was desperately short of capital at the time of ADB's establishment. Japan had joined OECD by 1964, but still incurred constant current account deficits until the mid-1960s. Nonregional membership in ADB by developed countries was essential to enhance the credibility of ADB as a borrower. President Watanabe insisted on sound banking principles and it took more than one year before ADB approved its first loan. Indeed, the importance of "economic considerations" is mentioned in the ADB Charter and analysis of the economic value of individual projects has been an integral part of ADB's operations right from the start. ADB could successfully launch an ADB bond in Germany in 1969, in Austria and Japan in 1970, and in the US (with a AAA rating) in 1971.

When ADB commemorated its 20th anniversary in 1986, it commissioned a corporate history book, *A Bank for Half the World* (published in 1987). I thought we should publish another book to commemorate our 50th anniversary. Since 1986, Asia has changed a lot. So has ADB. The region has gathered growth momentum and achieved further poverty reduction thanks to a more market-oriented approach, open trade and investment regimes, investments in infrastructure and human capital, and more prudent macroeconomic policies especially after the Asian financial crisis of 1997–1998. Asia as a whole also has become more stable after conflicts in many parts of the region.

But we cannot be complacent. Asia is facing remaining and new challenges. Still 330 million people live in absolute poverty on less than $1.90 a day. Large infrastructure gaps constrain economic development and people's welfare. Implementing the Sustainable Development Goals adopted by world leaders at the United Nations in 2015 and the climate change actions agreed at COP21 are collective priorities for Asian countries. The private sector should be further promoted. Gender equality should be enhanced. Asia is also facing such challenges as urbanization, aging, and widening inequalities.

ADB should continue to play an important role to address these challenges. In doing so, ADB will draw on our partnership, built over the past 50 years, with member countries, multilateral and bilateral development agencies, civil society organizations, the private sector, and academia from within and outside the region.

Peter McCawley, an academic from the Australian National University in Canberra, who also knows ADB from within as a former Executive Director and former Dean of the Asian Development Bank Institute, was commissioned to write this book. Without his relentless enthusiasm, the book would not have become a reality. He was supported by an ADB interdepartmental secretariat for the work. This book also benefited from comments and inputs by numerous people, including former staff of ADB. I would like to thank Peter McCawley, the secretariat, and all other collaborators.

I strongly believe that it is the duty of any institution, especially a public one, to keep a good, objective, and comprehensive record of its history, preferably in a book which is interesting to read. I hope this book will serve that purpose, help us to understand the important characteristics and culture of ADB, and provide insight for us to consider how ADB can best serve the region in the future.

Takehiko Nakao
President and Chair of the Board of Directors
Asian Development Bank

PREFACE

The origins of this book lie in plans to mark the 50th anniversary of the establishment of the Asian Development Bank (ADB). The Inaugural Meeting of the Bank opened on 24 November 1966 in Tokyo, so 24 November of 2016 marked the official 50th birthday of the institution. Another key event is the 50th ADB Annual Meeting being held in Yokohama, Japan, in May 2017. The first 20 years were chronicled in an earlier book, *A Bank for Half the World*.[1] As the Bank was turning 50, it seemed time to take stock again to look at how the organization has changed and how it has participated in the remarkable transformation in Asia during the last 50 years.

The story of an international organization like ADB might be written in various ways. And the approach taken determines the personality of the narrative. One approach would be to focus mainly on the achievements of the Bank with only a brief discussion of the institution itself. Another approach would be to highlight the activities of the people in the organization, drawing on stories about prominent personalities. The team working on this study carefully discussed these and other possibilities. The President of the Bank, Takehiko Nakao, set down a challenge when he said that he hoped the book would be informative, a narrative, and an archive.

We decided to set out, first, the story of the institution itself, focusing on the way ADB has evolved over time. The Bank has expanded from a newly established financial institution into a full-fledged multilateral development bank. This is an account of change and evolution in an international institution in Asia. It is also an account of economic diplomacy in the region because all of the countries who are members of ADB have interests in the work of the organization. But as we worked on the project, it became increasingly clear that the leadership of the Bank has been a key factor influencing the growth of the institution. Running through this story of ADB, therefore, is also a discussion of the role of its nine Presidents.

In parallel, economic and social changes across the region and international trends in thinking about development are set out. The aim is to show how growth and change in ADB has been influenced by many factors, both within the organization itself and across Asia, and also by international events as well.

---

[1] Wilson, 1987, *A Bank for Half the World*.

Underpinning the narrative and serving as anchors to help define the story are three themes which reflect the nature of the institution as a multilateral development bank: finance, development activities, and support for regionalism. ADB is a bank so its financial activities are central to the operations of the organization. But it is more than a bank because it has steadily widened its development activities, increasingly emphasizing the importance of knowledge and information for borrowing countries. And in its support for regionalism, ADB has drawn on its strengths as a multilateral organization to encourage cooperation across Asia and the Pacific.

ADB President Takehiko Nakao has a strong personal enthusiasm for exploring the history of ADB and hopes that the institution will draw on the lessons of history. The team working on the book had numerous meetings with the President between 2014 and 2017 to discuss many matters in detail. He provided valuable feedback on many aspects of the Bank's history as well as on the history of Asia's development over the past 50 years. He read the entire draft closely several times during weekends and made a number of specific comments. He wanted to make the book not just about the history of ADB, but also about how Asian countries have achieved growth and development in the face of various difficulties, and how international circumstances have affected Asia.

A small and dedicated team of colleagues worked on the book project. Edeena Pike, Planning and Policy Specialist in the Strategy and Policy Department (SPD), first joined the team in 2014 to conduct the initial background research for the book. She has continued to play a key role in coordinating the project and peer reviewing numerous manuscripts throughout the drafting, review and editing stages. Jade Tolentino is a highly capable and always cheerful project researcher who produced exceptional written research outputs as well as tables, graphs, and boxes throughout the book. This is in addition to her contributions in revising Chapters 2–4, in particular. Ananya Basu, Principal Economist in the Pacific Department, joined the team when the drafting was at an intensive stage. She is a fast thinking and skillful colleague, making substantial contributions in drafting book materials for Chapters 11–14. The fourth team member, Valerie Hill, Director of the Strategy, Policy, and Business Process Division in SPD, was an integral part of the Team during the inception year. She led the Secretariat during the book's formative phase, and made critical contributions in developing the annotated book outline and reviewing early drafts.

Common factors uniting these colleagues are their commitment and strong interest in the history of Asia and ADB. In the process of preparing background materials and researching for the project, the team produced, in parallel to the book work, a five-volume chronicle on 50 years of the Bank's history containing detailed information on institutional changes, operations, and finance. The chronicle has been published as *ADB through the Decades*.[2] A comprehensive survey of financial management in the organization was also coordinated by the Treasury Department and available as *A History of Financial Management at the Asian Development Bank*.[3] Both these publications tell the rich history of ADB and have provided valuable background materials to the ADB history book.

Xianbin Yao, Director General of the Pacific Department, as leader of our team guided this work. He has set aside a large amount of time since 2014, including many hours over weekends, to read numerous drafts of the chapters. His knowledge of both the overall literature of international development and of ADB's work in Asia is remarkable. This study reflects a strong imprint of Xianbin Yao's deep knowledge of development in Asia during the past five decades.

In addition to this core team directly involved in producing the book, this work could not have been completed without the generous support of numerous former and present ADB staff, Management, and Board members. So many people have helped that it is not possible to list them all but I wish to note a few who have made special contributions.

Kazu Sakai, before his retirement in 2015 as Director General of SPD, was a key supporter of the preparation of this history book. He assisted with many thoughtful comments and met with the team on several occasions during the progress of finalizing the draft.

Close to fifty formal interviews were conducted during two ADB Annual Meetings (Baku in 2015 and Frankfurt in 2016) as well as in Tokyo and Manila, including with former ADB Presidents Masao Fujioka (fourth President, 1981–1989) and Haruhiko Kuroda (eighth President, 2005–2013). In addition, all of the ADB Presidents have left records of various kinds of their work with ADB which have been consulted in the preparation of this book. The first President, Takeshi Watanabe, published his memoirs

---

[2] ADB, 2016, *ADB through the Decades*. Volumes 1–5.
[3] Erquiaga, 2016, *A History of Financial Management at the Asian Development Bank*.

as *Towards a New Asia*.⁴ Other Presidents made numerous speeches which are a running record of their views about events of the day. The fourth President, Masao Fujioka, prepared a diary which provides many glimpses of the role of ADB in the Asia and Pacific region during the 1980s.⁵

In addition to the formal interviews, a wide range of current and former ADB staff provided observations and in some cases valuable notes. Rajat M. Nag, former ADB Managing Director General, met with the team to share his views on earlier drafts. Paul Dickie, former Director General of the Infrastructure, Energy and Financial Sector Department; Robert Boumphrey, former Advisor (Finance and Governance) in the Southeast Asia Department; and Khaja Moinuddin, former Director General of the Southeast Asia Department, helped greatly with detailed comments on Chapter 10. Christopher MacCormac, former Deputy Director General of SPD, peer reviewed an earlier draft and, with Robert Wihtol, former Director General of the East Asia Department, took part in many discussions about the role of ADB in Asia.

A senior staff working group, including Satinder Bindra, Principal Director of the Department of External Relations; Indu Bhushan, Director General of the Strategy, Policy and Review Department; Woochong Um, The Secretary; and Juzhong Zhuang, Deputy Chief Economist and Deputy Director General of the Economic Research and Regional Cooperation Department reviewed several drafts of the book. The manuscript also benefited from comments received from various departments and offices as well as thematic and sector groups across ADB during several rounds of interdepartmental review. Lei Lei Song from the Office of the President provided strong support during successive rounds of drafting. Technical inputs were provided by staff from SPD; the Treasury Department; Controller's Department; the Budget, Personnel, and Management Systems Department; the Economic Research and Regional Cooperation Department; and the Office of Cofinancing Operations in checking the data in the book. Colleagues from the Records and Archives Unit, Library Services and the Office of the Secretary were always quick and resourceful in sourcing historical documents.

The work was supported by excellent administrative assistance, particularly from Rowena Agripa and Lorena Catap. Peter Stalker provided two rounds

---

4   Watanabe, 1977, *Towards a New Asia*.
5   Fujioka, 1986, *ADB President's Diary*.

of editorial assistance to help tighten the presentation and sharpen the content. The Department of External Relations, with support from Robert Davis, April Gallega, and Rommel Marilla in particular, supervised the overall book production.

In writing an account such as this, it is often necessary to choose between strict accuracy and readability. Few readers are likely to want to keep seeing the phrase "Asia and the Pacific" constantly repeated throughout the text. To improve readability, "Asia" has mainly been used, although hopefully it will be clear that the intent is generally to refer to the whole of the Asia and the Pacific region. Similarly, efforts have been made to streamline references to a range of technical and operational matters such as the ordinary capital resources (OCR) of the Bank, the Asian Development Fund (ADF), program lending, arrangements for loan guarantees, and so on. Where appropriate, an effort has been made to include a crisp explanation in the text. However, readers who would like additional information should consult the very comprehensive resources on the ADB website (www.adb.org).

Finally, I should mention that the views set out here are my own. They are not the official views of the the Bank. The dedicated team which helped prepare this study worked with remarkable commitment. A large number of other ADB colleagues assisted in many other ways. Nevertheless, mistakes and errors of judgment that readers may identify are mine.

Peter McCawley

CONTRIBUTORS

Ananya Basu is Principal Economist in the Pacific Department at the Asian Development Bank (ADB). Previously, she worked on debt sustainability and operations coordination in the Strategy and Policy Department and also in the Office of the President. She has over 14 years of experience with the World Bank in the processing and implementation of projects in the South Asia region. She has a doctoral degree in economics from Harvard University.

Edeena Pike is Planning and Policy Specialist of ADB's Strategy and Policy Department where she has been involved in the development and review of the Bank's corporate strategies and policies in the past 8 years. Before joining ADB in 2004, she was managing development projects in the Philippines for the United Nations Development Programme. She has a background in economics and holds a master's degree in development administration from the Australian National University.

Jade Tolentino is Project Researcher for the ADB History Book. She was a banking and finance professional prior to joining the Institute for Development and Econometric Analysis (IDEA) as Industry Studies Head in 2011 and later served as its Executive Director in 2013. IDEA is a nonprofit research organization based at the University of the Philippines School of Economics, where she is currently completing a master's degree in development economics. She holds a bachelor's degree in economics and a master's degree in finance from the same university.

Xianbin Yao is Director General of ADB's Pacific Department, responsible for the Bank's operations for its 14 small island developing member countries across the Pacific. Prior to this, he was the Director General of the Regional and Sustainable Development Department and Deputy Director General of the Central and West Asia Department. He joined ADB in 1991 under the Young Professionals Program and holds a doctoral degree in agricultural economics from Michigan State University.

ABBREVIATIONS

ADB	Asian Development Bank
ADBI	Asian Development Bank Institute
ADF	Asian Development Fund
AFIC	Asian Finance and Investment Corporation
AIIB	Asian Infrastructure Investment Bank
AIF	ASEAN Infrastructure Fund
AITF	Afghanistan Infrastructure Trust Fund
AMF	Asian Monetary Fund
ARIC	Asia Regional Integration Center (formerly Asia Recovery Information Center)
ASEAN	Association of Southeast Asian Nations
ASF	Agricultural Special Fund
BIMSTEC	Bay of Bengal Initiative for Multi-Sectoral Technical and Economic Cooperation
CAREC	Central Asia Regional Economic Cooperation
CAR	Central Asian republic
CMI	Chiang Mai Initiative
CMIM	Chiang Mai Initiative Multilateralization
COP	Conference of the Parties
CSF	Countercyclical Support Facility
DFI	development finance institution
DMC	developing member country
ECAFE	Economic Commission for Asia and the Far East
FDI	foreign direct investment
GCI	general capital increase
GDP	gross domestic product
GMS	Greater Mekong Subregion
HIPC	Heavily Indebted Poor Countries
IAE	internal administrative expenses
ICT	information and communication technology
IFCT	Industrial Finance Corporation of Thailand
IMF	International Monetary Fund
IMT-GT	Indonesia–Malaysia–Thailand Growth Triangle
IsDB	Islamic Development Bank
ISI	import substitution industrialization
JFPR	Japan Fund for Poverty Reduction
Lao PDR	Lao People's Democratic Republic
LIBOR	London interbank offered rate
LCL	local currency lending
LTSF	Long-Term Strategic Framework

MDG	Millennium Development Goal
MfDR	Managing for Development Results
MFF	multitranche financing facility
MPSF	Multi-Purpose Special Fund
MTR	Midterm Review of Strategy 2020
MTS	medium-term strategy
NDB	New Development Bank
NGO	nongovernment organization
NIE	newly industrialized economy
OCR	ordinary capital resources
OECD	Organisation for Economic Co-operation and Development
OPEC	Organization of the Petroleum Exporting Countries
PPP	public–private partnership
PRC	People's Republic of China
PRS	Poverty Reduction Strategy
REMU	Regional Economic Monitoring Unit
SARS	severe acute respiratory syndrome
SASEC	South Asia Subregional Economic Cooperation
SDG	Sustainable Development Goal
SMEs	small and medium-sized enterprises
TFP	Trade Finance Program
UK	United Kingdom
UN	United Nations
UNFCCC	United Nations Framework Convention on Climate Change
US	United States
WTO	World Trade Organization

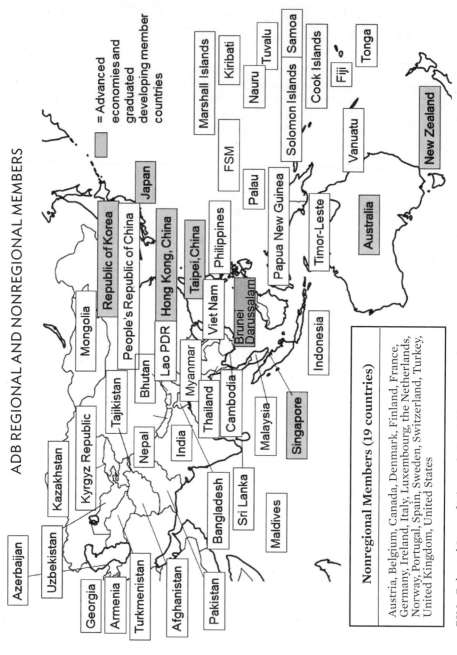

ADB TIME LINE

	1970s: Rise of NIEs ("4 Asian Tigers")	1980s: Asia's Miracle in full recognition	1990s: End of cold war	2000s: Emerging India and ascending PRC	2010s: Asia as engine of global growth
1960s: Asia's Green revolution	Oil shock (1973)	Oil shock (1979)	APEC established (1989)	Asian financial crisis (1997–1998)	Global financial crisis (2008–2009)
	End of Viet Nam war (1975)				

Timeline years: 1970 — 1980 — 1990 — 2000 — 2010

Presidents

- T. Watanabe (1966–1972)
- S. Inoue (1972–1976)
- T. Yoshida (1976–1981)
- M. Fujioka (1981–1989)
- K. Tarumizu (1989–1993)
- M. Sato (1993–1999)
- T. Chino (1999–2005)
- H. Kuroda (2005–2013)
- T. Nakao (2013–present)

Institutional Highlights

- ADB established (1966)
- First ADB headquarters inaugurated (1972)
- First Field Office—Dhaka (1982)
- PRC joins ADB (1986)
- CARs join ADB (1990s)
- Poverty reduction as overarching goal (1999)
- Strategy 2020 (2008)
- MTR (2014)

Boxed (1966): 31 member economies (1966); 40 staff, end of year (1966); 10 EDs, 10 AEDs (1966); $1 billion authorized capital (1966)

Boxed (2016): 67 member economies (2016); 3,092 staff, end of year (2016); 12 EDs, 12 AEDs (2016); $143 billion authorized capital (2016)

Operational Highlights

- First loan—Thailand (1968)
- Lending reaches $1 billion (1978)
- First program loan—Bangladesh (1978)
- First direct equity investment—Republic of Korea (1983)
- First nonsovereign loan—Pakistan (1986)
- GMS Program (1992)
- Asian financial crisis support—$7.8 billion (1997–1999)
- Operations in Afghanistan resume (2002)
- First MFF projects for Pakistan (2005)
- Asian Tsunami Fund (2005)
- Countercyclical Support Facility (2009)
- Reengagement with Myanmar (2012)
- First RBL—Sri Lanka (2013)
- OCR and ADF Merger (2015)[a]

Financing Highlights

- First bond issue (Germany) (1969)
- First bond issue in Asia (Japan) (1970)
- First bond issue in the US (1971)
- First bond issue in the Middle East (Kuwait) (1974)

GCI / ADF

GCI I (1971)	GCI II (1976)	GCI III (1983)			GCI IV (1994)				GCI V (2009)		
ADF I established (1974)	ADF II (1976–78)	ADF III (1979–82)	ADF IV (1983–86)	ADF V (1987–90)	ADF VI (1992–95)	ADF VII (1997–2000)	ADF VIII (2001–04)	ADF IX (2005–08)	ADF X (2009–12)	ADF XI (2013–16)	ADF 12 (2017–20)

ADF I (1973–75)

[a] Approved 2015; effective January 2017.

ADB = Asian Development Bank, AED = alternate executive director, ADF = Asian Development Fund, APEC = Asia-Pacific Economic Cooperation, CAR = Central Asian republic, ED = executive director, GCI = general capital increase, GMS = Greater Mekong Subregion, MFF = multitranche financing facility, MTR = Midterm Review of Strategy 2020, NIE = newly industrialized economy, OCR = ordinary capital resources, PRC = People's Republic of China, RBL = results-based lending, US = United States.

Sources: ADB Annual Reports; ADB.2016. ADB Through the Decades. Volumes 1–5; ADB website (www.adb.org).

CHAPTER 1

Introduction

"The purpose of the Bank shall be to foster economic growth and co-operation in the region of Asia and the Far East ... and to contribute to the acceleration of the process of the developing member countries in the region, collectively and individually."

– Article 1, ADB Charter, 1966

The Asian Development Bank (ADB) was established 50 years ago. On 24 November 1966, the Inaugural Meeting of the Bank opened at the Tokyo Prince Hotel in Shiba Park, Tokyo. Since then, 24 November has been regarded as the Bank's birthday. To mark the 50th anniversary, this book about banking on the future of Asia and the Pacific tells the story of this multilateral development bank and how it has worked with national governments and other international partners to promote development across the region.

ADB was established in the mid-1960s by Asian leaders who believed that regional cooperation supplemented with international financial resources would help promote development in Asia. Several ideas underpinned the establishment of the Bank. One was that Asian countries needed to join together to promote progress. A second was the realistic recognition that additional resources "both from within and outside the region" (as the ADB Charter put it) were needed to promote development. A third idea was that the establishment of a strong and credible regional bank would be an effective organization to support these goals.

The progress of ADB is inextricably linked with that of the Asia and Pacific region. In parallel with the story of ADB, therefore, this history outlines the region's economic and social development over the past 50 years while also tracking changes in international development thinking. The discussion about the Bank's work in each of the five decades reflects several main questions. These are: What are the outstanding features of the development process in Asia that ADB has needed to respond to? How has ADB grown and evolved in these changing circumstances?

A Multilateral Agency

The book emphasizes ADB's characteristics as a multilateral development bank. Each of these features—multilateralism, development, and its role as a bank—is essential to the work of the organization. And as the activities of the institution throughout each of the past 5 decades are discussed in the chapters below, it will become clear that ADB has steadily broadened the range of programs carried out under these three features of its operations.

ADB is multilateral in the sense that the members of the institution are governments both from across the Asia and Pacific region and from nonregional countries. In the early 1960s when the Bank's formation was being discussed, one suggestion was that full participation should be restricted to Asian countries. But the realistic view prevailed that ADB would attract greater international recognition—and funding—if membership was extended to countries in North America and Europe. When the Bank was established in 1966, it had 31 members: 19 from the Asia and Pacific region and 12 from elsewhere. By 2016, it had 67 members: 48 in the Asia and Pacific region and 19 elsewhere, all with equal legal standing in the Bank. However, to protect the Asian influence in key decisions in the organization, it is set down in the ADB Charter that regional members must always hold at least 60% of the capital stock. Nonregional members, therefore, may never hold more than 40% of the authorized stock.

ADB is also multilateral in the sense that it has numerous international partners. As set out in its Charter, ADB is "Asian in its basic character." But it is also international in outreach and cooperates with a wide array of stakeholders. The principal groups with whom ADB must interact constantly are the official representatives of member governments. Other important partners include agencies and firms, in both the public and the private sectors, as well as many organizations of civil society that have a direct interest in ADB projects in the field. A third key group includes the many stakeholders at the regional and global levels with whom ADB engages in discussions about development issues.

Over the years, the number of potential partners has increased dramatically. By 2006, around the world there were 225 bilateral agencies and 242 multilateral agencies. Of these, 40 were United Nations (UN) agencies and 24 were development banks.[1] Added to this list are thousands

---

[1] Estimates from OECD, 2011, *The OECD at 50*, 35.

of nongovernment organizations and other community organizations in both industrial and developing countries, and myriad private sector firms of consultants and contractors. All these bodies—agencies, firms, and groups—jostle with each other, competing for publicity and influence.

ADB's activities with all of these numerous institutions vary widely: in many cases, ADB joins with other agencies, both in borrowing countries and with bilateral or multilateral bodies, to implement projects; in other cases, meetings are held to consider strategy and conduct policy dialogue; numerous conferences and seminars are held with participants from universities and think tanks to strengthen the knowledge base of discussions about development policy in the Asian region; and, on other occasions, ADB staff meet with donors or the international financial community to raise funds to support the Bank's grant and loan programs in borrowing countries. ADB staff, therefore, must spend a good deal of time on liaison and coordination. Some of the issues which need to be discussed are sensitive and sharply contested although in many areas there is wide agreement between development partners.

A Development Organization

The ADB Charter sets out that one of the Bank's main purposes "shall be to foster economic growth" in Asia and the Pacific. Implicit in this purpose is the expectation that ADB will both promote change and adapt to it. This is especially demanding in a region that over the past 50 years has experienced astonishing changes. In the 1950s and early 1960s, prospects for developing countries in Asia and the Pacific were not encouraging. Indeed, between 1900 and 1950, average living standards in the three most populous countries—the People's Republic of China (PRC), India, and Indonesia—hardly increased at all. When ADB was established in 1966, Asia and the Pacific was a region largely defined by poverty, insecurity, and uncertainty.

Over the next half century, the picture was dramatically transformed. During the 1970s and into the 1980s, living standards rose on a strong tide of economic growth—propelled in many countries by the Green Revolution and export-oriented industrialization (Figure 1.1). This progress was underpinned by major economic reforms—from the late 1970s in the PRC, for example, and later in India. Despite the 1997–1998 Asian financial crisis and the 2008 global financial crisis, this momentum was sustained in the 1990s and 2000s.

Figure 1.1: Per Capita Gross Domestic Product in the People's Republic of China, India, Indonesia, and Japan, 1900–2010
(in 1990 international Geary–Khamis dollars)

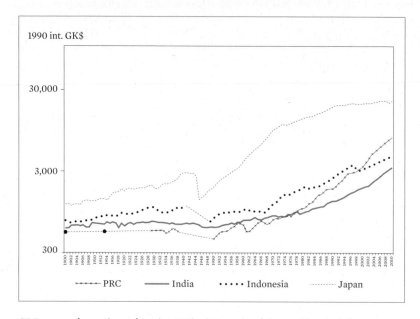

GDP = gross domestic product, int. GK$ = international Geary–Khamis dollars, PRC= People's Republic of China.
Notes:
1. GDP in long-term constant prices (1990 int. GK$).
2. Data for Indonesia are unavailable from 1942 to 1948.
3. Data for the PRC are unavailable from 1901 to 1912, from 1914 to 1928, and from 1939 to 1949. Single-year estimates for 1900 and 1913 are from the Maddison Project.
Source: The Maddison Project. 2013. New Maddison Project database. http://www.ggdc.net/maddison/maddison-project/home.htm (accessed 14 February 2017).

There has also been marked progress in people's quality of life. In 1966, average life expectancy in developing Asia was around 50 years. Between 1966 and 2014, however, life expectancy soared; in Bhutan, for example, from 35 to 69 years; in Hong Kong, China, from 70 to 84 years; and in Timor-Leste, from 37 to 68 years. By the end of 2014, the region's lowest life expectancy was in Afghanistan, at 60 years. Average life expectancy had risen to 71 years.

Three broad themes reflecting trends across the region emerge as the story unfolds in the chapters that follow. The first theme is that of transformation. The transformation across developing countries in Asia during the past 50 years has been astonishing. The earlier story of modern development in Asia began with the Meiji Restoration in Japan in 1868. However, strong progress toward development did not begin to take hold across most of the rest of the region until the 1950s. Then, throughout the 1960s and the succeeding decades, a determination to promote change began to spread across developing Asia. The vibrant developing Asia of 2016 presents a picture entirely different from the discouraging scene of the mid-1960s.

The second theme points to the importance of resilience. Many shocks of various kinds have brought confusion and distress in developing Asia during the past 50 years. Nevertheless, countries struck by these shocks have been remarkably resilient. Whether the shocks have been economic, financial, or humanitarian, developing countries in Asia have rebounded. Thus, resilience has been a second feature of the region during the past 50 years.

The third theme relates to stability. One element of stability has been attention to the maintenance of careful fiscal and monetary policies. But another element has been the spread of peace and increasing cooperation. In the mid-1960s, much of developing Asia was marked by regional instability and open conflict. During the succeeding decades, many successful steps were taken to reduce conflict and encourage regional cooperation. The result is that across developing Asia there is now a strong sense of the need for countries to cooperate to promote development and of the benefits of supporting programs to strengthen stability in the region.

The following chapters outline ADB's participation in this remarkable period of change. In the early years, loans were mainly for public sector projects such as agricultural development, roads, industrial programs, and finance institutions. Later, the Bank expanded into other areas, introducing new forms of loans and other financial assistance. Nowadays, ADB offers developing member countries access to a wide range of loans and grants as well as equity investments and bank guarantees.

This support has been adapted to countries at differing levels of economic development. Some have large and dynamic economies; others, such as countries in the Pacific, are small and still face difficult challenges. The Charter established that ADB should have "special regard to the needs of the smaller or less developed members in the region." Even as membership grows and becomes more diverse, the Bank's work continues to be guided by this principle. All these activities involve policy dialogue and technical assistance. For each country program, ADB engages with stakeholders in discussions on overall economic management while also offering specialist advice on sectoral issues and other forms of assistance.

To guide this work, ADB maintains an extensive database of knowledge and information. In the early 1980s, the fourth President, Masao Fujioka, planned for the Bank to become a "development resources center for Asia and Pacific." ADB publications include regular surveys of regional economic trends and key sectoral issues. These international public goods inform and contribute to an Asian perspective on regional and global policy.

Another central purpose of ADB is to foster regional economic cooperation. To support this activity, in the early years the Bank undertook a series of strategic studies—the Asian Agricultural Survey, the Asian Transport Survey, and the Asian Energy Survey—which identified opportunities for regional countries to work together. In the 1990s, ADB focused on programs for subregional cooperation. For the 21st century, it has set out a four-pillar strategy for regional cooperation: supporting infrastructure connectivity, expanding intraregional trade and investment, coordinating financial and monetary policy, and providing regional public goods.

A Financing Institution

The founders of ADB aimed to establish a bank to mobilize resources to finance the large development needs of Asia. Asia was poor and had a desperate shortage of capital. ADB was to be an institution to leverage the money of shareholders (provided by taxpayers) by issuing bonds in global capital markets, including the United States (US) and Europe. Engagement of nonregional advanced economies was important so as to have the strong creditworthiness required to borrow in international markets.

At the broadest level, the main banking function that ADB performs is as a financial intermediary, mobilizing funds to support development projects and programs in borrowing member countries. Traditionally, the Bank has mainly provided loans and other assistance for public sector (especially sovereign) activities, although work with nonsovereign (including private sector) partners has expanded in recent years.

Sound banking principles apply to ADB's financial operations. The first President, Takeshi Watanabe, emphasized the importance of prudent considerations of lending and it took more than 1 year to approve the first loan. The Charter clearly provides the need for due attention to economy and efficiency. The initial responsibility for the economic analysis of projects was assigned in 1966 to the Operations Department. Later, in 1969, the newly formed Projects Department took over the role. Today, this task of economic analysis of projects is conducted in collaboration with regional departments and the Economic Research and Regional Cooperation Department. As a development bank, ADB looks not only at financial returns but also at broader economic benefits and the development impact of its projects.

To mobilize funds, ADB maintains a sophisticated borrowing program in capital markets. In parallel, the Bank works to raise financial resources in other ways, such as through cofinancing and partnering with bilateral donor agencies. In using the funds, ADB takes care to design high-quality projects and programs so as to maintain its AAA rating in international markets and its reputation as a reliable bank with sound assets on its balance sheet.[2]

In the years since the first loan was approved in 1968, ADB has offered both nonconcessional loans from its ordinary capital resources (OCR) as well as highly concessional soft loans (originally funded from Special Funds and later from the Asian Development Fund [ADF]) to borrowing countries in Asia (Grant operations from ADF were added in 2005). OCR operations have been supported by the authorized capital from shareholders and leveraged by the issuance of ADB's AAA bonds. The authorized capital, which includes both paid-in and callable capital, has ensured the creditworthiness of ADB as a borrower. In the Charter, it is provided that the outstanding level of loans (and equity investments and guarantees) cannot exceed the total amount of authorized capital plus reserves (accumulated income). More recently, the ratio of equity (paid-in capital plus reserves arising from income of OCR) to loans outstanding, set at a minimum of 25%, has underpinned the AAA rating of OCR borrowings. Separately, ADF low-interest long-term loans and grants have been provided from funds contributed by donor countries supplemented by finance from ADB itself from net income.

---

[2] Erquiaga, 2016, *A History of Financial Management at the Asian Development Bank.*

When the Bank was established in 1966, it had an initial authorized capital of $1 billion. By the end of 1967, members had subscribed $970 million of this amount, only 50% of which was "paid-in." The other half was in the form of "callable" shares.[3,4] Compared to the needs for finance to support investment in developing countries in Asia, these amounts were modest. As the institution expanded, it needed more capital. Subsequent increases in subscribed capital, along with contributions from donor countries, allowed ADB to expand its lending. By 2009, the members had agreed to five general capital increases (GCIs). At the end of 2016, the total authorized capital was $143 billion; the subscribed capital was $142.7 billion, of which only $7.2 billion was paid-in.[5] Separately, through 12 rounds of ADF replenishment, 34 donors had contributed $35 billion (Appendix Table A2.15).

In the early years, ADB's lending was around $100 million per year. By 2005, annual approvals were $6.3 billion ($4.7 billion in OCR loans, $1.4 billion in ADF loans, $247 million in ADF grants), and by 2016 they had reached $17.5 billion ($14.4 billion in OCR loans, $2.6 billion in ADF loans, plus another $518 million in ADF grants).[6]

To put these operations in context, it helps to appreciate that the role of ADB in providing finance to developing Asia (along, indeed, with all of the rest of the official assistance provided by the international community) is limited. In fact, the great bulk of investment in developing countries in Asia is funded from within these countries themselves. However, to supplement domestic investment—with knowledge as well as finance—one of the original Charter goals set for the Bank was to mobilize additional financial resources from outside developing Asia. On a long-term basis, in recent years, the Bank's financial operations (annual approvals of loans and grants) have varied from around 0.5% to 0.8% of gross domestic product

---

[3] Payment for the callable amount was only due from members in the event ADB faced an urgent financial problem.

[4] The original authorized capital of ADB was $1 billion in terms of US dollars of the weight and fineness in effect on 31 January 1966. Of this amount, $500 million was paid-in shares and another $500 million was callable. In November 1966, the Board of Governors approved an increase of $100 million of authorized capital. As of 31 December 1967, the subscribed capital was $970 million, of which $485 million was paid-in, while the rest was callable shares.

[5] Given that ADB capital is denominated in special drawing rights (SDR), the reported US dollar level of capital stock fluctuates constantly, reflecting changes in the US dollar–SDR exchange rate.

[6] Here "loans" include gross approvals of loans, equity investments, and guarantees.

Figure 1.2: Share of ADB's Operations to Total Gross Domestic Product of Developing Asia (excluding the People's Republic of China), 1968–2015

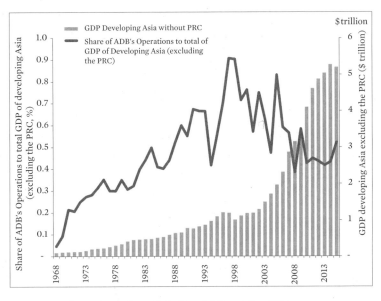

GDP = gross domestic product, PRC = People's Republic of China.

Source: Adapted from ADB. 2016. *Corporate Evaluation Study: The Asian Development Bank's Engagement with Middle-Income Countries.* Manila. p. 30.

(GDP) in borrowing countries excluding the PRC (Figure 1.2). ADB's role in supporting investment flows in Asia, therefore, needs to be focused just as much on strengthening the quality of investment in the region through the provision of knowledge as well as on the quantity of finance provided to borrowing countries.

Reflecting this approach, ADB in its banking activities has aimed to provide finance supplemented with activities designed to improve the quality of investment programs. The Bank has always emphasized prudence as well. Takeshi Watanabe frequently spoke of the importance of maintaining sound banking principles. These principles included the careful selection of projects in borrowing countries; to this end, ADB staff were expected to spend considerable time in borrowing countries, listening and observing so that they could prepare high-quality lending programs.

In response to the evolving needs of borrowers, ADB has adopted many changes in its financial and lending programs. Over its 50-year history, the menu of financial products has been continuously updated. The early lending program was made up of project loans provided in the form of foreign exchange to help finance specific sovereign project activities. Before long, program loans which did not finance a specific project were introduced, and then the objectives of program lending were revised in response to requests from borrowing countries. Program loans were first approved in 1978 to supply foreign exchange to fund imports of agricultural inputs. Between 1987 and 1996, program loans were used to support policy reform in a widening range of sectors. In 1999, they were approved to respond to exceptional large-scale crises. And in 2011, they were used for medium-term programmatic budget support.

Meanwhile, after initially providing only sovereign loans during the first decade of operations, ADB broadened activities into nonsovereign approvals in the early 1980s. In 1983, a direct equity investment—a first for the Bank—was approved for an investment in the private sector. This was to provide finance for a corporation in the Republic of Korea. Several years later, in 1986, ADB began direct lending to private sector enterprises without the benefit of any government guarantee. The first loan was to the National Development Leasing Corporation in Pakistan.

Concessional sovereign loans were also strengthened. In 2005, with the support of industrial donor countries, ADB provided the first grants from the ADF program.

There have been numerous other changes in ADB's lending and financial programs as well. In 2005, for example, learning from the Asian financial crisis, the Bank introduced local currency loans for sovereign borrowers to help address the potential "double mismatch" between borrowing in foreign currency and earning income in local currency. The following year, ADB started lending without sovereign guarantees to public sector borrowers (such as state-owned enterprises or municipalities) that are separate from the sovereign or central government.

Cofinancing with other multilateral and bilateral agencies as well as the private sector has increased. In 2016, notwithstanding global fiscal constraints, ADB supplemented its own financing of $17.5 billion with $14.1 billion in cofinancing (including trust funds)—an increase of 31% over the previous year.

In 2013, ADB, despite the fact that it is often regarded as a conservative financial institution, decided to initiate discussions on a remarkably innovative restructuring of its balance sheet. The plan met with a degree of skepticism from some member countries at first, but was unanimously approved in 2015 and came into effect on 1 January 2017. The financial implications of the restructuring for the Bank, and for its capacity to support expanded operations, are far-reaching. The change merges its concessional ADF loan resources with nonconcessional OCR. As a result of this startling piece of financial engineering, equity was boosted from $17.2 billion to more than $48 billion, well placing ADB to respond to growing requests for support from borrowing countries.

ADB has also had to be cost-effective and efficient. In its earliest days, Takeshi Watanabe warned about excessive bureaucracy. "Organization," he said, "even begun in the simplest manner, often becomes very complex… I wished to see the ADB take advantage of compactness from its very beginning."[7] All subsequent Presidents have kept close control over the Bank's administration and expenses and have kept ADB one of the most efficient multilateral development banks. Nevertheless, as its lending and other activities increased, ADB needed more staff. In 1966, the Bank had 40 employees in Manila, both international and national staff, drawn from six member countries. By 2016, it had almost 3,100 staff members coming from 60 countries. Over the same period, ADB's internal budget grew from less than $3 million to around $636 million.

The Leadership Succession

The following chapters tell the story of ADB as an evolving institution. Organized chronologically by decade, the book traces major developments in the Asia and Pacific region and shows how ADB responded.

The influence that the Presidents have had is emphasized. Since its establishment in 1966, ADB has had nine Presidents. There are clear patterns of both continuity and change in the different approaches that different Presidents have brought. Continuity is reflected in the way each President set out to implement the key ideas about ADB's role set out in the original Charter of the Bank. Each President highlighted the Bank's multilateral nature—and each President spent considerable time

---

[7] Watanabe, 1977, *Towards a New Asia*, 27.

visiting developing countries across the region, meeting policy makers, and visiting ADB projects. As well, each new President has aimed to build on the priorities of previous Presidents, promoting reform. However, in encouraging change, none of the Presidents has had a free hand. Because ADB is a multilateral organization, it has been necessary to negotiate reforms with multiple stakeholders including the Board of Directors, the Board of Governors, and sometimes directly with governments of member countries.

But there have been important changes as well. Each President has brought his own personal style: some have been more formal and alert to protocol, while others have been inclined to be more informal. And during the past five decades, both the nature of many of the challenges for the Bank in Asia has changed as have the responses that have been needed. Further, ADB itself has become a much more complex institution as reforms have been introduced and as the international development agenda has evolved. Over time then, Presidents have had to take on widening roles, guiding ADB in a region where rapid development and globalization has been taking place.

Takeshi Watanabe (who was President for 6 years from 1966 to 1972) has often been called the "Father of the Bank." This special recognition reflects the remarkable role that he played in the establishment of the institution. Watanabe participated in Tokyo in the early 1960s in the initial meetings to discuss the idea of the Bank (Chapter 3). He was then active between 1963 and 1965 in planning for the formation of ADB. And then he became the first President and played a decisive role in helping form the essential character of the institution.

The second President, Shiro Inoue (from 1972 to 1976), a banker from the Bank of Japan, the Japanese central bank, arrived just as there were early hopes for peace in Viet Nam (Chapter 5). But very soon, his attention to peace in Indochina was overtaken by the first oil shock in 1973–1974. Inoue found himself needing to guide ADB through the first regionwide economic crisis that the Bank had experienced.

During ADB's second decade, Taroichi Yoshida (from 1976 to 1981) initiated measures to widen the Bank's role. When he became President in 1976, developing countries in Asia were still coping with the adjustment challenges resulting from the first oil shock. There were, however, growing pressures for the Bank to expand its role as well. Then, in 1979, the second major oil shock transformed the economic outlook in Asia once again.

In response to these developments, Yoshida's legacy was to commission a major report on a *Study of Operational Priorities and Plans of the Asian Development Bank for the 1980s*.

Masao Fujioka (from 1981 to 1989) adopted the program set out in the Operational Priorities study. The recommendations became, in effect, a "Fujioka agenda" for institutional reform in ADB during the 1980s (Chapter 7). He was especially keen to see the organization widen its activities beyond a focus on banking and play a role as a wider development institution. In addition, the two giant countries of Asia, India and the PRC, became borrowing members of the Bank while Fujioka was President. He regarded this change as being of great importance for the organization and was very closely involved in the lengthy negotiations needed between various countries to complete the process.

In 1987, to encourage discussion about further change, Fujioka invited an external group of five experts to prepare a study on the work of the Bank. The final document, *Report of a Panel on the Role of the Asian Development Bank in the 1990s*, provided an agenda for reform for the next President, Kimimasa Tarumizu (from 1989 to 1993), who arrived on the Bank's birthday, 24 November 1989.

Tarumizu took up his position just a few weeks after the Berlin Wall had fallen. Thinking about international issues soon began to change quickly so he needed to guide ADB in adapting to a new development agenda. There were rapidly expanding demands on the organization from emerging economies as well. Within the Bank, Tarumizu's decision in 1992 to introduce a strategic planning process set the framework for continuing institutional reform throughout the 1990s.

The sixth President, Mitsuo Sato (from 1993 to 1999), arrived just as ADB was running out of lending headroom (that is, the amount of lending that can still be approved without breaching the legal ceiling of permissible lending, or without losing the AAA credit rating). A general capital increase (GCI), which would provide for more headroom, had been under discussion for some time but agreement was delayed. Sato immediately gave top priority to reaching agreement on a GCI, which was approved in May 1994 (Chapter 9). A second priority for Sato throughout his 5 years as President was to strengthen ADB as (to use the phrase he often preferred) a "fully-fledged development institution."

However, perhaps the single most challenging task for Sato as President was to guide the institution through the Asian financial crisis in 1997 (Chapters 10 and 11). Sato was immensely concerned by the effects of the crisis. He led ADB's responses in the crisis-affected countries and then supported the expansion of a range of new programs within ADB designed to strengthen financial systems in Asia so as to help guard against similar events in the future.

Tadao Chino (from 1999 to 2005) preferred a modest and low-key style as President. Soon after arriving, he initiated a major review of ADB's work, which led to the introduction of a new Poverty Reduction Strategy (Chapter 12). Poverty reduction became the "overarching goal" for ADB. Later, new corporate strategies—a 15-year Long-Term Strategic Framework and a 5-year Medium-Term Strategic Framework—were introduced to support the Poverty Reduction Strategy. Another of Chino's lasting contributions was his attention to fragile and conflict-affected states. He also took steps to raise the proportion of women in senior and professional positions in the Bank. ADB's first woman Vice-President was appointed in 2003 while he was President.

Chino's work prepared the groundwork for a capital increase. The next President, Haruhiko Kuroda (from 2005 to 2013), built upon these plans. Kuroda arrived with strong and broad experience, both in Japan and in international organizations, took a close personal interest in economic issues, and was well-connected in global financial circles. During his first few years in the Bank, he gave strong support to an expansion of ADB's regional activities. He also drew attention to the fact that ADB lending had been "stagnating" (as he put it) at around the level of $5 billion–$6 billion per year. Kuroda made it clear that he saw it as a priority for ADB to expand both the quantity of lending as well as the quality of its work.

However, during 2007 and into 2008, a global financial crisis began to spread across industrial countries. Just as Sato had needed to lead ADB through the unexpected Asian financial crisis in 1997–1998, so Kuroda faced the task of guiding the Bank through the unexpected 2007–2008 global financial crisis. In response, Kuroda pressed the case with member countries for a GCI. Under the urgent circumstances of an unfolding crisis, a GCI was quickly approved. He also guided the Bank to set a new corporate plan, Strategy 2020, in 2008.

In February 2013, Prime Minister Shinzo Abe of Japan nominated Kuroda as the Governor of the Bank of Japan in Tokyo. Following Kuroda's appointment, Takehiko Nakao was nominated as the ninth President of ADB (Chapter 14).

Takehiko Nakao (2013 to present), also with long and extensive experience in international finance, made it clear that he welcomed the opportunity to work on development issues in Asia. He would become known for his direct and hands-on management style. Nakao believed that additional efforts to reform the Bank were needed and urged ADB to be "stronger, better, faster." He revised Strategy 2020 through a midterm review and began considering a new "Strategy 2030." Then, in August 2013, he initiated the innovative ADF–OCR merger to reform the finances of the Bank in a way that will permit a sharp increase in operations (loans and grants) by 50% toward an annual level of around $20 billion within a few years. He also strengthened sector and thematic groups to share experiences as "one ADB" and announced a doubling of ADB's climate finance ahead of the UN Climate Change Conference (COP21) in Paris in late 2015.

The Challenge of Development

Development is a continuing journey—a transforming process—which emerging countries in Asia are currently embarked upon. An appreciation of the significance of this development journey is fundamental to an understanding of the sweeping processes of change taking place across the region.

Many forces that have influenced this process in the recent past will continue to exert their influence in the coming decades. New factors will emerge along the way as well. Collectively, countries in Asia have shown the commitment and capacity to manage the transformative process—not with any uniform model, but in ways that vary and are seen to be appropriate in the different situations that different countries face.

As a multilateral development bank, ADB has also shown its commitment and capacity to change—to anticipate and respond to the emerging priorities of its developing member countries.

We invite the reader to join us in exploring the history of ADB which, reflecting the journey of the region, began 50 years ago.

CHAPTER 2
Beginnings (Until 1966)

Asia in the 1960s: Ferment and Transformation

"Asia is now experiencing one of her most difficult periods since the end of the Second World War. ... In this context, it is gratifying to note that the Asian Development Bank has been created as a result of Asian initiative and cooperation, with the close support of countries in other parts of the world."

– U Thant, Secretary-General of the United Nations,
Message to ADB Inaugural Meeting, 24 November 1966, Tokyo

The post-World War II era was tumultuous. The colonial period was rapidly drawing to a close. One after another, countries across the region gained their independence, for instance, Indonesia in 1945, India in 1947, and Myanmar and Ceylon (later Sri Lanka) in 1948. The People's Republic of China (PRC) was proclaimed in 1949. The years of war had fermented the individual hopes of developing countries in Asia. There was a pent-up demand for nation building and construction, so after gaining independence, each country embarked upon a deep process of change. Countries across Asia were full of hope for a bright future, but before long they found the outlook for economic development and progress more sobering.

Almost a century earlier, during the Meiji Restoration, Japanese leaders had already committed themselves to development in the modern sense. But elsewhere in Asia, progress had been held back by colonialism, wars, and political instability. By the late 1950s and early 1960s, despite an urge to move forward, the prospects for sustained progress in the larger developing countries of Asia were still not encouraging. This chapter discusses the hopes for modernization—and the impetus for regional cooperation that led in 1966 to the establishment of the Asian Development Bank (ADB).

Japan and the Flying Geese

For centuries, markets in Asia had been connected with those in Europe. In the 16th and 17th centuries, European powers along with traders from China, India, and elsewhere had strengthened their trading links with Asia. However, this did little to stimulate Asia's economic development. The great global trade boom in the 18th and 19th centuries brought little benefit to most of the people of Asia and colonization hampered indigenous development in the region. The exception to this picture of arrested development was Japan. After the Meiji Restoration in 1868, Japan experienced a surge of development—demonstrating that, for Asian countries, sustained economic development as well as independence from European colonial powers were a realistic goal.

By the 1960s, the success of Japan's development path had served to provide encouragement to many other countries in Asia. One of the best-known development paradigms that emerged in Asia was that of the "flying geese." In this view, discussed in detail by Kaname Akamatsu,[1] countries in earlier stages of development were aligned behind industrial nations in "wild-geese formation."[2] Countries behind the leaders benefited from lower wage costs for the production of commoditized goods, but as their costs rose, they in turn passed this type of production of commoditized goods to countries further behind. Within Asia, the leader of this formation was Japan, the first Asian country to successfully industrialize its economy. It would be the first country to see rising labor costs, followed by the newly industrialized economies (NIEs)—Hong Kong, China; the Republic of Korea; Singapore; and Taipei,China—and subsequently by the main Association of Southeast Asian Nations (ASEAN) member states—Indonesia, Malaysia, Thailand, and others. Predictions by other scholars were more cautious, but the flying geese paradigm, with various modifications, would turn out close to the actual course of events.

The Four Tigers

Across much of developing Asia in the 1960s, the situation looked grim. But the picture was more positive in some countries. Scarcely noticed at first, as early as the mid-1950s, the four most dynamic economies were

---

[1] Akamatsu, 1962, *Historical Pattern of Economic Growth*.
[2] For a summary of the critiques of the flying geese paradigm, see Kasahara, 2004, *Flying Geese Paradigm*.

poised for liftoff. Owing to their rapid growth, these NIEs would later become known as the "four tigers." Before ADB's establishment, however, they were just four "cubs"—all determined not only to survive, but to grow and thrive.[3]

Singapore's pursuit of development was fueled by the political independence it gained in 1965 after a failed merger with Malaya (later Malaysia). The Republic of Korea was motivated by the need to rehabilitate after the Korean War in the 1950s and the installation in the country in 1961 of a new government bent on promoting export-driven growth. These developments would pave the way for rapid industrialization. Taipei,China had a similar economic agenda in the 1960s, focusing on manufacturing and expanding quickly on the strength of growing exports. The Republic of Korea and Taipei,China had also undertaken significant land reforms and continued to pay major attention to education and skills development.

In many respects, the development paths in the four NIEs were similar. All had restructured their economies, achieved high rates of savings and investment, and remained open to the world economy. In some respects, however, their strategies diverged—particularly in their relationships between the state and the market. In Hong Kong, China, for example, the state left much to market forces. In the other three economies, the state aimed to promote growth via comprehensive development strategies and strong guidance to players in markets.

The transformation was impressive. In 1953, the Republic of Korea had been one of Asia's poorest countries. Following policy reforms in the late 1950s, however, the economy began to grow rapidly. For the two decades to 1980, growth averaged over 8% per year (Table 2.1). There has been much debate about the source of this economic success but two elements stand out: an activist state and strong links with the global economy. Singapore took a similar approach.

Taipei,China also followed an export-oriented path. Exports grew at over 20% per year (Table 2.1). However, manufacturing had a different structure in Taipei,China. Exporting companies tended to be small. In contrast, in the Republic of Korea, output was mostly from the industrial conglomerates—the *chaebol*.

---

[3] Hughes, 1995, *Why Have East Asian Countries Led Economic Development?*, 88–104.

Table 2.1: Gross Domestic Product and Export Growth of the "Four Tigers" and Japan, 1953–1980 (% per year)

Economies	1953–1962	1963–1972	1973–1980
Hong Kong, China			
GDP	12.8	11.7	10.1
Exports	6.9	14.0	9.8
Korea, Republic of			
GDP	3.8	9.1	8.3
Exports	16.1	30.3	17.6
Singapore			
GDP	...	10.3	8.1
Exports	0.3	6.0	29.1
Taipei,China			
GDP	7.3	10.9	8.4
Exports	18.0	27.6	22.6
Japan			
GDP	8.3	9.4	4.1
Exports	16.3	15.8	6.2

... = not available, GDP = gross domestic product.

Source: Adapted from A. O. Krueger. 1995. East Asian Experience and Endogenous Growth Theory. In T. Ito and A. O. Krueger, eds. *Growth Theories in Light of the East Asian Experience*. Chicago: University of Chicago Press.

Corresponding to the flying geese paradigm, Indonesia, Malaysia, and Thailand would adapt these different approaches to their own circumstances and followed the four leaders, with the effects being more pronounced in later decades. Nevertheless, across the rest of Asia, the outlook in the early 1960s was less optimistic.[4] India, for instance, with its vibrant and seemingly chaotic democracy, seemed to have limited prospects for economic growth, and the PRC, one of the world's newest and certainly the largest communist country, was politically and economically isolated from the rest of the world. Meanwhile, in a number of countries in Southeast Asia, local independence movements were struggling to establish new states—leading to instability and open conflict.

---

[4] A useful summary of developments in the region in the late 1940s and 1950s is in the various economic and social surveys published by the United Nations Economic and Social Commission for Asia and the Pacific since 1947 available on the ESCAP website at http://www.unescap.org/publications/survey/#70s (accessed 17 January 2017).

Instability in Southeast Asia

Prospects looked difficult in Southeast Asia in the post-World War II period. The region was buffeted by international power struggles. Former colonial countries—France and the United Kingdom—were reluctant to accept the waning of their influence in the region. France only agreed to withdraw its forces from Indochina in 1954 after defeat in the battle of Dien Bien Phu. The United Kingdom was similarly reluctant to depart from Southeast Asia: throughout the 1950s, British and Commonwealth troops fought a long anti-insurgency campaign in Malaysia. Independence was achieved in 1957, but an attempt to establish a federation of Malaysia failed in 1965 when sharp policy disagreements led to Singapore's painful exit. The federation had also been strongly opposed by Indonesia's President Sukarno who regarded it as an attempt to preserve colonialist influence in the region—resulting in a period of sharp *Konfrontasi* (confrontation) between Indonesia and Malaysia.

But just as the former colonial powers were exiting, Southeast Asia was attracting growing attention from the United States (US). Foreign policy strategists in the US and other Western countries were worried about the perceived threat of communism and the domino effect in Viet Nam, Cambodia, and Laos (later the Lao People's Democratic Republic or Lao PDR), and argued that this should be stemmed by strong action. In the early 1960s, the US government made the fateful decisions first to increase military support, and then become directly involved. By 1969, the US had half a million troops serving in South Viet Nam. The ongoing war had widespread political and economic implications, including for ADB. US policy makers, keen to encourage peace and stability in Southeast Asia, responded favorably to the proposal to establish an Asian development bank.

There was also turmoil in Indonesia. The former colonial power, the Netherlands, had been reluctant to leave but Indonesian leaders declared independence in 1945. By the 1960s, however, Western observers and many Indonesians had become alarmed by the growing influence of the large Indonesian Communist Party. A showdown came in September 1965: in a terrible period of confusion and conflict, about half a million Indonesians are estimated to have died.[5] The subsequent change of leadership led to large reforms in both domestic and foreign policy, making

---

[5] Wanandi, 2012, *Shades of Grey*.

it difficult for Indonesia to participate in discussions on the establishment of ADB. Nevertheless, the new government was keen to join the Bank and in 1966 became a founding member.[6]

Meanwhile, the Philippines, which had taken advantage of the postwar boom, was an exception to the grim picture of Southeast Asia in the 1950s and early 1960s. It was among the most progressive economies in Asia and, for a time, had a higher per capita income than Taipei,China or the Republic of Korea.[7] The Philippines would play a major part in establishing the Bank, particularly when it set out to win the coveted role of hosting the permanent headquarters. However, the Philippines was overtaken by an authoritarian and protectionist regime and in the 1970s and early 1980s was beset by problems of crony capitalism and rising foreign debt. The result was that the Philippines fell behind its neighbors and settled in one of the rear rows of the flying geese formation.

Stagnation in South Asia

Prospects were also difficult in South Asia. By this time, India had experienced a long period of stagnation. In the three decades to independence in 1947, national income had grown by only 1% per year—barely sufficient to match population growth, so there was very little increase in per capita income.[8] After independence and the introduction of a series of 5-year plans, progress accelerated somewhat: by the 1960s, growth was around 4% per year.[9] However, these plans were directed largely to basic and heavy industries—providing less priority to the production of food and of consumer goods such as textiles that would offer more immediate benefits to the mass of the population.

Contemporary observers expressed disappointment. In 1954, the distinguished Indian economist V. K. R. V. Rao said that his country was "a static economy in progress."[10] In 1968, Swedish economist Gunnar Myrdal in his classic study *Asian Drama: An Inquiry into the Poverty of*

---

[6] Watanabe, 1977, *Towards a New Asia*, 19.
[7] Maddison, 2013, *Maddison-Project*. http://www.ggdc.net/maddison/maddison-project/data.htm
[8] Sivasubramonian, 2001, *Twentieth Century Economic Performance*, 103; Manish, 2011, *Central Economic Planning*, 199.
[9] For a detailed discussion as well as a summary of views held by various well-known scholars, see Manish, 2011, *Central Economic Planning*.
[10] Higgins, 1959, *Economic Development*, 40.

Nations observed that, "All the new nations in South Asia are now pledged to the promotion of economic development through the planned and coordinated efforts of governments. Only a few, however, have come far in this direction. Even India has been unable to register a rate of progress comparable to that in the Western countries, either now or in earlier stages of their economic development." Indeed, throughout the 1960s and into the 1970s, the Indian economy continued to grow slowly.

Myrdal ascribed the stagnation in India to the "social indiscipline" widespread in most countries of South Asia, reflected in corruption, deficiencies in legislation, and lack of law enforcement. He referred to these countries as "soft states" and saw them as unable to impose effective development policies.[11]

Elsewhere in South Asia, the prospects were mixed. Pakistan made progress during the 1950s but was hindered in the late 1960s by simmering internal political tensions that led to the secession of East Pakistan as Bangladesh in 1971. Development was faster in Ceylon (later Sri Lanka), which in the 1950s was widely regarded as a "model developing country, with functioning democracy, working institutions and good economic growth."[12] On a visit to Colombo in the early 1950s, Lee Kuan Yew, later Prime Minister of Singapore, commented that the capital was orderly, clean, and prosperous and that he wished Singapore could achieve the same standard. But after 1956, the Ceylon government started to intervene more directly in the economy and pursued more inward-looking policies so that the share of international trade in gross domestic product declined markedly.

Isolation of the People's Republic of China

The outlook was also unpromising in the PRC. In 1949, when the PRC was proclaimed, average incomes perhaps were 20% lower than those in India.[13] Nor did things improve quickly during the next few decades. Externally imposed economic blockages by major Western powers and an internally focused drive for self-reliance and self-sufficiency caused the PRC to be increasingly cut off from the world economy. Throughout the 1960s, the PRC would be isolated economically, technologically, and militarily.

---

[11] Myrdal, 1968, *Asian Drama: An Inquiry into the Poverty of Nations*.
[12] Abeyratne, 2002, *Economic Roots of Political Conflict: The Case of Sri Lanka*.
[13] Figures are provided by Desai, 2003, *India and China: An Essay in Comparative Political Economy*.

Its launch of the Great Leap Forward from 1958 to 1961 turned out to be a disastrous attempt to shift the economy from agriculture toward industrial production. Agriculture stagnated resulting in famines that destroyed the lives of millions of people.[14]

A subsequent campaign in 1966, the Cultural Revolution, invoked revolutionary change through class struggle. The Cultural Revolution plunged the PRC into a decade of social and political turmoil. During this difficult time, the country's leaders largely focused on internal affairs. So when discussions started on establishing ADB, the PRC did not participate, nor did it become a founding member. Indeed, it was not until the end of the 1970s, more than a decade after the Bank's establishment, that the PRC introduced sweeping reforms and began to build wider links with the international community.

Delayed Independence in the Pacific

In the early 1960s, the Pacific island countries had not joined in the postwar drive for national growth. They largely remained dependent on external powers for strategic and economic support. In 1962, Western Samoa (later Samoa) was the first small Pacific island country to gain independence and later became a founding member of ADB. The Cook Islands was a New Zealand colony until 1965. In 1968, Nauru became the world's smallest independent republic. The other Pacific island countries would achieve independence from 1970 onward. These countries would progressively join the Bank as new members. Timor-Leste in 2002 and then Palau in 2003 became members. By then, ADB had 14 Pacific developing member countries.

Other Economic Challenges

In the post-World War II period, each country in Asia faced its own particular economic problems. However, a common preoccupation was the risk of food shortages, and even famine. In South Asia in the early 1950s, for example, average caloric intake was often 10% or more below minimum needs. Food supplies were also unreliable in other parts of Asia, such as the Philippines (Table 2.2). The United Nations Economic Commission for Asia and the Far East (ECAFE) estimated that in 1957 per capita food

---

[14] de Wilde, Defraigne, and Defraigne, 2012, *China, the European Union and the Restructuring of Global Governance*, 16–18.

Table 2.2: Post-World War II Food Supplies in Selected Countries
Average Calories per Person per Day

Countries	Years	Average Calories per Person per Day	Deficit (%)
Ceylon	1952–1953	1,990	13
India	1949–1950	1,630	29
Pakistan	1949–1950	2,010	9
Philippines	1952–1953	1,790	18

Source: United Nations data quoted in G. Myrdal. 1968. *Asian Drama: An Inquiry into the Poverty of Nations.* New York: Pantheon. p. 544.

grain production across the Asian region was still 7% below prewar levels. Food was not just in short supply, it was also distributed very unequally, so a substantial proportion of the population received much less than the average.

In the most extreme cases, the result was famine. In the north of Viet Nam in 1954, thousands of people died. In the PRC between 1959 and 1961, food shortages led to the deaths of tens of millions of people.[15] Famine also threatened India—in Bihar in 1966–1967, for example, and in Maharashtra in 1973. These disasters, and broader concerns about food supplies, led ADB to give high priority to agriculture in its first decades of work.

Apart from food shortages, the region was also facing other postwar development concerns, described in detail in annual economic surveys prepared by ECAFE (Table 2.3).

These studies highlighted Asia's scarcity of domestic and foreign capital—for immediate reconstruction needs and for achieving long-term, stable growth. Asian economic managers also needed to deal with the threat of inflation, unstable export markets for primary products, unemployment and population pressures, and slow improvement in the agriculture sector.

During this time, the drive for industrialization in Asian developing countries was seen as an "expression of the freedom to shape their own economic destiny."[16] Many of these countries embraced import substitution

---

[15] Asia Society, 2005, *Amartya Sen: What China Could Teach India, Then and Now.*
[16] United Nations, 1958, *Economic Survey of Asia and the Far East.*

Table 2.3: Studies of the United Nations Economic and Social Survey of Asia and the Pacific

Survey Year	Theme
1957	Postwar problems of economic development
1958	Review of postwar industrialization
1959	Foreign trade of ECAFE primary exporting countries
1960	Public finance in the postwar period
1961	Economic growth of ECAFE countries
1962	Asia's trade with Western Europe
1963	Import substitution and export diversification
1964	Economic development and the role of the agriculture sector
1965	Economic development and human resources
1966	Aspects of the finance and development

ECAFE = United Nations Economic Commission for Asia and the Far East.
Source: United Nations. 1978. *Economic and Social Survey of Asia and the Pacific 1977*. p. ii.

industrialization (ISI) strategies. This approach required four things: local skilled and productive labor, technical know-how, the availability of markets, and capital. These strategies proved very costly. ISI required countries to produce their own goods—increasing imports of materials and the demand for foreign exchange. Asian countries soon realized that if they were to become stronger in these areas they would need to collaborate.

Regional Cooperation

When ECAFE was created in the late 1940s, non-Asian members of the United Nations aimed to limit the work of the ECAFE Secretariat to research and study. Over time, however, as the number of Asian members within ECAFE increased and governments in the region gained more confidence, ECAFE began to play an expanded role. From 1957 onward, ECAFE not only studied Asian developing countries' problems, it also encouraged countries in the region to collaborate in addressing common development challenges. Moreover, after the war, there was growing support for the idea that the weaker countries of Asia should band together to boost growth and achieve higher levels of economic independence from Europe and North America. As an "economic parliament in Asia," ECAFE supported these aspirations. U Nyun, its Executive Secretary from 1959 and 1973, was from Myanmar and argued that Asian countries should synchronize national development plans to achieve regional economic integration.[17]

In the years leading to the establishment of ADB, ECAFE would work to bring Asian economic managers together to talk over shared concerns.[18] ECAFE countries discussed programs for technical cooperation, operational cooperation, and consultation on development plans.[19] And they agreed that they would need to intensify such cooperation, with or without the assistance of ECAFE.

Channels for technical cooperation included discussion forums, regional seminars, and industrial missions. A number of technical and research institutions were also established, including the Asian Institute for Development and Planning in Thailand, the International Rice Research Institute in the Philippines, and the Asian Productivity Organization in Japan. ECAFE countries would also later welcome the establishment of the Asian Institute of Management in the Philippines to train managerial staff for large enterprises and the Asian Institute of Technology in Thailand to provide training in special production techniques.

There was also support for the promotion of industrialization in the smaller countries. To this end, a working group of experts commissioned by ECAFE proposed the establishment of a regional development bank to channel investment funds into industrial projects. This regional bank could be expanded into an "Asian Trade and Development Bank" to finance intraregional trade. An institution of this kind could also improve the coordination of national development plans. Previously, a lack of coordination had led to costly mistakes in several Asian countries such as overproduction of textile products and undercapacity of steel mills and petroleum refineries.

---

[17] Huang, 1975, *The Asian Development Bank: Diplomacy and Development in Asia*, 3–23.
[18] In 1963, the developing ECAFE members included Afghanistan; Brunei Darussalam; Myanmar; Cambodia; Sri Lanka; Taipei,China; Hong Kong, China; India; Indonesia; Iran; the Republic of Korea; Laos; Malaysia (and Singapore); Pakistan; the Philippines; Thailand; and Viet Nam.
[19] United Nations, 1963, *Economic Survey of Asia and the Far East*. pp.101–118.

International Trends

The regional programs supported by ECAFE were influenced by international events and by the changes occurring in the post-World War II global aid architecture.[20] Postwar development had been stimulated by programs of international assistance. In some respects, these programs were an extension of the Marshall Plan through which, in the late 1940s, the US provided large flows of finance to Europe.[21] In the immediate postwar period, the US and the World Bank also provided economic support to Japan. Encouraged by the success of these programs, leaders in industrial countries concluded that developing countries in Asia and elsewhere would benefit from similar flows. In addition, both donors and recipients were becoming increasingly aware of the advantages of establishing multilateral programs.

There was assistance from within the region as well, especially from Japan. When the US occupation ended in 1952, Japanese foreign policy aimed to reengage with Asian countries peacefully through trade and development assistance after the war had left serious scars in the region. Initially, Japan's assistance took the form of postwar reparations to countries such as the Philippines, Indonesia, and Myanmar as well as technical assistance beginning in 1955 as a new member of the Colombo Plan, an international organization established in 1951 to promote cooperative economic and social development in Asia and the Pacific. Later, the assistance developed into a more comprehensive official aid program.[22]

Japan's official development assistance in the early days was characterized by a focus on Asia, support for infrastructure to promote broad economic development, and assistance with concessional loans to encourage discipline in borrowing countries.[23] Following the success of these bilateral programs, Japan and other countries started to consider the establishment of new institutions to attract international capital to Asia and strengthen regional cooperation.

---

[20] According to Huang, the motivations behind the development of regional cooperation in Asia and the roots of the establishment of ADB included the rise of foreign economic assistance to Asia, growing Asian regionalism, and the increasing influence of ECAFE. Huang, 1975, *The Asian Development Bank: Diplomacy and Development in Asia*.
[21] Behrman, 2007, *The Most Noble Adventure*.
[22] Furuoka, Oishi, and Kato, 2010, *From Aid Recipient to Aid Donor*.
[23] Akiyama and Nakao, 2006, *Japanese ODA – Adapting to the Issues and Challenges of the New Aid Environment*.

The value of intraregional arrangements as instruments of cooperation was also encouraged by the expansion of regional groupings in other parts of the world. Three main regional development banks were formed. In 1959, the Inter-American Development Bank was established in Washington, DC to provide development financing for Latin America and the Caribbean. In 1964, the African Development Bank was established in Abidjan in the Ivory Coast. And in 1966, there was an agreement to create the Asian Development Bank with headquarters in Manila.

On the eve of ADB's establishment, the economies of developing Asia were at differing stages of development, depending on local circumstances and the policies pursued by their leaders. Nevertheless, in the early 1960s, they had much in common: the influence of colonial legacies, common ambitions for prosperity, and a similar set of broad economic concerns. At this point, they entered into formal discussions about the formation of a regional development bank—in and for Asia.

CHAPTER 3
Beginnings (Until 1966)

Establishing the Bank

"The establishment of the Asian Development Bank is a great step forward in the economic history of Asia ... The astonishing and inspiring pace with which the establishment of the Bank has been carried through must never be slackened."

– U Nyun, Executive Secretary of the United Nations Economic Commission for Asia and the Far East, ADB Inaugural Meeting, 24 November 1966, Tokyo

Late in 1962, Kaoru Ohashi, a well-regarded economist from a research institute in Tokyo, paid Takeshi Watanabe a visit. Watanabe was then a private financial consultant in Tokyo's Marunouchi district. Ohashi suggested to Watanabe that a small study group be formed to explore the prospect of establishing a regional development bank. Watanabe agreed and, although he could not have known it then, so began one of the first detailed considerations of a proposal that would soon shape the Asian Development Bank (ADB) Charter—which Watanabe would later describe as the Bank's "heartbeat."[1]

Earlier Proposals

The idea of an Asian development bank was not new. As early as 1956, Japanese Finance Minister Hisato Ichimada had suggested to United States (US) Secretary of State John Foster Dulles that development projects could be supported by a new financial institution for Southeast Asia.[2] Dulles merely promised to study the matter.

In 1957, during an overseas visit in Asia, Japanese Prime Minister Nobusuke Kishi announced that Japan intended to sponsor the establishment of a

---

[1] Watanabe, 1977, *Towards a New Asia*, 1–2.
[2] Huang, 1975, *The Asian Development Bank*, 16–17.

regional development fund to provide long-term, low-interest loans to Asian developing countries. The resources would come largely from Japan and other industrial countries such as Australia, Canada, and the US. Upon returning to Tokyo, Kishi handed a detailed prospectus to US Ambassador to Japan Douglas MacArthur II. One Japanese newspaper noted that "... the basic point of the Plan is to draw much dollars from the US and let them be disbursed in Southeast Asia."[3] Kishi's plan also referred to an "Asian Commercial Fund" which would operate along commercial banking principles to provide developing countries with import finance.

But the US government did not warm to the Kishi Plan—or to similar suggestions from other Japanese policy makers—so the proposals did not move ahead. Nevertheless, there was still support in Japan for the principle of financial assistance for development programs in Asia and for new institutions. This broad approach would be a central element of Japanese economic diplomacy in Asia for decades to come.[4]

Outside Japan, other Asian countries had also backed the idea of a regional development bank. In 1959, in Ceylon (later Sri Lanka), Prime Minister Solomon Bandaranaike suggested that an international meeting might be held in Colombo to discuss, among other things, the possibility of establishing such a bank. However, after his assassination in September 1959, the idea was not pursued. In 1962, a Ceylonese banker, C. Loganathan, was asked to contribute a paper to an Asian bankers' seminar and chose as his subject "Regional Economic Cooperation in Asia: A Case for a Development Bank for United Nations Economic Commission for Asia and the Far East (ECAFE) Countries." In the end, the talks in New Delhi, where the paper was scheduled to be presented, were cancelled due to clashes between India and Pakistan.

Asian policy makers had been considering the establishment of a regional bank for a number of reasons. They were committed to economic progress. They believed that Asians should control their own destiny. And they felt that existing international economic institutions were not really attuned to the needs of Asia's developing countries. Toyoo Gyohten, who would become one of the first ADB staff members, recounted his experiences as a Japanese representative in international meetings. In 1964, Japan joined

---

[3] Huang, 1975, *The Asian Development Bank*, 17.
[4] Orr discusses Japan's economic relations with Asia as a major aid donor to the region and notes that one influence on Japanese foreign policy is an emotional commitment to Asia. Orr, 1990, *The Emergence of Japan's Foreign Aid Power*.

the Organisation for Economic Co-operation and Development (OECD), and when the Japanese delegation entered the elegant OECD conference room in Paris, Gyohten observed: "... they would have seen that they were the only delegation whose members were so different, so non-Caucasian."

Gyohten also remembered attending a meeting of international bankers at the Bank for International Settlements (BIS) in Basel. This was a tumultuous time in Asia: the Cultural Revolution was sweeping the PRC and the war in Viet Nam was reaching a critical phase. Gyohten found, however, that the bankers in the BIS had little interest in such events and he thought uneasily that "for those bankers, the world seemed still to end somewhere near the Dardanelles."[5]

Takeshi Watanabe and the Tokyo Study Group

In Tokyo, Ohashi had discussed the idea of a regional bank in a meeting with friends from banking circles and the Ministry of Finance. He was encouraged to develop his plan. He was joined by Makoto Watanabe (no relation to Takeshi), who was then Vice-Director of the International Finance Bureau in the Ministry of Finance. The group decided that they needed another figure with credibility at the highest levels in government and invited Takeshi Watanabe to be their chair.

Watanabe proved an excellent choice. He graduated from Tokyo Imperial University (later renamed the University of Tokyo) in 1930, joined the Ministry of Finance, and went to the United Kingdom to study. After the war, he was appointed Vice-Minister of Finance for International Affairs in 1949 and then a Japanese executive director at the World Bank and the International Monetary Fund (IMF). He was a fair and broad-minded person. After retiring from the government, while working as a private consultant, he had supported education of children whose parents were working abroad. Moreover, he came from a distinguished family with a long career of service in government; his grandfather had been minister of finance and his father had been minister of justice.

The group first met on 6 February 1963 and subsequently once or twice a month.[6] They started with many questions. How would the proposed bank fit with existing multilateral financial institutions? Would it duplicate

---

[5] Gyohten, 2007, *The Future of Asia*, 49.
[6] Watanabe, 1977, *Towards a New Asia*, 1.

the functions of national development banks? Would it compete with the World Bank for the limited funds available for investment in developing countries? Further, would a bank financing less developed countries not come under pressure to lower its lending standards and support projects of doubtful quality? Such questions were not surprising.

To explain the relationship with the development banks, Watanabe drew on his experience at the World Bank. "We felt that the requirements of Asian development were too large to be met solely by the World Bank whose activities in Asia—except in India and Pakistan—were far from adequate. We also agreed that the creation of an institution which would concentrate its efforts specifically on the development of Asia would have the advantage of providing encouragement to the peoples of Asia."[7]

The group considered various possibilities for the bank's operations. Ohashi suggested, for example, that it could be a private commercial bank based in Hong Kong, China. Other members of the group proposed regional development banks to be financed by private capital or funded by bond sales in industrial countries, or supported by governments.[8]

By August 1963, the group had reached sufficient agreement to be able to draft a brief document, *Private Plan for the Establishment of the Asian Development Bank*.[9] The bank would contribute "to the economic development of the Asian region by supplying funds for development and by offering development techniques and other means, with the cooperation of all concerned countries."

The plan was well received by senior Japanese government officials.[10] However, the proposal initially met a cool response in World Bank circles. Watanabe sounded out colleagues in Washington, DC in September 1963 during the World Bank–IMF annual meetings. He was disappointed to find little support. Watanabe returned to Tokyo discouraged. The other members of the Tokyo study group, after listening to him, decided that their idea "seemed rather academic and unreal."[11]

---

[7] Watanabe, 1977, *Towards a New Asia*, 1.
[8] Huang, 1975, *The Asian Development Bank: Diplomacy and Development in Asia*, 21.
[9] The full text is in Watanabe, 1977, *Towards a New Asia*, 2.
[10] Huang notes that one of the main reasons that the idea of establishing an Asian development bank succeeded while other plans for new institutions failed was that because it was a bank and "dealing in a commodity of nearly universal appeal—money." Huang, 1975, *The Asian Development Bank: Diplomacy and Development in Asia*, 112.
[11] Huang, 1975, *The Asian Development Bank: Diplomacy and Development in Asia*, 23.

Help from the United Nations Economic Commission for Asia and the Far East

In fact, the seeds of an idea of an Asian regional bank had been growing elsewhere in Asia as well, notably at ECAFE in Bangkok. As early as 1961, ECAFE invited three Asian experts to study the matter. But ECAFE's "three wise men"—K. B. Lall from India, Luang Thavil Setaphanichkarn from Thailand, and Saburo Okita from Japan—were not convinced an Asian bank was feasible then. They decided instead to support the creation of an Asian development organization modeled along the idea of the OECD in Paris.

A little later, in January 1963, a 28-year-old Thai economist, Paul Sithi-Amnuai had more success. He presented a proposal for an Asian bank during an ECAFE conference on intraregional trade. The meeting's final resolution recommended that high priority be given to the establishment of such a bank.[12] The suggestion was given a pivotal push in March 1963 in Manila at the 19th annual session of ECAFE. Delegates called for accelerated measures for regional economic cooperation for the development of trade and industry and suggested that ECAFE call a meeting of representatives of member and associate member countries of the region.[13] ECAFE Executive Secretary U Nyun quickly welcomed the proposal. He directed his staff to prepare for a high-level meeting later that year (Table 3.1).

Preparatory meetings were held in September and October 1963. These meetings focused on regional cooperation and discussed in detail issues of trade, economic planning, and industrialization. It was recommended that the question of creating an Asian development bank be examined by an expert group with the assistance of the World Bank.

The high-level Ministerial Conference for Asian Economic Cooperation was held in Manila in December 1963. Significantly, the meeting was also the first ministerial-level ECAFE meeting in which participation was confined to Asian governments.[14] The conference did not consider the establishment of an Asian bank in any detail, focusing instead on broader

---

[12] Huang, 1975, *The Asian Development Bank: Diplomacy and Development in Asia*, 28. Later in the year, at the request of ECAFE staff, Paul Sithi-Amnuai prepared a paper on The Case for a Regional Bank for the ECAFE Region—with Special Reference to the Development of Intra-Regional Trade. Wilson, 1987, *A Bank for Half the World*, 5.

[13] Huang, 1975, *The Asian Development Bank: Diplomacy and Development in Asia*, 29–30.

[14] Huang, 1975, *The Asian Development Bank: Diplomacy and Development in Asia*, 32; Krishnamurti discusses the conference in some detail. Krishnamurti, 1977, *The Seeding Days*, 5–11.

Table 3.1: Establishment of ADB—Chronology of Official Meetings

1963	
5–18 Mar, Manila	**ECAFE, 19th Session**
	A resolution recommended the adoption of accelerated measures for regional economic cooperation. ECAFE Executive Secretary U Nyun called for the preparation of a high-level meeting later in the year.
15 Aug–13 Sep, Bangkok	**Working Group of Experts on Regional Economic Cooperation**
	The Expert Group on Regional Cooperation (convened by the ECAFE Executive Secretary) proposed the establishment of an Asian development bank.
21–26 Oct, Bangkok	**Preparatory Meeting for the First Ministerial Conference on Asian Economic Cooperation**
	Ministers from the Asian region met to discuss the expert group's recommendations. It was proposed that another expert group be constituted to study the matter and report its findings to ECAFE.
3–6 Dec, Manila	**First Ministerial Conference for Asian Economic Cooperation**
	Two resolutions were passed: (i) endorsing the establishment of a regional development bank for Asia and (ii) requesting the ECAFE Executive Secretary to undertake the necessary investigations and to recommend the institutional arrangements needed to establish the bank.
1964	
2–17 Mar, Tehran	**ECAFE, 20th Session**
	By February, R. Krishnamurti, Chief of ECAFE's International Trade Division, had organized a panel of experts.[a] ECAFE's 20th session endorsed the establishment of the Asian Development Bank, otherwise to be known as ADB.
20–31 Oct, Bangkok	**Expert Group on ADB**
	Ten members of ECAFE's Working Group of Experts met formally for the first time, including Japan's Takeshi Watanabe. They discussed major issues (purpose and character of ADB, capitalization, membership, etc.). Conclusions of the group were circulated to ECAFE member governments.

continued on next page

Table 3.1 *continued*

1965	
16–29 Mar, Wellington	**ECAFE, 21st Session**
	A resolution was passed requesting the ECAFE Executive Secretary to give top priority to the ADB project and convene a high-level consultative committee of experts to study the matter. The committee was directed to report to the upcoming Second Ministerial Conference on Asian Economic Cooperation.
23 Jun–4 Aug, Bangkok	**Consultative Committee on ADB**
	The nine-member consultative committee held its first meeting on 23 June. The United States and Japan would later announce their planned monetary contribution ($200 million each). The committee then embarked on a tour around the world to solicit support for the project and convince other countries to join.
21 Oct–1 Nov, Bangkok	**Preparatory Committee on ADB**
	A preparatory committee consisting of 31 regional and nonregional countries met and took final decisions on ADB's goals and structures. The ADB Charter was finalized during the meeting.
29 Nov–1 Dec, Manila	**Second Ministerial Conference on Asian Economic Cooperation**
	Membership of countries and the amount of their subscriptions were formalized. After three voting rounds, Manila was selected as the site of the ADB headquarters.
2–4 Dec, Manila	**Conference of Plenipotentiaries on ADB**
	Twenty-two governments signed the Charter during the Manila meeting in December 1965; another nine countries signed before the prescribed deadline of January 1966 (Bangkok meeting). A committee was set up and instructed to "initiate, devise and undertake the necessary steps for the establishment of the Bank, including the preparation for the Inaugural Meeting of the Board of Governors for the Bank."
1966	
28 Jan–21 Nov, Bangkok, Manila, and Tokyo	**Committee on Preparatory Arrangements for the Establishment of ADB**
	The committee met for several days on five occasions. A report was completed in November for submission to the Inaugural Meeting in Tokyo.

continued on next page

Table 3.1 *continued*

24–26 Nov, Tokyo	**Inaugural Meeting of the Board of Governors of ADB**
	Japan's Takeshi Watanabe was unanimously elected President of ADB. A resolution was passed increasing the Bank's authorized capital from its original $1 billion to $1.1 billion. Ten members of the ADB Board of Directors were elected: seven representing regional members and three representing nonregional members.
19 Dec, Manila	**Opening Ceremonies of ADB**
	The Bank commenced operations. Representatives from the Bank's 31 members gathered at the site of the Bank's temporary headquarters for the opening ceremonies.

ECAFE = United Nations Economic Commission for Asia and the Far East.

[a] D. L. Wilks (New Zealand), Kraisri Nimmanahaeminda (Thailand), and Amada Castro (Philippines).

Sources: R. Krishnamurti. 1977. *ADB: The Seeding Days*. Manila: ADB. p. 1; D. T. Yasutomo. 1983. *Japan and the Asian Development Bank*. New York: Praeger. p. 31; P. W. Huang. 1975. *The Asian Development Bank: Diplomacy and Development in Asia*. New York: Vantage Press. pp. 1–109; A. Chalkley. 1977. *Asian Development Bank: A Decade of Progress*. Manila: ADB. pp. 50–53.

issues of regional cooperation. Nevertheless, the broad idea of establishing a bank attracted much attention. As one commentator noted: "nearly every delegate had something to say about the proposal for a regional bank" and "almost everyone considered the idea a good one."[15] The conference supported the setting up of an expert group to consider the suggestion in detail—a proposal formally endorsed in Tehran in March 1964 at the 20th annual session of ECAFE.

By this time, there was broad agreement that such a bank would attract additional funds to the region. Asian capital markets were underdeveloped, while the major financial markets in Europe or North America rarely considered developing countries in Asia as investment opportunities. There was also a strong feeling, especially in countries such as Ceylon, that European and North American development institutions tended to focus on India and other large Asian countries. A new regional bank would therefore help change the picture and improve the way international markets and institutions channeled funds to developing Asia.

There were also other suggestions about what the proposed bank would do. The ECAFE working group took the view that the new bank should

---

[15] Huang, 1975, *The Asian Development Bank*, 33.

emphasize regional trade and liberalization and help coordinate plans for economic development. Some members thought that the new bank should provide trade credit. Others were less enthusiastic, arguing that trade finance was better suited to commercial banks. There was, however, strong support in principle, for financing industrial development—even if, as yet, there were few sound industrial projects. There was similar agreement on the need for infrastructure. Though, given the shortage of well-designed infrastructure projects, it was thought the bank should focus initially on preinvestment activities. It was also suggested that the bank should support agriculture.

Two Streams Merge

Despite mixed opinions, support for the establishment of a new bank continued to grow. The 20th Session of ECAFE in Tehran in March 1964 concluded that an expert group should further consider the idea. The Chief of ECAFE's International Trade Division, R. Krishnamurti, was given the responsibility for selecting the experts. To get Japan's support, he wrote to Saburo Okita, one of ECAFE's "three wise men" tasked in 1961 to study the idea of creating a regional bank. On the question of who would best represent Japan, Okita recommended someone who would be pivotal to the history of ADB: Takeshi Watanabe of the Tokyo study group.

After careful selection, 10 experts met officially for the first time in Bangkok in October 1964. Watanabe had been unaware of the ECAFE interest, but when he was invited to join this expert group, the two streams of thought—from ECAFE and from Japan—came together. Watanabe came from North Asia while other financial experts attended from elsewhere in Asia—including India, Iran, Pakistan, and the Philippines. When the invitation arrived, he said: "At the time I was an independent financial consultant engaged in business such as negotiating bond issues in foreign capital markets. I was completely free to express my own views, having no government status...I was in a relaxed mood and felt no obligation to come to any agreement."[16]

For 2 weeks, the group met in ECAFE headquarters, joined by advisers from the International Finance Corporation and the Inter-American Development Bank. They sifted through the numerous issues and produced the first detailed, semiofficial proposal for a multilateral development bank

---

[16] Watanabe, 1977, *Towards a New Asia*, 5.

for Asia.[17] ECAFE staff were sufficiently encouraged by their progress to suggest that they also draft a formal charter for the bank. Watanabe was more cautious; he felt this would be premature before prospective member governments had been consulted. In the end, the group produced a report agreeable to all participants—and incorporated most of the proposals set out earlier by the Tokyo study group.[18]

The Scope of Membership

The next step was to invite potential member countries to participate in arrangements to establish the bank. But, as is often the case with international discussions, there were differing views about who should be invited. Because the bank would be an Asian institution, one view was that full membership should be limited to Asian countries. Another view—supported by Watanabe—was that it should also include nonregional countries, especially the developed countries in North America and Europe. Such a wider membership would allow the bank to have easier access to major global capital markets—and thus attract additional finance flows to Asia. This would increase the flow of useful ideas and technology to the region while also offering industrial countries a better understanding of Asia's development challenges.

Ultimately, there was strong support for a bank that had a well-defined Asian character but was also outward-looking and multilateral.[19] The plan for the bank would thus have to strike a balance: its shareholding and governance arrangements should strengthen the bank's Asian character but should also be sufficiently inclusive to encourage participation by nonregional members. This inclusiveness reflected a general approach of openness toward the global economy—a path the region's most successful countries would subsequently follow.[20] Indeed, this arrangement was an encouraging early indication of how economic policies would evolve over much of Asia and the Pacific in later decades.

---

[17] Krishnamurti, 1977, *The Seeding Days*, 11–15.
[18] Watanabe, 1977, *Towards a New Asia*, 7.
[19] Watanabe, 1977, *Towards a New Asia*, 7.
[20] The report from the World Bank-supported Commission on Growth and Development, after surveying the experience in 13 countries which grew rapidly for extended periods between 1960 and 2005 (nine of which were in Asia) concluded that "During their periods of fast growth, these 13 economies all made the most of the global economy. This is their most important shared characteristic and the central lesson of this report." World Bank, 2008, *The Growth Report,* 21.

Japan and the United States

The report from the expert group was formally presented to the 21st Annual Session of ECAFE in March 1965 in Wellington, New Zealand. It received an encouraging response. Nearly every Asian nation was enthusiastic about the proposal.[21] ECAFE therefore established a high-level consultative committee to take soundings from potential member governments in Asia and the Pacific and in developed countries outside the region.

Further progress, however, would require support from two major powers—Japan and the US. Japan had already pledged support in principle. At a speech at the Foreign Correspondents' Club of Japan in Tokyo on 16 February 1965, Prime Minister Eisaku Sato had said, "I look forward eagerly to the realization of this project, which is bound to contribute, through economic development, to strengthening the sense of collaboration in Asia." He said that Japan would spare no effort toward the establishment of an Asian development bank.[22]

In the case of the US, things were about to move quickly. At the ECAFE meeting in Wellington, US representatives did not oppose a new bank, but neither could they pledge support.[23,24] Former World Bank President Eugene Black described the US attitude as: "Not 'No,' but not 'Yes.'"[25] Although not ready to commit financial support, the US chief delegate voted in favor of the resolution to establish a consultative committee and said that his delegation was happy to support the Asian development bank resolution.[26] For other delegates, this was encouraging.

Then, in April 1965, US President Lyndon B. Johnson took a series of key steps. On 7 April, in a major policy speech at Johns Hopkins University in Baltimore, he announced a new program of aid for Southeast Asia. To balance the growing US military support for the Government of South Viet Nam, Johnson said that the US was ready to contribute $1 billion toward economic and social development in the region. He also pledged

---

[21] Huang, 1975, *The Asian Development Bank*, 48.
[22] Krishnamurti, 1977, *The Seeding Days*, 21.
[23] Krishnamurti, 1977, *The Seeding Days*, 17.
[24] At the time of the ECAFE meeting in Wellington, talks were taking place within the US administration in Washington, DC to decide whether the US would support the establishment of the new bank. Geyelin discusses the views held by different departments and by President Johnson. Geyelin, 1966, *Lyndon B. Johnson and the World*, 276–283.
[25] Huang, 1975, *The Asian Development Bank*, 47.
[26] Huang, 1975, *The Asian Development Bank*, 48.

support for stronger regional cooperation: "We would hope that North Viet Nam would take its place in the common effort just as soon as peaceful cooperation is possible."[27] Johnson subsequently nominated Eugene Black as the head of the US team to carry the effort forward.

In his Baltimore speech, Johnson made no reference to an Asian development bank. However, during the next few weeks Eugene Black had discussions with UN officials who explained the ECAFE proposal. Black attended a meeting of the ECAFE committee and reported back to Johnson that an Asian development bank would fit with his broader program of assistance to Asia. On 20 April, Johnson said:

> I have had a good talk with Mr. Eugene Black on our efforts to assist in the economic progress of Southeast Asia. He has given me an encouraging report on the discussions which he had in New York with the Secretary General and other leaders in the UN.
>
> Mr. Black tells me that those discussions strongly support our view that this is centrally a matter for Asian leadership. Our hope is to act in cooperative support of the efforts of the Asian peoples themselves.
>
> Mr. Black has also discussed with me the project for an Asian Development Bank. He reports that after discussions both in New York and Washington, he finds agreement within this Government that under appropriate conditions and with sound management such a bank would be of considerable value in promoting regional development in Asia. I agree with this position and believe that the United States would wish to participate if such a bank can be established.[28]

With this statement, the US joined Japan in declaring support for the establishment of ADB.

Serious Preparations

For the members of the proposed consultative committee, it was as if a logjam had broken. The idea of establishing an Asian development bank was no longer a dream: it was now a real proposal. A flurry of preparations

---

[27] Krishnamurti, 1977, *The Seeding Days*, 22.
[28] Johnson, 1965, *Statement by the President*.

immediately got under way. When the nine-member consultative committee met for the first time in Bangkok in late June 1965, they would be contributing to an important part of ADB's history. Watanabe attended, this time with full official status as a Counselor of the Government of Japan.[29] One of the junior staff members accompanying him, Tadao Chino, would 30 years later become the seventh ADB President in 1999. Black attended as a special envoy of the US President.

Cornelio Balmaceda from the Philippines, who would play a central role in supporting the formation of ADB during the preparatory period, served as the committee's chair.[30] Masao Fujioka, another assistant to Watanabe who would later become the fourth President of ADB, recounted in his diary: "I can't think of the hardship associated with the establishment of the ADB without thinking about Mr. Balmaceda ... there is no denying that the ADB owes a lot to him."[31] Other members of the consultative committee included important future staff members of the Bank: C. S. Krishna Moorthi from India and Douglas Gunesekera from Ceylon, who would later become the first ADB Vice-President and Secretary, respectively.

On the second day of the meeting, Watanabe announced that the Government of Japan was prepared to subscribe $200 million as capital. A few days later, Black too pledged strong support, saying that the US was also ready to subscribe $200 million or 20% of the envisaged initial capital. In addition, Black said that the US would contribute $100 million to a special fund for the bank's concessional work. As things turned out, the US Congress later approved the proposed capital subscription but not the grant for concessional funds. Nevertheless, the pledges from Japan and the US got the detailed preparations for the bank off to a strong start.

The consultative committee then considered various organizational issues so that potential members would know what they were signing up to. They also planned meetings with national representatives. All of this was working toward a high-level preparatory conference in October 1965, just 4 months away. This work required intense, careful diplomacy that respected the opinions of each country and took into account their financial and economic interests. Members of the consultative committee visited many Asian countries. They also considered which nonregional

---

[29] Watanabe, 1977, *Towards a New Asia*, 8.
[30] Balmaceda played a major role in persuading Asian countries that the headquarters of ADB should be in the Philippines. Gozum, 2013, A Legacy of Honor, Chapter 17.
[31] Fujioka, 1986, *ADB President's Diary: Return to Manila*.

countries to visit, as well as deciding on those that might be visited later. The committee was keen to invite socialist countries such as the Soviet Union and Czechoslovakia to join as well, so in July 1965 a team visited Moscow.[32]

Prospective country members asked detailed questions about how the bank would operate. It was inevitable that many matters would have to be left to subsequent meetings. At this stage, prospective members could therefore express interest in membership while not committing themselves. In the end, the Soviet Union and Czechoslovakia did not join, nor did Iran, which had taken an active part in the early preparations.

Drafting the Charter

The consultative committee prepared a report. A charter that defined the relationship between the leadership of the bank and its member countries was drafted; it set down the rules for governance and management. The charter benefited from Chino's pioneering labors and from the inputs of the Tokyo study group before him. However, it was a Filipino lawyer, Florentino P. Feliciano, who would weave the ideas together, drafting and redrafting the charter's provisions, based on diverse country opinions and drawing from the experience of other institutions such as the World Bank.[33, 34]

The ECAFE Secretariat invited all its regional and nonregional members to the high-level preparatory committee, as well as a number of non-ECAFE developed countries. It circulated the draft charter in advance and gathered initial responses.

In October 1965, the high-level preparatory committee met in Bangkok for 10 days of intensive negotiations. As one observer noted: "The meeting of the preparatory committee was, in some ways, to be the most crucial of the conferences concerned with the Asian Development Bank's establishment. At this meeting, final decisions on the Bank's goals and structure would be made, and its charter put into finished form—all this only after every implication had been subjected to the hard, purposeful scrutiny of all interested parties."[35] Nevertheless, K. Farmanfarmaian from Iran ("a

---

[32] Krishnamurti, 1977, *The Seeding Days*, 51–53.
[33] Wilson, 1987, *A Bank for Half the World*, 16.
[34] Krishnamurti, 1977, *The Seeding Days*, 29.
[35] Huang, 1975, *The Asian Development Bank*, 82.

lively character who claimed he had 40 brothers and sisters"[36]) headed the discussions involving over 100 delegates from 31 countries with "great efficiency, fairness, skill, expedition and charm."[37]

The preparatory committee had three main tasks. First, to prepare the bank's legal instrument—the Charter. Second, to determine the conditions that needed to be met for the Charter to come into force—such as capital subscriptions and ratification arrangements. Third, to prepare a program for establishing the new institution.

The committee's work proceeded smoothly. After considerable debate, the delegates settled everything by consensus.

The Charter provides that, as in other multilateral development banks, the Board of Governors (usually ministers of finance or development, or governors of central banks) representing each member has the ultimate power over the management and affairs of the Bank. The Board of Governors shall have annual meetings and, when necessary, vote in person or through communication. The Board of Directors (10 members in the beginning and 12 since 1971) is resident in the Headquarters, and exercises powers assigned expressly by the Charter or delegated to it by the Board of Governors. The voting power for each member is assigned according to the shares of capital held by it, but in order to give more voting power to smaller economies, 20% of the total votes are allocated equally among members as "basic votes."

ECAFE had wished for a legal relationship with ADB. However, this idea was rejected because delegates preferred to maintain the full independence of the Bank's operations. They also agreed that the new institution would be a development bank (not a commercial or export finance bank or an aid agency) and that it would promote investment and projects in developing countries in Asia. In addition, it would support broader activities such as regional cooperation.

These objectives were spelled out in the preamble and the first articles of the Charter of the Bank (Box 3.1). The Charter specified that ADB should have "… regard to the needs of the smaller or less developed member countries in the region." The Charter also provided, in Article 2, wide flexibility for the Bank to design further programs as the institution grew: "to undertake

---

[36] Watanabe, 1977, *Towards a New Asia*, 13.
[37] Krishnamurti, 1977, *The Seeding Days*, 29.

Box 3.1: Agreement Establishing the Asian Development Bank (The Charter)

Article 1: Purpose

The purpose of the Bank shall be to foster economic growth and co-operation in the region of Asia and the Far East (hereinafter referred to as the "region") and to contribute to the acceleration of the process of economic development of the developing member countries in the region, collectively and individually. [...]

Article 2: Functions

To fulfill its purpose, the Bank shall have the following functions:

(i) to promote investment in the region of public and private capital for development purposes;

(ii) to utilize the resources at its disposal for financing development of the developing member countries in the region, giving priority to those regional, sub-regional as well as national projects and programmes which will contribute most effectively to the harmonious economic growth of the region as a whole, and having special regard to the needs of the smaller or less developed member countries in the region;

(iii) to meet requests from members in the region to assist them in the coordination of their development policies and plans with a view to achieving better utilization of their resources, making their economies more complementary, and promoting the orderly expansion of their foreign trade, in particular, intra-regional trade;

(iv) to provide technical assistance for the preparation, financing and execution of development projects and programmes, including the formulation of specific project proposals;

(v) to co-operate, in such manner as the Bank may deem appropriate, within the terms of this Agreement, with the United Nations ... and with public international organizations and other international institutions, as well as national entities whether public or private, which are concerned with the investment of development funds in the region ...; and

(vi) to undertake such other activities and provide such other services as may advance its purpose.

Source: Extracts from ADB. 1966. *Agreement Establishing the Asian Development Bank*. Manila.

such other activities and provide such other services as may advance its purpose."

The preparatory committee also considered the issue of membership using ECAFE's classification of regional and nonregional countries. There were suggestions to include other non-ECAFE countries such as Israel, Kuwait, and Saudi Arabia, all of whom had expressed interest. Such a wider membership was firmly opposed by a number of Asian countries, which wanted to guarantee that the Bank would be, as specified in the preamble to the Charter, "Asian in its basic character." When Australia; the United Kingdom; the US; and Taipei,China unexpectedly raised the issue again, the preparatory committee agreed that membership would be open to "other regional countries and nonregional developed countries."[38]

The Charter also aimed to ensure that the new bank would be a sound financial institution that followed prudent policies for raising and investing funds. It therefore specified the Bank's borrowing procedures as well as its operating principles for lending. It was agreed, for example, that loan proposals would be submitted to the Board of Directors and that approvals would take into account the situation of borrowing countries.

Two of the most difficult issues concerned the composition of the Board of Directors and the way that votes would be allocated between member countries.[39] Smaller Asian countries wanted to ensure that the Bank would not be controlled by a few larger countries. In the end, the preparatory committee was unable to come to an agreement on this. It was decided, instead, to make provision for further discussions while setting out an initial arrangement that would enable the Bank to be established without delay. These two issues would be solved by the time of the Inaugural Meeting held in November 1966 in Tokyo.

Considering the complexity of the issues and the potential for sharp differences, the preparatory committee achieved a great deal. In just 10 days, it considered, negotiated, and unanimously accepted the entire text of the Charter. As one author observed, the process was a remarkable testimony "to the firm determination of the regional and nonregional governments to finalize the draft agreement."[40] At the end of the meeting, only two more steps remained: a second ministerial conference and a special conference of plenipotentiaries.

---

[38] Krishnamurti, 1977, *The Seeding Days*, 48.
[39] Krishnamurti, 1977, *The Seeding Days*, 64, 75.
[40] Krishnamurti, 1977, *The Seeding Days*, 29.

Headquarters of the Bank

The Government of the Philippines had taken a close interest in the plans and had offered to sponsor the second ministerial conference. The conference was held in style in Manila in November 1965 with the opening address delivered by the President of the Philippines, Diosdado Macapagal.

The conference needed to agree on remaining issues about membership and capital subscriptions—and also choose the Bank's location. Japan hoped that the ADB offices would be in Tokyo. However, eight other cities had also expressed an interest: Bangkok, Colombo, Kabul, Kuala Lumpur, Manila, Phnom Penh, Singapore, and Tehran. The Philippines had presented a strong case for Manila so, as the delegates started to consider the issue, the outcome was far from clear.

As a first step, it was decided that 18 prospective regional members (not including Indonesia which had not yet become a signatory to the Charter) would choose the location of the headquarters. ECAFE Executive Secretary U Nyun suggested that the issue be settled in an "Asian way" by consensus.[41] But it quickly became clear that there was no consensus; there would need to be a formal vote. In any case, the Philippines delegates, who had worked hard to take advantage of the fact that the meeting was in Manila, did not necessarily favor a consensus decision. From the start of the conference, they had lobbied each country delegation. With characteristic Filipino enthusiasm, they had even arranged for a large sign to be erected over the land they were offering for the bank which confidently declared that the site was the "Permanent Site of the Asian Development Bank."

The first round of voting was held on 30 November in a small room in the Department of Foreign Affairs. The atmosphere was tense.[42] Colombo and Kabul withdrew from the list, and Phnom Penh had not supplied the required background information. This left six contenders. Delegation leaders wrote their choices on ballot slips and dropped them into a hat held by U Nyun who walked from one to the other.

The results, which came within a few minutes, were unexpected. Japan had hoped to win in the first round, but found it had only eight votes, one short of a majority. Iran had four votes; the Philippines three; and Thailand, Malaysia, and Singapore one each. The countries with only one

---

[41] Huang, 1975, *The Asian Development Bank*, 94.
[42] Details are drawn from Huang (1975, pp. 94–97) and Wilson (1987, pp. 17–20).

vote gracefully withdrew. U Nyun announced that he would conduct a second ballot the following morning, giving delegates from the remaining three cities—Manila, Tehran, and Tokyo—an opportunity to gather further support overnight. The delegates then enjoyed an evening of lively entertainment—until almost 2 a.m.—on board the S. S. Roxas, one of the presidential yachts. The incoming President of the Philippines, Ferdinand Marcos, stayed up until 4 a.m. to lend his support for Manila and keep in touch with wavering delegates.[43]

The next day, around noon on 1 December, the delegates again gathered for a vote. Once again, U Nyun collected the votes. Again, no country had a majority. Surprisingly, however, Japan still had only eight votes, while the Philippines now had six. Iran had four and retired from the contest. U Nyun announced that the final ballot would be held after lunch. The third vote delivered a swift result. Japan still had only eight votes. The Philippines had gained support from three more delegates to reach nine votes, and there was one abstention. "Manila wins," U Nyun ruled. To the surprise of many delegates, it was thus decided that the headquarters of ADB would be in one of the region's developing countries.

The Japanese delegates were mystified and deeply disappointed. Watanabe later said: "I felt as if the child I had so carefully reared had been taken away to a distant country."[44] But the Government of Japan had pledged support to the bank and accepted the decision. A few days later, when the leader of the Japanese delegation, Aiichiro Fujiyama, signed the Articles of Agreement to Establish the Asian Development Bank there was loud applause. The Government of the Philippines, in the meantime, moved quickly to show that it was ready to begin work on the headquarters. On 3 December, the government held a ceremony to lay the cornerstone of the new building.

As it turned out, over the succeeding years it became clear that the choice of Manila as the headquarters of the Bank had many advantages. In 2016, at the year-end cocktails to commemorate ADB's 50th anniversary, President Nakao said to staff and Board members: "It was a good decision. Manila has brought ADB closer to its developing member countries. ADB has benefited from warm hospitality of the Philippines' people and a strong pool of English-speaking professionals to draw on."

---

[43] Wilson, 1987, *A Bank for Half the World*, 20.
[44] Watanabe, 1977, *Towards a New Asia*, 16.

Table 3.2: First Signatories of the Articles of Agreement

Date Signed	Member
4 Dec 1965	Afghanistan; Australia; Cambodia; Canada; Ceylon (later Sri Lanka); West Germany (later Germany); India; Iran; Japan; Republic of Korea; Laos (later Lao People's Democratic Republic); Malaysia; Nepal; Netherlands; New Zealand; Pakistan; Philippines; Western Samoa (later Samoa); Taipei,China; Thailand; United Kingdom; United States
28 Jan 1966	Denmark, Finland, Norway, Viet Nam, Singapore
31 Jan 1966	Austria, Belgium, Italy, Sweden

Source: R. Krishnamurti. 1977. *ADB: The Seeding Days.* Manila: ADB. p. 32.

The ministerial conference was, in effect, extended to become a Conference of Plenipotentiaries to establish the Bank. The delegates needed to be accredited as plenipotentiaries with full legal powers to sign documents on behalf of their governments. On 4 December 1965, representatives of 22 economies signed the Articles of Agreement, which would remain open for further signatures until the end of the following month. Nine more governments would sign to meet this deadline (Table 3.2). To carry on the detailed work needed throughout 1966 to form the Bank, the conference appointed a committee on preparatory arrangements.

By the end of September 1966, these economies, except for Iran, would become the first members of ADB. Indonesia would become the 31st member during the Inaugural Meeting of the Board of Governors in Tokyo in November 1966. There were 19 regional members and 12 nonregional members.

Iran was the exception. After initially indicating strong support for the establishment of the Bank, it lost interest. Iran participated actively in the meetings leading up to the formation of ADB in 1965. But when it became clear that there was little support for locating the headquarters of the Bank in Tehran or in appointing an Iranian as President, enthusiasm from Iran waned. Iran allowed its plan for membership to lapse and did not attend the Inaugural Meeting in Tokyo.[45]

---

[45] Wilson, 1987, *A Bank for Half the World*, 25.

The First President

Intensive work was needed during 1966 to prepare for the opening of the Bank. High on the agenda was the choice of the first President. Watanabe was reluctant to be nominated but when he returned to Tokyo, Prime Minister Sato asked him to be a candidate. Watanabe initially declined, but the pressure continued and came from other countries, including Germany, the Republic of Korea, and the US. Eventually, Watanabe relented and let Prime Minister Sato know that he was prepared to be nominated. Later that year, he visited the US and Mexico to attend meetings of the World Bank and the Inter-American Development Bank to gather information about how they were run.

The Inaugural Meeting of ADB was to be held in Japan at the end of 1966. As the time approached, Watanabe's daily schedule increasingly resembled that of the head of a major international organization. As word spread that he was likely to be the first President, many people wanted to meet him—some to express interest in working in the Bank; others to explore business opportunities.

The Inaugural Meeting took place on 24 November 1966 at the Tokyo Prince Hotel. It was addressed by Prime Minister Sato and other senior figures, including Japanese Finance Minister Takeo Fukuda and ECAFE Executive Secretary U Nyun. When the time came to select a President, Takeo Fukuda, who chaired the meeting, called for nominations. Finance Minister of Thailand Serm Vinicchayakul nominated Watanabe.[46] After a pause, it became clear that there were no other candidates. Fukuda continued: "In the absence of any other nominations, I have great pleasure in declaring Mr. Takeshi Watanabe duly elected President of the Asian Development Bank."[47]

The characteristics of the new bank—the culture, the relationship with member countries, and the approach to operations—would only evolve over time. But Watanabe was to set the direction, even in his first remarks. After taking the rostrum to accept the presidency, he addressed the ADB Board of Governors and outlined his priorities. He mentioned the importance of recruiting competent staff and said the two main objectives must be to mobilize as much capital as possible and use it effectively.

---

[46] The nomination speech is in the Summary of Proceedings of the Meeting. ADB, 1967, *Inaugural Meeting*, 92.
[47] ADB, 1967, *Inaugural Meeting*, 81.

Table 3.3: Board of Directors and Voting Groups, 1966

Director	Members Represented
Cornelio Balmaceda	Philippines, Pakistan
Byung Kyu Chun	Republic of Korea; Taipei,China; Viet Nam
Masaru Fukuda	Japan
J. M. Garland	Australia
Kam-Poh Ng	Malaysia, New Zealand, Singapore, Thailand, Western Samoa
P. V. R. Rao	India
Byanti Kharmawan	Indonesia, Afghanistan, Cambodia, Ceylon, Laos, Nepal
Helmut Abramowski	Austria, Belgium, West Germany, Italy, Netherlands
W. K. Wardroper	Canada, Denmark, Finland, Norway, Sweden, United Kingdom
Bernard Zagorin	United States

Source: ADB. 1967. *Inaugural Meeting of the Board of Governors, Tokyo, 24–26 November 1966*. Manila. p. 3.

In addition, to guide him on his leadership "and the breathtaking challenge it affords,"[48] 10 directors would be elected by the Board of Governors on Watanabe's second day as President (Table 3.3).

Watanabe would expand on his ideas in the months to come, emphasizing the need for sound internal management, the importance of careful project preparation, and the need for ADB to serve developing member countries effectively through such activities as support for regional cooperation. With these thoughts in mind—and the dream of a regional bank now a firm reality—the first President of the new Asian Development Bank made plans to travel to the Philippines in mid-December 1966 to begin his work.

---

[48] Watanabe, 1977, *Towards a New Asia*, 20.

CHAPTER 4
First Decade (1967–1976)

Asia: Building Momentum and Facing Shocks

"We are studying the problems that would seem to be of greatest importance to the countries of Southeast Asia in the 1970s. What will be the effects of the so-called 'green revolution'? ... What will be the effects of the pressures of population? ... What will be the causes of further industrial development in the region?"

– *Takeshi Watanabe,*
Address to the ADB Annual Meeting, 1970

When the Asian Development Bank (ADB) began operations in late 1966, several key Asian countries had already adopted post-World War II structural transformation programs. In these countries, output and employment were shifting away from agriculture into industry and services. Earlier, Japan had led the way and was now being followed, reflecting the flying geese paradigm, by four East Asian economies: Hong Kong, China; the Republic of Korea; Singapore; and Taipei,China. Structural reform in these economies involved increasing domestic investment, boosting levels of education and skills, and promoting labor-intensive manufactured exports. By the mid-1970s, similar shifts were under way in Indonesia, Malaysia, and Thailand.

For most Asian governments, a primary concern in the mid-1960s was feeding their people (Chapter 2). The more successful economies, however, had showed that a prerequisite for structural transformation was often a highly productive agriculture sector. Among Asian "monsoon economies"— economies in Asia characterized by a distinct rainfall pattern—some developed more rapidly than others.[1] For the winners, rural development had been an integral part of the structural changes as it stimulated both off-season and off-farm economic activities. These activities helped absorb surplus labor, generated surpluses for investment in other sectors,

---

[1] The monsoon belt runs through Japan and the Republic of Korea in the North, the PRC and Southeast Asia, across the Indian Ocean, and through southern India and Pakistan. The rainy season (brought about by the monsoon winds) lasts for about 4–5 months, before the dry season ensues. This had profound effects on the economic activity of monsoon Asia and nurtured the seasonality of demand for labor for thousands of years.

and strengthened domestic demand to support overall economic growth. As will be seen in the next chapter, much of the Bank's work during the first ADB decade gave special attention to agricultural development along with financing industrial projects.

From 1967 to 1976, the drive for industrialization and development in developing Asia would be jolted by a series of shocks. Some were political and regional, such as the widening conflict in the Mekong area. Others were economic and global: in 1971, the postwar Bretton Woods international monetary system began to break down, and in 1973 the first oil shock threatened energy and food security and ushered in a long period of stagflation—economic stagnation combined with inflation—in industrial countries. These events would serve to underscore the resilience of developing countries in Asia in a changeable global environment. ADB, too, would be encouraged to reassess the strategic priorities it had pursued during the first 10 years of its operations.

Strengthening Agriculture

In the mid-1960s Asian developing economies continued to rely heavily on agriculture, which often provided employment for more than half of the labor force. However, rather than being market-oriented, most of the activities in agriculture involved village-level subsistence production that provided inadequate food supplies and low incomes. Asia in the 1960s had widespread poverty and high population growth rates, conditions which frequently led to social and political tension.[2] It was apparent that strengthening agriculture was necessary to ensure greater food security and stability. In 1965 and 1966, the impetus for greater food production would be bolstered by a marked fall in rice output in many Asian countries and a resulting spike in international rice prices. In the late 1960s, a number of Asian governments, therefore, aimed to expand food production and, if possible, achieve self-sufficiency.[3]

At this time, Asia saw the arrival of the Green Revolution, a set of innovative research and technology transfers designed to lift output of food grain production. International organizations such as the World Bank and the United States Agency for International Development, along with the Ford and Rockefeller foundations, provided strong support through the establishment in 1960 of the Philippines-based International Rice Research Institute

---

[2] ADB, 1969, *Asian Agricultural Survey*.
[3] Wihtol, 1988, *The Asian Development Bank and Rural Development*.

(IRRI). IRRI worked on breakthrough programs to develop new varieties of rice including the IR8 "miracle rice" introduced in 1966, just 6 months before ADB was created.

The miracle rice was an immediate success. Over the next decade, numerous countries in developing Asia would adopt modern strains of rice at rates that exceeded even those in developed nations.[4] By the late 1970s, high-yielding varieties would expand to cover over 70% of the rice areas of the Philippines and Sri Lanka, and over half of rural Pakistan and Indonesia.[5] There was similar progress in India introducing new varieties of wheat developed at the International Maize and Wheat Improvement Center in Mexico.

The Green Revolution was, in effect, an immense experiment. It soon became clear that its success would depend on a complex program of interventions, notably the rehabilitation and expansion of irrigation systems and the widespread application of fertilizers and pesticides.[6] These interventions were, however, costly and required the development of new rural credit programs to offer finance to farmers and to suppliers of agricultural inputs. There was also the cost of improving marketing infrastructure to reduce postharvest losses in food storage, transport, and processing.

The various gains from the Green Revolution would become clearer over time. Between 1970 and 1995, cereal yields doubled across developing Asia. Although the population increased by around 60% over this period, average per capita calorie consumption rose almost 25%. More intensive farming also created jobs for landless laborers. And poor families who often spent a large share of their family incomes on food benefited from greater food supplies and lower prices.[7]

Nevertheless, in the early 1970s, before the Green Revolution had taken hold, food shortages remained a pressing concern in many developing countries. Food self-sufficiency was threatened by natural disasters, droughts, pest infestations, and inadequate support for rural services. In 1973, all of this was aggravated by the oil price shock.[8] Later in the 1970s, the focus of agricultural policy began to broaden from increasing food output and achieving self-sufficiency in grain production to the wider goals of

---

[4] Sicat, 2014, *Cesar Virata: Life and Times: Through Four Decades of Philippine Economic History*, 80–84.
[5] James, Naya, and Meier, 1987, *Asian Development*, 169.
[6] Sicat, 2014, *Cesar Virata: Life and Times: Through Four Decades of Philippine Economic History*, 80–84.
[7] Borlaug, 1996, *The Green Revolution*, 9.
[8] James, Naya, and Meier, 1987, *Asian Development*.

promoting rural employment and development. This shift coincided with an increased international emphasis on growth with equity.[9] Wider rural development would depend not just on the technological solutions of the Green Revolution but also on improvements in rural infrastructure, institutions and financing that would support off-season, nonfood, and off-farm economic activities. Better rural infrastructure included large irrigation systems and roads as well as the development of communications systems, power supplies, and health and educational facilities.[10]

During this period, policy makers, especially in Asia's monsoon economies in Southeast Asia and South Asia, became increasingly aware that national development required boosting agricultural production and rural incomes so as to sustain vibrant rural economies. They looked at the earlier success stories of Japan; the Republic of Korea; and Taipei,China in the agriculture sector. In monsoon economies, seasonal winds brought heavy rain during half of the year but little rain during the other half. For thousands of years, this feature of the region made Asia's agriculture systems highly labor-intensive.

These characteristics of monsoon economies also encouraged high population growth because farming families with more children meant more help in paddy farms during the rainy season. There were also implications for off-farm employment because employers were reluctant to hire unskilled personnel during the dry season knowing that they would leave to return to nearby farm work during the next wet season. In the case of Japan; the Republic of Korea; and Taipei,China, the cycle of rural poverty had been broken by enhancing agricultural productivity and promoting agriculture-led industrialization. This process, aided by support for skills development and vocational training, had provided important opportunities for increases in income in rural areas.

The Drive for Industrialization

The shift from agriculture to industry and services which had happened earlier in Japan was followed by similar changes in the Republic of Korea and Taipei,China (Table 4.1). (The economies in Singapore and Hong Kong, China, in contrast, were not reliant on agriculture to begin with.) The Republic of Korea and Taipei,China illustrated that boosting agricultural productivity and developing the industry sector needed to go hand in hand. A productive agriculture sector not only provided increased food supplies but also supplied raw materials for agro-industry exports.

---

[9] Wihtol, 1988, *The Asian Development Bank and Rural Development*, 58.
[10] ADB, 1979, *Sector Paper on Agricultural and Rural Development*.

Table 4.1: Structure of Production in Selected Economies, 1960–1985
(% of GDP)

Economies	Agriculture			Industry			Services		
	1960	1970	1985	1960	1970	1985	1960	1970	1985
Japan[a]	13	6	3	45	47	41	43	47	56
NIEs									
Hong Kong, China[a]	4	2	1	38	37	30	55	56	68
Korea, Republic of	37	27	14	20	30	41	43	44	45
Singapore	4	2	1	18	30	38	79	68	61
Taipei,China	29	16	6	29	41	50	43	45	44
ASEAN-4									
Indonesia	54	47	25	14	18	36	32	35	39
Malaysia	36	31	20	18	25	37	46	44	43
Philippines	26	28	27	28	30	33	46	43	40
Thailand	40	28	17	19	25	30	42	46	53
South Asia									
Bangladesh	58	55	48	7	9	15	36	37	37
Myanmar	33	38	48	12	14	13	55	48	39
India[a]	47	43	35	19	20	27	28	28	28
Nepal[b]	...	68	58	...	11	14	...	21	27
Pakistan	44	33	25	15	20	28	36	37	47
Sri Lanka	32	27	24	20	23	27	48	46	50

... = not available, ASEAN = Association of Southeast Asian Nations, GDP = gross domestic product, NIE = newly industrialized economy.
[a] Figures for 1985 are from nearest year available—1984.
[b] Figures for 1985 are from nearest year available—1983
Source: Adapted from James, Naya, and Meier. 1987. *Asian Development.* p. 12.

These transformations were achieved first by technological innovations that allowed for multiple cropping and dry season cultivation that enabled full employment in the rural areas. With year-long employment, farmers had more income that they could use to purchase urban goods and services. In addition, farmers invested in additional agricultural equipment which, in turn, led to higher productivity per worker. The higher incomes were then reflected in rising food consumption, savings, and further investment in both physical and social capital.

At the same time, the export pessimism and protectionist policies of the 1950s were replaced by a growing interest in market-oriented policies. In the 1960s, there was a shift toward the mass production of simple manufactured items, particularly for export.[11] The newly industrialized economies (NIEs)—Hong Kong, China; the Republic of Korea; Singapore; and Taipei,China—realized that their industry sectors were constrained by their limited domestic markets. Moreover, with few natural resources of their own, they had little choice but to increase exports to import the resources they needed. To make better use of capital and become globally competitive, they invested in new technologies and developed trained, highly flexible, and low-cost labor forces.[12] In the Republic of Korea and Taipei,China, the industry sector completely absorbed the annual rise in the labor force and also drew labor from other sectors.[13]

The success of the NIEs was not due to the invisible hand of the market alone. In the 1960s, governments in these economies often intervened to promote labor-intensive manufacturing. They also played a crucial part in promoting human resources policies and in encouraging entrepreneurs. In subsequent decades, from around the mid-1970s, further structural change took place as output in capital- and technology-intensive sectors, such as automobiles, aircraft, and electronics, expanded rapidly.[14]

In contrast, the transition to industrialization did not proceed as smoothly in the monsoon economies in South Asia and in some parts of Southeast Asia. These countries found it difficult to achieve full rural employment. This was mostly due to a bias against agriculture. In the 1950s, many policy makers had misguidedly believed that manufacturing was "uniquely capable of providing the dynamic force for economic development" and adopted pro-manufacturing protectionist policies.[15] The Philippines, for example, restricted imports and applied tariffs to protect domestic industries,[16] as did Thailand. A prolonged period of import substitution policies reduced incentives for entrepreneurs to boost productivity and become internationally competitive. In fact, these countries also had limited scope for import substitution because there were only small domestic markets for manufactured goods. In addition, manufacturing firms found it difficult to pay for the imports they needed because of a scarcity of foreign exchange.[17]

Throughout the 1970s, exports of both agricultural and mineral primary commodities continued to account for a large share of the exports of

---

[11] ADB, 1971, *Southeast Asia's Economy in the 1970s*, Part One.
[12] Oshima, 1993, *Strategic Processes in Monsoon Asia's Economic Development*, 1–16.
[13] James, Naya, and Meier, 1988, Executive Summary: *Asian Development*, 8.
[14] James, Naya, and Meier, 1987, *Asian Development*.
[15] ADB, 1971, *Southeast Asia's Economy in the 1970s*, Part One.
[16] Sicat, 2014, *Cesar Virata: Life and Times,* 126–133.
[17] Myint, 1972, *Southeast Asia's Economy,* 62.

resource-rich countries in Southeast Asia such as Indonesia, Malaysia, the Philippines, and Thailand. In some cases, this emphasis on resources reflected colonial legacies. However, by the 1970s, it was becoming increasingly apparent that relying heavily on primary commodities to provide exports had its drawbacks. Interest groups were able to exploit the situation for rent-seeking behavior and, in addition, the extractive enterprises provided limited job opportunities. Further, the ability to generate exports from natural resources sometimes reduced the incentive for policy makers to develop labor-intensive manufactured exports.[18] In Indonesia, the Philippines, and Thailand, employment in manufacturing grew less than 5% annually in the 1970s.[19]

As a result, the industry sector in Southeast Asia was unable to absorb urban nor rural surplus labor. However, in the mid-1970s, learning from their East Asian neighbors, the Philippines and Thailand aimed to increase manufactured exports by relaxing export controls and abolishing export taxes—although keeping the incentives for capital-intensive industrial activities. Malaysia had much success in creating industrial jobs by creating free trade zones. By the 1980s, as wages rose in the NIEs and they lost their comparative advantage in unskilled labor-intensive goods, the prospects for more advanced manufactured exports became increasingly encouraging.[20]

South Asia, however, from the 1950s into the 1970s remained toward the back of the flying geese flock. For over two decades, development in much of the subcontinent was hindered by inward-looking and autarkic industrial policies. In India, for example, economic strategies leaned toward large-scale capital- and technology-intensive investments which failed to generate significant employment. Southeast Asia had had similar policies, but the consequences were worse in South Asia because many of the large state-owned corporations were given preferential treatment though they performed poorly. Progress was also held back by distorted prices and burdensome bureaucratic inefficiencies. These policies discouraged foreign capital inflow and hampered international competitiveness. It would not be until the 1980s that some South Asian countries, particularly India and Sri Lanka, would put more emphasis on market-based economic growth and become more open to international markets.[21]

Between 1967 and 1976, various Asian countries continued to explore opportunities for regional cooperation in the hope that joint industrial

---

[18] James, Naya, and Meier, 1988, Executive Summary: *Asian Development*, 46–47.
[19] James, Naya, and Meier, 1988, Executive Summary: *Asian Development*, 5–29.
[20] James, Naya, and Meier, 1988, Executive Summary: *Asian Development*.
[21] James, Naya, and Meier, 1988, Executive Summary: *Asian Development*.

projects would enable them to achieve economies of scale and help them compete successfully in world markets.[22] Later, the same approach would be invoked as part of the program of regional cooperation of the Association of Southeast Asian Nations (ASEAN).

Coping with Economic Shocks

The development performance of countries in Asia was partly influenced by the initial conditions they faced at the end of World War II and the colonial era. But more important was their choice of policies. Across the region, one common ingredient of success was economic policies. The countries that have performed well in the past 50 years are those that have adapted flexibly to sharp changes in international economic conditions.

One major test of Asia's resilience in the postwar period occurred in the early 1970s when plans for industrialization had to accommodate major changes in the global economic environment. First, in 1971, the Bretton Woods system of international monetary management began to break down. A period of global economic instability occurred following the announcement by President Richard Nixon in August 1971 that the United States would no longer support the direct convertibility of the US dollar into gold. The Smithsonian exchange rate arrangements, agreed to in December 1971, caused many Asian economies to falter—particularly those whose external reserves were in currencies which subsequently depreciated.[23]

Two years later, a second event—the first oil crisis—would lead to even greater changes across Asia. In late 1973, political tensions in the Middle East led to sharp increases in the world price of oil. During the next few years, the surge in oil prices triggered sharp inflation in the industrial world followed quickly by recession. Industrial countries soon became more protectionist and less willing to support international aid programs, leaving fewer resources available for developing countries and for replenishments for multilateral banks such as ADB. Within a few years, industrial countries moved into the uncharted policy waters of stagflation. For the rest of the 1970s, Asian policy makers would struggle to respond to this unfamiliar economic environment.

The 1973–1974 oil shock served to divide developing countries in Asia into two groups. Oil-importing countries (such as India and the Philippines) were hard hit, while oil-exporting ones (such as Brunei Darussalam,

---

[22] Krishnamurti, 1977, *The Seeding Days*, 3.
[23] Wilson, 1987, *A Bank for Half the World*, 57.

Malaysia, and Indonesia) benefited. But the change in oil prices was so sudden that both groups found it hard to adjust. Oil-importing countries suffered not just from the rising prices of energy but also from increases in the prices of oil-based inorganic fertilizers, affecting food security. At the same time, the recession in industrial countries reduced the demand for Asia's exports and some countries suffered a rapid deterioration in their balance-of-payments. External debt rose and unemployment increased. Oil importers responded by temporarily cutting overall demand to curb the domestic use of oil and other forms of energy.

An immediate effect of the first oil crisis was to redistribute income from oil-importing countries to those who were members of the Organization of the Petroleum Exporting Countries (OPEC). OPEC countries soon had large increases in export revenues which they wished to invest overseas. This provided an opportunity for international financial institutions such as ADB to create arrangements for recycling petrodollars back to Asia.

The new economic environment was also difficult for Asia's oil-exporting countries. They had an unexpected windfall from rising export receipts but nevertheless needed to find ways to use these funds effectively. On the whole, they used their oil revenues more productively than some countries in Africa and Latin America—by increasing spending on rural development, infrastructure, and industrial development.

Across Asia, these rapid economic changes hit poor communities hard. This directed attention to the issue of poverty. Later in the decade, international development thinking began to focus on meeting "basic human needs" such as food, clothing, and shelter. By the mid-1970s, Asian governments were increasingly recognizing the plight of the rural and urban poor and the unemployed.

This was the complex environment for the Bank's work during the first ADB decade. The decade began amid the optimism sparked by the Green Revolution; in the first 10 years of operations, ADB would provide loans for agricultural production and rural development and for investment in industry. The Bank also needed to help oil exporters restructure their economies and improve the quality of their public expenditures. In addition, in countries in Indochina—even before the end of the conflict—ADB began to explore opportunities for postconflict development.

The development challenges in Asia in the late 1960s would also pose a major test to Takeshi Watanabe's vision (Chapter 5) of ADB becoming a "family doctor" to developing countries in the region.

United Nations Economic Commission for Asia and the Far East (UN ECAFE) holds a meeting to lay the groundwork for ADB with future ADB President Tadao Chino (*left*), and U Nyun (*standing*), Executive Secretary of the Commission, 19 October 1964.

Consultative Committee of Experts for the Establishment of ADB, Manila, Philippines, 26 November 1965. (*left to right*) Sommai Hoontrakool (Thailand), Anwar Iqbal Qureshi (Pakistan), Nguyen Cao Hach (Viet Nam), (unidentified), (unidentified), ECAFE Executive Secretary U Nyun, Cornelio Balmaceda (Philippines, Chair of the Committee), Takeshi Watanabe (Vice-Chair of the Committee and later ADB President), Khodadad Farmanfarmaian (Iran), (unidentified), C. S. Krishna Moorthi (India, and later ADB's first Vice-President), Douglas Gunesekera (Sri Lanka, and later ADB's first Secretary), (unidentified).

Early support for the creation of a regional development bank came from the UN ECAFE, Wellington, New Zealand, 16–29 March 1965. (Photo courtesy of the United Nations)

Philippine President Diosdado Macapagal lays the foundation for the first ADB headquarters, Manila, Philippines, 3 December 1965.

Inaugural Meeting of the ADB Board of Governors at the Tokyo Prince Hotel, Tokyo, Japan, 24–26 November 1966.

The first technical assistance is provided to Indonesia for improving food production, 1967. (*The Philippines Herald*, 1 September 1967)

ADB's first President, Takeshi Watanabe, and General Manager of Industrial Finance Corporation of Thailand, Kraisri Nimmanahaeminda, sign the Bank's first loan agreement, 25 January 1968.

ADB President Takeshi Watanabe signs the first ADB bond issued in Frankfurt, Germany, 10 September 1969.

The first loan to the Pacific island countries is granted for the construction of Faleolo Airport in Apia, the capital of Samoa, 16 December 1969.

First ADB Vice-President C. S. Krishna Moorthi (*seated, center*) signing the first Co-Financing Agreement, Manila, Philippines, 5 June 1970. With him are Ambassador Major-General Kusno Utomo, Republic of Indonesia (*seated, left*); and ADB Alternate Director Long Boret of Cambodia (*seated, right*).

Education sector loan for the expansion of Ngee Ann Technical College, Singapore, 23 December 1970.

Board of Directors meeting with ADB President Takeshi Watanabe (*front row, center*), with Secretary Douglas Gunesekera (*front low, left*) and Vice-President C. S. Krishna Moorthi (*front row, right*) and ADB General Counsel Lewis Carroll (*far right*), ADB headquarters, 1972, Manila, Philippines.

Republic of Korea's President Park Chung-hee addressing ADB Board of Governors at the Annual Meeting in Seoul, Republic of Korea, 9 April 1970.

Yangmei freeway project in Taipei,China, 30 March 1970.

Philippine President Ferdinand Marcos (*right*) hands a symbolic key of the new ADB headquarters to ADB President Takeshi Watanabe, with Cornelio Balmaceda, Chair of the Ministerial Conference on Asian Economic Cooperation and Philippine Secretary of Commerce and Industry, 18 November 1972.

The first ADB headquarters, Manila, Philippines, inaugurated on 18 November 1972.

United Nations Secretary-General Kurt Waldheim with ADB President Shiro Inoue (*second from left*) at ADB headquarters, together with Mrs. Elisabeth Waldheim and daughter Christa Waldheim, 12 February 1976.

ADB President Shiro Inoue (*front row, second from left*) at a heads of regional banks meeting, Manila, Philippines, October 1976.

CHAPTER 5
First Decade (1967–1976)

ADB: The Character of the Bank

"The progress of underdeveloped nations depends on the will of those nations themselves ... It was never conceived, of course, that the Asian Development Bank alone could act as a panacea for Asian poverty. We are one alone among many actors in this drama."
– Shiro Inoue, Speech, Role of the Asian Development Bank in the Development of Asia and the Far East, 14 June 1973

The early priority of the Asian Development Bank (ADB) was to establish itself as a bank with sound credentials in the international community. The first two Presidents, Takeshi Watanabe and Shiro Inoue, had strong banking backgrounds. Before the institution took on a wider development role, both wanted ADB to build its reputation as a sound development bank. In this, they succeeded. By the end of the first ADB decade, the Bank was seen in global markets as a solid financial institution which allocated its funds in Asia with prudence.

In the initial stages of its work, ADB emphasized sectors of key importance to borrowing countries—energy, transport, manufacturing, and agriculture. During this early period, the Bank was concerned with building its reputation. ADB staff therefore set out to prepare a pipeline of carefully designed project loans for industrial and infrastructure development. And reflecting the concern about the need to promote agriculture, the Bank expanded lending for irrigation and rural development.

ADB also widened the way it mobilized funds—raising loans in capital markets in Europe, Japan, and North America. The Bank also reformed the management of the soft loan concessional funds. In 1973, donors agreed in Bonn to establish the Asian Development Fund (ADF), a major soft loan fund for borrowing by the poorest ADB member countries. The ADF soon became an integral part of the Bank's operations and bolstered the position of industrial donor countries as stakeholders.

The first test of the Bank's ability to deal with a major challenge was the international oil shock in 1973–1974. To assist developing countries in responding to the changed circumstances, ADB needed to extend loans and develop new approaches, notably to help bolster energy security. The Bank learned the importance of flexibility when systems come under strain.

This chapter tells the story of how the character of ADB was formed and molded during its first decade, initially by Takeshi Watanabe and then by his successor, Shiro Inoue.

A Vision for the Bank

The early days—the first few months and years—are a formative time for people and for institutions. Important relationships are established. Styles of life and work begin to develop. Even in the first few weeks, Takeshi Watanabe put his stamp on the way the new organization would operate.

When Watanabe arrived at Manila airport on 15 December 1966, he was met by a small team of Bank staff and held a press conference.[1] He then went to his ADB official residence which had been prepared by a young ADB staff member on leave from the Japanese Ministry of Finance, Masao Fujioka. Fifteen years later, Fujioka himself would become President of ADB.

The following day, Watanabe went to the temporary ADB headquarters in the nearby commercial area of Makati. He met staff, conducted some immediate business, and met the new Board members. The next day, Watanabe chaired the first meeting of the Board. In later years, Board meetings would usually last no longer than 3 hours. But this first meeting needed to address such initial matters as the appointment of a vice-president and some of the rules of the Bank so it lasted until 6 p.m.

Two days later, on 19 December, the Bank's official opening ceremony was held in the open near the temporary headquarters. President of the Philippines Ferdinand Marcos, still in his first year in office, attended, along with other dignitaries from the Philippines and international agencies.

In his first public address as ADB President, Watanabe talked about the key strategic issues the new organization would need to address. He was well prepared. He had been a board member of the World Bank in Washington, DC and had spent much time with his colleagues in the study group in Tokyo

---

[1] Watanabe, 1977, *Towards a New Asia*, 43.

considering the role of a new Asian bank. Further, during the previous few years he had been closely involved in planning its establishment.

In setting out his agenda, Watanabe took up themes he would repeatedly return to in the next few years in his visits to many countries.[2] Two of the most important were regional cooperation and multilateralism. He described ADB as a clearinghouse of common understanding. He pointed to the advantages of multilateral arrangements. "There is no question," he said, "that it is more palatable to the developing countries to accept funds from a multilateral institution. This type of organization does not seek public acclaim for its services, nor are there liable to be the onerous strings attached, which may accompany bilateral aid."

He also noted, realistically, that there were limits to what a multilateral bank could achieve. Most of the effort would need to come from developing countries themselves. Watanabe then outlined the principles that would guide ADB's work. First, it was important that staff listen carefully to the views of all stakeholders, and learn before teaching so as to be responsive to local needs. He planned to visit the countries himself as soon as possible to familiarize himself with their economic issues. To describe the relationship between Bank staff and member countries, Watanabe used the metaphor of a "family doctor"—an image that would later become part of the way the Bank described itself (Box 5.1).

Watanabe emphasized that the "family doctor" idea called for ADB staff to establish close relationships with their colleagues in developing countries in Asia. He explained that:[3]

> There was a case where this spirit was exemplified by deed. In Nepal, accommodations for visitors are limited with only a few first-class hotels available. Foreign missions often hesitate to visit the country unless reservations are confirmed with good hotels. But when the ADB staff arrived, neither first nor second nor even third-class hotel rooms were available. They stayed in a hotel without electricity and prepared their report by candlelight. After exhausting all the candles, they completed the report using the headlights of a car. I was moved by their dedication.

---

[2] Watanabe, 1966, *Pattern for Prosperity*.
[3] Watanabe, 1977, *Towards a New Asia*, 36.

> **Box 5.1: ADB as a Family Doctor to Developing Countries in Asia**
>
> "It is my ardent desire that the member countries will come to look upon the ADB as a kind of 'family doctor', who is ready to lend assistance whenever and wherever the need arises. This posture demands a thorough familiarity with the economic attitudes and environment of each developing country. I believe this familiarity can best be bred by endowing the Bank basically with a regional character, in terms of its personnel."
>
> —Takeshi Watanabe, ADB Opening Ceremony, 1966, quoted in ADB. 1968. *Summary of the Proceedings of the First Annual Meeting of the Board of Governors.* p. 14.
>
> "Like an oriental family doctor, the Bank is eclectic, non-intellectualized and deeply pragmatic. To the problems each country faced, the Bank seeks to provide not intellectual or rationalized answers but rather positive and practicable, down to earth solutions, taking the life of nations simply as they are, with all their individual complexities, confusions, incompatibilities and contradictions. Because of this, the Bank favors an empirical and inductive style. Instead of approaching from the general to the particular, the Bank prefers to start with individual projects to increase its knowledge from practical experience on the spot, to spread its influence and move upwards. Depending on circumstances, the Bank does not hesitate to change priorities or objectives."
>
> —Farewell speech for President Watanabe by Alternate Executive Director from Viet Nam Buu Hoan on 23 November 1972.

Watanabe also noted the need for sound management. Especially in the early years, the Bank should be a simple yet flexible organization. "It is far easier," he said, "to progress from simplicity to complexity than it is to go from complexity to simplicity." He also emphasized the importance of designing high-quality loans. "There is only one basic policy to which I firmly adhere: namely, to ensure that each loan conforms to the principles of sound banking. ... this is the only way to establish the good credit of the Bank, and to thereby assure the continuous flow of funds through our organization." He would emphasize this again and again during the next few years.

Looking further ahead, Watanabe envisaged ADB as a reliable adviser. "It is my belief that, in many instances, sound advice is a far more welcome and valuable antidote than hard cash." Thus, even in these early days, plans were being laid for the Bank to take on a wider development role.

Finally, there was the question of resources. ADB could only assist member countries if it had sufficient funds. Watanabe spoke of the need to establish a Special Fund with contributions from donors to support soft loan concessional lending. These Special Funds resources would soon become an important source of finance for low-income countries. He also flagged the need for ADB to prepare to issue bonds in capital markets to raise funds for ordinary nonconcessional loans.

A Careful Start

ADB began its operations in a modest way. ADB's original members totaled 31 (19 regional and 12 nonregional), compared with today's 67 members (48 regional and 19 nonregional). At the end of 1966, ADB had 20 Board members (10 directors and 10 alternate directors), and yet only 40 staff (President, 1 Vice-President, 11 international staff, and 27 national and administrative staff). At the end of 2016, ADB would have 24 Board members (12 directors and 12 alternate directors) and 3,092 staff (President, 6 Vice-Presidents, 1,103 international staff, and 1,982 national and administrative staff). Fifty years ago, there were only 3 departments and 5 offices, compared with 15 departments and 12 offices today (Appendix Table 2.22). ADB started with small office space in Makati, spread across several buildings. Today, ADB has offices in 31 countries including in Manila.

Watanabe spent the next year, 1967, putting his agenda into place. He traveled widely to developing and industrial countries and strengthened contacts with other multilateral agencies in Asia and across the international community. ADB staff too were soon on the move, undertaking survey missions in developing countries to help analyze problems, suggest solutions, and start projects.

Back at the new headquarters, it was also important that the organization was well-run. On 17 December 1966, at its first meeting, the new ADB Board appointed C. S. Krishna Moorthi as Vice-President. He would be a key figure in the Bank, developing a reputation as a decisive, even intimidating, administrator. Before joining ADB, Krishna Moorthi had served at the top levels of the Indian Civil Service. He had also been India's Executive Director at the World Bank in Washington, DC when Watanabe was on its board so the personal links between the two went back a long time. For the 6 years of Watanabe's presidency, Krishna Moorthi served as his right-hand manager. Indeed, Krishna Moorthi would continue to exercise a strong influence within the Bank for 12 years, working with the first three Presidents: Watanabe, Shiro Inoue, and Taroichi Yoshida.

Watanabe was also careful in recruiting staff. He explained that "one easy way was to ask other organizations to spare some of their personnel … I could have saved a lot of effort in staffing the ADB had I followed the same practice, by asking each member country to recommend a certain number of people."[4] But he said that if he had done this, he might have ended up with someone recommended solely because they were the friend of the head of the country. He preferred to interview candidates for professional positions himself. This approach received strong support from member countries. At the second ADB Annual Meeting in Sydney in April 1969, delegates noted satisfactory progress. Governor for the United States David M. Kennedy spoke of the impressive beginnings of the Bank and referred to an organization which had "a staff distinguished by professional competence and broad regional experience." By the end of 1967, the number of staff increased to 190, and gradually to 551 by the end of 1971.

In terms of its operations, ADB was initially cautious. Watanabe said: "There were those who urged me to take an early decision on one or two loans for demonstration purposes, but I was not in favor of rushing things as I thought it more important to make good loans so that the bank could establish a high credit standing."[5] It was important to show that the new institution was committed to high-quality projects. In fact, during its first year ADB made no loans at all. The Bank's initial steps were to support several advisory and technical assistance activities, the first of which was approved in August 1967.

Research Activities

One of the first problems for the staff was a shortage of information. It was difficult to design sound projects when basic statistics were hard to come by. For example, in Indonesia, which soon became one of the main borrowers, the national statistical service had fallen into disarray during

---

[4] Watanabe, 1977, *Towards a New Asia*, 24.
[5] Watanabe, 1977, *Towards a New Asia*, 45.

the difficult years of the 1960s. Data on such things as agricultural output and irrigation systems were quite unreliable.

Faced with this situation, ADB staff started to gather the basic data needed. The immediate focus was on agriculture which was the mainstay of many of the region's economies—and for which funds were already being requested. In December 1966 in Tokyo, a major conference on agricultural development in Southeast Asia had asked ADB "to start immediately deliberations on the various problems concerning the establishment of a Special Agricultural Fund." Watanabe suggested to the ADB Board of Directors that they accept in principle the idea of Special Funds but emphasized that to attract sufficient support there would need to be a convincing case. The Bank, he said, would need to base appeals to donors on a "clear, coherent and well-documented program of action."

The information underpinning the plan of action came from the first Asian Agricultural Survey launched in 1967. The survey, approved in May 1967, was ADB's first technical assistance activity. The terms of reference for the survey were drawn up by a committee co-chaired by Kazushi Ohkawa of Hitotsubashi University, Tokyo and T. W. Schultz of the University of Chicago. Ohkawa was an eminent development economist, and later in 1979 Schultz was awarded the Nobel Prize in economics for his studies of developing countries.

The survey was supported through a regional technical assistance which was designed to support work across a number of participating nations rather than in just one member country. In later years, ADB would support many more regional technical assistance projects to promote regional cooperation in Asia.

The survey team worked quickly. In early 1968, the team presented a report that dramatically highlighted the potential for new agricultural technology to boost food production: "The story of the rice breakthrough is a story written in the first half of this decade. It can be matched in time and substance by the story of hybrid and synthetic maize, hybrid grain sorghum, and hybrid millet ... The development of new varietal materials of high yield potential opens the road to modernization ... farmer acceptance of this material has been as overwhelming as it was unexpected."[6] The Asian Agricultural Survey provided additional impetus to the Bank's early focus on agriculture.

---

[6] ADB, 1969, *Asian Agricultural Survey*, 39.

Welcoming the report, at the first ADB Annual Meeting in 1968 in Manila, Watanabe summarized other main themes: "This promise [of agricultural progress] is attributable primarily to the raft of revolutionary technologies introduced in the past several years—technologies which have opened a vast frontier of productive capacity for Asian agriculture. Most encouraging are the host of new inputs—new and improved seed varieties, better fertilizers, more effective pesticides—which, when properly implemented, generate considerably higher yields and facilitate multiple cropping. ... It is the considered opinion of the Survey that priority emphasis on the rapid adoption of these modern technologies can engender immediate impacts on agricultural growth."[7] The survey also pointed to the importance of well-functioning agricultural markets and infrastructure.

The following year, at the second ADB Annual Meeting in April 1969 in Sydney, the Government of Australia joined with the Bank to sponsor a regional seminar on agriculture to discuss the results of the agricultural survey. Participants, including international experts on agriculture in developing countries, noted that the Bank's resources were very limited compared to the needs of farmers in Asia so, to be effective, ADB would need to be selective. And to design effective projects, ADB would also need to strengthen its in-house skills. The results of the seminar, published later in the year, helped guide the Bank's early operations in agriculture.[8]

Another major priority was transport. In 1968, responding to requests from governments in Southeast Asia, ADB initiated the Southeast Asian Regional Transport Survey.[9] The survey report, completed in early 1971, outlined an ambitious regional investment program for several decades to come. Watanabe observed that it presented an attractive agenda but injected a note of realism saying that: "building the bridges needed to join human, physical and institutional resources will not be easy."[10]

The growing emphasis on the need for information and research to support the Bank's work soon pointed to the importance of strengthening ADB's

---

[7] From the opening address by President Takeshi Watanabe delivered at the First Annual Meeting of the ADB Board of Governors, 1968. ADB, 1968, *Proceedings of First Annual Meeting*, 19.

[8] A detailed summary of the seminar is provided in the papers and proceedings. ADB, 1969, *Regional Seminar on Agriculture*.

[9] ADB, *Annual Report 1970*, 46.

[10] From the opening address by President Takeshi Watanabe delivered at the Fifth Annual Meeting of the ADB Board of Governors, 1972. ADB, 1972, *Proceedings of Fifth Annual Meeting*, 18.

own capacity to conduct economic analysis. In 1969, the Economic Office was established within the organization. The new office included a group of economists headed by a Chief Economist. The main responsibilities of the office were to carry out action-oriented research on development problems and to make evaluations of the growth experience in individual developing member countries. A Statistics Section was also established within the Economic Office to compile data on major economic problems of interest to the Bank. During the next few decades, the Bank would increasingly emphasize the importance of knowledge activities in its development work in the region.

Other Main Studies

Another major ADB-supported study was *Southeast Asia's Economy in the 1970s*. This was produced in response to a request in 1969 from the Fourth Ministerial Conference for Economic Development of Southeast Asia. At the time, there was relatively little information about the region's development prospects.[11] The study was supervised by a group which included Paul Streeten from the University of Oxford, Albert Hirschman from Harvard University, and Saburo Okita from the Japan Center for Economic Research. They were joined by other Asian scholars Sixto K. Roxas, Subroto, and Suparb Yossundara as well as Sam-Chung Hsieh, Head of Economic and Technical Assistance Department. The economist Hla Myint from Myanmar led the team.

The study incorporated six surveys. These addressed major issues in the region such as the Green Revolution, industrialization, foreign trade, foreign private investment, aspects of population growth, and the expected impact of the end of hostilities in Viet Nam and the British military withdrawal from Southeast Asia. Published in 1972, *Southeast Asia's Economy in the 1970s* soon became a widely quoted source. The study marked a key change in thinking about the strategy of development in Asia. Hla Myint and his colleagues argued that Southeast Asian countries could expect to enjoy rapid economic growth through export expansion—provided, however, that governments took steps to link the region's natural resources with expanding world demand.[12] Rather than being inward-looking and protectionist, the study urged that pro-market and export-oriented

---

[11] ADB, *Annual Report 1970*, 47.
[12] A useful summary of the study is provided in ADB, *Annual Report 1970*, 47.

policies should be introduced. Throughout the 1970s, many policy makers in Southeast Asia adopted this outward-looking approach. This strategy of development was a key factor underpinning strong growth across the region in the following decades.[13]

The First Technical Assistance and Loans

In the early years, ADB Management was keen to establish a pipeline of high-quality loans. Before it made its first loan, however, the Bank supported several technical assistance activities. The first, approved in the middle of 1967, was in Indonesia for a report on improving food production. Following the effective change of government in 1966, the new government in Indonesia attempted to stabilize food supplies throughout the vast archipelago. In January 1968, ADB prepared a report on food policy issues and later provided additional technical assistance for agricultural policies and for a study of the rural credit system.[14]

The first project loan in 1968 was a milestone for ADB as a new institution. The $5 million loan was provided to Thailand to support industrial development (Box 5.2). In the same year, 6 other loans quickly followed: to the Republic of Korea to build an expressway, to Malaysia to help improve water supplies, and to Pakistan to finance small private sector firms. All of the loans in 1968 were small; the largest was for $10 million to provide finance to an industrial plant in Taipei,China.

This cautious approach was adopted at first because the financial resources for the loans which came from the Bank's ordinary capital resources were quite limited. ADB was still finding its way. It was thought best to start with small loans that would build up a portfolio of project activities across several countries.

The following year, 1969, the first concessional loan from the Special Funds was approved for agriculture infrastructure in Indonesia. In 1969, ADB also began activities in the South Pacific by approving a concessional low-interest loan to Western Samoa for Faleolo Airport which serves the capital, Apia. From modest beginnings in the first 5 years of operations, the Bank's lending activities quickly accelerated in the second half of the decade, reflecting growing confidence among staff.

---

[13] James, Naya, and Meier, 1987, *Asian Development*, 11.
[14] Details of the plans for the technical assistance mission to Indonesia are in ADB, *Annual Report 1967*, 21.

> **Box 5.2: ADB's First Loans**
>
> **Industrial Finance Corporation of Thailand.** The first loan of the Asian Development Bank (ADB) was to a development finance institution in Thailand, guaranteed by the government. The assistance was funded from the ordinary capital resources (OCR) of the Bank.
>
> Approved in January 1968, the loan provided a $5 million line of credit. The Industrial Finance Corporation of Thailand (IFCT) was seen as being able to play a useful role in supporting Thailand's industrial policy. In contrast to the activities of Thai commercial banks that mainly engaged in short-term lending, IFCT extended medium- and long-term loans. ADB's loan supported IFCT's efforts to assist the expansion of Thai local industries. Seven subloans were issued which augmented IFCT's foreign exchange resources. From this modest beginning, the network of development finance institutions supported by ADB would steadily expand during the coming decade.
>
> **Tajum Irrigation Project in Indonesia.** The Tajum Irrigation Project loan, approved in June 1969, was a key step for the Bank. It was the first ADB loan for agriculture infrastructure, the first loan to Indonesia, and the first loan financed from the Bank's Special Funds (which later became the Asian Development Fund). The project was in a relatively less developed area in Central Java and aimed to help the Government of Indonesia strengthen its irrigation system. The project supported the introduction of improved agricultural methods and encouraged an efficient water management system. At that time, irrigation systems in Central Java were rather simple and crops in paddy fields were often reliant on rain-fed farming methods.
>
> Source: ADB. 2016. *ADB through the Decades: ADB's First Decade (1966–1976)*. pp. 18–20. https://www.adb.org/sites/default/files/publication/216111/adb-first-decade.pdf (accessed 20 December 2016).

Early Priorities

From the beginning, the loan portfolio was quite diverse. Main sectors included energy, agriculture, and transport. The lending strategy also included the provision of loans to development finance institutions (DFIs) guaranteed by governments.

Most energy loans were for electricity systems. At the time, many systems in developing countries in Asia suffered from high power losses. ADB loans were either for rehabilitating existing transmission and distribution facilities, or for investments in new generation plants. ADB also supported rural electrification. In some parts of the region, fewer than 10% of people in village areas had access to electricity; for modest sources of light at night, they typically used candles or kerosene lamps. Activities in the power sector were stepped up after the first oil shock in late 1973 when countries became preoccupied with energy security and aimed to reduce their dependence on imported oil by developing indigenous sources of energy.

In transport, the main investments were in roads—primarily for new highways to enhance economic growth, as well as rural roads to improve access to markets and other facilities in nearby towns.

Initially, ADB support for agriculture was largely for strengthening food security; later, it would be for promoting rural employment. One main area of focus was irrigation—a key input for the Green Revolution needed to improve agricultural productivity by expanding areas under cultivation and improving cropping intensities.

There was also support for the finance sector. The aim was to strengthen local DFIs so that they could mobilize long-term capital for private investment, provide advisory services to private enterprises, and help develop local securities markets. It was hoped that DFIs could also transfer resources, through onlending, to small and medium-sized enterprises (SMEs). ADB lending that directly flowed on to SMEs through DFIs accounted for 14% of total lending in the finance sector.

The Bank's early credit lines to development banks supported the provision of subloans to SMEs in manufacturing activities such as textiles, food processing, and engineering. This helped countries in the early stages of industrialization substitute local goods for imports and then boost exports. Later in the first decade, other subloans were supplied to support the manufacture of capital goods and intermediate goods, particularly in the chemical and engineering industries. This approach was in line with the strategies in some countries of shifting manufacturing production away from consumer goods to capital goods (Chapter 4).

The support in Asia for DFIs was also reflected in regional conferences on DFIs arranged by Asian leaders even before ADB was established. In September 1966 in Tokyo, during the third regional conference of development banks in Asia, participants suggested that the new bank could assume responsibility for convening such conferences. In response, between 1969 and 1976, ADB sponsored the fourth, fifth, and sixth regional conferences of development banks. In these meetings, delegates tackled such issues as implementing investment projects (fourth conference), promoting industrial development (fifth conference), and regional cooperation among DFIs (sixth conference).

Even with this support, however, DFIs in Asia often failed to achieve their goals. Too many institutions were held back by institutional weaknesses, mismanagement, political pressures, and a difficult economic environment. Over time, ADB decided to scale back its involvement with DFIs in the region.[15]

Trends in Lending

After some years, the main trends of the Bank's loan operations began to emerge. During the first 4 years, more loans went to more developed and creditworthy economies such as the Republic of Korea; Singapore; and Taipei,China. However, as the program expanded, lending increased to countries in South Asia such as Ceylon and Pakistan and others in Southeast Asia such as Indonesia, Malaysia, the Philippines, and Thailand.

In the early days, the main borrowers were larger countries. ADB staff were aware, however, that they should also support smaller countries. The Charter specified that the Bank should pay "special regard to the needs of the smaller or less developed member countries in the region." Representatives from these countries frequently reminded the Bank of their needs. Addressing the first ADB Annual Meeting in April 1968, ADB Governor for Western Samoa Gustav Betham said: "Western Samoa is the smallest member of this Bank and is probably also the least developed. ... I would like to remind members of the Bank of the provisions in the Charter relating to the smaller and less developed countries of the region. I sincerely trust that these provisions will be borne in mind when loan requests are received from the smaller countries."[16]

Operating in smaller countries was often difficult, particularly because of the lack of local expertise. In the South Pacific, government agencies

---

[15] A survey of ADB's experience in supporting financial intermediation for private sector development and small and medium-sized enterprises is in ADB, 2008, *Support for Financial Intermediation*.
[16] ADB, 1968, *Proceedings of First Annual Meeting*, 68.

were often severely understaffed and not used to delivering the types of investment projects which ADB hoped to support. Other obstacles were isolation from markets and closely bound community cultures which could complicate project design.

Nevertheless, even in the first few years, there were some activities in smaller countries. In Ceylon in 1968, there was a project for modernizing tea factories. In Nepal in 1969, ADB supplied funds for technical assistance to support a project for air transport infrastructure. In 1970, the first ADB activity in Afghanistan was a concessional loan for $5.1 million to fund the foreign exchange costs of expanding irrigation systems in the Gawargan and Chardarrah areas in the mid-Kunduz Basin.

The Bank also responded to the needs of countries in special circumstances. Bangladesh became independent in 1971 and joined ADB in 1973. Two loans were quickly approved: one for a fisheries project to improve marketing facilities and the other for development financing to provide credit to a wide range of local firms producing jute, cotton textiles, and other manufactured goods. Two more loans, for electric power and for a Chittagong port project, were approved before the end of the year. The Bank's approach in Bangladesh in these early years was to provide assistance "as swiftly as possible, in increasing amounts, and on the softest possible terms."[17]

A practical problem in quite a few countries was a shortage of "shovel-ready" projects. Even in the larger countries, many government agencies found it hard to prepare projects. One official quoted in the *Asian Agricultural Survey* reported that "we seem unable to formulate and prepare agricultural projects to the standards required for foreign aid and support."[18] In response, ADB adopted a two-step approach: first, technical assistance for project preparation would be provided; second, funds for the project itself would be approved.

This two-step approach helped fill the project pipeline. At the Annual Meeting in 1970, ADB Governor for Western Samoa Tofa Siaosi discussed the Western Samoa airport loan: "... The loan was the result of technical assistance, which made possible in large measure the final technical investigations and designs, after the identification and appraisal of the project itself. With the lack of the necessary expertise in my country for

---

[17] Inoue, 1975, *Bangladesh: Statement to Press*.
[18] ADB, 1969, *Asian Agricultural Survey*, 39.

these preliminary investigations and preparations, technical assistance was of paramount importance and was indispensable in the successful negotiations with the Bank for the loan."[19] To improve the capacity of small Pacific island countries to use development assistance, a review of the Bank's approach in these countries was prepared in 1974. New measures adopted included the provision of technical assistance to help prepare local development plans and an emphasis on the identification of high-priority projects.[20]

Sources of Finance

Watanabe also needed to spend considerable time fundraising and building relations with stakeholders. To support its loan pipeline and other activities, ADB needed reliable sources of funds. At first, the Bank's activities were funded from the initial capital subscribed by its members. However, it was clear from the outset that ADB would need to raise more money. At the first Annual Meeting in Manila in April 1968, Australian Governor Billy McMahon said: "We should keep in mind that the initial subscribed capital of the Bank, although large in itself, is not large in relation to the work to be done." Indian Governor and Deputy Prime Minister Morarji Desai agreed, saying: "The Bank's financial resources are… hardly of a magnitude to make any impact, on their own, on the capital needs of the region. The resources of the Bank are a form of 'seed money.'"

ADB provided nonconcessional loans from its ordinary capital resources (OCR) and soft loans from the concessional Special Funds. Watanabe worked with senior staff to expand both sources. To expand the pool of OCR funds in these early days, ADB could look to increases in the capital subscribed by member countries or the issuance of bonds in international capital markets. To increase the Special Funds, the Bank needed to approach donors for additional support. During the next few years, the staff designed programs to tap these sources.

Raising funds in each of these ways called for different approaches. Over time, ADB staff became more experienced. They realized, for example, that asking countries to increase their capital subscriptions had implications for the Bank's ownership: countries that contributed more capital would have a greater voting share—an issue often raised during

---

[19] ADB, 1970, *Proceedings of Third Annual Meeting*, 76.
[20] ADB, *Annual Report 1974*, 18; ADB, *Annual Report 1975*, 11.

discussions about capital increases. Subsequently, ADB also expanded its activities in international bond markets. ADB staff thus needed to develop specialized expertise to ensure that the Bank became a respected borrower in global bond markets. There were also some tricky issues when it came to mobilizing Special Funds from donors. Donors frequently attached conditions to their contributions leading to complex discussions between teams of delegates from the capitals.

Increases in Capital

Just as any company might be, ADB had been established with equity capital provided by the owners. For the Bank, this was made up of capital subscriptions from member countries. The member countries owned shares in ADB which, in 1966, amounted to authorized capital of $1 billion. A key aspect of this authorized capital was that not all of it was paid-in. The Charter established that the authorized capital would be of two types: part in the form of paid-in shares which members subscribed to on joining and the other in the form of callable shares which members would only be required to pay for if ADB faced an urgent financial problem. When the Bank was established, each of these two types of capital comprised half the subscribed capital. This approach had the advantage of providing the Bank with authorized capital while reducing the immediate demands on member countries; the member governments were viewed by the international money markets as extremely creditworthy so the Bank's callable capital was regarded as of equal worth to the capital that had actually been paid in.[21]

Another way in which the Charter aimed to reduce the financial burden for potential members, especially developing countries, was to allow for some of the payment to be made in local currency. Thus, members could pay with a combination of a convertible currency, such as the US dollar, and their country's own currency, which in some cases was not convertible in international money markets. Cambodia, for example, could pay for half of its paid-in shares in Cambodian riel. Many developing countries

---

[21] The idea of providing part of the subscription to ADB in callable capital rather than paid-in capital was widely understood and accepted by member governments. President Johnson in recommending that Congress approve participation in ADB noted that "The callable shares will constitute a guarantee for borrowings by the Bank in private capital markets. They would be drawn on only in the unlikely event that the Bank were unable to meet its commitments." Government of the United States, 1966, *Public Papers of the Presidents*, 28.

took advantage of this option. The result was that in the early stages, ADB Treasury Department staff found themselves with the unexpected headache of juggling a wide range of convertible and nonconvertible currencies. Over time, however, the Bank was able to make use of the nonconvertible currencies in various ways such as paying for local expenses incurred during ADB activities.

Within a few years, it had become clear that the initial level of authorized capital of $1.1 billion (a slight increase had been agreed in 1966) was too small. At the fourth ADB Annual Meeting in Singapore in April 1971, Watanabe said: "the importance of increased resources for ADB cannot be exaggerated." He asked that the Board of Directors be authorized to explore the possibility of increasing the Bank's capital stock. This request was approved and, for the rest of 1971, the Board and staff spent much time considering the first general capital increase (GCI I).

Discussions about GCI I were a complex exercise in economic diplomacy. The devil was in the detail. Throughout the talks, member countries carefully watched what other countries were aiming for as various contentious issues cropped up. The rate of interest, for example, that ADB charged for hard OCR loans became, over time, a matter which borrowing countries watched closely. By November 1971, after a series of negotiations, the Board of Governors agreed to increase the capital stock by 150% (Appendix Table A2.14). But to reduce the immediate cost to member countries, they also decided to reduce the paid-in proportion to 20%. The Board also agreed on a timetable for payments of the paid-in shares; in the end, only the United States (US) fell behind this. At one stage, the US voting share briefly dropped below those of Japan, India, and Australia. Looking to the future, the Board also recommended a further reassessment of the level of capital stock before the end of 1975.

ADB Bonds

Another potential source of funding was from borrowings in international financial markets through issuance of bonds. At first, international market conditions were not encouraging, especially for a new institution without an established track record. In 1966, Watanabe said that although he had been encouraged by the interest shown by the investment banking community "… in light of the exceedingly tight market conditions at present, I do not think it is practical for us to consider this source of capital for the immediate future." He noted, however, that "when the climate is more favorable, the Bank will be in a position to issue bonds on favorable terms."[22]

By late 1969, the time seemed right for ADB to borrow. In September, the Bank's first bond was offered on the West German market: a 15-year loan, for 60 million deutsche marks (around $16 million) through an international syndicate of 69 banks from 13 countries. This was the Bank's first entry into the market so it was important that the legal and administrative processes went smoothly—which they did. These ADB deutsche mark bonds were subsequently listed on the stock exchanges of Frankfurt, Düsseldorf, and Vienna. To support further activities in financial markets in Europe, in 1971 a financial adviser was appointed in Zurich, Switzerland. This office was kept open until 1974 when the function was reintegrated into the duties of the Treasury Department in ADB headquarters in Manila.

After this first bond issue in Europe, ADB staff planned to widen the borrowing program to financial markets in Asia and North America. This was partly to diversify across different markets but also because ADB, as a multilateral institution, was expected by member countries to have a borrowing program across various countries and in a range of currencies. In 1970, following the West German bond issue, ADB floated schilling bonds in Austria in April and yen bonds in Japan in November. The latter was significant. It was the Bank's first bond issue in Asia and it was the first public issue of yen bonds in Japan by a foreign entity.

The yen offering was also notable in financial circles because ADB was stealing a march on the World Bank. ADB, with Japanese support, was entering the Japanese market for 6 billion yen (around $16.7 million equivalent) before the World Bank, which would not issue its first bonds in Japan until the following year. For this and other bond offerings in Asia, ADB was aiming not just to raise funds for the Bank but also to establish new forms of bond offerings in capital markets across the region.

In North America, the process was more complicated. For ADB bonds to be treated as equal to those of the World Bank and the Inter-American Development Bank, ADB needed specific legislative approval in different states. During 1968 and 1969, therefore, legislation was enacted in 12 states, and in a further five in 1970. This process of bond qualification set

---

[22] Statement at the Opening Ceremony of the Asian Development Bank in Manila by Takeshi Watanabe in Watanabe, 1966, *Pattern for Prosperity*. Also found in ADB, 1969, *The Doors Are Open*.

the basis for the successful entry of ADB into the US financial market. In 1971, the Bank was able to float its first dollar-denominated bonds.[23] Underwritten by a nationwide syndicate and listed on the New York Stock Exchange, these bonds received a AAA rating. Following these successful bond offerings in Europe, Japan, and North America, ADB had established itself by the end of 1971 as a reputable borrower in international markets.

Borrowing in capital markets in industrial countries to support projects in Asian developing countries fulfilled one of the original purposes of ADB. The Bank's Charter spoke of the importance of mobilizing funds from "outside the region" and of fostering a "greater flow of development funds into the region." By taking early steps to issue bonds in international financial markets, ADB was moving quickly to encourage a flow of funds from capital-rich industrial countries to capital-poor developing countries in Asia.

Special Funds

The other main source of financial support that ADB planned to expand during the early years was Special Funds. These funds allowed the Bank to make soft loans—with long payback periods of up to 40 years and at low interest rates of 1.5%—for activities that promised high social gains but no immediate financial profit. In 1966, at the ADB Opening Ceremony in Manila, Watanabe had highlighted the importance of Special Funds saying that "...many countries are anxious to obtain soft loans ... We must therefore rely on the creation of Special Funds, i.e., capital resources over and above that subscribed. Toward that end, I will actively solicit contributions to this Fund."[24]

In fact, it had always been expected that the Bank would have Special Funds. Article 19 of the Charter discussed their establishment. Their expansion had also been anticipated by donors. In 1967, in recommending to Congress that the US contribute to the Special Funds of ADB, President Johnson had said that, based on the experience of the World Bank, development finance would require not just ordinary capital but special funds "for

---

[23] The 12 states where legislation was enacted in 1968 and 1969 were California, Colorado, Connecticut, Hawaii, Illinois, Maine, Massachusetts, New Jersey, New York, Ohio, Pennsylvania, and Washington. The five states where legislation was approved in 1970 were Iowa, Kentucky, Louisiana, Virginia, and Wisconsin. ADB, *Annual Report 1970*, 54.
[24] Watanabe, 1966, *Pattern for Prosperity;* ADB, 1969, *The Doors Are Open.*

longer-term loans at lower interest rates to finance the foreign exchange costs of projects such as schools and roads which do not yield immediate financial returns, but which add powerfully to economic growth." For this purpose, in September 1967, Johnson proposed that the US pledge up to $200 million to be provided over 4 years.[25]

In the end, Congress did not approve this proposal. When Richard Nixon became US President after the election in 1968, the new administration reviewed all US foreign assistance. It was not until 1972 that the US was able to make a reduced contribution of $100 million to ADB's Special Funds.

During its first 5 years, ADB established Special Funds for a number of purposes. They included the Agricultural Special Fund (with assets of almost $40 million), the Multi-Purpose Special Fund (almost $280 million), and the Technical Assistance Special Fund (with $6 million). Initially, the Agricultural Special Fund (ASF) was set up in 1968 following a contribution from Japan (7.2 billion yen, or $20 million equivalent) to finance special projects in agricultural development. A similar agreement was signed with Canada for its contribution to the Multi-Purpose Special Fund (MPSF) (for $25 million equivalent).

At the second ADB Annual Meeting in 1969, Watanabe reaffirmed the need for Special Funds. He noted that a number of countries had already contributed to various funds but he asked for more support—an appeal he repeated at the third Annual Meeting in 1970.[26] Financing for these funds was largely provided by donors but there were also contributions from ADB itself. Some of the OCR activities had begun generating surpluses when borrowers repaid. Rather than declare a profit, the Bank transferred the surplus to the Special Funds.

These Special Funds provided ADB with useful resources. However, before long, the proliferation of arrangements surrounding the use of the funds began to pose problems—for donor countries, for developing member countries, and for ADB itself. Access to the Agricultural Special Fund and to the Multi-Purpose Special Fund was often tied to procurement from donor countries. The conditions attached to the use of the funds made their administration extremely complicated.

---

[25] Government of the United States, Senate, 1967, *ADB Special Funds Hearing*, 3.
[26] Address by President Takeshi Watanabe delivered at the Third Annual Meeting of the ADB Board of Governors. ADB, 1970, *Proceedings of Third Annual Meeting*, 21.

The growing complexity suggested the need for a more streamlined and flexible system: a single large Special Fund with untied contributions from all donors. At the Annual Meeting in 1972, Watanabe said: "Our hope is to consolidate all our concessional loan monies into a single fund of maximum flexibility, contributed on standard terms to avoid the administrative and accounting nightmares of juggling a dozen pocketfuls of different currencies which must each be spent under different criteria." This issue would be addressed under President Inoue, and the Asian Development Fund (also classified as a Special Fund) would be established in 1974.

Transition of the Leadership

By mid-1972, after almost 6 years with ADB, Watanabe decided to hand over to a new President. As one of the original founders, Watanabe left a deep imprint on the Bank. On becoming the first President, in speech after speech, he had carefully laid out the essential principles that he insisted on while he was President—of care, prudence, attention to the needs of borrowing countries, and proper management.[27] Indeed, in many ways, Watanabe established the essential character of ADB. The Bank's official portrait of him, hanging on the eighth floor of ADB headquarters, shows a secure and dignified individual gazing back in a measured way—a person who believed that the task he had in mind had been done.

The Ministry of Finance of Japan wanted a strong candidate to succeed Watanabe and settled on Shiro Inoue, an executive director of the Bank of Japan and its representative for international affairs. Inoue was chosen because, among other things, he was very knowledgeable about international capital and financial markets.

Watanabe and Inoue worked closely to arrange a smooth transition. In August 1972, they spent time together in the resort area of Hakone, near Tokyo, discussing priorities for the Bank.[28] But before he left, there was one final thing that Watanabe wanted to see: for almost 6 years since ADB had begun operations in late 1966, the organization had worked out of offices scattered around the commercial area of Makati. During this time, the Government of the Philippines had supported the construction of a new ADB headquarters building. This was to fulfill the implicit promise made in November 1965 when delegates to the meeting in Manila to choose a

---

[27] In extensive speeches are in ADB, 1969, *The Doors Are Open*.
[28] Additional details are in "The Oil Crisis: The Inoue Years 1972–76" (Chapter 3) in Wilson, 1987, *A Bank for Half the World*.

site for the Bank had been greeted with a sign declaring that a designated plot of land was the "Permanent Site of the Asian Development Bank." By late 1972, the new building was ready. On 18 November 1972, as Takeshi Watanabe was finishing his 6 years with ADB, Philippine President Ferdinand Marcos inaugurated the new headquarters on Roxas Boulevard in front of Manila Bay.

Watanabe's last day as President, 24 November 1972, was, as he noted himself, the Bank's sixth birthday. The following day, Shiro Inoue arrived in Manila. Just 2 months earlier, on 21 September, Marcos had declared martial law in the Philippines. Inoue thus began work in an atmosphere in which Bank staff wondered what lay ahead.

In the farewell speeches for Watanabe, his colleagues spoke with affection about his work. One Board member, Buu Hoan from Viet Nam, recalled that there had been three different Boards since 1966 (Board members are subject to election every 2 years) and that each Board had a different collective personality. A challenge for Watanabe as chair of the Board had been to channel, as Buu tactfully put it, the "complex and divergent opinions and moods" of the Board into meaningful decisions. This had required considerable skills of persuasion and listening, especially since it was not easy to understand "all the varieties of English as practiced by Board members." Further, Buu recalled, Watanabe had once humorously noted that he sometimes chose "to pretend to understand when you are not so sure, especially when you could guess that the speaker was not saying something really important."[29]

Watanabe responded to these speeches with self-deprecating humor. In paying tribute to Vice-President C. S. Krishna Moorthi, he observed: "By the way, I never learned what his initials C and S stand for." He expressed warm thanks to Krishna Moorthi saying that "[c]onfidentially, I must confess that I could also save lots of my breath because of his extraordinary ability to talk." Watanabe spoke of the earthquakes, fires, typhoons, floods, riots, and martial law that had occurred during his 6 years with ADB. He added, "I shall never forget the signing ceremony for an electricity project by candlelight, and the Board meeting while typhoon Yoling was raging outside."[30]

---

[29] Buu, 1972, *Farewell Speech*.
[30] Address by President Takeshi Watanabe at a Farewell Reception for him and Mrs. Watanabe at the Convention Hall, Asian Development Bank, on 24 November 1972, Manila.

Shiro Inoue

Many challenges lay ahead for the new President. Although he had a strong banking background and knowledge of financial matters, he had little direct experience of development issues. Inoue had never been on business to a developing country, nor had he worked in any detailed way on North–South issues which involved relationships between industrial and developing countries.[31] Indeed, during his 4 years as President, he often described himself as "a banker." Nevertheless, on arrival in Manila, he committed himself fully to the affairs of the Bank and the development challenges in the region. Many of his efforts as President would be focused, first, on the region's key priority of achieving peace in Viet Nam and, second, on mobilizing additional resources for the Special Funds. A third and entirely unforeseen priority would emerge within a year: responding to the consequences of the 1973–1974 oil shock.

In November 1972, when Inoue took up the presidency, there were new hopes that a peace agreement could be negotiated in Viet Nam. The previous month, the US and North Viet Nam had arrived at a draft peace agreement. In mid-November, at one of his last Board meetings, Watanabe had outlined a possible role for ADB in supporting reconstruction in the war-torn region. He said he was confident that his successor would want these plans carried forward.

On becoming President, Inoue took up these proposals. He noted that ADB had already provided technical assistance and loans to Viet Nam: "We felt the need in this region was too urgent for us to wait for peace." He also said he hoped the Bank could play a leading role in the reconstruction process. To emphasize his commitment, Inoue included Viet Nam in his first international trip as President and followed this up with consultations with the United Nations, the World Bank, and other international agencies to discuss an international aid program in the region.

Inoue also supported plans for international funding for the second Nam Ngum hydropower project in Laos. This would be the country's largest ever development project and have regional significance because surplus power would be sold to Thailand—thus strengthening economic links in Indochina. Nine donor countries had agreed to assist the project, so no funding was required from ADB. Instead, the Bank provided secretarial

---

[31] Wilson, 1987, *A Bank for Half the World*, 66.

support for the administration of the Second Nam Ngum Development Fund Agreement established in 1974.[32] In Viet Nam, however, the situation remained highly uncertain so it proved difficult to arrange a meeting of donors for Indochina as a whole. It was not until April 1975 that the World Bank and ADB were able to organize a meeting on aid to Laos. This was held in Manila with a senior ADB official in the chair.[33] And it would not be until 1993 when ADB could resume lending to Viet Nam.

Since 1966, the Bank had nurtured a more ambitious goal—initiating a development program in the Mekong region. However, this would not be achieved until the early 1990s when ADB established the Greater Mekong Subregion Economic Cooperation Program (Chapter 9).

Inoue's early focus on Indochina was overtaken in late 1973 by the unforeseen consequences of the first oil shock. Global energy prices began to rise quickly. By mid-1974, it was becoming clear that the impact on the international economy would be serious. Inoue soon became very concerned at the way the crisis was unfolding. At the ADB Annual Meeting in Kuala Lumpur in April 1974, he said that the era of cheap and easily available petroleum had ended and that there was now a "real threat" to continued economic growth.

Inoue described the situation in the Asian region in grim terms: "Nations whose growth is now strong will be slowed." He said, "Nations still in the early stages of development—or highly dependent on imported energy—may well fall back in 1974, traditional nitrogen-exporting countries may find it difficult to maintain their fertilizer exports, while increasing world-wide demand may push the price of the fertilizer that is available to several times the 1972 price…. Food itself, the most basic of necessities, will be scarce."

This was the first regionwide economic crisis that ADB had been called upon to respond to. Until then, the Bank had focused largely on providing foreign currency loans for industrial and infrastructure projects. Suddenly, it was being asked to offer new forms of assistance. Responding to the crisis would take up much of the rest of Inoue's time as President.

---

[32] The nine donor countries were Australia, Canada, West Germany, India, Japan, the Netherlands, New Zealand, the United Kingdom, and the United States. Details of the complex set of international arrangements surrounding the Fund are set out in UK Foreign Secretary, 1974, *Second Nam Ngum*.
[33] ADB, *Annual Report 1975*, 10.

The ADB response was essentially twofold. On the one hand, the Bank quickly designed programs to meet the crisis-related needs of borrowing countries. At the same time, it made vigorous efforts to raise additional external resources for programs.

Crisis-Related Programs

The 1973–1974 oil shock was a major test: borrowing countries needed additional resources quickly, but they also needed assistance tailored to the changed economic environment. Developing countries in Asia now had to adjust to a sharp rise in global energy prices which raised costs of imports of fuel and petroleum-based nitrogen fertilizers, thus fueling inflation. Higher prices of fertilizers in turn threatened to disrupt the Green Revolution. At the same time, many countries faced balance-of-payments pressures and had little choice but to borrow more—leading to worryingly high levels of international debt.

As things turned out, over the next few years, the Bank would be sufficiently flexible and pragmatic to respond to the crisis-related needs of borrowing countries. Moreover, this experience would prove valuable when the Bank subsequently widened the way it worked in Asia—designing new approaches to lending and resource mobilization. Following many suggestions and requests from member countries, ADB lending and resource mobilization would become much more sophisticated.

The Bank's first response to the oil shock was to increase lending quickly. In the 4 years leading up to 1976, lending rose by an average of around 25% per year, from $316 million in 1972 to over $770 million in 1976 (Figure 5.1). In these early days, ADB was still a project bank, lacking the flexible program-based loan arrangements that could allow for rapid disbursements in large tranches. These would come later. Nevertheless, ADB staff aimed to tailor the project loans to meet priority needs.

There were also changes in the sector balance of loan approvals. Responding to concerns about the impact of the oil crisis on food supplies, ADB increased lending for agriculture whose share of the loan program rose from 11% in 1973 to over 24% in 1974.

Because of the sharp rise in world fertilizer prices, ADB expanded its lending for domestic production of fertilizers. In 1975, for example, a concessional loan was provided to Bangladesh for the Ashuganj plant whose fertilizer manufacture was based on natural gas. Inoue traveled to

Figure 5.1: Operational Approvals by Fund Type, 1968–1976
($ million)

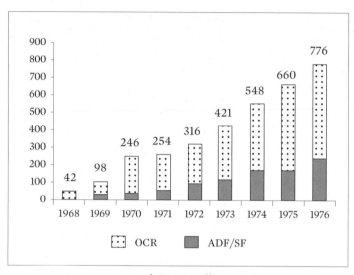

Total: $3,361 million

ADF = Asian Development Fund, OCR = ordinary capital resources, SF = Special Funds.
Note: Operational approvals include loans, grants, equity investments, and guarantees.
Source: ADB loan, technical assistance, grant, and equity approvals database.

Bangladesh to sign the loan agreement. While he was in Dhaka, he noted that Bangladesh was the first new member that had joined ADB since he became President and spoke of the "staggering problems" that the young nation faced. This project—and other fertilizer projects in Sri Lanka and Pakistan—relied on joint financing with other lenders, including members of the Organization of the Petroleum Exporting Countries (OPEC) in the Middle East. ADB also supported infrastructure development to facilitate easier movement of basic commodities such as food. The first loan for a rail project was in 1974, also in Bangladesh, for rehabilitating the Dhaka–Chittagong line and other parts of the national rail system.

Borrowing countries were also concerned about the spiraling costs of oil imports and took steps to generate more power domestically, through hydropower, coal, lignite, or natural gas. In response, the Bank made loans for hydropower and other projects such as the Sui–Karachi gas pipeline in Pakistan in 1974.

To assist lenders, ADB also changed some of its loan mechanisms.[34] It simplified arrangements for the concessional Special Fund loans. In addition, more local cost financing began to be provided to support projects. This was an important change. Previously, the Bank had only financed the foreign exchange costs of projects; all local costs had to be met by borrowing countries. The first ADB loan which provided financing for local costs was to Viet Nam for the Tan An Integrated Agricultural Project in the Mekong Delta approved in December 1974. A third change was to make it easier for borrowing countries to use part of their ADB loans to cover the interest costs and other charges attached to loans. Overall, the aim was to simplify loan procedures and make processes more flexible.

Second General Capital Increase and Establishment of ADF

The rapid expansion of the loan program imposed considerable pressures on the Bank. As an experienced banker, Inoue knew that ADB needed to move quickly to mobilize additional financial resources. One option was to raise more capital. Since there had been a GCI just a few years earlier, in 1971, it was unlikely that member countries would agree to another GCI so soon. But new member countries were still joining, and some existing members had not yet fully subscribed to the 1971 GCI. Inoue was thus able to tap these sources to raise additional modest amounts.

Inoue was also able to work toward a second general capital increase (GCI II). This was agreed just before he finished his term as President. In October 1976, member countries voted to raise the authorized capital of the Bank from by 135%. As with GCI I, the proposal was adjusted to make it easier for members to subscribe: the share of the capital that needed to be paid-in was reduced to 10%, and 4 years were allowed for the payments to be made. For most countries, therefore, the immediate cost of supporting GCI II was quite small. All member countries, with the exception of the US which had fallen behind in its subscription to GCI I, voted in favor of the increase.

Inoue also sought to mobilize more resources for ADB concessional funds. Following up on Watanabe's observation at the 1972 Annual Meeting that the management of a number of diverse Special Funds was a "nightmare," Inoue supported the proposal to establish one main concessional fund (Box 5.3). Discussions with donor countries throughout 1972 led to the

---

[34] ADB, *Annual Report 1974*, 17.

Box 5.3: Establishment of the Asian Development Fund

Manila, Dec 1968	**Establishment of the Agricultural Special Fund and the Multi-Purpose Special Fund**[a]
	The Agricultural Special Fund (ASF) was set up in 1968 following a contribution from Japan (7.2 billion yen, or $20 million equivalent) to finance special projects in agricultural development. A similar agreement was signed with Canada for its contribution to the Multi-Purpose Special Fund (MPSF) (for $25 million equivalent). These were voluntary and often tied to procurement in contributing countries.
Washington, DC, Sep 1972	**Meeting of developed member countries to review Special Funds**
	A meeting was held to discuss the proposed restructuring of the Bank's Special Funds. Preliminary proposals envisioned the creation of a special unified fund—later called the Asian Development Fund (ADF)—that would be governed by uniform regulations reflecting the operational arrangements of the Asian Development Bank (ADB). The ADF would untie resources under agreed multilateral arrangements and be periodically replenished.
Nov 1972	**Appointment of John Chadwick as the Bank's Special Funds Ambassador**
	ADB appointed John Chadwick as special advisor to President Shiro Inoue to help with resource mobilization for the unified Special Funds. On 30 November, Chadwick began his travels to 17 developed countries to gather support for the ADF.
London, 15 Mar 1973	**Special Funds meeting**
	The first meeting of all prospective donors was held in London. Main issues discussed included the amount to be mobilized, the amount of individual contributions, and the regulations of the Fund. Proposals to establish the unified Special Fund were accepted in principle.

continued on next page

Box 5.3 *continued*

Manila, 28 Apr 1973	**Adoption of resolution on ADF Establishment**
	On the last day of the Sixth ADB Annual Meeting, the Board of Governors adopted Resolution No. 62 authorizing the establishment of the ADF.
22 May 1973	**Termination of the Agricultural Special Fund**
	With the repayment of a small amount still due to Denmark for its original loan contribution, the way was clear for the formal termination of the ASF. Earlier, Japan and the Netherlands had transferred their ASF contributions to the MPSF.
Bonn, Oct 1973	**Final meeting on the establishment of ADF**
	The arrangements for ADF I were jointly accepted by 14 developed member countries. The amount agreed ($525 million) was to be paid in two stages: $350 million by 30 June 1975 and $175 million by the end of March 1976. Regional donors would contribute around 40% of the total, of which more than 80% was provided by Japan.
28 Jun 1974	**ADF formally established**
	Contributions to the initial mobilization reached $260 million, triggering the conditions for the Fund to be legally effective.
Manila, 26 Apr 1975	**Adoption of resolutions on review of ADB's resources and transfer of set-aside resources to ADF**
	On the last day of the Eighth Annual Meeting, the Board of Governors adopted Resolution No. 84 approving the examination of the Bank's resource requirements (including the need for early ADF replenishment) and Resolution No. 85 arranging transfer of all set-aside resources from the MPSF to the ADF.
Washington, DC, 30 Aug 1975	**Request for reduction of replenishment**
	Potential donors were asked to consider revised arrangements for an $830 million replenishment (a reduction from the original proposal of $1 billion).

continued on next page

Box 5.3 continued

Brussels, Sep 1975	**Final meeting on the first ADF replenishment (ADF II)**
	A draft Board resolution was prepared and discussed. The reduced amount was accompanied by a reduction in the United States share from 29% to 22%. Canada increased its share substantially. Australia and Sweden became new donors.
Jun 1976	**ADF II made effective**
	The replenishment was made effective after 18 months of negotiations.

ADF = Asian Development Fund.

[a] Between December 1968 and the end of 1972, ADB received contributions to the ASF and MPSF from nine other developed member countries for a total of $198 million. The ASF was to wind down in early 1973 and its resources consolidated with those of the MPSF. Nearly all the MPSF resources were eventually transferred to the ADF.

Source: ADB. 2016. *ADB Through the Decades: ADB's First Decade (1966–1976)*. Manila.

proposal for a new Asian Development Fund (ADF). Most of the details were settled at a meeting in London in early 1973. The proposal was endorsed later that year at the Annual Meeting in Manila. The ADF was formally established when contributions to the initial mobilization became effective in June 1974.

Following the oil shock, low-income countries were keen to borrow from the new ADF and it soon seemed likely that the first round of contributions to the Fund would be exhausted by the end of 1976. But this problem had been anticipated. No sooner had the ADF been established than discussions started on the first replenishment (ADF II). When negotiations proved difficult, ADB asked a former British diplomat John Chadwick to act as a special advisor.

Meanwhile, ADF funds were running down quickly. At the Annual Meeting in Jakarta in April 1976, Inoue spoke of an "agonizing slowdown" of concessional lending: "Our uncommitted Special Funds resources have dwindled to $23 million and we have had to postpone consideration of certain projects for lack of resources. This indeed is a precarious state." ADB initially proposed a replenishment of $1 billion—an amount which would have allowed for around $250 million of soft loans to be approved in 1975, rising to about $400 million in 1978.

But donors did not agree and settled on a replenishment of $830 million. The ADF II replenishment became effective in mid-1976. Following ADF II, regular replenishment of the Fund by donor countries would become the main source of finance for concessional soft loan activities.

Borrowing in Capital Markets, Cofinancing, and Recycling of Oil Money

A third main source of funding which Inoue looked to was further borrowing in international capital markets, including through the issuance of bonds. In 1975, the Bank sharply expanded its borrowing activities. In the 6 years to 1974, ADB had borrowed over $291 million in total. However, the level rose to over $310 million in 1975 and to almost $530 million in 1976. By the end of 1976, ADB had issued around $1,100 million in bonds in 12 countries and in 11 currencies—much of which was used to support ADB infrastructure investments and some crisis-related activities.

An important new source of potential funding was the pool of petrodollars that had been building up in the Middle East. In the wake of the oil shock, the major petroleum-producing nations (mainly OPEC members) had amassed large financial surpluses. During the 1974 Annual Meeting, Inoue spoke of the opportunity to recycle some of these funds to borrowing countries in Asia.

However, among the international finance institutions, ADB was the only one without a capital-exporting OPEC country as a member. Hence, it took time for ADB to build up its relationships with OPEC countries. In 1974, the Bank was able to issue its first bonds in a Middle East country—in Kuwait for the equivalent of about $17 million. The first ADB Treasurer, Wolf Preuss, recounted that tapping the capital markets of OPEC countries for the first time was a tedious process. In 1975, ADB issued bonds in Saudi Arabia for 50 million Saudi Arabian riyals (equivalent to $14.6 million). In addition, ADB was able to arrange private placements with institutions such as the Saudi Arabian Monetary Agency and investors in Kuwait. Despite the difficult conditions, ADB succeeded in expanding its borrowings in Middle East capital markets.

As another means of attracting petrodollar funds, ADB explored joint financing for its projects. By the mid-1970s, the flow of finance from ADB's own resources and borrowings was being supplemented with cofinancing from multilateral and bilateral sources, including from oil-exporting countries. In 1970, the first Bank cofinancing agreement was arranged. This was for a fertilizer plant in Indonesia with funding from Japan, the US, and the International Development Association of the World Bank. Cofinancing was also used to help finance fertilizer projects in Bangladesh, Pakistan, and Sri Lanka.

As part of the program to build up its links with institutions in the Middle East, the Bank provided technical support to the new Islamic Development Bank (IsDB) established in 1973. ADB helped the IsDB organize its operations (including the Saudi Fund for Development) and discussed institutional collaboration such as cofinancing of projects in countries where both ADB and the IsDB operated. When the inaugural meeting of the IsDB Board of Governors was held in Riyadh in July 1975, Inoue attended to extend a "welcome to the new bank to the growing family of development financial institutions."

Operational Summary

By the end of the first ADB decade, over $3 billion of loans had been approved for 23 countries. The total loan commitments had reached three times the Bank's 1966 initial capital subscription of $1 billion. Of this, over a quarter was on concessional terms to the poorest borrowing members—a significant achievement.

During this first decade, ADB provided 23% of its total lending for energy, 20% to transport and information and communication technology (ICT), 19% to agriculture, and 18% to finance. Most of the remainder was lent to industry (10%) and water (9%) (Figure 5.2). Of this total, ADF lending was more heavily concentrated in agriculture at 34%, followed by energy at 19%, industry at 15%, and transport and ICT at 14%. The rest went to finance (10%), water (7%), and education (1%).

More than half of the lending went to Southeast Asia (52%). The rest was shared by East Asia (21%), Central and West Asia (15%), South Asia (11%), and the Pacific (2%) (Figure 5.3). The top five country recipients were the Republic of Korea (16%), the Philippines (14%), Pakistan (13%), Indonesia (11%), and Thailand (9%).

Figure 5.2: Operational Approvals by Sector, 1968–1976
(%, $ million)

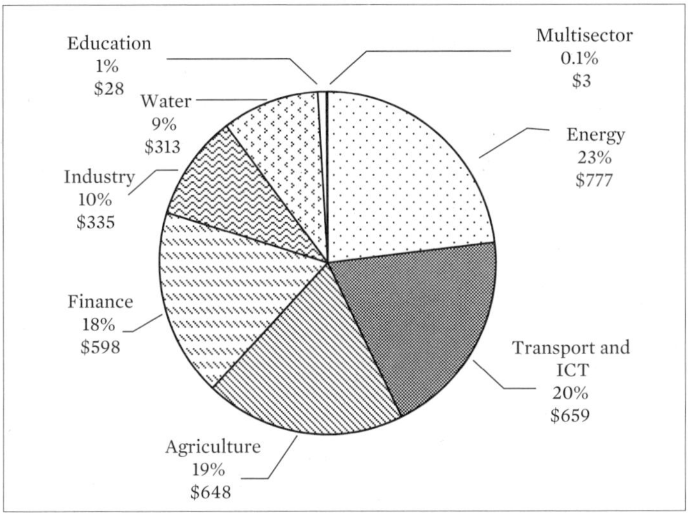

- Education 1% $28
- Water 9% $313
- Industry 10% $335
- Finance 18% $598
- Agriculture 19% $648
- Transport and ICT 20% $659
- Energy 23% $777
- Multisector 0.1% $3

Total: $3,361 million

ICT = information and communication technology.

Note: Operational approvals include loans, grants, equity investments, and guarantees.

Source: ADB loan, technical assistance, grant, and equity approvals database.

Technical assistance operations during these 10 years reached $25.4 million. Technical assistance projects helped expand lending, often being used to prepare projects and build up institutions and skills in borrowing countries. Regional technical assistance was also used to finance major regional surveys. Almost half of technical assistance operations went to agriculture, while more than a sixth supported activities in transport and ICT. The remainder went to finance (12%), energy (9%), water (5%), public sector management (4%), industry (4%), and education (1%). The top five country recipients of technical assistance were Indonesia (18%), Bangladesh (12%), Afghanistan (10%), Nepal (9%), and the Philippines (9%).

From 31 founding members, 11 new members joined ADB during the first decade: Switzerland (1967); Hong Kong, China (1969); Fiji and France (1970); Papua New Guinea (1971); Tonga (1972); Bangladesh, Myanmar, and Solomon Islands (1973); Kiribati (1974); and the Cook Islands (1976).

Figure 5.3: Operational Approvals by Region, 1968–1976
(%, $ million)

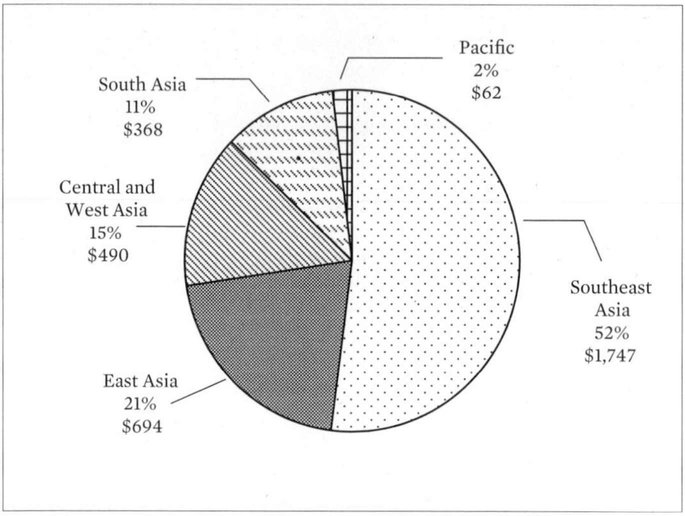

- Pacific 2% $62
- South Asia 11% $368
- Central and West Asia 15% $490
- East Asia 21% $694
- Southeast Asia 52% $1,747

Total: $3,361 million

Notes: Regional breakdown is based on current country groupings of ADB. Operational approvals include loans, grants, equity investments, and guarantees.

Source: ADB loan, technical assistance, grant, and equity approvals database.

By 1976, membership had grown to 42 members (29 regional and 13 nonregional). The internal administrative expenses budget had grown from $3.04 million in 1967 to $19.7 million by 1976 (Appendix Table A2.8). Efforts to recruit highly competent staff continued as well. By the end of the first decade, there were 760 staff—290 international and Management staff from 33 member countries and 470 supporting staff (Table 5.1).

Ten Years Old

By 1976, ADB was approaching its teenage years. At the Annual Meeting in Jakarta in April 1976, Inoue announced that he would not seek reelection at the end of his term in November. Soon a third President would arrive. The first two, Takeshi Watanabe and Shiro Inoue, had established firm foundations and shaped the organization as a development bank and a regional development institution. The Bank now had a strong loans program with many technical assistance projects, and it was supporting regional cooperation.

Former World Bank President Eugene Black had predicted: "...it will be five to seven years before the real personality of the ADB emerges."[35] Watanabe, too, noted that in the early years the Bank had spent some time finding its way. "Because of the variety of projects to which our assistance has been given," he said to the Third Annual Meeting, "it has not always been easy to describe the ADB."

Watanabe had envisaged ADB as Asia's family doctor, attuned to and quick to respond to the region's problems, but within the discipline and prudence of a sound bank. By the end of its first decade, the Bank's profile was clearer. When Inoue took over in 1972, he inherited a bank that had "established itself for the world to see, for the financial community to trust, for the countries and peoples of developing Asia to rely upon." At the Annual Meeting in 1972, Inoue underlined the Bank's distinctive Asian character: "There is a willingness to find new paths towards development, to move beyond precedents, to establish Asia's own way of meeting Asia's problems."

The next two Presidents, Taroichi Yoshida and Masao Fujioka, would carry these legacies forward. The second ADB decade would bring challenges that would force further large changes. The Bank would also attract new members, including the largest country in the world, the People's Republic of China.

---

[35] Quoted by Watanabe in his speech during the 1970 Annual Meeting. ADB, 1970, *Address by President at Third Annual Meeting*; also in ADB, 1970, *Proceedings of Third Annual Meeting*.

Table 5.1: Selected Operational, Institutional, and Financial Information, 1966–1976

	1966–1967 (Start of the First Decade)	1976 (End of the First Decade)	1967–1976 (Total, First Decade)
A. Operational Highlights ($ million)			
Total operational approvals[a]	–	776	3,361
By fund source			
Ordinary capital resources	–	540	2,466
Asian Development Fund	–	236	895
By operations			
Sovereign	–	776	3,361
Nonsovereign	–	–	–
Technical assistance approvals[b]	0.2 (1967)	3	25
Technical assistance projects	0.1 (1967)	2	21
Regional assistance	0.2 (1967)	1	4
Outstanding loan portfolio	–	1,079	
Ordinary capital resources	–	881	
Asian Development Fund	–	198	
Total loan and grant disbursements	–	327	1,159
Ordinary capital resources	–	263	948
Asian Development Fund	–	63	211
Official cofinancing[c]	–	–	29
Commercial cofinancing	–	–	–
B. Institutional Highlights			
Staff information (end of year)			
Total staff	40 (1966)	760	
International staff [d]	13 (1966)	290	
Women staff	14 (1966)	308	
Women international staff	1 (1966)	5	
Staff in field offices	–	–	

continued on next page

Table 5.1 continued

	1966–1967 (Start of the First Decade)	1976 (End of the First Decade)	1967–1976 (Total, First Decade)
Member countries	31 (1966)	42	
Field offices	–	–	
Internal administrative expenses budget ($ million)	3 (1967)	20	102
C. Financial Highlights ($ million)			
Authorized capital[e]	1,000 (1966)	3,707	
Subscribed capital[e]	1,000 (1966)	3,688	
Paid-in	500 (1966)	1,183	
Callable	500 (1966)	2,506	
Borrowings ($ million)	–	529	1,133

– = nil, SDR = special drawing right.

[a] Figures refer to loan, grant, equity investment, and guarantee approvals, net of terminations (they exclude operations approved by the Board of Directors but terminated before they were deemed effective). The first loan from ordinary capital resources was approved in 1968. Concessional financing operations began in 1969.

[b] Technical assistance operations cover grants funded by the Technical Assistance Special Fund only. The first technical assistance project was approved in 1967.

[c] Includes trust funds and cofinancing of loans, grants, and technical assistance.

[d] International staff data include Management.

[e] The original authorized capital of ADB was $1 billion in terms of US dollars of the weight and fineness in effect on 31 January 1966. In November 1966, the Board of Governors approved an increase of $100 million of authorized capital. As of 31 December 1967, the subscribed capital was $970 million, of which $485 million was paid-in, while the rest was callable shares.

Sources: ADB Annual Reports; ADB Budget, Personnel, and Management Systems Department; ADB Controller's Department; ADB's Strategy and Policy Department; ADB loan, technical assistance, grant, and equity approvals database; ADB Cofinancing database.

CHAPTER 6
Second Decade (1977–1986)

Asia: Transformation in the Region

"The economic record of 1979 foreshadows the kinds of challenges which developing member countries must be prepared to face during the 1980s. … The most formidable challenge is posed by the world energy situation. … A second major challenge for developing countries is to ensure a sustained increase in agricultural production. … A third major challenge of the 1980s will be the provision of productive employment …"

– *Taroichi Yoshida,*
Address to the ADB Annual Meeting, 1980

During the second ADB decade, there were major economic changes across the international economy and within Asia. At the global level, policy makers in industrial countries were deeply divided on how to respond to the unfamiliar challenges posed by stagflation—the strange combination of stagnant economic growth and high inflation. Global monetary policy tightened sharply after the announcement of new measures in the United States (US) in late 1979 which led to sharp increases in interest rates and disruptive realignments in exchange rates. These changes contributed to the Latin American debt crisis which lasted for much of the 1980s leading to a "lost decade" for international development.

While these events were occurring at the international level, key changes were taking place in Asia. In contrast to Latin America, Asia was powering ahead. The newly industrialized economies (NIEs) continued to grow strongly. But more importantly, dramatic reforms began to take hold in the People's Republic of China (PRC) after 1978 with the introduction of new pro-market policies. The far-reaching impact of these reforms would only become clearer later, during the third ADB decade and after 2000. Development prospects also continued to strengthen in Southeast Asia and in South Asia.

Consequences of Stagflation

The first oil shock at the end of 1973 disrupted national economies and international markets, but after several difficult years international conditions began to improve. By the beginning of the second ADB decade in 1977, the most uncertain period seemed to have passed.

This stability was to be short-lived. In 1979, international markets experienced a second oil shock triggered by the revolution in Iran and other events in the Middle East. Oil prices rose sharply, from around $13 per barrel in 1978 to over $30 by the end of 1979. Oil exporters in Asia, such as Indonesia and Malaysia, enjoyed further windfall gains, but oil-importing countries in developing Asia were hard hit. As will be seen in the next chapter, ADB needed to respond quickly to the changed situation with new programs and loan products.

In the early 1980s, the second oil shock led to a deep recession in industrial countries as they sought policies to combat stagflation. There was also a marked fall in the international demand for commodities. This damaged the terms of trade for many resource-exporting countries. In 1981, for the first time in many years, the volume of world trade declined. Governments in developing countries in Asia struggled to respond. Frequent changes in policy were necessary. The uncertain environment also created problems for ADB. Many borrowing countries requested loans to help respond to the crisis—just when volatile international conditions were making it more difficult for ADB to raise additional resources in global financial markets.

Nevertheless, despite the widening recession, the new chair of the US Federal Reserve, Paul Volcker, decided to give priority to fighting inflation, rather than stimulating the economy. On 6 October 1979, though the economy was beginning to slow sharply, he announced that monetary policy would be tightened—an announcement immediately dubbed the "Volcker Shock." The federal funds rate, a key tool of monetary policy, rose sharply from around 11% in 1979 to over 20% in 1981.

The abrupt tightening of monetary policy in the US quickly spilled over to the global economy. Interest rates soon began to rise across the world. Over the next few years, the changes in US monetary policy, along with uncertainty in international markets, led to strong appreciation of the US dollar. It was not until 22 September 1985, when the Plaza Accord was signed in New York, that agreement was reached between finance ministers and central bank governors of the Group of Five (G5) leading industrial countries (France, West Germany, Japan, the United Kingdom, and the US) to encourage a depreciation of the US dollar. Following the Plaza Accord, the value of the US dollar fell quickly until ministers and central bank governors of the G7 countries (including Canada and Italy) met again in Paris in February 1987 to sign the Louvre Accord to agree to coordinate policies to stabilize the value of the US dollar.

Higher interest rates also contributed to an international debt crisis. The crisis had a particularly severe impact in Latin America after 1982 when Mexico defaulted on its debt. African economies, too, became deeply enmeshed in a series of debt crises, though in Africa much of the debt was not to private banks but to official bilateral and multilateral lenders. Asian developing countries also found it more difficult to service international debt but managed it comparatively well, reducing the risk that excessive debt would hamper growth.[1]

Basic Human Needs and Structural Adjustment

Over this period, there were also changes in development thinking. The international community was increasingly divided on the question of whether rapid economic growth would "trickle down" to provide benefits to the poor. In 1976, for example, the International Labour Organization World Employment Conference emphasized the importance of meeting "basic human needs." Another landmark was the 1980 report of the Brandt Commission on global inequity and poverty. The report addressed major global issues such as hunger and food, population, the environment, industrialization, trade, energy, and the international monetary system. It also considered what developing countries could do for themselves and the need for more development funds, including foreign aid.

Just as the Brandt Commission was issuing its report, new issues were being added to the global development agenda—notably the debt crisis in Latin America and pressures for structural adjustment. For the rest of the 1980s, development policy focused on the risks of indebtedness and the need to monitor borrowing more carefully. Attention shifted away from redistribution and basic needs and back toward traditional questions of how to achieve overall growth and development. US President Ronald Reagan and United Kingdom Prime Minister Margaret Thatcher argued for supply-side economic reforms.

---

[1] James, Naya, and Meier, 1987, *Asian Development*.

By the mid-1980s, the conventional wisdom was that developing countries should be more market oriented and undertake "structural adjustment" to be able to respond quickly to changes in international circumstances. There was also an emphasis on outward-looking industrialization, as countries abandoned the import substitution industrialization policies of the 1960s and 1970s.

These changes in development thinking had implications in Asia and for ADB, which in the latter part of the 1970s was being pressed to respond to social and equity issues (Chapter 7). At the ADB Annual Meeting in 1978, for example, the US representative J. Fred Bergsten said that he was pleased that the Bank had focused the lending program on "growth with equity."

Another implication was that structural adjustment in Latin America began to influence policy discussions in Asia. International institutions such as the World Bank and ADB were moving beyond simply financing projects and engaging more in policy dialogue with borrowing countries. Developing countries were also designing structural adjustment programs, especially in view of the rapid changes taking place across the international economy.

A third influence on policy discussions in Asia throughout the 1980s and into the 1990s was the Reagan–Thatcher emphasis on the "magic of the market." Many Asian policy makers took a pragmatic approach, agreeing that pro-market policies were often appropriate but also emphasizing the importance of the state in the development process.

Geese Become Tigers

Amid the difficult international environment, development in the region gathered pace—though progress differed across countries. The fastest-growing were the four NIEs: Hong Kong, China; the Republic of Korea; Singapore; and Taipei,China. By the time of the first oil shock, these "geese," flying in formation behind Japan, had already been pursuing export-led industrial development and later would become known as the four Asian "tigers." In broad terms, their government policies, although often interventionist, were pro-market—they avoided distorting relative prices and instead encouraged private firms to adjust to domestic and international markets. Governments also supported markets by investing in better social and physical infrastructure.

Economic growth in the NIEs slowed following the first oil shock but soon rebounded. From 1976, as the industrial world emerged from recession, the NIEs' export growth resumed and for the rest of the 1970s would generally be over 20% per year.[2] But it soon became apparent that the NIEs would need to revise their industrial strategies. They had started out as exporters of low-skill, labor-intensive goods such as textiles, clothing, footwear, and toys, but as real wages grew, they found it more difficult to compete in world markets. Moreover, the industrial countries were becoming more protectionist for these products:[3] in 1979, for the Republic of Korea, nearly 50% of exports to industrial countries were affected by trade restrictions, almost double the proportion just 4 years earlier.[4]

By the early 1980s, policy makers in the NIEs were giving greater emphasis to skill- and capital-intensive manufactured goods. One ADB study noted: "All of them have embarked on policies of adjustment towards skill-intensive and/or heavy industries. The large well-trained labor force available... suggests that these countries can attain a high degree of international competitiveness in the production of relatively human-capital intensive products, such as the more sophisticated kinds of electrical and mechanical engineering, shipbuilding and the manufacture of parts and components for heavy engineering products."[5]

Each of the NIEs encouraged structural change.[6] In the Republic of Korea, the government initially promoted light industry in the 1960s and heavy industry in the 1970s under the strong leadership of President Park Chung-hee (1963–1979). Preferential trade and security arrangements with the US as well as financial assistance ($300 million grants and $200 million concessional loans) and technology transfer from Japan after the signing of the treaty normalizing relations in 1965 also helped. In addition, West Germany played a key role in supporting the Republic of Korea's rapid growth in the 1960s and 1970s by providing policy advice, financial assistance, and technology. In the early 1980s and later, automobiles and electronics would become the focus of policies.

---

[2] Naya, 1983, *Asian and Pacific Developing Countries*, 5.
[3] The "new protectionism" mainly took the form of quantitative restrictions. However, it also included a range of other measures such as countervailing and anti-dumping steps and assistance to ailing industries. Commonwealth Secretariat, 1980, *The World Economic Crisis*, 33.
[4] Commonwealth Secretariat, 1980, *The World Economic Crisis*, 33.
[5] Naya and James, 1982, *Developing Asia*.
[6] James, Naya, and Meier, 1987, *Asian Development*, 41–43.

Singapore and Taipei,China pursued a different approach—encouraging exports of standardized product cycle goods (such as radios and color televisions) along with heavy engineering goods. In 1979–1981, Singapore, under the leadership of Prime Minister Lee Kuan Yew, aiming to shift from unskilled to skilled activities, raised legal wages by around 80%. Initially, this was only partially successful because less educated workers found it difficult to make the transition. However, the government continued to pursue a high wages policy into the mid-1980s, encouraging a movement to capital-intensive sectors. Nevertheless, when Singapore found itself less competitive than the other NIEs, the government changed direction again and brought labor and other costs into line with those in international markets.

Unlike the other NIEs, Hong Kong, China did not aim for changes in manufacturing but moved to develop highly competitive services. The global recession in 1982 caused a sharp fall in exports and growth, but Hong Kong, China took advantage of the beginning of liberalization in neighboring PRC in trade and services including financial services. Residents of Hong Kong, China quickly began to invest in the new special economic zones.

By the end of the second ADB decade, the performance of the NIEs as a group was attracting growing international attention. In 1987, a major study on trends in Asia, *Asian Development,* which grew out of research carried out in ADB, noted that the growth rates of these countries were virtually without historical precedent.[7] A range of factors contributed to their success. These economies benefited from sound management, well-developed institutions, and strong entrepreneurial skills. Moreover, the governments in all four NIEs supported pro-market and export-oriented economic change. In addition, they pursued prudent international borrowing policies and used foreign capital effectively so they did not run into debt problems.

Southeast Asia: Swings of Fortune

Even if they were not as adaptable as the NIEs, most developing countries in Southeast Asia coped well under the difficult circumstances during the second ADB decade. Of these, Indonesia and Malaysia were oil exporters

---

[7] James, Naya, and Meier, 1987, *Asian Development,* 10. The earlier research in ADB was set out in Naya and James, 1982, *Developing Asia.*

and benefited from the first and second oil shocks—although they found it difficult to adjust in the 1980s when international oil prices fell quickly.

In the mid-1970s, the largest country, Indonesia, still gave high priority to agriculture and only later paid more attention to manufacturing. After the first oil shock in 1973, Indonesia benefited from a large windfall of income from commodity exports and rapidly increased government development spending on such things as rural infrastructure (irrigation and local roads), health, and education. But balance-of-payments pressures prompted a devaluation of the rupiah in 1978. Unexpectedly, the second oil shock in 1979 transformed the situation again and boosted revenues. In the 1980s, Indonesia expanded its development activities, including the ambitious transmigration program aiming to shift several million people from Java to the outer islands. At the same time, growth slowed sharply in industrial countries in the early 1980s, and international oil prices began to weaken, bringing renewed strains on the balance-of-payments. Indonesian policy makers responded with frequent adjustments in economic policy and in the 1980s introduced policy packages to promote structural adjustment. Indonesia again devalued its currency in 1983 and 1986.

Malaysia, also an oil exporter, experienced similar swings of fortune, but under the leadership of Prime Minister Mahathir Mohamad weathered economic challenges well. After the second oil boom, the government implemented expansionary fiscal policies in the early 1980s for which it borrowed extensively in international markets. However, economic management was complicated by the spillover effects from the Volcker Shock, reflected in increases in international interest rates and appreciation of the US dollar. Malaysia was more successful than Indonesia with its industrial policies and established several export processing zones where multinational companies, especially from Japan, produced goods such as textiles and electronics. Later, in the 1990s, the Malaysian manufacturing sector would become part of the rapidly growing network of value-added chains with strong links to East Asia.

Thailand, as an oil importer, was affected by the oil price shocks. Thai policy makers responded pragmatically, relying on a dynamic domestic private sector and foreign investment policies which were pro-market and export oriented. The political situation was generally stable and engendered confidence in the business and financial community. As a result, growth throughout the late 1970s into the 1980s was around 7% per year, though the economy slowed during the global recession in the early 1980s. Later in the 1980s and onward, rapid structural transformation took place in the Thai economy led by the industry sector, including car and auto parts manufacturing, supported by strong inflows of foreign investment.

The Philippines, also an oil importer, suffered economic setbacks during the periods of high oil prices. Compared with Thailand, however, economic performance was disappointing. The main difference was in economic policy. From the late 1960s, the Philippines had embarked upon inward-looking import substitution. By the early 1980s, protection for manufacturing had become an increasing burden on the economy and was holding back international competitiveness. Economic development was also hampered in the 1980s by political upheaval and changes in government. The economy contracted around 7% in 1984 and again in 1985. The transition from a martial law regime to a new democratic government in 1986 brought widespread hopes for reform. Nevertheless, political instability, power shortages, and natural disasters (such as the major volcanic eruption at Mount Pinatubo in 1991) held back progress for almost a decade after 1986.

One of the important drivers of higher growth and industrial transformation in the ASEAN-4 countries (Indonesia, Malaysia, the Philippines, and Thailand) of the Association of Southeast Asian Nations (ASEAN) was increased foreign investment, especially from Japan. The flow of outward investment from Japan was induced by the sharp appreciation of the yen to the US dollar after the Plaza Accord,[8] rising wages,[9] and a domestic and foreign investment boom during the bubble period up to 1990. The result was that Japanese foreign direct investment to the ASEAN-4 countries increased from $5.3 billion in 1980–1984 to $6.9 billion in 1985–1989, and then to $15.8 billion in 1990–1994.[10] Among the ASEAN-4 countries, the Philippines found it difficult to take advantage of the massive investment flow because of the political instability at the time.

In the Mekong countries too, efforts to promote development were held back by internal conflict. In Cambodia, for example, where the brutal rule of the Khmer Rouge claimed millions of lives in the late 1970s, life expectancy at 21 years was the lowest in the world in 1976. One out of four children died before their fifth birthday. The story was more positive in Viet Nam

---

[8] The average exchange rate appreciated from around 238 yen to the US dollar in 1985 to 128 yen in 1988.
[9] Japan's per capita GDP in dollar terms surpassed that of the US in the late 1980s.
[10] JETRO Trade and Investment Statistics, https://www.jetro.go.jp/en/reports/statistics

where, despite conflict, the economy made considerable progress following liberalization in agriculture and industry. In agriculture, the government introduced greater scope for farmers to use land on a private basis and to keep a share of increases in production. The result was that rice output began to expand rapidly in the early 1980s. In 1986, the Government of Viet Nam introduced further pro-market *Doi Moi* (renovation) reforms which, over subsequent decades, transformed economic prospects not just in Viet Nam but across the wider Mekong region.

South Asia

All South Asian countries were oil importers, so the two oil shocks, along with the recession in industrial countries, had severe consequences. In these generally agricultural countries, the impact of the oil shocks was exacerbated in the early 1980s by widespread droughts. The economies of South Asia had large informal sectors and the smaller formal sectors were dominated by state-owned enterprises. Governments also gave high priority to economic planning and regulating markets and to specific industries. Throughout much of the 1970s, overall development performance often fell below expectations. The countries of South Asia found it difficult to achieve structural change. As a result, the development gap between the countries in the subcontinent and the PRC, the NIEs, and countries in Southeast Asia widened.

The United Nations in 1979 summarized the daunting range of problems holding back much of South Asia in its annual *Economic and Social Survey of Asia and the Pacific*:[11] "The main causes of shortfalls in growth in South Asia differ from country to country. But in general they would include: (a) low saving and investment rates, (b) low (and in some countries even falling) productivity of investment, particularly public investment ..., (c) recurring shortages of agricultural and industrial inputs ..., (d) restricted participation of the vast small farm sector in the green revolution due to the failure to implement land reforms and other institutional reforms, (e) continuing high population growth rates, (f) declining foreign assistance/investment ratios, (g) declining terms of trade, increasing barriers faced by exports and (h) the aggravation of these long-term difficulties by the energy crisis and stagflation in the developed economies." In addition, other potential important factors included inadequate policies and poor governance.

---

[11] United Nations, 1980, *Economic and Social Survey of Asia and the Pacific*, 83.

Toward the end of the second ADB decade, there were signs of greater commitment to change. At various times, most governments in South Asia announced market-oriented reforms—reducing discrimination against private firms and improving the management of the public industry sector.[12] Sri Lanka, for example, encouraged the production of traditional light consumer goods. India became somewhat less interventionist and growth accelerated during the 1980s, but it was not until 1991 that an economic crisis prompted far-reaching changes in development policy.

Pacific Island Countries

In the Pacific island countries, policy makers grappled with challenges of nation building. Papua New Guinea, for example, the largest country in the region, had become independent in 1975. The young nation's leaders gave priority to strengthening the systems of government. In many of the Pacific island countries, economic affairs and international relations were still strongly influenced by linkages to former colonial countries.

The unique challenges in the Pacific island countries complicated their responses to the changes in the global economy during the second ADB decade.[13] The South Pacific island countries were particularly exposed to international markets. Between 1980 and 1986, some of the countries in the South Pacific experienced low or even negative economic growth with large trade and current account deficits and high inflation.

People's Republic of China

During the early part of the second ADB decade, one of the greatest economic transformations in history got under way in Asia: a period of remarkable reform began in the PRC that would lead to the emergence of the nation as one of the world's leading economies.

After the establishment of the PRC in 1949, its leaders had experimented with different approaches to development—largely based on self-reliance, with relatively few links with the international community. But these strategies, along with industrial policies, had not resulted in sustained growth. As one analysis put it: "When China started its transition in 1978,

---

[12] Naya and James, 1982, *Developing Asia*, 55.
[13] Tsusaka, 1984, *South Pacific Developing Countries*, 65–81.

Table 6.1: Major Reform Steps in the People's Republic of China, 1978–1986

Year	Reforms
1978	Communique of the Third Plenary Session of the 11th Central Committee of the Communist Party initiating the "four modernizations"
1979	"Open door" policy initiated, with foreign trade and investment reforms
	Law on Joint Venture Companies passed
1979	Limited official encouragement of household responsibility system in agriculture
1979	Three specialized banks formed separate from the People's Bank of China (the central bank)
1980	First four special economic zones created
1980	"Eating from separate kitchens" reforms in intergovernmental fiscal relations
1984	Individual enterprises with fewer than eight employees officially allowed
1984	Tax for profit reforms of state-owned enterprises
1986	Provisional bankruptcy law passed for state-owned enterprises

Source: B. Hofman and J. Wu. 2009. Explaining China's Development and Reforms. *Working Paper No. 50*. Washington, DC: World Bank on behalf of the Commission on Growth and Development.

it was a desperately poor, predominantly rural, agricultural country with a highly inefficient industry sector oriented to heavy industry."[14]

In 1977, it was declared that the Cultural Revolution spanning the period from 1966 to 1976 had ended. In late 1978, the Third Plenary Session of the 11th Central Committee of the Communist Party of the People's Republic of China set out a program of reform which was carried out carefully, deliberately, and in stages (Table 6.1). The first stage involved introducing the household responsibility system and free markets in rural areas which allowed farmers to benefit more from their own efforts. The role of collectives was greatly reduced.

---

[14] Hofman and Wu, 2009, *Explaining China's Development and Reforms*, 16.

This new approach encouraged a burst of entrepreneurship, especially in rural areas. While later changes would be directed more toward the internationalization of the economy, the first round of pro-market reforms liberalized domestic markets. As these reforms took effect, the pace of rural activity picked up.[15] Rural workers diversified their incomes, engaging in more non-agricultural activities, often in "town and village enterprises," many of which were privately owned.[16] The result was a rapid increase in rural incomes and output.

Another important element of the new strategy was the establishment of special economic zones. In 1980, the government established zones in four coastal cities. In 1984, the open door policies of these zones were extended to 14 coastal cities. In 1985, special zones were established in the Yangtze, Pearl, and Minnan river deltas.[17] Liberalization was more gradual in the finance sector. At the start of the reform, only the central bank, the People's Bank of China, could conduct business in foreign currency. By 1986, all domestic banks could do so, introducing much more competition into the foreign exchange business.

Combined with these key reform policies and the opening up of the economy, foreign direct investment from advanced economies played a crucial role during the next four decades of strong growth. Assistance from the World Bank and later from ADB were important sources of development finance. Bilateral assistance from Organisation for Economic Co-operation and Development (OECD) countries also helped. In particular, following the Japan–PRC Treaty of Peace and Friendship signed in 1978, Japan provided concessional loans (yen credits) amounting to 3.3 trillion yen, grant support of 157 billion yen, and technical assistance of 182 billion yen between 1979 and 2016.[18]

Within a few years, the impact of the new strategy was reflected in economic growth. Growth of national output accelerated from around 5% in 1966–1978 to almost 10% between 1979 and 1988. For a time, the change did not attract much attention outside the PRC. The international community was slow to realize that a dragon had awoken in Asia. But the

---

[15] Du, 2006, *Course of Rural Reform*, 7.
[16] Huang, 2010, *China Boom*.
[17] Hofman and Wu, 2009, *Explaining Development and Reforms*, 27.
[18] Government of Japan, Ministry of Foreign Affairs, 2016, Overview of Official Development Assistance (ODA) to China, February. http://www.mofa.go.jp/policy/oda/region/e_asia/china/ (accessed 12 January 2017).

new policies were of enormous importance. Over the coming decades, they would transform the economy and dramatically alter the PRC's economic influence both within Asia and across the wider international community.

Growth Continues

Three main changes in the pattern of development across Asia became clearer during the second ADB decade. One was the increasing differences in the pace of growth between the different subregions. The four NIEs adopted adjustment strategies more quickly than the more resource-abundant countries of Southeast Asia. The PRC, still inward-looking at the beginning of the period, introduced reform measures in 1978 which soon began to stimulate rapid development. Development prospects lagged, however, in South Asia and in the Pacific island countries.

A second feature was that reforms in the successful countries were generally pro-market and export oriented. Moreover, countries in the region were increasingly trading with and learning from each other. The NIEs, for example, were displacing Japanese low-end manufacturing goods in the US market as well as in Japan and Europe. At the same time, they were sharply increasing their imports of capital and intermediate goods from advanced economies. Supply chain networks, especially in East Asian and Southeast Asian countries, began to emerge. Opportunities for resource-abundant countries such as Indonesia and Malaysia were widening as well, and prospects for labor surplus countries to develop manufacturing sectors were opening up.

The third and most important feature of development in Asia during this second ADB decade was that despite the difficult international environment, transformation in the region proceeded apace. The international development community, deeply concerned with economic challenges in industrial countries and the Latin American debt crisis, was still only dimly aware of the dramatic changes taking place in Asia. Meanwhile, in the NIEs, in Southeast Asia, and especially in the PRC, the outlines of sustained change were becoming clearer. Across Asia, confidence was growing and would strengthen in the third ADB decade into the 1990s.

CHAPTER 7
Second Decade (1977–1986)

ADB: Toward a Broader Development Bank

"When I took my post in late 1981, it had been 15 years since the Asian Development Bank (ADB) was established ... However, as with any organization, inevitably it was beginning to have, after 15 years of rapid growth, some fatigue and strains. It was time to overhaul the ADB."

– *Masao Fujioka,*
ADB President's Diary, 1986.

During the second decade of the Asian Development Bank (ADB), beginning in 1977, the Bank's operations began to widen out. Taroichi Yoshida, the third President, introduced measures to broaden ADB's role. Later, the fourth President, Masao Fujioka, welcomed these ideas and strongly promoted a more active development role for the Bank throughout the 1980s.

During his 5 years as President, Taroichi Yoshida faced two major issues. First, in 1977, there were plans for ADB to widen its agenda from its early focus on infrastructure projects and pay more attention to wider social goals. Second, in 1979 and 1980, ADB needed to respond to the pressures for adjustment resulting from the second oil shock.

Yoshida was succeeded by the fourth President, Masao Fujioka, who arrived in November 1981. Fujioka knew ADB well. Over a decade earlier, in 1966, he had been the first Director of Administration. Fujioka had firm views about the directions in which he wanted to take the institution. His major achievements included arranging for both India and the People's Republic of China (PRC) to become borrowing members.

Taroichi Yoshida

At the ADB Annual Meeting in Jakarta in April 1976, Shiro Inoue had announced that he would not seek reelection as President when his 5-year term ended later that year. Nevertheless, he had taken the opportunity to outline future directions. Inoue envisaged continuing support for the production of key goods such as food, fertilizer, and fuel. But he also talked of a new direction for ADB. He spoke of the need for more attention to social issues such as health and family planning. He also said that while he had been President, the Bank's role in developing human capital—through, for example, support for the education sector—had been "disappointing to me." In talking of these matters, Inoue was outlining issues that the next President would soon take up.

In 1976, Taroichi Yoshida had just retired as Vice-Minister of Finance for International Affairs in the Ministry of Finance in Tokyo when he was pressed to take up the position of ADB President. He accepted the candidacy despite some initial hesitancy. One challenge for Yoshida was that he had worked primarily on domestic issues in Japan. His international experience had been limited to one posting to the International Monetary Fund (IMF) in Washington, DC in the late 1950s until he became Vice-Minister in 1974. Many development issues were therefore new to him although he quickly became familiar with ADB's work in development in the region.

When Yoshida became President on 24 November 1976, the Bank's birthday, the institution was facing pressures to change. One set of pressures came from challenges in Asia. Another came from the international community which, during the mid-1970s, had been discussing the need to look beyond economic growth and widen the approach to development.

During his first year as President, Yoshida often spoke of the challenges for Asia. He pointed, especially, to four problem areas: food supplies, exports, jobs, and the need for external resources. For food production, he drew on the results of the recently completed ADB-supported Asian Agricultural Survey which suggested that by the mid-1980s the region could face a food grains deficit of 20 million metric tons. Yoshida believed the outlook was worrying. In various speeches during 1977, he outlined the problems in some detail. "Regional food deficits of this order," he told the ADB Annual Meeting in 1977, "cannot be sustained without affecting economic and social stability."[1] He noted that the Green Revolution had been especially successful in irrigated areas but that more research was needed to help lift output on farms in dryland and upland areas.

---

[1] Address by President Taroichi Yoshida delivered at the 10th Annual Meeting of the ADB Board of Governors. Manila. 21–23 April 1977. Also in ADB, 1977, *Proceedings of the 10th Annual Meeting*, 36.

Yoshida also noted that countries in the region needed to promote exports. Some had serious balance-of-payments deficits—often financed in part through short-term international borrowing—so they were faced with rising external debt and high debt service payments. These countries would need to reduce imports of nonessential goods while broadening their export bases.

He was also concerned about finding jobs for the growing rural labor force. He argued that the unemployed and the underemployed represented a waste of a major resource in the Bank's region. It would be important to strengthen links between agriculture and industry, and between rural and urban areas but the top priority was the rural sector. "Agricultural and rural development," Yoshida said, "should provide the base of the strategy."

Responding to these problems would require more resources. Yoshida argued for greater international assistance: "The flow of assistance into the Asian region is by no means commensurate either with its needs or with the technical capacity of the region to absorb such assistance. The region accounts for 57% of the population of the developing world, but it receives less than a quarter of the external resources provided by the developed countries to the developing world."

Widening Agenda for ADB

These were Yoshida's personal views but he was also identifying needs in Asia and responding to ideas being discussed in the international community. These issues, along with numerous others, were taken up in 1977 at the 10th Annual Meeting of the Bank in Manila—his first as President. The meeting was important because it set out much of the agenda that ADB would implement during Yoshida's presidency.

The meeting agreed that ADB should broaden its activities. Members wanted the Bank to take on a wider role. In his opening address, the Chair of the Board of Governors, Tengku Razaleigh Hamzah from Malaysia, suggested a seven-point program of action. He urged ADB to move more effectively into the more challenging and rewarding fields of socioeconomic development projects and programs. He noted, specifically, that lending for agriculture and agro-based industries should be expanded because only 26% of ADB loans in 1976 had been for these activities—which was "inadequate."

There was wide support for more socially oriented programs. In the United States (US), the Carter administration had come into office just a few months earlier. Reflecting a key change in policy under the new administration, the US delegate to the 1977 meeting, Arnold Nachmanoff, said that the US wanted to see more support for lower-income groups "through the Bank's emphasis on employment and other social purposes, particularly in the rural areas." Other delegates said similar things.

A second conclusion from the meeting was that ADB needed to reform its operations—by introducing program loans (budget support for the implementation of policy reforms), expanding the use of local currency financing, and improving the procurement of goods and consultants. Further, borrowing countries noted—as they would in later years—that the Bank was slow to disburse funds because of its complicated procedures. Although these were technical matters, they were seen as important by borrowing countries.

In fact, the Bank was already considering many of the social impacts of its activities. In 1973, the previous President, Shiro Inoue, had spoken of the way fisheries loans were "aimed at improving both the income of small and medium fishermen and the protein intake of the citizens ...." He had said that development needed to be brought "directly to the people." And at international meetings in 1974, Inoue warned that following the first oil shock there could be disastrous effects to the developing economies. He noted that the problem of high oil prices "will be compounded by the shortage in supply and inflated prices of fertilizer and basic foods ... and of costs of manufactured imports from the industrialized countries."

A third main topic at the meeting was mobilization of resources. Chair of the Meeting Tengku Razaleigh Hamzah lifted the bar for the Bank in saying: "ADB should ... set new and much higher goals for raising new resources." In response, Yoshida pointed to strong support from donor countries for the Asian Development Fund (ADF) as well as the agreement on the second general capital increase. In addition, Yoshida promised that the Bank would look for cofinancing to support large projects from Organization of the Petroleum Exporting Countries (OPEC) members, the European Economic Community, and Japan.

Yoshida also pointed to two matters ADB had often overlooked in the past. One was the environmental impact of expanding agricultural output. "Environmental conditions must be viewed as an essential part of agricultural development." He emphasized the importance of watershed management and reforestation. These and other environmental matters would become major priorities for the Bank in coming decades.

The other matter was one that Yoshida himself took a special interest in: the need to adapt traditional rural institutions to modern agricultural technology. He said, "Traditional institutions that have evolved over the years usually have very deep and sound roots." Nonindigenous modern agricultural systems might not be easily assimilated and "could prove to be counterproductive." Summarizing his views on these matters, Yoshida spoke of the need to see agricultural development as part of a wider process of rural development.

During the next few years, Yoshida's agenda was to implement the approach discussed at the 1977 Annual Meeting. Traditional loan operations continued for a while, but soon other changes were introduced. Later, the loan operations were reviewed as well.

In early 1978, there was an important change at the top of ADB when the first Vice-President, C. S. Krishna Moorthi, retired. C. S. Krishna Moorthi had been appointed in 1966. He had worked closely with the first two Presidents, including on the arrangements for the establishment of the Bank with Takeshi Watanabe. At the last senior staff meeting that C. S. Krishna Moorthi attended, Yoshida noted that he had served ADB "longer than anyone."[2]

During his long period as Vice-President, Krishna Moorthi had become something of a legend. He had strict standards for staff. Yoshida spoke of "his thorough grasp of facts and figures, his eye for both substance and detail, and his tireless search for perfection." Both Watanabe and Inoue had relied on him to provide strong administrative guidance and to monitor the preparation of Board documents. When Krishna Moorthi retired there was a large gap.

The gap was filled by the appointment of two new Vice-Presidents. At Yoshida's request, C. S. Krishna Moorthi suggested that one successor could be A. T. Bambawale who, like him, had been a senior civil servant in India. Yoshida immediately accepted the suggestion. Bambawale was a very different character. Whereas quite a few staff had been intimidated by C. S. Krishna Moorthi, Bambawale was charming and easy to approach.

The other new Vice-President was S. Stanley Katz who had been a senior official in the US Department of Commerce. He also had strong experience of multilateral affairs, having worked in the World Bank in Washington, DC and the Organisation for Economic Co-operation and Development (OECD)

---

[2] President's Remarks at the Senior Staff Meeting, 15 March 1987.

in Paris. Katz added to the multilateral balance in senior management since he was knowledgeable about the workings both of the US administration and of Congress. Bambawale and Katz would have many years of service and ensure continuity of senior management. Later, in April 1983, the Bank appointed a third Vice-President, Günther Schulz from West Germany. He too would remain for a considerable period, working for three Presidents into the 1990s.

Creating New Loans

During the next few years, ADB lending continued to expand—exceeding $1 billion for the first time in 1978. Loans also went to a widening range of sectors. From 1977, these included forestry, urban housing, vocational education, and skills training. In 1978, ADB provided a loan to Hong Kong, China for the Sha Tin Hospital Polyclinic in the New Territories, the first loan for a health project (Box 7.1). However, the Bank continued to give priority to agriculture, especially in lower-income countries that relied on soft ADF loans. By the end of 1977, nearly 50% of ADF loans had been for agriculture or agro-industry.

The Bank was also providing new loan types (Box 7.2). During the first decade of operations, ADB had been a project bank; loans had been provided for individual projects. But it had become clear that some countries needed to borrow for other purposes—for example, to buy essential equipment or raw materials needed to make better use of productive capacity. Beginning in 1978, the Bank began to provide program loans (Box 7.3). However, staff had little experience in managing program loans so the initial steps were cautious. It was expected that program loans would be less than 5% of total ADB annual lending and normally not exceed 10% of annual lending to any single country.

Another innovation was the "multiproject" loan which financed a group of projects that individually would be considered too small for Board review. Multiproject loans were particularly useful in smaller countries such as those in the South Pacific. The first multiproject loan was to Tonga in 1979 for developing wharves and landing facilities.

In 1980, ADB introduced sector lending which could be used to finance a group of subprojects in a specific sector. Too often, individual projects had provided limited benefits because overall sector policies were badly designed. Sector loans would enable the Bank to focus on that sector,

Box 7.1: ADB's Health Sector Projects

The Asian Development Bank (ADB) has a long history of supporting the health sector. Early projects helped build clinics and hospitals. The first one was the Sha Tin Hospital Polyclinic in Hong Kong, China in 1978. Since then, ADB's health sector projects have evolved from single-hospital support to strengthening health systems and achieving universal health coverage at the country level. ADB has also supported health issues through its subregional initiatives.

In Bangladesh, ADB, together with Swedish International Development Cooperation Agency and other development partners, has supported the Urban Primary Health Care Project since 1998, amounting to $191 million. It aimed at strengthening primary care provided by public health centers in urban areas. It targeted the poor and the needs of women and children. This project has adopted a public–private partnerships (PPP) modality in the delivery of primary health services and has innovative features such as active involvement of the community in governance and the piloting of green clinics with solar panel renewable energy.

ADB's notable activities in the health sector include subregional programs to fight against communicable diseases. In the Greater Mekong Subregion, ADB's concessional loans and grants have aimed at strengthening the capacity of health systems to address public health threats including HIV/AIDS, malaria, and dengue in border areas in Cambodia, the Lao People's Democratic Republic, Myanmar, and Viet Nam. The Bank has helped the governments to strengthen surveillance and reporting systems, human resource training, laboratory testing capacity, and infection prevention and control of hospitals. An ADB-managed trust fund contributed by Australia and the United Kingdom augmented resources for technical assistance.

ADB is also responding to the increasing challenges of ageing. In 2016, ADB approved a PPP-based elderly care services project in Yichang, Hubei Province of the People's Republic of China (PRC). The ADB assistance will develop the capacity of the municipal government to design, procure, manage, and deliver effective services through private elderly care providers. This $50 million results-based sovereign loan was ADB's first one in the PRC to promote PPPs. The usage of PPP in elderly care would provide a replicable model in Asia.

Source: ADB.

engaging in policy dialogue with governments on sector policies and the capacities of local institutions to manage the necessary activities. Sector loans were expected to be large. For example, for transport, they might cover a network of secondary feeder roads.

Box 7.2: Project, Program, Multiproject, and Sector Loans

Project loans. These loans provided finance for specific projects, both for infrastructure and social sectors. Project loans provided in the early 1970s tended to be for new investments in large, capital-intensive activities rather than for small projects or for investments intended to make better use of existing assets.

Program loans. These quick-disbursing loans were initially designed to help borrowing countries increase productive capacity in high-priority activities. The loans from 1978 were to countries lacking the foreign exchange needed to import key inputs, particularly for agriculture. The first program loan was provided to Bangladesh in 1978 for the Low-Lift Pump Maintenance Program. Later, from 1987, program loans were given primarily to provide budget support for the implementation of policy reforms based on policy matrices which listed an agreed set of changes along with the actions needed to implement the reforms. Even compared to project loans, program loans often required close monitoring of implementation and broad-based evaluation.

Multiproject loans. These loans provided funds for projects that individually would normally be considered too small for Board review. Under the new arrangements, several activities were grouped under one overall loan agreement. Multiproject loans were introduced in 1979 for small island economies.

Sector loans. These loans financed the capital requirements of specific sectors or subsectors. Introduced in 1980, they had several advantages over project loans. They could be larger and be used for institution building and policy support, and could be disbursed quickly. Sector lending was particularly useful for agriculture and rural development, water supply and sanitation, and education and health, as well as for small industry where a number of small investment activities could be combined under one loan. The first two sector loans were approved in 1980—for water supplies in Indonesia and to support the highway sector in Thailand.

Sources: ADB. 1978. *Program Lending*. R10-78. Manila; ADB. 1983. *A Review of Program Lending Policies*. R21-83. Manila; ADB. 1980. *Sector Lending*. R52-80. Manila.

> **Box 7.3: First Program Loan**
>
> **Low-Lift Pump Maintenance in Bangladesh.** The first program loan was approved in 1978 for a low-lift pump maintenance program in Bangladesh. Farmers in the Dhaka area had low-lift irrigation pumps that were not being fully utilized. The $8.9 million program loan (funded from the Asian Development Fund) supported the repair and maintenance of pumps. This program enabled farmers to irrigate an additional 40,000 hectares of land during the dry season. The succeeding program loans in these early days remained mainly targeted at activities in the agriculture sector which financed fertilizers and other inputs needed to boost output.
>
> Source: ADB. 2016. *ADB Through the Decades: ADB's Second Decade (1966–1976)*, p. 21. https://www.adb.org/sites/default/files/publication/216246/adb-second-decade.pdf (accessed 20 December 2016).

Just as ADB was introducing these new types of loans, there were further pressures on Bank operations. In 1979, the second oil shock hit non-oil developing countries hard with rising prices for oil and other imports. At the same time, growth was slowing in industrial countries. These problems were compounded by concerns about food supplies: world production of food grains declined in 1979 causing serious food shortages in several countries. Before long, policy makers in Asian developing countries were worrying about food and energy security—issues which would be major concerns well into the next century.

The Bank responded by expanding lending for agriculture and energy. There was also more support for projects in social sectors such as water supply, housing, and health. In 1979, nearly a third of ADB loans were in agriculture, and lending for energy had expanded quickly. Lending to the social sectors rose from around 10% of lending in 1976 to nearly 22% in 1981. In 1980, around $90 million was approved for loans to Indonesia for irrigation projects, and loans to both Pakistan and the Philippines were authorized for power projects. In his speech to the Annual Meeting in Honolulu in 1981, his last as ADB President, Yoshida said that the Bank continued to accord the highest priority to agriculture and rural development. ADB lending for indigenous energy resources and social infrastructure had remained high as a share of total lending. Lending to the energy sector rose sharply from around $380 million in 1980 to $480 million in 1981.

Surveys and Reviews

A range of surveys and reviews were commissioned to guide the institution through this period of rapid change. Several of the most important focused on agriculture. The first Asian Agricultural Survey had been in 1967; the second was published in early 1977.[3] The 1976 survey recalled the original hopes that the Green Revolution would create abundance of food in Asia. However, it noted that: "If the general mood today is more chastened, it is surely not due to cynicism or disillusionment. The events of the last decade have forced us to re-examine the assumptions on which the earlier optimism was based. The first to go was the euphoria of plenty. ... the availability of food since 1968 has barely improved even in per capita terms while the nutritional status of large portions of the population has declined. ... the 'green revolution' is not providing the expected impetus to production ... It has become clear that, except in a few areas, introduction of the new technology has not brought about widespread improvement in the general economic status of the population."

The survey identified deep-seated rural problems. First, there were worrying signs that the Green Revolution might be slowing down. Second, the main beneficiaries of the new agricultural technology were farms with access to good irrigation in lowland areas who could cultivate high-yielding varieties of rice, while many millions of farmers in upland areas, or who grew other crops, were receiving few gains. Third, marginal farmers and landless laborers were often affected by social problems arising from joblessness, malnutrition, and hunger.[4] Drawing on the survey, in 1978, the ADB Board agreed to increase lending for agriculture and rural development by 20% per year until 1982.

Other studies in the late 1970s included a review of the Bank's financial policies and the criteria for soft loan ADF lending. There were also reports on improving operations in the South Pacific and, specifically, on its work in agriculture in small island countries.

Another major sector report was on energy. In response to the second oil crisis, the 1981 *Regional Energy Survey* highlighted three major issues. One, for oil-importing developing countries, high energy prices were

---

[3] ADB, 1977, *Asian Agricultural Survey 1976: Rural Asia: Challenge and Opportunity*.
[4] Speech delivered by Taroichi Yoshida, President, Asian Development Bank, at the Sub-Regional Seminar on the Second Asian Agricultural Survey (Manila/Los Baños, 9–13 January 1978).

causing severe balance-of-payments problems. A second issue was that many countries were struggling to develop alternatives to imported oil—hampered by the costs of developing domestic energy sources such as coal-fired power stations and hydroelectricity plants. Third, faced with rising costs for commercial fuels, households were putting increasing pressure on traditional noncommercial sources of energy such as fuelwood and charcoal.

ADB decided to increase and diversify its energy lending—for developing renewable and domestic energy resources such as hydropower, natural gas, and coal, as well as for biomass and other nonconventional energy sources. The Bank also started to promote energy conservation and explore the potential for regional cooperation in energy development.

Pressures for Fundraising

Like other Presidents, Yoshida gave priority to fundraising. And he was effective in mobilizing resources. Between 1977 and 1981, gross borrowings rose from $117 million to $668 million. Nevertheless, for Yoshida and the staff, mobilizing funds was a never-ending task.

The second general capital increase (GCI II) came into effect on 30 September 1977, raising the authorized capital by 135% (Appendix Table A2.14). Even so, in the face of the need for loans following the second oil shock in 1979, this ceiling of authorized capital soon seemed low. Before long, there was talk of another capital increase.

There were also growing demands for ADF funds. In 1978, donors had agreed to a second replenishment (ADF III) with donors' contributions of $2.15 billion (Appendix Table A2.17). But some of these funds were slow to arrive, particularly from the US. One of the main problems with ADF resources—and a recurring problem in the years to come—was that while the US administration supported the ADF program, its participation was sometimes hampered by the complicated legislative processes in the US Congress. This limited the way ADB could draw on ADF resources. In frustration, Yoshida judged that the risks of being blunt were less than the costs to the Bank of continual delays. He told the 1980 Annual Meeting that:[5]

---

[5] Address by President Taroichi Yoshida delivered at the 13th Annual Meeting of the ADB Board of Governors. Manila. 30 April–2 May 1980. Also in ADB, 1980, *Proceedings of the 13th Annual Meeting*, 29.

> ...I must point out ... that loans approved in 1979 have all but depleted Asian Development Fund resources. ... As a result, it has been necessary to defer the signing of loan agreements for several projects in the Bank's poorer developing member countries which were approved in the early months of 1980 ... this situation arises from the delay in the authorization for the US contributions to the second replenishment of the Asian Development Fund and the payment of its first installment.

Nevertheless, full US participation in ADF III would continue to be held up. The result was that disbursements of soft loan funds were delayed for several years.

Masao Fujioka

There were further pressures for change within ADB. Across the region, developing countries were faced with the rise in the value of the dollar and high global interest rates. The Bank also had to adjust to changes in development thinking. The 1980 Brandt Commission report, *North–South: A Programme for Survival*, called for a renewed global development effort. The view was also growing that institutions such as the World Bank and regional development banks should go beyond providing finance. To initiate a reform program, Yoshida announced at the Annual Meeting in 1981 that ADB would carry out its first major strategic review. He also said he would not seek another 5-year term and would leave in November. These changes ushered in the Fujioka era.

During his 5 years with the Bank, Taroichi Yoshida, like the two previous Presidents, had aimed to drive change within ADB. In 1977, in his first year as President, he had responded to calls for ADB to widen its role and pay increasing attention to social issues of development. Yoshida's departing legacy carried the Bank through to the next decade. Just as Presidents Watanabe and Inoue had passed on a reform agenda when they left, Yoshida in turn, through announcing a strategic review, passed on a plan for his successor.

Masao Fujioka became the fourth President of ADB on 24 November 1981. He attended the University of Chicago in the early 1950s and had rich experience in international finance. He had been Director-General of the International Finance Bureau at the Ministry of Finance in Tokyo and an executive director of the Japan Export–Import (EXIM) Bank. Moreover, Fujioka already had a strong background in the work of the Bank; in

1966, he had been one of the first staff members, appointed Director of Administration. During his 8-year presidency, he would bring a forceful style of management and oversee large organizational changes.

Even before arriving in Manila, Fujioka had signaled that he would set his own priorities. Unlike the three previous new Presidents, he did not travel directly to Manila. Instead, he made short official visits to Myanmar and to Thailand to talk to senior officials about their priorities and to gain an impression of economic progress in Southeast Asia. After several days, he continued on to the Philippines. On the way, he came face to face with some of the human problems arising from conflict in the region: his Air France flight from Bangkok was unexpectedly delayed by an hour to board over 100 Vietnamese refugees heading for Manila.

Fujioka's arrival in Manila has become part of ADB folklore. Instead of going to his house to unpack, Fujioka planned to begin work at once. He scheduled a press conference for his arrival at Manila airport at 3 p.m., after which he planned to go directly to Bank headquarters to meet senior staff and the Board of Directors at 3:30 p.m. These plans were somewhat disrupted by the late arrival of his flight, but nevertheless his intentions were quite clear.

Fujioka had thus signaled that he would be an action-oriented President and would move firmly into the Bank's leadership. At his first meeting with the Board, he reaffirmed the priority for the three sectors listed by Yoshida: agriculture, alternative energy, and social infrastructure. He was also keen to see more cofinancing, especially with the private sector, and to promote the private sector generally. He wanted ADB to carry out more economic research and to be recognized as an information hub for Asia's economies. He also spoke of the need to improve the image of ADB, saying that while the Bank was well known in major financial markets in Tokyo and Germany, "... in Switzerland and other markets, investors still don't know where the ADB is located and have a wrong idea that the ADB provides loans only to the agriculture sector."

In addition to his first official duties, Fujioka had some personal links he wanted to pursue after arriving in Manila. One person he wanted to get in touch with was Cornelio Balmaceda. In 1965 Balmaceda, who later became a senior minister in the Philippines, had been chair of the preparatory committees in Bangkok and Manila planning the establishment of ADB. Fujioka had worked closely with Balmaceda in those days and wanted to renew contacts with him. After asking around among friends, Fujioka finally learned that Balmaceda, now 84, and his wife were living quietly in retirement in Pasay City, not far from where Fujioka himself lived. The day before Christmas 1981, he arranged to visit the Balmacedas with a bouquet of flowers. Mrs. Balmaceda, in a wheelchair, welcomed him in the front yard as he arrived and Cornelio Balmaceda, cane in hand, greeted him as soon as he entered the house. The small group of three were able to go out into the garden and enjoy the open air, recalling their activities in the mid-1960s.

Priorities in the 1980s

Fujioka had his own definite views about the Bank's work. He chose to wait for the outcome of the Yoshida-commissioned study to set strategic goals but nevertheless quickly pressed ahead with immediate reforms. He had heard, for example, that the Board discussion of the 1981 ADB budget had been contentious and had gone on for 2 days. Fujioka did not favor, as he put it, "excessively inefficient deliberations." As Chair of the Board, he ruled that the budget for 1982 would be discussed in summary fashion. It was quickly approved. This approach foreshadowed the brisk and sometimes controversial management style that marked Fujioka's presidency.[6]

The long-term strategic study of ADB's operations initiated by Yoshida was carried out by a Bank task force, coordinated by a newly created Development Policy Office with guidance from an advisory group of five development experts. Chaired by John P. Lewis from Princeton University and including Asian specialists such as Kiyoshi Kojima from Hitotsubashi University, the group also prepared its own commentary on the report.

The report was submitted to Fujioka on 29 October 1982, almost a year after he had arrived in ADB. It was later published under the uninviting title *Study of Operational Priorities and Plans of the Asian Development Bank for the 1980s*. In fact, the title was misleading. The report set out a surprisingly ambitious program for change. What might be called the "Fujioka agenda" argued for better country programming, additional types of assistance, and better efforts to mobilize resources. It also pointed bluntly to the need to improve the management and administration of loans. Overall, the study recommended that the work of ADB should be broadened into a wider range of development activities.

The study was refreshingly frank about the Bank's problems. One was a short-term approach. In the 1970s, ADB had typically sent missions to

---

[6] Fujioka, 1986, *ADB President's Diary*, Chapter 1.

borrowing countries to prepare a pipeline of projects, usually for a 4-year period. Based on the pipeline, ADB staff would prepare country programs. However, this approach encouraged ADB staff to focus on the current year rather than on the longer-term pipeline. This short-term emphasis tended to exacerbate end-of-the-year "bunching," with a sudden rush of projects presented to an often irritated Board for approval to meet annual lending targets. Bunching became a serious problem for Fujioka a few years later in 1986 when 77% of the year's lending commitments were approved in the last quarter. The Board asked Management to review the problem. However, bunching continued to occur.[7] Another problem was inadequate economic analysis. "The Bank's knowledge base with regard to the sectors in which projects are currently funded," the study noted, "appears to be weak. ... there is thus no clear direction as to what the Bank should try to achieve in its country operational programs."

To respond to these issues, the study made two main recommendations. First, that ADB country programming should be more rigorous. Second, ADB should move beyond the use of short-term annual targets and adopt multiyear time frames. The study also called for greater flexibility in the types of ADB assistance, arguing that while most loans should still be for projects, greater flexibility and better country programming could be achieved if there was more use of other types of lending—such as program, multiproject, and sector loans.

The task force also concluded that ADB should be ready to finance more local costs. In the early years, reflecting contemporary thinking about the role of international development banks, ADB had mainly financed the foreign exchange costs of projects. But this approach often caused delays. Low-income countries often found it hard to fund the local currency share of projects. To reduce the mismatch, the report proposed that the Bank should be more willing to make loans to finance local costs. The international advisory group supported this suggestion.

Another central idea of the study was that ADB needed to broaden out its range of development activities. Fujioka and others had already taken note of the work of the Paris-based Organisation for Economic Co-operation and Development (OECD) which coordinated policy discussion between industrial countries. In 1982, in his first speech as President at the ADB Annual Meeting, Fujioka said: "As an institution established to promote the economic development of the region, the Bank should also aim at

---

[7] ADB, *Annual Report 1986*, 2.

becoming an acknowledged center of expertise in identifying the problems and potentials of its DMCs [developing member countries]."

However, there were differing views about how far ADB should go in becoming a broad based regional resource center. The study itself noted that "Improving the role of the Bank as a regional development institution is a complex matter as the results are not always tangible and the costs generally high." Nevertheless, the international advisory group strongly supported the idea. Commenting on the report as a whole, the advisory group said: "…during its first 15 years the ADB has been a good and sound development projects bank …the attached study advances the thesis that the time has come for the Bank to become a considerably more active and versatile development promoter. We fully endorse this view."

Increasing Lending and First Private Sector Operations

Fujioka would spend much of the next decade implementing his reform agenda. At the Annual Meeting in Amsterdam in 1984, he reported on progress: "In 1983, the Bank responded to the needs of developing countries with: a special assistance program to help complete ongoing projects; a move into equity investment operations; more liberal policies on local cost financing; increased program lending; supplementary financing for cost overruns; and more systematic financing of interest during construction."

One way of promoting the reform agenda was to ensure that Bank lending continued to grow. Over the second ADB decade, annual lending rose from nearly $890 million in 1977 to just over $2 billion in 1986. Of this, around a third was concessional ADF loans.

The scale of lending reflected both demand and supply. On the demand side, much depended on the willingness and capacity of developing countries to borrow. This, in turn, often varied according to economic and budgetary conditions and the ability of implementing agencies (such as departments of agriculture or public works) to manage projects effectively. On the supply side in ADB, lending was influenced by the Bank's capacity to manage loans. To improve the supply side, ADB in 1983 liberalized some of its policies on program lending and on the provision of local cost finance. As a result of these changes, as well as a more flexible approach to multiyear programming and approvals for some large loans, lending in 1984 surged to over $2.2 billion (Figure 7.1).

Figure 7.1: Operational Approvals by Fund Type, 1977–1986
($ million)

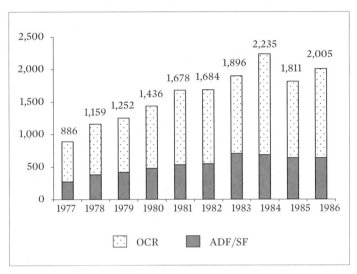

Total: $16,041 million

ADF = Asian Development Fund, OCR = ordinary capital resources, SF = Special Funds.
Note: Operational approvals include loans, grants, equity investments, and guarantees.
Source: ADB loan, technical assistance, grant, and equity approvals database.

ADB's lending approvals leveled off leveled off slightly in 1985 and 1986 reflecting generally slower world economic conditions as well as high debt levels and budgetary constraints in many borrowing countries. The decline was more pronounced for ordinary capital resources (OCR) because lending was lower to most traditional major borrowers. Fujioka explained in 1986 that this was because "Constraints on the availability of development funds have made our DMCs [developing member countries] more selective in choosing projects, and greater emphasis is being placed on the efficiency and productivity of investment." In fact, the slowdown proved temporary because India and the PRC soon began to borrow. Fujioka later said that without the two countries, ADB would have remained a small bank.

An important aspect of the reform agenda were efforts to strengthen links with the private sector. ADB's early emphasis during the 1970s had been on supporting development finance institutions (DFIs) to help small and

> **Box 7.4: First Loans without Government Guarantee**
>
> **Cherat Cement Company and the National Development Leasing Corporation of Pakistan.** The policy on lending to the private sector without government guarantee was approved in 1985. The following year, the first loan to a private sector enterprise without government guarantee was approved for the Cherat Cement Company in Pakistan to assist the company in doubling its capacity. The loan, given in Swiss francs, amounted to $5 million. The first loan to a financial institution without government guarantee was also approved in 1986 for an activity in Pakistan. The loan, $5 million provided in Swiss francs to the National Development Leasing Corporation, helped cover the foreign exchange cost of directly imported equipment. The equipment was intended to be supplied to the leasing company's private sector customers, mainly in the manufacturing sector.
>
> Source: ADB. 1987. *ADB 1986 Annual Report*. Manila. p. 1.

medium-sized enterprises (SMEs). Fujioka himself was eager to see the Bank widen its work with the private sector. Indeed the first ADB loan, in 1968, had been to provide a line of credit to a Thai DFI for onlending to SMEs. In Fujioka's first speech to the Board in 1981, he outlined steps to promote private investment. Among other things, he suggested an equity investment facility to allow direct investments in equity in the private sector.

Over the next few years, various options were considered and, in 1983, the Board approved a new policy which enabled the Bank to invest in the equity capital of institutions and firms in the private sector. In 1983, two equity investments were approved—one to take up share capital in the Korea Development Investment Corporation and another in Pakistan for Bankers Equity to facilitate investments in industrial SMEs. This is the beginning of ADB nonsovereign operations.

Then in 1985, the policy on lending to the private sector without government guarantee was approved. The following year, the first loan to a private sector enterprise without government guarantee was approved (Box 7.4). Following these moves, ADB's Private Sector Division was established in 1986.

Shortly before leaving ADB, Fujioka was able to support the establishment of an agency designed to expand operations in the private sector. In

1989, along with private financial institutions from within and outside the region, the Bank created a new organization, the Asian Finance and Investment Corporation (AFIC), which was approved as a merchant bank in Singapore.[8] ADB made an initial equity investment of $35 million in AFIC. The expectation was that AFIC would be able to mobilize funds to provide long-term loans and equity investments to private sector medium-sized industrial enterprises in developing countries in Asia.

However, for a range of reasons, ADB's support for AFIC ran into problems. And then, following the Asian financial crisis in 1997, there was a sharp deterioration in AFIC's investment portfolio. Following these problems, ADB scaled back involvement in AFIC and eventually exited from the troubled investment.

Staff and First Resident Mission

Another part of the reform agenda was the recruitment of promising young staff. In the early years, throughout the first ADB decade and into the 1980s, many professional staff were civil servants seconded from their governments to the Bank. Their average age was 40 years or older, with most having perhaps 15 years of professional experience. Over 95% were men. Fujioka thought it important for the Bank to build up professional skills. In 1984, the Young Professionals Program was introduced. Five men and one woman, all under 30, were recruited from Canada, France, Japan, Sri Lanka, and Thailand.

There were some settling-in hiccups in the Young Professionals Program as older hands and the new young staff learned to work with each other. However, the scheme quickly proved successful. There was strong demand across the Bank for the young professionals, so new batches were recruited annually. Over time, many were promoted to senior positions. The earliest group spoke of the "incredible opportunities to be assigned to projects, missions, and training." By 2015, nearly 170 young professionals had been recruited, 45% of whom were women.[9]

The Bank also established closer partnerships with borrowing countries. In 1982, the first resident mission was opened in Dhaka, Bangladesh. A regional office was also planned for the South Pacific because it was

---

[8] ADB, *Annual Report 1991*, 61.
[9] Details here are drawn from Bouvery et. al. 2015, *ADB@50—The Young Professionals Program (YPP)*.

difficult from Manila to maintain close links with the dispersed countries across the vast Pacific Ocean. But Fujioka was less concerned about geographic proximity than the need for ADB staff to understand local development issues "through both heart and mind." One key aim of opening regional offices, he said, was to "achieve mental proximity" with borrowing countries.[10]

Agreeing on Country Strategies and Flexible Lending Arrangements

The Operational Priorities study also recommended that the Bank should strengthen country programming. Program documents should not consist just of a project pipeline but should also establish the ADB strategy in borrowing countries. This approach would call for a different mix of staff skills. The Bank prepared its first country strategy in 1984—for Pakistan—followed by strategies for Sri Lanka and Indonesia, but it would not be in a position to prepare country programs for most borrowing member countries until the third ADB decade.

ADB had made its first program loans in the late 1970s. In 1983, the program loan policy was reviewed with the aim of improving sector plans through better dialogue with countries while also strengthening institutions through technical assistance.[11] In 1984, a review of sector lending also suggested strengthening policy dialogue while building capacity in borrowing countries.[12]

Throughout the decade, the Bank also paid more attention to loan administration. In 1978, as part of a reorganization ADB established the Central Projects Services Office. The procurement guidelines, which had often caused delays, were reconsidered. However, the Bank remained under pressure, especially from industrial countries, to maintain close controls over procurement arrangements.

Rules for local cost financing were also liberalized. After pilot trials in some low-income countries, special financing arrangement for shortfalls in local-cost funding in priority cases were introduced in early 1983.

---

[10] Address by President Masao Fujioka delivered at the 16th Annual Meeting of the ADB Board of Governors. Manila. 4–6 May 1983. Also in ADB, 1983, *Proceedings of the 16th Annual Meeting*, 25.
[11] ADB, 1983, *Review of Program Lending Policies*.
[12] ADB, 1984, *Review of Sector Lending Operations*.

Nevertheless, with a close eye to preserving its AAA rating in international capital markets, ADB remained cautious. Fujioka told the Annual Meeting in Manila in 1983 that "financing under this scheme will be consistent with stabilization and structural programs being pursued by developing countries in agreement with the IMF and the World Bank." The policy was reviewed again later in 1983 when the scope was widened to include most developing country borrowers and most sectors.[13]

These changes to lending arrangements provided greater flexibility. The Bank was, for example, able to respond quickly to problems in the Philippines. For most of 1985, the government was hampered by political turmoil and no loans were approved. In early 1986, however, after Ferdinand Marcos had been replaced as President by Corazon C. Aquino, ADB was able to move swiftly. Local cost financing arrangements were approved to provide Special Project Implementation Assistance loans of $100 million for 36 delayed projects. Recognizing that the Philippines was passing through a period of special difficulty and that the international community was keen to assist, half the loans were on concessional ADF terms.

Indonesia was also in difficulty. Sharp declines in oil and commodity prices were causing severe budgetary problems that were delaying six education projects. To speed these up, in December 1986, the Board approved a Special Project Implementation Assistance loan for $30 million.

Raising Funds in Hard Times

For most of the second ADB decade, especially in the second half, the Bank found it a continual challenge to mobilize funds. At the Annual Meeting in Amsterdam in 1984, Fujioka spoke of the "new protectionism" and the "deepest recession since the 1930s" which were constraining the flows of aid and private capital into Asia. In May 1980, a review recommended a substantial increase in OCR operations although this would require more subscribed capital. The Bank prepared plans to step up the OCR lending program to over $11 billion over 1983–1987. But this level of lending would require a third general capital increase (GCI III).

Discussions about GCI III took place throughout 1981 and 1982. Member countries were prepared to consider an expansion of capital but, before they agreed to the increase, they wanted ADB to improve loan administration and to strengthen the preparation of country and sector plans. Members

---

[13] ADB, 1983, *Review of Lending Foreign Exchange.*

also wanted the Bank to mobilize finance from other sources, including private capital. In April 1983, satisfied with ADB commitments on these issues, member countries approved GCI III, increasing the authorized capital by 105% (Appendix Table A2.14). This opened the way for ADB to expand bond operations in international capital markets: in 1978, annual borrowings were $390 million but by the end of the decade were more than $800 million.

The expansion in authorized capital did not, however, increase the resources available for soft loan activities. This would require further replenishments of the Asian Development Fund. During the second ADB decade, there were two rounds of replenishment negotiations—ADF III and ADF IV. Before agreeing to additional contributions, however, donors wanted assurances from the Bank about a range of policy matters. After discussion, in 1978 donors agreed to provide $2.15 billion for ADF III (covering the period 1979–1982). In 1982, donors approved a further replenishment under ADF IV of $3.205 billion to support lending over 1983–1986 (Appendix Table A2.17).

The Bank also widened its cofinancing operations. In 1981, a review had concluded that while ADB had satisfactory cofinancing arrangements with official agencies, it had been less successful in working with commercial partners. To address the problem, a cofinancing unit was established in 1982 which worked to expand operations with official aid agencies and export credit institutions as well as commercial sources such as banks. Cofinancing was also used to recycle petrodollars from the Middle East. The Bank partnered with institutions such as the OPEC Fund for International Development and the Islamic Development Bank.

A Regional Development Institution

The Operational Priorities study envisaged ADB as a development institution and as a regional resource center. To move in this direction, ADB needed to strengthen analytical capacity and extend its outreach. In fact, in 1980 even before the study, the Bank had expanded the Economic Office under a newly appointed Chief Economist (the first was US professor Seiji Naya from the University of Hawaii) and had assigned economic analysts to country departments. Policy dialogue with borrowing countries was also beginning to be established.

ADB had built up practical knowledge through experience in financing projects. Now it needed to strengthen its capacity for long-term research and analysis and initiated specific studies of the region's development problems. In 1981, the Bank launched the Economic Staff Papers series.

In his first main statement to the ADB Board in 1982, Fujioka announced his intention to establish the *Asian Development Review* journal, the first issue of which appeared in 1983. In a foreword to the first issue, he said: "I see the Bank as a center of information on economic issues and potentials of the region. In this way the Bank can further contribute to the efforts of its developing member countries in assessing strategies, formulating policies and in implementing effective development programs. The *Asian Development Review* is a part of that endeavor."

In 1982, again at Fujioka's suggestion, ADB launched its Distinguished Speakers Series. Eminent economists were invited to deliver lectures on socioeconomic development issues. In 1983, the Bank began the ADB Development Roundtable series: an annual gathering of senior policy makers and resource persons who focused on key development issues. In 1983, they considered financial policies and external debt management. In 1984, they discussed industrial development and trade policy and held a seminar on domestic resource mobilization through financial development. In 1985, they focused on the private sector. Over this period, ADB also intensified joint research with national institutions.

The move to become a regional resource center marked a new role for ADB. As Fujioka said during the Annual Meeting in Bangkok in 1985, "We have been a 'family doctor' always taking the best interest of the developing countries to heart. Now we must play a more complex and sophisticated role, combining financial assistance and policy advice on key development issues." One of these was environmental pressures. In 1980, the Board discussed a paper on environmental considerations in Bank operations and had agreed on measures to ensure that environmental implications would be considered in ADB project activities.[14] In 1986, the Bank reviewed the arrangements for managing environmental aspects of its project work. The study suggested that ADB should aim to become a regional resource center for environmental activities.[15]

Another major concern was gender. In 1985, the Board approved the policy on the role of women in development which recommended that ADB should specifically consider the role of women in its activities.[16] From 1986, staff

---

[14] ADB, 1979, *Environmental Considerations in Bank Operations*.
[15] ADB, 1986, *Review of the Bank's Environmental Policies and Procedures*.
[16] ADB, 1986, *Role of Women in Development*.

worked on guidelines for incorporating gender issues in the preparation of projects in major sectors, such as rural development, education, water supply, and sanitation.[17] Work also commenced on disaggregating data by gender in key development indicators. Early in 1987, a project specialist was recruited to serve as a focal point for ADB efforts to promote women in development. These and other issues would add to the expanding international development agenda that ADB was expected to address.

The People's Republic of China Joins the Bank

Overshadowing these developments, however, were remarkable changes in the relationship between the Bank and Asia's two giant nations, the PRC and India. At the beginning of the second ADB decade, neither was a borrowing member. For various reasons, India had chosen to abstain from borrowing, and the PRC had not yet joined the Bank. However, by the end of the second ADB decade, both countries had entered into borrowing programs. During the third ADB decade, their participation as major borrowers would help transform the multilateral nature of the Bank.

In 1971, the United Nations "restored the lawful rights" of the PRC.[18] Following this change, there was much speculation during the 1970s about the possibility of the PRC joining ADB. Expectations rose when the PRC "assumed responsibility" for relations with the IMF and the World Bank in 1980.[19] However, the first official discussions about ADB membership did not begin until 1983—and then lasted 3 years. In February 1983, the PRC contacted ADB Management to express interest in joining the Bank following the same approach as by the IMF and the World Bank.[20] This arrangement, however, would require that the membership of Taipei,China in ADB be terminated. Fujioka took the view that this would not be possible as the ADB Charter does not have a provision for terminating members in good standing.

For a time, there was a stalemate. But then, the PRC indicated that it was willing to search for a solution. The PRC suggested that Taipei,China could

---

[17] ADB, 1986, *Role of Women in Development*.
[18] United Nations General Assembly Session 26 Resolution 2758, 1971. *Restoration of the Lawful Rights of the People's Republic of China in the United Nations A/RES/2758(XXVI)*, 25 October, 1. http://www.un.org/ga/search/view_doc.asp?symbol=A/RES/2758(XXVI) (accessed 30 January 2017).
[19] International Monetary Fund. *At a Glance—China and the IMF*. https://www.imf.org/external/country/chn/rr/glance.htm (accessed 30 January 2017).
[20] Fujioka, 1986, *ADB President's Diary*, Chapter 4.

Chapter 7—ADB: Toward a Broader Development Bank 145

remain a member, provided a satisfactory compromise could be found over the name used in the Bank. Fujioka continued with negotiations holding over 20 meetings with officials from Taipei,China and over 30 meetings with representatives of the PRC.

In June 1984, the PRC sent a mission to Manila to discuss membership.[21] Among the issues to be considered was the possibility of amending the ADB Charter to make Taipei,China an "associate member." This option was not supported by ADB Management. In August and December 1984 and in January 1985, Fujioka stopped over in Taipei,China on a mission. He also had intensive meetings with officials of the PRC and Taipei,China on the occasion of the ADB Annual Meeting in Bangkok in May 1985. After long and detailed negotiations, ADB reached an agreement with the PRC in November 1985. At the recommendation of the Board of Directors, the Board of Governors approved the PRC's membership on 17 February 1986.[22] Taipei,China's designation would be changed from "Republic of China" to "Taipei,China" by administrative arrangement.

In March 1986, after the domestic procedures, the PRC became a member of ADB. Taipei,China did not attend either the 1986 or 1987 ADB Annual Meetings. It resumed sending a delegation in 1988. In the Board of Directors today, Taipei,China belongs to a constituency with six other members including the Republic of Korea, while the PRC is in a one-member constituency. Hong Kong, China has belonged to a constituency with other members including Australia since 1971 (Appendix Tables A2.3 and A2.4).

Before entry into the ADB, the Government of the PRC requested that the flag of Taipei,China be removed from ADB headquarters. The position of Taipei,China was that all national flags of members should be displayed. To solve the impasse, after careful thought, Fujioka decided that no national flags would be displayed in front of ADB headquarters. Only one flag, the official ADB flag, would be hoisted on the main flagpole. Since then, at both the old and new headquarters buildings, this practice of hoisting only ADB's flag has been maintained. But at the new ADB headquarters building in Mandaluyong, there is a particular item of architecture which reflects this history: accompanying the solitary plinth which carries the ADB flag each day, there are over 50 other plinths which await the hoisting

---

[21] Wang, 2007, *ABA Journal*.
[22] The ADB Charter requires, for new members, a vote of Governors comprising at least a two-third majority in number and a three-quarter majority in voting power. This requirement was met for the PRC's entry.

of other flags at some time in the future. These additional plinths, largely unnoticed, are part of the architectural history of the Bank.

India as a Borrower

While the PRC was applying to become a member of ADB, India had begun moves to begin borrowing from the Bank. In August 1981, India requested the initiation of lending. This was a significant change in India's relationship with the Bank. It would lead to a marked increase in the calls on ADB's resources.

India's decision was a departure from the informal understanding that it would only look to the World Bank for multilateral financial support. When ADB was established, smaller developing countries in the Asia and Pacific region had argued that the World Bank was already providing considerable support to India so it would be appropriate for ADB to give more attention to other countries in Asia, especially to smaller borrowing countries.

The US had come to see this informal arrangement as a useful division of effort between the World Bank and ADB and was not comfortable with the proposed change. At the ADB Annual Meeting in Amsterdam in 1984, US delegate David C. Mulford said: "The World Bank, with its longer history, greater resources and institutional specialization, is best equipped to assist the development efforts of the larger countries in the region. ... Efficiency dictates that both organizations should cooperate and concentrate on their areas of greater strength."

India's request brought unexpected problems for Fujioka. To his surprise, the US seemed more concerned about India than about the PRC.[23] He met with both Indian and US officials on numerous occasions. He found that reaching agreement on this issue was even more difficult diplomatically than negotiating the PRC's entry to the Bank.

In the end, sufficient agreement had been reached by 1985 for ADB to dispatch staff from Manila to New Delhi for discussions about loan arrangements. India's priority was rapid industrialization. The Bank's first project loans to India were designed to support this strategy. In 1986, ADB began lending with $250 million on OCR terms for private enterprises in the industry sector and for investment in a power project

---

[23] Wilson, 1987, *A Bank for Half the World*, 274.

in Tamil Nadu. Over the next few decades, India would become the Bank's largest borrower.

Operational Summary

In the second decade, ADB financing operations expanded rapidly. In 1978, annual lending exceeded $1 billion for the first time. For the entire second decade, ADB operational approvals reached over $16 billion, an almost fivefold increase from the previous decade. A third of this amount was sourced from the ADF.

Reflecting the priorities of borrowing countries, loans were largely for agriculture and energy. These sectors accounted for over half of total lending. The rest went to transport and information and communication technology (ICT) (12%), finance (10%), water (10%), education (5%), industry (3%), and health (2%). Aside from greater emphasis placed on agriculture, significant changes compared to the previous decade included an increase in the share of lending going toward social sectors (education and health) with a corresponding reduction in the share going to transport, finance, and industry (Figure 7.2).

In terms of geographic distribution, ADB lending remained heavily concentrated in Southeast Asia with more than half of the total (Figure 7.3). South Asia and Central and West Asia, however, overtook East Asia, each accounting for 18%. Singapore and Hong Kong, China received relatively modest amounts of OCR lending consistent with their increased ability to borrow from private capital markets. These economies stopped borrowing from ADB over the decade. Meanwhile, the Pacific member countries remained the smallest borrowing region collectively accounting for only 2% of total ADB lending. The top five borrowers over the decade were Indonesia (21%), Pakistan (17%), the Philippines (12%), Bangladesh (11%), and the Republic of Korea (9%).

Overall, technical assistance operations increased fivefold during the second decade to $125 million. The top five recipients were Indonesia (15%), the Philippines (12%), Pakistan (9%), Bangladesh (8%), and Nepal (8%). ADB also continued to provide technical assistance to Pacific island countries. By sector, 41% of technical assistance operations went to agriculture, while 14% went to energy, 10% to transport and ICT, 9% to public sector management, and 7% to industry and trade. The Bank was taking more interest in policy issues and institutional development

Figure 7.2: Operational Approvals by Sector, 1977–1986
(%, $ million)

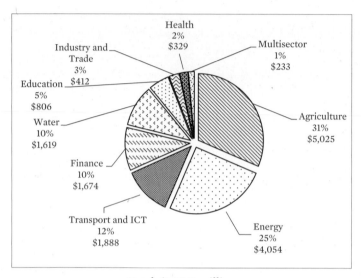

Total: $16,041 million

ICT = information and communication technology.
Note: Operational approvals include loans, grants, equity investments, and guarantees.
Source: ADB loan, technical assistance, grant, and equity approvals database.

activities in borrowing countries so there was more emphasis on advisory and technical assistance programs. At the same time, there were efforts to expand project-specific technical assistance activities to strengthen project preparation and implementation. ADB's new role as a regional development resource center led to an increase in technical assistance to finance studies related to region, sector, and issues.

These activities placed increasing demands on the staff and budget of the Bank. Between 1976 and the end of 1986, the number of staff increased from 760 to 1,604 while the internal administrative expenses budget increased from almost $20 million to just under $90 million. There was also pressure on office space. In 1976, ADB had decided, in principle, to construct a new office building. In the interim, the Government of the Philippines offered temporary rent-free space in the nearby central bank complex though ADB had to rent additional accommodation nearby. By then, the Bank's offices were scattered around a range of buildings in the Pasay City area near Manila Bay.

Figure 7.3: Operational Approvals by Region, 1977–1986
(%, $ million)

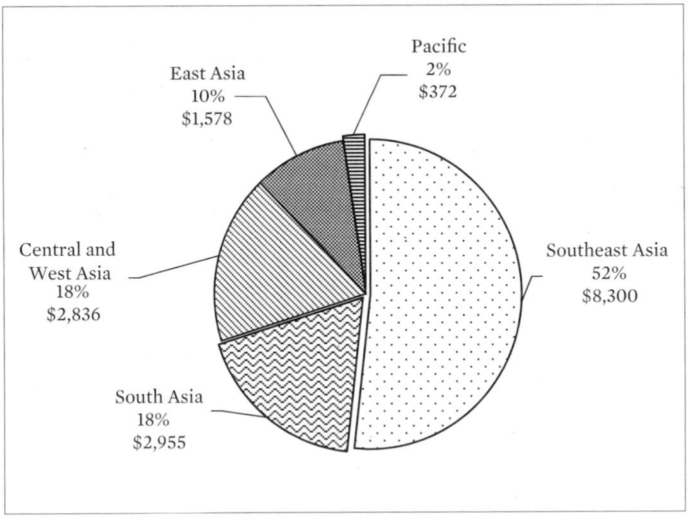

- East Asia: 10%, $1,578
- Pacific: 2%, $372
- Central and West Asia: 18%, $2,836
- South Asia: 18%, $2,955
- Southeast Asia: 52%, $8,300

Total: $16,041 million

Notes: Regional breakdown is based on current country groupings of ADB. Operational approvals include loans, grants, equity investments, and guarantees.

Source: ADB loan, technical assistance, grant and equity approvals database.

Five new members joined over this period. These are: the Maldives (1978), Vanuatu (1981), Bhutan (1982), and Spain (1986). The PRC also became a member in 1986. Unlike other agencies related to the United Nations, ADB retained the membership of Taipei,China under its current designation.

Into a Third Decade

The second ADB decade saw many changes within the Bank and across Asia. At the beginning of the decade in 1977, ADB was still mainly a project-oriented bank, largely focused on the tasks involved in working on project loans. But Shiro Inoue, who left the Bank in November 1976, had already pointed toward change. The next two Presidents, Yoshida and Fujioka, carried the process forward. The 1982 *Study of Operational Priorities and Plans of the Asian Development Bank for the 1980s* provided Fujioka with an agenda for much of the rest of the 1980s. ADB also had to respond to difficult times in the global economy and changes in the region—providing assistance to borrowing countries concerned with food and energy security and faced with the need for structural adjustment.

By the end of the second decade, the Bank had been transformed. The number of member countries had grown from 42 to 47. India, meanwhile, had become an active borrower. While ADB loans would continue to focus on infrastructure, the Bank would broaden the range of development activities during the next decade. ADB had also designed new lending products which strengthened its capacity to mobilize financial resources.

During the next and third ADB decade, Masao Fujioka would continue to promote reform until the end of his presidency in November 1989. Two further Presidents, Kimimasa Tarumizu and Mitsuo Sato, would lead the Bank into the mid-1990s.

Table 7.1: Selected Operational, Institutional, and Financial Information, 1967–1986

	1967–1976 (Total, First Decade)	1976 (end-year)	1986 (end-year)	1977–1986 (Total, Second Decade)
A. Operational Highlights ($ million)				
Total operational approvals[a]	3,361	776	2,005	16,041
By fund source				
Ordinary capital resources	2,466	540	1,369	10,758
Asian Development Fund	895	236	636	5,283
By operations				
Sovereign	3,361	776	1,993	16,022
Nonsovereign	–	–	12	19
Technical assistance approvals[b]	25	3	24	125
Technical assistance projects	21	2	17	96
Regional assistance	4	1	6	29
Outstanding loan portfolio		1,079	8,749	
Ordinary capital resources		881	5,998	
Asian Development Fund		198	2,751	

continued on next page

Table 7.1 continued

	1967–1976 (Total, First Decade)	1976 (end-year)	1986 (end-year)	1977–1986 (Total, Second Decade)
Total loan and grant disbursements	1,159	327	1,024	7,317
Ordinary capital resources	948	263	612	5,145
Asian Development Fund	211	63	413	2,173
Official cofinancing[c]	29	3	30	576
Commercial cofinancing	–	–	5	36
B. Institutional Highlights				
Staff information				
Total staff		760	1,604	
International staff[d]		290	603	
Women staff		308	740	
Women international staff		5	25	
Staff in field offices		–	23	
Member countries		42	47	
Field offices		–	2	
Internal administrative expenses budget ($ million)	102	20	89	588
C. Financial Highlights ($ million)				
Authorized capital[e]		3,707	19,663	
Subscribed capital[e]		3,688	19,476	
Paid-in		1,183	2,354	
Callable		2,506	17,122	
Borrowings	1,133	529	813	6,418

– = nil, SDR = special drawing right, US = United States.

[a] Figures refer to loan, grant, equity investment, and guarantee approvals, net of terminations (they exclude operations approved by the Board of Directors but terminated before they were deemed effective).

[b] Technical assistance operations cover grants funded by the Technical Assistance Special Fund and the Japan Special Fund only.

[c] Includes trust funds and cofinancing of loans, grants, and technical assistance.

[d] International staff data include Management.

[e] Values are US dollar equivalents based on US dollar/SDR exchange rate on 31 December 1976 (for 1976 capital) and 31 December 1986 (for 1986 capital).

Sources: ADB Annual Reports; ADB Budget, Personnel, and Management Systems Department; ADB Controller's Department; ADB Strategy and Policy Department; ADB loan, technical assistance, grant, and equity approvals database; ADB Cofinancing database.

ADB President Taroichi Yoshida greets Australian Prime Minister Malcolm Fraser at ADB headquarters, Manila, Philippines, 10 May 1979.

Construction of the ADB-financed Sha Tin Hospital Polyclinic Project (Prince of Wales Hospital) in Hong Kong, China began in 1979. A nurse cares for a premature infant inside the intensive care nursery of the Department of Paediatrics.

14th Annual Meeting of the Board of Governors, Honolulu, Hawaii, United States, 30 April–2 May 1981.

Indian Prime Minister Indira Gandhi signs the guest book with ADB President Taroichi Yoshida, 9 October 1981.

The agreement establishing ADB's first resident mission, the Bangladesh Resident Office (now known as Bangladesh Resident Mission), was signed on 16 July 1982. Seated from left: Executive Director G. Ramachandran; Alternate Executive Director for Bangladesh, Kafiluddin Mahmood; ADB President Masao Fujioka; ADB Vice-President Ashok T. Bambawale; and ADB Vice-President S. Stanley Katz. Standing from left: ADB Senior Counsel, Office of the General Counsel, Desha-Priya Cuthbert Amerasinghe; and first Country Director of BRM Song Chil Lee.

Canadian Prime Minister Pierre Trudeau visits ADB, 14 January 1983.

ADB President Masao Fujioka (*right*) finalizing the first loan to the People's Republic of China with Chen Muhua, State Councilor and Governor of the People's Bank of China, 9 November 1987.

The Rajasthan Urban Infrastructure Development Project is an ADB-financed sewage treatment plant in Delawas, Jaipur. ADB gave its first loan to India on 3 April 1986.

Construction of the second ADB headquarters in Mandaluyong City, Philippines began in 1986. The exterior was completed in 1988.

The ADB-funded Second Compensatory Forestry Sector Project established fast-growing, high-yielding forest plantations on degraded forestlands covering seven states in Malaysia, 17 November 1988.

Pakistan Prime Minister Benazir Bhutto with ADB President Masao Fujioka at the opening of the Pakistan Resident Mission in Islamabad, Pakistan, 18 July 1989.

ADB President Kimimasa Tarumizu (*right*) visits a tea plantation project site in Sri Lanka, February 1991.

CHAPTER 8
Third Decade (1987–1996)

Asia: Reemergence of the Region

"The new decade has opened with far-reaching changes in virtually all parts of the world. The political and economic changes taking place in Eastern Europe may result in a redirection of attention from Asia. ... the momentum for Asian development may have to come increasingly from within. This presents Asian countries and the Bank with new opportunities."

– Kimimasa Tarumizu,
Address to the ADB Annual Meeting, 1990

The late 1980s saw dramatic political and economic developments across the world. The most significant was the collapse of communism in the Soviet Union and Eastern Europe. This event triggered major shifts, among other things forcing the governments of centrally planned economies to rethink the balance between states and markets. Meanwhile, global investors were seeking more opportunities in developing Asia, and the World Trade Organization was reshaping international trade. Development organizations were also reconsidering the role of states and markets, and focusing on issues of sustainable economic growth and poverty reduction.

The fall of the Berlin Wall toward the end of 1989 ushered in the end of the Cold War which had dominated North–South relations since the end of World War II. The swift change in international relations had reverberations across Asia. During 1990 and 1991, the Central Asian states declared their independence from Soviet rule. And in December 1991, the Soviet Union itself was formally dissolved. Although many policy makers did not fully appreciate it at the time, this was the end of an era. Global communism would no longer hold sway over countries within the socialist orbit. The centralized state-led communist paradigm was largely discredited. Some observers even drew sweeping conclusions about "the end of history," arguing that Western liberal democracy would now be the norm across the world.¹ The upheaval in Eastern Europe also heightened competition for aid funds, especially among European donors who were giving large-scale assistance to countries that had broken away from the socialist bloc.

Developing countries in Asia would also be affected by developments in the Middle East, especially the war in the Gulf in 1990 and the conflict in Iraq in 1991.² They felt the impact through rising oil prices and disruption to their export markets—as well as through losses in remittances from Asian contract workers of up to $750 million per year. The Gulf conflict also reminded the international community of the risks of instability in the developing world and the need to address the deeper factors that fueled the problems.

Changes in Capital Flows

The early part of the period saw a slowdown in capital flows to East Asia and Southeast Asia. Investors in industrial countries, concerned by the debt crisis in Latin America, became more cautious about emerging markets. The main exceptions were Japanese investors (Chapter 6). They still had confidence in developing Asia and in the latter part of the 1980s rapidly increased their direct investments in the newly industrialized economies (NIEs) in Southeast Asia, as well as in the People's Republic of China (PRC), helping these economies transform and weather the fluctuations in international capital markets.³

Official capital flows proved more stable. Indeed, official development assistance rose steadily across the world. This was strongly influenced by Japan, which was moving to expand its international role and had major trade and investment links in Asia.⁴ In 1988, Japan announced the Miyazawa Plan, a debt management proposal designed to help developing countries dealing with heavy debt problems. By 1989, Japan had surpassed the United States (US) as the world's largest official donor. It maintained the top position throughout the 1990s, especially by supporting infrastructure in Southeast Asia and the PRC.

---

1. Fukuyama, 1992, *The End of History and the Last Man*.
2. ADB, *Asian Development Outlook 1991*, Box 1.1.
3. ADB, *Asian Development Outlook 1989*, Box 1.6.
4. Ichimura discusses the *kokusaika* (internationalization) approach to international economic policy pursued during the 1980s. Ichimura, 1998, *Political Economy*, 8.

In the early 1990s, developing countries in Asia saw a revival in private capital flows. International investors were encouraged by the liberalization of capital markets and the easing of restrictions on foreign investment. Portfolio investment flows to the region increased. There was also a sharp rise in foreign direct investment (FDI): between 1994 and 1995, FDI flows to Indonesia, Malaysia, the Philippines, and Thailand rose from $8.6 billion to $14.1 billion.[5] In the mid-1990s, European transnational corporations and international banks also began to pay increasing attention to Asia and the Pacific. These activities fueled a boom in regional stock markets. Although it was not obvious at the time, these flows were helping to inflate a financial bubble.[6] Before long, the bubble would burst.

New Trade Arrangements

The 1990s also saw renewed efforts to reduce barriers to trade. Previously, the only multilateral agreement governing international trade had been the 1948 General Agreement on Tariffs and Trade. In January 1991, this arrangement was replaced by the establishment of the World Trade Organization (WTO). Negotiations for the WTO had been protracted and had highlighted policy differences between developing and industrial countries.

Even at the WTO inaugural meeting in Singapore in 1996, leaders from developing and industrial countries disagreed over such matters as government procurement, trade and investment, and competition policy—topics which became known as the "Singapore issues." Developing countries in Asia were especially concerned that tightened patent protection for pharmaceutical products would lead to higher prices for consumers. Nevertheless, the establishment of the WTO reflected the continuing drive toward globalization. And when the PRC joined the WTO in 2001, it was signaling its commitment to structural change and deeper integration into the world economy.

Regional institutions in Asia were also evolving. The changes in the region reflected policies adopted in Asia but they were also influenced by the establishment of new international institutions such as the single market in Europe and the WTO. Moves toward a single market in Europe had been carried forward decisively when the Maastricht Treaty was signed

---

[5] ADB, *Asian Development Outlook 1997*, Box 1.1.
[6] ADB, *Asian Development Outlook 1994*, Box 1.2.

in February 1992. The treaty set up the European Union and led to the creation of the euro.

Since the 1950s, there had already been strong interest in regionalism in Asia and this increased during the 1990s. The establishment of the European Union reminded leaders in Asia and the Pacific that strengthening the international voice of developing countries of Asia would require unified regional policies. In 1989, the Asia-Pacific Economic Cooperation (APEC) forum was formed to discuss ways of improving cooperation. In 1993, heads of government met for the first time within the APEC framework when US President Bill Clinton invited leaders to a summit in the US. Other regional activities expanded as well: in Southeast Asia, the Association of Southeast Asian Nations (ASEAN) was widening its activities and membership (Viet Nam joined in 1995, the Lao People's Democratic Republic and Myanmar in 1997, and Cambodia in 1999). As will be seen in the next chapter, the Asian Development Bank (ADB) actively supported the creation of new regional groupings.

A Broadened International Development Agenda

By the late 1990s, the international development agenda was broadening out and becoming more comprehensive. Many new priorities had branched out into a "Christmas tree" of issues.[7] These included governance and corruption, women and gender, environmental impacts, population growth, and the interests of indigenous people and communities subject to involuntary resettlement. The issues were reflected in publications of the United Nations. In 1990, the United Nations Development Programme (UNDP) began publishing an annual *Human Development Report* which broadened international discussion into areas such as human security, women's equality and gender, and cultural diversity.[8]

There was also increasing attention to the idea of sustainable development. The suggestion that development should be sustainable was hardly new. For many years, numerous authors and reports had pointed out that rapid

---

[7] Numerous commentators on the changes in aid policy following the end of the Cold War have discussed these issues. These include Love (OECD, 1991, *Development Co-operation*, 11), the Swedish Ministry for Foreign Affairs (1999, *Our Future with Asia*, 2), and Nekkers and Malcontent (2000, *Fifty Years of Dutch Development Cooperation*, 49). Meier provides a survey of changes in development thinking, mainly in Western countries, over the post-World War II period (Meier, 2005, *Biography of a Subject*).

[8] Jolly, Emmerij, and Weiss, 2005, *Power of UN Ideas*, 11.

economic growth could cause serious social and environmental damage. In the mid-1960s, Ezra Mishan's book *The Costs of Economic Growth* had set out the key issues.[9] However, sustainable development began to receive more emphasis after 1987 when the World Commission on Environment and Development (Brundtland Commission) released its report *Our Common Future*. These principles were reiterated in 1992 when the United Nations Conference on Environment and Development (Earth Summit) in Rio de Janeiro agreed to Agenda 21, a plan to make sustainable development a central part of global development policy for the 21st century.

Toward the end of the 1980s, the needs of the world's poorest people moved up the global agenda. The concept of poverty itself was broadening to include empowerment of people in terms of factors such as education, health, and gender equity. In 1988, after speakers at the Annual Meeting called for more action on poverty, ADB established an internal Task Force on Poverty Alleviation to identify ways of prioritizing attention to poverty within its projects.[10] The Bank also supported new studies: in 1990, for example, the *Asian Development Review* sponsored a collection of articles on poverty by scholars such as Shahid Javed Burki, Toshiyuki Mizoguchi, H. T. Oshima, and Montek K. Ahluwalia.[11]

Toward the end of the third ADB decade, in 1995, a sharp controversy broke out about the role of international development banks. The row centered on the work of the World Bank, although the controversy reflected concerns that went well beyond the activities of the World Bank. The World Bank was established in 1945 and its 50th anniversary prompted a coalition of nongovernment organizations and numerous other citizens' groups in the US to mount a highly critical campaign against it based on the arresting theme "50 Years Is Enough."

Their argument was that the model of development promoted by the World Bank, the International Monetary Fund (IMF), and similar institutions was doing great harm.[12] The campaign was well organized and made a range of sharp criticisms—that the World Bank was too project-oriented, too secretive and bureaucratic, and too comfortable in dealing with governments in developing countries. Moreover, it failed to consider the interests of women, marginalized groups, minorities, and ordinary people

---

[9] Mishan, 1966, *The Costs of Economic Growth*.
[10] ADB, 1988, *Annual Report*, "Poverty Alleviation," 29.
[11] ADB, 1990, *Asian Development Review*.
[12] Danaher, 1994, *50 Years Is Enough*.

displaced by large-scale projects. Other charges were that the World Bank too easily supported economic structural adjustment programs that caused widespread unemployment, that it promoted the free flow of international capital which damaged local industries in developing countries, and that it encouraged policies which aggravated problems of high debt in borrowing countries.

The campaign attracted much attention and led the World Bank to reconsider many of its policies. As will be seen in Chapter 9, other international institutions such as ADB responded to the "50 Years Is Enough" campaign by reviewing their own programs. Among other things, these criticisms encouraged a focus on aid effectiveness which would become a major issue for donor countries in their work with multilateral banks.

States and Markets

Influenced by the Reagan and Thatcher administrations in the US and the United Kingdom during the 1980s, the expanding international development agenda gave more weight to the private sector and to markets.[13] These supply-side Anglo-Saxon policies promoted smaller government and encouraged skepticism about government action (Chapter 6). The end of the Cold War and the collapse of the central planning paradigm served to reinforce these views.

In the US, discussions about policies in Latin America evolved into the "Washington Consensus" reflecting neoliberal pro-market views supposedly held by the IMF, the World Bank, and the US Treasury.[14] In some quarters during the early 1990s, views about the private sector verged on a form of market fundamentalism. Some neoliberals also questioned the need for multilateral development banks such as ADB on the grounds that developing countries should be able to get adequate finance from efficient international markets.

In Asia, senior policy makers had their own views about these issues. Many agreed that more needed to be done to support the private sector, but also insisted that markets should operate within clear rules set by governments and societies. After all, some of the region's most successful countries had

---

[13] Meier, 2005, *Biography of a Subject*, 83.
[14] Meier, 2005, *Biography of a Subject*, 92.

relied on strong and effective states—for example, the PRC, the Republic of Korea, and Singapore. This more balanced view, which reaffirmed the importance of governments and states, was supported by leading Asian policy makers and scholars, including Mohammad Sadli from Indonesia, Amartya Sen from India, and Lee Kuan Yew from Singapore.

In 1993, with the support of the Government of Japan, the World Bank published a report, *The East Asian Miracle*.[15] It examined the public policies of eight high-performing Asian economies (the four NIEs, Indonesia, Japan, Malaysia, and Thailand) from 1965 to 1990. It found that the foundations of macroeconomic stability and development of human and physical capital were key factors underpinning dramatic and sustainable growth. The report also highlighted the importance of policies to ensure more equitable income distribution, to promote rapid capital accumulation by making banks more reliable and encouraging high levels of domestic savings, to increase the skilled labor force by providing universal primary schooling and better primary and secondary education, and to implement agricultural policies supporting productivity. These eight economies kept price distortions in check and welcomed new technology. Legal and regulatory structures created a positive business environment. Cooperation between governments and private enterprises was fostered. In short, the report discussed the important role of governments and institutions although it was not so supportive of proactive intervention by government targeting certain industrial sectors.

The Influence of Globalization

Across Asia, the third ADB decade was a time of widespread economic reform and strong growth, not only in the PRC and India but also in many other countries. The process differed considerably from country to country, but in broad terms involved encouraging globalization and relying more on markets and on flows of international trade and capital. Much of the capital flow was from Japan to the NIEs, Southeast Asia, and the PRC.

Flows from Japan were supplemented by additional investments from the NIEs, especially to Southeast Asia.[16] NIEs such as the Republic of Korea and Taipei,China were attracted to Southeast Asia where they could capitalize on the valuable technological and marketing knowledge they had gained

---

[15] World Bank, 1993, *The East Asian Miracle*.
[16] ADB, 1996, *Asian Development Outlook 1996 and 1997*, 194.

from their own experience in labor-intensive manufacturing. Direct investment from these economies was consistent with the earlier flying geese paradigm. Now that their comparative advantage in labor-intensive manufactures was being eroded by rising real wages and appreciating exchange rates, the NIEs were keen to invest in lower-wage countries such as Indonesia which were ready to expand employment, particularly in manufacturing.[17] The Republic of Korea and Taipei,China could then redeploy their workforces toward more capital-intensive activities.

These changes were facilitated by the currency realignments following the 1985 Plaza Accord and led to major shifts in the geographic pattern of exports.[18] Previously, developing countries in Asia depended on export markets in North America, Europe, and Japan.[19] However, from around 1986, they started trading much more with each other. Asia was rapidly becoming its own most important and rapidly expanding market.

Another major factor underpinning regional transformation was the scale of reform in the Russian Federation and the PRC—both of which were shifting away from centralized economic planning and toward market mechanisms.[20] These changes had important implications for Asia. In the early 1990s, the Russian Federation withdrew economic assistance from countries such as Viet Nam and Mongolia which previously had strong links with the former Soviet Union. At the same time, policy makers in Asia, especially in Viet Nam and the Lao PDR, were noting the experience of the PRC where pro-market agricultural reforms had led to very rapid growth and boosts in productivity.[21]

Just as striking as the scale of change was its speed. The achievements of the eight high-performing Asian economies studied in the 1993 World Bank report *The East Asian Miracle* boosted performance in other countries in the region as well. The report noted that from 1965 to 1990, the group of 23 economies of East Asia grew faster than all other regions of the world.[22] In 1997, ADB published *Emerging Asia: Changes and Challenges*

---

[17] ADB, *Asian Development Outlook 1991*, 48.
[18] ADB, *Asian Development Outlook 1991*, 43.
[19] Japan was the most important export destination for the Republic of Korea; Taipei,China; Indonesia; Malaysia; and Thailand in the early years of their industrialization. It was also the second largest export destination, after Hong Kong, China, for the PRC until 1996.
[20] ADB, *Asian Development Outlook 1991*, Box 1.3.
[21] ADB, *Asian Development Outlook 1989*, 38.
[22] World Bank, 1993, *The East Asian Miracle*, 1.

which described the transformation as "unrivaled in history" noting that Asians had rapidly become richer, healthier, better fed, and more educated.[23] But the study also noted that there were consequences from the transformation—demographic, social, and environmental—that would create problems in the decades ahead.

The Newly Industrialized Economies

The overall thrust of economic policy in East Asia and Southeast Asia during this period was for the NIEs to move into high-value manufacturing and service activities. All the NIEs remained oriented toward exports, but each had distinctive features. Hong Kong, China, for example, was increasingly influenced by market reforms in the PRC. During the late 1980s, there was a dramatic increase in investment from Hong Kong, China into the PRC.[24] In Hong Kong, China, the service sector expanded rapidly. By 1996, services accounted for over 80% of the economy. In the mid-1990s, however, investors began to worry about the implications of the impending reunification with the PRC in 1997.

Meanwhile, the Republic of Korea was moving on from labor-intensive manufacturing. Facing shortages of unskilled workers and higher labor costs, enterprises aimed to become more capital intensive. The level of investment rose to very high levels, nearly 40% of GDP. This strategy shifted the balance of industrial output toward heavy and chemical industries whose exports began to grow strongly—increasing by over 30% in 1995. The Republic of Korea prepared for joining the Organisation for Economic Co-operation and Development (OECD) in 1996 and also stepped up its foreign direct investment, especially to Southeast Asia and the PRC.

Progress was also extremely rapid in Singapore. In the early 1980s, the government had announced plans to promote more advanced technologies while continuing to be open to international trade and investment. Initially, progress was slow. However, by the 1990s, the strategy was bearing fruit, with overall economic growth of over 10% per year, the main engines of growth being manufacturing as well as financial and business services.

Taipei,China similarly aimed to become a high-skilled, technology-intensive economy while also investing in neighboring economies such as

---

[23] ADB, 1997, *Emerging Asia*.
[24] ADB, 1991, *ADF VI: Report of Donors*, Box 2.1.

the PRC; Hong Kong, China; and countries in Southeast Asia. Taipei,China also faced political uncertainties, notably about whether it could join the WTO. This issue was not decided until December 2001—in favor of admitting Taipei,China—when the PRC became a member.

People's Republic of China

The transformation which had begun in the late 1970s gathered pace. Nevertheless, it was sometimes "piecemeal, partial, incremental, and often experimental."[25] Compared with the top–down "big bang" transition in Eastern Europe, the approach in the PRC was more bottom–up, prompting a debate as to which model of reform in transitional economies was likely to be more successful.[26]

It was clear, however, that in the PRC a long period of almost continuous structural adjustment was accompanied by high levels of investment and increases in productivity. The government carefully but progressively opened up the economy to foreign trade and investment while reducing regulations and subsidies and relying more on markets.[27] Liberalization was phased. For a time, for example, the government allowed a dual-track price system which gave state-owned enterprises partial freedom to sell output in excess of official quotas at market prices.

After the mid-1980s, the process of change widened out from rural and agricultural reforms to urban areas and to small-scale manufacturing. As a result, rural and urban districts increased their production of labor-intensive, light consumer goods. Soon, the PRC became the world's largest producer and exporter of textiles, cotton, furniture, and toys. This process was supported in Guangdong province and nearby areas by FDI—especially from Hong Kong, China and from Taipei,China. Between 1991 and 1994, FDI in the PRC rose from $4 billion to $30 billion.[28] In the spring of 1992, Deng Xiaoping made his famous trip to the southern parts of the country where he spoke about the importance of further economic reform and opening up and criticized those who did not support these changes.

---

[25] Lin, Cai, and Li, 1996, *Lessons of China's Transformation*, 201.
[26] For a summary of the debate, see Lin, Cai, and Li, 1996, *Lessons of China's Transformation*, 201, 225.
[27] ADB, 1989, *Asian Development Outlook 1989*, Box 2.1.
[28] ADB, 1996, *Asian Development Outlook 1996 and 1997*, 20.

Nevertheless, there were periods of difficulty when rapid structural reform led to macroeconomic problems. There were, for example, several episodes of rising inflation and slower growth during the third ADB decade.[29] Policy makers became concerned that rapid microeconomic change was leading to a "boom and bust" pattern of development and were determined to ensure that pro-market liberalization did not lead to economic instability.

During the early 1990s, the PRC entered a period of sustained development which was encouraged by further policy shifts. In 1994, the government made the renminbi convertible for current account transactions, strengthened the central bank and widened the commercialization of the banking system, and introduced a package of fiscal reforms.[30] During the latter part of the third ADB decade, average growth in the PRC rose to 10% per year and more. This period of rapid transformation continued well into the new century.

Southeast Asia

Transformation accelerated in most countries in Southeast Asia influenced, first, by domestic reforms; second, by open trade and investment relations with other countries; and third, by international factors such as the changes taking place in the NIEs and the PRC.

At the beginning of the third ADB decade, Indonesia and Malaysia both faced the need to make major changes in policy. Following the dramatic increases in world oil prices in the 1970s, they had benefited from a windfall in export revenues and tax collections. But when the international price of oil collapsed in 1986, Indonesia and Malaysia were forced to introduce sweeping reforms.

In Indonesia, a series of economic policy packages was introduced to promote restructuring and deregulate parts of the economy. By the early 1990s, these had helped reduce the dominance of the oil sector and encouraged rapid growth in labor-intensive manufacturing. There were also important changes in the finance sector. Deregulation in the late 1980s had encouraged a proliferation of commercial banks—from 110 in 1988 to 240 in 1995.[31] But the financial authorities lacked the capacity to monitor

---

[29] ADB, 1990, *Asian Development Outlook 1990*, Box 2.1.
[30] ADB, 1996, *Asian Development Outlook 1996 and 1997*, Box 2.1.
[31] Hamada, 2003, *Transformation of the Financial Sector in Indonesia*.

the rapid changes and there were serious consequences when the Asian financial crisis unfolded in 1997 (Chapter 10).

Similar changes occurred in Malaysia. The combination of effective macroeconomic policy, comparatively good infrastructure, and a strong resource base ensured that international trade grew quickly and that Malaysia remained an attractive destination for foreign investors. Export-oriented manufacturing grew strongly, with large investments in information technology. Output of electrical and electronic goods, for example—by far the largest manufacturing subsector—grew by over 20% in 1995.

Growth was even stronger in Thailand, reaching double digits between 1988 and 1990. This was a period of transformation. In the 1970s, the economy had relied heavily on primary commodities but was becoming increasingly diversified—with rapidly growing manufacturing output alongside strong agricultural industries and an expanding service sector. Supported by foreign investment, Thailand diversified its exports. Nevertheless, by the mid-1990s, the current account deficit was beginning to widen significantly, climbing to over 7% of GDP in 1995. At the time, this large external deficit appeared sustainable.[32] But as would become clear when the Asian financial crisis emerged in mid-1997, the growing imbalance had left Thailand vulnerable to unpredictable fluctuations in international capital flows.

In the Philippines, the development process continued to lag. The contrast with nearby ASEAN member states was striking. The end of the Marcos era in 1986 encouraged a tentative recovery. However, the new government under Corazon C. Aquino found it difficult to overcome the legacies of the previous 20 years which included a high burden of debt, rapid population growth, and difficulties of implementing reform within a cumbersome governance system. In 1991–1992, the economy slipped back into recession before a new President, Fidel Ramos, took office and started to promote investment.[33]

In the late 1980s, there was a sustained period of change in the transitional Mekong economies of Viet Nam, Cambodia, and the Lao PDR. In Viet Nam,

---

[32] ADB, 1996, *Asian Development Outlook 1996 and 1997*, 107.
[33] Sicat provides a thorough survey of the changes during this period (Sicat, 2014, *Cesar Virata*). Balisacan and Hill also provide a valuable overview of development policies in the Philippines (Balisacan and Hill, 2007, *The Dynamics of Regional Development*).

the *Doi Moi* reforms, announced in December 1986, reflected changes in the PRC as liberalization in domestic markets in agriculture resulted in sharp increases in rice output.[34] Nevertheless, it was proving difficult to transition from a controlled economic system to a market economy. Similar changes were introduced in Cambodia and the Lao PDR. When the Paris Peace Accords to settle the conflicts in Cambodia were signed in 1991, all three countries rapidly increased their engagement with the international community. In contrast, Myanmar remained inward-looking and development was held back by heavy regulation and control of political and economic activities.

South Asia

In South Asia during the third ADB decade, the pace of change accelerated. India and Bangladesh especially, for different reasons, were becoming more open to the international economy. In India, a turning point was a sweeping policy package introduced in 1991 under the leadership of Prime Minister P. V. Narasimha Rao and Finance Minister Manmohan Singh.[35] There had been incremental reforms in the 1980s,[36] but in the late 1980s faster growth had led to economic difficulties, with rising levels of debt as well as rising balance-of-payments and fiscal deficits. In response, in July 1991, the government introduced a major reform package—supported by the IMF delicensing much industrial activity, liberalizing foreign investment procedures, and reforming trade and financial policies.[37] The new policies led to a marked acceleration of long-term economic growth, as well as a change in attitudes; henceforth, political leaders would find themselves under pressure to support reform. By the end of the third ADB decade, there was a strong commitment in India to growth-oriented policies.

Elsewhere in South Asia, development performance was mixed. In Pakistan, periods of strong growth were interrupted by episodes of political and economic instability. In 1989, ethnic violence in Karachi, the only large port and the financial and industrial center, created uncertainty and held back investment. Development was also affected by frequent power shortages and difficulties in the agriculture sector. In Bangladesh, the prospects improved somewhat. In the mid-1980s, the economy had been dominated

---

[34] ADB, 1991, *Asian Development Outlook 1991*, Box 1.3.
[35] Panagariya, 2001, *India's Economic Reforms*.
[36] ADB, 1989, *Asian Development Outlook 1989*, Box 2.5.
[37] ADB, 1992, *Asian Development Outlook 1992*, Box 2.5.

by agriculture while formal manufacturing was underdeveloped. A decade later, some reforms, such as substantial liberalization of trade and changes in taxes, had helped promote growth and reduce excessive dependence on agriculture. Nevertheless, investment levels remained among the lowest in South Asia.

In the smaller countries—Sri Lanka, Nepal, and Bhutan—policy makers were generally cautious of outward-looking, trade-oriented policies. Levels of foreign investment were low. Governments did relax some inward-looking and regulatory policies but did not aim for the kind of structural change taking place in East Asia and Southeast Asia.

Central Asian Republics

Three of the Central Asian republics (CARs)—Kazakhstan, the Kyrgyz Republic, and Uzbekistan—joined the Bank toward the end of the third ADB decade. Several more would join within the next few years.

The breakup of the Soviet Union in 1991 brought a period of extreme economic and social difficulty for the CARs. All of the countries declared independence from the Soviet Union and were affected by severe reductions in real output during the following structural adjustment period. Between 1990 and 1996, real output fell by over 40% in the CARs. Uzbekistan, however, escaped a difficult adjustment process because the local economy was less directly affected than economies in the other former Soviet republics.

In Kazakhstan, the collapse in output was largely due to the interruption of oil and gas production, loss of subsidies from the Soviet Union, and the exit of Russian technicians and managers. The Kyrgyz Republic was less dependent on natural resources but was more dependent on support from the Soviet Union. Both countries left the ruble zone in 1993 and established their own currencies. Rampant inflation followed. The inflation rate was over 1,000% in each of the 3 years to 1994 in Kazakhstan and rose to almost 1,000% in the Kyrgyz Republic in 1992 and in 1993.

All of the countries faced difficult transition challenges which required strict stabilization measures, structural reforms, and the development of effective markets. Fiscal problems were acute for a number of years following independence. As a result, there were deep cuts in government-provided social services. The severe economic difficulties led to sharp increases in poverty. People living in isolated industrial centers and rural areas were especially affected. In Kazakhstan in mid-1995, for example, approximately 37% of the total population was estimated to have fallen below the poverty line compared with 20% in 1992.[38]

Pacific Island Countries

The Pacific island countries are very diverse. The broadest categorization is by size. Most of the land-based resources, and over 90% of the Pacific population, are in the four Melanesian states: Fiji, Papua New Guinea, Solomon Islands, and Vanuatu. In contrast, most of the smaller Polynesian and Micronesian states rely largely on marine resources.[39] Throughout the third ADB decade, most of the Pacific island countries experienced periods of boom and bust and most had high fiscal and balance-of-payments deficits.

Their economies are sharply dualistic with large subsistence sectors and small formal sectors, of which a large part comprised government activities. As a result, higher economic growth does not necessarily improve living standards for the majority of people. For example, in 1992, Papua New Guinea experienced a boom in the mining and petroleum sector where output surged by 30%. However, in the same year, production in the non-mining parts of the economy rose by just 4%. Boosting economic growth would require improving performance in the government sector, promoting private enterprise, and lifting rates of both savings and investment. Throughout the decade, most of the Pacific island countries made only modest progress in these respects. Both Australia and New Zealand maintained long-established development assistance programs to the Pacific island countries. However, the challenges of development in the region were such that international aid programs could only help address some of the barriers holding back growth in these countries.

Increasing Strength in Asia

The third ADB decade thus saw key changes which affected thinking about development policy and about the way development programs were designed. Many countries in Asia were reaping a reform dividend through faster growth and more were adopting outward-oriented market-friendly

---

[38] ADB, 1996, *Asian Development Outlook 1996 and 1997*, 68.
[39] ADB member countries which are generally regarded as falling into the Polynesian part of the Pacific are the Cook Islands, Nauru, Samoa, Tonga, and Tuvalu. The Micronesian area includes Kiribati, the Federated States of Micronesia, the Marshall Islands, and Palau.

policies. Rapid increases in exports were helping finance imports of world-class technologies and capital goods. High savings, often supported by frugal fiscal policies, were supporting investment in infrastructure and in the private sector. Some of the lower-income countries were increasing labor-intensive manufacturing while higher-income countries such as the NIEs were producing more high-technology industrial goods.

The structural adjustments in Asia were supported by large increases in outward capital flows from Japan and the NIEs. This flood of capital was welcome. The foreign direct investment transfers provided packages of finance, technology, and management know-how. However, in 1997 when the Asian financial crisis erupted, it quickly became clear that opening their capital markets, especially allowing the rapid liberalization of short-term portfolio investment, had exposed borrowing countries to sudden shifts in investor sentiment.

During this period, ADB spoke of the emergence of Asia—or, more accurately, the reemergence of Asia. The region grew in confidence and contributed a rising share of the world economy.[40] This trend accentuated as the third decade proceeded. While industrial countries grew sluggishly, developing Asia continued to do well. The transformation in the PRC showed no sign of slowing and indeed gathered pace as reforms in one part of the huge country judged to be successful were adopted elsewhere. It became increasingly clear that if Asian countries adopted appropriate domestic policies they could expect sustained development even when there were uncertainties in international markets. Another feature of the growing confidence in the region was the insistence that the pro-market views reflected in the Washington Consensus needed to be tempered by Asia's own experiences.

Regional institutions were also coming to the fore. Organizations such as ASEAN were building institutional strength, and there was an expansion of cooperation schemes such as the ADB Greater Mekong Subregion Economic Cooperation Program and later the Central Asia Regional Economic Cooperation (CAREC) Program. The South Asia Subregional Economic Cooperation (SASEC) Program was also initiated (Chapter 12).

During the third ADB decade, the Bank needed to respond to these and other developments. As will be seen in the next chapter, the end of the Cold War led to numerous changes in the international development agenda— and to new expectations of ADB.

---

[40] ADB, 1997, *Emerging Asia*, xi.

CHAPTER 9
Third Decade (1987–1996)

ADB: New Members and New Regions

"I have long stressed, the Bank must accelerate its transformation from a project financier to a broad-based development institution ... our basic mandate is to maximize our development impacts, not just maximizing the lending volume."

– Mitsuo Sato,
New Year's Message, end of 1997

In 1987, at the beginning of the third decade of the Asian Development Bank (ADB), the Bank held its 20th Annual Meeting in Osaka, Japan. This was a significant event—the first ADB Annual Meeting held in Japan since the Inaugural Meeting in Tokyo in November 1966—and the opening ceremonies were held in the presence of the Crown Prince and Princess of Japan. In his formal address, Masao Fujioka recalled that first ADB meeting and then provided a summary of growth and development in the region over the period.

Looking ahead, it was clear that ADB faced numerous challenges. One was the slowdown in Bank lending—just when many developing countries were facing sharp declines in export commodity prices and rising levels of debt and had to cut back on government spending on new projects. Fujioka also expected ADB operations to become more complex as the institution responded to the widening expectations of its development role.

ADB was also under pressure from member countries, though the industrial countries and the borrowing countries were often pushing in different directions. The United States (US), for example, was pressing for an expansion of the Bank's work with the private sector and was sometimes critical of ADB management practices. These views were forcefully expressed by Joe Rogers, the US Executive Director in 1985 and 1986, and then by his successor, Victor Frank, between 1987 and 1993—

both of whom had close personal links with the Reagan administration.[1,2] Other nonregional countries had different priorities. Several European countries, for example, pressed ADB to increase lending to the People's Republic of China (PRC) and India, and to work more with nongovernment organizations and pay greater attention to the role of women in development.

Developing member countries had other concerns and were generally more worried about the volume and terms of lending. At the Annual Meeting in 1987, India drew attention to the slowdown in ADB lending, urging the Bank to provide larger loans and reduce "complex procedural requirements" that delayed the disbursement of funds. Indonesia called for technical assistance to strengthen national institutions and for more projects that would specifically benefit the poor.

Managing Member Priorities

Fujioka needed to respond to these and numerous other issues in his final 3 years as President. He set three major priorities: expanding ADB links with India and the PRC, strengthening the Bank as a development resource center, and redefining the institution's role for the 1990s.

Fujioka's attention to the first of these issues would soon bring important changes. In 1986 and 1987, India and the PRC received their first loans and, as their borrowings surged, the ADB lending program moved into a new phase of growth. Cooperation with these two countries would be a key feature of the Bank's work during its third decade.

The new programs helped overcome the worrying problems caused by the sluggish lending in the early 1980s and expanded the Bank's balance sheet. This, in turn, soon prompted discussion about a general capital increase.

Fujioka had worked hard to arrange to bring India into ADB as a borrower. From India's perspective, ADB provided additional, albeit modest, external finance. The Bank's first loan to India, for the Industrial Credit

---

[1] Roy, 1985, *The Struggle of Mr Fujioka*, 60; Rogers, 1985, "The Problem Is, They Don't Understand Business," 68.
[2] Sherk provides a useful summary of his experience of the way the US works with multilateral organizations, including ADB. He was an Alternate Executive Director at ADB from June 1982 to August 1985. Sherk, 2008, Multilateralism and US Foreign Economic Policy.

and Investment Corporation of India in 1986, was to support onlending to private sector industrial firms.

Fujioka was keen to see the Indian program grow quickly. However, for this purpose, the Bank would need to learn more about specific sectors and establish itself as a useful partner. Borrowing agencies in India often had difficult relationships with donors from whom they did not always welcome advice. Indeed, the political environment in India was generally not conducive to policy discussions with external organizations. However, as the Bank's program grew, ADB staff gradually began to expand the opportunities for policy dialogue at the sector level.

Fujioka also aimed to expand the Bank's program in the PRC. ADB and the PRC both perceived substantial advantages in working together. ADB saw an opportunity to establish itself as a major development institution in the region. The PRC saw a useful way of strengthening its international economic diplomacy: joining the Bank sent a signal—an important one for the PRC in the mid-1980s—that the nation was opening up to the global community and was ready to cooperate with Asian neighbors in regional development. Work with the PRC began in 1986. The first loan, approved in 1987, was for $100 million for the China Investment Bank to provide assistance to small and medium-sized industrial enterprises. As in India, the first few years were a formative stage in the relationship. Initially, the PRC borrowed mainly for industrial development in the eastern coastal seaboard region which the government had chosen as a growth corridor. By and large, the PRC authorities chose the projects for which they would borrow from ADB.[3]

Two monumental projects financed by ADB in the early years in the PRC were the Nanpu and Yangpu bridges in Shanghai (Box 9.1). In Shanghai, the Suzhou Creek rehabilitation and cleaning project was another successful project for the Bank. Later, when President Takehiko Nakao visited Shanghai in November 2016 to attend the symposium for commemorating 30 years of partnership between ADB and the PRC, he was impressed by the remark of a long-serving senior official in the municipal government. The official remarked that ADB's projects had been, and still were, vital to the development of the country because they combined finance with new technologies and expertise on the ground to design and implement projects.

---

[3] ADB, 1998, *Country Assistance Program Evaluation in the PRC*, iv.

> **Box 9.1: Two Bridges in Shanghai**
>
> **Nanpu Bridge.** The project helped restructure Shanghai's economic base by supporting the construction of the first bridge across the Huangpu River, transforming the Pudong New Area into a business and financial center. The bridge was opened in December 1991, 2 years ahead of schedule. Traffic grew quickly. During the first month, around 12,000 vehicles crossed the toll bridge daily; this rose to 17,000 the following month. A decade later, about 120,000 vehicles were passing over the Nanpu Bridge each day. ADB shouldered a little less than a third ($70 million) of the total project cost of about $227 million. The rest was shared by commercial cofinancing sources and the Municipality of Shanghai.
>
> **Yangpu Bridge.** The Yangpu Bridge, the sister bridge to the Nanpu Bridge, was opened in 1993. At the time, it was among the world's longest bridges. It has a total length of more than 8,000 meters and is one of the longest cable-stayed bridges in the world. Use of the facility grew rapidly. By 2000, around 100,000 vehicles were crossing the Yangpu Bridge each day. ADB financed $85 million of the total cost of the project of around $267 million.
>
> Both the Yangpu and Nanpu bridges were showcases for technological achievements in Shanghai. The Nanpu Bridge, made of high-strength materials, was designed by the Shanghai Municipal Engineering Design Institute and was modeled after the Alex Fraser Bridge in Vancouver. To promote the adoption of lessons from the experience, ADB provided a technical assistance program to bring an international group of world-class engineers to review the Nanpu Bridge. Learning from this experience, Chinese technicians took charge of the construction of the Yangpu Bridge themselves.
>
> Sources: I. Gill. 2011. Bridges Bring Boom. *Impact Stories from the People's Republic of China*. Manila: ADB. pp. 4–6. https://www.adb.org/sites/default/files/publication/28883/prc-impact-stories.pdf (accessed 20 December 2016); ADB. 1999. *Project Performance Audit Report: Shanghai-Nanpu Bridge Project*. Manila.

The Government of the PRC was keen to take advantage of ADB membership and agreed to host the Bank's Annual Meeting in Beijing in 1989. The gathering was eventful. In addition to taking up the recommendations of a major report about the Bank's role in the 1990s, delegates considered the rapidly evolving political events in the PRC. They also speculated as to who would be the next ADB President because during the meeting Fujioka officially announced that he would resign at the end of 1989.

During his last 3 years as President, Fujioka also strengthened the Bank as a development institution. Because financial assistance alone was not sufficient to support all-round development, he wanted ADB to be a development resource center for Asia by providing information and knowledge to borrowing countries. In pointing to the importance of knowledge and intellectual capital, Fujioka was foreshadowing the knowledge-based approaches to development that would gain prominence later in the mid-1990s when the new president of the World Bank, James Wolfensohn, announced that the World Bank would become a "knowledge bank."

In 1989, Fujioka launched the first issue of the *Asian Development Outlook*. It has subsequently become one of the Bank's most important regular publications. He also lent his personal support to a series of Roundtables on Development Strategies which began in 1989 and would provide a forum where participants from Asian borrowing countries could discuss development issues.[4]

Responding to calls for further reform in 1987, Fujioka invited an external panel of five experts to consider the role of the Bank in the 1990s. The panel came from within and outside Asia, though, reflecting the Charter, it was "Asian in its basic character." The chair was Saburo Okita, a distinguished Japanese economist and policy maker who also had a strong interest in environmental issues. There were two other well-known development economists from Asia, Mohammad Sadli from Indonesia and Amartya Sen from India. Two senior policy makers from industrial countries, John M. Hennessy from the US and Emile van Lennep from the Netherlands, also joined the group. They met delegations from many countries and in early 1989 issued their final document, *Report of a Panel on the Role of the Asian Development Bank in the 1990s*.[5]

The panel report reflected the changes in thinking at the time (Chapter 8). The report confirmed that ADB should be a sound financial institution whose overriding aim was to promote the development of its developing member countries.[6] However, development was defined broadly to include not only sustainable economic growth but also social and environmental goals. This approach, the panel emphasized, would mean striking a balance:

---

[4] Fujioka, 1989, *Development Strategies for Growth with Equity*.
[5] ADB, 1989, *Report of a Panel on the Role of the Asian Development Bank in the 1990s*.
[6] ADB, 1989, *Report of a Panel on the Role of the Asian Development Bank in the 1990s*, 2.

"From Asia's recent experience, one lesson stands clear. For successful and sustained development, nothing is more important than the achievement of the right balance – between the scope and roles of the public and private sectors, between government planning and the judicious use of market mechanisms, between policies that directly promote growth and those that pay attention to social questions."[7] The panel members thus distanced themselves from the neoliberal pro-market policies espoused in some quarters in the 1980s.

The panel offered specific recommendations. One main suggestion was that while the Bank should continue to concentrate on lending to the public sector infrastructure investments, it should offer more support for social sectors—such as public health, including family planning, and education (Box 9.2). The panel also said that ADB should do more to address poverty: ADB should support social investments that provide direct benefits to the poor and pay special attention to the impact of projects on employment, especially informal employment. And when appraising projects, it should always consider the impact on the poor. Also, ADB should follow the suggestions of the report of the Brundtland Commission by making "a fundamental commitment to sustainable development."

Strong support for public sector investments was balanced with the suggestion for more support for the private sector. ADB, the panel observed, had a very limited direct role in private sector activities. The panel also recommended that the Bank expand its policy dialogue with borrowing countries. Following the earlier 1983 study on operational priorities, ADB had increased its policy dialogue during the 1980s.[8] But the panel was keen to see ADB do more, particularly through multilateral cooperation, engaging with representatives of both regional and nonregional countries.

In 1992, many of the suggestions of the panel report would be incorporated into a new medium-term strategic framework.[9] The report gave impetus to Fujioka's efforts to promote ADB as a broader development financial institution. But this created a dilemma. As the Bank embraced a more diverse agenda, its resources remained constrained. Indeed, within a few years, the Bank would reach a "headroom problem" as lending programs ran up against the authorized ceiling on loans.

---

[7] ADB, 1989, *Report of a Panel on the Role of the Asian Development Bank in the 1990s*, 3.
[8] ADB, 1983, *Study of Operational Priorities and Plans of ADB for the 1980s*, 12.
[9] ADB, 1992, *Medium-Term Strategic Framework*, 1992.

Box 9.2: ADB's Education Sector Projects

Education has been a priority sector from the beginning for the Asian Development Bank (ADB). ADB's focus has been on improving vocational education, strengthening science and technology education, and enhancing the quality of basic education.

ADB's first loan for education was approved in 1970 to Singapore to expand the capacity of Ngee Ann Technical College. Initially, ADB's support to vocational education focused on East Asian and Southeast Asian countries including the Republic of Korea, Malaysia, and Thailand. But the demand for technical and vocational education and training (TVET) has grown rapidly. Over the past 50 years, ADB has supported over 90 TVET projects in 26 countries.

Recognizing its importance in national development, ADB has been very active in supporting science and technology in secondary and higher education from the earliest stages of operations. For example, in the Republic of Korea, ADB supported upgrading and strengthening of six research and development institutes including the Korea Institute of Science and Technology and the Korea Standard Research Institute in the late 1970s. ADB also provided significant support for strengthening several universities in Indonesia in the 1980s and 1990s.

ADB's involvement in basic education during the past decades has led to significant progress in access, quality, and gender equality. For example, ADB-supported stipend programs for girls were instrumental in Bangladesh becoming a globally recognized early achiever in gender parity up to secondary education. Quality has been improved through teacher training and textbook support in Mongolia, Uzbekistan, and Viet Nam. ADB has also helped government-led comprehensive sector-wide approaches in Nepal, Samoa, and other countries.

Building on the experience and progress made, ADB is now focusing on four areas: enhancing access for hard-to-reach populations (including continued support to gender equality and for disadvantaged groups); improving teaching and learning; ensuring job ready graduates; and preparing for knowledge-based economy in Asia through innovation and cross-sectoral collaboration.

Source: ADB.

In the ADB Charter, specific limitations are laid down which set a ceiling on the amount of ordinary capital resources (OCR) loans that may be approved. The total outstanding of OCR loans, equity investments, and guarantees may not exceed ADB's subscribed capital (paid-in and callable) and reserves.[10] The borrowing policy, annually approved by the Board, provides that the total outstanding borrowing should not exceed ADB's callable capital from non-borrowing members and ADB's capital (paid-in and reserves). In later years, lending would also be constrained by the conditions the Bank needed to meet to preserve its AAA credit rating; for this purpose, a strict ceiling of the ratio of equity (paid-in capital and reserves, but not including callable capital) to outstanding loans on the OCR balance sheet needed to be observed. Because of these constraints, ADB would need a new capital increase to expand the amount of headroom from time to time.

Kimimasa Tarumizu

In November 1989, an era came to an end when Masao Fujioka retired. He had arrived in 1981 ready to promote change, though before pressing ahead had waited for the 1983 *Study of Operational Priorities and Plans of the Asian Development Bank for the 1980s*.

Fujioka's relations with the Board were not always easy. A group of Board Directors regularly took issue with his decisions. These Directors were usually from the US, Australia, the United Kingdom (UK), and Canada—and often promoted their own priorities. Despite these difficulties, Fujioka had been a strong and effective President with clear ideas and a disciplined management style. Because of his efforts, ADB had expanded its activities as a regional resource center and a repository of knowledge and had extended its work into policy development. And ADB was now lending to India and the PRC, following Fujioka's extended efforts to arrange for them to become borrowing members.

Fujioka's successor, Kimimasa Tarumizu, who became President in November 1989, had a very different approach to management. Like most other ADB Presidents, he had worked at the Ministry of Finance in Tokyo. He had also served as Minister at the Embassy of Japan in Washington, DC and had been Director General of the Customs and Tariff Bureau. Tarumizu had a conciliatory, consensus-driven style that transformed relations

---

[10] Article 12 of the Charter provides details of the limitations on OCR lending.

between the Bank's Management and the Board of Directors. At the Annual Meeting in New Delhi in May 1990, numerous representatives welcomed his appointment. The Governor from Afghanistan described him as having a "gentlemanly character."

Tarumizu was a gentle, self-deprecating man. He also had an impish sense of humor. Much of the time he kept this under control, realizing that as the head of an international agency he was expected to maintain official decorum. But to the dismay of his close advisers, he sometimes let his guard down. He quite enjoyed, for example, sparring with Victor Frank, the US Executive Director. Frank brought a direct and no-nonsense conservative Republican style to ADB Board meetings, but outside the office he was much more easy-going.

At the 1991 Groundhog Day party hosted by Frank in the garden of his residence in Manila,[11] when invited to speak, Tarumizu began by modestly observing: "Most Japanese begin their speeches with either a 'thank you' or an 'apology.' But my nationality is no longer 'Japanese' but rather 'ADB.' So perhaps I should begin my speech with a question. The question is whether I am the appropriate person to be making this speech—especially since I have never seen a groundhog." But he said that after studying Frank's briefing notes on groundhogs, "I think I understand, better, the tradition of Groundhog Day. And, once 'internationalization' of this day spreads to Japan, I have no doubt that someone in Japan will invent an 'electronic' groundhog." He closed by saying that, "rain or shine, the groundhog could not find more enthusiastic supporters than Mr. and Mrs. Frank."[12]

When Tarumizu arrived in ADB on Friday 24 November 1989, the Bank's birthday, he was confronted with a pressing agenda. Some issues had been anticipated: the need to mobilize both Asian Development Fund (ADF) and OCR financial resources and to implement the recommendations of the Okita panel. Others were less predictable, such as the changes following the fall of the Berlin Wall and the rapidly expanding demands from India and the PRC. But before Tarumizu could begin to deal with these issues, he was faced with a much more immediate problem—leading the Bank during the events of the December 1989 coup attempt in the Philippines.

---

[11] Groundhog Day is a traditional event celebrated in some parts of the US and other countries to mark the arrival of spring. According to tradition, the groundhog emerges from its burrow on this day. Depending on whether the groundhog sees its shadow or not, spring will arrive soon or late.

[12] Quotes are from the official notes of Tarumizu's speech, 31 January 1991.

Just a week after Tarumizu arrived, on 1 December, a dissident faction of the Philippines armed forces attempted a coup against the President, Corazon C. Aquino. The international airport was closed and there was chaos in Metro Manila, including in areas close to ADB. The atmosphere was tense. ADB was closed, although to protect staff and property, the Bank maintained high-level contact with the government. President Aquino received US military assistance, including airpower, and within a week the coup had collapsed.

Shortly afterward, in reviewing events with staff, Tarumizu talked of how the ADB Crisis Management Committee, which he chaired, met every day during the crisis.[13] With this rather sobering experience behind him, and as a very uncertain calm settled on a troubled Manila, Tarumizu turned his attention to the regular affairs of ADB.

New Resources

One of Tarumizu's first tasks was to mobilize more financial resources to meet the constant pressure from member countries to expand programs—either with ADF funds or OCR resources. Negotiations for the fifth replenishment of the Asian Development Fund (ADF VI) had started in early 1990. Unfortunately, this was just after the fall of the Berlin Wall. Donors were now facing requests for support from Eastern Europe and said that the initial amount proposed by the Bank was unrealistic. At the same time, donors wanted a more diverse program. As suggested by the Okita panel, they asked for greater attention to poverty reduction, economic growth, environmental improvements, the role of women in development, and population issues.

The donor community was also pressing ADB to support policy reforms in borrowing countries. The formal *ADF VI: Report of Donors* agreed to in 1991 was assertive about the responsibilities of borrowing countries: "Donors believe that DMC [developing member country] governments must be committed to the policy changes agreed upon. Reform packages needed to be realistic and capable of implementation and to justify fully the assistance provided."[14]

---

[13] Tarumizu, 1989, *Speech to Staff*.
[14] ADB, 1991, *ADF VI: Report of Donors*.

Such views were not always readily accepted by governments and other stakeholders from developing countries. At Annual Meetings of the Bank, borrowing countries had sometimes urged for policy dialogue between ADB and developing countries to be conducted in a careful way. They were also concerned about suggestions from donor countries that priorities for ADF programs should be implemented across all ADB activities. In the *ADF VI: Report of Donors*, for example, it said: "Donors noted that while these undertakings relate primarily to ADF operations, they also involve issues which should apply, where relevant, to ordinary capital resources (OCR) operations of the Bank."[15] Directors from developing countries on the ADB Board did not warm to this approach. When reports from donor meetings were presented to the Board, these Directors reminded Tarumizu that Bank policies should reflect the views of all members, not just those of donor countries.

Negotiations for a general capital increase (GCI) proved even more difficult. In principle, these should have been easier since contributions would largely be in the form of callable capital to be paid in only if needed and so would impose relatively small financial burdens on member countries. Most member countries recognized that the budgetary load would be fairly light and were ready to begin discussions by 1991 or 1992.

The US, however, was in no hurry to start negotiations. And being in no hurry, it was in a strong position. At the ADB Annual Meeting in Hong Kong, China in 1992, the US outlined an extensive list of requirements that might need to be considered before a GCI could be agreed to: a strategy for encouraging private sector development, arrangements for cofinancing, a medium-term lending strategy, addressing the issue of lending to "countries with high current account surpluses" (with an eye toward the PRC), and an estimate of the Bank's long-term "sustainable level of lending." The last topic was a signal that the US wanted a firm ceiling on ADB lending so that further GCIs would not be needed. Other member countries soon added further suggestions.

Tarumizu's repeated efforts to reach agreement on a GCI before the end of 1993 were thus frustrated. This was worrying. The authorized capital serves to set upper limits on both the Bank's borrowing from capital markets and the loans that can be approved. When Tarumizu arrived, there was still some remaining authorization headroom for OCR lending,

---

[15] ADB, 1991, *ADF VI: Report of Donors*.

but this was rapidly running out. Without a GCI, there would soon be a freeze on new lending.

Strategic Planning

Another issue Tarumizu needed to address was implementing the recommendations of the 1989 Okita panel. Tarumizu made it clear that he supported the priorities of the panel: alleviating poverty, addressing social problems, and protecting the environment; promoting expansion of the private sector; and supporting improved policy environments in borrowing countries.

Tarumizu also took the major step of introducing strategic planning into the Bank. ADB had never developed a strong strategic planning framework. But support had been growing for such plans. In 1990, the Development Policy Office had begun work on a planning process. Further impetus to these changes was given in 1991 when delegates at the ADB Annual Meeting in Vancouver spoke of the importance of strategic planning and a Strategic Planning Unit was created reporting directly to the President.[16]

In early 1992, Tarumizu recommended the introduction of strategic planning. The proposed change would offer a process for implementing the recommendations of the Okita panel and also reinforce the role of the Board and Management in setting the directions of the Bank's work. Steps in this direction received strong support at the ADB Annual Meeting in Hong Kong, China in May.

Over the next few years, the strategic planning process was strengthened. ADB was coaxed and cajoled into adopting new ways and focusing more on strategic goals. There was organizational change too. New sections were created to ensure that the strategic goals received priority.

During the Bank's third decade, the strategies would be overseen by three Presidents. In November 1993, Tarumizu was succeeded by Mitsuo Sato. There was also considerable turnover among the three Vice-Presidents. Long-standing Vice-Presidents S. Stanley Katz and Günther Schulz both

---

[16] The Strategic Planning Unit was created in 1991. It was renamed the Strategy and Policy Office (SPO) in 1994 when it was merged with the then Development Policy Office. This was upgraded into the Strategy and Policy Department (SPD) in 2000. Over time, the functions of the department expanded into, among other things, the oversight of dialogue with the Bank's shareholders for resource mobilization efforts.

retired. Each had contributed steady guidance for around 12 years, bringing institutional continuity. Henceforth, Vice-Presidents would hold office for shorter periods and their roles would change considerably, reflecting increasing political pressures from member countries.

Reverberations from Europe

A few weeks before Tarumizu arrived in Manila in late 1989, the world had witnessed historic events in Europe. The Berlin Wall had fallen. For a time, the implications for Asia and for ADB were uncertain. By May 1990, however, at the Bank's Annual Meeting in New Delhi, the international donor community was considering how the unfolding changes in East–West relations might affect their programs in Asia and with ADB. One consequence would be greater competition for funds as donors reallocated aid budgets toward priorities in Europe. Donors had, for example, pledged substantial amounts for the European Bank for Reconstruction and Development which had been established in London a month before the ADB Annual Meeting. European delegates at the New Delhi meeting said they were still committed to Asia but that there would certainly be greater pressures on aid budgets.

For Asia, the changes in Europe would also have political implications. In her statement to the 1990 ADB Annual Meeting, UK Governor Lynda Chalker said: "It is no coincidence that everywhere in Latin America, Africa and now Eastern Europe, the watchwords are greater freedom, privatization, and liberalization. The countries of Asia should also take these to heart ...." Other participants said the changes in Europe highlighted the importance of democracy and of market-oriented policies. Over the next few years, the expectations of international donors of the Bank would widen to reflect these and other changes in development thinking.

Transition Economies

The end of the Cold War also greatly diminished the international influence of global communism. Before long, countries in the Mekong subregion and Central Asia began to reduce their links with Eastern Europe. Even in the 1980s, countries in the Mekong subregion—Cambodia, the Lao People's Democratic Republic (Lao PDR), and Viet Nam—had been adopting market-oriented policies. The reforms gathered pace after the *Doi Moi* reforms in Viet Nam in 1986 but received a further impetus from the collapse of the Soviet Union in 1991. Soon, these too were considered "transitional economies," moving from central planning toward market-based economic systems.[17]

ADB had long wanted to provide more support in the Mekong countries but had been held back by conflict in the subregion. In 1973, the cease fire agreements created brief windows of optimism but did not lead to sustained peace. Throughout the long period from 1974 to the early 1990s, no ADB loans were approved for Viet Nam. It was not until October 1991, when the Paris Peace Accords settled the conflict in Cambodia, that countries in the subregion were able to focus more on development. Viet Nam, especially, was keen to mobilize external investment. In 1993, ADB lending operations resumed in Viet Nam after a hiatus of almost two decades. A loan for Irrigation and Flood Control Protection Rehabilitation for $76.5 million was approved in October. Two more loans for a total of $185 million (for road improvements and for water supply in Ho Chi Minh City) were agreed to before the end of the year.

In 1992, ADB was finally able to begin a program in the Greater Mekong Subregion (GMS), cautiously at first, to support the transition process and to strengthen regional cooperation by encouraging cross-border economic and trade relations.[18] The chief architect was the Director General of the Programs Department (West), Noritada Morita. He recalled the first low-key official gathering at ADB headquarters in Manila in October 1992: "It was probably the first meeting where all the countries previously in conflict in the subregion got together in a room to talk about cooperation for common development."[19]

Gradually, ADB activities in the GMS expanded. Initially, in 1992, the program began in six countries: Cambodia, the PRC (focusing on Yunnan Province), the Lao PDR, Myanmar, Thailand, and Viet Nam. In 2004, Guangxi Zhuang Autonomous Region of the PRC joined the group. During the fourth ADB decade, the GMS program would expand to become one of the Bank's most effective programs of regional cooperation.[20] Over time, some of the features of the GMS program were adopted by other subregional programs ADB supported. These features included efforts to strengthen

---

[17] "Economies in Transition: The Asian Experience" in ADB, *ADB Annual Report 1995*, 19–39.
[18] ADB, 2012, *Greater Mekong Subregion: Twenty Years of Partnership*.
[19] Morita, 2012, "The Greater Mekong Subregion."
[20] ADB, 2009, *ADB Reflections and Beyond*, "Economic Corridors," 113.

bilateral relations, promotion of connectivity through investments in infrastructure, and a focus on economic rather than political relationships.

The Central Asian republics (CARs) were also embarking on economic transition. Here, however, ADB took longer to get going. Nevertheless, early programs had started even before the first two CARs, Kazakhstan and the Kyrgyz Republic, joined in 1994.

Asia's Giant Economies

ADB was also expanding in India and the PRC. However, operations in these two countries were different to those in smaller borrowing countries. The governments in India and the PRC had quite clear ideas about their own priorities. Although they were prepared to enter into policy dialogue with the Bank, they emphasized the importance of addressing their domestic goals. Further, a main objective for policy makers in these countries was to obtain ADB-funded projects to support their national investment programs. But the Bank too had policies to adhere to. Agreement on these activities often required careful consultation.

By 1990, ADB had built up a substantial pipeline of projects in India, mostly supporting one of the government's most important objectives, rapid industrialization.[21] At the time, the government was moving toward market-oriented economic management so ADB approved projects to strengthen private sector manufacturing. The Bank also provided loans for energy and transport, such as a $250 million loan in 1991 for the hydrocarbon sector and two loans for over $550 million in 1993 for gas projects.

In mid-1991, India was hard hit by an unprecedented economic crisis.[22] Foreign exchange reserves fell sharply—to the equivalent of only 2 weeks of imports. The government swiftly implemented a stabilization and reform program, supported by the International Monetary Fund (IMF), the World Bank, ADB and Japan. As part of its contribution, in December 1992, ADB authorized a $300 million Financial Sector Program Loan which covered 58 measures to support market-based policies. Of these measures, 20 were to be completed before the ADB Board approved the loan; the rest by the end of the loan period in March 1996.[23] Under Tarumizu's guidance,

---

[21] Box 2.5 in ADB, *Asian Development Outlook 1989*, 119.
[22] Vikraman, 2016, "25 Years On, Manmohan Singh Has a Regret."
[23] ADB, 2000, *Program Performance Audit: Financial Sector Program Loan (India)*.

ADB provided strong support to India during this difficult time with lending averaging over $900 million per year during 1991–1993.

In the mid-1990s, ADB also started working at the subnational level with state governments in India. With support from the central government, ADB began a partnership with Gujarat, widely regarded as a progressive and reform-minded state with a culture of market orientation, private entrepreneurship, and good administration. In December 1996, the Board approved the first program loan from a multilateral development bank to a subnational government—$250 million to support a public sector management program.[24] In later years, there would be similar loans to Assam, Kerala, Madhya Pradesh, and West Bengal.

The shift to support state-level operations, particularly in the northeastern and other poorer states, strengthened relations between India and the Bank. This, in turn, helped ADB address policy issues more directly through program loans and project assistance. Over the whole of the third ADB decade, the Bank financed projects worth over $6 billion in India.

At the same time, ADB was also increasing support for the PRC. Here, however, activities were complicated by political events. Following incidents in Beijing and other cities in May and June 1989, multilateral agencies such as the World Bank and ADB were pressed by some member countries to restrict lending to the PRC. This was difficult for ADB whose Charter, as the Government of the PRC pointed out, required it not to interfere in the political affairs of any member and to take decisions based only on economic considerations. Yet, feelings in Western capitals were running high. For a time, the Bank held back on activities in the PRC but, after a period of restraint, rapidly expanded its program in the early 1990s. ADB provided support for well-known projects such as the Nanpu and Yangpu bridges in Shanghai as more activities got under way (Box 9.1).

One issue was the program mix because ADB policies required a balance between traditional growth activities and social and environmental projects. The PRC authorities had given more emphasis to infrastructure and rural development. In financing these infrastructure projects, the Bank and the government worked together to address cross-cutting issues such as poverty and environmental protection. For example, the government prioritized road infrastructure projects linking to poorer areas and

---

[24] ADB, 2007, *Country Assistance Program Evaluation for India*.

building feeder roads to the poorest villages. Power projects addressed environmental concerns by closing old, inefficient, and polluting thermal plants. The government gradually added water supply and wastewater treatment projects to the lending program.[25]

In 1992 and 1993, the ADB Board approved substantial lending to the PRC to assist with market-oriented reforms as well as geographically more balanced growth. For example, reforms to introduce appropriate pricing and distribution policies and to improve incentives for state enterprises were taken up under the Fertilizer Industry Restructuring (Sector) Project agreed to in 1993. With the support of the government, ADB gradually moved its activities from better-off coastal regions to the poorer inland provinces. Another feature of the Bank's operations in the PRC was their speed. In some borrowing countries, there could be long delays. However, in the PRC, agencies were often ready to proceed with agreed activities even before loans were approved.[26] As a result, ADB projects were generally carried out on schedule.

Mitsuo Sato

At the end of 1993, after an eventful period as President, Tarumizu decided to step down. His successor was Mitsuo Sato who, like most previous Presidents, came from the Japanese Ministry of Finance. Sato had worked on tax policies and had a particular interest in international tax issues. He was a graduate of the Faculty of Law at the University of Tokyo, had worked for 3 years in the IMF in Washington, DC, and had served, as Tarumizu had done, as Director General of the Customs and Tariff Bureau in the Ministry of Finance. After retiring from government, Sato became Deputy President of the Tokyo Stock Exchange. He also had followed development issues closely.

Sato would provide firm and effective leadership well into the fourth ADB decade. He had a reserved and self-disciplined style, often preferring to listen carefully during meetings without saying much himself. He had the habit, which some found unnerving, of closing his eyes to concentrate when others were speaking. One ADB staff member recalled that, "When

---

[25] ADB, 1998, *Country Assistance Program Evaluation in the PRC*, 13.
[26] One important reason for this was that in the PRC, most of the key design issues were decided upon by the PRC authorities before the involvement of external funding agencies such as ADB (ADB, 1998, *Country Assistance Program Evaluation in the PRC*, v).

I first started to deal with him, I thought he was asleep. He would use this as a technique to focus on what you were saying. When you realized that, it was even more frightening to deal with him because you knew he was trying to digest and understand every single word."[27]

Sato acted swiftly when it became clear that a rapid response was needed to the Asian financial crisis (Chapter 10). Nevertheless, his preferred approach was to spend time considering the pros and cons of issues needing a Management decision. He took care to think both about the details of ADB operations and about the broad policy issues of development in Asia. Within the Bank, he took a close interest in arrangements for projects being proposed to the Board. He regarded the formal process of discussing projects carefully at pre-Board Management Committee Meetings as important. He gave priority to attending such meetings to satisfy himself that the projects were ready to present to the Board.

Sato also kept abreast of broader economic policy issues. In the wake of the Asian financial crisis, he believed it was urgent that ADB and the international community move to build institutions to help countries in the region avoid future financial crises (Chapter 12). He argued that the crisis had been a capital account crisis which was "an entirely new form of financial turmoil."[28] To help prevent such crises occurring again, he urged that arrangements such as the regional surveillance of monetary policies and the strengthening of Asian capital markets be expanded rapidly.[29]

Running Out of Headroom

When Sato arrived in November 1993, the Bank was running out of headroom for lending. Member countries, particularly the US, were not yet ready to agree to a new GCI. They continued to bargain over policy changes. By early 1994, the Board had approved loans up to the ceiling allowed by the Bank's rules. It was touch and go. In the end, the Bank ran out of headroom. For the first time in ADB history, there was a temporary freeze on lending. There were tense moments as the Board tried to reach final agreement. Sato was new in the job but he was blunt with the Board. He made it clear that he expected all member countries to agree to a GCI quickly.

---

[27] Purdue, 2009, "BP on President Sato," in ADB, *ADB Reflections and Beyond*, 157.
[28] Sato, 1999, Capital Flow Reversal, Not Cronyism, Caused Asian Financial Crisis.
[29] Sato, 1998, The Asian Development Bank View, 83.

One issue that had delayed negotiations was project quality. As projects had become more complex, their design and implementation had become more difficult. Under pressure to consider a widening range of cross-cutting issues, particularly in the agriculture and social sectors, ADB had sometimes prepared projects with rather ambitious objectives. Multiple goals, numerous components and executing agencies, and overlapping coordination arrangements were some of the characteristics of projects less likely to succeed.[30]

Responding to these concerns, in April 1993, Tarumizu had appointed a senior task force on project quality. Chaired by Vice-President Schulz, the task force included two external experts, both former Board members.[31] In March 1994, Sato received the report of the task force on improving project quality. It recommended that less priority be given to higher volumes of lending and that more attention be given to the implementation of projects on the ground.[32] This would mean moving away from an "approval culture" which encouraged staff to get loans accepted and looking closely at local needs and the capacity in borrowing countries. To do this, ADB would need to give more support to building institutional capacity in borrowing countries. It also recommended that the Bank itself should change by introducing better systems of internal accountability to give equal weight to project processing and implementation. The report recommended a one-time "spring cleaning" to weed out ADB's problem projects.

Operations were reviewed to encourage a stronger country focus. In 1995, a new organizational structure with two regional East and West Vice-Presidents was established.

In the end, a diplomatic deal was struck. Sato pointed out that addressing the concerns of the US and some other countries would take time and that ADB could not wait. He gave a personal assurance that these concerns would be addressed within the Bank's strategic planning process. On this basis, all member countries agreed to increase the authorized capital by 100% (Appendix Table A2.14). Voting by the Board of Governors closed on 22 May 1994 and the capital increase became effective immediately, although subscription of capital and the budget for paid-in capital would still be subject to legislative approval in member countries.

---

[30] ADB, 1994, *Report of the Task Force on Improving Project Quality*, 11.
[31] ADB, 1994, *Report of the Task Force on Improving Project Quality*.
[32] A discussion about "Improving Project Quality" is in ADB, *Annual Report 1995*, 78.

Resource Mobilization

Resource mobilization also expanded through the Bank's borrowing program. During the Bank's third decade, the level of ADB's borrowings increased to nearly $12.2 billion. The program had also become more sophisticated, with a wider range of activities. In the first ADB decade, the main concern had been to establish a sound reputation in as many markets as possible. In the second decade, when interest rates started to rise, the Bank concentrated its borrowings in low-interest currencies. The third stage came in 1986 with the introduction of pool-based variable lending rates. Under this system, the Bank used financial engineering techniques such as swaps. These allowed ADB to borrow in low-coupon currencies, offering flexibility to borrow in a wider range of international markets.

The Bank did not borrow only for its own needs. It also aimed to stimulate the development of Asian financial markets by, for example, introducing the concept of a "dragon bond"—a fixed income security usually denominated in US dollars. The first dragon bond issue—for $300 million—was launched in 1991 simultaneously in Hong Kong, China; Singapore; and Taipei,China. This approach would subsequently be replicated by top-rated issuers such as international and regional financial institutions in the US and Europe. Previously, in Japan in 1970, ADB initiated the issuance of yen-denominated "samurai bonds."

Other measures to mobilize private resources included loan guarantees by ADB. A review in 1994 enlarged the scope for the Bank to provide loan guarantees to the private sector. There were also efforts in 1995 to attract cofinancing. And in 1996, the Bank established the Office of Cofinancing Operations.

New Ways of Working

Sato's time was a period of active policy reform within the Bank. In the earlier part of the third ADB decade, a number of policy papers had been approved. In 1987, these included policies on cooperation with nongovernment organizations and on disaster and emergency assistance for small island countries. In 1988, the Bank reviewed its private sector operations and over the next few years issued policy statements on education and telecommunications.

During the ADF VI negotiations in 1991, there was growing pressure to strengthen policies across a range of cross-cutting topics. In the negotiations, donors had shown strong interest in such issues as women in development, population, the environment, and support for the private sector. Member countries continued to emphasize these issues in 1994 during the negotiations for the GCI. Bank staff prepared numerous policy papers, many of which were approved by the Board during 1994 and 1995 (Box 9.3).

One of the main concerns was gender. In 1985, a policy on women in development aimed to integrate gender considerations into all aspects of ADB operations—addressing the role of women and the effects on them at every stage of the project cycle. This approach would also involve

---

Box 9.3: Selected Policy Papers, 1987–1996

1987	A Review of Program Lending Policies
	An Interim Review of Bank Policy and Procedures for Private Sector Operations
	Rehabilitation Assistance to Small Developing Member Countries Affected by Natural Disasters
	The Bank's Cooperation with Nongovernment Organizations
1988	Bank Guarantee Operations
	A Review of Private Sector Operations
	Task Force Report on the Bank's Role in Poverty Alleviation
1989	Education and Development in Asia and the Pacific
	The Asian Development Bank in the 1990s: Panel Report
1990	Second Review of Private Sector Operations
1991	Report of the Task Force on Strategic Planning
1992	Report of the Private Sector Task Force
	The Bank's Medium-Term Strategic Framework (1992–1995)
1993	Guidelines for Incorporation of Social Dimensions in Bank Operations
	Human Resources Development and Management Operational Study
	Medium-Term Strategic Framework (1993–1996)
	Review of Bank's Major Financial Policies

continued on next page

Box 9.3 continued

1994	Bank Support for Regional Cooperation
	Confidentiality and Disclosure of Information: Information Policy of ADB
	Medium-Term Strategic Framework (1994–1997)
	Framework for Bank Assistance to the Population Sector
	Report of the Task Force on Improving Project Quality
	Review of the Bank's Guarantee Operations
	The Bank's Future Direction and Operational Agenda for the 1990s
	Women in Development: Issues, Challenges and Strategies in Asia and the Pacific
1995	Bank Policy Initiatives for Energy Sector
	Establishment of an Inspection Function
	Governance: Sound Development Management
	Involuntary Resettlement
	Review of Lending Foreign Exchange for Local Currency Expenditures on Projects
	Strategy for the Bank's Assistance for Private Sector Development
	The Bank's Cofinancing Strategy
	Medium-Term Strategic Framework (1995–1998)
	The Bank's Policy on Agriculture and Natural Resources
1996	Review of the Bank's Program Lending Policies

Source: ADB, *Annual Reports*, 1987 to 1996.

projects that provided direct benefits to women, such as those in the social sectors, as well as those that would be likely to provide women with employment in areas such as agriculture, rural development, and small-scale industries. In addition, there should be stand-alone women-targeted projects—such as the 1989 Primary Education Project in Pakistan designed to provide education for girls. To monitor changes in women's status and participation, the collection of sex-disaggregated data was expanded.

Over time, however, the emphasis shifted from specific projects toward mainstreaming issues of women in development across all projects. This change was based on a new operational framework which stressed the importance of gender analysis and improved project components to create jobs for women, as well as women-friendly macroeconomic policies. The policy paper on women in development was updated in 1994.

There was also increasing interest in good governance. In February 1994, Sato issued interim instructions to staff on ADB's approach to governance. In 1995, a governance policy was approved by the Board which stressed the importance of sound institutions in borrowing countries that could absorb development assistance effectively. To operationalize this policy—the first for a multilateral development bank on governance—there were four areas of focus: accountability, participation, predictability, and transparency.

ADB also strengthened its own governance. In 1994, the new Policy on Confidentiality and Disclosure of Information and the Information Policy and Strategy were approved. The following year, the Inspection Function was established. This created an independent forum to which project beneficiaries could appeal if they believed that the Bank was not complying with its own policies or procedures regarding social and environmental impacts of ADB-financed projects.

Earlier, during its second decade, ADB had expanded its work with the private sector. In 1988, a review of private sector operations was issued. In 1989, private sector activities were reorganized within the newly created Private Sector Department, upgraded from the Private Sector Division. Another review was undertaken in 1990. Despite these efforts, the Bank remained largely a public sector institution that found it hard to work with private enterprises. Among the industrial countries, the US, especially, continued to press for more private sector work. The Bank aimed at integrating its private sector operations more closely with the public sector program. In addition, staff of the Private Sector Department were instructed to work more closely with ADB country offices.

This brisk program of policy reform generated a plethora of policy documents—38 during the 5 years of Sato's presidency. This was partly a consequence of the post-Cold War burst of enthusiasm among donors for new international development policies. But it was also driven by Sato himself who wanted ADB to become, as he frequently said, "a broad-based development institution."[33]

---

[33] Sullivan, 1999, Official Farewell to President Mitsuo Sato.

New Lending Instruments and Scholarships

To undertake the increasingly complex forms of assistance, ADB developed new types of loans and programs. Earlier, in 1978, the Bank had started with a first type of program loan. In 1987, an expanded form of program loan was introduced to allow greater flexibility and more support for policy reforms. The scope of program lending was broadened to include a wider range of sectors such as the financial, energy, transport, telecommunications, and social sectors.[34]

Another lending facility was a Special Interventions Project Loan for activities that needed rapid expenditures to help alleviate poverty. The facility was first used in 1990 when a $10.5 million loan was approved for Papua New Guinea, part of a multidonor effort to mitigate the social costs of a structural adjustment program. Activities implemented through the loan arrangements needed a strong poverty focus. Funds were expected to be spent quickly to create jobs.

Further, in 1987, some Pacific countries proposed setting up a special facility to assist those affected by cyclones or other natural disasters in small member economies. This request triggered the creation of the Bank's first policy on disaster rehabilitation for small countries. In 1989, the Bank's new disaster policy and rehabilitation loans extended the scope to all other members and covered response as well as disaster risk reduction.

Yet another innovation was the introduction of a scholarship program. In the late 1980s, Japan established several international scholarship programs through the World Bank and ADB. Scholarships were offered for study in a wide range of countries. In 1988, with finance from the Government of Japan, the Japan Scholarship Program was established in ADB. In the first year, 49 scholarships were awarded. Over the next several decades, over 3,000 students from Asian developing countries undertook studies in development-related fields at regional and international institutions.[35] Also in 1988, ADB launched the Scholarship Program for Smaller DMCs, financed by the Bank, to sponsor short-term scholarships in specific fields for candidates from Bhutan, the Lao PDR, the Maldives, and eight Pacific island countries. After the ADB official website was established in the 1990s, the scholarship pages scored among the highest hits across all Bank pages.

---

[34] ADB, 1987, *Annual Report 1987*, 43.
[35] ADB, 2016, *Japan Scholarship Program 2014 Annual Report*.

New Offices Abroad and the ADB Institute

Changes in Bank policy were accompanied by key changes in the approach to management. During the 1990s, there was growing international interest in the ideas of "new public management" and in measuring results and effectiveness. During the next ADB decade, into the new century, donors would increasingly press the Bank to provide evidence of the effectiveness of its work. At the ADB Annual Meeting in Auckland in 1995, Sato spoke of the need for the Bank to be "effective, efficient and accountable." To improve effectiveness, he said, the recommendations of the 1994 Task Force on Improving Project Quality had been implemented. To increase efficiency, a major reorganization had been introduced in January 1995. And to improve accountability, he pointed to the new Policy on Disclosure and Information and the establishment of the Inspection Function.

Rapid institutional growth occurred during the third ADB decade. To encourage closer relationships with borrowing countries, the Bank opened more resident missions: in 1987 in Jakarta; in 1992 in New Delhi; and in 1996, reflecting the growing program in the Mekong area, in Phnom Penh and Ha Noi (Figure 9.1).

In 1994, it was decided to establish offices in industrial countries. Some Board members were skeptical, questioning whether the benefits were worth the costs. But the representatives from the US, Japan, and Europe had reached an agreement, so the proposal was approved. The first office, for North America, was opened in Washington, DC in 1995, followed by one for Japan in Tokyo and one for Europe in Frankfurt. In 1996, the Board also approved the establishment of the ADB Institute (ADBI) in Tokyo as a think tank to carry out research and training to support the Bank's programs in Asia. Initially, the operations of the Institute were funded by Japan, although later other countries, such as the Republic of Korea, Australia, and Indonesia, also contributed to the Institute's budget. In 2016, PRC also expressed its intention to contribute to ADBI. With these steps, ADB was expanding its international presence, not only in borrowing countries but in donor countries as well.

Before becoming ADB President, Sato had built up extensive experience on financial policy issues in Japan and Washington, DC (at the IMF). Not surprisingly, he took a special interest in the way financial systems worked in the region. In the numerous regional and international meetings he attended, he often spoke of the importance of improving financial

Figure 9.1: Establishment of Field Offices

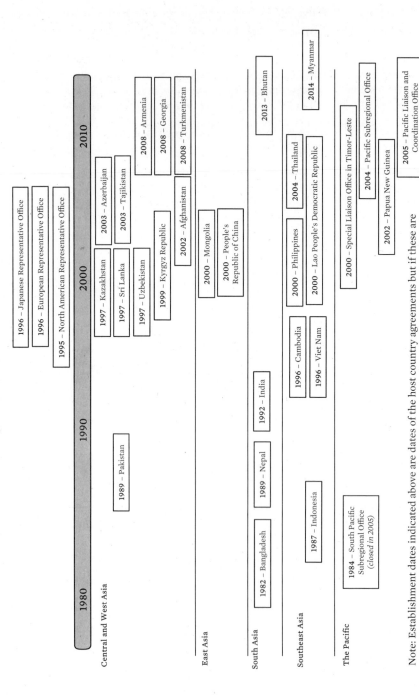

Note: Establishment dates indicated above are dates of the host country agreements but if these are not available, establishment dates based on R-papers circulated/approved by the Board of Directors were used.

Source: ADB. 2016. Establishment of Field Offices. *The ADB Archives Gallery*. https://www.adb.org/sites/default/files/publication/176469/adb-archives-gallery.pdf

markets.[36] Sato noted that during the 1970s and 1980s, many governments in developing countries had viewed financial markets as little more than convenient sources of finance and had frequently intervened in market operations to direct credit to their own priorities. They failed to strengthen domestic banking systems or develop securities markets, such as the bond markets which underpinned industrial economies.[37] Later, when the 1997 Asian financial crisis unfolded, it would become clear that his concerns had been well-placed.

Sato was also keen to strengthen the Bank's identity as an Asian institution. At the time, there were differing views across the international community of how multilateral development banks should operate. One view was that the banks should prioritize interbank coordination, even coming close to uniformity. Another view was that each bank should make its own distinct contribution. In 1996, the Development Committee of the World Bank issued a report, *Serving a Changing World: Report of the Task Force on Multilateral Development Banks,* on the subject. The report reflected the World Bank's preferred approach of intensifying coordination and paying less attention to the individuality of the regional banks.[38]

Serving a Changing World was published in March 1996. Sato soon provided a carefully worded response. Addressing the ADB Annual Meeting in Manila in May, he said that the report's call for closer cooperation was well taken. But coordination should not mean unification, he said. Instead, Sato favored an approach of "competitive pluralism" which would allow ADB to fashion its own distinctive niche, reflecting its Charter as an institution that is "Asian in its basic character." Sato's response drew a line in the sand between the work of ADB and the World Bank.

Operational Summary

Operational approvals continued to expand in the third decade, reaching a total of $43 billion, an almost threefold increase from the second decade, with 30% of lending financed from the ADF. Public sector and government-guaranteed loans accounted for 96%, with the rest going to direct loans to

---

[36] For example, Sato's comments at the Pacific-Basin Finance Conference in Manila in July 1995 in Sato, 1995.
[37] "The Financial Sector and Asian Development: Historical Experiences and Prospects" in ADB, 1995, *Asian Development Outlook 1995 and 1996.*
[38] World Bank, 1996, *Serving a Changing World,* 24.

Figure 9.2: Operational Approvals by Fund Type, 1987–1996
($ million)

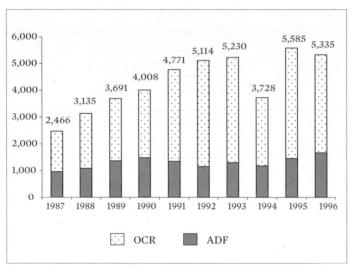

Total: $43,063 million

ADF = Asian Development Fund, OCR = ordinary capital resources.

Note: Operational approvals include loans, grants, equity investments, and guarantees.

Source: ADB loan, technical assistance, grant, and equity approvals database.

private sector firms or equity investments in them. Annual approvals grew at an average rate of 14% from 1987 to 1993 (Figure 9.2). In 1994, however, they dropped by 29%. At the Annual Meeting in Auckland in 1995, several delegates commented on this sharp decline. There were various reasons for it. As noted earlier, lending was suspended early in 1994 during the uncertainty over negotiations for a GCI. The main factor was the Bank's efforts to consolidate its lending program and to spend more time further improving the quality of projects. In subsequent years, operational approvals bounced back above the $5 billion mark.

During this period, there was also a marked shift in the geographical pattern of lending (Figure 9.3). The PRC and India became active borrowers, each accounting for 15% of total lending over the decade. Consequently, the share of lending going to South Asia and East Asia increased. ADB resumed

Figure 9.3: Operational Approvals by Region, 1987–1996
(%, $ million)

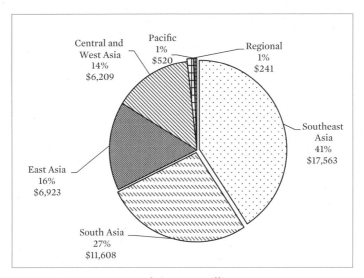

Total: $43,063 million

Notes: Regional breakdown is based on current country groupings. Operational approvals include loans, grants, equity investments, and guarantees.

Source: ADB loan, technical assistance, grant, and equity approvals database.

lending to Cambodia and Viet Nam after a hiatus of almost two decades. New ADB members (Kazakhstan, the Kyrgyz Republic, and Uzbekistan) borrowed for the first time in the latter part of the decade. Afghanistan stopped borrowing in 1979 and would not resume activities until 2002. The Pacific continued to account for the smallest share of lending. The top five borrowers over the third decade were Indonesia (22%), the PRC (15%), India (15%), Pakistan (13%), and the Philippines (9%).

There were also marked changes in the sector spread of ADB activities (Figure 9.4). As was the case in the second decade, the three major sectors were energy, transport, and agriculture. But in the third decade, there were significant shifts. The share of transport expanded (from 12% to 24%) while that of agriculture fell (from 31% to 16%), and energy remained much the same (around 25%).

Figure 9.4: Operational Approvals by Sector, 1987–1996
(%, $ million)

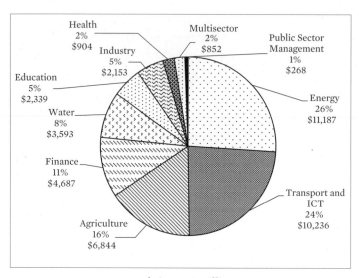

Total: $43,063 million

ICT = information and communication technology.

Note: Operational approvals include loans, grants, equity investments, and guarantees.

Source: ADB loan, technical assistance, grant, and equity approvals database.

These shifts were driven less by the policies of ADB than by the changing preferences of borrowers—in particular the expanding programs in India and the PRC. ADB, being a bank, needed to be responsive to the demands of its borrowers.

The expanding activities in the transport sector reflected many requests for loans for road projects. For ADB, the priority was to upgrade existing roads, improve maintenance, and encourage private sector participation which included using public–private partnerships (PPPs) such as "build, own, transfer" and "build, operate, own" arrangements. Nevertheless, for a range of reasons, using PPPs remained limited. The Bank also encouraged the financing of transport infrastructure through user charges. However, there was widespread resistance in the region to the introduction of user charges.

The move away from lending for agriculture was quite marked. And the decrease in lending became even more pronounced throughout the decade. The decline partly reflected the considerable practical difficulties ADB had experienced in supporting agriculture projects and partly also the preferences of borrowing countries such as India and the PRC which generally preferred to borrow for projects in energy and transport.

The continuing demand for energy loans reflected the growing use of energy and electricity in Asian borrowing countries. Per capita consumption of energy was still quite low in developing countries but was expanding rapidly. ADB operations focused on supporting local oil supplies rather than relying on imports and on promoting more efficient use of fuel. In 1995, to encourage investment in energy and attention to environmental issues, the Bank prepared a new energy sector policy paper. The new policy focused on increasing private sector participation in large-scale energy investments, improving energy efficiency, and integrating environmental considerations in energy development.[39]

Over the third decade, the Bank offered more technical assistance, which became a vital element of its development strategy. ADB wanted to move on from being a project financier to providing integrated services of financing, policy support, and capacity building as appropriate for a broad-based development institution. During 1987–1996, technical assistance operations increased dramatically, reaching $882 million, a sevenfold increase from the previous decade. The top five country recipients were the PRC (14%), Indonesia (12%), the Philippines (8%), Bangladesh (6%), and Pakistan (5%). Assistance in the agriculture and energy sectors decreased, while support for public sector management, transport and information and communication technology, and social sectors expanded.

During this period, the ADB internal administrative expenses budget grew modestly at an annual average of 8%. In 1996, this budget was $190 million. By the end of the decade, there were 1,961 ADB staff from 43 member countries, including 673 international and Management staff and 1,288 local staff (Table 9.1). This represented a 22% increase compared to the previous decade. Along with the change in focus, there was a change in the skill requirements with ADB looking for staff with expertise in economic planning and policy analysis as well as people with interdisciplinary backgrounds. Women were also encouraged to apply for professional positions.

---

[39] ADB, 1995, *Bank Policy Initiatives for the Energy Sector*.

Nine new members joined the Bank over the period. With the collapse of the former Soviet Union in December 1991, the Asia and Pacific region gained six independent states, three of which would become ADB members during the period: Kazakhstan and the Kyrgyz Republic (1994) and Uzbekistan (1995). Four Pacific island countries also joined: the Marshall Islands and the Federated States of Micronesia (1990), Nauru (1991), and Tuvalu (1993). The other new members were Mongolia and Turkey (1991). This brought membership to a total of 56 countries (41 regional and 15 nonregional).

Calm before the Storm

In the third ADB decade, as in the first two decades, the Bank grew and changed in response to both external and internal pressures. External pressures included the dramatic transformation that was taking place across Asia and the widening international agenda. Within ADB, each of its three Presidents during the decade promoted reform. ADB staff also supported the widening development role.

The founders of ADB had set down in the Charter that the organization should be "Asian in its basic character." Indeed, that had become one of the distinguishing characteristics of the Bank. For ADB staff, the challenges of development in Asia were real. Many staff were recruited from Asian countries and they lived in Manila or other parts of the region. Every day, at work and at home, their lives involved dealing with both the benefits and the costs of rapid development.

The pace of change in the Bank accelerated during the third decade. The numerous external and internal pressures for reform increased. India and the PRC became borrowing members and the international environment changed following the end of the Cold War. Throughout its history, the Bank had always emphasized the need for prudence in its operations. But while ADB had always exercised prudence when managing its finances, during the third decade it became bolder in its role as a multilateral development institution.

At the end of the decade, the outlook for ADB seemed promising. There was strong support from member countries, a large capital increase had been approved, and a clear set of new policies had been introduced. At the Annual Meeting in Manila in May 1996, Sato told Governors that the Bank faced the challenges ahead "with confidence and enthusiasm."

But this was the calm before the storm. Very soon, as the next chapter shows, the Bank would find itself caught up in the turmoil of the Asian financial crisis. Again, ADB would need to quickly design flexible programs to respond to new demands for assistance in the region.

Table 9.1: Selected Operational, Institutional, and Financial Information, 1977–1996

	1977–1986 (Total, Second Decade)	1986 (end-year)	1996 (end-year)	1987–1996 (Total, Third Decade)
A. Operational Highlights ($ million)				
Total operational approvals[a]	16,041	2,005	5,335	43,063
By fund source				
Ordinary capital resources	10,758	1,369	3,669	30,082
Asian Development Fund	5,283	636	1,666	12,981
By operations				
Sovereign	16,022	1,993	5,156	41,813
Nonsovereign	19	12	179	1,250
Technical assistance approvals[b]	125	24	138	882
Technical assistance projects	96	17	106	727
Regional assistance	29	6	31	155
Outstanding loan portfolio		8,749	28,577	
Ordinary capital resources		5,998	16,109	
Asian Development Fund		2,751	12,468	
Total loan and grant disbursements	7,317	1,024	3,797	27,751
Ordinary capital resources	5,145	612	2,563	18,154
Asian Development Fund	2,173	413	1,234	9,597
Official cofinancing[c]	576	30	397	4,018
Commercial cofinancing	36	5	92	560

continued on next page

Table 9.1 continued

	1977–1986 (Total, Second Decade)	1986 (end-year)	1996 (end-year)	1987–1996 (Total, Third Decade)
B. Institutional Highlights				
Staff information				
Total staff		1,604	1,961	
International staff [d]		603	673	
Women staff		740	1,023	
Women international staff		25	100	
Staff in field offices		23	144	
Member countries		47	56	
Field offices		–	11	
Internal administrative expenses budget ($ million)	588	89	190	1,411
C. Financial Highlights ($ million)				
Authorized capital[e]		19,663	50,103	
Subscribed capital[e]		19,476	49,368	
Paid-in		2,354	3,472	
Callable		17,122	45,896	
Borrowings	6,418	813	584	12,166

– = nil, SDR = special drawing right, US = United States.

[a] Figures refer to loan, grant, equity investment, and guarantee approvals, net of terminations (they exclude operations approved by the Board of Directors but terminated before they were deemed effective).

[b] Technical assistance operations cover grants funded by the Technical Assistance Special Fund and the Japan Special Fund only.

[c] Includes trust funds and cofinancing of loans, grants, and technical assistance.

[d] International staff data include Management.

[e] Values are US dollar equivalents based on US dollar/SDR exchange rate on 31 December 1986 (for 1986 capital) and 31 December 1996 (for 1996 capital).

Sources: ADB Annual Reports; ADB Budget, Personnel, and Management Systems Department; ADB Controller's Department; ADB Strategy and Policy Department; ADB loan, technical assistance, grant, and equity approvals database; ADB Cofinancing database.

CHAPTER 10
Fourth Decade (1997–2006)

The Asian Financial Crisis

"The [East] Asian financial crisis of 1997 will, I believe, go down in history as an important watershed in our economic development. A wake-up call for several countries ... Just as our countries undergo reform, the development agencies themselves, including ADB, must also reexamine their own roles ..."

– Chuan Leekpai, Prime Minister of Thailand,
Opening Address to the ADB Annual Meeting, Chiang Mai, 2000

The 1997 Asian financial crisis was one of the most significant episodes in the 50 years of the work of the Asian Development Bank (ADB) in Asia. The crisis was a dividing line. It separated the first 30 years from the subsequent 20 years. The optimism in the region following the development successes since the 1950s was reflected in the ADB study *Emerging Asia: Changes and Challenges* published in early 1997. The study outlined Asia's rising prosperity and emphasized that "Asia is not emerging so much as reemerging."[1] At the time, the process of globalization that had gathered pace during the early 1990s appeared to be a powerful force helping sweep the region forward. Trade was expanding rapidly, and greater global financial integration was making it easier for local investors in Asia to borrow funds in international markets. The *Emerging Asia* study emphasized the need for developing countries in Asia to prepare for globalization and declared that, "Greater internationalization will also render old economic strategies redundant."[2]

Then, quite suddenly, after decades of strong growth, output plummeted in a number of countries, leading some observers to wonder whether the Asian miracle was over. In a little more than a year, the five crisis-affected countries—Indonesia, the Republic of Korea, Malaysia, the Philippines, and Thailand—experienced a combined loss of around 30% of gross domestic

---

[1] ADB, 1997, *Emerging Asia*, 10.
[2] ADB, 1997, *Emerging Asia*, 9.

product (GDP).[3] The region was again faced with issues of poverty and unemployment.

The crisis unfolded rapidly, catching policy makers and multilateral development finance institutions, including ADB, by surprise. It began with the collapse of the Thai baht in July 1997. Within weeks, the financial problems in Thailand had widened to become a regional crisis that soon engulfed Indonesia, the world's fourth most populous country, and the Republic of Korea, the world's eleventh-largest economy.[4] The crisis undermined economies and governments, threatened seemingly well-established firms and institutions, and imposed severe hardship on hundreds of millions of people.[5]

The international response was swift and unprecedented. The highest-profile—and often controversial—interventions were from the International Monetary Fund (IMF). But there were also key regional initiatives, many of which would form the cornerstone of subsequent regional financial and economic cooperation programs.[6] The crisis was also a watershed for ADB. The Bank needed to design new programs to support the IMF-driven responses and, in so doing, further evolve from a project-financing bank to a fully-fledged development agency.

Thailand: The Crisis Erupts

Strong economic growth in Thailand during the early 1990s was accompanied by a widening deficit in the balance-of-payments, although at the time the growing imbalance seemed sustainable (Chapter 8). Some signs of economic difficulties began to appear in Thailand early in 1997. At first, the problems did not seem severe, but as concerns grew the markets began to lose confidence. Soon there were speculative attacks on the Thai baht, which for over a decade had been pegged to the US dollar.[7] By the end of June 1997, transactions in financial markets were beginning to spin out of control. On 2 July, the Thai authorities bowed to the inevitable and stopped defending the peg—allowing the baht to float and rapidly lose

---

[3] ADB, "Corporate and Financial Sector Reform," 21.
[4] ADB, "The Financial Crisis in Asia," *Asian Development Outlook 1999*, 21.
[5] ADB, "The Financial Crisis in Asia," *Asian Development Outlook 1998*, 19–37.
[6] These are discussed in some detail in the ADB study *Emerging Asian Regionalism* (ADB, 2008).
[7] ADB, 1997, Box 2.2 Financial Problem and Response. *Asian Development Outlook 1997 and 1998*.

value. What followed was a deep economic recession in Thailand and a contagion that would spread across the region and beyond.

The economic turmoil was exacerbated by widening political difficulties. Before the devaluation, Thailand's Prime Minister, Chavalit Yongchaiyudh, had insisted that the value of the currency would not change. Following the devaluation and the rapid deterioration in the economy, he came under increasing pressure to resign. In early November, he was replaced by Chuan Leekpai who remained as Prime Minister for the next 3 years.

Faced with these difficulties, the Government of Thailand sought assistance from the IMF and other international donors at a meeting held on 11 August 1997 in Tokyo. This meeting led to agreement about a rescue package equivalent to $17.2 billion announced on 20 August. Much of the assistance was from the IMF and other multilateral donors, including $1.2 billion from ADB (Table 10.1). Notably, over 60% of the package was made up of bilateral pledges from countries in Asia and the Pacific including Japan and Australia.

The crisis hit Thailand hard: through much of the 1980s and 1990s, GDP growth had been strong, but in 1998 the economy shrank by over 10%. Unemployment climbed sharply. Thailand would not see its prospects significantly improve until 4 years later.

Republic of Korea: A Rapid Response

Just a year after being admitted as a member of the Organisation for Economic Co-operation and Development (OECD) in 1996, the Republic of Korea was engulfed by the Asian financial crisis. The crisis in the country was triggered by a series of excessive borrowings by *chaebols* (conglomerates). As the foreign exchange crisis swept through other countries in the region, international creditors refused to roll over the *chaebols*' foreign exchange-denominated short-term loans, triggering a series of bankruptcies.

To stop a drain on currency reserves and an economic collapse, the monetary authorities requested urgent support from the IMF. Intense negotiations followed which were not made any easier by political uncertainty surrounding the presidential elections taking place at the time. However, the main opposition candidate and subsequent President, Kim Dae-jung, confirmed that he would support an agreement with the

Table 10.1: Currency Stabilization Support Programs during the Asian Financial Crisis ($ billion)[a]

	Thailand	Indonesia	Republic of Korea[b]
Multilateral Agencies	6.7	18.0	35.0
IMF	4.0	10.0	21.0
World Bank	1.5	4.5	10.0
ADB	1.2	3.5	4.0
Bilateral Support	10.5		
Japan	4.0		
PRC	1.0		
Australia	1.0		
Hong Kong, China	1.0		
Malaysia	1.0		
Singapore	1.0		
Republic of Korea	0.5		
Indonesia	0.5		
Brunei Darussalam	0.5		
Indonesia: Emergency Reserve		5.0	
Subtotal	17.2	23.0	35.0
Second-Line Defense[c]		16.2	23.0
Japan		5.0	10.0
United States		3.0	5.0
Singapore		5.0	
Others		3.2	8.0
Total	17.2	39.2	58.0
Date of agreement	Aug 97	Oct 97	Dec 97

IMF = International Monetary Fund, PRC = People's Republic of China.

[a] The composition of the financial packages was complex and was subject to agreements reached with agencies providing support. Timing also varied. For these reasons, different sources may record differences in the size of the packages.

[b] In addition to the official package shown here, the official international package for the Republic of Korea was greatly strengthened by the agreement of private sector international banks in the United States and Europe to support the efforts to restore stability in financial markets in the Republic of Korea.

[c] To be used if needed.

Sources: ADB and IMF.

IMF. In December 1997, the government agreed to an assistance package of $58 billion, including $4 billion from ADB.

The markets quickly delivered judgment on the package. From 8 December, the won began to fall sharply again. At this point, the United States (US) Treasury stepped in and persuaded American and other international banks to collectively call a halt to capital flight from the Republic of Korea, thus largely stemming the outward flow of capital. This, along with other emergency measures, bought sufficient time to prepare a more orderly plan and strengthen local financial markets. By late January 1998, the government had managed to reschedule much of the debt.

The subsequent adjustment process was difficult: in 1998, national output declined by almost 7% and unemployment rose rapidly. Nevertheless, by 1999, the recovery was well under way and the economy grew strongly. Many factors contributed to this success, not least the actions taken by national policy makers with strong support from the international community, including ADB.

Indonesia: Political Upheaval

In early 1997, the Indonesian economy appeared robust with the rupiah trading comfortably within the official market range. But in the second week of July 1997, following the floating of the Thai baht, the rupiah began to weaken. Faced with jittery financial markets, on 11 July, Indonesian monetary authorities widened the range in which the rupiah could trade.[8] Unexpectedly, there were soon signs of capital flight. On 14 August, the government floated the rupiah and to bolster confidence also introduced a package of economic measures. But these were not effective. To the surprise of most observers, the rupiah began to fall quickly.

The Government of Indonesia turned for support to the IMF, which on 31 October announced an initial $23 billion rescue package that also

---

[8] Similar arrangements had been made several times before. Previously, when changes of this kind had been announced, the rupiah had strengthened. But on this occasion, the rupiah began to weaken. The Governor of Bank Indonesia at the time, J. Soedradjad Djiwandono, has noted that it soon became apparent that "[a] contagion effect was in progress" because the "herd instinct" of international creditors, worried by events in Thailand, was to move their investments out of Asia (Djiwandono, 2000, *Bank Indonesia and the Recent Crisis*, 52). He provides additional comment in his book on the contagion phenomenon in Southeast Asia at the time (Djiwandono, 2005, *Bank Indonesia and the Crisis*, 26).

involved ADB, the World Bank, and various bilateral donors. Despite this and other efforts to restore confidence, speculation against the currency continued. Confidence was ebbing away. By January 1998, the rupiah entered a dizzy fall against the US dollar. Faced with an escalating crisis, the government on 15 January agreed to a new IMF agreement which involved a controversial program of structural reform.[9] But this too failed to stabilize the markets or halt the collapse of the rupiah.

Over the next few months, the economic and political situation continued to deteriorate. On 4 April 1998, the government agreed to another IMF assistance package totaling $3 billion. However, uncertainty continued. In May 1998, the political crisis peaked when President Soeharto, the leader of Indonesia for 30 years, resigned. GDP declined by around 13% in 1998 and there was a significant increase in poverty.[10] Despite continuing political instability, the economy gradually improved. However, it would take almost a decade for real income per person to return to precrisis levels and for Indonesia to achieve sustained economic growth once again.

Other Asian Neighbors

The financial turmoil spread well beyond the three main crisis-affected countries—though the impact was smaller. In the Philippines, the economy was severely buffeted in 1998, with large outflows of short-term capital that put strains on the banking sector. To counter this, the government took a series of measures to mitigate the impact, including drawing on funds from the IMF, the World Bank, and ADB.

Malaysia, too, managed to contain the damage, though in a distinctive and unorthodox fashion under the leadership of Prime Minister Mahathir. In 1998, after more than a decade of impressive growth, the Asian crisis pushed the Malaysian economy into recession. The ringgit depreciated and official interest rates were sharply increased, reducing output and imposing severe strains on the corporate and finance sectors.

---

[9] Extensive details are provided in an IMF evaluation report prepared in 2003 (IMF, *IMF and Recent Capital Account Crises*, 15). A comprehensive time line of events is included in the same evaluation report (IMF, 2003, *IMF and Recent Capital Account Crises*, 91). A memorandum accompanying the agreement set out the policies that Indonesia intended to follow as part of the arrangement with the IMF (IMF, 1998, *Indonesia – Memorandum*).

[10] Booth discusses trends in poverty levels in Indonesia during this period (Booth, 2016, *Economic Change in Modern Indonesia*, 173–176).

Initially, the government responded with an IMF-endorsed contractionary economic policy. But policy makers soon decided that restricting domestic demand was not the solution and reversed the policy—aiming instead for economic expansion. And in September 1998, the authorities startled markets by introducing exchange and capital controls. This flew in the face of conventional wisdom and drew considerable criticism. But the Malaysian economy soon began to recover strongly, demonstrating that at times of financial crisis governments could usefully apply capital controls.

The ADB Response

ADB, like the rest of the international community, was caught unawares by the scale of the crisis. The Bank was not prepared to provide emergency programs in the crisis-affected countries. In the Republic of Korea, ADB had been scaling down activities during the 1990s. The last loan for the country, for the Fifth Road Improvement Project for $100 million, had been approved almost a decade earlier in 1988. Since then, the tacit understanding had been that since the Republic of Korea was growing strongly and was moving rapidly toward middle-income status, it would abstain from borrowing from ADB. When the financial crisis unfolded, Bank staff needed to swiftly reestablish links with colleagues in Seoul to design an emergency package (Table 10.2).

In Indonesia in 1997, ADB had a large loans and technical assistance program. However, these activities were mostly in nonfinancial sectors such as schools, urban development, and agriculture. ADB staff in Jakarta did not have well-established contacts in the finance sector to draw on for preparing a support program at short notice. Similarly, in Thailand, most activities were for social sectors and for physical infrastructure, such as energy and telecommunications.

However, though the Bank normally operates as a prudent institution that considers new activities carefully, in this case it had to respond quickly. Fortunately, ADB operational systems had become more flexible during the 1990s. Having evolved into a broad-based development institution, ADB had the staff resources to monitor the situation closely and to liaise with member countries, the IMF, the World Bank, and bilateral donors. As a result, the Bank was able to contribute to the IMF-driven emergency assistance packages, not just financially but also by guiding developing member countries toward reforms in the public sector and the financial

Table 10.2: Main Crisis-Related Loans and Technical Assistance, 1997–1999

Date[a]	Loan	Amount[b] ($ million)
Thailand		
19 Dec 1997	Financial Markets Reform Program	
	Program loan	300.0
	Technical assistance grant	2.0
12 Mar 1998	Social sector program	
	Program loan	500.0
	Technical assistance grant	2.1
25 Mar 1998	Export Financing Facility	
	Loan to Export–Import Bank of Thailand	50.0
	Partial credit guarantee	950.0
23 Sep 1999	Agriculture sector program	
	Program loan	300.0
	Technical assistance grant	1.7
Republic of Korea		
19 Dec 1997	Financial Sector Program	
	Program loan	4,000.0
	Technical assistance loan	15.0
Indonesia		
25 Jun 1998	Financial Governance Reforms Sector Development Program	
	Program loan	1,400.0
	Development finance institution loan	47.0
	Equity investment	3.0
	Technical assistance loan	50.0
9 Jul 1998	Social Protection Sector Development Program	
	Program loan	100.0
	Project loan	200.0
	Technical assistance grant	2.90
	Supplementary technical assistance grant	3.00
23 Mar 1999	Power Sector Restructuring Program	
	Program loan	380.0
	Technical assistance loan	20.0

continued on next page

Table 10.2 continued

Date[a]	Loan	Amount[b] ($ million)
25 Mar 1999	Health and Nutrition Sector Development Program	
	Program loan	100.0
	Project loan	200.0
	Technical assistance grant	2.0
	Supplementary technical assistance grant	1.0
25 Mar 1999	Community and Local Government Support Sector Development Program	
	Program loan	200.0
	Project loan	120.0
	Technical assistance grant	2.5

[a] The date is that of ADB Board approval.

[b] Amounts noted here are the funds provided by ADB; in some cases, additional cofinancing was provided by other institutions, particularly for technical assistance grants.

Source: *ADB Annual Reports* for 1997, 1998, and 1999.

capital markets. This required detailed work on financial market regulation, governance, and capacity building—all of which consolidated the Bank's capacity to provide a broadening range of services to member countries.

Just as important, the Bank recognized the need to respond to severe social problems. Unemployment was rising sharply, children were dropping out of school, and there were rising levels of malnutrition. ADB President Mitsuo Sato, writing in the *International Herald Tribune*, in March 1998 pointed to the social costs of the crisis and the need to address the emerging social problems.[11] In Thailand and Indonesia, ADB programs (such as the health and nutrition sector loan for Indonesia) financed social safety nets to mitigate the damage. In the circumstances, the Bank had to set aside normal procedures to respond quickly. Different dimensions of the crisis called for a different focus in each country.

Programs in Thailand

In August 1997, following the Tokyo pledging meeting, responsibility for overseeing the $17.2 billion international rescue package for Thailand was divided among the international institutions. ADB agreed to focus

---

[11] Sato, 1998, "Workers of Asia Need Social Security," *International Herald Tribune*.

on capital market reforms and on supporting the social sector. The Bank was able to start quickly on these programs partly because earlier in 1997, before the onset of the crisis, it had already agreed to provide a loan for the Rural Enterprise Credit Program that could supply immediate liquidity assistance.

During the next 6 months, ADB made three more crisis-related loans. The principal one, as part of the IMF-coordinated response, was the Financial Markets Reform Program Loan for $300 million. This loan, among other things, aimed to strengthen financial regulation and supervision as well as improve risk management.

But as the crisis unfolded, many people argued that the response to the crisis should go beyond monetary and fiscal structural adjustment programs and support the poorest people most directly affected. Shortly afterward, therefore, ADB followed up the first loan with a Social Sector Program Loan—a step toward a social safety net. This loan included a scholarship fund for students who had dropped out of school and a component to extend health coverage to 3 million people and provide milk for disadvantaged children. Another loan, approved in March 1998, was the Export Financing Facility, one of the Bank's largest syndicated loans to an Asian borrower, which signaled Thailand's return to international financial markets.

Programs in the Republic of Korea

ADB's response to the crisis in the Republic of Korea was even more rapid although it was confined to the finance sector. As part of the international support program, the Bank processed its largest-ever assistance package, a $4 billion Financial Sector Program Loan which offered foreign exchange to respond to the currency and liquidity problems. This loan was 10 times larger than any previous ADB loan. Under normal circumstances, such a large loan at such short notice would have been unthinkable. But the circumstances were not normal. The Republic of Korea, a major country in Asia, was facing an unprecedented crisis.

The process of preparing an emergency loan started on 29 November 1997 when an ADB team arrived in Seoul. The team could not base the loan on an approved country strategy because since 1988 the Republic of Korea had been a non-borrowing ADB member. Nevertheless, fact-finding preparations which normally took months were completed in just 11 days.

It helped that the ADB mission had access to plans for financial sector reforms prepared by local experts.

The Government of the Republic of Korea was dismayed by the tough conditions proposed by the international community. Nevertheless, the authorities wanted to reach a quick agreement and did so in just 2 days. By 11 December, the ADB team produced a $4 billion loan proposal. The loan was approved by the Board—under the circumstances—just 8 days later.

The ADB Financial Sector Program Loan for the Republic of Korea aimed to encourage the finance sector to rely more on market forces. A later ADB evaluation study concluded that "The design of the FSPL [Financial Sector Program Loan] had several positive features that enabled it to achieve many of its envisaged impacts. It was processed in a timely manner and had a very high level of government ownership of the reforms. It used the window of opportunity to address fundamental structural weaknesses in the finance sector. The coverage of the reforms and the sequencing were appropriate."[12] In retrospect, it is clear that the ADB participation in the international program was an effective response to the crisis in the Republic of Korea.

Programs in Indonesia

Managing the ADB response in Indonesia proved much more difficult. The program was delayed because of sharp differences on important policy issues—not just within the government but also between the international agencies. The ADB team in Jakarta at the time, for example, disagreed with the IMF's decision to create a "bad bank" to deal with the problem of settling bad loans that surfaced during the crisis.

In October 1997, an ADB team arrived in Jakarta shortly after the main IMF mission. The plan was that the teams from ADB, the IMF, and the World Bank would coordinate their work. But coordination proved difficult. The problems were partly practical since the three teams worked out of different offices making it hard to convene multiple meetings at short notice. But there were also disagreements about policy and the negotiating stance with the Indonesian authorities. Compared with their colleagues in the World Bank and ADB, the IMF team in Jakarta had little flexibility in day-to-day matters and needed to clear their main decisions

---

[12] ADB, 2006, *Program Performance Evaluation Report*, v.

with a disciplined hierarchy in Washington, DC.[13] They were also bound by strict rules of confidentiality which allowed little scope for sharing of information even with partner international agencies.

Before long, the problems of coordination in Jakarta came to the attention of ADB Management in Manila. Eventually, ADB Vice-President Peter Sullivan took the unusual step of sending a firm letter to his counterpart in the IMF, Stanley Fischer.

These disagreements were apparent to their Indonesian colleagues. One Indonesian official was reported as chiding a World Bank staffer that, "The patient is dying, and the three doctors are fighting." Despite the difficulties, the three organizations worked as best they could within the fraying administrative and political situation in Jakarta. As part of a coordinated approach, they agreed that ADB would focus on the private banks while the IMF would give priority to state-owned banks. In December 1997 and January 1998, including over the Christmas season, an ADB mission visited to prepare for a $1.4 billion loan for the Financial Governance Reform Program.

The ADB program was almost in place when it was thrown entirely off course. On 15 January 1998, President Soeharto and IMF Managing Director Michel Camdessus signed an agreement in Jakarta. The IMF team in Jakarta, bound by strict confidentiality rules, had not shared any information with ADB about this plan. But the arrangements set out in the IMF agreement clashed with the ADB program that had already been negotiated with the Indonesian Minister of Finance. Given the unexpected terms of the IMF program, ADB plans for a loan needed to be withdrawn from consideration by the ADB Board and completely redesigned.[14]

The redesign took up valuable time. There was increasing political uncertainty in Indonesia which delayed the presentation to the Board. Management took the unusual step of scheduling two Board meetings to consider the Financial Governance Reform Program. A preliminary discussion was held on 21 April 1998 to obtain Board feedback on the main issues of concern. One month later, on 21 May, Soeharto resigned. The following month, on 25 June, after the incoming President, B. J. Habibie, had formed a new cabinet in Jakarta and the prospects of stability had improved, the Board approved a revised version of the loan document.

---

[13] Blustein, 2001, *The Chastening*, 104.
[14] ADB, 2005, *Country Assistance Program Evaluation for Indonesia*.

In all, between June 1998 and March 1999, ADB approved support for Indonesia, including five crisis support loans, totaling $2.8 billion with the overall aim of providing liquidity and budgetary support (Table 10.2). Because the crisis had led to rising unemployment and increasing poverty, the Bank also offered several loans to support social protection for the poor.[15] Equally important, extensive policy support was provided. ADB committed additional staff resources through frequent visits and prolonged stays, including establishing extended missions to Indonesia (and to the Republic of Korea). The ADB program in Indonesia lasted well past 2000.[16]

Implementation was further complicated between 1999 and 2001 by a radical program of decentralization to over 500 subprovincial governments across Indonesia.[17] In 2003, Indonesia finally graduated from the main IMF stabilization program, the last of the three main crisis-affected countries to do so.[18]

Impact on ADB

ADB was greatly affected by the crisis, both immediately and in succeeding years. ADB had, in a short time, moved well beyond its traditional role as a development bank focusing on longer-term projects to provide the type of short-term emergency financial support normally supplied by the IMF. Nevertheless, there was a key difference between the support provided by ADB and the IMF. In supporting crisis-hit countries, ADB programs focused on budget support to maintain national expenditures, especially for social sectors and for structural reform, while IMF programs were for balance-of-payments support.

As the crisis unfolded, ADB Board Directors took a close interest in the way the Bank responded in each country. They generally strongly supported the Bank's responses but also made many comments when the loans came before the Board: loans for Thailand were approved in December 1997, for the Republic of Korea in December 1997, and for Indonesia in June 1998.

---

[15] For information on ADB's approach, ADB, 2001, *Crisis Management Interventions in Indonesia*.
[16] ADB, 2001, *Crisis Management Interventions in Indonesia*.
[17] Booth outlines the major steps in decentralization of government which began in 1999 (Booth, 2016, *Economic Change in Modern Indonesia*, 211–218).
[18] ADB, 2005, *Country Assistance Program Evaluation for Indonesia*, 4.

Directors emphasized, for example, that governments in the crisis-affected countries should be committed to reform. Management had anticipated this. Before the loan for Thailand was considered, ADB Vice-President Bong-Suh Lee had visited Thailand. He was able to tell the Board that he had received strong assurances from the Government of Thailand. Similarly, senior Korean leaders had guaranteed their support for the IMF-driven program to which the ADB loan was linked. But in Indonesia, the political situation remained changeable until mid-May 1998 when a new president committed to international programs took office.

Some Board members also referred to the difficulties of coordination between the different organizations. Nevertheless, they emphasized that the Bank's programs should be closely coordinated with those of the IMF and the World Bank. ADB Management, in response, said that the Bank's programs would indeed be aligned with the work of other international agencies and that procedures for better coordination would be discussed with the IMF.

ADB Directors also noted that coordination within the Bank had worked well. This was because Management and staff had established a task force to design and coordinate various types of loans across the crisis-affected countries. ADB's North American office was also closely involved because of the need to keep in touch with US and international agencies in Washington, DC.

The problems to be tackled in each of the main countries—Thailand, the Republic of Korea, and Indonesia—were quite different. Programs and loans needed to be tailored accordingly. In Thailand and Indonesia, the important challenges were financial sector reforms and the need to respond to the social impact of the crisis. The countries also differed in their institutional capacities, so technical assistance needed to reflect local circumstances.

The emergency lending in 1997 and the following year had a dramatic impact on the financial operations of ADB. Throughout November and December 1997, staff in the Treasury Department kept a close watch on what these changes meant for the Bank's financial accounts. ADB had always given top priority to the protection of its financial reputation and the maintenance of its AAA ratings in international financial markets.

To maintain an adequate buffer of resources for its various needs, the Bank rapidly expanded its international borrowing program. In December 1997, the Board agreed—though it really had little choice—to a sharp increase in the borrowing program by over 100% from $2.6 billion to $5.6 billion. Despite the turmoil in the finance sector in Asia, and because ADB had a sound reputation, it could raise these funds at short notice in major international markets. In 1998 the borrowing program was increased yet again, leading the Bank to raise around $9.6 billion.

The Bank also needed to make other changes in financial arrangements. Following the crisis, it soon became clear that ADB was facing greater risks in its loan portfolio. And because of expenses associated with the higher borrowing levels, the Bank's operating expenses rose markedly following the crisis. These and other factors led to increasing pressure on the net income of ADB. After a review in 1999, the Bank in January 2000 introduced a new loan charge policy. This involved an increase in the lending spread (the difference between the cost to borrowers and funding cost to ADB) and a new front-end fee to borrowers of 1% on new loans.[19] Although the changes were not presented in this way, in effect the Bank was increasing loan charges to cover costs arising from the Asian financial crisis.

These changes proved controversial. For a time, they sparked vigorous discussions between the Board and ADB Management. Borrowing countries argued that loan charges should be as low as possible and that the Bank should find other ways of covering the increased costs arising from the Asian financial crisis. Management responded that it was in the interests of all members that the sound financial reputation of the institution be protected. In the end, amid some acrimony, the Board approved increases in loan charges. The impact of the financial crisis in the region was far-reaching. But for ADB, the impact on the financial policies of the institution was far-reaching as well.

Over time, these higher loan charges were progressively reduced. The lending spread for most borrowers was reduced in 2004, and in 2007 the Board approved the elimination of front-end fees for new sovereign loans based on the London interbank offered rate (LIBOR), the benchmark rate for short-term interbank loans set on a daily rate in London.

---

[19] These issues are discussed in Chapter VI in Erquiaga, 2016, *A History of Financial Management at the Asian Development Bank*.

Graduation of Newly Industrialized Economies

Board discussion about a hardening of ordinary capital resources (OCR) loan terms were not made any easier by the approach of donor countries during Asian Development Fund (ADF) negotiations. Some borrowing countries took the view that when OCR and ADF policies were being discussed, Management ceded too much ground to industrial countries. They pointed to the recent ADF VII negotiations in which donors had insisted that ADB introduce initiatives to use ADF resources more effectively and had argued that the long-term goal should be for ADF to become self-funding. Donors had suggested, for example, transferring some of the Bank's own net income into the ADF, and preparing a graduation policy for borrowing countries.

The first suggestion was quickly adopted. Following a ruling from the internal Office of the General Counsel that transfers from net income to the ADF were consistent with the Bank's Charter, in May 1997 the Board of Governors authorized a transfer of $230 million. Since then, ADB has regularly made transfers from the net income of OCR to ADF.

The second issue—preparing a graduation policy—was more difficult. Since 1977, ADB has (up to the present) classified developing member countries into three main groups: Group A countries are fully eligible for ADF (for concessional loans, and for grants introduced in 2005); Group B covers "blend countries" which borrow from both OCR and ADF; and Group C countries are eligible for only OCR loans.[20] While the 1977 approach had worked well for two decades, donors believed it was time to develop a more formalized approach to allow for the transition of countries from one group to another and for countries graduating from ADB borrowing. For one thing, no borrowing country had ever moved from one group to the next. For another, no country—not even the successful newly industrialized economies (NIEs) of East Asia—had ever formally graduated from being eligible for access to OCR loans. Indeed, the policy did not envisage a stage beyond Group C. Donors wanted this situation to change.

During 1997, formulation of a new policy was complicated by the turmoil of the Asian financial crisis. The need to provide the Republic of Korea with an emergency loan of $4 billion underscored the necessity for any

---

[20] The 1998 graduation policy classified borrowing countries into four categories with blend countries falling under either Group B1 (ADF with limited amounts of OCR) or Group B2 (OCR with limited amounts of ADF).

new policy to be flexible. It was almost 2 years before the ADB Board could agree to approve a new classification and graduation policy.

The new policy covered reclassification from one group to another, and graduation from regular (OCR) Bank assistance. Under the policy, transitions from Group A to B, and then Group B to C, would be determined by two main country criteria: per capita gross national product and the debt repayment capacity of the borrowing country. Graduation from OCR borrowing would be based on per capita gross national product, availability of commercial capital flows on reasonable terms, and the attainment of a certain level of capacity by key economic and social institutions.

It was agreed that while the four NIEs (Hong Kong, China; the Republic of Korea; Singapore; and Taipei,China) would formally graduate from regular Bank lending, they would remain eligible for emergency assistance if needed.[21]

However in graduating the NIEs even from OCR borrowing, the key question arose of the nature of ADB's changed relationship with these countries after graduation. The Bank's revised policy emphasized that graduated countries could receive expert services and technical assistance. They would also be encouraged to participate in subregional activities and the cofinancing of development projects. Further, traditional donors certainly hoped that these countries would soon contribute to the ADF and other regional funds. Today, all of these graduated countries, as well as some borrowing countries, contribute to the ADF.

Policy Reforms, Research, and Advocacy

In response to the Asian financial crisis, ADB also expanded its activities to strengthen institutions across the region. Early in 1999, it formed the Regional Economic Monitoring Unit (REMU), whose tasks included working with the ASEAN+3 countries (the 10 members of the Association of Southeast Asian Nations plus the People's Republic of China, Japan, and the Republic of Korea) to carry out regional monitoring of economic policies and financial conditions. REMU was also tasked with operating the new Asia Recovery Information Center (ARIC). Developed with support from the Government of Australia, the ARIC website provided information about countries most affected by the crisis and about programs to assist recovery.

---

[21] ADB, 1993, *A Graduation Policy for the Bank's DMCs*.

In 2000, REMU launched a new publication, *Asia Recovery Report*, later renamed *Asia Economic Monitor*. The unit also organized workshops on topics such as private capital flows, developed a prototype early warning system of financial crises at the request of ASEAN+3 finance ministers, and assisted several ASEAN member states in establishing surveillance units in ministries of finance. REMU also supported the Asian Bond Markets Initiative and developed the AsianBondsOnline website with the aim of promoting the development of local currency bond markets to address one of the causes of the Asian financial crisis—so-called currency and maturity "mismatch." In April 2005, the unit was upgraded to become the Office of Regional Economic Integration. Over the next decade, it would play a key role within ADB supporting regional economic cooperation throughout Asia.

In other activities during the crisis period, ADB supported a regionwide process of reflection about experiences in different countries—sponsoring seminars, books, workshops, and articles. Much of this activity was carried out by the Economic Development Resource Center. In 1998, to improve understanding of the sources of the crisis, the center initiated a study of financial markets.

During the crisis years 1998 to 2000, ADB continued to produce its flagship publication, the *Asian Development Outlook*, which included commentary about regional economic developments and a special theme chapter on key development issues at that time. In addition, a series of *Briefing Notes* on economic issues was prepared and many of these covered key topics relating to the financial crisis.

Another initiative was the establishment of the ADB Institute (ADBI) in Tokyo. With finance from the Government of Japan, the Institute was set up as an ADB subsidiary to carry out policy research and build capacity in developing countries. ADBI was officially inaugurated on 10 December 1997 with a symposium titled "The Currency Crisis and Beyond."

In 1998, ADBI organized a series of roundtables on the Asian financial crisis—in Manila, San Francisco, Singapore, and Tokyo—with subsequent seminars to promote the findings. The following year, ADBI together with the Financial Supervisory Agency of Japan sponsored a dialogue in Tokyo where central bankers and senior regulators from crisis-hit economies met their counterparts from Japan, the United Kingdom, and the US to review changing banking regulations and the measures to prevent future crisis. Other ADBI studies were carried out on exchange rate regimes for emerging economies and on banking regulations with the Bank for International Settlements.

Turmoil in Asia: What Went Wrong?

The Asian financial crisis had some of its origins in the zealous promotion of pro-market policies during the 1990s. A number of developing countries in Asia had liberalized their capital markets after, as Toyoo Gyohten (a close adviser to the first ADB President, Takeshi Watanabe) put it, "incessant prodding by US advocates of globalization."[22] These countries became magnets for footloose private capital.[23] Global investors including hedge funds, aiming for higher investment returns and seeking to diversify, were drawn to Asia. They were attracted by high interest rates underpinned by pegged exchange rates that encouraged a false sense of security. In the years preceding the crisis, much of this capital arrived as short-term bank lending or portfolio investment; more than as long-term foreign direct investment. In Indonesia, a considerable share of the inflow was in the form of direct lending from international banks to Indonesian conglomerates. These capital movements were difficult to monitor, making it hard to coordinate policy responses across the region.

The surge of private capital inflows pushed up prices, particularly for real estate. These developments, in turn, encouraged further capital inflows which by mid-1996 reached an all-time high. But then, following a cyclical downturn in the global demand for electronic goods, the bubble burst. The slowdown in exports widened the current account deficit, eventually putting pressure on exchange rates and then leading, in July 1997, to the float and collapse of the Thai baht (Figure 10.1).

The depreciation of currencies undermined economic confidence and there was a fall in equity and real estate prices. This, in turn, put banks and many corporates under strain because of a serious "double mismatch"— in both currencies and maturities. Many investors in Asia had borrowed overseas in foreign currency (usually US dollars) and used the funds to invest in long-term and illiquid projects which often provided revenue flows in local currencies. When overseas lenders lost confidence, they

---

[22] Gyohten, 2007, *The Future of Asia*, 51.
[23] This section is largely drawn from ADB, "The Asian Financial Crisis," *ADO 1998*, 19–37.

Figure 10.1: Selected Indicators in the Republic of Korea, Indonesia, Malaysia, the Philippines, and Thailand, 1992–2002

(1) Portfolio Equity, Net Inflows ($ billion)

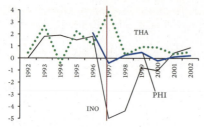

INO = Indonesia, PHI = Philippines, THA = Thailand.
Note: Data are unavailable for Malaysia and the Republic of Korea.
Source: World Bank.

(2) Exports, Annual Growth Rate (%)

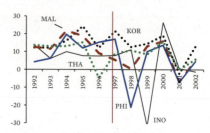

INO = Indonesia, KOR = Republic of Korea, MAL = Malaysia, PHI = Philippines, THA = Thailand.
Source: World Bank.

(3) Real Effective Exchange Rate
2010 = 100

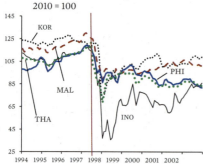

INO = Indonesia, KOR = Republic of Korea,
MAL = Malaysia, PHI = Philippines, THA = Thailand.
Source: Bank for International Settlements.

(4) Gross Domestic Product, Annual Growth Rate (%)

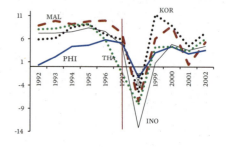

INO = Indonesia, KOR = Republic of Korea, MAL = Malaysia, PHI = Philippines, THA = Thailand.
Source: ADB.

(5) Nonperforming Loans Ratio

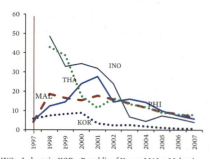

INO = Indonesia, KOR = Republic of Korea, MAL = Malaysia, PHI = Philippines, THA = Thailand.
Note: Comparable and accurate data on nonperforming loans prior to 1997 are not unavailable. They are often underreported at the beginning or prior to a crisis.
Source: World Bank.

(6) Unemployment Rate
1997 = 100

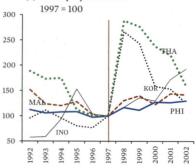

INO = Indonesia, KOR = Republic of Korea, MAL = Malaysia, PHI = Philippines, THA = Thailand.
Source: ADB.

refused to roll over the short-term debt, sharply reducing private capital flows and exacerbating pressures on the region's currencies.

The financial crisis in Asia was thus a currency crisis that led to a banking crisis. These events created a downward spiral that imposed severe economic and social costs: GDP growth slowed significantly, particularly in 1998, causing widespread unemployment and rising levels of poverty.

Weak Fundamentals or Investor Panic

Following the crisis, there was widespread debate about the underlying causes.[24] Two principal explanations were offered: weak fundamentals and investor panic. The weak fundamentals approach identified a range of underlying problems in the crisis-affected countries, such as structural and policy distortions as well as weak governance which eventually undermined market confidence. The investor panic approach, on the other hand, put the blame on erratic shifts in market expectations, with subsequent regional contagion. This view also acknowledged structural and governance problems but pointed out that these economies had previously been strong and suggested that the crisis and the capital flight were due more to herd behavior. Many Asian observers also blamed speculative attacks including by hedge funds.

Both explanations contributed to an understanding of the crisis. Many developing countries had structural and policy weaknesses. And in Indonesia, for example, where the crisis widened into an overall crisis of governance, it seems clear that the financial weaknesses were exacerbated by fundamental economic and political problems.[25] In Indonesia, there had been a dramatic increase in the number of banks following a liberalization of the banking sector in 1988. The number of banks more than doubled to reach 240 in 1996, causing major regulatory problems.[26] Nevertheless, the immediate trigger in all three countries was the collapse of investor confidence that caused rapid and unexpected capital flight.

---

[24] Mitsuo Sato, the former President of ADB, took a close personal interest in the discussions about the crisis. He emphasized the capital account nature of the problems at the time and described the crisis as "an entirely new type of financial turmoil" (Sato, 1999, Capital Flow Reversal, Not Cronyism, Caused Asian Financial Crisis, *The Korea Herald*).

[25] Djiwandono provides an authoritative discussion of the causes of the crisis in Indonesia (Djiwandono, 2005, Bank Indonesia and the Crisis, 22–75).

[26] Pangestu and Habir, 2002, The Boom, Bust, and Restructuring of Indonesian Banks, *IMF Working Paper;* Hamada, 2003, "Transformation of the Financial Sector."

The Asian financial crisis was thus not a traditional current account crisis but a capital account crisis. Some borrowers, lenders, and international organizations were slow to acknowledge this. Moreover, governments and international organizations had vigorously promoted open financial markets, holding a sanguine view of the benefits of free capital flows and greatly underestimating the difficulties of managing such flows in developing countries in Asia.[27]

Criticism of International Rescue Operations

This crisis was largely unforeseen. There were soon sharp disagreements on the best way to respond. The IMF, drawing on its experience in crises in Latin America during the 1980s and the crisis in Mexico in 1994, prescribed restrictive economic and financial policies and pressed for structural reforms. But there were important differences between the Latin American and Asian situations. Latin American countries often had lax fiscal and monetary policies which had led to unsustainable balance-of-payments deficits. Asian countries, however, had maintained conservative fiscal and monetary policies and did not generally have current account deficits caused by imprudent macroeconomic policies.

In a number of Asian countries, large and growing capital inflows—consisting especially of short-term portfolio investment and bank lending from abroad underpinned by virtually fixed exchange rates—had caused overheating. The result was large capital account surpluses accompanied by current account deficits. The boom in financial flows was often associated with overinvestment and price hikes in real estate. Then, when observers began to question the sustainability of the boom, there was a sudden reversal in capital flows from inflows to outflows leading to balance-of-payments and financial crises. The Asian financial crisis was seen as a new type of crisis because it originated from the volatility of capital accounts. Following the massive capital outflows, domestic liquidity in the crisis-affected countries dried up quickly sending the economies into recession and resulting in a liquidity crisis in the financial systems.

In that sense, tight monetary and fiscal policies that might have been appropriate for current account problems in Latin America were the wrong prescription for capital account crises in Asia. The tight policies which

---

[27] Villafuerte and Yap, 2015, "Managing Capital Flows in Asia."

were quickly implemented restricted aggregate demand even though some of the Asian economies were already in recession. These policies brought further damage to the balance sheets of banks and nonfinancial corporations and created widespread unemployment and needless social damage.

There was also controversy over the IMF insistence that stringent structural adjustment be introduced in countries such as Indonesia.[28] The disagreements were not just about the relevance and design of the programs. There were also disagreements about the idea of implementing such measures during a crisis while presenting the measures as a long-term package of comprehensive and stringent banking sector reforms. Over time, these criticisms would lead the international community to reassess its responses to financial crises. These changes mainly affected programs introduced by the Washington-based Bretton Woods institutions.

Regional Initiatives

Policy makers in various countries in Asia were concerned about the IMF's approach to the crisis. They considered alternatives and announced their own programs in response. The crisis had demonstrated to Asian policy makers that they should not rely solely on IMF support but also strengthen their own policies and institutions. Moreover, since financial systems and economic conditions in neighboring countries were now more closely interconnected, national governments were interested in considering regionwide mutual self-help mechanisms for crisis prevention and management.

One of the earliest and most controversial of these alternatives was a proposal by Japan for an Asian Monetary Fund (AMF) to pool East Asian foreign exchange reserves in a fund that could be used to deter currency speculation and to mobilize resources during crisis. Japanese Vice-Minister of Finance Eisuke Sakakibara announced the proposal at the IMF–World Bank meeting in Hong Kong, China in September 1997. This caught many observers by surprise—though the idea had been under discussion for at least a year by senior advisers in Japan and raised with some Asian countries informally. Some observers noted that the IMF had provided strong support during the 1994 financial crisis in Mexico but were

---

[28] Sakakibara, 1999. Reform of the International Financial System, Speech at the Manila Framework Meeting in Melbourne.

not confident that financing from the IMF would be sufficient to respond to the crisis in Asia.[29] These concerns turned out to be correct, especially in the case of the crisis in Thailand.

The AMF proposal included complementing IMF resources by establishing the following: a regional pool of foreign exchange reserves amounting to as much as $100 billion (not including US participation), macroeconomic surveillance arrangements by the AMF (in coordination with IMF surveillance), and a permanent secretariat. However, the proposal did not receive sufficient support in the meeting in Hong Kong, China. It was vigorously opposed by the US Secretary of the Treasury Lawrence Summers on the grounds of risks of moral hazard and of duplicating IMF functions so the plan was diplomatically set aside.[30, 31] Nevertheless, the suggestion had established the principle of expanding regional self-help mechanisms.

The discussion about the AMF was followed by another proposal, subsequently dubbed the Manila Framework. In November 1997, in response to the talk about the AMF, senior officials of the Asia-Pacific Economic Cooperation (APEC) forum meeting in the Philippines agreed on a framework to strengthen regional banking and financial systems. The draft statement was considered overnight by officials including Timothy Geithner from the US, later Secretary of the Treasury, and Takehiko Nakao from Japan, later President of ADB. The agreed statement of this framework, including the US as a member, gave more clearly a central role to the IMF. It included enhanced regional surveillance to complement global surveillance by the IMF, intensified economic and technical cooperation to improve financial regulatory capacities, new IMF mechanisms for adjustment programs, and a cooperative financing arrangement which would supplement IMF resources.

The Manila Framework was endorsed by the 18 APEC leaders on 25 November 1997. This idea was similar to that of the AMF proposal except that the framework did not suggest the establishment of a permanent

---

[29] Blustein, 2001, *The Chastening*, 165; Grenville notes that the US was "less highly motivated" in responding to the financial crisis in Indonesia than was the case when the crisis occurred in Mexico in 1994 (Grenville, 2004, *The IMF and the Indonesian Crisis*).

[30] Blustein, 2001, *The Chastening: The Crisis That Rocked the Global Financial System and Humbled the IMF*, 162.

[31] Lipscy, 2003, Japan's Asian Monetary Fund Proposal, *Stanford Journal of East Asian Affairs*, 94.

secretariat or propose the creation of a regional pool of funds based on a treaty. Manila Framework meetings were held semiannually for a period, then annually, before they were terminated in 2004. By then, other initiatives such as the Chiang Mai Initiative (CMI), introduced by the ASEAN+3 countries, would become more important (see discussion on the CMI in Chapters 11 and 13).

Japan was particularly active in promoting measures in Asia to respond to the crisis. In October 1998, the government announced a $30 billion support package, the New Miyazawa Initiative. This provided $15 billion to meet medium- to long-term financial needs in Asian countries, and another $15 billion for their possible short-term capital requirements while implementing economic reforms. Explaining the plan at the Foreign Correspondents' Club of Japan in Tokyo in December 1998, Minister of Finance Kiichi Miyazawa outlined three fundamental issues for the international financial system: the problems caused by large-scale, short-term capital movements; the determination of exchange rates; and the provision of liquidity to crisis-affected countries.[32]

Miyazawa explained that problems caused by short-term capital movements often arose because of herding, which could trigger large and abrupt movements that did not reflect economic fundamentals. Flows of this kind could ruin a nation's economy so they should be more carefully monitored. Miyazawa also pointed to the need for better arrangements to determine appropriate exchange rates, both in the major industrial countries and in developing countries in Asia. But there was no simple formula: some cases required greater stability; others more flexibility.

A third priority was to provide adequate liquidity in times of crises. During the Asian financial crisis, the affected countries had essentially lost access to capital markets leading to an extreme shortage of liquidity. In these circumstances, international financial institutions such as the IMF could have provided liquidity support more quickly and sufficiently. Miyazawa outlined a range of measures that could be taken in future to provide greater liquidity. Indeed, in setting out such an approach, he was foreshadowing the types of policies that the IMF and Western central banks would pursue vigorously in industrial countries in 2007 and 2008. As part of the New Miyazawa Initiative, Japan established the $3 billion Asian Currency Crisis Support Facility within ADB in March 1999. This

---

[32] Miyazawa, 1998, *Towards a New International Financial Architecture*.

included guarantees and interest subsidies to help crisis-affected countries raise funds in international financial markets.

Subsequent developments took place at meetings of the ASEAN+3 regional grouping. In November 1999, the ASEAN+3 leaders met in Manila and issued a statement on the need for coordination and collaboration on financial, monetary, and fiscal issues of common interest. Soon after, the ASEAN+3 finance ministers embarked on several other initiatives. One was the Economic Review and Policy Dialogue Introduced in May 2000, it would be used to analyze economic and financial conditions at the global, regional, and national levels. Based on peer review and policy dialogue, it would monitor capital flows and developments in financial markets, help manage risks, and recommend policies and joint action. The expectation was that peer pressure would stimulate better macroeconomic and financial policies and encourage regional cooperation.

But a significant form of cooperation was the CMI. Introduced in May 2000, the initiative was established as a network of bilateral swap arrangements between ASEAN+3 countries to provide short-term US dollar liquidity to member countries experiencing balance-of-payments crises. It was hoped that the CMI would supplement existing international financial arrangements, and the initiative was cautiously welcomed by the US and the IMF. ADB actively supported both the Economic Review and Policy Dialogue and the CMI.

Asia and ADB after the Crisis

Initial speculation in much of the international media suggested that the financial crisis showed that the Asian miracle was a mirage. Subsequent events proved this conclusion wrong. The crisis did not diminish the drive in Asia for sustained growth. By 1999, the crisis had abated and confidence had largely returned. The crisis stalled progress for a time in some countries but most of the region recovered strongly.

Nevertheless, the wrenching experience offered valuable lessons. One was that large and complex financial crises require effective coordination across numerous national and international institutions. The scale of the required financing is likely to be beyond the resources and traditional instruments of the IMF as well as those of other institutions such as the World Bank, ADB, and major bilateral aid agencies. It requires strong, collective actions involving central banks as well as creative and flexible responses.

For policy makers across the region, the crisis also provided an opportunity to reassess their economic policies and address structural weaknesses. They reconsidered the importance of prudent macroeconomic policies including the role of central banks, of closer monitoring of capital accounts and asset prices, and of stronger financial sector supervision and policies. The crisis also exposed the reality that many millions still lived in very precarious conditions and that it was important to deal with the social fallout of crises and address poverty. More generally, the crisis highlighted Asia's common vulnerabilities and shared interests and provided an impetus for regional cooperation.

For ADB, the Asian financial crisis was a severe test from which it emerged stronger as a multilateral development institution. The Bank had teamed up with the international community and in so doing had widened its banking operations and used new financial instruments. Nevertheless, like other organizations, it had been caught off guard and would need to consider how to respond to unexpected financial crises and be ready to work with other partners.

ADB would draw on these lessons from the crisis as it moved toward a new presidency. When Tadao Chino took over from President Sato in January 1999, he inherited a wider and more complex agenda.

CHAPTER 11
Fourth Decade (1997–2006)

Asia: A New Century Dawns

"Asian economies have generally been successful in harnessing the benefits of globalization to achieve rapid economic growth and reduce poverty. On the other hand, globalization also involves risks that have to be managed. Globalization can generate social and economic stresses as well as financial volatility."

– Tadao Chino,
Address to the ADB Annual Meeting, 2001

As the Asian Development Bank (ADB) entered the new century, the effects of the financial crisis dissipated and strong growth began to gather pace. The crisis had held back progress in some countries, but recovery was quicker and stronger than anticipated (Chapter 10). The region powered ahead—fueled by the rise of the People's Republic of China (PRC), the emergence of India, and improving performance in parts of Central Asia and Southeast Asia. Greater globalization in international trade, cross-country capital flows, and migration facilitated the changes.

At the same time, globalization had its discontents. These groups provoked sharp policy debate and often organized protests.[1] Persistent poverty, rising inequality, financial contagion and geopolitical insecurity were seen by many as downsides of globalization. For the benefits to outweigh the costs, it was believed that globalization had to be carefully managed. This view contributed to a considerable rethinking of development policy. Key international conferences generated a widening global agenda. Policy makers continued to aim for rapid growth, and also tried to address complementary priorities such as reducing inequality, promoting social development, and building safeguards against financial instability.

---

[1] Stiglitz, 2002, *Globalization and Its Discontents*.

Recovery and Ascent in Asia

The new millennium ushered in a period of strong development in Asia. Within 2 years of the crisis most of the affected countries had largely recovered. Robust growth in developed economies, coupled with competitive exchange rates, provided the initial impetus for export-led recovery. A buoyant economy in the United States (US) grew more than 4.0% annually during 1998–2000. In the eurozone, growth exceeded 3.5% in 2000, reinforced by domestic demand and exports. And after recession during the Asian financial crisis, the Japanese economy grew about 2.0% in 2000, partly as a result of macroeconomic stimulus. Growth in ADB developing member countries had slumped to 0.2% in 1998 but by 2000 had rebounded to over 7.0%.[2]

The growth in industrial countries began to slow. In early 2000, the dot-com crash in the US led to a slowdown that soon widened to other industrial countries. In September 2001, the 9/11 terrorist attacks in the US further shook investor confidence. Recovery was constrained throughout 2002 by the looming conflict in Iraq. Stronger growth would not resume in industrial countries until after 2004.

Turbulent as things may have seemed at the time, since the mid-1980s the advanced economies had experienced a period often described as the "great moderation." Into the early 2000s, there had been a distinct pattern of moderating swings in both quarterly real output growth and quarterly inflation.[3] This was attributed to a combination of "structural change, improved macroeconomic policies, and good luck."[4] The relatively mild recession in the early 2000s, coming after a long period of expansion in advanced economies, reinforced the view that policy makers were now better able to control macroeconomic fluctuations.

In this changing economic environment, much of developing Asia continued to grow well although there was considerable diversity. The balance of international economic influence was now shifting because Asia's share in global economic output continued to rise. A key factor was the performance of the PRC. Policy makers in the PRC had worried about spillover effects from the Asian financial crisis but as it turned out, the country was largely unaffected. In 2001, the PRC's accession to

---

[2] ADB, 2001, *Asian Development Outlook 2001*.
[3] Blanchard and Simon, 2001, The Long and Large Decline in US Output Volatility,.
[4] Bernanke, 2004, "The Great Moderation."

the World Trade Organization (WTO) further expanded its economic influence. Negotiations over entry had lasted 15 years, during which the government agreed to implement a wide range of market-oriented reforms in agriculture, energy, banking, and retailing.[5] Helped by these changes, annual growth in the PRC exceeded 10% during 2002–2006.

South Asia was also largely unaffected by the Asian financial crisis. India's program of structural reform and liberalization, launched in 1991, was at last bearing fruit.[6] By 2003, economic growth had reached 7% per year, a rate sustained for the rest of the fourth ADB decade. Prospects were also improving elsewhere in South Asia. After relatively sluggish growth earlier in the decade, growth picked up to around 6% by 2004–2006 in Bangladesh, Pakistan, and Sri Lanka.

In the Mekong region, countries making the transition toward greater market orientation needed to overcome difficult economic legacies. For five decades, they had been constrained by war and strife, but following the 1991 Paris Peace Accords (Chapter 8), Viet Nam, Cambodia, and the Lao People's Democratic Republic started to grow rapidly relying more on manufacturing and exports. For most of the fourth ADB decade, the Mekong countries expanded by around 6%–7% per year.

By 2000, growth had started to pick up in the crisis-affected countries of Southeast Asia. Governments continued to address the structural weaknesses that had triggered the earlier financial collapse—through corporate and financial reforms, including restructuring insolvent financial institutions, improving corporate governance, reducing labor market rigidities, and deregulating domestic markets.[7]

The outlook improved in many Central Asian republics (CARs) as they emerged from the centralized economic controls of the Soviet era. Transition to market-oriented policies in the early 1990s was painstaking. The change involved reducing structural and pricing distortions, improving budgetary processes and statistical systems, and controlling off-budget spending. In the midst of continued macroeconomic stabilization, countries such as Azerbaijan and Kazakhstan were able to grow rapidly, benefiting from the emerging global resource boom. The CARs which were

---

[5] An indicative sample list of the PRC's commitments on entering the WTO and the outcome at the end of 2004 after 3 years is in Box 2.1 in ADB, *Asian Development Outlook 2005*.
[6] ADB, 1994, *Asian Development Outlook 1994*.
[7] ADB, 2000, *Asian Development Outlook 2000*.

poorer in natural resources, however, had a more difficult time. Expansion in the islands in the Pacific was also relatively modest.

The Asian financial crisis highlighted the issues of chronic and transient poverty. Since the 1960s, there had been a steady decline in poverty in developing Asia. This trend was interrupted by the crisis. In Indonesia, the $1.25-a-day poverty rate rose from 11% in 1996 to 16%–20% in 1998. There was a similar surge in unemployment, which during the crisis rose to 5.5% in Indonesia, 9.6% in the Philippines, and 5.3% in Thailand.[8] These shocks precipitated social turmoil with food riots and labor unrest.

As governments responded with expanded social safety nets, and growth resumed after the crisis, poverty started to fall again. Between 1999 and 2005, the $1.25-a-day poverty headcount rates in ADB developing member countries fell from almost 40% to below 27%; more than 300 million people exited absolute poverty.[9] But inequality was rising in several large economies—including the PRC, India, Indonesia, and Bangladesh.[10] These poverty and inequality outcomes would have major implications for the ADB corporate strategy (Chapters 12 and 14).

Growing Intraregional Trade and Capital Flows

The recovery in the region from the Asian financial crisis was accompanied by strengthening of intraregional trade and capital flows. Between the mid-1990s and mid-2000s, intraregional trade more than doubled with a small dip during 1997–1999.[11] Intraregional cross-border capital inflows more than tripled during the fourth decade. The richer Asian countries that grew rapidly in the 1980s and 1990s found themselves with low unemployment and attracted a steady flow of migrants from poorer countries in the region.

The PRC, especially after joining the WTO in 2001, emerged as the nexus between intraregional trade within Asia and interregional trade with the rest of the world.[12] The PRC imported increasing amounts of intermediate goods from other Asian countries, processed them, and exported finished goods to the rest of the world, especially to the US, the European Union,

---

[8] ADB, *Annual Report 1998*, 104.
[9] ADB, 2014, *Midterm Review of Strategy 2020*, 14.
[10] ADB, *Asian Development Outlook 2012*.
[11] Author's estimates using data from ADB, Asia Regional Integration Center database (accessed 23 December 2016).
[12] ADB, *Asian Development Outlook 2004*, Box 1.1.

and Japan. The backward linkages which expanded as the imports of intermediate goods grew from economies such as the Republic of Korea; Malaysia; and Taipei,China provided a strong stimulus to growth in these nations.

These patterns of growth were another instance of the flying geese paradigm. Growth in Japan had earlier been supported by expansion in the manufacturing of processed goods and labor-intensive products but had then moved on to more capital-intensive industries. First, the newly industrialized economies, and then other Asian countries, had followed suit (Chapter 2). In the fourth ADB decade, other Asian countries similarly moved up the value chain from the manufacture of textiles, clothing, and footwear toward more sophisticated products. The PRC was now opening up opportunities for relatively lower-income countries like Malaysia, Thailand, and Viet Nam to further expand their manufacturing sectors, especially in parts and components of electrical machinery and transportation.

Following the Asian financial crisis, policy makers realized that external shocks associated with globalization could be moderated by establishing regional economic initiatives. Before the crisis, economic cooperation in Asia had largely focused on trade linkages. Now there was growing interest in strengthening financial cooperation. The crisis led to the formation of the ASEAN+3 group—comprising the Association of Southeast Asian Nations (ASEAN) member states along with the PRC, Japan, and the Republic of Korea. In May 2000, the ASEAN+3 finance ministers established a network of bilateral currency swap agreements known as the Chiang Mai Initiative. The Economic Review and Policy Dialogue was introduced to monitor economies, detect financial vulnerabilities, and consider corrective action. This initiative had mixed success in surveillance but in recent years there have been gradual improvements. Another significant measure, endorsed in 2003 at the ASEAN+3 Finance Ministers Meeting in Manila, was the Asian Bond Markets Initiative to support the development of local currency bond markets.

Making Globalization Work

Globalization was not a new phenomenon. During the fourth ADB decade, the pace of globalization accelerated, supported by the spread of information and communication technology. Globalization soon became the subject of intense debate. Some observers felt that the process had contributed to "a growing divide between the haves and have-nots."[13] Even as world income grew 2.5% a year over the period 1990–2000, critics pointed out that world poverty had decreased less than 1.0% a year.[14] They saw this as a consequence of privatizing public firms, opening markets to foreign investment and competition, removing controls on capital, reducing tariffs and other trade barriers, and removing protection for local industries. Globalization, in their view, was creating sweatshop working conditions, threatening environmental sustainability, and endangering indigenous cultures.

Moreover, a rapid expansion in global financial flows had financed investment but had also heightened risks of instability. These risks became evident during the 1994 Mexican financial crisis and the 1997 Asian financial crisis. Similarly, while international migration had opened up employment opportunities for millions of people, it caused some anxiety among workers and citizens in countries receiving migrants. While trade and transportation had increased employment and made consumer goods cheaper and more widely available, it is a reality that some people lost jobs, at least during the transition.

This debate about globalization coincided with changing perspectives on development policies. In the late 1980s, there had been discussion about a "Washington Consensus" which was often regarded as outlining a neoliberal pro-market agenda (Chapter 8). However, many policy makers in Asia argued that reliance on markets needed to be balanced with appropriate regulation. In this view, globalization could be a force for good, with the potential to enrich everyone, including the poor. But globalization had to be managed if it was to be universally beneficial. To manage and take advantage of globalization, national governments would need to implement appropriate domestic policies and build institutions to ensure that benefits were evenly shared. Governments also had to be prepared to respond to unexpected international events.[15] The finance sector would need supervision to reduce risks posed by short-term capital movements.

In parallel, discussions were under way to improve the international financial architecture because it was agreed that global markets needed

---

[13] Stiglitz, 2002, *Globalization and Its Discontents*.
[14] World poverty based on the $1.90-per-day rate fell from 1,840 million in 1990 to 1,691 million in 2000, based on World Bank PovcalNet data accessed 10 January 2017.
[15] "Minimizing the Risks" in ADB, *Asian Development Outlook 2001*, 179–189.

global governance.[16] Some scholars pointed out that "global governance without global government" could lead to international policies that favored developed countries to the detriment of developing ones.[17] In particular, it was argued that external agencies, including international financial institutions, should not try to impose inappropriate reforms on developing economies. And the multilateral development banks needed to realign their activities to better meet the needs of their borrowers.

The influence of civil society and nongovernment organizations increased during this period. These institutions were generally regarded as taking a close interest in the problems of the poor. They were often involved in a wide range of activities such as relief and rehabilitation, social development, human rights, and environmental issues. The series of international development conferences that took place in the 1990s and 2000s provided wider opportunities for cooperation between governments, donor agencies, and these civil society groups.

There were numerous organized protests against globalization while these debates were taking place. The 50th anniversary of the Bretton Woods institutions in 1995 sparked criticism, including from nongovernment organizations who launched the "50 Years Is Enough" campaign. Many institutions, notably the International Monetary Fund (IMF) and the World Bank, were viewed as promoting market-driven capitalism and were targeted by antiglobalization groups. Demonstrations in 1999 at the WTO Ministerial Conference in Seattle gained widespread media attention. The movement continued—in 2001 at the Genoa Group of Eight (G8) Summit and in 2002 at the annual meetings of the World Bank and the IMF, along with local demonstrations in many developing countries.

There were other concerns about international development assistance as well. In industrialized countries where national budgets were being tightened, the value and effectiveness of aid programs came under close scrutiny. Many donors seemed to be concentrating their aid on better-performing countries to the detriment of the poorest ones. Development agencies were also being criticized for trying to impose their own preferred objectives on borrowing countries. To serve the interest of borrowers and to make best use of constrained development resources, these agencies would need to collaborate more. And since aid was most effective when

---

[16] Miyazawa, 1998, *Towards a New International Financial Architecture*.
[17] Stiglitz, 2002, *Globalization and Its Discontents*.

provided within a sound policy environment, agencies were encouraged to work closely with developing country governments to improve local institutions and strengthen policies.

The debate on globalization continued through the fourth ADB decade. In 2001, WTO members began negotiations in the Doha Round, aiming to lower barriers and facilitate global trade. There were some positive outcomes. In December 2005, for instance, the Sixth WTO Ministerial Conference in Hong Kong, China created a new Aid for Trade program. However, the Doha negotiations remain stalled due to disagreements between developed and developing countries on a range of tariff and nontariff barriers, stemming partly from developing country apprehensions about the possible collapse of their local industries. Further antiglobalization protests would spread from developing to developed countries during the fifth decade (Chapter 13).

Broader View of Development and Millennium Development Goals

In response to this more complex environment, the international community increasingly took a broader view of development. Following the Millennium Summit of the United Nations (UN), the Millennium Development Goals (MDGs) were officially adopted by the international community in 2001. The MDGs reflected a wide agenda. They encapsulated eight goals to be achieved by 2015. Supporting the goals were 17 targets and 48 indicators covering social and human development. All UN member states and over 20 international organizations committed to achieving the MDGs.

The MDGs were not new. However, they were an attempt to refocus attention on the economic and social development of poor countries. Objectives like poverty reduction, universal primary education, and gender equality had long been promoted by the UN. In fact, development had first become a central theme for UN action in the 1960s which had been declared the first "UN Development Decade." Subsequently, similar campaigns were launched. The MDGs were an attempt to bring these various initiatives together within one platform.

By the turn of the century, with the ongoing debates on globalization and development assistance, poverty reduction became the top priority and the concept of poverty was widened. The first MDG target was to halve

$1-a-day poverty. Nevertheless, poverty alleviation was only one part of a multidimensional view of development—reflected in the breadth and ambition of the other MDGs. Likewise, the *World Development Report 2000/2001* viewed poverty as a set of multiple deprivations resulting from economic, political, and social processes. To tackle poverty, the report called for action to increase the opportunities, empowerment, and security of the poor.[18]

Adding to the objectives for global development was a concern to assist "fragile states." Faced with multiple international crises, the international community turned its attention to peacekeeping, conflict resolution, and postconflict reconstruction. The agenda gained added impetus after the 9/11 terrorist attacks in the US. In their international development programs, especially in bilateral assistance, US and Western foreign policy agencies began to pay greater attention to issues related to security and conflict. It was also clear that achieving the MDGs would require special efforts in countries with disappointing development performances, many of which were affected by fragility and conflict.[19]

There were also growing concerns about natural disasters. Early in the new century, developing countries in Asia were hit by a series of catastrophic events. In January 2001, an earthquake in Gujarat, India, left around 19,000 dead and 200,000 people injured. Then, in December 2004, the great Asian tsunami swept away over 230,000 people. And in October 2005, more than 80,000 people died and around 2.8 million were left homeless when an earthquake struck in Pakistan.

These events led to increased international attention to disaster risk management. The First World Conference on Natural Disaster Reduction was held in 1994 in Yokohama, Japan. And the Second World Conference on Disaster Reduction was held in 2005 in Kobe, Japan. Initially, the preparations for the conference had attracted little international attention. However, the Asian tsunami—just a month before the conference— prompted a dramatic increase in interest. Over 4,000 participants attended the opening ceremony addressed by Emperor Akihito.

The international community was also beginning to pay increasing attention to the human security implications of health issues. In 2003 and

---

[18] World Bank, 2001, *World Development Report 2000/2001*.
[19] Cammack et al., 2006, *Donors and the "Fragile States" Agenda: A Survey of Current Thinking and Practice*.

2004, there was widespread public concern across Asia about diseases such as severe acute respiratory syndrome (SARS) and avian influenza. Although these risks soon abated, the outbreaks highlighted the need to strengthen national health systems and ensure a coordinated international response.

The criticism faced by development agencies and the broader international agenda provided a fresh impetus for the aid effectiveness movement, starting in the mid-1990s. To improve the impact of assistance, donor governments and aid agencies resolved to work more closely with each other and with developing countries. At the International Conference on Financing for Development in Monterrey, Mexico, in 2002, the international community agreed to increase its funding for development, while also ensuring that aid would be used more effectively.

A series of international conferences and declarations followed (Table 11.1). The discussions culminated in the 2005 High Level Forum on Aid Effectiveness which endorsed the Paris Declaration, establishing principles on numerous issues including country ownership, harmonization, managing for results, and mutual accountability for the use of aid. These efforts to improve aid effectiveness would continue well into the fifth ADB decade, adding to the already multipronged development agenda (Chapter 13). ADB participated in these forums and committed itself to these principles.

Changing Finance Architecture

The proliferation of development goals was accompanied by increasing diversity in sources of finance.[20] Traditional actors in the aid industry found themselves competing with new agencies providing alternative types of funding. Some of the new activity was South–South cooperation between developing countries themselves supported by middle-income countries seeking to bolster their influence through aid to leverage trade and investment links with other developing countries. There was also a surge in philanthropy with the creation in 2000, for example, of the Bill & Melinda Gates Foundation which received a large donation in 2006 from the renowned global investor Warren Buffett. Another major source of finance was international remittances sent home by workers.

---

[20] Kharas and Rogerson, 2012, *Horizon 2025: Creative Destruction in the Aid Industry*.

Table 11.1: Key International Steps toward Development Effectiveness

Date	Place	Event
1996	Paris	***Shaping the 21st Century: The Role of Development Cooperation*** **is issued** The report by the OECD Development Assistance Committee (DAC) establishes a set of basic goals based on UN conference outcomes for well-being, social development, and environmental sustainability.
2000	New York	**Millennium Declaration signed at the United Nations** This led to the establishment of the eight Millennium Development Goals (MDGs) in 2001.
2002	Monterrey	**International Conference on Financing for Development** The Monterrey Consensus was agreed to which set funding targets to achieve the MDGs and called for a more effective way of using these resources.
2003	Rome	**First High Level Forum on Aid Effectiveness** Donors agreed to improve in-country coordination and to reduce transaction costs for aid recipients.
2005	Paris	**Second High Level Forum on Aid Effectiveness** Donors and developing countries endorsed the Paris Declaration with 56 action-oriented commitments to improve aid quality to be monitored against 14 targets.
2008	Doha	**Second International Conference on Financing for Development** The Doha Conference was a follow-up to the first conference held in 2002 intended to monitor the implementation of the Monterrey Consensus.
2008	Accra	**Third High Level Forum on Aid Effectiveness** A wide range of participants from donor and developing countries and civil society agreed on the Accra Agenda for Action, a framework to support the achievement of the Paris commitments.

continued on next page

Table 11.1 *continued*

Date	Place	Event
2011	Busan	**Fourth High Level Forum on Aid Effectiveness**
		Steps were taken to evaluate progress already made toward achieving aid delivery and to define an agenda for the future.
2015	Addis Ababa	**Third International Conference on Financing for Development**
		The conference reflected a considerable shift from the 2002 Monterrey Consensus by considering a much broader approach to development financing based on tax, investment, and international public finance.
2015	New York	**Sustainable Development Goals established**
		These encompass 17 goals and 169 targets agreed at the United Nations summit.

OECD = Organisation for Economic Co-operation and Development.
Sources: Reports on aid effectiveness at OECD, Development Co-operation Directorate. Effective Development Co-operation. http://www.oecd.org/dac/effectiveness/

The widening agenda gave greater importance to organizations concerned with the social impact of development. A more diverse set of institutions, including donors and civil society, came to be better placed to exert their influence on the management of multilateral development banks. On the one hand, this put pressure on multilateral development banks to reform. On the other, this further exposed them to expanding demands which stretched their capacity and diffused their operational focus. ADB was expected to respond to these pressures.

A major issue for development finance in the 1990s was the accumulated debt owed to multilateral and bilateral aid agencies. The poorest countries had little prospect of repaying this debt. Prompted partly by advocacy from civil society, in 1996, the IMF and the World Bank proposed the Heavily Indebted Poor Countries (HIPC) Initiative which offered debt relief and low-interest loans to the most indebted countries.[21] But one-off relief was no guarantee against future debt buildup. In 1999, the HIPC Initiative was

---

[21] The only ADB member qualifying for HIPC debt relief was Afghanistan (ADF borrower).

modified to incorporate additional objectives of debt sustainability and poverty reduction—requiring beneficiary countries to prepare "poverty reduction strategy papers" indicating plans to reduce poverty and stimulate growth.[22]

The concerns about debt buildup, combined with rising demands for funds to achieve the MDGs, intensified the debate on whether development assistance should be provided as loans or grants. Previous loans had sometimes saddled countries with large amounts of debt. However, shifting toward grants would also have disadvantages: in the recipient countries, it may mean smaller amount of financing for projects and a higher grant element could increase aid dependency; in donor countries, it could reduce public support for overseas aid. This debate would affect the work of the multilateral development banks, encouraging them to modify the terms of their financial assistance and to provide more grants and debt relief (Chapter 12).

The Fourth ADB Decade

ADB thus began its fourth decade against a background of strengthening confidence in Asia, growing globalization, and a widening development agenda. Following the serious but temporary setback of the Asian financial crisis, the Bank designed strategies to respond to rapid changes in the region while also adjusting to new international development thinking and balancing the objectives of poverty reduction and economic growth. In view of the widespread criticism of international finance institutions in the 1990s, ADB would also need to demonstrate greater effectiveness in aid delivery. Moreover, since many borrowing countries were at or approaching middle-income levels, policies were required that considered the needs of expanding numbers of these borrowers. ADB's work would therefore not only have to respond to the increasing demand for funds but also address the revolution of rising expectations in Asia.

---

[22] The same documents were subsequently used to anchor IMF-supported programs for low-income countries to allow for the implementation of strategies to achieve sustained poverty reduction and growth. With the HIPC Initiative almost completed, and the World Bank delinking its concessional financing support to the International Development Association (IDA) countries from the poverty reduction strategy approach in 2014, in June 2015 the IMF adopted a more flexible poverty reduction strategy policy for its engagement with low-income countries.

Philippine President Corazon C. Aquino inaugurates the second ADB headquarters with President Kimimasa Tarumizu, Manila, Philippines, 31 May 1991.

Nanpu Bridge project, cofinanced by ADB in Shanghai, People's Republic of China. Project approved 28 May 1991.

The Lao Bao International Border Gate between Viet Nam and the Lao People's Democratic Republic is part of an ADB-funded project for the Greater Mekong Subregion (GMS) economic cooperation program, which began in 1992. It promotes economic cooperation between six GMS countries through improved connectivity and competitiveness.

The ADB-funded Kali Gandaki "A" Hydroelectric Project in Nepal has effectively contributed to economic growth by producing approximately 592 gigawatt-hours annually which benefits 4,142 households connected to the grid. Project approved 23 July 1996.

The Central Asia Regional Economic Cooperation (CAREC) Program was formed in 1996 as part of the Regional Cooperation and Integration Program. ADB staff visit the Taraz–Korday road section of the CAREC Transit Corridor 1, Zhambyl Oblast, Kazakhstan.

United Nations High Commissioner for Refugees Sadako Ogata visits ADB, 5 January 1998.

ADB President Mitsuo Sato (*left*) meets World Bank President James Wolfensohn, Manila, Philippines, 6 February 1998.

The Tonle Sap Poverty Reduction and Smallholder Development Project in Cambodia, cofinanced by the Government of Finland, helped farmers generate more income through increased agricultural production. Poverty reduction became ADB's primary goal in 1999.

ADB President Tadao Chino visits urban communities in Muntinlupa, Philippines, 2 April 2002.

Hamidullah Durrani (*right*) of the Afghanistan Resident Mission visits a concrete pole factory in Kabul. ADB's reengagement with Afghanistan began in 2002.

ADB President Tadao Chino visits a water project in the Kyrgyz Republic, 5 November 2004.

Nam Theun 2 Hydroelectric Project, Lao People's Democratic Republic. Project approved 4 April 2005.

CHAPTER 12
Fourth Decade (1997–2006)

ADB: The Widening Development Agenda

"Dynamic changes in the region also mean that ADB must change. To assist our developing member countries in achieving the Millennium Development Goals, the new era of development requires that ADB become more relevant, more responsive, and more focused on results."

– Haruhiko Kuroda,
Address to the ADB Annual Meeting, 2005

The fourth decade was a period of important change for ADB. The institution needed to respond to multiple demands. The Asian financial crisis had highlighted the plight of the poorest people in the region. This encouraged the development community to focus on poverty. But poverty-focused interventions did not always meet the expectations of middle-income borrowers. As the international development agenda evolved, the Bank needed to do more to support human development, protect the environment, promote economic growth, and strengthen regional programs. There was also criticism of the Bank's effectiveness, especially as lending stagnated. Relations with stakeholders were sometimes difficult.

ADB had three Presidents during the decade. Mitsuo Sato guided ADB through the Asian financial crisis (Chapter 10). The postcrisis period was managed by Tadao Chino, who became President in 1999 and introduced key internal reforms. Haruhiko Kuroda, who became President in 2005, consolidated the changes to make ADB "a more relevant, responsive, and results-oriented institution."

Tadao Chino

Tadao Chino arrived in Manila in January 1999 when Mitsuo Sato retired after 5 years as President. Like his predecessors, Chino had spent most of his career in Japan's Ministry of Finance. He had held several posts in the banking, budget, and international finance bureaus in the ministry. In 1991, he became Vice-Minister of Finance for International Affairs. He left the ministry in 1993 but continued to hold the post of special advisor.

Chino had been closely involved in the establishment of ADB when he was seconded to the United Nations Economic Commission for Asia and the Far East (ECAFE) in the 1960s. In his remarks to the Board when he assumed office, Chino recalled his early days in ECAFE, preparing documents for the expert group discussion in 1964 on the establishment of the Bank. He spoke of his strong emotion later watching the proceedings of the ADB Inaugural Meeting in 1966 on television while on assignment in northern Japan. When nominated as a candidate for President, Chino felt this was his destiny.

Chino's presidency was especially welcomed in the Mekong and Central Asian member countries. In the early 1990s, as Japan's Vice-Minister of Finance, Chino had overseen bilateral assistance to these countries. He was warmly received on his official trips. On one occasion, he was presented with a horse when he visited the Kyrgyz Republic—though he did not take the horse back to Manila. Senior Uzbek officials noted his personal style; compared with visiting representatives of multilateral development bank from Washington, DC who were inclined to begin lecturing on policy issues, Chino took care to listen to the government's concerns. Indeed, this is the tradition from the first President Watanabe's time.

Chino brought a new approach to the leadership in ADB—modest and low-key. As he said to Julian Payne, then Dean of the ADB Board of Directors: "I live in this huge house; nobody needs a big house. I sometimes wonder. When I go back to Japan I would like to live in my little hut on the river. My bedroom is bigger than the hut I need."[1] Chino was comfortable when visiting developing countries and meeting groups of street children in Asia. Staffers recall him as personable and friendly—willing to take part in karaoke singing. He was also prepared to be flexible in order to achieve corporate goals. He was sincere and hardworking, often staying late in the office, sometimes (to the dismay of his personal staff) even until 3 a.m.

Chino led ADB through a difficult period. Buoyed by its rapid response to the Asian financial crisis, the Bank went through what some staff referred to as a "self-congratulatory" phase. After the crisis, the organization flirted with the idea of going back to "business as usual," not appreciating that

---

[1] ADB, 2009, *Reflections and Beyond*, 156.

large borrowing members like the People's Republic of China (PRC), India, and Indonesia wanted different products and lower transaction costs. Facing greater public scrutiny from civil society and contentious relations with donors, Chino often had to address internal and external pressures. In doing so, he succeeded in introducing reforms which future Presidents would build on.

Immediately into his tenure, Chino needed to address the Bank's tight financial position. In response to the 1997 crisis, ADB had needed to raise more funds and the borrowing program had increased from $2.6 billion to $5.6 billion (Chapter 10). ADB raised a record $9.6 billion in capital markets in 1999. Meanwhile, the Bank's own net income was under pressure, partly due to a fall in yields on its liquid asset investments and the higher cost of borrowing.

To strengthen the finances, ADB either had to increase its capital base or raise loan charges. Management sought Board approval to increase loan charges by 20 basis points beginning in 2000.[2] This was not an easy decision. Developing country members were especially concerned. Chino realized that if ADB was to respond to the region's growing investment needs he would need to build support for another general capital increase (GCI)—after the last one in 1994.

At the same time, while Asia had recovered more quickly from the crisis than expected, millions had slipped back into poverty. Even countries not directly hit by the crisis still had significant numbers of poor. Chino knew that ADB would have to pay more attention to poverty reduction. For him, the need to focus on the issue was much more than an intellectual response to the growing importance of poverty in the global development agenda (Chapter 11). Chino was a devout Buddhist who felt deeply for the poor. He believed that poverty reduction needed to be the core purpose of development finance.

---

[2] ADB, 1999, *Review of OCR Loan Charges*. The Board of Directors concluded that the lending spread would be raised by 20 basis points, from 0.4% to 0.6% per year, on all outstanding pool-based loans (both existing and new loans). The increased spread would also apply to new public sector loans under the market-based lending window. A new front-end fee of 1% per year would be charged on new loans, with borrowers retaining an option to include this charge in the loan. And the commitment fee for new program loans would carry a flat 0.75% annual fee instead of the progressive rate, as before. The commitment fee for new project loans would remain as before. The new loan charge policy would take effect from 1 January 2000.

A Corporate Strategy

Soon after assuming office, Chino initiated a major review of the Bank's work. Following the review, the Board in November 1999 approved the new Poverty Reduction Strategy (PRS). The PRS approach introduced a major change into ADB's strategic framework. Henceforth, poverty would not just be one of many objectives but, rather, the "overarching goal." The achievement of this goal would be based on three strategic pillars: pro-poor sustainable economic growth, social development, and good governance. Staff privately observed that Chino may have personally preferred to focus on infrastructure for sustained economic growth and perhaps did not believe in setting multiple pillars. But he adopted the PRS with the aim of building donor support for Asian Development Fund (ADF) replenishments.

After the PRS was approved, Chino declared that "this single-mindedness of approach is radically changing how ADB does business, with all ADB staff members making poverty reduction their priority." The Bank prepared an action plan and increased the emphasis on poverty reduction in country partnership agreements and project proposals. By 2001, the target was to have least at 40% of new public sector lending be poverty interventions. This was an attempt to cut through the growing problem of goal congestion in the widening international development agenda (Chapter 11).

In reality, ADB could not be quite as single-minded as Chino intended. The Bank was also expected to incorporate the objectives of the eight Millennium Development Goals (MDGs) into its programs.[3] This meant looking beyond income poverty to take into account non-income considerations such as deprivations in health, education, water, and sanitation. To do this, ADB identified priority sectors. As part of the PRS, four cross-cutting concerns were promoted: environmental sustainability, gender equality, good governance, and private sector development.[4]

About 4 years after the approval of the PRS, a review was undertaken in 2004 to assess progress. The review questioned the 40% target, pointing out that some projects not primarily envisaged as antipoverty measures might turn out to have a greater impact on poverty than those that were. Moreover, the target tended to encourage the incorporation of poverty

---

[3] ADB formally adopted the MDGs in its operations in 2002 (ADB, 2003, Annual Report for 2002, 36).

[4] The priority sectors were agriculture and rural development, social sectors (education, health and population, social protection, and urban development), infrastructure (transport, communications, and energy), and finance.

activities into projects in a somewhat artificial way and focus attention on project inputs rather than outcomes. As a result, in 2004, the Board approved the Enhanced Poverty Reduction Strategy. The enhanced strategy retained the three main strategic pillars of the PRS and added a new thematic priority of capacity development. Importantly, the enhanced strategy did not include the 40% target.[5]

While implementing the PRS, the Bank was also preparing its Long-Term Strategic Framework (LTSF).[6] This was part of Chino's objective of building support for a GCI. Following earlier efforts in the 1980s (Chapters 7 and 9), the LTSF would be ADB's third major corporate strategy document. As with previous reviews, the process of preparing the new strategy involved extensive stakeholder consultations and was guided by an external advisory panel of eminent persons. As well as drawing on the PRS and a private sector development strategy formulated in 2000, the LTSF took up findings from its recent studies of developing Asia such as the 1997 review of *Emerging Asia: Changes and Challenges*.

The new framework was published in 2001 as *Moving the Poverty Reduction Agenda Forward in Asia and the Pacific*.[7] The LTSF, being a corporate strategy, was a high-level document. It addressed the recently endorsed MDGs and set out the broad directions for ADB's work until 2015. The LTSF retained the vision of "an Asia and Pacific free of poverty" and focused ADB interventions in three core areas: sustainable economic growth, inclusive social development, and governance for effective policies and institutions. It also identified three cross-cutting themes similar to the pillars in the PRS.[8]

The Bank originally planned to implement the LTSF through three 5-year medium-term strategies (MTSs). Two were subsequently implemented: MTS I, for the period 2001–2005, was approved in 2001; MTS II, for the period 2006–2010, would be adopted in 2006 during the tenure of Haruhiko Kuroda.

---

[5] ADB, 2004, *Review of the Asian Development Bank's Poverty Reduction Strategy*.
[6] ADB, 2001, *Moving the Poverty Reduction Agenda Forward in Asia and the Pacific: The Long-Term Strategic Framework of the Asian Development Bank (2001–2015)*.
[7] ADB, 2001, *Moving the Poverty Reduction Agenda Forward in Asia and the Pacific: The Long-Term Strategic Framework of the Asian Development Bank (2001–2015)*.
[8] The LTSF identified three cross-cutting themes: (i) promoting the role of the private sector in development, (ii) supporting regional cooperation and integration, and (iii) addressing environmental sustainability. It further specified four operating principles: (i) ensuring country leadership and ownership of the development agenda, (ii) taking a long-term approach to development assistance, (iii) enhancing strategic alliances and partnerships, and (iv) measuring development impact.

The LTSF reflected the development priorities of the period. But the combination of the LTSF and the PRS, the review of the PRS, and the two MTS documents created overlapping goals. Sometimes, Bank staff found it hard to fit all of these goals together.

Organizational Changes

Soon after assuming office, Chino realized that the institution needed a fundamental reorganization. ADB members were faced with a more complex development agenda. Borrowers and donor countries expected the Bank to be more responsive to their concerns. In addition, other multilateral and bilateral organizations wanted ADB to enter into stronger partnerships with them. In response, Chino initiated a series of reforms, the first of which was to increase the Bank's presence in borrowing countries.

ADB had long endorsed the principle of country focus and had made efforts to engage with borrowers more closely. Nevertheless, many of its activities still seemed to be determined by decisions taken in Manila rather than in the borrowing countries. The Bank's sector divisions, which looked after operational matters like physical infrastructure and social sectors, agriculture, and finance, still largely drove the programming of assistance to countries.

To move ADB closer to member countries, Chino expanded the role of resident missions. In 2000, he issued the first policy on resident missions since 1986.[9,10] Rather than being concerned primarily with project administration, resident missions would now be expected to engage in broad strategic and policy support.[11] Over time, the changes began to take effect. Although not all of aims of the policy were achieved quickly, by the end of the fourth ADB decade, the Bank had become more responsive. to the needs of borrowing countries with whom ADB would do its work. Reflecting this approach, ADB renamed its country strategy documents as country partnership strategies in the early 2000s.

The number of resident missions grew rapidly with more staff and higher budgets, allowing a decentralization of functions. During the fourth decade,

---

[9] ADB, 1986, *Establishment of Bank Resident Offices in DMCs*.
[10] ADB, 2000, *Resident Mission Policy*.
[11] ADB, 2000, *Resident Mission Policy*.

ADB established 14 resident missions.[12] The opening of an offices in the PRC in 2000 was a significant step. The PRC was among the largest borrowers. The new resident mission helped ADB strengthen relationships with the government, the local funding community, and other key organizations. The same year, ADB also opened the Philippines Country Office in its headquarters in Manila.

In 2004, to work more closely with Pacific island countries, the Bank replaced the South Pacific Regional Mission in Vanuatu with the South Pacific Subregional Office in Fiji and in 2005 opened the Pacific Liaison and Coordination Office in Sydney. Other forms of local presence including extended missions in Jakarta and Seoul in the wake of the financial crisis in 1997 and in Gujarat following the earthquake in 2001.

Strengthening resident missions was part of Chino's plan to boost ADB's organizational capacity to deliver the new agenda. In January 2001, Chino oversaw a review that would form the basis for a major reorganization.[13] At the heart of the institutional change, which took effect in January 2002, was the creation of five new regional departments—for East and Central Asia, the Mekong, the Pacific, South Asia, and Southeast Asia. Sector divisions were grouped within the regional departments. Instead of having to deal with separate contact points for country programs and projects, government officials could now deal with one focal point in ADB.[14]

In addition, following approval of the Private Sector Development Strategy, the Private Sector Operations Department was established in January 2002. The new Department recruited new staff, most of whom were from the private sector with commercial banking experience. As a result of this and other changes after the adoption of a new private sector strategy, the volume of transactions began to pick up in 2003.

The LTSF envisaged ADB as a regional knowledge leader. The 2001 reorganization introduced changes to promote this approach. In 2002, the Regional and Sustainable Development Department was established. This knowledge center was expected to encourage technical excellence and strengthen sector and thematic work as well as support ADB regional

---

[12] These were in Kazakhstan, Uzbekistan, and Sri Lanka in 1997; the Kyrgyz Republic in 1999; Mongolia, the PRC, the Philippines, and the Lao People's Democratic Republic in 2000; Afghanistan and Papua New Guinea in 2002; Azerbaijan, Tajikistan, and Timor-Leste in 2003; and Thailand in 2004.

[13] ADB, 2001, *Reorganization of Asian Development Bank*.

[14] ADB, 2003, *Implementation of the Reorganization of Asian Development Bank*.

development functions. To oversee its knowledge products, the Bank established sector and thematic committees. In 2003, a fourth Vice-President was appointed to guide activities in knowledge management and sustainable development.

Chino was also concerned about staffing. As the Bank went beyond being a project finance bank to becoming a more broad-based development institution and addressing multiple goals, there were increasing pressures on staff. A human resources strategy had been prepared in 1996, but it needed to be revised.[15] In 2004, the Board approved a new strategy aiming for more merit-based and transparent human resources policies.[16] The MDGs had endorsed gender equality targets, so ADB came under scrutiny for gender balance within the institution. In 2003, therefore, Chino had introduced the Bank's second gender action program. He would later take pride in raising the representation of women within ADB during his 6-year tenure—from 19% to 30% among international staff and from 5.1% to 8.6% among senior staff. The first woman Vice-President, Khempheng Pholsena from the Lao People's Democratic Republic, was appointed in 2004 during Chino's presidency.

Assisting Fragile States

The growing country focus of Bank activities was reflected in support for activities in postconflict situations. During the fourth ADB decade, the international community gave increasing priority to issues of security and peace (Chapter 11). This shift in priorities became one of Chino's abiding concerns. One of his lasting contributions was to focus attention on problems in fragile and conflict-affected states. He participated in several international conferences on these issues and visited many affected countries.

In Sri Lanka, for example, following almost 20 years of armed conflict between the government and the Liberation Tigers of Tamil Eelam, ADB helped with the rehabilitation of infrastructure from 2001 to 2005. Immediately after the February 2002 cease-fire, Chino visited Sri Lanka, including conflict-affected areas and did so again in March 2003. He was struck by the improvements he witnessed even in a short time. At the 2003 Annual Meeting in Manila, he noted that peace dividends had

---

[15] ADB, 1996, *Human Resources Strategy Paper*.
[16] ADB, 2004, *Human Resources Strategy*.

been realized but more needed to be done to achieve a better future for the country. In Tajikistan, following independence after the breakup of the Soviet Union in 1991 and the havoc during the 1992–1997 civil war, the Bank encouraged the transition to a market economy, assisted postconflict rehabilitation, and helped rebuild infrastructure. In Timor-Leste, ADB first provided assistance as part of the UN-administered postconflict support program, and then provided support for reconstruction after Timor-Leste joined the Bank in 2002.

Of all ADB's postconflict programs, the assistance to Afghanistan after December 2001 was the most significant. Afghanistan, a founding member of ADB in 1966, received a total of over $95 million in concessional funding until 1979. However, ADB operations were suspended following the Soviet occupation in 1979. For 2 decades, Afghanistan was ravaged by external aggression and civil war. In December 2001, following the signing of the Bonn Agreement which led to the establishment of an interim administration in Afghanistan following the fall of Taliban rule earlier that year, ADB moved quickly to provide assistance to Afghanistan.

ADB returned to Afghanistan on a cold, misty morning in February 2002. A Bank team arrived in Kabul for the first formal meetings with an administration in the country in 23 years. Soon after, Chino visited Afghanistan to meet with Chairman Hamid Karzai. ADB reengaged with the country amid severe security risks. In September 2003, an antigovernment group attacked and killed several members of Afghan security forces protecting an ADB contractor's road construction team on the Kabul–Kandahar road. Not long after in November 2003, a bomb exploded at the Intercontinental Kabul where Bank staff were staying although no one was hurt. The Bank enhanced security measures and continued to do so.

Over the years, Afghanistan had built up arrears with ADB. To pay these off, in 2002, the Government of the United Kingdom stepped in with a special contribution of $18 million. This cleared the way for the Bank to approve a $150 million postconflict program (the amount was later revised to $167.5 million) in December 2002—the first for Afghanistan by an international financial institution for over 20 years. In the same year, ADB established a resident mission in Kabul. Between 2002 and 2006, the Bank provided $1 billion in financial assistance, almost 90% of which came from the ADF. Subsequently, during Kuroda's term, ADB participated in an international program of debt relief for Afghanistan (Chapter 14).

The international community also expected quick responses following mega disasters in the region (Chapter 11). In January 2001, after a major earthquake in Gujarat, ADB sent an emergency mission. Within 2 months, the Board had approved a $500 million loan to finance urgent reconstruction and help restore economic activities—the largest ADB loan for earthquake recovery in a single country. But the most severe natural disaster to hit the region in many years was the Asian tsunami of December 2004 which affected 14 countries. The tsunami struck at the end of Chino's tenure, so the main ADB response came during the leadership of President Kuroda.

During Chino's presidency, ADB stepped up support for health-related crises. In 2003, the severe acute respiratory syndrome (SARS) epidemic sent shock waves through the world and even affected the region's growth projections (Chapter 11). The Bank provided regional technical assistance to strengthen the capacity of health systems to control outbreaks of SARS as well as assistance to combat HIV/AIDS.

ADB became increasingly involved in addressing challenges in fragile states. A new policy paper, *Approach to Weakly Performing Developing Member Countries*, was prepared for an ADF donor meeting in Lisbon in 2004. The aim of the revised approach was to make ADB activities more effective in countries where progress had been slowed by conflict and other disruptive events. In 2004, ADB adopted its new Disaster and Emergency Assistance Policy.[17] This policy discussed the Bank's planned interventions in emergency preparedness and response to natural and nonnatural disasters such as conflicts, food prices, and health crises.[18]

Concerns for Sustainable Development and Governance

The PRS and the LTSF highlighted themes cutting across operational sectors such as good environmental practices, improved governance, and gender equality. The Bank aimed to incorporate these in its operations through the preparation of a series of policy and strategy documents. Shifts in ADB's approach toward cross-cutting concerns were part of efforts to address criticisms that the multilateral development banks were contributing to globalization risks (Chapter 11).

---

[17] ADB, 2004, *Disaster and Emergency Assistance Policy*.
[18] In 2003, for example, ADB provided support to help member countries respond to the avian influenza.

ADB's policies on environmental issues had evolved along with international thinking. During the 1980s, the aim was mostly to ensure that Bank activities would cause "no significant harm." During the 1990s, however, environmental concerns began to attract much more attention in international discussions about development policy. In response, ADB became increasingly active in promoting sustainable development. A 2000 review of the energy policy committed the Bank to promoting clean energy, supporting Kyoto Protocol mechanisms for greenhouse gas abatement, and financing renewable energy projects.[19] Part of ADB's work was carried out in collaboration with the Global Environment Facility, an international partnership of official agencies, civil society organizations, and the private sector which funds projects to improve the global environment.

In 2002, ADB introduced an environmental policy that required it to go beyond an emphasis on safeguards and to offer support on environmental management to key development sectors.[20] The objective was to support national institutions and build capacity for environmental and natural resource management. The policy committed ADB to integrating environmental considerations across its operations.

Another cross-cutting issue was good governance, particularly strengthening collaboration with civil society (Chapter 11). In 1998, the 1987 policy on cooperation with nongovernment organizations (NGOs) was updated.[21] Other governance concerns included corruption and money laundering. A 1998 policy addressed ways of dealing with identified cases of corruption and led to the establishment in 1999 of the Anticorruption Unit, now renamed the Office of Anticorruption and Integrity.[22]

Over the years, ADB further broadened the governance agenda it aimed to address. The first governance action plan was approved in 2000.[23] This led

---

[19] ADB, 2000, *Energy 2000*.
[20] To reduce poverty through environmentally sustainable development, the policy highlighted five main elements: (i) promoting environment and natural resource management interventions to reduce poverty directly, (ii) assisting developing member countries to mainstream environmental considerations in economic growth, (iii) helping maintain global and regional life support systems that underpin future development prospects, (iv) building partnerships to maximize the impact of ADB lending and non-lending activities, and (v) integrating environmental considerations across all ADB operations.
[21] ADB, 1998, *Cooperation between the Asian Development Bank and Nongovernment Organizations*.
[22] ADB, 1998, *ADB Anticorruption Policy*.
[23] ADB, 2000, *Promoting Good Governance: ADB's Medium-term Agenda and Action Plan*.

to the Bank preparing general country governance assessments to increase opportunities for dialogue. A 2005 review found that these assessments were rather broad, so a second plan was approved in 2006.

The approach to gender had shifted even before the PRS came into effect. ADB established its first gender policy, called the Role of Women in Development, in 1985. This policy was designed to focus on well-being and empowerment of women through such projects as girls' education and women's health. It was under the policy that ADB hired its first gender specialist. In 1998, the Board approved a new policy on gender and development in which the emphasis was on the "mainstreaming" of gender considerations.[24] This policy recognized gender as a cross-cutting issue influencing all social and economic processes. For instance, the design of rural road projects should consider the needs of women, such as their access to jobs, markets, education and health services, to maximize benefits to the community. The policy provided an impetus for change and the proportion of ADB loans and grants addressing gender concerns rose from less than 40% in 1998 to 70% in 2003. Further efforts, including the setting of corporate targets, led to this ratio averaging about 70% during 2013–2015.

More Accountable and Effective Assistance

ADB thus attempted to involve civil society and address international criticism by incorporating key cross-cutting themes into its work. But relations with some stakeholders remained uneasy, especially early in the decade.

In 2000, at the Annual Meeting in Chiang Mai, Thailand, almost 3,000 Thai activists, farmers, and students gathered, chanting slogans like "ADB go to hell" and blocking traffic. They were protesting what they saw as threats to their livelihoods caused by ADB-funded projects, particularly dams that had displaced farmers and fisherfolk, and a large wastewater treatment plant planned for Klong Dan, near Bangkok, under the Samut Prakarn Wastewater Management Project. They demanded that ADB stop funding the plant. During a news conference Chino promised that he would study their demands. The Bank undertook its first ever independent inspection case into problems for this project in 2001 and 2002. The project was later cancelled by the Thai government.

---

[24] ADB, 1998, *The Bank's Policy on Gender and Development*.

The episode reinforced the need for ADB to enhance accountability and respond better to stakeholder complaints. Chino set up a high-level committee in the Bank to consider the issues. Subsequently, ADB took steps to strengthen its cooperation with NGOs. In 2001, the Bank established the NGO Center in its headquarters which organized consultations at the 2001 Annual Meeting in Honolulu.[25] The meeting was attended by 92 NGO representatives.

In 2003, the Bank introduced its new Accountability Mechanism which had two complementary phases: an informal consultation phase for people affected by ADB projects and a compliance review phase to investigate alleged violations of operational arrangements.[26] ADB was the first multilateral development bank to establish such a two-phase mechanism for both private and public sector operations.[27] Speaking at the 2003 Annual Meeting in Manila, Chino said that the mechanism would "improve ADB's development effectiveness, project quality, and accountability by enhancing our responsiveness to the concerns of project-affected people and ensuring fairness to all stakeholders."

ADB continued to engage with civil society to achieve environmental and social objectives. Measures would later be strengthened under Haruhiko Kuroda and Takehiko Nakao through improved public communications and disclosure. Nonetheless, like other international financial institutions, the Bank can expect criticisms that challenge the organization to improve its performance (Box 12.1).

The development community was also facing criticisms that aid programs were not delivering results (Chapter 11). A series of international conferences discussed ways of addressing these problems by emphasizing "results-based management." In 2003, following the 2002 International Conference on Financing for Development in Monterrey, Mexico, ADB introduced its Managing for Development Results (MfDR) framework.[28] The aim was to monitor performance and align the Bank's approach with a set of well-defined results.

---

[25] The NGO and Civil Society Center serves as a window for ADB's engagement with civil society organizations and works closely with operations in strengthening civil society participation in ADB programs and projects.

[26] ADB, 2003, *Review of the Inspection Function*.

[27] The compliance advisor ombudsman of the International Finance Corporation was the first to introduce problem solving for private sector operations. ADB was the first to introduce problem solving for both public and private sector operations.

[28] A discussion of the steps ADB took toward strengthening effectiveness is in "Policy Overview: Improving Effectiveness" in ADB, *Annual Report 2006*, 21–35.

Box 12.1: Working with Stakeholders: Example of the Nam Theun 2 Project

During its fourth decade, the Asian Development Bank (ADB) supported major projects which brought together many cross-cutting issues. One of these was the 2005 Nam Theun 2 Hydroelectric Project in the Lao People's Democratic Republic (Lao PDR). This was one of the first major operations cofinanced with the World Bank. The project was funded by a total of 27 international institutions. ADB financing included a $20 million public sector loan to the Government of the Lao PDR along with $100 million loan and guarantee to the project company.

A key feature of the Nam Theun 2 project was a comprehensive set of environmental and social measures designed to ensure compliance with safeguards. Since about 6,300 local people were to be displaced, communities living near the project began providing inputs to planning in 1996 and were consulted in several hundred public meetings. Communities benefited from high-standard resettlement programs and contributed to the design of their new houses and villages.

The project has operated since 2010. The largest hydroelectric project so far in the Lao PDR, it exports power to Thailand as well as to local areas. The $1.25 billion project set a standard for the construction of good dams and underscored the importance of the private sector, regional cooperation, and stakeholder consultations between development institutions. Some revenues are earmarked for environmental purposes. For example, the project helps preserve the Nakai Nam Theun National Protected Area, one of Southeast Asia's few remaining intact tropical rainforests.

The Nam Theun 2 project has its critics. During the development phase, civil society organizations questioned whether the dam would meet the standards set for the project. More recently, in 2015, a group of nongovernment organizations cited evidence to show that the project "has failed to bring intended development benefits, and instead has unleashed a range of negative impacts on the affected populations."[a] Regular socioeconomic monitoring updates on the project are issued by the World Bank and ADB outlining ongoing measures to support local communities affected by the project. In 2013, household surveys indicated that the majority (86%) of resettled families felt that they were better off than before resettlement with primary school enrollment up threefold and child mortality cut by more than half. A 2014–2015 survey confirmed that the average consumption of resettled communities significantly exceeds the rural average.

[a] *The Nation*. 2015. "Ten Years after Nam Theun 2, Development Banks Back in Spotlight." 8 April. http://www.nationmultimedia.com/opinion/Ten-years-after-NAM-THEUN-2-development-banks-back-30257606.html

Source: ADB project documents and updates.

In February 2004, the Results Management Unit was established and the first MfDR action plan was approved. Henceforth, programs were increasingly defined in terms of expected outputs, outcomes, and impacts. MfDR action plans would increasingly be seen as important documents within the organization.

An essential component of large development programs is evaluation. In 1978, ADB had established a postevaluation office. In 1999, its mandate was expanded and it was renamed the Operations Evaluation Office. In March 2001, the office was upgraded to become the Operations Evaluation Department. In 2003, the Board approved a new evaluation policy through which the department would report not to the President but, rather, to the Board Development Effectiveness Committee.[29] Management responses to the department's recommendations evolved over time from a "no comment" nature to carefully considered commitments to specific improvements which would be monitored through the Management Action Record System.[30] In 2009, reflecting its increasing independence, the Operations Evaluation Department was renamed the Independent Evaluation Department.

In response to concerns of borrowing countries and donors, in 2003 the Bank launched its Innovation and Efficiency Initiative to help make the organization more results oriented. A working group identified bottlenecks in the operational cycle. Country strategies needed to focus more on project pipelines and on results. It was also seen as important to simplify internal procedures to reduce the high transaction costs of dealing with ADB. In 2004, the Bank further streamlined its business processes—in particular, simplifying procurement and documentation requirements. Kuroda's presidency saw further innovation and efficiency measures, particularly for lending instruments and modalities.

Three Asian Development Fund Replenishments

To finance the various multiple development objectives, ADB needed resources. During the fourth ADB decade, three ADF replenishments were completed: ADF VII in 1997 for an agreed total replenishment amount of $6.3 billion (of which $2.61 billion were pledged donor contributions); ADF VIII in 2000 for an agreed total replenishment amount of

---

[29] ADB, 2003, *Enhancing Independence and Effectiveness*.
[30] This system was under the leadership of the Managing Director General.

$5.645 billion (of which $2.905 billion were pledged donor contributions); and ADF IX in 2004 for an agreed total replenishment amount of $7.035 billion (of which $3.347 billion were pledged donor contributions) (Appendix A2.17). But successive rounds of negotiations were becoming more complex and there were tensions between Bank Management and donors. Donor delegations steadily widened the scope of the discussions, often raising issues that went beyond broad policy matters to include the Bank's internal management. This led to some difficult ADF meetings.

Negotiations for ADF VII (1997–2000) spanned a total of seven meetings before being completed in 1997. For the first time, regional and nonregional members contributed similar amounts. Following the negotiations, in December 1998, the Bank adopted a policy for borrowing members to graduate from different forms of assistance—from ADF to ordinary capital resources (OCR) lending, and eventually out of OCR lending (Chapter 10).[31] This policy recognized that access to concessional funds should gradually be reduced and eventually cease as countries developed. As a result, the status of eligibility for both ADF and OCR changed for many borrowers. In particular, four members (Hong Kong, China; the Republic of Korea; Singapore; and Taipei,China) graduated out of regular Bank assistance although they remained eligible for emergency assistance.

The seventh ADF replenishment round (ADF VIII, 2001–2004) involved negotiations during five meetings. From the outset, donors established their priorities. As part of the PRS process, they wanted to see greater support for activities such as private sector development, gender issues, and the environment. They also called for stronger partnerships with other development organizations and recipient governments. Overall, they wanted ADB to improve its internal governance with the introduction of better evaluation systems and greater delegation to resident missions.

Donors were also concerned about the way ADF resources were allocated. There was increasing interest in the idea of adopting "performance-based allocation" approaches in the delivery of aid. Reflecting the assessment that assistance is most effective in countries which have strong policies and institutions, donors stressed that scarce resources should be allocated according to performance as well as need. In March 2001, ADB introduced a performance-based allocation policy to direct ADF resources to poor

---

[31] ADB, 1998, *A Graduation Policy for the Bank's DMCs*.

countries and to situations where the funds would be used most effectively.[32] Donors also agreed that ADB should devote ADF resources to subregional cooperation.

Negotiations over the eighth ADF replenishment (ADF IX, 2005–2008) opened uneasily in late 2003. Donors continued to doubt the Bank's effectiveness. Anticipating donor concerns, Chino in his opening statement explained what ADB had done to make itself more accountable, transparent, and efficient and detailed the impact of the recent reorganization. He outlined commitments for further reform in such areas as project quality, human resources, the devolution of responsibility to resident missions, and transparency in Management appointments. The statement got the negotiations off to a good start. Chino's speech was well received. Donors, however, promptly asked that a time-bound agenda for implementation be provided.

In 2004, negotiations for ADF IX were completed. The most important change for the ADF IX was establishing a grant program. This change was controversial. Some sharp differences of view emerged during discussions between delegates attending the ADF meetings. Offering grants rather than concessional loans would benefit borrowers and reduce the prospect of debt accumulation although there was a risk of encouraging dependency.[33] These views reflected the international discussions of the time (Chapter 11).

The grant framework initially applied only to ADF IX although it was subsequently extended and aligned more closely with that of the World Bank's International Development Association. Grant operations from the ADF commenced in 2005. Almost $250 million was approved in ADF grants that year, of which $100 million went to Afghanistan. By the end of 2016, cumulative ADF grant approvals totaled $7 billion.

During ADF IX period (2005–2008), ADB committed to a Bank-wide 19 reform initiatives that brought together various changes already under way. All were included in a framework for monitoring.[34] The performance-based allocation policy was also reviewed.[35] The allocation formula was

---

[32] ADB, 2001, *Policy on Performance-Based Allocation for Asian Development Fund Resources.*
[33] ADB, 2004, *Eighth Replenishment of the ADF.*
[34] A list of the 19 initiatives is in "The Reform Agenda" in ADB, *Annual Report 2004*, 4. Part 1 on "Institutional Effectiveness" in this annual report provides an extended discussion of the efforts being made by ADB at the time to improve the effectiveness of the Bank's operations (ADB, *Annual Report 2004*, 32–47).
[35] ADB, 2004, *Policy on Performance-Based Allocation of ADF Resources.*

revised to strengthen links with needs and performance. A separate mechanism was introduced for allocation to postconflict countries.

Ordinary Capital Resources Operations and Funding

The concessional ADF was replenished three times during the fourth ADB decade. But there was no increase in the Bank's OCR capital base for over 10 years. A review of ADB's capital stock was long overdue: the Charter provides that the Board of Governors should review the capital stock at intervals of not less than 5 years. Past reviews had resulted in regular increases, the previous one being in 1994. Staff close to Chino said that he wanted to arrange a GCI and that he had designed his reform efforts as a way of building support for one. Nevertheless, the Bank was unable to obtain sufficient support. The fourth ADB decade remains the only one in which there was no GCI.

Although no capital increase was imminent, important reforms were introduced into the OCR lending program. Early in Chino's tenure, in 2000, loan charges were increased with the lending spread widening by 20 basis points.[36] In 2001, loans based on the London interbank offered rate (LIBOR) were introduced.[37] This approach provided loans on more competitive terms, and introduced rebates and surcharges: a surcharge would arise if ADB's actual average funding cost was above the 6-month

---

[36] At the time, ADB had three OCR lending windows: (i) the pool-based multicurrency loan window established in July 1986, where loan disbursements were made in a variety of currencies of the Bank's choice; (ii) the pool-based single currency loan window in US dollars established in July 1992; and (iii) the market-based loan window established in 1994, which provided single currency loans (in US dollars, Japanese yen, or Swiss francs at either fixed or floating rates) to private sector borrowers and to financial intermediaries in the public sector.

[37] ADB, 2001, *Review of Financial Loan Products*. The LBL had market-based features, including a fixed spread and pricing relative to standard market references. With LBL, a high degree of flexibility was given to borrowers in terms of choice of currency and interest rate basis, options to link repayment schedules to actual disbursements for financial intermediary borrowers, the ability to change the original loan terms (currency and interest rate basis) at any time during the life of the loans, and options to purchase a cap or collar on a floating lending rate at any time during the life of the loans. A unique characteristic of LBLs was the introduction of rebates and surcharges. Since the concept of automatic cost pass-through pricing was maintained, a surcharge would arise if ADB's actual average funding cost was above the 6-month LIBOR, while a rebate would be given if ADB's actual average funding cost was below the 6-month LIBOR. Lending charges were regularly reviewed to ensure that funds were provided at the lowest possible costs to ADB's borrowers.

LIBOR, while a rebate would be given if ADB's actual average funding cost was below the 6-month LIBOR. Subsequently, the Bank no longer offered the pool-based multicurrency loans formerly provided, under which disbursements were made in a variety of currencies of the Bank's choice.

The Asian financial crisis taught Asian policy makers an important lesson about risk management. ADB itself also undertook measures to strengthen its corporate risk management systems, improve liquidity portfolio management, and introduce new tools to better measure risk. Kuroda would build on these reforms. In August 2005, during his tenure, the ADB Risk Management Unit was created. The unit was later upgraded to the separate Office of Risk Management covering management of credit risk of all nonsovereign transactions, market risks in ADB's treasury portfolio, and operational risk across different organizational lines.

To supplement the Bank's own financing for projects, ADB actively sought to mobilize cofinancing from other sources such as bilateral and multilateral partners and private financing institutions. ADB had begun cofinancing activities in 1970 and expanded these arrangements in the 1980s and into the 1990s.[38] Now the situation was more complex, with new sources, new players, and new requirements. In 1995, a review of cofinancing had recommended that the Bank be more active in designing activities with cofinancing partners.

ADB also encouraged individual countries—or sometimes groups of countries—to contribute to trust funds for specific purposes managed by the Bank. In the early years of operations, the Bank was cautious about taking on the management of small trust funds because the administration of dozens of separate funds seemed likely to be a challenging task for a new organization. But from around 2000, there was a flurry of activity with the creation of a number of new trust funds. Some were established by individual donor countries to promote nominated activities; others were thematic funds designed to support activities in renewable energy, water, climate change, poverty reduction, and governance. The Water Financing Partnership Facility was established in 2006 with initial contribution from Australia, the Netherlands, and Norway. In subsequent years, Austria, Spain, Switzerland, and the Gates Foundation joined the financing partnership with additional contribution. The same year, the Republic of Korea established the e-Asia and Knowledge Partnership Fund to improve access to information and communication technology in the region.

---

[38] ADB, 2006, *ADB's Financing Partnership Strategy*.

Another major development was the establishment of the Japan Fund for Poverty Reduction (JFPR). Created in May 2000 in support of the Bank's new PRS, the fund continued the Japanese tradition of helping ADB develop bankable projects and strengthen human resources[39] (Chapter 14).

Haruhiko Kuroda

In early 2005, Tadao Chino left ADB and returned to Japan. The 6 years of his presidency had been turbulent, subjected to numerous internal and external pressures. Nevertheless, Chino had achieved a great deal. He had reorganized ADB, decentralized its operations, and made it more country focused. He was leaving ADB with 24 resident missions in place compared with 11 at the beginning of his tenure. He had also strengthened the approach to conflict situations and fragile states. But he would be most remembered for his work to make poverty reduction the Bank's overarching goal. While he did not achieve the capital increase he had hoped for, he successfully laid the groundwork for many important reforms that Kuroda would build on.

Haruhiko Kuroda arrived in 2005 with impressive experience in international finance. He studied law in the University of Tokyo and obtained a master's degree in economics at the University of Oxford. He was a staff member at the IMF in the 1970s. In his work with the Ministry of Finance he had helped coordinate the regional response to the Asian financial crisis. As Vice-Minister of Finance, Kuroda had visited ADB in 2000 to speak on the role of regional development banks— where he warmly supported the PRS and called for ADB to play a more central role in the region. He urged ADB to become an "even more active institution, while the World Bank [was] asked to be more humble in Asia and the Pacific." Kuroda's appointment reflected strong support for ADB at the highest political and administrative levels in Japan.

Kuroda was highly literate in economics, and well connected globally. A profile article by the International Monetary Fund (IMF) in 2006 described him as "bookish and thoughtful, rather than charismatic" and recognized that he delighted in intellectual discussions.[40] For recreational reading, aside from detective novels, he read books on mathematics and physics. He was thoughtful, discreet, and soft-spoken, preferring

---

[39] ADB, 2000, *Cooperation with Japan: Japan Fund for Poverty Reduction.*
[40] IMF, 2006, People in Economics: The Quiet Integrationist, *Finance and Development.*

understatement to flamboyance, and selected his words with academic precision. He was comfortable with international speaking engagements and during his tenure participated in numerous high-level conferences, summits, and symposia.

Kuroda took the challenge of guiding the Bank's diverse and often opinionated Management team in his stride. His management style was traditional and formal. At internal meetings, Kuroda would seek views by going around the table. He would usually conclude meetings by saying "we have now reached a consensus" and then state his decision. Once he had made a decision, he normally stuck to it—unless it became very clear that the idea was not working. He was instrumental in eventually securing GCI V and pushing through important internal reforms.

On 1 February 2005, his first day as President, Kuroda addressed a meeting of the Board, Management, and staff, setting out his views on development issues in Asia and the role of ADB. He said that "the primary challenge facing the region is poverty reduction." He also drew on Watanabe's idea, repeated by later Presidents that "the role of ADB as the region's 'Family Doctor' should be reinforced." But Kuroda also signaled change: the Bank must be more relevant and responsive and focus more on results. And reflecting his previous academic papers and newspaper articles, Kuroda signaled his commitment to greater Asian regional integration.

While continuing with Chino's reforms, which in some quarters were still viewed with skepticism, Kuroda worked to improve the sometimes tense relations with stakeholders. He recognized the concerns of donor countries set out at several ADF replenishment meetings. He also understood the position of OCR borrowers, as expressed in a 2006 survey: the borrowers found the Bank to have a limited choice of instruments and modalities, while the costs of doing business with ADB were increasing and the quality of services was deteriorating.[41] Another problem was that since 1998, annual lending levels had stagnated at around $5 billion–$6 billion. Despite uncertainties about donor support, Kuroda decided to plan for increases in ADB lending—supported by ADF replenishments, and, subsequently, a GCI.

---

[41] ADB, 2006, *Enhancing Asian Development Bank Support to Middle-Income Countries and Borrowers from Ordinary Capital Resources.*

Building on Past Measures

As soon as he became President, Kuroda had to deal with ADB's response to natural disasters of a staggering scale. At the beginning of 2005, the international community was mobilizing to help survivors of the 2004 Asian tsunami. Later, at the end of the year, large assistance was needed to help provide shelter to the millions whose homes were destroyed in October by the earthquake in Pakistan. Kuroda's immediate priority was to implement the ADB response to the tsunami initiated by Chino. In February 2005, within 6 weeks of the disaster, the Bank had set up the $600 million multidonor Asian Tsunami Fund grant facility—the largest grant program in ADB's history at the time. In March, around $775 million was earmarked for emergency relief ($600 million in new loans and grants and $175 million redirected from ongoing projects and programs)—the Bank's largest response to a single natural disaster. And after the earthquake in Pakistan in 2005, ADB provided more than $400 million in emergency assistance to help rehabilitation and infrastructure.

Kuroda also continued Chino's Innovation and Efficiency Initiative to meet the needs of borrowers and reduce project transaction costs. In 2005, ADB piloted and expanded financial instruments that would become part of its regular lending modalities (Box 12.2).

Also in 2005, the Bank reviewed its policy on supplementary financing. When originally adopted in 1973 in the wake of the first oil shock, the instrument was to meet project cost overruns and close financing gaps. ADB had introduced several improvements since then, such as reducing restrictions on access, simplifying business processes, and expanding the scope to include operations that were performing well. After these modifications, supplementary financing increased somewhat.[42] In particular, the policy allowed scaling up assistance to successful projects. This instrument was not as widely used as initially anticipated, partly because supplementary financing was often viewed as being synonymous with financing due to cost overruns. Subsequently, in 2010, this instrument was superseded by the policy for additional financing. Using simplified business processes, additional financing enabled scaling up and modifying well-performing projects for greater impact, without any restrictions being imposed on the amount, duration, and number of provisions.

---

[42] ADB, 2005, *Review of the Policy on Supplementary Financing: Addressing Challenges and Broader Needs*.

Box 12.2: Important Instruments under the Innovation and Efficiency Initiative

Multitranche Financing Facility. This allows the Asian Development Bank (ADB) to offer financial resources to clients for an agreed investment program, or a set of interrelated investments, in a series of tranches over a fixed period. The multitranche financing facility (MFF) helped reduce uncertainty in country programming and assured clients that ADB could be part of their long-term financing plans. Two MFFs were approved on a pilot basis in 2005, totaling $1.52 billion. These were $770 million to Pakistan for the National Highway Development Sector Investment Program and $750 million to India for the Rural Roads Sector II Investment Program. Loans from these facilities were approved starting in 2006. The MFF proved popular among clients, so in 2008 the Board approved this as a generally available instrument.

Nonsovereign Public Sector Financing. This was adopted as a pilot instrument in 2006 to allow ADB to provide loans and guarantees directly to selected nonsovereign public sector entities, without requiring a central government or sovereign guarantee. Within a year, as part of the pilot, the Private Sector Operations Department processed two nonsovereign public sector financing facilities: the National Thermal Power Corporation Capacity Expansion Financing Facility in India and the South Sumatra to West Java Phase II Gas Pipeline Project in Indonesia. Both clients were state-owned enterprises. In 2011, the Board made the instrument generally available.

Local Currency Lending for the Public Sector. The Innovation and Efficiency Initiative called for the expansion of the ADB product portfolio to include local currency lending (LCL). Traditionally, loans by ADB had been offered exclusively in foreign currency, backed by sovereign guarantees. To meet borrowers' evolving financial needs, ADB introduced the LCL product for the public sector in August 2005. Public sector entities including local governments and public sector enterprises could avail themselves of LCLs. LCLs aimed to address the potential mismatch between borrowing in foreign currency and having income streams in local currency. In 2005, ADB extended a 15-year LCL equivalent of about $70 million Indian rupees to Powerlinks, a public limited company incorporated in India. This was funded by proceeds of the inaugural ADB rupee bond issue in 2004. The same year, Bayerische Hypo- und Vereinsbank received an LCL denominated in Philippine pesos, to acquire a nonperforming loan portfolio from a bank in the Philippines. ADB sourced the required local currency by means of a cross-currency swap with a commercial counterparty.

Source: ADB. 2005. *Innovation and Efficiency Initiative*. Manila.

In the same year, the Board approved a new policy framework on cost sharing, expenditure eligibility, and local cost financing for public sector assistance. Thus far, cost-sharing limits had been fixed up front for all projects, based on the member country's lending classification. Now, cost-sharing ceilings and financing arrangements for each borrower would be established in conjunction with the country partnership strategy. This policy brought ADB practices in line with those of other development institutions.[43]

Kuroda took external relations very seriously, especially in view of the recent controversies about accountability and transparency, including those relating to public inspection. In 2005, ADB introduced a new Public Communication Policy to improve disclosure of information including, reflecting past controversies, during project preparation and implementation.[44] Among the new features, the policy would take the initiative to make information publicly available by posting early details on the web, and not just after a request had been received from stakeholders. In a departure from past practice, if the information ADB held was not subject to clear confidentiality criteria, the new policy required that it had to be disclosed. Announcing the new policy at the 2005 Annual Meeting in Istanbul, Kuroda said that it would improve public access to documents and commit ADB to greater openness and dialogue.

The policy also called for more robust external communications—through public speaking events and media outreach. The ADB Office of External Relations was upgraded to a department and resident missions were encouraged to promote communications at the field level.

To better understand stakeholders' perceptions of ADB, regular independent surveys were introduced. The first survey was undertaken in 2006, polling more than 700 opinion leaders from government, civil society, the private sector, and development partners in 30 ADB member countries. According to the report from the survey, stakeholders "acknowledge ADB's contribution to the development progress of the Asia and Pacific region ... However, opinion leaders also found that ADB lacked capacity or is spread too thinly. Other weaknesses identified were its procedures, which

---

[43] In the past, cost-sharing limits were fixed up front and equally for all projects based on the member country's classification. The new policy harmonized ADB's approaches and practices with those of other development institutions.
[44] ADB, 2005, *Public Communications Policy*.

some opinion leaders characterized as too bureaucratic."[45] Subsequent perception surveys would be conducted in 2009 and 2012.

Kuroda promoted further reforms in the institution. In 2006, business processes were reviewed and measures were introduced to enhance "quality-at-entry" for country strategies and projects.

Revitalizing Regional Cooperation

Kuroda would become known for revitalizing ADB in regional cooperation activities. The first sentence of the ADB Charter refers to "the importance of closer economic cooperation." Kuroda lost little time in redirecting attention to regional cooperation, transcending this agenda across regional departments. Speaking at the Asian Institute of Management in Manila in 2005, Kuroda noted that his objective was not a "fortress Asia" but an integrated region that was open to the rest of the world. "Asia," said Kuroda, "should increasingly act regionally while continuing to think globally."

During Chino's term, the regional cooperation agenda had expanded as Asian countries tried to develop regional linkages to guard against volatility (Chapter 11). ADB has implemented its regional cooperation and integration (RCI) agenda mostly through subregional cooperation programs (Box 12.3). Moreover, in 1999, in response to the impact of the Asian financial crisis on developing countries in Asia, ADB established the Regional Monitoring Unit (REMU). The main activities of REMU were to support the overall response process of the Association of Southeast Asian Nations (ASEAN), to provide inputs to meetings and discussions in the region, and to operate the new Asia Recovery Information Center (ARIC). REMU also assisted in establishing surveillance units in the respective ministries of finance in Indonesia, the Philippines, and Thailand.

In 2004, ADB initiated local currency borrowings, which would contribute to the development of regional bond markets. Inaugural bond issues were launched in the domestic capital markets of India; Hong Kong, China; Malaysia; and Singapore—with subsequent issues in 2005 and 2006 in Thai baht, renminbi, and Philippine pesos.

Overall, however, it was during President Kuroda's tenure that ADB's regional cooperation activities widened markedly. In April 2005, just 2 months

---

[45] ADB, 2006, *ADB Perceptions Survey: Multinational Survey of Opinion Leaders 2006.*

Box 12.3: ADB Subregional Cooperation Programs

The Asian Development Bank (ADB) implemented its regional cooperation and integration (RCI) agenda, mostly through subregional cooperation programs. The first subregional program, the Greater Mekong Subregion (GMS) Economic Cooperation Program, was established in 1992, predating the launch of ADB's first RCI policy in 1994. The GMS Program was followed in quick succession by the Brunei Darussalam–Indonesia–Malaysia–Philippines East ASEAN Growth Area (BIMP-EAGA) program in 1995 and by the Central Asia Regional Economic Cooperation (CAREC) and Bay of Bengal Initiative for Multi-Sectoral Technical and Economic Cooperation (BIMSTEC) programs in 1997. The South Asia Subregional Economic Cooperation (SASEC) program was established in 2001 followed by the Indonesia–Malaysia–Thailand Growth Triangle (IMT-GT) program in 2006.

Greater Mekong Subregion Economic Cooperation. In 1992, six countries—Cambodia, the People's Republic of China (PRC) (focusing on Yunnan Province), the Lao People's Democratic Republic, Myanmar, Thailand, and Viet Nam—established the program. Guangxi Zhuang Autonomous Region of the PRC joined the program in 2004. It focuses on (i) increasing connectivity through sustainable development of physical infrastructure and economic corridors; (ii) improving competitiveness through efficient facilitation of cross-border movement of people and goods, integration of markets, and enhancing value chains; and (iii) building a greater sense of community through shared concerns. The GMS Program paid particular attention to building strategic alliances, especially with the Association of Southeast Asian Nations (ASEAN), ASEAN+3 (ASEAN, plus the PRC, Japan, and the Republic of Korea), and the Mekong River Commission.

Brunei Darussalam–Indonesia–Malaysia–Philippines East ASEAN Growth Area. The BIMP-EAGA program was launched in 1995 to address subregional inequalities in development. The program comprised the entire sultanate of Brunei Darussalam; the provinces of Kalimantan, Sulawesi, Maluku, and West Papua of Indonesia; the states of Sabah and Sarawak and the federal territory of Labuan in Malaysia; and Mindanao and the province of Palawan in the Philippines. ADB has been BIMP-EAGA's regional development advisor since 2001. The program focuses on five strategic pillars: (i) connectivity, (ii) food basket, (iii) tourism, (iv) environment, and (v) trade and investment facilitation. Its long-term goal has been to ensure that non-resource-based industries are established in the subregion. BIMP-EAGA cooperation aims to increase trade, tourism and investments within and outside the subregion, and take full advantage of the subregion's resources and the existing complementarities.

continued on next page

Box 12.3 *continued*

Central Asia Regional Economic Cooperation. The program was established in 1997 to promote economic cooperation in central Asian countries. Initial members included Azerbaijan, the PRC (through Xinjiang Uygur Autonomous Region), Kazakhstan, the Kyrgyz Republic, Mongolia, Tajikistan, and Uzbekistan. In 2005, Afghanistan, Pakistan, and Turkmenistan joined the program, enabling a North–South opening to the Arabian Sea through Pakistan. The program design also involved a partnership between member countries and a group of multilateral development partners. Besides ADB, the European Bank for Reconstruction and Development, the International Monetary Fund, the Islamic Development Bank, the United Nations Development Programme, and the World Bank were included. ADB serves as the CAREC secretariat, which started functioning in 2000. The sector focus of the program has been on transport, energy, and trade (both trade facilitation and trade policy).

Bay of Bengal Initiative for Multi-Sectoral Technical and Economic Cooperation. The program was launched in 1997 and comprised Bangladesh, Bhutan, India, Myanmar, Nepal, Sri Lanka, and Thailand. Trade-led economic integration through the BIMSTEC Free Trade Area was one of the key objectives of the program. ADB support has facilitated subregional strategies for transport and energy trade.

South Asia Subregional Economic Cooperation. The program was established in 2001 as a project-based initiative that initially promoted economic cooperation through the enhancement of cross-border connectivity and facilitation of trade between Bangladesh, Bhutan, India, and Nepal. Sri Lanka and the Maldives later joined the program in 2014. Originally, the priority areas for cooperation were transport, trade facilitation, energy, and information and communication technology (ICT). Subsequently, the ICT focus area was dropped from the program.

Indonesia–Malaysia–Thailand Growth Triangle. The program began in 1993 as a subregional framework for accelerating economic cooperation and integration of the member states and provinces in the three countries. The program currently covers 14 provinces in southern Thailand, 8 states of Peninsular Malaysia, and 10 provinces of Sumatra in Indonesia. The strategic objectives of the program relate to (i) facilitating trade and investment; (ii) promoting agriculture, agro-industry, and tourism; (iii) strengthening infrastructure linkages and supporting integration of IMT-GT subregion; (iv) addressing cross-sector concerns such as human resources development, labor, and the environment; and (v) strengthening institutional arrangements and mechanisms for cooperation.

Source: ADB. 2015. *Thematic Evaluation Study on ADB's Efforts on Regional Cooperation and Integration*. Manila.

after he arrived, Kuroda announced the establishment of the new Office of Regional Economic Integration. In 2006, the Board approved the Regional Cooperation and Integration Strategy based on four pillars: subregional economic cooperation on cross-border infrastructure and related software, trade and investment cooperation and integration, monetary and financial cooperation and integration, and cooperation in regional public goods.[46] The RCI strategy envisaged ADB playing four distinct roles: as a money bank, as a knowledge bank, as a capacity builder, and as an honest broker. Together with Strategy 2020, the corporate strategy plan which was later released in 2008, this approach significantly expanded the Bank's RCI activities over its fifth decade (Chapter 14).

In 2006, Kuroda also announced a realignment of regional departments. To achieve economies of scale for staff resources, as well as better cooperation with ASEAN, the Mekong and Southeast Asia departments were merged into the Southeast Asia Department. A new Central and West Asia Department was established to work with countries in the Caucasus and Central Asia together with Afghanistan and Pakistan.

The same year, Brunei Darussalam (already active in the ADB-supported BIMP-EAGA program; see Box 12.3) formally joined ADB as a regional member.[47]

New Corporate Directions

Kuroda then turned his attention to the resource issues which had constrained Chino. After the 1997 crisis response, lending had stagnated (Figure 12.1). This was a matter of serious concern for the Bank. But lending then picked up in 2006 with eight multitranche facilities approved—for India, Bangladesh, the PRC, and Pakistan—totaling $3.8 billion. That year, ADB increased its own prudential minimum liquidity levels to ensure that even in difficult financial conditions, the institution would be able to meet its normal cash requirements. By 2007, however, just a year later, the financial situation had become very tight, so Kuroda asked the Treasury and the Strategy and Policy departments to study the Bank's future resource requirements. This, in effect, marked the start of the process that would lead to a large fifth general capital increase (GCI V) in 2009 (Chapter 14).

---

[46] ADB, 2006, *Regional Cooperation and Integration Strategy*.
[47] ADB, 2006, *Membership of Brunei Darussalam*.

Figure 12.1: Operational Approvals by Fund Type, 1997–2006
($ million)

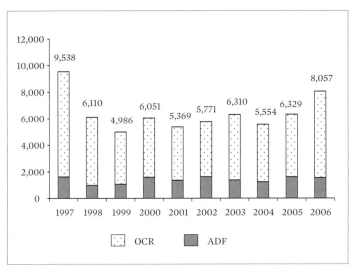

Total: $64,075 million

ADF = Asian Development Fund, OCR = ordinary capital resources.

Note: Operational approvals include loans, grants, equity investments, and guarantees.

Sources: ADB Operations Dashboard eOperations database; ADB Strategy and Policy Department.

Cutting across all these changes was the need for the Bank to take stock of its priorities. When he arrived as President in early 2005, Kuroda had realized that to build support for the additional resources, a review of the corporate strategy would be needed. He signaled his intention to conduct a corporate review in his first speech as President at the 2005 Annual Meeting in Istanbul. He pointed out that, faced with a broadening list of international development goals, the Bank had taken on what staff called a "multifaceted policy agenda"—with around 30 sector and thematic policies. This multiplicity made it difficult to run well-defined programs. Kuroda argued for greater focus and selectivity. For this purpose, he announced that the Bank would clarify its priorities through the second medium-term strategy (MTS II).

Originally, the MTS II was to cover the period 2006–2010. Subsequently, however, a more ambitious two-track approach was adopted. The first track would be an MTS for a shorter period, 2006–2008; the second track would be a longer-term plan to cover the period to 2020, based on an assessment by an external eminent persons group. They would consider the future of the region—and ADB—as more countries moved into the middle-income category. The group, which was appointed in June 2006, was chaired by Supachai Panitchpakdi, a senior Thai policy maker, then Secretary-General of the United Nations Conference on Trade and Development. He was supported by five experienced scholars and practitioners: Isher Judge Ahluwalia from India, Nobuyuki Idei from Japan, Caio Koch-Weser from Germany, Justin Lin from the PRC, and Lawrence Summers from the US. They presented their report the following year (Chapter 14).

At the 2006 Annual Meeting in Hyderabad, in his second Annual Meeting speech as President, Kuroda presented the new Medium-Term Strategy (MTS II). This document supported the broad approach of the 1999 PRS in that the main approach set out was: "to strengthen the poverty reduction impact of ADB's assistance programs in the context of the key challenges facing the region." But the Medium-Term Strategy also addressed the growth of middle-income countries, which "is likely to profoundly change how the world does business and establish a new international division of labor."[48] Kuroda spoke of "the two faces of Asia." One was middle class; the other was poor—and the gaps between them were widening. He said, "Poverty—in all its aspects—is still our region's most daunting problem."

The MTS II set out to balance selectivity and diversity. Kuroda believed that ADB should avoid spreading itself too thinly and concentrate on a limited number of priorities. But many stakeholders had their own wish lists. The Bank was thus again pulled in different directions. After extensive consultations, the MTS II attempted to capture—or at least summarize—the collective concerns of shareholders. The strategy had five priorities: catalyzing investments, strengthening inclusiveness, promoting regional cooperation and integration, managing the environment, and improving governance and preventing corruption. Later, in the fifth decade, ADB would consciously shift back toward providing assistance based on client demand rather than trying to be fixed on selected sectors and priorities based on corporate strategy.

---

[48] ADB, 2006, *Enhancing Asian Development Bank Support to Middle-Income Countries and Borrowers from Ordinary Capital Resources.*

Operational Summary

During the fourth ADB decade, financing operations expanded by about 50% compared with the levels in the previous decade, with total financing of $64 billion for 1997–2006. Lending had peaked in 1997 when large financial sector loans to the Republic of Korea and Thailand financed from OCR boosted total lending for the year to $9.5 billion (Chapter 10). The postcrisis years saw the annual level of lending at around $5 billion–$6 billion before activities picked up again in 2006.

In geographical terms, compared to the third ADB decade, lending was more equally distributed across regions, with Southeast Asia, South Asia, and East Asia each accounting for more than a quarter of total lending (Figure 12.2).[49] Lending to East Asia increased significantly reflecting the large crisis loan provided to the Republic of Korea and continued increases in lending to the PRC. Lending to Central and West Asia also rose as additional members from the former Soviet Union joined the Bank and ADB resumed operations in Afghanistan in 2002. Lending to South Asia grew as well, particularly to India. By contrast, lending to Southeast Asia declined as a share of the total. No loans had been made to Malaysia since 1997 and no new public sector lending had been provided to Thailand since 1999. The top five borrowers in this decade were the PRC (19% of total lending), India (16%), Indonesia (13%), Pakistan (12%), and the Republic of Korea (6%).

Following the approval of the PRS, ADB diversified its activities into a broader range of sectors. Transport and information and communication technology accounted for more than a quarter of total lending followed by finance and energy (Figure 12.3). Compared to the third ADB decade, transport overtook energy as the largest sector. Lending for the finance sector and public sector management surged in response to the crisis.[50]

ADB operations continued to be supported by technical assistance. Compared to the level of $882 million in the previous decade, technical assistance approvals between 1997 and 2006 reached $1.4 billion. Of the total, 77% was allocated to specific countries, while the remaining 23% funded regional technical assistance. Excluding regional technical assistance, the top five country recipients of technical assistance were

---

[49] Figure 9.3 has the breakdown of lending by region in 1987–1996.
[50] Figure 9.4 has the composition of lending by sector in 1987–1996.

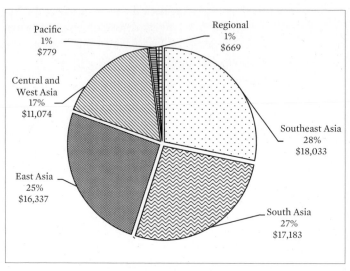

Figure 12.2: Operational Approvals by Region, 1997–2006
(%, $ million)

Total: $64,075 million

Notes: Regional breakdown is based on current country groupings. Operational approvals include loans, grants, equity investments, and guarantees.

Sources: ADB Operations Dashboard; ADB Strategy and Policy Department.

the PRC (14%), Indonesia (9%), Viet Nam (6%), Pakistan (6%), and the Philippines (5%). Technical assistance operations covered a multitude of sectors and subsectors. Compared to the third ADB decade, there was large increase in support for public sector management following the Asian financial crisis, while the share of technical assistance going to agriculture declined significantly.

Ten new members joined the Bank, bringing the membership by the end of 2006 to 66 (47 regional and 19 nonregional).[51] Four of the new members were from Central and West Asia, and, as ADB's operations expanded in the subregion, a new department for Central and West Asia was established as part of the 2006 organizational realignment. Because of a cautious

---

[51] There were six new regional and four new nonregional members: Tajikistan (1998), Azerbaijan (1999), Turkmenistan (2000), Portugal and Timor-Leste (2002), Palau and Luxembourg (2003), Armenia (2005), and Brunei Darussalam and Ireland (2006).

Figure 12.3: Operational Approvals by Sector, 1997–2006
(%, $ million)

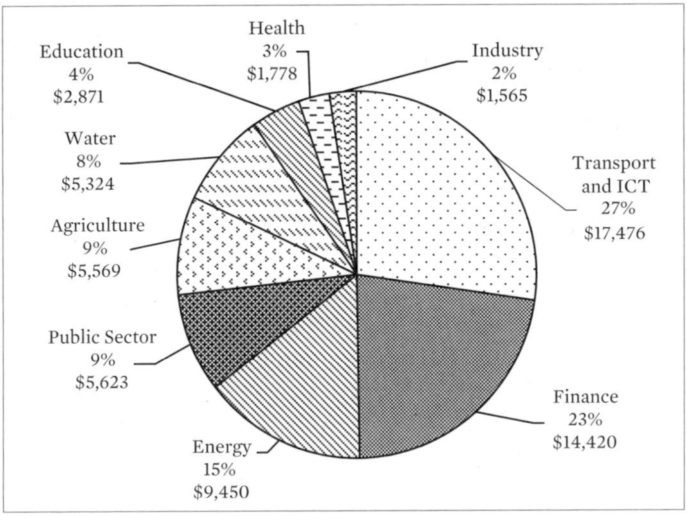

- Education 4% $2,871
- Health 3% $1,778
- Industry 2% $1,565
- Water 8% $5,324
- Transport and ICT 27% $17,476
- Agriculture 9% $5,569
- Public Sector 9% $5,623
- Energy 15% $9,450
- Finance 23% $14,420

Total: $64,075 million

ICT = information and communication technology.

Note: Operational approvals include loans, grants, equity investments, and guarantees.

Sources: ADB Operations Dashboard; ADB Strategy and Policy Department.

approach, particularly during the crisis, the Bank's internal administrative expenses budget grew modestly. Compared with annual average growth of 8% in the third decade, the growth rate during 1997–2006 was 5%. The number of staff grew steadily: by the end of the fourth decade, the total was 2,405, including 861 international and Management staff and 1,544 national and administrative staff—from 54 member countries.[52]

A Challenging and Transformative Decade

The fourth decade was thus a period of rapid change. The Bank was expected to achieve multiple objectives with limited resources and tools at its disposal. President Chino had introduced important organizational reforms, laying the groundwork effectively for further change and

---

[52] This represented a 22% increase compared to the previous ADB decade (1987–1996).

expansion. Kuroda would take these forward while also using the upcoming Strategy 2020 to clarify the objectives.

The decade closed on an optimistic note for the region, amid rapid growth. At the 2007 Annual Meeting in Kyoto, Kuroda signaled changes forthcoming for the institution when he recognized that ADB would need to transform itself to meet the region's needs. "The challenge," he said, "will be to define how we will make that transition. Our process of change has already begun through our Medium-Term Strategy II. And we will be deepening our work further, as we review our Long-Term Strategic Framework." He identified three core areas: promoting regional cooperation and integration, mobilizing and intermediating financial resources, and creating and disseminating knowledge. These areas would come to be strongly reflected in ADB's work in its fifth decade.

Table 12.1: Selected Operational, Institutional, and Financial Information, 1987–2006

	1987–1996 (Total, Third Decade)	1996 (end-year)	2006 (end-year)	1997–2006 (Total, Fourth Decade)
A. Operational Highlights ($ million)				
Total operational approvals[a]	43,063	5,335	8,057	64,075
By fund source				
Ordinary capital resources	30,082	3,669	6,502	50,013
Asian Development Fund	12,981	1,666	1,554	14,062
By operations				
Sovereign	41,813	5,156	7,096	60,042
Nonsovereign	1,250	179	960	4,033
Technical assistance approvals[b]	882	138	148	1,383
Technical assistance projects	727	106	94	1,063
Regional assistance	155	31	54	320
Outstanding loan portfolio		28,577	47,714	
Ordinary capital resources		16,109	26,192	
Asian Development Fund		12,468	21,522	
Total loan and grant disbursements	27,751	3,797	5,793	48,062

continued on next page

Table 12.1 continued

	1987–1996 (Total, Third Decade)	1996 (end-year)	2006 (end-year)	1997–2006 (Total, Fourth Decade)
Ordinary capital resources	18,154	2,563	4,420	36,551
Asian Development Fund	9,597	1,234	1,373	11,511
Official cofinancing[c]	4,018	397	891	5,091
Commercial cofinancing	560	92	315	642
B. Institutional Highlights				
Staff information				
Total staff		1,961	2,405	
International staff [d]		673	861	
Women staff		1,023	1,358	
Women international staff		100	249	
Staff in field offices		144	474	
Member countries		56	66	
Field offices		11	26	
Internal administrative expenses budget ($ million)	1,411	190	313	2,441
C. Financial Highlights ($ million)				
Authorized capital[e]		50,103	53,169	
Subscribed capital[e]		49,368	53,169	
Paid-in		3,472	3,740	
Callable		45,896	49,429	
Borrowings	12,166	584	5,576	45,412

SDR = special drawing right, US = United States.

[a] Figures from 1997 to 2006 are based on gross approvals of loans, grants, equity investments, and guarantees. Due to data unavailability, data from 1987 to 1996 are net of terminations (they exclude operations approved by the Board of Directors but terminated before they were deemed effective).
[b] Technical assistance operations cover grants funded by the Technical Assistance Special Fund and the Japan Special Fund only.
[c] Includes trust funds and cofinancing of loans, grants, and technical assistance.
[d] International staff data include Management.
[e] Values are US dollar equivalents based on US dollar/SDR exchange rate on 31 December 1996 (for 1996 capital) and 31 December 2006 (for 2006 capital).

Sources: ADB Annual Reports; ADB Budget, Personnel, and Management Systems Department; ADB Controller's Department; ADB's Strategy and Policy Department; ADB loan, technical assistance, grant, and equity approvals database; ADB Cofinancing database.

CHAPTER 13
Fifth Decade (2007–2016)

Asia: Growth in Uncertain Times

"As the world begins to emerge from recession, it is clear that Asia is leading the global recovery. ... Despite a robust recovery, challenges remain.... And with uncertainty still present in industrial countries, nothing can be taken for granted."

– Haruhiko Kuroda,
Address to the ADB Annual Meeting, 2010

The fifth ADB decade started with the region growing strongly; output expanded by over 10% in 2007. The 2008–2009 global financial crisis slowed progress somewhat, but the damage in Asia was less than in many developed countries in other parts of the world. In 2010, growth rebounded in Asia. With industrial economies continuing to face weaker and riskier growth prospects after the crisis, strategy in Asia needed to focus more on developing growth drivers in the region.

During this fifth decade, the global development agenda and development financing architecture evolved rapidly. The Sustainable Development Goals (SDGs), which replaced the Millennium Development Goals (MDGs), gave increased emphasis to inclusiveness, sustainability, and resilience. New institutions, particularly two new multilateral development banks, started their operations, providing financing to the region. All of these changes presented the Asian Development Bank (ADB) with challenges to respond to needs of the diverse group of borrowers in Asia.

Progress with Variations, but Growth Gathering Momentum

By the start of the decade, Asia's growing role in global affairs was widely recognized. Earlier, developing Asia's prospects had been closely linked to economic conditions in the main industrial countries. Now the relationship was changing. Asia was a major driver of global growth.[1] Developing Asia had become the world's largest net exporter of capital as a result of its large current account surplus and was providing much of the demand in world commodity markets.[2]

Asia's growth led to much optimism that the 21st century would be an "Asian century." This was not a new idea. But past discussion had generally focused on a Pacific century—comprising Pacific Basin countries, including Japan, the newly industrialized economies (NIEs), made up of Hong Kong, China; the Republic of Korea; Singapore; and Taipei,China), and the ASEAN-4 (Thailand, Malaysia, Indonesia, and the Philippines).[3] In contrast, by the fifth ADB decade, the idea of an Asian century was a pan-Asian concept embracing countries in South Asia, Southeast Asia, and Central Asia.

At the start of the fifth ADB decade, there were still wide differences between Asian countries. As the *Asian Development Outlook 2007* observed: "Asia's stellar economic growth disguises wide variation and distracts attention from the full extent of the gap that is still to be bridged."[4] There were countries that had caught up with or were converging rapidly on economies of the Organisation for Economic Co-operation and Development (OECD). These included the NIEs, which had already substantially closed the gap and were high-income. There were also middle-income countries, such as the People's Republic of China (PRC), Malaysia, and Thailand, which, although some way behind, had made significant gains. Performance in other countries, however, was somewhat lagging.

Growth in Asia gathered momentum during the decade. Middle-income countries with large populations such as Bangladesh, India, Indonesia, the Philippines, and Viet Nam continued solid and more broad-based growth reflecting a market-based approach. Many of the young Central Asian countries capitalized on their natural resource industries and market-oriented reforms, although their growth was often volatile due to changes in commodity prices. And they still faced institutional challenges. Countries such as the Kyrgyz Republic, Myanmar, Nepal, and Pakistan, which had been converging more gradually for various reasons, including

---

[1] "The Growing Weight of the South" in Part 2: South–South Economic Links in ADB, *Asian Development Outlook 2011*, 39.
[2] ADB, *Asian Development Outlook 2011*, 12.
[3] Oshima, 1990, *Strategic Processes in Monsoon Asia's Economic Development*.
[4] ADB, *Asian Development Outlook 2007*.

moves to overcome political conflicts, were heading for stability, reform, and more robust growth. In the Pacific island countries, while growth had been volatile and the economies remained vulnerable to external shocks, many had benefited from larger investments from abroad in such sectors as tourism and mining (notably natural gas in Papua New Guinea).

Global Financial Crisis and Asian Resilience

At the start of the fifth decade, as the center of the world economy was shifting eastward, economic clouds were gathering. Major industrial economies moved into their most difficult period for a generation. The West was sliding toward a "great recession," suggesting that the "great moderation" had been the calm before the storm (Chapter 11). Conditions began to deteriorate in the latter part of 2007. Stock markets peaked in North America and then began to fall. At first, there appeared no cause for concern; the Dow Jones Industrial Average had almost doubled in the previous 6 years, so an adjustment seemed overdue.

The decline gathered pace. Before long, major financial institutions in the United States (US) were writing down the value of their assets. The problems widened to other countries, with signs of a worldwide credit crunch. One of the first casualties was in the United Kingdom: in September 2007, Northern Rock, a highly leveraged medium-sized mortgage lender, suffered a bank run. Difficulties rippled out across financial markets as it became clear that many financial institutions held undeclared "toxic" assets in the form of subprime, securitized mortgage loans of doubtful value. Then, in September 2008, with no notice, an iconic institution of the US financial system, Lehman Brothers, filed the largest bankruptcy in US history.

Despite turmoil in industrial countries, growth in Asia initially remained strong. The PRC and India were performing well and encouraging expansion across the rest of developing Asia. In 2007, the region registered its highest growth in almost two decades, even creating concerns that some economies were growing too rapidly with the risk of inflation. The fundamentals of banking systems were seen as sound as well—a consequence of extensive restructuring and reform after the 1997–1998 crisis. Between 1999 and 2007–2008, throughout the region, the incidence of nonperforming loans had come down and the rate of return on bank assets had risen.

Nevertheless, for Asian countries the scale of the slowdown in industrial economies was disturbing. The optimistic view was that Asia had decoupled from growth in industrial countries and could pursue robust growth on its own. Indeed, the region's financial institutions, unlike their counterparts in the US and Europe, had only limited exposure to subprime and related products. But another view was that the widening problems in the US and Europe were bound to hurt Asia. Indeed, by mid-2008, it was clear that the slowdown in OECD countries would have spillovers for developing Asia largely through lower levels of global trade and investment. In 2008–2009, growth in developing Asia fell to 6%–7%.

In the early years of the fifth ADB decade, there was a dramatic surge in food and fuel prices in the region. In late 2006, rising oil prices, combined with droughts in grain-producing nations and inflationary pressures following turbulence in global markets, pushed up food prices. The *Asian Development Outlook 2008* noted that "many years of robust growth supported by accommodative monetary policies buttressed excessive aggregate demand that nurtured price pressures."[5] In the first quarter of 2008, world rice prices more than doubled compared with the previous year—exacerbated by export restrictions in key rice-producing countries and panic buying in major rice-importing countries. Prices rose for wheat, cotton, and soybeans and for fertilizers.

On the whole, developing countries in Asia coped with these economic headwinds fairly well. Governments could consider various options for mitigating the impacts, including the implementation of swift expansionary policies to stimulate domestic demand. Initial responses aimed to safeguard the stability of banking and financial systems, particularly following the turmoil after the collapse of major investment banks in the US.[6] To reduce the risk of bank runs, the authorities increased maximum amounts covered by deposit insurance and the blanket guarantees for the liabilities of major banks. Many of the region's central banks followed up by providing liquidity and by easing credit and monetary policy, including by cutting interest rates.

Several countries introduced fiscal stimulus packages to offset falling demand for exports and rebalance growth toward domestic demand. The PRC announced dramatic increases in spending on infrastructure and

---

[5] ADB, *Asian Development Outlook 2008*.
[6] ADB, *Asian Development Outlook 2009*.

housing and on social development. In India, the government expanded infrastructure investment while reducing several taxes. In the Philippines, spending on infrastructure and social programs was increased. Similarly, Indonesia announced measures involving tax cuts, infrastructure projects, and assistance for those hurt most by declines in income. Thailand's package included tax cuts and cash assistance to low-income households. Many other developing countries also adopted fiscal packages and stabilization programs.

These stimulus packages were generally effective. The PRC and India grew strongly throughout 2009 and into 2010, encouraging growth in neighboring countries.[7] Even as global trade fell, developing Asia's exports expanded. The Central Asian republics also generally fared well, benefiting from rising prices for their main exports—oil and gas, metals, cotton, and gold. In 2010, growth in developing Asia recovered to more than 9.4% as Asia became the first region to emerge from the global turmoil. The global economic slowdown had also brought down food and oil prices. The IMF observed that "although Asia's GDP [gross domestic product] trend growth has exceeded that of advanced economies over the last three decades, this is the first time that Asia's contribution to a global recovery has outstripped that of other regions."[8]

Rebalancing Growth to Sustain Development

By the beginning of 2011, however, risks appeared to be rising again. In March 2011, an extremely powerful earthquake and tsunami caused devastation in Tohoku, Japan, and set back the country's economic prospects. In addition, there were pressures on global oil and food prices, with the risk of a wage inflation spiral. As things turned out, commodity price pressures subsided quite quickly and the threat of inflation receded. Nevertheless, there were still many financial difficulties elsewhere in the world. North America was showing signs of recovery, but several eurozone countries, notably Greece, had severe sovereign debt problems.

In Asia, volatile and destabilizing capital flows were causing increasing concern. In 2011, short-term capital had flowed out of Asian markets,

---

[7] Harris provides a summary of recent and current economic foreign policy in the PRC. Harris, 2014, *China's Foreign Policy*.
[8] IMF, 2010, *Regional Economic Outlook: Asia and Pacific. Leading the Global Recovery: Rebalancing for the Medium Term*.

but then flowed back—partly in response to quantitative easing in the US where interest rates dropped to new lows. Then in mid-2013, with the prospect of a "tapering" of quantitative easing, capital flowed out of Asia again causing a "taper tantrum." The abrupt changes in short-term capital flows led to erratic movements in Asian currencies. And in 2014 and 2015, the overall global economic environment remained difficult, with continuing uncertainty across international financial markets accompanied by sharp falls in commodity prices.

In this new and unfavorable global economic climate, policy makers in developing Asia considered ways to sustain growth. They sought to reduce their dependence on industrial countries and strengthen South–South linkages through increased cross-border flows of trade, capital, and labor.[9]

Asian regional cooperation was largely driven by trade (Chapter 11). Between 1990 and 2009, global trade among developing countries grew from 7% to 17% of world nonfuel merchandise trade.[10] Much of this growth was in developing Asia, particularly through trade of intermediate goods across "factory Asia." By 2010, developing Asia accounted for about three-quarters of South–South trade, and the PRC alone accounted for roughly 40%. Further efforts to reduce trade barriers and promote interregional trade seemed a promising way forward.

Asian capital flows became more intraregional as well. Various countries adopted policies to improve the investment climate with the aim of attracting foreign investment, developing equity and bond markets, and promoting openness of capital accounts. Partly as a result of these policies, more than half of the total foreign direct investment inflows to developing Asia now originate in the region compared with less than 30% in 2007. Capital outflows from the relatively high savers like the PRC, India, and ASEAN member states have also been increasingly invested within the region.

Just as globalization opened up markets for goods and capital, so labor markets expanded as well. Asian migrant workers headed for East Asia and Southeast Asia, notably to the NIEs and emerging economies such as Malaysia and Thailand. Growing migration stimulated rising remittances. India, the PRC, the Philippines, and Bangladesh are among the world's top

---

[9] An extended discussion of South–South issues is in Part 2: South–South Economic Links in ADB, *Asian Development Outlook 2011*, 37–86.
[10] ADB, *Asian Development Outlook 2011*, xvi.

remittance-receiving countries with more than half of their total inflows coming from developing Asia. As a share of GDP, remittance receipts are especially important for Tajikistan, Nepal, the Kyrgyz Republic, Bangladesh, and the Philippines, as well as for several Pacific island countries where they are a major source of income for the migrants' families.

Another factor which helped Asia to rebalance growth toward domestic markets was the rise of the middle class, which increasingly drove consumption and domestic demand. Developing Asia's middle class, with per capita incomes between $2 and $20 a day, grew threefold—from 565 million in 1990 to 1.9 billion in 2008.[11] Looking ahead, over the next decade, the bulk of the growth of the global middle class is projected to be in Asia. In 2009, Asia was home to 28% of the global middle-class population but by 2030 the region is expected to be home to around 66% of this group.[12] In several countries, the aspirations of the emerging middle class prompted market-oriented reforms.

Activities to promote monetary and financial cooperation have also continued. These expanded in the aftermath of the 1997–1998 crisis and gained momentum during the fourth ADB decade (Chapter 11). In 2010, the Chiang Mai Initiative was extended to become the Chiang Mai Initiative Multilateralization (CMIM), a multilateral currency swap arrangement under a single contract among the ASEAN+3 countries (ASEAN members plus the PRC, Japan, and the Republic of Korea) instead of a network of bilateral swap arrangements. CMIM started with a total amount of $120 billion and expanded to $240 billion in 2014. To support the CMIM, the ASEAN+3 Macroeconomic Research was established in Singapore in 2011 to analyze regional economies, detect risks, and recommend appropriate action. The CMIM was a start, but financing through currency swaps has yet to be used. The Republic of Korea and Singapore, for example, when faced with shortfalls in liquidity after the global financial crisis, instead signed a series of bilateral swap agreements with major central banks, including the US Federal Reserve.

In 2012, the prospects for regional linkages were boosted by the emergence of Myanmar from decades of isolation, largely through lifting of US financial sanctions and reengagement with multilateral and bilateral

---

[11] ADB, 2010, *Key Indicators for Asia and the Pacific 2010*, The Rise of Asia's Middle Class.
[12] Kharas, 2010, The Emerging Middle Class in Developing Countries, *Development Center Working Papers*.

donors including ADB. This was enabled by efforts of the government, starting in 2010, to accelerate democratization and ethnic reconciliation, improve macroeconomic policies (such as removal of plural exchange rates), implement structural policies, reduce trade barriers, and open up commercial activities. These contributed to large inward foreign direct investment and growth rates of 7%–9%. Myanmar is part of the Greater Mekong Subregion and is strategically located between two economic giants, the PRC and India. The opening up of Myanmar presents expanded opportunities for greater connectivity between South Asia, East Asia, and Southeast Asia. As the PRC moves up the global value chain, manufacturing firms are encouraged to relocate to other countries, including Myanmar.

By the middle of the fifth ADB decade, therefore, developing countries in Asia—helped by stronger regional ties—were adjusting to new opportunities closer to home. This encouraged more moderate but more sustainable development: in nearly every year of the postcrisis period, growth exceeded 7% in eight economies across the region, including in the PRC, the Lao People's Democratic Republic, and Sri Lanka.[13] Although growth slowed in the PRC toward the end of the decade from double-digit levels in the previous ADB decade to below 7%, this was counterbalanced by growing strength in India where growth accelerated past 7% in 2015. During 2012–2016, ADB developing economies expanded by an average of more than 6% a year. Excluding the NIEs, the growth rate was even higher. In contrast, growth in the Group of Seven (G7) economies over the same period averaged about 1.5% and in the European Union about 1.0%.

Rising Inequality and Pressure on Environment

Was the world indeed on the verge of a pan-Asian century? A study commissioned by ADB in 2011, *Asia 2050: Realizing the Asian Century*, concluded that the Asian century scenario was plausible but not preordained. It warned of obstacles—including rising inequality, environmental degradation, changing demographics, and inadequate governance.

At the 2007 Annual Meeting in Kyoto, ADB President Haruhiko Kuroda had highlighted two of these concerns. The first was inequality, which threatened social cohesion and could hamper growth. Asia, he said, "…is increasingly a region of two faces—the shining Asia of vitality and

---

[13] ADB, *Asian Development Outlook 2015*, 10.

wealth, and its shadows, where desperate poverty persists." The second was environmental degradation and climate change. He said that countries would need to use natural resources wisely "so that the poor do not bear the brunt of the environmental impacts of growth."

It was clear that the gains from the social and economic transformation occurring in Asia had not been equally shared. After 50 years of progress since the mid-1960s, millions of people had received no more than modest gains. In many Asian countries, the Gini coefficient—a widely used measure of inequality—had been rising. Societies were becoming more unequal. Between the mid-1990s and the late 2000s, the Gini coefficient for Asia as a whole increased from 39 to 46, or by 1.4% a year. In 1999, over 1 billion people lived on less than $1.90 per day.[14] By 2012, this number had fallen to about 450 million. However, only six countries in Asia—Bangladesh, the PRC, India, Indonesia, Pakistan, and the Philippines— accounted for almost half of the measured poor across the globe[15] while these countries are now considered middle-income countries.

These trends gave rise to yet another debate: whether development assistance should focus on poor countries or, rather, on poor people.[16] In 1990, more than 90% of the world's poor lived in low-income countries. But by 2010, almost three-quarters of the world's poor lived in middle-income countries. This shift had been brought about by fast growth in countries that had large numbers of poor people, notably India and the PRC. Some argued that development assistance for middle-income countries should be reduced because these countries had the resources to take care of their own poor. Others felt that development assistance should instead consider the nature of poverty as well as the institutional context in the aid recipient countries.

---

[14] Estimates of global poverty incidence require the use of internationally comparable poverty lines. Until recently, the most widely used international poverty line was $1.25 a day measured in 2005 purchasing power parity (PPP). This poverty line was based on the average of 15 national poverty lines from some of the world's poorest countries converted to a common currency using 2005 PPP exchange rates. In 2015, the international poverty line was updated to $1.90 a day using 2011 PPP. The real value of the poverty line remains the same, i.e., $1.90 in 2011 buys the same basket of goods and services as $1.25 did in 2005 prices.

[15] World Bank, PovcalNet Database (downloaded 8 October 2015) based on 2011 PPP adjustment.

[16] Kanbur and Sumner, 2012, Poor Countries or Poor People? Development Assistance and the New Geography of Global Poverty, *Journal of International Development*, 686–695.

Expectations were rising as well. More people in Asia were becoming aware of inequalities within and across countries. Globalization, and the associated spread of information and communication technology meant that news and knowledge circulated much more rapidly. Millions of young people in Asia had high expectations of schooling and careers. They could easily compare standards in their own countries with those elsewhere. Often, they were not satisfied, putting political and economic institutions under pressure. Dramatic political change occurred, for example, in Myanmar, when Aung San Suu Kyi's National League for Democracy won a sweeping election victory in 2016 and formed the first civilian government in the country for over 50 years. In Southeast Asia, the ASEAN Economic Community came into effect at the end of 2015, putting pressure on all member governments to open their markets to neighboring ASEAN countries.

Asia's economic growth, accompanied by rapid urbanization, had put great pressure on the environment. Added to this was the impact of climate change. Asia and the Pacific has extensive coastal areas with high concentrations of people and economic activities which are vulnerable to the likely impacts of climate change. Between 1976 and 2015, 1.5 million natural hazard-related deaths were recorded in the region, more than half of the global total. A number of major weather-related and destructive events occurred during the fifth ADB decade. In 2008, more than 130,000 people died when cyclone Nargis swept into southern Myanmar; and in 2013, typhoon Haiyan in the Philippines killed at least 6,000 people and caused damage worth $13 billion. Major typhoons, floods, and droughts also caused much damage in other countries including India, Indonesia, the PRC, and several Pacific island countries.

Actions Needed for Climate Change

With scientific studies predicting that environmental pressures would intensify, it was clear that climate change could seriously hinder sustainable development and poverty eradication. Previously, the philosophy of "grow now, clean up later" had been widely held across developing Asia. By the fifth ADB decade, this approach was giving way to the idea that high economic growth needed to be combined with efforts to improve the environment. Countries were beginning to invest in clean energy, conserve biodiversity and forest communities, and aim for cleaner urban air by introducing improved public transport systems and cleaner vehicles. Green finance—for environment-oriented technologies, projects, and industries—began to emerge as an alternative to traditional financing models. At the same time, developing countries in Asia faced a growing need to expand energy output despite the environmental costs.

The climate was also increasingly recognized as a public good. Since carbon dioxide production has global environmental implications, responses to climate change would have to be international, requiring global solutions built on common but differentiated responsibilities among economies. Countries would need to work together to promote climate-resilient, low-carbon development.

This would not be easy, as numerous efforts at conducting international negotiations indicated. The 1992 Earth Summit in Rio de Janeiro, Brazil resulted in the United Nations Framework Convention on Climate Change (UNFCCC), an international treaty aimed at limiting greenhouse gas emissions. Since the Earth Summit, there have been annual climate change conferences bringing together UNFCCC parties, known as the Conferences of the Parties (COPs), to assess progress. While most of these conferences did not lead to binding or enforceable action, they served to highlight climate-related issues.

One of the most important attempts was set out in the Kyoto Protocol, an international agreement linked to the UNFCCC adopted in December 1997 at COP3. It committed developed country parties by setting internationally binding emission reduction targets.[17] Recognizing that developed countries are principally responsible for the current high levels of greenhouse gas emissions in the atmosphere as a result of more than 150 years of industrial activity, the Kyoto Protocol places a heavier burden on developed nations under the principle of "common but differentiated responsibilities." But this agreement was not regarded as a major success since the US did not ratify it. Moreover, large developing countries such as the PRC and India did not enter into any emissions reduction commitments.

At the 2007 conference in Indonesia (COP13), the Bali Road Map was adopted. This was to lead to the discussions of binding agreements in 2009 in Copenhagen, covering issues such as nationally appropriate mitigation actions and commitments, adaptation measures for poor countries and the reduction of global emissions. However, the 2009 conference in

---

[17] United Nations, 1998, Kyoto Protocol. http://unfccc.int/kyoto_protocol/items/2830.php. (accessed 13 November 2016).

Copenhagen (COP15) was plagued by disagreement with a deep divide remaining between industrial and developing countries. Developing countries understandably argued that the main responsibility for tackling global environmental issues largely lay with the industrial countries whose centuries of emissions had created most of the current problems. Industrial countries, on the other hand, took the view that it was unhelpful to talk about the past and that policies should focus on the future. Since carbon dioxide emissions were now likely to grow fastest in developing countries, it was vital to curb emissions in both industrial and developing countries. The media reported that the conference ended "in disarray" with parties blaming each other.

The 2009 conference led to the Copenhagen Accord which was "taken note of" but not adopted unanimously by participating countries. The document recognized climate change as one of the world's greatest challenges and called for action to keep temperature increases below 2°C. The Copenhagen Accord was an important building block, prompting voluntary nonbinding mitigation commitments by major countries. It was agreed that developed countries would mobilize $100 billion a year by 2020 for developing countries to mitigate and adapt to climate change. For their part, the PRC and India agreed to lower carbon dioxide emissions per unit of GDP by 40%–45% and 20%–25%, respectively, by 2020 compared to the 2005 levels. Uzbekistan adopted energy efficiency measures, Armenia and the Philippines introduced laws on renewable energy, and Indonesia resolved to reduce deforestation.

Six years later, the 2015 conference (COP21) was held in Paris. In efforts to forge a consensus, COP21 was preceded by several meetings, including the October 2015 session of the Ad Hoc Working Group on the Durban Platform for Enhanced Action in Bonn which prepared a draft agreement. Around the world, there were demonstrations in favor of a strong agreement. The French Presidency of COP21 skillfully avoided the bitterness of the Copenhagen conference and steered the negotiations to an approval of the Paris Agreement, through which participating countries agreed to a global peaking of greenhouse gas emissions "as soon as possible" and to do their best to keep global warming "to well below 2 degrees C...and pursuing efforts to limit the temperature increase to 1.5°C....." Some delegates considered the Agreement a historic turning point. Others were less impressed, noting that much of the agreement recorded promises rather than commitments. Nevertheless, there was now greater pressure for international action. The Paris Agreement entered into force in November

2016 after 74 countries, representing almost 60% of the global greenhouse gas emissions, ratified the agreement.

Sustainable Development Goals

The ideals of environmental protection and sustainability came to be more strongly reflected in new global development goals adopted in 2015. In 2001, the international community had adopted the eight Millennium Development Goals (MDGs) setting out 18 targets to be achieved by 2015 (Chapter 11). In addition to focusing on poverty, the MDGs had given priority to social objectives. While it was hard to judge precisely how useful the MDGs had been in achieving their aims, they served to bring the global development community together around common objectives. As the target date for the achievement of the MDGs of 2015 approached, there was widespread support for the idea of setting new goals.

In 2012, the Secretary-General of the United Nations appointed a high-level panel to prepare a new list of Sustainable Development Goals (SDGs). The panel included Indonesian President Susilo Bambang Yudhoyono as one of the three co-chairs.[18] The panel worked with many other organizations to arrive at a list of SDGs. In September 2015, the SDGs were unanimously adopted by 193 member states of the United Nations, supporting a bold new global agenda to end poverty by 2030 and pursue a sustainable future.

The SDGs were broader and more extensive than the MDGs. The SDGs embraced a triple bottom line, combining economic development, environmental sustainability, and social inclusion. In particular, compared with the MDGs, the SDGs raised the profile of environmental objectives. However, some critics argue that having 17 SDGs and 169 related targets led to a loss of focus (Figure 13.1).[19] Reflecting the development issues of the period, 11 of the 17 SDGs refer to sustainability.

New Sources of Development Finance

As was the case in the previous ADB decade (Chapter 11), new sources of development finance became available during the fifth decade. While traditional donors were splintering into many specialized agencies, new

---

[18] The other co-chairs were President Ellen Johnson Sirleaf of Liberia and Prime Minister David Cameron of the United Kingdom.
[19] Kenny, 2015, MDGs to SDGs: Have We Lost the Plot? *Centre for Global Development Essays*.

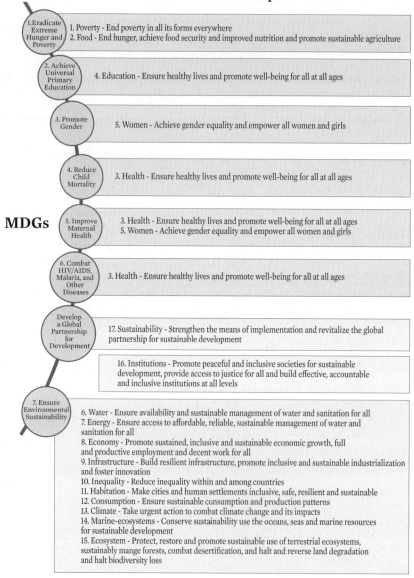

Figure 13.1: Comparing the Millennium Development Goals and the Sustainable Development Goals

MDG = Millennium Development Goal, SDG = Sustainable Development Goal.

Source: Asian Development Bank and Millennium Development Goal targets along with Sustainable Development Goal targets. See (a) http://www.un.org/millenniumgoals/ and (b) http://www.un.org/sustainabledevelopment/sustainable-development-goals/

bilateral donors were emerging from the South, each with its own approach to development cooperation. Developing countries now had access to more diverse sources of financing including market-based resources. Private organizations, including philanthropic foundations, nongovernment organizations, and religious or community-based groups provided more financing, but at the same time added to fragmentation and volatility.[20] Meanwhile, official development assistance to Asia stagnated as donor industrial countries faced fiscal pressures and, in Europe toward the end of the decade, a migrant crisis led to sharply increased calls on funding.[21]

In 2015, choices for borrowing countries in Asia widened when two new institutions for financing infrastructure were established. One was the Asian Infrastructure Investment Bank (AIIB), headquartered in Beijing. The other was the New Development Bank (NDB), headquartered in Shanghai and established by Brazil, the Russian Federation, India, the PRC, and South Africa—the first multinational development bank set up entirely by emerging economies.

Both institutions have adopted standards for safeguarding environmental and social impacts of projects as well as for a fair and transparent procurement system which are at par with those of existing multilateral development banks. In 2016, the NDB approved four renewable energy projects for India, the PRC, Brazil, and South Africa. The Indian project provided a multitranche loan of $250 million to the nationalized Canara Bank for lending to renewable energy ventures. AIIB has approved projects in Bangladesh, Indonesia, Pakistan, and Tajikistan, covering slum development, highway construction, and electricity grid development, many of which are cofinanced with the World Bank, ADB, and the European Bank for Reconstruction and Development.

Issues Surrounding Globalization

The end of the fifth ADB decade saw increasing uncertainty—and what some viewed as a reversal of globalization. Globalization is facing even greater criticisms, regarding such issues as rising inequality, job losses in certain sectors, increasing financial volatility, and environmental degradation. The UK vote to leave the European Union (popularly known

---

[20] Kharas, 2007, *The New Reality of Aid*.
[21] Center for Global Prosperity, 2013, *The Index of Global Philanthropy and Remittances with a Special Report on Emerging Economies*.

as Brexit) and the US presidential election, both in 2016, were reminders of widespread concerns about globalization.

Indeed, large segments of the population in advanced countries did not benefit from globalization. It has been observed that: "In the US, the bottom 90% has endured income stagnation for a third of a century. Median income for full-time male workers is actually lower in real (inflation-adjusted) terms than it was 42 years ago. At the bottom, real wages are comparable to their level 60 years ago."[22] There is evidence that the main winners in terms of income between 1998 and 2008 were the richest 1% of the world's people, and the middle class in emerging economies. The losers included the middle and working classes in advanced countries.[23]

The second "dagger penetrating globalization" is a growing fear of immigration.[24] Although many developed countries have opened their doors to refugees from the Middle East, public resentment has been fanned by sporadic terrorism. With the inconclusive results from the World Trade Organization Doha Round and political hurdles to proposed trade deals involving developed countries, such as the Transatlantic Trade and Investment Partnership and the Comprehensive Economic and Trade Agreement, there are growing fears that opposition to globalization may widen in the coming years.

The debate about globalization is still unfolding. For many policy makers, the solution lies in managing globalization better so that it does not lose public support. Many scholars believe that globalization is a positive-sum game that serves the common interest but that institutions must be developed to ensure that everybody benefits.[25] Globalization still brings many benefits to developing countries in Asia, but greater attention should be paid to issues arising from these changes.

Solid Growth of Asia

At the end of the ADB's fifth decade, the Asian developing economy—covering ADB's 45 developing member economies including the NIES that have graduated from ADB assistance—has sustained a high overall annual growth rate of around 6%, even though it is slower than in some years

---

[22] Stiglitz, 2016, Globalization and Its New Discontents, Project Syndicate, web.
[23] Milanovic, 2016, *Global Inequality: A New Approach for the Age of Globalization*.
[24] Kharas, 2016, What Does Brexit Mean for Poor People? *Future Development*.
[25] Piketty, 2014, *Capital in the Twenty First Century*.

before the global financial crisis. ADB's ninth President Takehiko Nakao has emphasized that "excessive pessimism is unwarranted in Asia."[26]

Certainly, growth in the PRC economy is slowing due to its transition to a new economic model that focuses on consumption and services and that is more environmentally friendly. The country is also faced with a shrinking working-age population, rising wages, and the repercussions of massive investments made in the wake of the global financial crisis. Given its size, the PRC's slowdown is having an impact on the regional and global economies including through the declining price of resources and contracting trade. The PRC, however, is still a middle-income country with plenty of room to grow.

India, Bangladesh, Viet Nam, and Myanmar continue to grow their economies by around 7% per year through policies that focus on boosting the private sector and foreign direct investment. Indonesia, which has been hit by falling resource prices, is growing at about 5% annually, principally due to domestic demand. The Philippines is posting an annual growth rate of 6%, thanks to growth in consumption and the service sector. Since these countries have a large and young population, they can take advantage of the demographic bonus for a period of time if they can provide good education and job opportunities. Among smaller countries, Sri Lanka with the population of 20 million, after the long and deadly conflict ended in 2009, benefited from solid growth of 8–9% in 2010–2012 and around 5% thereafter. Bhutan, which became known as the inventor of "gross national happiness" index, also has enjoyed strong growth under the stable constitutional monarchy based on reformist policies.

In general, the growing middle class in Asia is providing impetus by keeping consumption strong. Once people's lifestyles have been bettered by access to such goods as air conditioners, cars, and cosmetics, the process is not reversible or stoppable. These are phenomena earlier experienced by Japan, the NIEs, and advanced economies in North America and Europe. Hence, growth in Asia has become more broadly based on domestic and regional demand, supported by regionwide supply chains. Growth and social development in Asia are also being encouraged by democratically elected new reformist leaders like Prime Minister Narendra Modi of India, President Joko Widodo of Indonesia, and State Counsellor and Union Minister for Foreign Affairs Aung San Suu Kyi of Myanmar.

---

[26] Nakao, 2017, *ADB's New Strategy in Asia: Helping Build Quality Infrastructure at Scale.*

For the region to continue growing steadily Asia should not be complacent. President Nakao has emphasized that strengthening appropriate policies is essential.[27] These include a steady macroeconomic policy, investments in infrastructure, investments in education and health, open trade and investment regimes, good governance, inclusiveness of society (addressing persistent poverty and gender issues) and sustainability (climate actions), a vision for the future, and political stability in countries and friendly relations with neighbors.

The Fifth ADB Decade

In the fifth ADB decade, Asia was still ascending. But the region was also settling into the realities of more moderate growth driven by regional and national factors, although some countries have maintained growth or even gathered more momentum. While absolute poverty declined, policy makers still needed to focus attention on the problems of persistent poverty, inequality, and environmental sustainability.

Moreover, the development paradigm became more ambitious. ADB members, particularly middle-income countries, expected the Bank to respond and adapt to their diverse needs. The Bank needed, therefore, to catalyze more resources for development, act as convener in regional activities, and provide knowledge and policy advice. ADB Management spent much of the fifth decade ensuring that the Bank remained the institution of choice for its developing member countries.

---

[27] Nakao, 2015, Eight Conditions for Economic Development, *Nikkei Asian Review*.

CHAPTER 14
Fifth Decade (2007–2016)

ADB: Stronger, Better, Faster

"I want ADB to be stronger, better, and faster. First, we will have stronger financial capacity, and we will use it well. Second, we will provide better knowledge services and innovative solutions. Third, we will be faster in responding to our clients."

– *Takehiko Nakao,*
Address to the ADB Annual Meeting, 2015

The Asian Development Bank (ADB) entered its fifth decade needing to meet the diverse needs of a dynamic region while aiming for higher standards of performance. At the 2007 Annual Meeting in Kyoto, President Kuroda recognized that "a dramatically transformed Asia will also require an equally transformed development partner in ADB." His successor, Takehiko Nakao, who arrived in early 2013, said that ADB would need to be "stronger, better, and faster."

By this time, ADB was already familiar with designing strategies to respond to rapid changes in the region and the evolution of international development thinking. The fourth ADB decade had witnessed upheavals with the 1997 Asian financial crisis and a widening global development agenda, including the emphasis on aid effectiveness, global environmental policies, and the Millennium Development Goals (MDGs). As pressures for change grew, both Presidents initiated further reforms in ADB and took steps to expand the Bank's capital.

New Long-Term Strategic Framework

President Kuroda had started work on a new corporate strategy in 2006 when he appointed an eminent persons group to make an assessment of possible directions (Chapter 12). The group presented their report, *Toward a New Asian Development Bank in a New Asia*, to him in March 2007 and it was discussed a few months later at the Bank's Annual Meeting in Kyoto.[1] The report envisaged that, by 2020, most countries in Asia would have conquered widespread absolute poverty though they would still be facing formidable economic and social problems. The report set out a framework for ADB's response noting that "In this transformed Asia, the traditional model of development banking—transferring outside official capital—will become redundant." In hindsight, such a view might have reflected the benign global financial conditions at the time. In any case, it urged ADB "to change radically and adopt a new paradigm for development banking."

The report recommended three complementary strategic reorientations: from fighting extensive poverty to supporting faster and more inclusive growth, from targeting economic growth to ensuring environmentally sustainable growth, and from a primarily national focus to a regional and ultimately global focus. It urged the Bank to be more selective and proposed changes in its business model. It questioned whether ADB should remain a "full service" development bank such as a "mirror image of a global institution like the World Bank," or whether it should become more specialized.[2]

Kuroda thought that the Bank needed a new corporate strategy. And the eminent group's report strengthened the case by emphasizing that ADB needed to adapt to rapid changes in Asia. The previous long-term strategy document had been prepared in 2001 when the region was still affected by the impact of the 1997 Asian financial crisis and, reflecting the priorities of the time, had focused on poverty reduction. Now the situation was different. Moreover, the Bank had accumulated a proliferation of strategy documents, leading to problems of overlap and confusion. Without a new central strategy statement, different sections of the institution could easily find a document to support the programs they favored. Kuroda also saw a new strategy as a way to build support for additional capital (Chapter 12).

To draft the strategy, the Bank established a task force which during 2007 engaged in extensive consultations. The outcome was a new long-term strategic framework, Strategy 2020, approved by the Board early in 2008 and discussed at the 2008 Annual Meeting in Madrid. Strategy 2020 emphasized the vision of an Asia and Pacific region free of poverty. However, it went beyond a focus on poverty alone to include broader issues as improving living conditions and the quality of life of citizens. These included such matters as governance and gender equity. Strategy 2020 set out three complementary

---

[1] ADB, 2007, *Toward a New ADB in a New Asia*.
[2] ADB, 2007, *Toward a New ADB in a New Asia*, 13.

agendas to support this approach: fostering inclusive growth, promoting environmentally sustainable growth, and encouraging regional cooperation and integration. To implement these, the strategy identified five core areas of operations: infrastructure, environment (including climate change), regional cooperation and integration, the finance sector, and education. Strategy 2020 also set out operational targets. Among them, ADB would seek by 2012 to maintain 80% of its operations in the five core operational areas.[3]

A notable feature of Strategy 2020 was that it changed the Bank's view on the approach to growth. Previously, ADB had espoused "pro-poor growth" (Chapter 12). Given widening inequality in the region, Strategy 2020 now aimed for "inclusive growth," a somewhat different concept which suggested that all segments of society should participate in and benefit from growth, especially the poor. Under Strategy 2020, the Bank's approach to inclusive growth would be based on three pillars. The first was high sustainable growth to expand economic opportunities. The second was broader access to these opportunities, by expanding human capabilities. And the third was social protection, including safety nets to prevent extreme deprivation.

The earlier corporate strategy had called for large investments in infrastructure and social sectors, directing resources at sectors such as rural development and agriculture which could have the greatest impact on poverty. Strategy 2020 now focused on food security, particularly for the poor, with an emphasis on a multisector perspective of food security going beyond agriculture and involving support for a wider range of sections including education, health, water, infrastructure, and disaster and emergency assistance.

There has been considerable debate within the Bank, however, on the approach to the idea of inclusive growth. On the one hand, there was concern that ADB's approach, combined with the dominance of lending to infrastructure, resulted in less attention to the social protection pillar of inclusive growth compared with the other two.[4] On the other, there was the view that, following Strategy 2020's approach of selectivity and focus, ADB did not need to address all elements of inclusive growth and should instead focus on areas where it could have a stronger impact. Donors also pressed the Bank to clarify its understanding and measurement of inclusiveness in its operations. In response, ADB has been trying in recent years to make

---

[3] Support for other areas of operation, such as health, agriculture, and disaster and emergency assistance, was to be selectively provided.
[4] ADB, 2004, *ADB's Support for Inclusive Growth*.

interventions more inclusive and has issued internal guidelines on the matter. However, this issue clearly still requires further attention.

To support sustainable growth, ADB stepped up the use of environmentally friendly technologies. Safeguards, along with systems for enforcement, were strengthened. Following the adoption of the Kyoto Protocol in 1997 and its subsequent ratification in 2005, ADB had increased climate change financing. The priority given to climate change issues gathered momentum in the fifth ADB decade. In 2009, the Board approved its new Energy Policy that set a clean energy (including renewable energy, energy efficiency, natural gas and clean coal) investment target of $2 billion per year to be reached by 2013. The Bank also aimed to reduce the vulnerability of developing countries to natural and environmental hazards by strengthening integrated disaster risk management and establishing a facility to provide post-disaster assistance in poor countries.[5,6]

There was greater prominence for regional cooperation activities during the Kuroda era. Previous ADB efforts had been fragmented across departments and had offered limited support for trade and investment. Strategy 2020 envisaged greater assistance in capacity building and in promoting economic corridors and regional value chains—while anticipating and mitigating external shocks. The Bank set a target of increasing support for regional cooperation to at least 30% of total assistance by 2020. By 2014–2016, the ratio was already 27%, so activities have been on on track to achieve the target. Along with the ADB Institute, the Bank undertook a trilogy of regional studies: on strengthening architecture for regional policy cooperation, on building physical infrastructure networks to support regional growth, and on strengthening institutions to support an Asian economic community.[7]

One of the major regional projects promoted by ADB is the Turkmenistan–Afghanistan–Pakistan–India Pipeline (TAPI) gas pipeline based on a public-private partnership framework (Box 14.1).

Strategy 2020 recognized that ADB would have to take different approaches to four broad categories of countries: graduated, middle-income, low-income, and fragile. Notably, Strategy 2020 advocated the development of a stronger relationship with graduated members, who could transfer best

---

[5] ADB, 2014, *Operational Plan for Integrated Disaster Risk Management*.
[6] ADB, 2012, *Piloting a Disaster Response Facility*.
[7] ADB, 2008, *Emerging Asian Regionalism*; ADB and ADBI, 2009, *Infrastructure for a Seamless Asia*; ADB, 2008, *Institutions for Regional Integration*.

Box 14.1: ADB Support to the Turkmenistan–Afghanistan–Pakistan–India Natural Gas Pipeline

The Asian Development Bank (ADB) is developing the Turkmenistan–Afghanistan–Pakistan–India (TAPI) Pipeline to transport natural gas from Turkmenistan through Afghanistan into Pakistan and India. The project, the total cost of which would exceed $10 billion, presents an opportunity for regional cooperation on an expanded scale linking the four economies. With the opening up of new markets, landlocked Turkmenistan will be able to diversify gas exports to the east. Afghanistan, Pakistan, and India will gain a steady supply of affordable gas to power their growing economies.

The project began in March 1995 with the signing of an inaugural memorandum of understanding between Turkmenistan and Pakistan. However, plans were held up because of Afghanistan's unstable political situation. With improved regional security after the fall of the Taliban, the countries in the region decided to push ahead with the ambitious plans for the 1,600-kilometer-long pipeline.

ADB has been the TAPI project's secretariat since 2003 at the request of the relevant governments. The project is being implemented in four phases with Bank support. Phase 1 was completed in December 2010 with the signing of the gas pipeline framework agreement. Phase 2 ended with the signing of the gas sales and purchase agreement in 2012. The parties asked ADB to continue as secretariat in phase 3 for establishing a special purpose consortium company to operate the TAPI project, select a commercial company as consortium lead, and finalize operational agreements. The pipeline will be constructed in phase 4; construction began in Turkmenistan in December 2015.

ADB, now involved in the project for 14 years, has been balancing the interests of the various parties. The Bank has organized minister-level steering committees and technical working groups. It has also financed technical studies and the drafting of agreements. ADB was appointed the transaction advisor for the project in November 2013 and advised on the establishment of the TAPI pipeline company. In 2015, ADB facilitated the endorsement of Turkmengaz as the project's consortium leader and the execution of the shareholders' agreement. During the financial arrangement stage, ADB may also play a role of a financier to lend to governments for their equity investments, or to private sector partners.

Sources: ADB. 2012. *Technical Assistance Report: Turkmenistan–Afghanistan–Pakistan–India Natural Gas Pipeline Project, Phase 3*. https://www.adb.org/sites/default/files/project-document/73061/44463-013-reg-tar.pdf (accessed 26 February 2017); ADB. 2016. *Infographic: ADB TAPI Gas Pipeline*. https://www.adb.org/news/infographics/tapi-gas-pipeline (accessed 26 February 2017).

practice approaches to policy reforms in other countries and provide direct financing of projects or cofinancing of ADB-assisted projects.

Strategy 2020 was a high-level corporate document. To guide staff on implementing it, more than a dozen operational plans and policies were prepared during the fifth decade. These documents often had multiple objectives, so staff often faced the challenge of ensuring consistency across the Bank's activities.

Global Financial Crisis and Response

No sooner had Strategy 2020 been prepared than headwinds began to blow the Bank's plans off course. Just as the strategy was being published, the 2008 global financial crisis took hold in industrial countries. Strategy 2020 had not given any particular attention to agriculture and provided little guidance on how the Bank should respond to the food and fuel price increases that suddenly affected the region (Chapter 13). To address these issues, a paper addressing the causes and impacts of price inflation and policy responses was hastily prepared before the 2008 Annual Meeting in Madrid.[8]

At the 2008 Annual Meeting when Strategy 2020 was adopted, Kuroda spoke of troubling times for the world economy and outlined the assistance the Bank could offer. By early 2009, the impact of the crisis was being felt across Asia, especially following the collapsing demand for regional exports. One year later at the 2009 Annual Meeting in Bali, Kuroda said: "There is no doubt that the global downturn has hit Asian economies hard. Access to finance has tightened. And a sharp drop in export demand seriously affects the region's production networks." Faced with a "triple F" crisis—of food, finance, and fuel—many countries in Asia looked to borrow from ADB.

ADB was able to respond because it had resources on hand. The Bank was able to draw on both the Asian Development Fund (ADF) for soft loan lending and the ordinary capital resources (OCR). In 2008, to help lower-income countries, donors had agreed to the ninth replenishment of ADF (ADF X). Even more important, ADB member countries had agreed in 2009 to the large general capital increase (GCI V) that both Kuroda and Tadao Chino before him had worked toward. Drawing on these resources, new activities were quickly approved. In 2008, lending approvals were $11.3 billion. In 2009, they rose sharply to $15.8 billion. Funds were used to provide loans for budget

---

[8] ADB, 2008, *Food Prices and Inflation in Developing Asia*.

support as well as for public and private sector projects to bolster demand, create jobs, improve social safety nets, and boost private sector confidence.

ADB used a range of instruments to respond quickly to prepare packages to suit the needs of borrowing countries. In June 2009, a new lending authority for OCR, the Countercyclical Support Facility (CSF), was introduced.[9] The facility offered time-bound budget support loans that provided fast-disbursing assistance to address liquidity difficulties. It was priced above regular OCR loans to help contain demands on the limited CSF pool of funds.[10] Since the CSF did not impose structural adjustment conditionalities, the higher price helped avoid the moral hazard risk of being regarded as "easy money." And CSF loans had a short maturity of 5 years to avoid any negative impacts on ADB's lending capacity.

Within a month, there were CSF applications from several developing members so a decision was taken to cap the amount available to each country. By December 2009, five CSF loans had been approved for the equivalent of $500 million each to Bangladesh, Indonesia, Kazakhstan, the Philippines, and Viet Nam. CSF was later mainstreamed.[11] In 2015, during Nakao's tenure, the Bank approved a $1 billion CSF to Kazakhstan to provide assistance in the face of fiscal problems arising from a steep decline in world oil prices and a slowdown in growth in neighboring countries. This was followed by a $500 million CSF to Azerbaijan at the end of 2016. The policy regarding CSF was updated in 2016,[12] clarifying the eligibility criteria and emphasizing the importance of comprehensive structural reforms for crisis-hit countries and close coordination with the IMF.

To help low-income countries without access to OCR funds, the Bank drew on ADF resources. In June 2009, an additional $400 million was approved to support economies facing fiscal strain. Armenia, Georgia, Mongolia, and Papua New Guinea received approval for front-loading beyond their maximum annual utilization.[13] ADB also made extra efforts to increase cofinancing with partner institutions from the PRC, Japan, and the Republic of Korea, as well as with the World Bank and the Islamic Development Bank.

---

[9] ADB, 2009, *Enhancing ADB's Response to the Global Economic Crisis: Establishing the Countercyclical Support Facility*.
[10] The terms comprised the interest rate with a spread of 200 basis points above the London interbank offered rate (LIBOR), with a provision of surcharge or rebate reflecting ADB's cost of funds; 5-year maturity, including a 3-year grace period; and the commitment charge at 75 basis points.
[11] ADB, 2011, *Review of ADB's Policy-Based Lending*.
[12] ADB, 2016, *Review of ADB's Lending Instruments for Crisis Response*.
[13] ADB, 2010, *Annual Report 2009*.

Access to trade finance was crucial for cushioning the impact of the global downturn on developing countries in Asia in 2008. As the crisis widened, banks and export–import agencies in industrial countries became increasingly risk averse. They began to restrict the finance they would approve for trade with developing countries, exacerbating an already grim situation for smaller enterprises. ADB already had set up a Trade Finance Program (TFP) in 2003 to provide banks with guarantees of repayment, a form of insurance, when they financed trade with selected developing countries. In 2009, the Bank increased the TFP's overall exposure limit from $150 million to $1 billion, making it a more effective countercyclical tool.[14] Access to the TFP grew quickly during 2009, supporting the international trading activities of many small and medium-sized firms in countries such as Nepal, Sri Lanka, and Viet Nam.[15]

The Bank also stepped up its support for policy discussion. Throughout 2009, ADB and the ADB Institute in Tokyo, often in association with other partners such as universities and think tanks, arranged more than 20 seminars in developing countries to discuss the crisis. These included several forums in South Asia on the impact of the crisis and a conference on poverty and sustainable development in Viet Nam. The Bank's resident missions also offered policy advice to individual countries.

As things turned out, the global financial crisis had less of an impact in Asia than had first been anticipated (Chapter 13). ADB had projected economic growth for developing Asia at 3.4% for 2009.[16] In fact, growth turned out to be 6.0% in 2009 and in 2010 accelerated to 9.4%. The new forms of lending supported by the Bank had helped strengthen economic performance across the region at a difficult time.

The General Capital Increase

Faced with growing demands on its resources, by 2008 it was clear that ADB needed an injection of capital—a capital increase—to support expanded activities. In fact, well before the global financial crisis, both Chino and Kuroda had taken steps to build support for a capital increase. Looking ahead, they wished to see Bank lending continue to grow and were concerned that unless there was a capital increase, ADB would face both headroom constraints and the prospects of stagnating lending. However, the previous

---

[14] ADB, *ADB Trade Finance Program*.
[15] ADB, 2012, *Evaluation Lessons of a Global Financial Crisis for Asia and ADB*.
[16] ADB, 2009, *The Fifth General Capital Increase of the Asian Development Bank*.

general capital increase (GCI IV) had been approved in 1994. Efforts to find agreement about another increase had met with a lukewarm response from some of ADB's main country shareholders (Chapter 12).[17]

Kuroda knew that ADB would require more resources to meet the needs of members. Even before the 2008 global financial crisis, OCR borrowers aiming to achieve the MDGs had an estimated large resource gap. By the end of the fourth decade, at Kuroda's instructions staff had prepared three financial scenarios for a capital increase of 100%, 150%, or 200%. Early expectations were quite modest and staff were encouraged to "think 100%." Initial discussions with shareholders, however, prompted an upward shift to a level of around 150%, although ADB expected that a compromise might result in a smaller increase.

The mood of shareholders, however, changed quickly in 2008 when the global financial crisis began to affect world markets. The prospect of an international recession led developing countries in Asia to look to ADB for support. In response, ADB offered an additional $7 billion–$8 billion of OCR funding to crisis-affected borrowers in 2009–2010, almost 50% more than the amount of lending originally planned. However, without GCI V, ADB estimated that OCR operations from 2010 onward would need to be cut back sharply to less than $4 billion.[18] This outlook—where the need for financial assistance in Asia was suddenly quite urgent but the prospects were that ADB's resources would be quite limited—quickly strengthened the case for a large GCI.

Around this time, in November 2008, Group of Twenty (G20) leaders from the world's largest economies met in Washington, DC and agreed that there should be a coordinated response to the global crisis from the multilateral development banks. Reflecting these international concerns, several ADB Board members expressed strong support for a substantial capital increase, perhaps as large as 200%. At a Board and management retreat at the Sofitel Hotel in Manila, some Board members were still reluctant. It was pointed out, however, that the paid-in portion of the capital increase would be only 4% and the remaining 96% would be callable capital, payable only in the event of a large-scale default by borrowers. The Bank had never made a call on its callable capital, so the risk was minimal. After some discussion, many donors decided that a large capital increase would be appropriate in view

---

[17] The need for a general capital increase was raised in 2006, but Management decided not to pursue the matter because several main countries were not supportive.
[18] ADB, 2009, *The Fifth General Capital Increase of the Asian Development Bank*.

of the unfolding international crisis and would be consistent with the G20 discussions. Japan threw its support behind the larger proposal. Kuroda himself visited the United States (US) Treasury to make the case and the US also agreed, though urging stronger institutional reforms.

In April 2009, ADB Management formally proposed a 200% increase which tripled the Bank's authorized capital (Table 14.1). The paid-in proportion would be 4%, raising the paid-in amount to $8 billion. To respond to the financial crisis, the increase would be front-loaded and its sector distribution would reflect the priorities in Strategy 2020. As part of the GCI V negotiations, ADB also agreed to introduce various institutional reforms including strengthening human resources, increasing organizational effectiveness, and strengthening safeguards.

Although the discussions for the GCI had been started before the global crisis, the crisis certainly helped to build support for the increase. In April 2009, an overwhelming majority of ADB members endorsed GCI V, the largest general capital increase in the Bank's history and the first secured by a major multilateral development bank following the crisis. At the 2009 Annual Meeting in Bali, Kuroda declared: "The tripling of ADB's capital resource base, confirmed just days ago, is a resounding vote of confidence in this region's ability to overcome obstacles on the path to economic growth and poverty reduction."

Table 14.1: General Capital Increases and Capital Composition (Authorized Capital Stock)

	Initial Subscription	GCI I	GCI II	GCI III	GCI IV	GCI V
Resolution Date	22 Aug 1966	30 Nov 1971	29 Oct 1976	25 Apr 1983	22 May 1994	29 Apr 2009
Capital Increase						
% increase	0	150	135	105	100	200
Number of new shares	110,000	165,000	414,800	754,750	1,770,497	7,092,622
Composition of Capital (%)						
Callable	50	80	90	95	98	96
Paid-in	50	20	10	5	2	4

continued on next page

Table 14.1 continued

	Initial Subscription	GCI I	GCI II	GCI III	GCI IV	GCI V
Components of Capital (%)						
Convertible currency	50	40	40	40	40	40
National currency	50	60	60	60	60	60
Composition of Capital, Increase						
in SDR million	1,100	1,650	4,148	7,547	17,705	70,926
Callable	550	1,320	3,733	7,170	17,351	68,089
Paid-in	550	330	415	377	354	2,837
in $ million	1,100[a]	1,650[b]	4,790[c]	8,163[d]	25,043[e]	106,272[f]
Callable	550	1,320	4,311	7,755	24,542	102,021
Paid-in	550	330	479	408	501	4,251
Composition of Capital, Cumulative[g]						
in SDR million	1,100	2,750	7,221	14,768	34,910	106,389
Callable	550	1,870	5,823	12,993	32,480	101,084
Paid-in	550	880	1,398	1,775	2,430	5,306
in $ million	1,100[a]	2,750[b]	8,338[c]	15,974[d]	49,378[e]	159,408[f]
Callable	550	1,870	6,724	14,054	45,941	151,459
Paid-in	550	880	1,614	1,920	3,437	7,950

GCI = general capital increase, SDR = special drawing right, US = United States.

Note: Numbers may not sum precisely because of rounding.

[a] Translated at the exchange rate of $1 per SDR as of 22 August 1966. At the time of ADB's inception, the original authorized capital of ADB was $1 billion in terms of US dollars. Of this amount, $500 million was paid-in shares, and another $500 million was callable. In November 1966, the Board of Governors approved an increase of $100 million of authorized capital.
[b] Translated at the exchange rate of $1 per SDR as of 30 November 1971.
[c] Translated at the exchange rate of $1.15471 per SDR as of 29 October 1976.
[d] Translated at the exchange rate of $1.08163 per SDR as of 29 April 1983. There are no daily rates in Bloomberg for 1983, only month-end rates.
[e] Translated at the exchange rate of $1.41445 per SDR as of 20 May 1994.
[f] Translated at the exchange rate of $1.49835 per SDR as of 29 April 2009.
[g] Includes special capital increases of new and existing members.

Sources: ADB Controller's Department and ADB Annual Reports.

Ninth and Tenth Asian Development Fund Replenishments

Two ADF replenishments took place during the fifth ADB decade allowing the Bank to mobilize additional concessional resources. During the fourth decade, discussions during ADF replenishments had often been contentious (Chapter 12). In response, the Bank, led by Chino, had agreed to implement a series of changes. By the fifth decade, donors had come to regard ADB more positively and expressed broad satisfaction with the reforms taking place.

In 2008, donors agreed on a total replenishment size of $11.3 billion for the ninth ADF replenishment (ADF X, 2009–2012). Of this amount, donors pledged a contribution of $4.2 billion. The negotiations had taken place while Strategy 2020 was being prepared so the ADF framework reflected the priorities in the strategy, including the three core items of inclusive growth, environmentally sustainable growth, and regional integration.[19] Donors also agreed with the five core operational areas of Strategy 2020. At their request, ADB joined with other organizations including the World Bank to provide debt relief to Afghanistan under the Heavily Indebted Poor Countries Initiative (Chapter 11).[20]

The next replenishment (ADF XI, 2013–2016) was concluded in 2012 and agreed on a total amount of $12.4 billion, of which donors pledged $4.6 billion. As was customary, donors took the opportunity to review the Bank's operations, policies, and effectiveness. They urged ADB to continue with the Strategy 2020 priorities and to address concerns about food security, fragile states, gender equity, and governance. Since this was the final replenishment before the MDG target date of 2015, ADB for its part called for generous contributions to ADF XI to help countries achieve the MDGs. Donors also noted growing risks from natural disasters and agreed to pilot the Disaster Response Facility during 2013–2016, which would provide resources outside a country's regular performance-based allocation. This facility would subsequently be regularized under ADF 12 (2017–2020). Resumption of

---

[19] ADB, 2015, *Asian Development Fund X and XI Operations: Opportunity Amid Growing Challenges,* Chapter 3.
[20] The International Development Association and the International Monetary Fund launched the Heavily Indebted Poor Countries (HIPC) Initiative in 1996 to reduce the excessive debt burden faced by the world's poorest countries. It stipulated a sunset clause to prevent the HIPC debt relief from becoming a permanent facility and minimize moral hazard. This sunset clause has been extended several times with the latest attempting to limit its application to countries satisfying the income and indebtedness criteria using data from the end of 2004. The only ADF borrower qualifying for HIPC debt relief was Afghanistan: while other ADF borrowers had met the HIPC indebtedness criteria, no others qualified for HIPC debt relief at that time.

lending to Myanmar was a particularly important development for ADB during the ADF XI period.

ASEAN Infrastructure Fund and Credit Guarantee and Investment Facility

ADB continued to promote cooperation in the Association of Southeast Asian Nations (ASEAN) and ASEAN+3 (ASEAN, plus the PRC, Japan, and the Republic of Korea) regions. For the implementation of the Chiang Mai Initiative Multilateralization, ADB supported the creation of the ASEAN+3 Macroeconomic Research Office, as well as the development of local currency bond markets under the Asian Bond Markets Initiative (Chapter 13).

In 2012, the Bank also worked with ASEAN on the establishment of the ASEAN Infrastructure Fund (AIF) which mobilizes regional savings (including foreign exchange reserves) for infrastructure development. All AIF-financed projects are cofinanced by ADB. The AIF supports the Master Plan on ASEAN Connectivity, designed to bring people, goods, services and capital closer together. As of December 2016, the AIF had financed seven projects in Indonesia, the Lao People's Democratic Republic, Myanmar, and Viet Nam.

In 2010, the Bank also worked with ASEAN+3 to establish the Credit Guarantee and Investment Facility (CGIF), an ADB trust fund to guarantee bonds in the region. As of December 2016, the facility had provided guarantees to support 16 issuances of corporate bonds by 12 issuers in five local currency bond markets (Thai baht, Indonesian rupiah, Singapore dollar, Vietnamese dong, and Philippine peso) in the ASEAN+3 region.

Improving Performance and Accountability

From its earliest days, donors had pressed ADB to constantly improve its performance. In 1974, at the Seventh Annual Meeting in Kuala Lumpur, the US Secretary of the Treasury George P. Shultz (also the US Governor for the Bank) had observed that the general attitude in the US toward development assistance was a questioning one and reminded the meeting, "… we cannot ignore the basic fact that support for these [international] programs depends upon a continuing record of performance by the ADB and all the assistance institutions—and our ability to demonstrate that performance in down-to-earth, understandable terms."

Aware of this international interest, each ADB President strived to make the Bank more efficient. Nevertheless, partly because of aid fatigue in donor countries, ADB remained under constant pressure to demonstrate how it was improving performance and achieving a "results revolution."[21] This drive for effectiveness received additional impetus in 2001. The adoption of the MDGs demanded regular assessments of progress toward targets. A succession of international conferences added to the pressures on international agencies to set measurable development goals and monitor progress through what was termed Managing for Development Results (MfDR) (Chapter 12).[22, 23]

ADB had adopted MfDR in its fourth decade but reinforced it through Strategy 2020. In 2008, ADB became the first multilateral development bank to adopt a corporate results framework. Earlier, in 2007, ADB launched the first in an annual series of Development Effectiveness Reviews. These reviews would be expanded over time both to track the region's progress and to assess the Bank's implementation of Strategy 2020. With the adoption of a scorecard, they quickly became a key part of ADB's annual corporate performance review and reporting system. Often blunt in noting deficiencies, the Development Effectiveness Reviews served as important sources of data for Management, shareholders, donors, and other stakeholders on the Bank's performance. By 2015 when the SDGs were adopted, the global community had come to regard the MfDR approach as a central part of the international development effort.

Kuroda continued to take the issue of accountability and transparency very seriously. Further changes to the Accountability Mechanism, originally introduced by Chino in 2003, were approved in 2012 (Chapter 12).[24] Reforms included direct access to compliance reviews for people adversely affected by projects, as well as appointing a complaint receiving officer as a single entry point for complaints. The 2005 Public Communications Policy was revised in 2011 to expand and speed up access to information.[25] Further improvements to disclosure are planned under President Nakao.

The Independent Evaluation Department was further strengthened following a review of its role in 2008. The Board would appoint the Director

---

[21] ADB, 2006, *An Introduction to Results Management: Principles, Implications, and Applications*, 3.
[22] Further details are in "Historical Context of Managing for Development Results" in ADB, 2011, *Special Evaluation Study on MfDR*.
[23] A summary of the MfDR approach is in OECD, 2009, *Managing for Development Results*.
[24] ADB, 2012, *Accountability Mechanism Policy 2012*.
[25] ADB, 2011, *2011 Public Communications Policy*.

General of the department upon the recommendation of the Development Effectiveness Committee, in consultation with the ADB President. Under Strategy 2020, ADB also committed itself to more actively involving civil society in the design and implementation of projects.

Human Resources

Just as previous Presidents had, Kuroda gave high priority to staffing issues. To implement the new strategy, he initiated a workforce planning exercise which soon made it clear that ADB would need more staff. The Bank had a strong case for an increase in staffing and budget resources. It could point to achievements such as the preparation of Strategy 2020, the adoption of a results framework, and the completion of GCI V. In 2009 therefore, after accounting for efficiency measures and internal staff redeployment, the budget incorporated a requirement for 500 additional positions during 2010–2012. As a result, from the end of 2009 to the end of 2012, the number of staff rose by 18%. The majority of these new positions were provided to regional departments and resident missions to support decentralization.[26]

There were also further efforts to improve staff quality. The Our People Strategy, adopted in 2010, framed "efforts to attract and retain highly motivated individuals and create an environment that enables them to give their best to the region's development."[27] To improve the gender balance, the Bank implemented a third gender action program in 2008–2012, which boosted the proportion of women across staff categories and levels.[28] From 2008, with help from external experts, ADB introduced regular, usually biennial, staff engagement surveys to identify organizational issues and staff satisfaction.[29] In 2012, the Office of the Ombudsperson was set up to

---

[26] The provision of a substantial number of new positions in resident missions was in response to the need to further strengthen them following the 2002, 2007, and 2008 reviews of the resident mission policy and as a response to the decentralization model. Further, several human resources reforms also contributed to successful implementation of the decentralization model. Incentives for posting international staff to resident missions were increased and career prospects for national staff were better defined. The institutional and management structure of resident missions has been improved by creating deputy country director positions, among others. The internal organization of resident missions is streamlined around three core functions: (i) country programming and economic analysis, (ii) country operations, and (iii) finance and administration.

[27] President Kuroda's opening address at the 43rd Annual Meeting of the Board of Governors, Tashkent, Uzbekistan, 2 May 2010.

[28] ADB, 2011, *Updating the Third Gender Action Program (GAP III): GAP III Extension, 2011–2012*.

[29] This followed the survey undertaken in 2003.

provide staff with confidential, impartial, and informal assistance to resolve workplace issues.

Two new vice-presidencies were established during Kuroda's tenure with the aim of improving Strategy 2020 implementation. In 2010, ADB created a new vice-presidency for private sector and cofinancing operations. Effective January 2013, the finance and administration vice-presidency was reorganized into two separate vice-presidencies—for finance and risk management[30] and for administration and corporate management.[31] These changes expanded the number of vice-presidencies to six.

Takehiko Nakao

In February 2013, Prime Minister Shinzo Abe of Japan nominated Kuroda as the next Governor of the Bank of Japan. This did not come as a surprise as the international press had been circulating rumors for some weeks. In mid-March, after a review by the parliament, the Government of Japan confirmed Kuroda's appointment, ending his term as the eighth ADB President.

Kuroda had held office for 8 years, becoming the longest-serving ADB President. He left a strong imprint on the organization. Under his leadership, the Bank almost doubled lending, formulated the long-term Strategy 2020, and carried out many internal reforms. Kuroda led the first general capital increase in 14 years, which tripled the ADB capital base (Table 14.1), and two replenishments of the ADF, which raised over $23.5 billion. He also led the response to the 2008 global financial crisis when ADB provided much needed assistance through the establishment of the Countercyclical Support Facility and expanding the Trade Finance Program. His other achievements included the resumption of operations in Myanmar after more than 20 years. He left ADB having engaged it more in regional cooperation and in international discussions about Asia's expanding role. During his tenure, ADB became more transparent and accountable.

Kuroda was succeeded in April 2013 by the ninth ADB President, Takehiko Nakao, who had extensive experience in international finance. During the 1990s, he had spent 3 years as a staff member at the International Monetary

---

[30] This consisted of the Treasury Department, the Controller's Department, and the Office of Risk Management.
[31] This consisted of the Budget, Personnel, and Management Systems Department; the Operations Services and Financial Management Department; the Office of Administrative Services; the Office of the General Counsel; and the Office of the Secretary.

Fund in Washington, DC, and, like several previous Presidents, had been Vice-Minister of Finance for International Affairs in the Ministry of Finance in Tokyo. He had dealt with issues such as the IMF, multilateral development banks, G7 and G20 meetings, exchange rates, foreign reserve management, and regional and bilateral financial cooperation in Asia. He studied Economics at the University of Tokyo, before obtaining a master of business administration degree from the University of California, Berkeley, and taught international economics to graduate students as a visiting professor at the University of Tokyo when he was Director General of the International Bureau at the Finance Ministry. He pays great attention to work-life balance, and cooks regularly on the weekend.

Nakao welcomed the opportunity to work on development at ADB. Just a few days after his arrival, at the 46th Annual Meeting in Delhi, he outlined his vision of a "more innovative, more inclusive, and more integrated" Asia with growing international influence. Nakao was eager to learn and collect information and proved a good listener. In Mongolia in June 2013, for example, a minister had mentioned that they considered ADB "too small, too slow, and too self-centered." The comment could have been lighthearted criticism, but Nakao took it as a serious signal of the need for change.

Indeed, Nakao has paid more visits than some of his predecessors to ADB developing member countries, including in the Pacific. He has also made multiple visits to large borrowers to have close dialogue with leaders, ministers, and other senior officials. For example, following the Bank's reengagement with Myanmar, Nakao visited the country twice in 2014, and again in June 2016 to meet State Counsellor Aung San Suu Kyi. He had also given special attention to visiting developed member countries regularly to discuss ADB's roles with officials as well as the private sector. He has regarded ADB interactions with the media as essential and is very mindful of wording and messages. He often writes opinion pieces on development topics and encourages staff to do the same. He has given lectures at think tanks, universities, and international forums.

In more than 3 years as President, Nakao has become known for his hands-on management style, his attention to detail, and his close involvement in reforms. In every country he visited, he has had press conferences and meetings with staff at the resident mission. He personally worked on the ADB corporate strategy and reforms through frequent interactions with staff. Executive Directors welcomed his style of engaging the Board early and closely in discussion of important issues. In August 2016, Nakao was unanimously reelected by the ADB Governors for a 5-year term starting November 2016.

Midterm Review of Strategy 2020

Upon assuming office in 2013, Nakao decided that ADB needed corporate and financial reforms. Strategy 2020 had served ADB well, but in the subsequent 5 years after its adoption there had been quite a few changes within the Bank and across the international economy. Nakao asked for a midterm review of Strategy 2020, starting with regional and country consultations and discussions with stakeholders and staff. These consultations generated significant feedback—some critical.[32] The consultations fed into the *Midterm Review of Strategy 2020* (MTR) published in April 2014.[33]

The MTR broadly endorsed and updated Strategy 2020 but noted that ADB would need to adapt to a fast-changing region. It outlined 10 priorities for improving services to member countries.[34] In July 2014, Nakao approved a corresponding action plan. The plan provided a detailed agenda to improve ADB operations, build skills, and provide better services to clients. Clear responsibilities and time lines, along with a transparent basis for monitoring the reforms, were set out.

The MTR did not introduce major changes away from Strategy 2020 but put greater emphasis on selected priorities. Given the serious environmental challenges facing the region, it emphasized climate change, clean energy, and energy efficiency.[35] It also envisaged that more attention would be paid to regional connectivity, including to reforms to facilitate trade harmonization, improve the investment climate, increase access to finance, and develop skills. Between 2003–2007 and 2008–2012, the share going to education and finance had declined. So the MTR proposed that greater attention be given to the social sectors—including the health sector, which was not among the five core areas, but where Nakao found during his visits that some countries

---

[32] ADB, 2014, *Summary of Stakeholder Consultations on the Strategy 2020 Midterm Review*.
[33] ADB, 2014, *Midterm Review of Strategy 2020*.
[34] The 10 strategic priorities were (i) poverty reduction and inclusive economic growth, (ii) environment and climate change, (iii) regional cooperation and integration, (iv) infrastructure development, (v) middle-income countries, (vi) private sector development and operations, (vii) knowledge solutions, (viii) financial resources and partnerships, (ix) delivering value for money in ADB, and (x) organizing to meet new challenges.
[35] ADB had been responding to these issues since the early the 1990s (ADB, 2007, *Background Paper on ADB's Approach to Climate Change*).

wanted ADB engagement and evolving development challenges like rapid urbanization (Box 14.2).

Compared with Strategy 2020, the MTR also paid more attention to middle-income countries. At the time of adopting Strategy 2020, the international community was debating whether development assistance should be provided only for poor countries or, rather, for poor people including those in middle-income countries (Chapter 13). Some Board members were also pressing ADB to implement its graduation policy (Chapter 10) and to reduce assistance to rapidly growing middle-income countries.

Before his arrival in ADB, Nakao himself had wondered if the provision of ADB assistance to upper-middle-income countries was the best use of scarce resources. After working with these countries at ADB, however, he became convinced that ADB should continue to assist these countries but do so more strategically in such areas as climate change, environmental protection, and other global or regional public goods. He thought that ADB's continued lending to middle-income countries including the PRC would provide an important and efficient way of engagement with these countries and also make ADB's lending portfolio more diversified.

Toward a "Stronger, Better, Faster" ADB

At the 2014 Annual Meeting in Astana, Nakao announced that he wanted to reform ADB to become "stronger, better, and faster" to provide better support to the Asia and Pacific region. His general stance was to stress concrete actions instead of rhetoric, effective and efficient work on the ground, and the "one ADB" approach across departments and between headquarters and resident missions. He particularly wanted innovation in three areas: mobilizing finance, processes and products, and the ideas and skills of staff. Toward this end, ADB introduced a variety of reforms across sectors and themes, in line with concrete ideas in the Midterm Review.

The Midterm Review noted that "[i]nfrastructure will remain the main focus of ADB operations." In the area of infrastructure, ADB has moved to give more attention to promoting innovative technologies (Box 14.2). On his visits to some of the Nordic countries, Spain, and Portugal, Nakao met with officials from companies using advanced technologies to build bridges, power plants, and water systems. They wanted closer engagement with Asian development. ADB client countries also wanted to use higher technical specifications in their infrastructure projects but were often unaware of the

Box 14.2: ADB's Urban Sector Projects

The Asian Development Bank (ADB) started its support for urban development in 1968 with a water supply project in Penang, Malaysia. Since then, ADB's support has evolved from financing specific urban infrastructure such as water supply, waste treatment, and road improvement to adopting a long-term and integrated approach to improving delivery of urban services. It aims at strengthening the ability of institutions to deliver services and providing cross-sector and thematic solutions. ADB's goal is helping build environmentally sustainable and resilient cities to address the impacts of rapid urbanization and climate change.

In Dhaka, Bangladesh, since 2008 ADB has provided a series of loans and technical assistances of $700 million to improve the operations of the Dhaka Water Supply and Sewage Association. They helped improve water availability to about 13 million people, and enhance the financial soundness of the operator. The projects reduced nonrevenue water from 50% to 15% through district metered areas and leakage rectification. Additionally, ADB syndicated cofinancing with Agence Française de Développement and the European Investment Bank to support the development of a water intake, treatment plant, and transmission facility to supply water to Dhaka. ADB has also supported the strengthening of staff capacity to provide better customer services and financial management, thereby improving revenue collection from 64% to 98%.

Since 2010, ADB has supported Tbilisi, Georgia to improve its urban transport systems and connectivity. Through a $300 million multitranche financing facility (MFF), ADB has been supporting the city's subway system extension by 2 kilometers (km) and connecting Tbilisi with its rapidly developing satellite city, Rustavi, by a 21 km access road. In collaboration with Austria and Germany, ADB commenced feasibility studies to develop an integrated public transport system in Tbilisi by connecting bus rapid transit to the subway.

Since 2010, in Viet Nam, ADB has adopted an integrated approach to urban services in Ho Chi Minh City (HCMC) by two MFFs totaling $1.5 billion. In the water sector, ADB has been supporting the construction of an 11 km water transmission pipeline, partially below the Saigon River, using advanced tunneling technology. In the transport sector, ADB will connect the Northwestern part of HCMC with the city center through a 13 km long mass rapid transit system (including a 9 km underground section). In the coming years, ADB plans new projects to improve wastewater and drainage in HCMC, helped by technical assistance from a trust fund supported by the United Kingdom, Switzerland, and the Rockefeller Foundation.

Source: ADB.

options available or were deterred by high initial costs. In 2016, the Bank started a new initiative of incorporating advanced technologies in projects by strengthening project design, putting more emphasis on quality in procurement procedures, and helping countries access the best expertise.

The MTR reconfirmed the importance of tackling climate change. Climate-related disasters were frequent and often devastating (Chapter 13). Early in his presidency, Nakao oversaw the ADB response to typhoon Haiyan, the strongest recorded typhoon to make landfall in the Philippines (Box 14.3). It was clear to him that the region as a whole needed stronger adaptation measures. Under the MTR, ADB committed to providing more support for adaptation through, for example, climate-proofed infrastructure, climate-smart agriculture, and better preparation for climate-related disasters. Climate risk screening was mandated for all projects. At the same time, ADB would strengthen support for mitigation through development of clean energy sources as well as projects for energy efficiency.

In September 2015, on the eve of adoption of the sustainable development goals and a couple of months before the Paris Climate Change Conference in 2015, Nakao announced, that by 2020 ADB would double its annual climate financing to $6 billion: $4 billion for mitigation and $2 billion for adaptation. During 2011–2015, $13.4 billion of climate finance was approved from the Bank's own resources. In 2016, ADB approved $3.7 billion in climate finance investments, of which $ 2.6 billion was for mitigation and $1.1 billion for adaptation, on track to achieve the goal in 2020.

A good example of ADB support was its policy-based loan of $300 million to the PRC approved in 2015 for air quality improvement in the Beijing–Tianjin–Hebei greater capital area. This loan supported policy actions such as enhanced monitoring of polluting industries and guidelines for converting coal to gas and also contributed to climate change mitigation.

Additional financing was mobilized through channels such as the Climate Investment Funds, Global Environment Facility and donor trust funds hosted by ADB. Climate Investment Funds based on contributions from 14 donors, for which the World Bank is the trustee and 5 multilateral development banks including ADB are the implementing agencies, have been the single largest source of cofinancing for ADB's climate operations.

In 2015, ADB became the first multilateral development bank accredited to receive financing from the Green Climate Fund (GCF) to tackle climate change. The GCF was established in 2010 under the United Nations

Box 14.3: ADB Response to Typhoon Haiyan, 2013

One of the most powerful storms on record, typhoon Haiyan (locally known as Yolanda), struck the Philippines on 8 November, 2013, claiming over 6,000 lives and inflicting catastrophic damage. Thousands were injured, millions were displaced, and infrastructure losses exceeded $13 billion.

The Asian Development Bank (ADB) moved swiftly to support its host country, activating its internal monitoring even before the typhoon made landfall. A team of more than 40 senior staff with experience in postdisaster situations was set up to coordinate responses. ADB President Takehiko Nakao promised: "ADB will provide full support to the people and the Government of the Philippines together with other development partners to speedily implement both needed relief and reconstruction—especially as the Philippines is our home."

To help restore life-saving services, ADB immediately offered a $3 million grant from its emergency assistance facility, the Asia Pacific Disaster Response Fund. Another $20 million grant was provided from the Japan Fund for Poverty Reduction, a trust fund financed by the Government of Japan. ADB was also ready to provide a $500 million quick-disbursing program loan to help postdisaster rehabilitation and reconstruction. Nakao met Philippines President Benigno S. Aquino III on 13 November to discuss the package.

Later in November, ADB completed its first mission to the hardest-hit areas, conducting rapid assessments in Leyte, Samar, Roxas, and Cebu. This approach formed the basis for a $500 million emergency assistance loan to cover immediate costs associated with rebuilding. An additional loan of $372.1 million was provided for basic social services in severely affected areas.

The overall response called for close coordination between donors. In all, 15 multilateral and bilateral agencies committed funds for reconstruction. The top three contributors were ADB, the World Bank, and the Japan International Cooperation Agency. ADB total assistance in 2013 amounted to $900 million.

Sources: ADB. 2014. *Typhoon Yolanda—One Year On: From Relief to Recovery to Reconstruction*. November. https://www.adb.org/sites/default/files/publication/154514/typhoon-yolanda-one-year.pdf (accessed 14 June 2015); ADB. 2014. *Typhoon Yolanda (Haiyan) Asian Development Bank Assistance*. November. https://www.adb.org/publications/typhoon-yolanda-haiyan-asian-development-bank-assistance (accessed 26 November 2015).

Framework Convention on Climate Change (UNFCCC) to serve as the central global investment vehicle for climate finance in developing countries. In 2015–2016, ADB approved two projects, one for adaptation and one for mitigation in Pacific island countries, to be cofinanced by the GCF.

ADB also raised $500 million from an inaugural Green Bond issue in 2015, based on the certified green bond principle and aimed at financing ADB projects which promote low-carbon and climate-resilient investment. In 2016, ADB issued additional green bonds worth $1.3 billion.

In 2016, ADB backed the first Climate Bond in Asia and the Pacific issued by a private company in the Philippines for expanding geothermal power generation, by providing credit enhancement in the form of a guarantee of 75% of principal and interest on the bond.

One of the agendas Nakao is strongly committed to is the promotion of quality knowledge services to developing country members and the integration of ADB's tacit and explicit knowledge in projects. ADB had reorganized its knowledge services as part of a plan to integrate Bank financing with additional resources and support for knowledge.[36] The Regional and Sustainable Development Department, established in 2002, was reorganized to strengthen linkages between knowledge and operations and in 2015 was renamed the Sustainable Development and Climate Change Department.

The same year, the Bank established seven sector groups (education, energy, finance, health, transport, urban, and water) and eight thematic groups (climate change and disaster risk management, gender equality, governance, social development, environment, rural development and food security, regional cooperation and integration, and public–private partnership). These groups, each equipped with a secretariat headed by technical advisors, are expected to share knowledge across operations departments, build staff expertise, provide specialized support to operations, and strengthen knowledge partnerships with centers of excellence of the world, academia, and the private sector.

In early 2016, at meetings with sector and thematic groups, Nakao mentioned "As ADB's developing many member countries have gained access to financing their needs through bond markets, unless we can

---

[36] ADB, 2013, *Knowledge Management Directions and Action Plan (2013–2015)*.

combine finance with strong sector and thematic expertise, knowledge and ideas, ADB will become less relevant. In this respect, the success of ADB's future will depend on the success of sector groups and thematic groups." To maintain the momentum, he regularly met each sector and thematic group to discuss progress.

To respond faster to clients, ADB introduced changes to improve its business processes. Stakeholders often complained that Bank procedures were cumbersome. To tackle these problems, a 10-point program was adopted in 2014 to reduce procurement time while maintaining fiduciary oversight. This led to the faster processing of procurement contracts and encouraged further policy reforms. As part of these changes, greater authority was delegated to resident missions to enable staff to work more closely with clients.

ADB has given more attention to the way it dealt with the private sector. In 2008, the Strategy 2020 plan set an ambitious target of scaling up total assistance for the private sector to 50% of OCR financing by 2020. This target included both direct private sector operations (which included ADB's equity investment, nonsovereign lending, and guarantees to private sector companies) as well as private sector development activities (especially sovereign operations, such as policy-based lending to improve the business climate). The target for private sector operations alone was subsequently set to 25%. However, during 2011–2013, this ratio was still only around 15%. The Private Sector Operations Department had been constrained by traditional annual OCR allocations, so in 2015 ADB decided to start applying an economic capital planning model in which the Bank would deploy its capital based on risk-based analysis of each asset. Under the new approach, the department would be provided with economic capital, allowing it to originate transactions based on multiyear capital availability rather than annual resource allocations.

In 2015, additional reforms were introduced to streamline processes for small private sector projects. Supported by these reforms, assistance for private sector operations rose to 20% of OCR financing in 2015. The dramatic increase of OCR capital from 2017 and onward, reflecting the financial innovation as discussed in the next section, will also provide much greater scope for nonsovereign operations.

The Bank has expanded its engagement with public–private partnerships (PPPs). This approach required quite specialized skills. The Midterm

Review of Strategy 2020 found that staff with the necessary skills were scattered across various departments and recommended centralizing the Bank's PPP services. A new Office of Public–Private Partnership (OPPP) was established in 2014 with additional staff. Operations commenced in 2015. Besides supporting PPP operations, the new office provides transaction advisory services (TAS) to countries.[37] Its first transaction advisory service was the agreement signed in 2015 for a railway project in the Philippines, the largest PPP tendered in the Philippines so far. ADB, through the OPPP, also manages the Asia Pacific Project Preparation Facility (AP3F). The facility was established in 2015 with contributions from Australia, Canada, and Japan to help channel private sector money toward bankable infrastructure development projects. The facility provides legal, technical, and financial expertise to countries with projects at early stages of development.

New lending instruments were also introduced. In 2013, ADB piloted a results-based lending approach which linked disbursements to results. The first such loan, for $200 million, was approved in June 2013 to help the Government of Sri Lanka modernize its secondary school system. Subsequently, results-based loans have been approved for Armenia, the PRC, India, Indonesia, the Philippines, Solomon Islands, and Sri Lanka. The results-based lending option quickly became a popular financing modality that was seen as reducing transaction costs and making program administration more efficient. Initial experience shows that it is critical to have the right choice of disbursement-linked indicators and close discussion with authorities about inputs, outputs, and results.

Nakao realized that implementing the MTR, as well as scaling up operations based on financial innovation, would require more staff. Like previous Presidents, Nakao believed that a "diverse and inclusive workforce makes ADB a more creative, collegial and productive workplace." Building on the success of the Gender Action Plans under Chino and Kuroda, a Diversity and Inclusion Framework was introduced for 2013–2016.[38] This framework included attention to nongender issues identified by staff engagement surveys, such as the need for greater respect in the workplace, and managerial competency. ADB is taking further concrete steps to strengthen institutional gender equality.

---

[37] Transaction advisory services are fee-based advisory services provided by ADB over the entire range of activities associated with the preparation, structuring, and procurement of PPP transactions.

[38] ADB, 2013, *Diversity and Inclusion Framework, 2013–2016*.

Financial Innovation: Combination of Asian Development Fund Lending Operations and Ordinary Capital Resources

By far the most striking initiative after Nakao arrived in the Bank was the proposal to combine the ADF's lending operations and OCR.

For ADB, a traditionally cautious financial institution, the idea of combining the ADF's lending operations and OCR funds was a startling suggestion. For decades, all the main multilateral development banks (MDBs) had drawn on the two streams of finance, one for ordinary operations using leverage (issuing bonds based on capital), and one for concessional operations (soft loans and grant) without using leverage (using donors contribution for lending without issuing bonds). No MDB had merged the two streams. Nakao encouraged discussion of this innovative idea.

The logic of the merger was straightforward and compelling. ADB could only leverage resources against the OCR balance sheet. It did not leverage resources in this way with the ADF, which had a separate set of donors, no callable capital, and no credit rating. When the ADF was first created in 1973, this was not seen as a limitation. At that time, few international investors would have been willing to purchase bonds linked to loans to poor countries in the region, and if ADB dared to finance by issuing bonds, the financing costs would have been much higher than the ADF loan pricing. However, since the ADF's establishment, its borrowers had demonstrated a strong track record of repayment. The inability to issue debt against the ADF balance sheet came to be seen as a missed opportunity. By moving the ADF's loan assets to OCR, the Bank would significantly expand its equity and thus expand the base for leveraging resources for operations. This, in turn, would reduce the ADF's dependence on donor contributions.

The Bank's Treasurer Mikio Kashiwagi first floated the possibility of merging the ADF and OCR in 2012 as one of several ways to reverse the Bank's projected decline in lending headroom. A wide range of options were proposed to implement such a combination. These included issuing ordinary or special shares to ADF donors on their previous ADF contributions and liquidating the ADF, distributing its assets to ADF donors and having the donors reconvey the assets to OCR.

The merger idea was unconventional. Not only was a merger apparently constrained by the Charter but numerous technical, accounting, and political obstacles appeared insurmountable as well. Issuing new shares to ADF donors was politically and strategically unworkable. It would have dramatically increased the voting shares of the largest and wealthiest members, and diluted the shares of other members.[39] And any structure that distributed assets to donors would require—typically through legislative action in donor countries—that they authorize budget expenditures to return the funds to ADB, a practical impossibility for many donor countries.

However, shortly after becoming President, Nakao sensed that there was a key opportunity for the Bank to merge the ADF and OCR balance sheets. With his fresh perspective and experience of dealing with legislators of the Japanese Diet, Nakao proposed a direct transfer of the assets of the ADF's lending operations to the OCR balance sheet and of the corresponding equity to the "reserves" portion of OCR capital, thus avoiding the impact on the voting shares. The merger would dramatically increase the capital of the Bank (paid-in equity and reserves) and enabled ADB to increase lending significantly without seeking a general capital increase or additional donor contributions to the ADF. Detailed discussions about the merger started in August 2013.

Nakao believed that, despite the complicated and technical challenges associated with the proposal, donors and shareholders would come to support it because of its win–win–win nature. First, the proposal would make it possible to increase support to low-income countries. This was because larger grant operations would be possible from the new ADF arrangements (including increased income transfer from expanded OCR operations) and because larger concessional lending would be possible from the expanded OCR balance sheet. Second, it would allow ADB to substantially increase lending, including nonconcessional OCR operations, using the expanded OCR balance sheet (even if the minimum required equity-to-loan ratio were increased to 35% from 25% in order to accommodate less creditworthy former ADF borrowers to OCR operations and to maintain the AAA rating). Finally, it would reduce the burden on ADF donors by reducing their future ADF replenishment contributions at a time when many countries were facing tight fiscal constraints.

In addition, Nakao understood that as the ADF was a Special Fund established within and managed by ADB (not as a separate legal identity as is the case of the International Development Association of the World Bank Group), this proposal would not require an amendment of the Charter. He also expected that so long as the ADF resources contributed by donors continued to be used

---

[39] For instance, Japan's cumulative contribution to the ADF is 36.3% of the total while its share in ADB's capital is 15.6% and its voting power is 12.8%.

to support poor member countries in line with the donors' original intention and purpose of those contributions, donor governments would not need to go back to their legislatures for new approvals.

In mid-September 2013, Nakao instructed staff to prepare the proposal in detail, internally dubbed "Project Galaxy." All relevant departments closely collaborated. General Counsel Christopher Stephens made a notable contribution by providing flexible and appropriate interpretations of the Charter. Nakao also wanted to ensure that the resources previously contributed by each ADF donor would continue to be reflected in ADB's financial statements even after they become part of OCR capital. Further, in case of a theoretical possibility of OCR being liquidated in the future, he instructed that past ADF contributions be noted separately next to the paid-in equity of donor shareholders.

Discussions with ADF donors started in the fall of 2013, but initial consultations did not go well. At one early meeting between Nakao and a senior US official in October 2013, the proposal was dismissed as a "nonstarter." Later, the US became one of the initiative's strong supporters. Several donors initially found it too good to be true. Nakao continued to push for it, and senior staff visited donor countries in 2013 and 2014 to build support. ADB simultaneously sought to build a consensus among developing members and to garner support through consultations with civil society.

Faced with a fundamental change to the Bank's financing model, ADF donors asked for an independent assessment. This was carried out in 2014 by the Center for Global Development (CGD) based in Washington, DC and came to a positive conclusion.[40] The review "...found that the main promises of the proposal are sound, and therefore [CGD has] encouraged the ADF's donors to move swiftly to approve it in order to take full advantage of the benefits that will come from greater leveraging of ADF resources. More fundamentally though, [CGD sees] the proposal as an impressive launching point for further innovations in the ADB's basic model, potentially paving the way for fresh thinking across the multilateral development banks."

The Bank also engaged a major rating agency to assess the impact of the merger on the Bank's coveted AAA credit rating. The agency concluded that not only would ADB retain its AAA rating, but the financial strength of ADB would actually be enhanced by the merger, largely due to the portfolio

---

[40] Birdsall, Morris, and Rueda-Sabater, 2014, *Review of "Enhancing ADB's Financial Capacity to Achieve the Long-Term Strategic Vision for the ADF."*

diversification resulting from the addition of the ADF loan portfolio to OCR. ADB also discussed with its auditors various accounting issues concerning the financial treatment and reporting of the asset transfers and valuations.

Momentum toward support steadily built from late 2013 and into 2014. By March 2015, ADB had obtained support for the proposal from all 67 ADB shareholders and all 34 ADF donors. The Board of Governors formally approved the change in April 2015 which took legal effect in January 2017.

The merger greatly increased the Bank's capacity to mobilize additional finance for borrowing countries in Asia. It transformed the ADB balance sheet and strengthened the Bank's ability to achieve the original Charter goal of "mobilizing ... funds and other resources both from within and outside of the region." The ADF–OCR combination was unique among multilateral development banks and stimulated discussions of similar approaches at other multilateral development banks. The G20 leaders endorsed the merger in their statements in November 2014, which indicated that the G20 would continue to work with multilateral development banks to "optimize use of their balance sheets to provide additional lending."

On 1 January 2017, OCR equity almost tripled, from $17.2 billion to $48 billion, as $30.8 billion of ADF loans and other assets were transferred from the ADF. Assets amounting to $2.5 billion remained in the ADF to support its grant operations. The newly enlarged OCR window would offer the poorer borrowing countries concessional lending on the same terms and conditions as before, while the ADF itself would provide only grant assistance going forward. This reform is expected to raise ADB annual loan and grant approvals by a targeted 50%—from $13.5 billion in 2014 to $20.0 billion in 2020.

The effects of the combination became evident even before it became effective. ADB immediately commenced efforts to increase operational approvals (including loans, grants, guarantees, and equity investments) in 2015 and 2016. Between 2014 and 2015, total approvals expanded by over 20% to $16.3 billion (Figure 14.1). The total increased by another 7% to $17.5 billion in 2016. Such increases in approvals ahead of the merger's effective date were possible because it would take some time to disburse approved amounts and because the constraints of the equity-to-loan ratio relate to outstanding disbursed amounts (minus repaid amounts) of loans (not approved amounts).

Figure 14.1: Operational Approvals by Fund Type, 2007–2016
($ million)

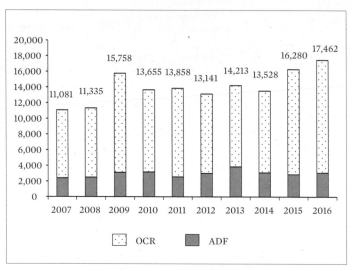

Total: $140,311 million

ADF = Asian Development Fund, OCR = ordinary capital resources.

Notes: Operational approvals include loans, grants, equity investments, and guarantees. Data are as of 20 January 2017.

Sources: ADB Operations Dashboard; ADB Strategy and Policy Department

Eleventh Asian Development Fund Replenishment

Nakao assumed office during the ADF XI period and oversaw the resumption of lending to Myanmar which led to record ADF approvals in 2013 (Box 14.4). Since 2015, he presided over the eleventh replenishment of the ADF (ADF 12). This was the first after the announcement of the combination of the ADF and OCR balance sheets, so to differentiate it from earlier replenishments, the suffix was no longer in Roman but in Arabic numerals.

At the ADF Donors' Meeting held in Frankfurt in May 2016, 32 donors agreed to the ADF 12 for the 4-year period from 2017 to 2020. This would provide $3.3 billion of new resources to the ADF and $0.5 billion to the Technical Assistance Special Fund. The total amount was considerably smaller than recent earlier replenishments, because ADF 12 would finance only grant

Box 14.4: ADB's Reengagement with Myanmar

Myanmar joined the ADB in 1973. From 1973 to 1986, ADB provided 32 loans totaling $531 million for 29 projects in the country. Processing of ADB loan and technical assistance (TA) projects in Myanmar was suspended in 1988. However, ADB staff visited Myanmar periodically to keep abreast of the situation and to join the annual IMF Article IV consultations. Government representatives continued to participate as observers in ADB's Greater Mekong Subregion (GMS) regional cooperation programs which allowed for ongoing dialogue on regional cooperation plans.

Framework for Reengagement Activities. Following comprehensive reform efforts and the reopening of Myanmar in early 2012, ADB began reengagement activities. An interim country partnership strategy for 2012–2014 was approved in October 2012, and subsequently, extended to 2016 to provide the framework for reengagement. It included the strategic goals of building human resources and capacity, promoting an enabling economic environment, and creating access and connectivity.

Clearance of Arrears. Generous development partner support was critical to enabling ADB's reengagement in Myanmar, leading to the resumption of lending in 2013. ADB coordinated closely with other major creditors to Myanmar, in particular Japan and the World Bank, to clear Myanmar's arrears in the context of the Paris Club official creditors' debt restructuring. The Japan Bank for International Cooperation provided bridging loans to the government in January 2013 to clear its arrears to ADB and the World Bank. This allowed the disbursement of policy-based loans from ADB and the World Bank to immediately repay the bridging loans. Arrears on Japanese concessional loans ("yen credits") were also cleared through bridging loans from several commercial banks along with a new program loan from Japan International Cooperation Agency, and arrangements for some debt reduction. ADB's $512 million policy-based loan from ADF, Support for Myanmar's Reforms for Inclusive Growth, helped clear arrears to ADB and provided the foundation for improved policy frameworks.

Asian Development Fund Special Allocations. ADF donors recognized the importance of reengagement with Myanmar. They responded with a special resource allocation. In view of its low per capita income, Myanmar was classified a group A country (ADF only, concessional loans). A special ADF allocation for a total of $1.024 billion for 2013–2016 (including the already-disbursed $512 million loan to clear arrears) was approved by donors, and confirmed by the Board in August 2013. During the Eleventh ADF

continued on next page

Box 14.4 *continued*

> replenishment (ADF 12) completed in 2016, donors and the Board agreed to an additional allocation of $1.4 billion of concessional loans for Myanmar for 2017–2020.
>
> **Field Office.** The Bank established its Extended Mission in Myanmar from 1 August 2012. The ADB Board of Directors, in October 2013, approved the establishment of a full resident mission in Myanmar with two offices: one in the capital Nay Pyi Taw, and the other in Yangon, the commercial center and base of most development partners.
>
> Source: ADB. 2014. Myanmar: Building the Foundations for Growth. Paper prepared for the ADF XI Midterm Review Meeting. Manila.

operations in the poorest and most debt-distressed member countries (rather than concessional lending as was the case for earlier replenishments).

The total replenishment amounting to $3.8 billion would be financed from new donor contributions ($2.5 billion), net income transfers from OCR ($1.0 billion), and income from ADF liquidity investments ($0.2 billion). One important feature of the ADF 12 replenishment was that the share of donor contributions from Asian emerging economies increased to 11.7% from 6.9% during the ADF XI period (2013–2016).

ADB grant support of $3.3 billion to the poorest countries represented an increase of 70% as compared to funding during the previous 4 years. ADF grants together with ADB's concessional loans delivered more than $16 billion in assistance to poor countries during the same period, an increase of more than 40%. Assistance to small island countries would rise by over 150%. At the same time, ADF 12 reduced donors' burden by about half. In addition to the $3.3 billion in new resources for the core activities of the ADF, some donors together agreed to contribute up to $150 million to an ADF facility for regional health security.

The replenishment meetings noted that ADB had been responding rapidly using the Disaster Response Facility piloted during ADF XI. During 2013–2014, the Bank had approved four projects and allocated $57 million in the aftermath of cyclone Evan in Samoa, flooding in Cambodia, cyclone Ian in Tonga, and cyclone Ita in Solomon Islands. Furthermore, in response to earthquakes in Nepal in 2015, ADB allocated $120 million from the facility for the reconstruction of roads, schools, and other public buildings. The

Bank also provided $3.0 million to Tuvalu and $5.6 million to Vanuatu for assistance after tropical cyclone Pam. Accordingly, from the ADF 12 period, the Disaster Response Facility became a part of regular operations.

In addition, recognizing the growing vulnerability to disasters, donors agreed to establish Disaster Risk Reduction Financing Mechanism. The Facility provides a total of up to $200 million of grant financing during the ADF 12 period to countries (except countries eligible for nonconcessional lending only) to incentivize investments in disaster risk reduction and mainstream it into their broader public expenditures.

Cofinancing and Trust Funds through the Decades

ADB has mobilized both "official cofinancing" and "commercial cofinancing" in support of its operations through the past five decades.

Partners for "official cofinancing" such as donor governments, bilateral aid agencies, multilateral development banks, and private foundations have provided support for ADB's sovereign operations (but also for nonsovereign operations starting during the last decade). Official cofinancing has been building on ADB's longstanding experience and in-depth knowledge of its client developing member countries.

Official cofinancing (based on approved allocations of resources) over the five decades has grown exponentially and amounted to $35.3 billion in the fifth decade (Table 14.2). The share of official cofinancing as a percentage of ADB's own financing has increased from less than 1% in ADB's first decade to 25% in its fifth.

Official cofinancing has been making essential contributions to ADB's core sectors: energy, transport, and education sectors.

On a cumulative basis, official cofinancing approvals over the five decades is $45.0 billion. This includes $2 billion cofinancing for technical assistance. Loan cofinancing comprises 83% of total official cofinancing, provided by such bilateral development institutions as the Japan International Cooperation Agency (JICA), Agence Française de Développement, KfW (Germany), and Korea Exim Bank; and multilateral development banks such as the World Bank, Islamic Development Bank, and the European Investment Bank. Grant cofinancing for investment projects composes 12% of official cofinancing with the governments of the United Kingdom, Australia, and Japan being the top three investment grant providers.

Table 14.2: Cofinancing in 1967–2016
($ million)

	1967–1976	1977–1986	1987–1996	1997–2006	2007–2016	Total
Total Cofinancing	29	612	4,578	5,733	68,301	79,253
Official Cofinancing	29	576	4,018	5,091	35,329	45,044
for Sovereign Operations	29	576	4,018	5,091	34,699	44,413
Trust Funds[a]		11	28	494	1,741	2,274
Bilateral	1	9	3,770	4,007	13,759	21,545
Multilateral	28	556	220	588	18,169	19,563
Others[b]				1	1,029	1,030
for Nonsovereign Operations				1	630	631
Trust Funds[a]		.		1	263	264
Bilateral					97	97
Multilateral					270	270
Commercial Cofinancing		36	560	642	32,972	34,209
ADB Financing[c]	3,386	16,166	43,945	66,139	142,058	271,695
OCR	2,466	10,758	30,082	50,013	110,663	203,983
ADF	895	5,283	12,981	14,062	29,648	62,868
TASF and other Special Funds	25	125	882	2,064	1,747	4,844
Total Cofinancing and ADB Financing[c]	3,416	16,778	48,523	71,872	210,359	350,948

ADB = Asian Development Bank, ADF = Asian Development Fund, OCR = ordinary capital resources, TASF = Technical Assistance Special Fund.

[a] Approved allocations to grants and technical assistance from trust funds.

[b] Others include private sector cofinancing through foundations and corporate social responsibility programs, and any public source such as national development banks.

[c] ADB loan, grant, equity, and guarantee operations (OCR and ADF) from 1997 to 2016 are based on gross approvals.

Sources: ADB Annual Reports; ADB. 2016. *ADB Through the Decades*. Volumes 1-5; ADB website (www.adb.org).

An important part of official cofinancing comes in the form of "trust funds" contributed by ADB member countries (single or multiple partners) and managed by ADB (Appendix Table A2.19). The first trust fund was established in 1980, contributed by Switzerland for technical assistance. Prior to this, there were "special funds" based on the Charter (Chapter 5). Special funds (except the Japan Special Fund) receive contributions from ADB through transfers from OCR. ADF and the Asia Disaster Response Fund are two of the special funds in the definition of the Charter.

By the fifth decade, ADB had instituted a number of trust funds covering issues such as health, regional cooperation, private sector development, disaster risk management, climate change, energy, water, urban development, finance, and the use of information technology. By 2016, total commitment from partners for trust funds was about $3.2 billion.

Among trust funds, the Afghanistan Infrastructure Trust Fund (AITF) was established in 2010 as a facility for development partners to work together to support infrastructure projects in transport, energy, and agriculture and natural resources. As of December 2016, the total amount pledged by AITF donors was $694 million.

The Urban Climate Change Resilience Trust Fund was established in 2013 with the support of the governments of Switzerland and United Kingdom, and the Rockefeller Foundation. This trust fund aims to help fast growing cities in 7 developing member countries become more resilient to the impacts of climate change such as floods and droughts.

The Regional Malaria and Other Communicable Diseases Threats Trust Fund, also established in 2013, is a multipartner trust fund with contributions from Australia, Canada, and the United Kingdom. It supports developing member countries especially those in the Greater Mekong Subregion to develop cross-border and multisector responses to drug-resistant malaria and other communicable disease issues.

The Japan Fund for Poverty Reduction (JFPR) is a trust fund created in 2000 in response to the devastating impact of the 1997 Asian financial crisis on vulnerable groups. JFPR augmented two Japanese funds set up in 1988. First, the Japan Special Fund (JSF) supported ADB's technical assistance program, with contributions of $1.1 billion. The second trust fund was the Japan Scholarship Program (JSP), which started with 46 scholars, and is now supporting about 150 scholars annually from ADB developing member countries to undertake postgraduate studies. To this date, JSP has more than 3,000 alumni helping toward their countries' development.

JFPR was established to provide grant assistance (and later also technical assistance) to promote use of innovative approaches that could later be scaled up or integrated into Bank operations. For example, a $3 million JFPR grant to Mongolia in 2009 built 135 *ger* (tent) kindergartens for nomadic children. As of 2016, JFPR has provided $789 million to 174 grant and 224 technical assistance projects, especially partnering with civil society. These include emergency assistance to Nepal for the earthquake in 2015, to the Philippines for Typhoon Haiyan in 2013, and for the Asian tsunami in 2004.

One of the innovative trust funds established in 2016 was the Leading Asia's Private Sector Infrastructure Fund (LEAP) with a committed $1.5 billion in capital from JICA to leverage and complement ADB's nonsovereign financing to private infrastructure projects in the region. Before the end of 2016, the LEAP cofinanced two ADB's clean energy projects in India and Indonesia.

Emerging government donors, such as such as the Republic of Korea and the PRC, have started to establish trust funds. Established in 2005, with total contributions of $40 million by the end of 2016, the PRC Regional Cooperation and Poverty Reduction Fund promotes innovation and regional cooperation. The Republic of Korea established the e-Asia and Knowledge Partnership Fund in 2006 with total contributions of $72 million to narrow the digital divide and promote knowledge sharing and partnerships for poverty alleviation. Private foundations have also contributed to trust funds more recently.

Commercial cofinancing has complemented ADB's nonsovereign operations. Cofinancing partners are commercial banks, insurance companies and other private entities, and multilateral development banks such as the European Bank for Reconstruction and Development. For private partners, cofinancing with ADB provides credit enhancement compared to lending on their own. Since the global financial crisis in 2008–2009, the Trade Finance Program partnering with local and international banks has become a major part of commercial cofinancing. The Private Sector Operations Department (PSOD) assumes primary responsibility for commercial cofinancing.

Strategy 2020 emphasized the importance of partnerships and cofinancing. It set an ambitious target of having total annual cofinancing (official and commercial combined) exceed the value of ADB's own financing by 2020.

ADB therefore stepped up efforts to partner with a wide range of institutions. In 2016, official cofinancing (excluding technical assistance) was $8.3 billion and commercial cofinancing stood at $5.6 billion. The total cofinancing of $13.9 billion amounted to 80% of ADB's own resources of $17.5 billion for loan and grant operations, so it is on track to reach the target. In addition, partners provided $148 million to ADB's technical assistance.

Cooperation with New Multilateral Development Banks

ADB started close cooperation with the recently established Asian Infrastructure Investment Bank (AIIB) and New Development Bank (NDB). These new institutions have created further opportunities for financing the large infrastructure needs of Asia (Chapter 13). ADB has shared with AIIB and the NDB its experiences and expertise in various areas including legal and treasury issues.

On the sidelines of the 2016 Annual Meeting in Frankfurt, Nakao signed a memorandum of understanding on joint financing with AIIB President Liqun Jin. In 2015–2016, Nakao and Jin had nine bilateral meetings and discussed not just cofinancing opportunities but also policy issues common to both institutions such as funding, private sector operations, local currency lending, safeguard policies for environmental and social impacts, and human resources management. Jin had previously been an ADB Vice-President, and visited ADB in December 2016. During a colloquium with ADB Board members, he emphasized that AIIB would focus on infrastructure investment and stay away from concessional operations, social sector, policy-based lending, and research work, and that AIIB would aim at being a leaner institution without a resident Board. Because of these different characteristics, there would be more scope to cooperate and complement each other.

Nakao and NDB President K. V. Kamath signed a memorandum of understanding in Manila in July 2016 setting out areas for cooperation. Kamath said that the memorandum "creates a platform for sharing knowledge and seeking cofinance opportunities."

In 2016, ADB approved two cofinancing projects with AIIB—a highway project in Pakistan with each institution providing $100 million and a natural gas project in Bangladesh with $167 million from ADB and an expected $60 million from AIIB.

Operational Summary

Compared with the level of lending in 1997–2006, operations over the period 2007–2016 almost doubled—from $64 billion to $140 billion, of which 21% was in ADF operations. Public sector and government guaranteed loans accounted for about 86% of total lending, with the rest being nonsovereign lending. Two years stand out: first, 2009, when lending approvals increased by 39% in response to the global financial crisis; second, 2015, when lending approvals reached a record high as ADB scaled up activities following the approval of the ADF and OCR merger.

The increased lending in 2015 reflected demand from borrowing countries for resources to respond to natural disasters, including the Nepal earthquake in April and the Vanuatu cyclone in March, and for support for fiscal measures in countries such as Kazakhstan and Mongolia suffering from lower commodity prices and volatility in financial markets. The large $1 billion countercyclical support loan to Kazakhstan, especially, was designed to help the government stabilize the currency and mitigate the impacts of a steep drop in oil prices. The first ADB policy-based loan to the PRC, for $300 million, was also approved in 2015. The loan was to help address the greater Beijing capital region's long-standing problems of air pollution. In 2016, Bank lending continued to expand reaching a record $17.5 billion.

In regional terms, the shares of lending going to South Asia and Southeast Asia were the highest during the decade (Figure 14.2). East Asia's share declined from 25% during 1997–2006 to 14% during 2007–2016 reflecting the cessation of lending to the Republic of Korea after emergency support during the fourth decade (Chapter 10). The share going to Central and West Asia increased as newer ADB members (Georgia, Kazakhstan, the Kyrgyz Republic, and Uzbekistan) became regular borrowers. The top five borrowers during 2007–2016 were India (18% of total lending), the PRC (13%), Pakistan (9%), Viet Nam (9%), and Indonesia (8%).

In 2013, classification of Brunei Darussalam as a graduated country was approved by ADB's Board.[41] In fact, the country had never borrowed from ADB since becoming a member in 2006. To sign a memorandum of understanding (MOU), Nakao visited the country in August 2016 and met with the Sultan of Brunei Darussalam and other senior figures. The memorandum set out continued collaboration in the areas of knowledge creation and capacity development to enhance education quality, support the private sector, and expand regional economic cooperation.

---

[41] Approval became effective with the signing of a memorandum of understanding in 2016.

Figure 14.2: Operational Approvals by Region, 2007–2016
(%, $ million)

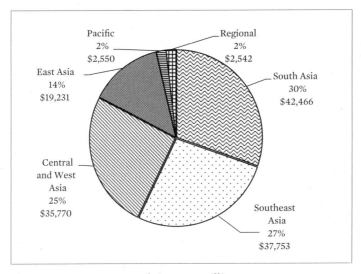

Total: $140,311 million

Notes: Regional breakdown is based on current country groupings.
Operational approvals include loans, grants, equity investments, and guarantees.
Data are as of 20 January 2017.

Sources: ADB Operations Dashboard; ADB Strategy and Policy Department

Sectoral patterns of operations reflected the corporate directions of the decade. The most important sectors for lending during 2007–2016 remained infrastructure, particularly transport and information and communication technology (ICT) as well as energy (Figure 14.3). Food security-related investments exceeded $2 billion a year. Since 2011, ADB has met the annual clean energy investment target of $2 billion a year.

During 2007–2016, technical assistance approvals were about $1.5 billion—somewhat higher than in the fourth ADB decade. Of this, 62% was allocated to specific countries, while the remaining funding was for regional technical assistance work. Excluding regional technical assistance, the top five country recipients were the PRC (18%), India (10%), Viet Nam (8%), Bangladesh (6%), and Pakistan (6%). Compared to the previous decade, there was a further shift away from agriculture, the most important sectors for technical

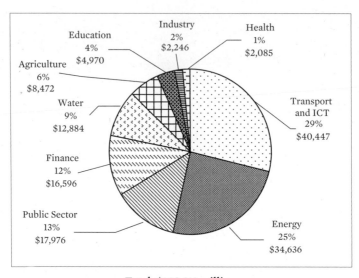

Figure 14.3: Operational Approvals by Sector, 2007–2016
($ million)

Total: $140,311 million

ICT = information and communication technology.

Notes: Operational approvals include loans, grants, equity investments, and guarantees. Data are as of 24 January 2017.

Sources: ADB Operations Dashboard; ADB Strategy and Policy Department.

assistance being public sector management, transport and ICT, multisector, and energy.

ADB staffing and membership also grew. Georgia joined the Bank in 2007 bringing the number of members to 67 (48 regional and 19 nonregional). During 2007–2016, the net internal administrative expenses budget grew at an annual rate of 7.4% compared with 5% during the fourth decade.[42] At the end of 2016, ADB had 3,092 staff from 60 member countries made up of 1,110 international and Management staff and 1,982 national and administrative staff.[43]

---

[42] During 2010–2012, internal administrative expenses grew 10%–13% as ADB filled about 500 new positions.
[43] By contrast, at the end of the fourth decade, there were 2,405 staff (including 861 professional and 1,544 support staff) from 54 member countries.

Looking Ahead

In 2015, at the first ADF 12 replenishment meeting in Manila, discussions began on a new corporate strategy for the Bank. At the 2015 Annual Meeting in Baku, President Nakao said: "[W]e will develop a concrete plan to scale-up our operations and start thinking about a new strategy beyond 2020." A new strategy was needed to guide expanded operations after the combination of OCR and ADF. It will also respond to the newly established Sustainable Development Goals and the goals set down at the 2015 Paris Climate Change Conference. ADB also needs to position itself in relation to new and emerging development partners, and to establish how best to work with middle-income countries.

In a change away from the approach adopted in Strategy 2020 in 2008, the new ADB corporate strategy is not expected to distinguish between core and other sectors. At a Board and Management retreat at the Taal Vista Hotel in Tagaytay in September 2016, Nakao said that ADB could not support every borrower in every sector in every year, but he believed that ADB needed to support clients based on their demands—as much as possible taking into account the Bank's financial and human resources.

Building on the culture of ADB as a "family doctor," Nakao believed that ADB could play a greater role as a premier development institution in the region, providing comprehensive services as a reliable financier, catalyzer of finance, and coordinator for regional cooperation. In addition, the institution could act as provider of integrated technology solutions, supporter of good policies, and promoter of collaboration with civil society organizations, the private sector, and other development partners.

The Bank has taken steps toward President Nakao's goal of becoming "stronger, better, and faster." It still needs to respond to major issues in the world's most dynamic region. In July 2016, Nakao presented his vision statement for seeking a new 5-year term in office, with 10 priorities for the institution.[44] Nakao aims to achieve—and even surpass—ADB's expanded annual approval targets and to use resources effectively to achieve poverty reduction and climate action objectives. He has promised to support high-priority infrastructure development, expand private sector operations, and enhance the Bank's credentials as a knowledge institution.

Nakao is also committed to maintaining high-level dialogue with national leaders and other authorities. He will further upgrade human resources

---

[44] Nakao, 2016, *Vision Statement for the New Term.*

management including enhancing mobility, advancing the gender balance, ensuring a respectful workplace, and fostering an innovative culture and the "one ADB" approach. He will also keep ADB efficient through prudent and careful management of the administrative budget, further streamlining procedures and greater use of country systems, more effective information technology systems, and stronger organizational resilience. Further, the Bank's compensation and benefit packages should be competitive enough to attract the best talent, but also sustainable and fair, consistent with ADB's mission and in line with international trends. And he will give priority to the preparation of a new long-term strategy. Finally, he has voiced his wish to maintain strong governance of ADB, including close coordination with development partners and enhanced external relations.

This agenda, set by President Nakao who was reelected for the term beginning 24 November 2016, will guide ADB's new corporate strategy and its role during the sixth ADB decade.

Table 14.3: Selected Operational, Institutional, and Financial Information, 1997–2016

	1997–2006 (Total, Fourth Decade)	2006 (end-year)	2016 (end-year)	2007–2016 (Total, Fifth Decade)
A. Operational Highlights ($ million)				
Total operational approvals[a]	64,075	8,057	17,462	140,311
By fund source				
Ordinary capital resources	50,013	6,502	14,389	110,663
Asian Development Fund	14,062	1,554	3,073	29,648
By operations				
Sovereign	60,042	7,096	14,960	120,902
Nonsovereign	4,033	960	2,502	19,409
Technical assistance approvals[b]	1,383	148	162	1,540
Technical assistance projects	1,063	94	89	948
Regional assistance	320	54	72	593
Outstanding loan portfolio		47,714	94,914	
Ordinary capital resources		26,192	67,547	
Asian Development Fund		21,522	27,367	

continued on next page

Table 14.3 continued

	1997–2006 (Total, Fourth Decade)	2006 (end-year)	2016 (end-year)	2007–2016 (Total, Fifth Decade)
Total loan and grant disbursements	48,062	5,793	12,253	93,746
Ordinary capital resources	36,551	4,420	9,763	71,433
Asian Development Fund	11,511	1,373	2,490	22,314
Official cofinancing[c]	5,091	891	8,464	35,329
Commercial cofinancing	642	315	5,596	32,972
B. Institutional Highlights				
Staff information				
Total staff		2,405	3,092	
International staff[d]		861	1,110	
Women staff		1,358	1,804	
Women international staff		249	375	
Staff in field offices		474	753	
Member countries		66	67	
Field offices		26	31	
Internal administrative expenses budget ($ million)	2,441	313	636	4,988
C. Financial Highlights ($ million)				
Authorized capital[e]		53,169	143,022	
Subscribed capital[e]		53,169	142,699	
Paid-in		3,740	7,154	
Callable		49,429	135,545	
Borrowings	45,412	5,576	22,932	143,685

SDR = special drawing right, US = United States.

[a] Figures from 1997 to 2016 are based on gross approvals of loans, grants, equity investments, and guarantees.

[b] Technical assistance operations cover grants funded by the Technical Assistance Special Fund and the Japan Special Fund only.

[c] Includes trust funds and cofinancing of loans, grants, and technical assistance.

[d] International staff data include Management.

[e] Values are US dollar equivalents based on US dollar/SDR exchange rate on 31 December 2006 (for 2006 capital) and 31 December 2016 (for 2016 capital).

Sources: ADB Annual Reports; ADB Budget, Personnel, and Management Systems Department; ADB Controller's Department; ADB's Strategy and Policy Department; ADB loan, technical assistance, grant, and equity approvals database; ADB Cofinancing database.

ADB President Haruhiko Kuroda surveying the damage of the tsunami in Banda Aceh, Indonesia, 9 March 2005.

ADB President Haruhiko Kuroda visits the Tsunami Emergency Assistance Project in Nagapattinam, India, 13 October 2007.

An ADB grant, the Rural Electricians Training Program, trained women to provide remote villages in Bhutan with solar-powered lighting. The women installed solar panels on the rooftops of 504 households in 46 villages, providing enough light for students to study in the evening and for families to cook dinners, 2008.

The Madrasah Education Development Project in Indonesia has improved teaching standards and upgraded facilities in a large number of *madrasah* schools, while supporting the implementation of a secular curriculum and the improvement of teachers' skills. Photo taken 2009.

ADB's Allan Lee (*left*) visits with local beneficiaries of the Highlands Region Road Improvement Investment Program in Papua New Guinea, 3 August 2009.

ADB is helping Uzbekistan boost the efficiency of its electricity supply by building an 800-megawatt combined cycle gas turbine power plant. Located 440 kilometers southwest of Tashkent, the new facility will increase energy efficiency through clean power generation, 20 April 2010.

Actress Michelle Yeoh, United Nations Ambassador for Global Road Safety, is received by ADB Director General Xianbin Yao of the Regional and Sustainable Development Department, Manila, Philippines, 26 May 2010.

Burmaa Nergui, a 22-year-old woman in the southern Mongolian town of Sainshand, and her 2-year-old daughter Bilguun obtain water from an ADB-supported kiosk, 30 September 2010.

ADB frequently hosts seminars and knowledge forums for staff to foster greater understanding of regional and global issues, institutional challenges, and other significant topics. At the lectern is ADB Vice-President for Knowledge Management and Sustainable Development Ursula Schaefer-Preuss, 28 June 2011.

The Theppana Wind Power Project, led by the Private Sector Operations Department, will diversify Thailand's energy mix through the addition of renewable energy capacity, helping the country achieve its 2021 target of 25% primary commercial energy coming from renewable sources, 20 November 2012.

The Ha Noi Metro Rail System Project in Viet Nam will provide integrated sustainable public transport in five districts. It was started in 2013.

President Takehiko Nakao visits an area in Tacloban, Leyte, Philippines struck by Typhoon Haiyan (locally known as Yolanda), 11 February 2014. ADB has provided nearly $900 million to help the government restore infrastructure in the areas affected by the typhoon.

ADB President Takehiko Nakao meets with Myanmar State Counsellor Aung San Suu Kyi, Nay Pyi Taw, 14 June 2016.

Aerial view of ADB headquarters, with solar panels on the right generating about 817 megawatt-hours of electricity annually. This accounts for 5% of total annual electricity usage at ADB headquarters, 14 April 2016.

ADB Board, 2016

Top row, left to right: Vice-Presidents Ingrid van Wees, Diwakar Gupta, Wencai Zhang, Stephen Groff, Bambang Susantono, Deborah Stokes; Managing Director General Juan Miranda. *Middle row, left to right:* Alternate Directors Muhammad Sami Saeed, Scott Dawson, Masashi Tanabe, Johannes Schneider, Wenxing Pan; The Secretary Woochong Um; Alternate Directors Mario Di Maio, Joar Strand, Philip Rose, Rokiah Hj Badar, Michael Strauss, Sharafjon Sheraliev. *Front row, left to right:* Directors Paul Dominguez, Mathew Fox, Koichi Hasegawa, Won-Mok Choi, Maurizio Ghirga, Zhongjing Wang; President and Chair of the Board of Directors Takehiko Nakao; Directors Bhimantara Widyajala, David Murchison, Philaslak Yukkasemwong, Swati Dandekar, Kshatrapati Shivaji (*not in photo:* Director Mario Sander), 12 December 2016.

ADB's 50th anniversary launch, ADB headquarters helipad, 20 April 2016.

CHAPTER 15

Epilogue: Looking beyond 50 Years

"Asia's development landscape has changed dramatically over the past several decades. Impressive growth has brought equally impressive poverty reduction ... Yet the region has a long way to go on its development journey ... A large proportion of the region's population lives on less than $2 a day and remains highly vulnerable to external shocks. ... As it continues to grow, Asia must increase its focus on environmentally sustainable development."

– Takehiko Nakao,
President's Message, ADB Annual Report 2013

The Asian Development Bank (ADB) was established on 24 November 1966, 50 years ago, at the Inaugural Meeting in Tokyo, Japan. At the Tokyo Prince Hotel in Shiba Park, the first Governors of the Bank met to make their formal statements, setting out their expectations of the new organization and to elect Takeshi Watanabe as the first President of ADB. Prime Minister Eisaku Sato of Japan, in welcoming Asian leaders and representatives of nonregional countries, delivered the opening address. He described the meeting as "an event which marks the brilliant opening of a new era in the history of Asia." He said that the idea of establishing a regional development bank had been a long cherished aspiration across Asia and that it was "a source of deep gratification for the peoples of this region that this aspiration is about to become a reality."[1]

Looking ahead, one can be equally optimistic about the prospects for developing countries in the Asia and Pacific region. There has been much talk of the "Asian century" and, during the past decade, growth in Asia has contributed well over 50% of global growth. Further, one recent ADB study, *Asia 2050: Realizing the Asian Century*, spoke of the historic transformation taking place in the region. The study noted that if growth

---

[1] ADB, 1967, *Inaugural Meeting*, 9.

in Asia follows recent trajectories, average per capita income could rise sixfold (in purchasing power parity terms) by 2050.[2] In this scenario, the Asian share of global gross domestic product will rise rapidly, from around 28% in 2010 to over 50% in 2050. It is a reasonable assumption that, with half of the world population in Asia, the region will regain the dominant economic position it held before the Industrial Revolution.

However, Asia's rise is not preordained. ADB President Takehiko Nakao has discussed eight policies which have been conducive to Asian development in the past 50 years and which will be required to sustain the momentum of growth in Asia. The list includes steady macroeconomic management, investment in infrastructure, spending for health and education, and the continued promotion of open trade and investment regimes. Good governance helps promote growth; social inclusiveness and environmental sustainability will not only improve the quality of economic outcomes, but also is a basis for solid and continued growth; and governments must provide a credible national vision along with a strategy to achieve the vision. Underpinning these factors is the need to maintain security and political stability, both across the region and within countries. Hard-won gains in growth and poverty reduction can be quickly lost if there is instability or conflict.[3]

Asian countries must maintain and strengthen these good policies and also address the many remaining and new challenges in Asia. There is still persistent poverty. Large infrastructure gaps constrain economic development, poverty reduction, and people's welfare. Implementing the Sustainable Development Goals adopted at the 2015 United Nations summit meeting and the climate change actions agreed at the Paris Climate Change Conference are collective priorities for Asian countries. The private sector should be further promoted. Asia is also facing challenges such as urbanization, aging, widening inequalities, health issues, and the middle-income trap.

ADB should help countries address these issues in the coming 50 years. The Bank should strengthen work in its three broad areas of achievement in Asia mentioned in President Nakao's foreword to this book: providing a combination of finance and knowledge for developing countries, promoting good policies, and expanding programs of regional cooperation.

---

[2] Kohli, Sharma, and Sood, 2011, *Asia 2050: Realizing the Asian Century*, 47.
[3] Nakao, 2015, Eight Conditions for Economic Development, *Nikkei Asian Review*.

And to play this role effectively, ADB should transform itself. It should have strong financial resources, upgrade human resources management, build up knowledge and expertise based on operations in member countries, speed up processes, and better engage partners including civil society organizations.

As this book has discussed, ADB has evolved in response to the region's changing needs in the past 50 years. The Bank was created by the collective aspiration of the people of Asia and should live up to their expectations. With sustained efforts to reform itself, ADB, as the premier multilateral development bank of the region, will continue in the next 50 years to play a critical role in building an Asia and Pacific that is vibrant, inclusive, and sustainable.

BIBLIOGRAPHY

Note: In preparing this book, a very large number of sources of many kinds were consulted. Items cited in the text are listed in this bibliography. In addition, a number of studies about Asian development issues not cited directly but which are key references and were used to help prepare this study are included.

Abeyratne, S. 2002. *Economic Roots of Political Conflict: The Case of Sri Lanka.* https://taxpolicy.crawford.anu.edu.au/acde/asarc/pdf/papers/2002/WP2002_03.pdf

Adams, C., and L. Song. 2012. Asia's Emerging Financial Safety Net. In R. Pringle and N. Carver, eds. *RBS Reserve Management Trends 2012.* London: Central Banking Publications.

Ahluwalia, M. S. 1990. Policies for Poverty Alleviation. *Asian Development Review.* 8 (1). pp. 111–132.

Ahluwalia, M. S., L. H. Summers, A. Velasco, N. Birdsall, and S. Morris. 2016. *Multilateral Development Banking for This Century's Development Challenges: Five Recommendations to Shareholders of the Old and New Multilateral Development Banks.* Washington, DC: Center for Global Development.

Akamatsu, K. 1962. A Historical Pattern of Economic Growth in Developing Countries. *Journal of Developing Economies.* 1 (1). pp. 3–25.

Akiyama, T., and T. Nakao. 2006. Japanese ODA – Adapting to the Issues and Challenges of the New Aid Environment. *FASID Discussion Paper on Development Assistance.* No. 8. October.

Amerasinghe, N. 2011. *International Financial Institutions and Development in Asia.* Manila: Asian Institute of Management.

———. 2015. *Design, Appraisal, and Management of Sustainable Development Projects.* Manila: Asian Institute of Management.

Asia Society. 2005. Amartya Sen: What China Could Teach India, Then and Now. 17 February. http://asiasociety.org/amartya-sen-what-china-could-teach-india-then-and-now (accessed 22 January 2017).

Asian Development Bank (ADB). 1966. *Agreement Establishing the Asian Development Bank.* Manila.

———. 1967. *Inaugural Meeting of the Board of Governors, Tokyo, 24–26 November 1966.* Manila.

———. 1968. *Summary of the Proceedings of the First Annual Meeting of the Board of Governors.* Manila.

———. 1969. *Asian Agricultural Survey.* Tokyo: University of Tokyo Press published for the Asian Development Bank.

———. 1969. *The Doors Are Open: Selected Addresses by Takeshi Watanabe*. August. Manila: ADB Office of Information.

———. 1969. *Regional Seminar on Agriculture Papers and Proceedings*. Hong Kong, China.

———. 1970. Address by President Takeshi Watanabe delivered at the Third Annual Meeting of the ADB Board of Governors in Seoul, 9–11 April. *Summary of the Proceedings of the Third Annual Meeting of the Board of Governors (Seoul, 9–11 April)*. Manila.

———. 1971. *Annual Report for 1970*. Manila.

———. 1971. *Southeast Asia's Economy in the 1970s*. London: Longman.

———. 1972. Opening Address by President Takeshi Watanabe delivered at the Fifth Annual Meeting of the ADB Board of Governors in Vienna, 20–22 April. Also in ADB, *Proceedings of the Fifth Annual Meeting* (1972).

———. 1972. *Summary of the Proceedings of the Fifth Annual Meeting of the Board of Governors (Vienna, 20–22 April)*. Manila.

———. 1977. Address by President Taroichi Yoshida delivered at the 10th Annual Meeting of the ADB Board of Governors in Manila, 21–23 April. *Proceedings of the 10th Annual Meeting*.

———. 1977. *Asian Agricultural Survey 1976: Rural Asia: Challenge and Opportunity*. Manila.

———. 1978. *Program Lending*. R10-78. Manila.

———. 1979. *Environmental Considerations in Bank Operations*. WP6-79. Manila.

———. 1979. *Sector Paper on Agricultural and Rural Development*. Manila.

———. 1980. Address by President Taroichi Yoshida delivered at the 13th Annual Meeting of the ADB Board of Governors. Manila. 30 April–2 May 1980. *Proceedings of the 13th Annual Meeting*, 29.

———. 1980. *Sector Lending*. R52-80. Manila.

———. 1981. *Regional Energy Survey*. Manila.

———. 1982. Developing Asia: The Importance of Domestic Policies. *ADB Economic Staff Paper Series*. No. 9. Manila.

———. 1983. Address by President Masao Fujioka delivered at the 16th Annual Meeting of the ADB Board of Governors in Manila, 4–6 May. *Proceedings of 16th Annual Meeting* (1983).

———. 1983. *A Review of Lending Foreign Exchange for Local Currency Expenditures on Projects*. R1-83. Manila.

———. 1983. *A Review of Program Lending Policies*. R21-83. Manila.

———. 1983. *Study of Operational Priorities and Plans of the Asian Development Bank for the 1980s*. Manila.

———. 1984. *A Review of Sector Lending Operations*. R186-84. Manila.

———. 1985. *Role of Women in Development*. R56-85. Manila.

———. 1986. *Establishment of Bank Resident Offices in DMCs.* R108-86. Manila.
———. 1986. *Review of the Bank's Environmental Policies and Procedures.* R120-85. Manila.
———. 1986. *Role of Women in Development.* IN.67-86. Manila.
———. 1989. *Report of a Panel on the Role of the Asian Development Bank in the 1990s.* Manila.
———. 1989. *Recent Policy Reforms in India.* Manila.
———. 1990. *Asian Development Review.* 8 (1). Manila.
———. 1991. *ADF VI: Report of Donors.* Manila.
———. 1992. *The Bank's Medium-Term Strategic Framework.* Manila.
———. 1993. *A Graduation Policy for the Bank's DMCs.* Manila.
———. 1993. *The Strategic Context of Bank Involvement in the Telecommunications Sector.* Manila.
———. 1994. *Report of the Task Force on Improving Project Quality.* Manila.
———. 1995. *Asian Development Outlook 1995 and 1996.* New York: Oxford University Press.
———. 1995. *Bank Policy Initiatives for the Energy Sector.* Manila.
———. 1995. *Establishment of an Inspection Function.* Manila.
———. 1996. *Asian Development Outlook 1996 and 1997.* New York: Oxford University Press.
———. 1996. *Human Resources Strategy Paper.* IN.120-96. Manila.
———. 1997. *Emerging Asia: Changes and Challenges.* Manila.
———. 1998. *ADB Anticorruption Policy.* R89-98. Manila.
———. 1998. *The Bank's Policy on Gender and Development.* R74-98. Manila.
———. 1998. *Cooperation between the Asian Development Bank and Nongovernment Organizations.* R54-98. Manila.
———. 1998. *Country Assistance Program Evaluation in the People's Republic of China.* Manila.
———. 1998. *A Graduation Policy for the Bank's DMCs.* R204-98. Manila.
———. 1998. *Review of the Loan Terms for the Asian Development Fund.* R205-98. Manila.
———. 1999. *Fighting Poverty in Asia and the Pacific: The Poverty Reduction Strategy.* Manila.
———. 1999. *A Review of OCR Loan Charges.* R205-99. Manila.
———. 2000. *ADF VIII Donors' Report: Fighting Poverty in Asia. Seventh Replenishment of the Asian Development Fund (ADF VIII).* Manila.
———. 2000. *Cooperation with Japan: Japan Fund for Poverty Reduction.* Manila.
———. 2000. *Energy 2000: Review of the Energy Policy of the Asian Development Bank.* IN.282-00. Manila.

———. 2000. *The Poverty Reduction Strategy of the Asian Development Bank. Asian Development Outlook 2000.* Manila.
———. 2000. *Program Performance Audit: Financial Sector Program Loan (India).* IN.47-00.
———. 2000. *Promoting Good Governance: ADB's Medium-term Agenda and Action Plan.* R229-00. Manila.
———. 2000. *Resident Mission Policy.* Manila.
———. 2000. *Rural Asia: Beyond the Green Revolution.* Manila.
———. 2000. *Special Evaluation Study Interim Assessment of ADB's Lending to Thailand during the Economic Crisis.* Manila.
———. 2001. *Moving the Poverty Reduction Agenda Forward in Asia and the Pacific: The Long-Term Strategic Framework of the Asian Development Bank (2001–2015).* Manila.
———. 2001. *Policy on Performance-Based Allocation for Asian Development Fund Resources.* R29-01. Manila.
———. 2001. *Reorganization of the Asian Development Bank.* R152-01. Manila.
———. 2001. *Review of Asian Development Bank's Financial Loan Products.* Manila.
———. 2001. *Special Evaluation Study of the Asian Development Bank's Crisis Management Interventions in Indonesia.* Manila.
———. 2001. *Special Evaluation Study on Program Lending.* Manila.
———. 2003. *Enhancing the Independence and Effectiveness of the Operations Evaluation Department.* R263-03. Manila.
———. 2003. *Implementation of the Reorganization of the Asian Development Bank: A Review of Progress after One Year.* Manila.
———. 2003. *Review of the Inspection Function: Establishment of a New ADB Accountability Mechanism.* R79-03. Manila.
———. 2004. *Disaster and Emergency Assistance Policy.* R71-04. Manila.
———. 2004. *Eighth Replenishment of the Asian Development Fund and Third Regularized Replenishment of the Technical Assistance Special Fund.* R111-04. Manila.
———. 2004. *Human Resources Strategy.* Manila.
———. 2004. *Review of the Asian Development Bank's Policy on the Performance-Based Allocation of ADF Resources.* R249-04. Manila.
———. 2004. *Review of the Asian Development Bank's Poverty Reduction Strategy.* R95-04. Manila.
———. 2005. *Country Assistance Program Evaluation for Indonesia.* Manila.
———. 2005. *Innovation and Efficiency Initiative.* Manila.
———. 2005. *Private Sector Development.* Manila.
———. 2005. *Public Communications Policy.* Manila.

———. 2005. *Review of the Policy on Supplementary Financing: Addressing Challenges and Broader Needs*. R303-05. Manila.
———. 2006. *ADB Perceptions Survey: Multinational Survey of Opinion Leaders 2006*. https://www.adb.org/publications/adb-perceptions-survey-multinational-survey-opinion-leaders-2006
———. 2006. *ADB's Financing Partnership Strategy*. June.
———. 2006. *Enhancing Asian Development Bank Support to Middle-Income Countries and Borrowers from Ordinary Capital Resources*. Manila.
———. 2006. *Further Enhancing Country Strategy and Program and Business Processes*. Manila.
———. 2006. *An Introduction to Results Management: Principles, Implications, and Applications*. Manila.
———. 2006. *Medium-Term Strategy II, 2006–2008*. Manila.
———. 2006. *Membership of Brunei Darussalam and Increase in Authorized Capital Stock*. Manila.
———. 2006. *Program Performance Evaluation Report: Financial Sector Program (Republic of Korea) and Institutional Strengthening of the Financial Sector (Republic of Korea)*. Manila.
———. 2006. *Regional Cooperation and Integration Strategy*. Sec.M30-06. Manila.
———. 2007. *Background Paper on ADB's Approach to Climate Change in Asian Development Fund Countries*. Manila.
———. 2007. *Country Assistance Program Evaluation for India*. Manila.
———. 2007. *Long-Term Strategic Framework: Lessons from Implementation (2001–2006)*. Manila.
———. 2007. *Project Performance Evaluation Report on India: Gujarat Public Sector Resource Management Project*. Manila.
———. 2007. *Toward a New Asian Development Bank in a New Asia: Report of the Eminent Persons Group to the President of the Asian Development Bank*. Manila.
———. 2008. *Emerging Asian Regionalism: A Partnership for Shared Prosperity*. Manila.
———. 2008. *Special Report. Food Prices and Inflation in Developing Asia: Is Poverty Reduction Coming to an End?* Manila.
———. 2008. *Support for Financial Intermediation in Developing Member Countries*. ADB Evaluation Study. Manila.
———. 2008. *Strategy 2020: The Long-Term Strategic Framework of the Asian Development Bank, 2008–2020*. Manila.
———. 2009. *ADB's Response to the Global Economic Crisis: An Update*. Manila. August.

———. 2009. *Enhancing ADB's Response to the Global Economic Crisis: Establishing the Countercyclical Support Facility*. Manila.

———. 2009. *The Fifth General Capital Increase of the Asian Development Bank*. Manila.

———. 2009. *Reflections and Beyond*. Manila.

———. 2010. Address by President Haruhiko Kuroda delivered at the 43rd Annual Meeting of the ADB Board of Governors in Tashkent, Uzbekistan, 2 May.

———. 2010. *Institutions for Regional Integration: Toward an Asian Economic Community*. Manila.

———. 2010. *Key Indicators for Asia and the Pacific*. Special Chapter: The Rise of Asia's Middle Class. Manila.

———. 2011. *2011 Public Communications Policy of the Asian Development Bank: Disclosure and Exchange of Information*. Manila.

———. 2011. *Review of ADB's Policy-Based Lending*. Manila.

———. 2011. *Special Evaluation Study on Managing for Development Results*. Independent Evaluation Department. Manila.

———. 2011. *Updating the Third Gender Action Program (GAP III): GAP III Extension, 2011–2012*. Manila.

———. 2012. *Accountability Mechanism Policy 2012*. Manila.

———. 2012. *Evaluation Lessons of a Global Financial Crisis for Asia and ADB*. Independent Evaluation. Manila.

———. 2012. *Greater Mekong Subregion: Twenty Years of Partnership*. Manila.

———. 2012. *Piloting a Disaster Response Facility*. Manila.

———. 2012. *Review of the ADB Results Framework*. Manila.

———. 2013. Address by President Takehiko Nakao at the Opening of the 46th Annual Meeting of the Board of Governors in New Delhi, India, 4 May. Manila.

———. 2013. *Diversity and Inclusion Framework, 2013–2016*. Manila.

———. 2013. *Food Security in Asia and the Pacific*. Manila.

———. 2013. *Knowledge Management Directions and Action Plan (2013–2015): Supporting "Finance ++" at the Asian Development Bank*. Manila.

———. 2013. *Piloting Results-Based Lending for Programs*. Manila.

———. 2014. *ADB's Support for Inclusive Growth*. Thematic Evaluation Study. Manila.

———. 2014. *Midterm Review of Strategy 2020: Meeting the Challenges of a Transforming Asia and Pacific*. Manila.

———. 2014. *Myanmar: Building the Foundations for Growth*. Paper prepared for the ADF XI Midterm Review Meeting. Manila.

———. 2014. *Operational Plan for Integrated Disaster Risk Management, 2014–2020*. Manila.

———. 2014. *Summary of Stakeholder Consultations on the Strategy 2020 Midterm Review.* Manila.
———. 2015. *2014 Development Effectiveness Review.* Manila.
———. 2015. *Asian Development Fund X and XI Operations: Opportunity Amid Growing Challenges.* Manila.
———. 2015. *The Strategic Agendas in the Independent Evaluation Department's Review.* Manila.
———. 2015. *Thematic Evaluation Study on ADB's Efforts on Regional Cooperation and Integration.* Manila.
———. 2016. *Asian Development Bank–Japan Scholarship Program: 2014 Annual Report.* Manila.
———. 2016. *ADB Through the Decades.* Volumes 1 - 5. Manila. https://www.adb.org/publications/series/adb-through-the-decades
———. 2016. *Effectiveness of Asian Development Bank Partnerships.* Independent Evaluation Department Thematic Evaluation Study. Manila.
———. 2016. *Mapping Fragile and Conflict-Affected Situations in Asia and the Pacific: The ADB Experience.* Manila.
———. 2016. *Review of ADB's Lending Instruments for Crisis Response.* R52.16.
———. All years. *Annual Report.* Manila.
———. All years. *Asian Development Outlook.* Manila.
Asian Development Bank (ADB) and Asian Development Bank Institute (ADBI). 2009. *Infrastructure for a Seamless Asia.* Manila.
———. 2014. *ASEAN, PRC, and India: The Great Transformation.* Tokyo. Asian Development Bank (ADB) and Korea Capital Market Institute. 2014.
———. 2014. *Asian Capital Market Development and Integration: Challenges and Opportunities.* New Delhi: Oxford University Press.
Asian Development Bank Institute (ADBI). 2000. *High-Level Dialogue on Development Paradigms.* Proceedings on the 2nd anniversary of the ADB Institute, 10 December 1999. Tokyo.
———. 2009. *Recommendations of Policy Responses to the Global Financial and Economic Crisis for East Asian Leaders.* March. http://www.adb.org/documents/recommendations-policy-responses-global-financial-and-economic-crisis-east-asian-leaders
———. 2010. *Policy Recommendations to Secure Balanced and Sustainable Growth in Asia.* http://www.adb.org/sites/default/files/institutional-document/159295/adbi-sustainable-growth-asia.pdf
Balisacan, A. M., and H. Hill. 2007. *The Dynamics of Regional Development: The Philippines in East Asia.* Cheltenham, UK: ADB Institute and Edward Elgar.
Behrman, G. 2007. *The Most Noble Adventure.* New York: Free Press.

Bernanke, B. 2004. The Great Moderation. Remarks by Governor Ben S. Bernanke at the meetings of the Eastern Economic Association in Washington, DC, 20 February. https://www.federalreserve.gov/BOARDDOCS/SPEECHES/2004/20040220/ (accessed 15 September 2015).

Birdsall, N., S. Morris, and E. Rueda-Sabater. 2014. *Review of "Enhancing ADB's Financial Capacity to Achieve the Long-Term Strategic Vision for the ADF."* Washington, DC: Center for Global Development. http://www.cgdev.org/sites/default/files/CGD-Assessment-Birdsall-MorrisRuedaSabater-ADB.pdf

Blanchard, O. J., and J. A. Simon. 2001. The Long and Large Decline in US Output Volatility. *Brookings Papers on Economic Activity*. 1. pp. 135–164.

Blustein, P. 2001. *The Chastening: The Crisis That Rocked the Global Financial System and Humbled the IMF*. Cambridge, MA: The Perseus Books Group.

Booth, A. 2016. *Economic Change in Modern Indonesia: Colonial and Postcolonial Comparisons*. Cambridge, UK: Cambridge University Press.

Borlaug, N. E. 1996. *The Green Revolution: Past Success and Future Challenges*. Convocation address at the 34th Indian Agricultural Research Institute in New Delhi, India.

Bouvery, P., J. Perumalpillai-Essex, K. Senga, K. Sophestienphong, and J. Sparrow. ADB@50—The Young Professional Program (YPP): The Beginning. Unpublished essay prepared as part of contribution of former ADB staff to the ADB@50 History Book.

Burki, S. J. 1990. Development Strategies for Poverty Alleviation. *Asian Development Review*. 8 (1). pp. 1–17.

Buu, H. 1972. Farewell Speech in Honor of President Watanabe. Manila. 23 November.

Byung-il, C., and C. Rhee. 2014. *Future of Factory Asia*. Manila: ADB and Seoul: Korea Economic Research Institute.

Cammack, D., D. McLeod, and A. Menocal with K. Christiansen. 2006. Donors and the "Fragile States" Agenda: A Survey of Current Thinking and Practice. Report submitted to the Japan International Cooperation Agency.

Center for Global Prosperity. 2013. *The Index of Global Philanthropy and Remittances with a Special Report on Emerging Economies*. Washington, DC: Hudson Institute.

Chalkley, A. 1977. *Asian Development Bank: A Decade of Progress*. Manila: ADB.

Cline, W. R. 1989. The Baker Plan: Progress, Shortcoming, and Future. *International Economics Department, Policy, Planning, and Research Working Papers*. Washington, DC: World Bank. http://www-wds.worldbank.org/external/default/WDSContentServer/WDSP/IB/1989/08/01/000009265_3960928040356/Rendered/PDF/multi0page.pdf

Commonwealth Secretariat. 1980. *The World Economic Crisis: A Commonwealth Perspective*. London.
Culpeper, R. 1997. *Titans or Behemoths? The Multilateral Development Banks, Volume 5*. Ottawa, Canada: The North–South Institute.
Danaher, K. 1994. *50 Years Is Enough: The Case against the World Bank and the International Monetary Fund*. Boston, MA: South End Press.
de Wilde, T., P. Defraigne, and J. C. Defraigne. 2012. *China, the European Union and the Restructuring of Global Governance*. Cheltenham, UK: Edward Elgar.
Desai, M. 2003. *India and China: An Essay in Comparative Political Economy*. Paper presented at an International Monetary Fund conference in New Delhi, November.
Djiwandono, J. S. 2000. Bank Indonesia and the Recent Crisis. *Bulletin of Indonesian Economic Studies*. 36 (1). pp. 47–72.
———. 2005. *Bank Indonesia and the Crisis: An Insider's View*. Singapore: Institute of Southeast Asian Studies.
Du, R. 2006. *The Course of China's Rural Reform*. Washington, DC: International Food Policy Research Institute.
Erquiaga, P. 2016. *A History of Financial Management at the Asian Development Bank: Engineering Financial Innovation and Impact on an Emerging Asia*. Manila: ADB.
Findlay, R. 1984. Trade and Development: Theory and Asian Experience. *Asian Development Review*. 2 (2). pp. 23–42.
Fujioka, M. 1986. *Ajia Kaigin sosai nikki: manira e no sato-gaeri* [ADB President's Diary: Return to Manila]. Tokyo: Toyo keizai shimposha. (Translated into English in 2016.)
———. 1989. Development Strategies for Growth with Equity. Speech at the First Round Table on Development Strategies in Manila, 10 January.
Fukuyama, F. 1992. *The End of History and the Last Man*. New York, NY: Free Press.
Furuoka, F., M. Oishi, and I. Kato. 2010. *From Aid Recipient to Aid Donor: Tracing the Historical Transformation of Japan's Foreign Aid Policy*. http://www.japanesestudies.org.uk/articles/2010/FuruokaOishiKato.html
Gang, F., D. H. Perkins, and L. Sabin. 1997. People's Republic of China: Economic Performance and Prospects. *Asian Development Review*. 15 (2). pp. 43–85.
Geyelin, P. 1966. *Lyndon B. Johnson and the World*. New York: Praeger.
Government of Japan, Ministry of Foreign Affairs. 2016. Overview of Official Development Assistance (ODA) to China. February. http://www.mofa.go.jp/policy/oda/region/e_asia/china/index.html (accessed 12 January 2017).

Government of Sweden, Ministry for Foreign Affairs. 1999. *Our Future with Asia: Proposal for a Swedish Asia Policy*. The Asia Strategy Project. Stockholm.

Government of the United Kingdom, Secretary of State for Foreign and Commonwealth Affairs. 1974. *Second Nam Ngum Development Fund Agreement, 1974*. Treaty Series. No. 45. London.

Government of the United States. 1966. Special Message to the Congress Recommending Approval of US Participation as a Member Nation in the Asian Development Bank. 28 January. *Public Papers of the Presidents of the United States: Lyndon B. Johnson*. Washington, DC.

Government of the United States, United States Senate, Committee on Foreign Relations. 1967. *Asian Development Bank Special Funds Hearing before the Committee on Foreign Relations United States Senate, Ninetieth Congress First Session on S. 2479 to Authorize the Appropriation of $200,000,000 for a United States Contribution to Multilateral Special Funds of the Asian Development Bank*. 3 October. Washington, DC: US Government Printing Office.

Gozum, G. B. 2013. *Cornelio Balmaceda—A Legacy of Honor and Integrity*. Manila: Cornelio Balmaceda Foundation.

Grenville, S. 2004. *The IMF and the Indonesian Crisis*. IEO Background Paper. Washington, DC: International Monetary Fund, Independent Evaluation Office. http://www.ieo-imf.org/ieo/files/completedevaluations/BP043.pdf

Gyohten, T. 2007. The Future of Asia. In I. Gill, Y. Huang, and H. Kharas, eds. *East Asia Visions: Perspectives on Economic Development*. Washington, DC: World Bank and Singapore: Institute of Policy Studies.

Hamada, M. 2003. Transformation of the Financial Sector in Indonesia. *Institute of Developing Economies Research Paper*. No. 6. Tokyo: Institute of Developing Economies.

Hamanaka S. 2009. Re-considering Asian Financial Regionalism in the 1990s. *ADB Working Paper Series on Regional Economic Integration*. No. 26. Manila: ADB.

Harris, S. 2014. *China's Foreign Policy*. Cambridge, UK: Polity Press.

Higgins, B. 1959. *Economic Development: Principles, Problems, and Policies*. New York, DC: W. W. Norton.

Hofman, B., and J. Wu. 2009. Explaining China's Development and Reforms. *Working Paper No. 50 Commission on Growth and Development*. Washington, DC: World Bank on behalf of the Commission on Growth and Development.

Huang, P. W. 1975. *The Asian Development Bank: Diplomacy and Development in Asia*. New York, NY: Vantage Press.

Huang, Y. 2010. China Boom: Rural China in the 1980s. Essays: The China Book Project. The Asia Society Center on US–China Relations. http://chinaboom.asiasociety.org/essays/detail/212

Hughes, H. 1971. The Manufacturing Sector. In ADB, *Southeast Asia's Economy in the 1970s*.

———. 1995. Why Have East Asian Countries Led Economic Development? *The Economic Record*. 71 (212). pp. 88–104.

Ichimura, S. 1998. *Political Economy of Japanese and Asian Development*. Tokyo: Springer.

Inoue, S. 1975. Bangladesh: Statement to Press. Statement on the occasion of his visit to Bangladesh. 6 May.

International Monetary Fund (IMF). 1998. *Indonesia—Memorandum of Economic and Financial Policies*. Jakarta. 15 January. http://www.imf.org/external/np/loi/011598.htm

———. 2003. *The IMF and Recent Capital Account Crises: Indonesia, Korea, Brazil*. Washington, DC.

———. 2006. People in Economics: The Quiet Integrationist. *Finance and Development*. 43 (1).

———. 2010. *Regional Economic Outlook: Asia and Pacific. Leading the Global Recovery: Rebalancing for the Medium Term*. Washington, DC.

———. At a Glance—China and the IMF. https://www.imf.org/external/country/chn/rr/glance.htm (accessed 30 January 2017).

International Rivers, Mekong Watch, Focus on the Global South, CEE Bankwatch, NGO Forum on ADB, and Both ENDS. 2015. Development Banks Urged to Review Support for Mekong Dams, 10 Years after Nam Theun 2. Press release. 1 April. http://www.bothends.org/uploaded_files/inlineitem/2Press_release_-_Dev_Banks_Should_Review_Support_for.pdf

James, W. E., S. Naya, and G. M. Meier. 1987, *Asian Development Economic Success and Policy Lessons*. Madison, WI: University of Wisconsin Press.

———. 1988. *Executive Summary: Asian Development: Economic Success and Policy Lessons*. Madison, WI: University of Wisconsin Press.

Japan External Trade Organization (JETRO). Japanese Trade and Investment Statistics. https://www.jetro.go.jp/en/reports/statistics

Johnson, L. B. 1965. Statement by the President Following a Meeting with Eugene Black to Discuss Economic Progress in Southeast Asia. 20 April. Online by G. Peters and J. T. Woolley, *The American Presidency Project*. http://www.presidency.ucsb.edu/ws/?pid=26906

Jolly, R., L. Emmerij, and T. G. Weiss. 2005. *The Power of UN Ideas: Lessons from the First 60 Years*. New York, NY: United Nations Intellectual History Project.

Kanbur, R., and A. Sumner. 2012. Poor Countries or Poor People? Development Assistance and the New Geography of Global Poverty. *Journal of International Development.* 24 (6). pp. 686–695.

Kasahara, S. 2004. *The Flying Geese Paradigm: A Critical Study of Its Application to East Asian Regional Development.* Discussion Paper. No. 169. Geneva, Switzerland: United Nations Conference on Trade and Development.

Kawai, M. 2015. From the Chiang Mai Initiative to an Asian Monetary Fund. *ADBI Working Paper Series.* No. 527. Tokyo: Asian Development Bank Institute.

Kawai, M., P. J. Morgan, and P. B. Rana. 2014. *New Global Economic Architecture: The Asian Perspective.* ADBI Series on Asian Economic Integration and Cooperation. Cheltenham, UK: Edward Elgar.

Kenny, C. 2015. MDGs to SDGs: Have We Lost the Plot? Centre for Global Development Essays. 27 May. http://www.cgdev.org/publication/mdgs-sdgs-have-we-lost-plot

Kharas, H. 2007. *The New Reality of Aid.* Washington, DC: Wolfensohn Center for Development at Brookings.

———. 2010. The Emerging Middle Class in Developing Countries. *Development Center Working Papers.* No. 295. Paris: OECD Publishing.

———. 2016. What Does Brexit Mean for Poor People? *Future Development.* 24 June. https://www.brookings.edu/blog/future-development/2016/06/24/what-does-brexit-mean-for-poor-people/

Kharas, H., and A. Rogerson. 2012. *Horizon 2025: Creative Destruction in the Aid Industry.* London: Overseas Development Institute.

Kohli, H. S., A. Sharma, and A. Sood. 2011. *Asia 2050: Realizing the Asian Century.* New Delhi: Sage.

Krishnamurti, R. 1977. *ADB: The Seeding Days.* Manila: ADB.

Krueger, A. O. 1995. East Asian Experience and Endogenous Growth Theory. In T. Ito and A. O. Krueger, eds. *Growth Theories in Light of the East Asian Experience.* Chicago, IL: University of Chicago Press.

Krugman, P. 1994. The Myth of Asia's Miracle. *Foreign Affairs.* 73 (6). pp. 62–78. In Kumar, D., ed. 1984. *The Cambridge History of India 1757–1970.* Cambridge, UK: Cambridge University Press.

Lee, B. S. 1998. *An Asian View of Asia's Crisis.* Remarks of Vice-President Bong Suh Lee at the SIT Investment Associates Annual Client Workshop in California, 14 February.

Lee, H., and C. Rhee. 2012. Lessons of China's Transition to a Market Economy. *ADB Economics Working Paper Series.* No. 298. Manila: ADB.

Lin, J. Y., F. Cai, and Z. Li. 1996. The Lessons of China's Transformation to a Market Economy. *Cato Journal.* 16 (2). pp. 201–231.

Lindblad, J. T. 1997. Survey of Recent Developments. *Bulletin of Indonesian Economic Studies*. 33 (2). pp. 3–33.

Lipscy, P. Y. 2003. Japan's Asian Monetary Fund Proposal. *Stanford Journal of East Asian Affairs*. 3 (1). pp. 93–104.

Maddison, A. 2001. *The World Economy: A Millennial Perspective*. Paris: Development Studies Centre, Organisation for Economic Co-operation and Development.

–––. 2013. The Maddison-Project. http://www.ggdc.net/maddison/maddison-project/home.htm

Manish, G. P. 2011. Central Economic Planning and India's Economic Performance, 1951–1965. *The Independent Review*. 16 (2). pp. 199–219. http://www.independent.org/pdf/tir/tir_16_02_3_manish.pdf

Meier, G. M. 2005. *Biography of a Subject: An Evolution of Development Economics*. New York, NY: Oxford University Press.

Milanovic, B. 2016. *Global Inequality: A New Approach for the Age of Globalization*. Cambridge, MA: Harvard University Press.

Mishan, E. 1966. *The Costs of Economic Growth*. London: Staples Press.

Miyazawa, K. 1998. *Towards a New International Financial Architecture*. Speech by Mr. Kiichi Miyazawa, the Minister of Finance, at the Foreign Correspondents' Club of Japan, 25 December. http://www.mof.go.jp/english/international_policy/new_international_financial_architecture/e1e057.htm (accessed 21 August 2016).

–––. 2000. Introduction: Postcrisis Development Paradigms. *High-Level Dialogue on Development Paradigms*. Tokyo: ADB Institute.

Morita. N. 2012. The Greater Mekong Subregion: My Memories and Expectations. In *Greater Mekong Subregion: Twenty Years of Partnership*. Manila: ADB.

Myint, H. 1971. Part One. Overall Report by Hla Myint. *Southeast Asia's Economy in the 1970s*.

Myint, H. 1972. *Southeast Asia's Economy in the 1970s*. London: Longman.

Myrdal, G. 1968. *Asian Drama: An Inquiry into the Poverty of Nations*. New York, NY: Pantheon.

–––. 1970. The "Soft State" in Undeveloped Countries. In P. Streeten, ed. *Unfashionable Economics: Essays in Honour of Lord Balogh*. London: Weidenfeld and Nicolson.

Nakao, T. 2015. Eight Conditions for Economic Development. *Nikkei Asian Review*. 5 February. http://asia.nikkei.com/Viewpoints-archive/Perspectives/Eight-key-conditions-for-economic-development

–––. 2016. Vision Statement for the New Term. 1 July. Manila. https://www.adb.org/sites/default/files/related/44029/Re-election-Vision-Statement-by-Takehiko-Nakao.pdf (accessed 30 August 2016).

———. 2017. *ADB's New Strategy in Asia: Helping Build Quality Infrastructure at Scale.* Manila. https://www.adb.org/news/op-ed/adbs-new-strategy-asia-helping-build-quality-infrastructure-scale

The Nation. 2015. Ten Years after Nam Theun 2, Development Banks Back in Spotlight. 8 April. http://www.nationmultimedia.com/opinion/Ten-years-after-NAM-THEUN-2- development-banks-back-30257606.html

Naya, S. 1983. Asian and Pacific Developing Countries: Performance and Issues. *Asian Development Review.* 1 (1). pp. 1–40.

Naya, S., and W. James. 1982. Developing Asia: The Importance of Domestic Policies. *ADB Economic Staff Paper.* No. 9. Manila: ADB.

Nekkers, J. A., and P. A. Malcontent, eds. 2000. *Fifty Years of Dutch Development Cooperation: 1949–1999.* The Hague: Sdu Publishers.

Organisation for Economic Co-operation and Development (OECD). 1991. *Development Co-operation.* Annual report of the Development Assistance Committee. Paris.

———. 2009. *Managing for Development Results.* Policy Brief. Paris. http://www.oecd.org/regional/searf2009/42577005.pdf

———. 2011. *The OECD at 50: Development Cooperation Past, Present, and Future.* In *Development Co-operation Report 2011: 50th Anniversary Edition.* Paris. http://dx.doi.org/10.1787/dcr-2011-7-en

Orr, R.M. 1990. *The Emergence of Japan's Foreign Aid Power.* New York, NY: Columbia University Press.

Oshima, H. T. 1990. Employment Generation: The Long-Term Solution to Poverty. *Asian Development Review.* 8 (1). pp. 44–70.

———. 1993. *Strategic Processes in Monsoon Asia's Economic Development.* Baltimore: Johns Hopkins University Press.

Panagariya, A. 2001. India's Economic Reforms: What Has Been Accomplished? What Remains to Be Done? *ADB Economics and Research Department Policy Brief.* No. 2. Manila: ADB.

Pangestu, M., and M. Habir. 2002. The Boom, Bust, and Restructuring of Indonesian Banks. *IMF Working Paper.* WP/02/66. Washington, DC: International Monetary Fund. https://www.imf.org/external/pubs/ft/wp/2002/wp0266.pdf (accessed 31 July 2016).

Payne, J. 2009. JP on Presidents Sato and Chino. *ADB Reflections and Beyond.*

Piketty, T. 2014. *Capital in the Twenty First Century.* Translated by Arthur Goldhammer. Cambridge, MA: The Belknap Press of Harvard University Press.

Prasad, E., R. Rajan, and A. Subramanian. 2007. The Paradox of Capital. *Finance and Development.* 44 (1).

Project Syndicate. 2016. Globalization RIP? https://www.project-syndicate.org/onpoint/globalization-rip-2016-08

Purdue, B. 2009. BP on President Sato. In, *ADB Reflections and Beyond*.

Rodrik, D. 1999. The New Global Economy and Developing Countries: Making Openness Work. Policy Essay No. 24. Washington, DC: Overseas Development Council.

———. 2008. The New Development Economics: We Shall Experiment, but How Shall We Learn? *Faculty Research Working Paper Series*. HKS Working Paper. No. RWP08-055. Cambridge, MA: John F. Kennedy School of Government, Harvard University.

Rogers, J. 1985. The Problem Is, They Don't Understand Business. *Asian Finance*. 15 April.

Roy, B. 1985. The Struggle of Mr. Fujioka. *Asian Finance*. 15 April.

Sakakibara, E. 1999. *Reform of the International Financial System*. Speech by Dr. Eisuke Sakakibara at the Manila Framework Meeting in Melbourne, 26 March.

Sato, M. 1995. Keynote Address by Mitsuo Sato, President, Asian Development Bank, to Seventh Annual PACAP Finance Conference. Capital Market Development in Asia and the Initiatives of the Asian Development Bank. 7 July. Manila.

———. 1998. The Asian Development Bank View. *Asian Affairs*. 1 (4).

———. 1998. The Workers of Asia Need Social Security Systems. *International Herald Tribune*. 16 March.

———. 1999. Capital Flow Reversal, Not Cronyism, Caused Asian Financial Crisis. *The Korea Herald*. 27 October.

Schenk, C. 2002. *Hong Kong as an International Financial Centre: Emergence and Development, 1945–1965*. London and New York: Routledge.

Schulz, G. 1993. *Farewell Address*. Remarks delivered by Vice-President Günther Schulz on the occasion of the staff's farewell ceremony for President Kimimasa Tarumizu. 23 November.

Sherk, D.R. 2008. Multilateralism and United States Foreign Economic Policy. *Kansas Journal of Law and Public Policy*. XVII (2). pp. 273–284.

Sicat, G. P. 2014. *Cesar Virata: Life and Times: Through Four Decades of Philippine Economic History*. Diliman, Quezon City: The University of the Philippines Press.

Singh, M. 1970. Regional Development Banks. *International Conciliation*. 576. January.

Sivasubramonian, S. 2001. Twentieth Century Economic Performance of India. In Maddison, *The World Economy*.

Soesastro, H., and M. C. Basri. 1998. Survey of Recent Developments. *Bulletin of Indonesian Economic Studies*. 33 (2). pp. 3–54.

Stiglitz, J. 2002. *Globalization and Its Discontents.* New York and London: W. W. Norton.

———. 2016. Globalization and Its New Discontents. Project Syndicate. https://www.project-syndicate.org/commentary/globalization-new-discontents-by-joseph-e--stiglitz-2016-08

Sullivan, P. H. 1999. Remarks by Peter H. Sullivan Vice-President, Asian Development Bank at the Bank's Official Farewell to President Mitsuo Sato, Auditorium, Bank Headquarters, 14 January.

Sumulong, L., and F. Zhai. 2008. Asian Workers on the Move. *Asian Development Outlook 2008.* Manila: ADB.

Sussangkarn, C. 2010. The Chiang Mai Initiative Multilateralization: Origin, Development, and Outlook. *ADBI Working Paper Series.* No. 230. Tokyo: Asian Development Bank Institute.

Tarumizu, K. 1989. Speech to Staff by President Kimimasa Tarumizu on the Occasion of the Bank's Annual Celebration and Presentation of Service Awards, Manila, 19 December.

Tsusaka, A. 1984. South Pacific Developing Countries: Development Issues and Challenges. *Asian Development Review.* 2 (1). pp. 65–81.

United Nations. 1958. *Economic Survey of Asia and the Far East.* Bangkok. www.unescap.org/publications/survey/surveys/survey1957-1.pdf

———. 1963. *Economic Survey of Asia and the Far East.* Bangkok. http://www.unescap.org/publications/survey/surveys/survey1964-1.pdf (accessed 26 May 2016).

———. 1971 *General Assembly Session 26 Resolution 2758. Restoration of the Lawful Rights of the People's Republic of China in the United Nations A/RES/2758(XXVI)* 25 October. http://www.un.org/ga/search/view_doc.asp?symbol=A/RES/2758(XXVI) (accessed 30 January 2017).

———. 1980. *Economic and Social Survey of Asia and the Pacific 1979.* Bangkok.

———. 1998. *Kyoto Protocol.* http://unfccc.int/kyoto_protocol/items/2830.php

United Nations Economic and Social Commission for Asia and the Pacific. 1978. *Economic and Social Survey of Asia and the Pacific 1977.* Bangkok.

———. 2014. *Asia and the Pacific: A Story of Transformation and Resurgence.* Bangkok.

Vientiane Times. 2000. 7 (36). 9–11 May.

Vikraman, S. 2016. 25 Years On, Manmohan Singh Has a Regret: In Crisis, We Act. When It's Over, Back to Status Quo. *India Express.* 6 July.

Villafuerte, J., and J. T. Yap. 2015. Managing Capital Flows in Asia: An Overview of Key Issues. *ADB Economics Working Paper Series.* No. 464. Manila.

Wanandi, J. 2012. *Shades of Grey: A Political Memoir of Modern Indonesia.* Singapore: Equinox.

Wang, H. S. 2007. *ABA Journal.* XXII (2). pp. 1–14.

Watanabe, T. 1966. Pattern for Prosperity. In ADB, *Inaugural Meeting of Board of Governors.*

———. 1977, reprinted 2010. *Towards a New Asia.* Manila: ADB.

Wihtol, R. 1988. *The Asian Development Bank and Rural Development: Policy and Practice.* Hampshire, UK: Macmillan Press.

Wilson, D. 1987. *A Bank for Half the World: The Story of the Asian Development Bank, 1966–1986.* Manila: ADB.

World Bank. 1993. *The East Asian Miracle: Economic Growth and Public Policy.* New York, NY: Oxford University Press.

———. 1996. *Serving a Changing World: Report of the Task Force on Multilateral Development Banks.* Washington, DC: Development Committee, Task Force on Multilateral Development Banks.

———. 1998. *Assessing Aid: What Works, What Doesn't, and Why.* New York, NY: Oxford University Press.

———. 2001. *World Development Report 2000/2001: Attacking Poverty.* New York, NY: Oxford University Press.

———. 2007. *Aid Architecture: An Overview of the Main Trends in Official Development Assistance Flows.* Washington, DC: International Development Association.

———. 2008. *The Growth Report: Strategies for Sustained Growth and Inclusive Development.* Washington, DC: Commission on Growth and Development. https://openknowledge.worldbank.org/handle/10986/6507

Yasutomo, D. T. 1983. *Japan and the Asian Development Bank.* New York, NY: Praeger.

Yoshida. 1977. Address at the 10th ADB Annual Meeting of the Board of Governors. Manila. 21–23 April.

———. 1978. *ADB at the Sub-Regional Seminar on the Second Asian Agricultural Survey.* Speech delivered at the Sub-Regional Seminar on the Second Asian Agricultural Survey in Manila/Los Baños, 9–13 January.

———. 1980. Address by President Taroichi Yoshida delivered at the 13th Annual Meeting of the ADB Board of Governors. Manila. 30 April–2 May 1980. Also in ADB, Proceedings of the 13th Annual Meeting, 29.

Yoshitomi, M., and ADBI Staff. 2003. *Post-crisis Development Paradigms in Asia.* Tokyo: Asian Development Bank Institute.

APPENDIXES

1 **Asia: Regional Overview Tables**
   - A1.1 Total Population
   - A1.2 Gross Domestic Product
   - A1.3 Gross Domestic Product per Capita
   - A1.4a Agriculture, Value Added
   - A1.4b Industry, Value Added
   - A1.4c Services, Value Added
   - A1.5 Exports of Goods and Services, as Share of Gross Domestic Product
   - A1.6 Imports of Goods and Services
   - A1.7 Poverty and Inequality
   - A1.8 Life Expectancy at Birth
   - A1.9 Mortality Rate, Aged 5 Years and Below
   - A1.10 Adjusted Net Enrollment Rate, Primary Education, Both Sexes

2 **ADB: Institutional, Operational, and Financial Highlights Tables**
   - A2.1 Regional and Nonregional Members, Years of Membership
   - A2.2 Share of Subscribed Capital and Voting Power
   - A2.3 Board Constituencies through the Years
   - A2.4 Board of Directors and Constituencies
   - A2.5 List of Presidents
   - A2.6 Annual Meeting Venues and Dates
   - A2.7 Staff Members
   - A2.8 Annual Number of Staff (end of year) and Internal Administrative Expenses Budget
   - A2.9 Establishment of Field Offices
   - A2.10 Selected Financial Highlights, 2012–2016
   - A2.11 Operational Approvals by Member and by Decade, 1967–2016
   - A2.12 Operational Approvals by Fund Source and Type, 1967–2016
   - A2.13 Outstanding Portfolio and Loan and Grant Disbursements
   - A2.14 General Capital Increases and Capital Composition
   - A2.15 Donor Contributions on Asian Development Fund by Replenishments
   - A2.16 Asian Development Fund Replenishments by Funding Sources

A2.17   History of Asian Development Fund Replenishments
A2.18a Official Cofinancing from Bilateral Partners, 1967–2016
A2.18b Official Cofinancing from Multilaterals, 1967–2016
A2.18c Official Cofinancing from Private Foundations, 1967–2016
A2.19   List of Active and Closed Trust Funds and Special Funds
A2.20   Annual New Borrowings
A2.21   First Organizational Structure, 1966
A2.22   Organization Chart, 2016
A2.23   ADB Sector and Thematic Group

3   ADB: Impact of the ADF–OCR Merger and ADB's Financial Statements
   A3.1   Asian Development Bank—Ordinary Capital Resources Summary Statement of Effect of Asset Transfer from ADF
   A3.2   Asian Development Bank—Asian Development Fund Summary Statement of Effect of Asset Transfer to OCR
   A3.3   Proportionate Share of Funding Sources of the ADF Assets Transferred to OCR

4   ADB: Time Line of Key ADB Milestones, 1950s to 2016

1. Asia: Regional Overview Tables

Table A1.1: Total Population (mid-year)[a]
(million)

Regional Member	1966	1976	1986	1996	2006	2015
Developing Member Economies						
Central and West Asia[b]	102.9	132.4	167.8	212.3	256.1	305.3
Afghanistan	10.1	12.8	11.4	17.5	25.2	28.6
Armenia	2.3	2.9	3.4	3.2	3.0	3.0
Azerbaijan	4.7	5.8	6.8	7.8	8.5	9.7
Georgia[c]	4.0	4.3	4.7	4.6	4.1	3.7
Kazakhstan	11.9	13.9	15.6	15.6	15.3	17.5
Kyrgyz Republic	2.7	3.4	4.1	4.6	5.2	5.9
Pakistan	52.2	68.8	95.2	125.7	156.5	191.7
Tajikistan	2.6	3.5	4.7	5.9	6.9	8.6
Turkmenistan	1.9	2.6	3.3	4.3	4.8	5.4
Uzbekistan	10.6	14.4	18.6	23.2	26.5	31.3
East Asia[b]	784.2	988.9	1,134.9	1,293.3	1,391.6	1,459.0
China, People's Rep. of	735.4	930.7	1,066.8	1,217.6	1,311.0	1,374.6
Hong Kong, China	3.6	4.5	5.5	6.4	6.9	7.3
Korea, Rep. of	29.4	35.8	41.2	45.5	48.4	50.6
Mongolia	1.1	1.5	2.0	2.3	2.6	3.0
Taipei,China	14.6 (1970)	16.3	19.3	21.4	22.8	23.5
South Asia[b]	589.0	736.9	929.0	1,141.2	1,353.2	1,491.0
Bangladesh	57.7	72.9	95.6	121.0	144.8	157.9
Bhutan	0.3	0.4	0.5	0.5	0.7	0.8
India	508.4	636.2	799.6	979.3	1,162.1	1,283.0
Maldives	0.1	0.1	0.2	0.3	0.3	0.5
Nepal	11.1	13.6	17.1	21.9	25.8	28.0
Sri Lanka	11.4	13.7	16.1	18.2	19.5	21.0

continued on next page

Table A1.1 continued

Regional Member	1966	1976	1986	1996	2006	2015
Southeast Asia[b]	252.4	326.0	407.7	490.9	567.1	626.1
Brunei Darussalam	0.1	0.2	0.2	0.3	0.4	0.4
Cambodia	6.6	7.4	8.0	11.0	13.5	15.1
Indonesia	103.1	134.0	168.4	199.9	229.3	255.2
Lao PDR	2.4	3.1	3.8	5.0	5.8	6.5
Malaysia	9.8	12.6	16.2	21.3	26.3	31.0
Myanmar	24.6	31.4	39.3	45.3	50.4	52.5
Philippines	31.9	42.5	55.8	71.4	87.6	101.0
Singapore	1.9	2.3	2.7	3.7	4.4	5.5
Thailand	32.8	43.4	53.0	59.9	66.2	67.2
Viet Nam	39.1	49.2	60.2	73.2	83.3	91.7
The Pacific[b]	3.81	4.86	6.07	7.59	9.35	11.83
Cook Islands	...	0.02 (1975)	0.02	0.02	0.02	0.02
Fiji	0.48	0.59	0.72	0.78	0.83	0.87
Kiribati	0.05	0.06	0.07	0.08	0.09	0.11
Marshall Islands	0.02	0.03	0.04	0.05	0.05	0.05
Micronesia, Fed. States of	0.05	0.06	0.09	0.11	0.11	0.10
Nauru	0.01	0.01	0.01	0.01	0.01	0.01
Palau	0.01	0.01	0.01	0.02	0.02	0.02
Papua New Guinea	2.21	2.89	3.77	4.84	6.24	8.23
Samoa	0.13	0.15	0.16	0.17	0.18	0.19
Solomon Islands	0.14	0.20	0.28	0.37	0.48	0.59
Timor-Leste	0.56	0.65	0.67	0.86	1.00	1.25
Tonga	0.08	0.09	0.09	0.10	0.10	0.10
Tuvalu	0.01	0.01	0.01	0.01	0.01	0.01
Vanuatu	0.08	0.10	0.13	0.17	0.21	0.28
Developing Member Economies[b,d]	1,732.2	2,189.1	2,645.5	3,145.2	3,577.4	3,893.3
Share of World (%)	51.0	52.9	53.7	54.3	54.2	53.0

continued on next page

Table A1.1 *continued*

Regional Member	1966	1976	1986	1996	2006	2015
Developed Member Economies[b]	114.1	129.9	140.8	147.8	152.7	155.3
Australia	11.7	14.0	16.0	18.3	20.7	23.8
Japan	99.8	112.8	121.5	125.8	127.9	127.0
New Zealand	2.7	3.1	3.2	3.7	4.2	4.6
Share of World (%)	3.4	3.1	2.9	2.6	2.3	2.1
Regional Members[b,e]	1,846.4	2,319.0	2,786.2	3,293.0	3,730.2	4,048.6
Share of World (%)	54.4	56.0	56.5	56.9	56.6	55.1
World Population (billion)	3.4	4.1	4.9	5.8	6.6	7.3

... = data not available, Lao PDR = Lao People's Democratic Republic.

[a] For 2015, population figures refer to estimates as of 1 January for Georgia and the Kyrgyz Republic, 1 May for Afghanistan, 30 September for the Federated States of Micronesia, 1 October for India and Myanmar, 7 November for Kiribati, and 31 December for the People's Republic of China. Where no data are available for the specific year headings, available data for the earliest and/or nearest years are reflected.

[b] Regional and subregional aggregates are calculated using data available for the respective year headings or nearest years given in the table. Moreover, aggregates are provided for subregions/region where at least two-thirds of the countries and 80% of the total population are represented.

[c] Population estimates for 2015 are based on the 2014 census. Revised estimates for years prior to 2014 are not yet available.

[d] Values are sum of the total population of ADB's developing member economies.

[e] Values are sum of the total population of ADB's developing and developed member economies.

Sources: Asian Development Bank. Statistical Database System. http://sdbs.adb.org (accessed 20 January 2017); World Bank. World Development Indicators Database. http://data.worldbank.org (accessed 20 January 2017); ADB estimates.

Table A1.2: Gross Domestic Product[a]
(2010 constant US$, million)

Regional Member	1966	1976	1986	1996	2006	2015
Developing Member Economies						
Central and West Asia	...	...	...	213,618	394,290	616,605
Afghanistan	...	...	...	...	10,305	20,737
Armenia	...	...	...	3,554	8,680	11,457
Azerbaijan	...	...	...	9,467	33,290	59,025
Georgia	7,539	13,664	20,046	5,325	9,903	14,754
Kazakhstan	...	...	...	59,422	121,197	186,232
Kyrgyz Republic	...	...	3,788	2,613	3,979	6,059
Pakistan	20,696	33,814	63,589	105,001	159,256	215,035
Tajikistan	...	...	6,454	2,138	4,388	7,913
Turkmenistan	...	...	9,506 (1987)	9,223	15,301	37,278
Uzbekistan	...	...	17,897 (1987)	16,875	27,989	58,114
East Asia	...	...	1,068,685	2,596,955	5,554,521	10,843,840
China, People's Rep. of	148,200	244,985	616,801	1,625,871	4,023,920	8,795,129
Hong Kong, China	17,964	36,557	79,674	140,520	201,916	264,271
Korea, Rep. of	41,411	113,680	257,792	590,829	941,020	1,266,580
Mongolia	...	...	3,507	3,428	5,702	11,694
Taipei,China	...	...	110,911	236,308	381,963	506,165
South Asia	196,863	279,010	430,882	742,648	1,380,088	2,554,298
Bangladesh	22,995	24,645	36,747	55,328	91,589	156,630
Bhutan	...	...	263	534	1,077	2,049
India	163,579	239,510	370,104	649,877	1,227,441	2,295,155
Maldives	...	...	...	...	1,845	2,905
Nepal	3,234	3,922	5,602	9,083	13,311	19,661
Sri Lanka	7,056	10,933	18,166	27,825	44,826	77,899

continued on next page

Table A1.2 *continued*

Regional Member	1966	1976	1986	1996	2006	2015
Southeast Asia	...	302,138	542,748	1,133,398	1,620,279	2,527,784
Brunei Darussalam	...	8,533	9,302	11,528	13,848	13,638
Cambodia	...	...	...	3,857	9,015	15,930
Indonesia	57,546	116,999	225,214	471,391	602,627	987,514
Lao PDR	...	...	1,672	2,840	5,266	10,378
Malaysia	17,276	33,900	59,387	141,477	216,303	329,954
Myanmar	3,916	5,504	8,831	11,325	33,103	70,538
Philippines	37,495	64,824	77,566	111,364	165,099	265,832
Singapore	8,170	22,839	45,289	109,941	185,843	287,018
Thailand	24,583	49,540	91,515	221,897	297,868	392,475
Viet Nam	...	...	23,972	47,778	91,308	154,509
The Pacific	...	...	...	12,208	17,447	24,639
Cook Islands	...	...	...	...	289	317
Fiji	812	1,561	1,990	2,538	3,088	3,844
Kiribati	...	183	129	129	155	182
Marshall Islands	...	...	104	145	155	177
Micronesia, Fed. States of	...	...	203	282	298	292
Nauru	...	...	...	...	...	114
Palau	...	...	...	194	207	222
Papua New Guinea	2,314	3,545	4,327	7,118	7,442	13,313 (2014)
Samoa	...	...	395	439	639	716
Solomon Islands	...	...	...	595	574	790
Timor-Leste	...	...	...	...	3,622	3,504 (2014)
Tonga	...	...	244	292	353	386
Tuvalu	...	...	...	23	30	37
Vanuatu	...	...	347	452	596	747
Developing Member Economies	...	...	...	4,698,826	8,966,625	16,567,166
Share of World GDP (%)	...	...	...	10.9	14.9	22.1

continued on next page

Table A1.2 continued

Regional Member	1966	1976	1986	1996	2006	2015
Developed Member Economies	1,631,831	2,887,908	4,381,487	6,038,018	6,918,006	7,103,321
Australia	253,862	390,415	523,795	714,579	1,021,939	1,301,412
Japan	1,377,970	2,497,493	3,773,795	5,220,783	5,752,856	5,632,781
New Zealand	...	...	83,897	102,656	143,211	169,128
Share of World GDP (%)	10.6	12.0	13.5	13.9	11.5	9.5
Regional Members[b]	...	...	...	10,736,844	15,884,632	23,670,487
Share of World GDP (%)	...	...	...	24.8	26.4	31.6
World GDP	15,402,533	24,019,438	32,529,704	43,300,988	60,229,092	74,888,840

... = data not available, GDP = gross domestic product, Lao PDR = Lao People's Democratic Republic.

[a] Where no data are available for the specific year headings, available data for the earliest and/or nearest years are reflected. Aggregates are provided for subregions/region where at least two-thirds of the economies and 80% of the total population are represented. No imputation for missing data was done in the calculation of regional and subregional aggregates. However, the aggregates for The Pacific, Developing Member Economies, and Regional Members in 2015 include data for Papua New Guinea (2014) and Timor-Leste (2014).

[b] Values refer to the sum of GDP of developing and developed members of ADB.

Sources: Asian Development Bank. Statistical Database System. https://sdbs.adb.org/ (accessed 20 January 2017); Directorate-General of Budget, Accounting and Statistics. http://eng.dgbas.gov.tw/mp.asp?mp=2 (accessed 21 February 2017); World Bank. World Development Indicators Database. http://data.worldbank.org (accessed 21 February 2017); ADB estimates.

Table A1.3: Gross Domestic Product per Capita[a]
(2010 constant US$)

Regional Member	1966	1976	1986		1996	2006	2015
Developing Member Economies							
Central and West Asia	...	...	...		1,097	1,540	2,019
Afghanistan	...	...	...		...	409	725
Armenia	...	...	...		1,120	2,891	3,813
Azerbaijan	...	...	...		1,220	3,924	6,117
Georgia	1,900	3,147	4,261		1,154	2,394	3,973
Kazakhstan	...	...	...		3,814	7,917	10,618
Kyrgyz Republic	...	...	931		565	763	1,028
Pakistan	397	491	668		835	1,017	1,122
Tajikistan	...	...	1,376		365	631	925
Turkmenistan	...	...	2,872	(1987)	2,161	3,187	6,935
Uzbekistan	...	...	960	(1987)	727	1,057	1,857
East Asia	...	...	942		2,008	3,991	7,432
China, People's Rep. of	202	263	578		1,335	3,069	6,398
Hong Kong, China	4,949	8,091	14,422		21,835	29,446	36,173
Korea, Rep. of	1,407	3,171	6,255		12,978	19,454	25,023
Mongolia	...	...	1,775		1,480	2,229	3,863
Taipei,China	...	...	5,733		11,021	16,736	21,573
South Asia	334	379	464		651	1,020	1,713
Bangladesh	399	338	385		457	632	992
Bhutan	...	...	544		1,043	1,615	2,706
India	322	376	463		664	1,056	1,789
Maldives	...	...	...		...	5,540	6,228
Nepal	291	288	328		415	516	703
Sri Lanka	617	797	1,130		1,528	2,296	3,716

continued on next page

Table A1.3 *continued*

Regional Member	1966	1976	1986	1996	2006	2015
Southeast Asia	...	1,135	1,358	2,309	2,857	4,038
Brunei Darussalam	...	51,008	40,547	38,115	37,614	32,689
Cambodia	...	...	...	350	667	1,058
Indonesia	558	873	1,337	2,358	2,629	3,870
Lao PDR	...	...	442	572	902	1,598
Malaysia	1,755	2,691	3,661	6,654	8,236	10,644
Myanmar	159	175	225	250	657	1,345
Philippines	1,177	1,527	1,390	1,559	1,885	2,632
Singapore	4,223	9,959	16,569	29,951	42,224	51,855
Thailand	750	1,142	1,727	3,706	4,501	5,837
Viet Nam	...	...	398	653	1,096	1,685
The Pacific	...	...	...	1,822	1,867	2,232
Cook Islands	...	...	...	...	12,144	16,855
Fiji	1,706	2,658	2,769	3,235	3,732	4,421
Kiribati	...	3,263	1,967	1,634	1,643	1,656
Marshall Islands	...	...	2,598	2,825	2,969	3,285
Micronesia, Fed. States of	...	...	2,310	2,606	2,817	2,853
Nauru	...	...	...	...	...	10,465
Palau	...	...	...	10,970	10,364	12,600
Papua New Guinea	1,048	1,227	1,147	1,471	1,193	1,784 (2014)
Samoa	...	...	2,463	2,564	3,531	3,698
Solomon Islands	...	...	...	1,611	1,194	1,332
Timor-Leste	...	...	...	...	3,636	2,891 (2014)
Tonga	...	...	2,588	3,033	3,477	3,706
Tuvalu	...	...	...	2,528	3,063	3,386
Vanuatu	...	...	2,611	2,631	2,778	2,692
Developing Member Economies	...	...	...	1,503	2,506	4,256

continued on next page

Table A1.3 continued

Regional Member	1966	1976	1986	1996	2006	2015
Developed Member Economies	14,643	22,775	31,128	40,853	45,294	45,728
Australia	21,789	27,821	32,700	39,025	49,374	54,713
Japan	13,809	22,147	31,062	41,515	44,996	44,367
New Zealand	...	...	25,844	27,507	34,223	36,801
Regional Members[b]	...	...	...	3,279	4,258	5,848
World GDP per capita	4,536	5,804	6,602	7,480	9,133	10,194

... = data not available, GDP = gross domestic product, Lao PDR = Lao People's Democratic Republic.

[a] Where no data are available for the specific year headings, available data for the earliest and/or nearest years are reflected. Average GDP per capita are provided for subregions/region where at least two-thirds of the economies and 80% of the total population are represented. No imputation for missing data was done and the subregional and regional averages refer to the average for economies with data for respective reference years. However, averages for The Pacific, Developing Member Economies, and Regional Members in 2015 include data for Papua New Guinea (2014) and Timor-Leste (2014).

[b] Values refer to the average GDP per capita of developing and developed members of ADB.

Sources: Asian Development Bank. Statistical Database System. https://sdbs.adb.org/ (accessed 20 January 2017); Directorate-General of Budget, Accounting and Statistics.http://eng.dgbas.gov.tw/mp.asp?mp=2 (accessed 21 February 2017); World Bank. World Development Indicators Database. http://data.worldbank.org (accessed 21 February 2017); ADB estimates.

Table A1.4a: Agriculture, Value Added[a]
(% of GDP)

Regional Member	1966	1976	1986	1996	2006	2015
Developing Member Economies						
Central and West Asia[b]	...	...	27.6	23.8	17.2	16.3
Afghanistan	...	...	...	38.5 (2002)	29.2	22.9
Armenia	...	...	17.4 (1990)	36.8	20.5	19.0
Azerbaijan	...	...	29.0 (1990)	27.5	7.5	6.8
Georgia	...	24.8 (1980)	26.8	34.1	12.8	9.2
Kazakhstan	...	...	26.7 (1992)	12.8	5.9	5.0
Kyrgyz Republic	...	...	33.5 (1990)	49.7	32.8	15.9
Pakistan	37.1	31.6	27.6	25.5	23.0	25.5
Tajikistan	...	32.7 (1985)	33.1	39.0	24.2	25.0
Turkmenistan	...	...	26.9 (1987)	13.3	17.4	8.5 (2014)
Uzbekistan	...	...	27.6 (1987)	26.1	27.9	19.0 (2013)
East Asia[b]	...	...	18.4	12.1	7.7	7.8
China, People's Rep. of	37.2	32.4	26.6	19.3	10.6	9.3
Hong Kong, China	...	...	0.4	0.1	0.1	0.1 (2014)
Korea, Rep. of	36.5	24.1	11.1	5.5	3.0	2.3
Mongolia	...	16.7 (1981)	18.7	41.0	19.6	14.8
Taipei,China	12.7 (1975)	11.4	5.4	3.1	1.6	1.8
South Asia[b]	...	...	30.3	26.8	18.3	16.7
Bangladesh	53.9	51.9	34.1	24.5	19.0	15.5
Bhutan	...	43.6 (1980)	42.1	31.2	22.1	17.7 (2014)
India	41.8	35.8	29.7	27.1	18.3	17.0
Maldives	...	...	11.5 (1995)	10.7	6.4	3.4 (2014)
Nepal	70.5	69.3	51.5	41.5	34.6	31.8
Sri Lanka	28.7	29.3	27.5	22.5	11.3	8.7

continued on next page

Table A1.4a *continued*

Regional Member	1966	1976	1986	1996	2006	2015
Southeast Asia[b]	...	...	22.6	20.3	10.7	11.2
Brunei Darussalam	1.3 (1974)	1.1	1.9	1.1	0.7	1.1
Cambodia	...	...	46.5 (1993)	46.6	31.7	28.2
Indonesia	50.8	29.7	24.2	16.7	13.0	14.0
Lao PDR	...	...	60.6 (1989)	53.3	35.3	24.8 (2014)
Malaysia	31.5	29.4	20.2	11.7	8.6	8.6
Myanmar	41.5 (1970)	46.6	50.2	60.1	43.9	26.7
Philippines	27.1	29.3	23.9	20.6	12.4	10.3
Singapore	2.2 (1975)	2.1	0.7	0.2	0.1	0.0
Thailand	33.4	26.7	15.7	9.1	9.4	9.1
Viet Nam	...	40.2 (1985)	38.1	27.8	18.7	18.9
The Pacific[b]	...	...	30.4	28.9	19.9	12.1
Cook Islands	...	14.5 (1985)	13.9	10.3	5.5	8.1
Fiji	32.0	25.8	20.9	20.1	14.5	11.5 (2014)
Kiribati	...	19.6 (1978)	26.8	27.4	23.2	23.5 (2014)
Marshall Islands	...	...	...	...	9.3	14.3
Micronesia, Fed. States of	...	...	25.3 (1995)	24.6	24.4	27.8
Nauru	...	...	27.9 (1987)	6.7 (1994)	7.8	2.6 (2012)
Palau	...	...	18.5 (1992)	3.9	4.8	3.4
Papua New Guinea	43.0	33.6	35.3	33.3	21.2	20.2 (2013)
Samoa	...	...	22.5 (1994)	18.5	12.0	9.3
Solomon Islands	...	...	28.9 (1990)	41.1	35.7	28.0 (2014)
Timor-Leste	...	...	...	...	5.1	6.7 (2014)
Tonga	50.1 (1975)	45.8	38.9	23.8	18.6	19.4 (2014)
Tuvalu	...	8.0 (1981)	18.4	25.1	24.1	24.5 (2012)
Vanuatu	...	22.0 (1979)	23.9	17.6	23.8	26.8 (2014)
Developing Member Economies[b]	...	...	22.5	16.8	10.2	9.6

continued on next page

Table A1.4a *continued*

Regional Member	1966	1976	1986	1996	2006	2015
Developed Member Economies[b]	...	4.8	2.8	1.9	1.5	...
Australia	7.0 (1972)	6.3	5.1	3.7	3.0	2.3
Japan	5.1 (1970)	4.4	2.5	1.7	1.2	1.2 (2014)
New Zealand	11.6 (1971)	10.9	6.2	7.0	5.4	6.1 (2012)
Regional Members[b]	...	...	9.2	7.4	6.3	...
World	...	...	5.8	4.1	3.4	4.3

... = data not available, 0.0 = magnitude is less than half of unit employed, GDP = gross domestic product, Lao PDR = Lao People's Democratic Republic.

[a] Where no data are available for the specific year headings, available data for the earliest and/or nearest years are reflected.

[b] Regional and subregional aggregates are calculated using data available for the respective year headings and no imputations are made for missing values. Moreover, aggregates are provided for subregions/regions where at least two-thirds of the countries are represented.

Sources: Asian Development Bank. Statistical Database System. sdbs.adb.org (accessed 19 January 2017); United Nations Statistics Division. UNDATA. http://data.un.org/ (accessed 27 December 2016); World Bank. World Development Indicators Database. http://data.worldbank.org (accessed 20 February 2017); ADB estimates.

Table A1.4b: Industry, Value Added[a]
(% of GDP)

Regional Member	1966	1976	1986	1996	2006	2015
Developing Member Economies						
Central and West Asia[b]	...	...	23.4	26.9	32.2	29.3
Afghanistan	...	...	...	23.7 (2002)	28.8	22.9
Armenia	...	...	52.0 (1990)	32.6	44.7	28.2
Azerbaijan	...	...	...	39.1	68.9	50.2
Georgia	...	35.2 (1980)	37.0	23.7	24.9	24.5
Kazakhstan	...	...	44.6 (1992)	26.9	42.1	33.2
Kyrgyz Republic	...	...	35.0 (1990)	18.3	20.1	26.9
Pakistan	20.6	24.3	23.4	24.2	20.9	19.0
Tajikistan	...	...	40.1	31.6	31.1	28.0
Turkmenistan	...	...	38.5 (1987)	68.8	36.3	63.0 (2014)
Uzbekistan	...	...	38.3 (1987)	30.5	29.9	33.2 (2013)
East Asia[b]	...	...	41.5	41.6	42.1	39.7
China, People's Rep. of	37.9	45.0	43.5	47.1	47.6	40.7
Hong Kong, China	...	...	30.5	14.7	8.2	7.2 (2014)
Korea, Rep. of	22.1	29.1	37.2	37.8	36.9	38.0
Mongolia	...	25.0 (1981)	28.3	25.2	43.0	34.1
Taipei,China	39.9 (1975)	43.2	45.8	32.5	32.4	35.4
South Asia[b]	...	...	25.4	26.2	28.5	29.5
Bangladesh	10.3	14.4	20.8	22.8	25.4	28.2
Bhutan	...	11.7 (1980)	20.1	33.8	39.0	42.9 (2014)
India	20.1	23.4	25.9	26.6	28.8	29.7
Maldives	...	...	13.5 (1995)	12.8	13.5	18.5 (2014)
Nepal	9.3	8.9	15.9	22.9	17.2	14.9
Sri Lanka	20.3	27.4	27.0	26.6	30.6	30.7

continued on next page

Table A1.4b continued

Regional Member	1966		1976		1986		1996		2006	2015	
Southeast Asia[b]	...		...		33.4		34.3		41.1	36.2	
Brunei Darussalam	90.5	(1974)	90.5		58.8		56.3		73.2	60.2	
Cambodia	...		...		13.0	(1993)	15.7		27.6	29.4	
Indonesia	11.9		34.1		33.7		43.5		46.9	41.3	
Lao PDR	...		...		13.4	(1989)	21.1		27.7	34.7	(2014)
Malaysia	29.6		37.3		39.2		43.5		46.1	39.6	
Myanmar	13.3	(1970)	11.5		12.2		10.4		19.2	34.5	
Philippines	30.9		36.2		34.6		32.1		33.5	30.8	
Singapore	32.4	(1975)	33.2		34.4		33.6		31.7	26.4	
Thailand	22.5		27.6		33.1		37.3		39.3	35.7	
Viet Nam	...		27.4	(1985)	28.9		29.7		38.6	37.0	
The Pacific[b]	...		...		26.5		29.6		27.8	17.3	
Cook Islands	...		8.5	(1985)	11.1		7.1		8.7	8.9	
Fiji	24.7		22.4		20.1		24.1		18.9	18.7	(2014)
Kiribati	...		57.0	(1978)	8.8		8.6		8.0	14.6	(2014)
Marshall Islands	...		...		...		...		12.1	10.6	
Micronesia, Fed. States of	...		...		7.3	(1995)	7.9		4.4	6.5	
Nauru	...		...		8.8	(1987)	14.5	(1994)	2.1	66.2	(2012)
Palau	...		...		12.6	(1992)	9.1		13.6	8.7	
Papua New Guinea	21.1		26.6		31.2		36.6		36.3	27.0	(2013)
Samoa	...		...		28.0	(1994)	27.4		29.7	24.2	
Solomon Islands	...		...		5.0	(1990)	15.8		6.8	15.0	(2014)
Timor-Leste	...		...		...		...		84.9	72.5	(2014)
Tonga	10.4	(1975)	10.6		14.6		22.3		18.2	18.2	(2014)
Tuvalu	...		9.8	(1981)	16.9		11.2		6.0	5.6	(2012)
Vanuatu	...		6.0	(1979)	10.2		10.6		9.2	8.7	(2014)
Developing Member Economies[b]	...		...		35.2		37.0		39.5	37.6	

continued on next page

Table A1.4b *continued*

Regional Member	1966		1976	1986	1996	2006	2015	
Developed Member Economies[b]	...		39.3	37.7	31.4	27.1	...	
Australia	39.1	(1972)	39.0	37.0	28.5	27.9	23.8	
Japan	43.7	(1970)	39.4	37.8	31.7	28.1	26.9	(2014)
New Zealand	35.9	(1971)	35.8	32.7	27.1	24.9	23.0	(2012)
Regional Members[b]	...		...	36.9	33.5	34.0	...	
World	...		...	...	29.8	29.4	26.3	

... = data not available, GDP = gross domestic product, Lao PDR = Lao People's Democratic Republic.

[a] Where no data are available for the specific year headings, available data for the earliest and/or nearest years are reflected.

[b] Regional and subregional aggregates are calculated using data available for the respective year headings and no imputations are made for missing values. Moreover, aggregates are provided for subregions/regions where at least two-thirds of the countries are represented.

Sources: Asian Development Bank. Statistical Database System. sdbs.adb.org (accessed 19 January 2017); United Nations Statistics Division. UNDATA. http://data.un.org/ (accessed 27 December 2016); World Bank. World Development Indicators Database. http://data.worldbank.org (accessed 20 February 2017); ADB estimates.

Table A1.4c: Services, Value Added[a]
(% of GDP)

Regional Member	1966	1976	1986	1996	2006	2015
Developing Member Economies						
Central and West Asia[b]	...	...	49.0	49.3	50.6	54.4
Afghanistan	...	...	...	37.8 (2002)	41.9	54.2
Armenia	...	...	30.7 (1990)	30.6	34.9	52.8
Azerbaijan	...	...	38.1 (1990)	33.4	23.6	43.0
Georgia	...	40.0 (1980)	36.2	42.1	62.3	66.3
Kazakhstan	...	...	28.7 (1992)	60.3	52.0	61.8
Kyrgyz Republic	...	...	31.4 (1990)	32.0	47.2	57.1
Pakistan	42.3	44.2	49.0	50.4	56.0	55.5
Tajikistan	...	25.0 (1985)	26.8	29.5	44.7	47.1
Turkmenistan	...	...	34.6 (1987)	17.8	46.3	28.6 (2014)
Uzbekistan	...	...	34.1 (1987)	43.4	42.2	47.8 (2013)
East Asia[b]	...	...	40.1	46.2	50.2	52.6
China, People's Rep. of	24.9	22.6	29.8	33.6	41.8	50.0
Hong Kong, China	...	...	69.1	85.2	91.8	92.7 (2014)
Korea, Rep. of	41.4	46.8	51.7	56.7	60.2	59.7
Mongolia	...	58.3 (1981)	53.1	33.8	37.4	51.1
Taipei,China	47.4 (1975)	45.5	48.7	64.4	66.1	62.8
South Asia[b]	...	...	44.3	47.0	53.2	53.8
Bangladesh	35.7	33.6	45.0	52.7	55.6	56.4
Bhutan	...	44.6 (1980)	37.8	35.1	38.9	39.4 (2014)
India	38.1	40.8	44.4	46.3	52.9	53.2
Maldives	...	...	75.0 (1995)	76.5	80.1	78.1 (2014)
Nepal	20.2	21.9	32.7	35.6	48.2	53.3
Sri Lanka	51.0	43.3	45.6	50.9	58.0	60.6

continued on next page

Table A1.4c continued

Regional Member	1966	1976	1986	1996	2006	2015
Southeast Asia[b]	...	...	44.0	45.3	48.2	52.6
Brunei Darussalam	8.1 (1974)	8.4	39.3	42.6	26.1	38.7
Cambodia	...	...	40.5 (1993)	37.7	40.8	42.3
Indonesia	37.3	36.3	42.0	39.9	40.1	44.7
Lao PDR	...	...	26.0 (1989)	25.6	37.0	40.5 (2014)
Malaysia	38.8	33.3	40.6	44.8	45.3	51.8
Myanmar	45.2 (1970)	41.9	37.6	29.5	36.8	38.7
Philippines	41.9	34.6	41.5	47.3	54.1	58.9
Singapore	65.4 (1975)	64.7	64.9	66.2	68.2	73.6
Thailand	44.1	45.7	51.3	53.6	51.3	55.1
Viet Nam	...	32.5 (1985)	33.1	42.5	42.7	44.2
The Pacific[b]	...	...	43.1	41.5	52.3	70.6
Cook Islands	...	77.1 (1985)	75.0	82.6	85.8	83.0
Fiji	43.3	51.8	59.0	55.9	66.6	69.9 (2014)
Kiribati	...	23.4 (1978)	64.4	64.0	68.8	62.0 (2014)
Marshall Islands	...	...	...	...	78.5	75.1
Micronesia, Fed. States of	...	...	67.3 (1995)	67.5	71.2	65.8
Nauru	...	...	63.3 (1987)	78.8 (1994)	90.1	31.2 (2012)
Palau	...	...	68.9 (1992)	87.0	81.6	87.9
Papua New Guinea	35.9	39.8	33.5	30.1	42.5	52.8 (2013)
Samoa	...	...	49.5 (1994)	54.2	58.3	66.6
Solomon Islands	...	...	66.1 (1990)	43.1	57.6	57.0 (2014)
Timor-Leste	...	...	...	...	10.0	20.8 (2014)
Tonga	39.5 (1975)	43.6	46.5	53.9	63.2	62.4 (2014)
Tuvalu	...	82.2 (1981)	64.7	64.0	69.9	70.0 (2012)
Vanuatu	...	72.0 (1979)	65.8	71.8	67.0	64.5 (2014)
Developing Member Economies[b]	...	...	42.3	46.2	50.3	52.8

continued on next page

Table A1.4c continued

Regional Member	1966	1976	1986	1996	2006	2015
Developed Member Economies[b]	...	55.9	59.6	66.6	71.5	...
Australia	53.9 (1972)	54.7	57.9	67.8	69.1	73.9
Japan	51.2 (1970)	56.2	59.7	66.6	70.7	72.0 (2014)
New Zealand	52.5 (1971)	53.3	61.1	66.0	69.7	70.9 (2012)
Regional Members[b]	...	...	54.0	59.1	59.7	...
World	...	...	...	66.1	67.3	...

... = data not available, GDP = gross domestic product, Lao PDR = Lao People's Democratic Republic.

[a] Where no data are available for the specific year headings, available data for the earliest and/or nearest years are reflected.

[b] Regional and subregional aggregates are calculated using data available for the respective year headings and no imputations are made for missing values. Moreover, aggregates are provided for subregions/region where at least two-thirds of the countries are represented.

Sources: Asian Development Bank. Statistical Database System. sdbs.adb.org (accessed 19 January 2017); United Nations Statistics Division. UNDATA. http://data.un.org/ (accessed 27 December 2016); World Bank. World Development Indicators Database. http://data.worldbank.org (accessed 20 February 2017); ADB estimates.

Table A1.5: Exports of Goods and Services, as Share of Gross Domestic Product[a] (% of GDP)

Regional Member	1966		1976		1986		1996	2006	2015	
Developing Member Economies										
Central and West Asia										
Afghanistan	8.6		13.2		...		...	24.9	7.0	
Armenia	...		...		35.0	(1990)	23.2	23.4	29.8	
Azerbaijan	...		...		43.9	(1990)	29.5	66.5	37.8	
Georgia	...		...		41.5	(1987)	13.3	32.9	45.0	
Kazakhstan	...		...		74.0	(1992)	35.3	51.0	28.5	
Kyrgyz Republic	...		...		29.2	(1990)	30.7	41.7	36.2	
Pakistan	9.2	(1967)	10.7		11.9		16.9	14.1	10.9	
Tajikistan	...		...		35.2	(1988)	76.6	58.2	11.3	(2014)
Turkmenistan	...		...		39.0	(1991)	74.6	73.1	73.3	(2012)
Uzbekistan	...		...		28.8	(1990)	27.7	37.0	19.3	
East Asia										
China, People's Rep. of	3.5		4.6		10.5		17.6	35.7	22.4	
Hong Kong, China	75.9		89.4		109.3		136.4	201.8	201.6	
Korea, Rep. of	10.0		28.3		33.1		25.7	37.2	45.9	
Mongolia	...		23.9	(1981)	30.2		35.5	59.4	44.9	
Taipei,China	...		51.5	(1980)	56.5		46.8	65.8	64.6	
South Asia										
Bangladesh	10.3		4.7		5.2		9.7	16.4	17.3	
Bhutan	...		13.6	(1980)	17.6		35.5	54.4	36.3	(2014)
India	4.1		6.6		5.1		10.2	21.1	19.9	
Maldives	...		153.5	(1980)	68.1		91.7	53.0	...	
Nepal	5.6		10.8		11.7		22.8	13.4	11.7	
Sri Lanka	22.4		29.0		23.7		35.0	30.1	20.5	

continued on next page

Table A1.5 *continued*

Regional Member	1966	1976	1986	1996	2006	2015
Southeast Asia						
Brunei Darussalam	...	93.7	61.8 (1989)	59.9	71.7	52.2
Cambodia	7.8	...	...	25.4	68.6	...
Indonesia	14.1	25.9	19.5	25.8	31.0	21.1
Lao PDR	...	...	3.6	22.7	40.4	...
Malaysia	43.4	52.1	56.5	91.6	112.2	70.9
Myanmar	...	...	...	...	0.2	17.4
Philippines	20.4	19.3	26.3	40.5	46.6	28.2
Singapore	123.3	149.5	148.9	176.1	230.1	176.5
Thailand	17.6	20.2	25.6	39.0	68.7	69.1
Viet Nam	...	...	6.6	40.9	67.8	89.8
The Pacific						
Cook Islands	...	...	...	...	...	...
Fiji	43.4	37.7	41.7	62.8	47.2	51.8
Kiribati	...	56.4	32.0	13.4	11.1	...
Marshall Islands	...	...	...	...	27.6	52.6 (2014)
Micronesia, Fed. States of	...	...	3.4 (1983)	...	...	...
Nauru	...	...	...	...	...	...
Palau	...	...	20.4 (1991)	12.9	43.0	...
Papua New Guinea	16.8	41.8	43.6	59.4	72.2 (2004)	...
Samoa	...	...	...	31.5	28.9	...
Solomon Islands	...	36.9 (1981)	36.7	34.4	35.4	54.4 (2014)
Timor-Leste	...	...	...	...	96.9	92.7 (2014)
Tonga	...	26.9	25.7	20.4	14.4	18.5 (2014)
Tuvalu	...	...	...	...	...	...
Vanuatu	...	33.2 (1980)	34.8	46.0	41.3	48.7 (2014)
Developing Member Economies[b]	8.4	16.8	21.6	35.7	46.3	32.7

continued on next page

Table A1.5 continued

Regional Member	1966	1976	1986	1996	2006	2015
Developed Member Economies[b]	10.6	13.6	11.6	10.7	17.0	17.8
Australia	12.9	13.5	15.0	18.9	19.6	19.8
Japan	10.6	13.3	11.1	9.7	16.2	17.9
New Zealand	...	26.7	26.6	28.3	29.6	28.1
Regional Members[b]	9.4	14.8	14.7	19.7	33.2	29.2
World	11.8	17.9	17.0	21.5	29.1	28.9

... = data not available, GDP = gross domestic product, Lao PDR = Lao People's Democratic Republic.

[a] Where no data are available for the specific year headings, available data for the earliest and/or nearest years are reflected.

[b] Regional and subregional aggregates are calculated using data available for the respective year headings and no imputations are made for missing values. Moreover, aggregates are provided for subregions/regions where at least two-thirds of the countries are represented.

Sources: Asian Development Bank. Statistical Database System. sdbs.adb.org (accessed 12 January 2017); World Bank. World Development Indicators Database. http://data.worldbank.org (accessed 12 January 2017); ADB estimates.

Table A1.6: Imports of Goods and Services[a]
(% of GDP)

Regional Member	1966	1976	1986	1996	2006	2015
Developing Member Economies						
Central and West Asia						
Afghanistan	18.6	14.9	...	...	69.6	49.3
Armenia	...	...	46.3 (1990)	56.0	39.3	42.0
Azerbaijan	...	...	39.2 (1990)	55.5	38.8	34.8
Georgia	...	...	40.8 (1987)	32.4	57.0	64.9
Kazakhstan	...	...	75.3 (1992)	36.0	40.5	24.7
Kyrgyz Republic	...	...	49.6 (1990)	56.6	79.0	72.2
Pakistan	...	19.4	22.7	21.4	21.5	17.1
Tajikistan	...	...	46.2 (1988)	80.0	83.0	58.5 (2014)
Turkmenistan	...	...	27.1 (1991)	75.4	34.9	44.4 (2012)
Uzbekistan	...	...	47.8 (1990)	34.2	30.1	18.5
East Asia						
China, People's Rep. of	3.2	4.3	11.2	15.9	28.4	18.8
Hong Kong, China	79.4	78.8	100.2	137.8	190.6	199.3
Korea, Rep. of	20.1	30.2	28.4	29.0	36.4	38.9
Mongolia	...	71.0 (1981)	81.4	42.4	53.5	42.0
Taipei,China	...	52.6 (1980)	37.7	43.5	60.0	51.6
South Asia						
Bangladesh	12.7	17.6	11.8	16.4	21.8	24.8
Bhutan	...	37.7 (1980)	52.4	45.7	59.2	57.3 (2014)
India	6.6	6.0	6.9	11.3	24.2	22.5
Maldives	...	205.1 (1980)	60.7	73.1	71.0	...
Nepal	8.8	14.2	20.3	35.6	31.3	41.7
Sri Lanka	25.8	31.4	35.3	43.9	41.1	28.0

continued on next page

Table A1.6 continued

Regional Member	1966	1976	1986	1996	2006	2015
Southeast Asia						
Brunei Darussalam	17.4 (1974)	18.3	35.2 (1989)	60.6	25.2	32.7
Cambodia	12.8	...	...	43.8	76.0	66.6 (2014)
Indonesia	20.9	21.5	20.5	26.4	25.6	20.8
Lao PDR	...	...	7.7	41.1	45.9	...
Malaysia	39.2	41.5	50.4	90.2	90.4	63.3
Myanmar	13.7	6.6	6.7	1.5	0.1	27.9
Philippines	18.3	25.2	22.4	49.3	48.4	33.5
Singapore	130.6	156.4	146.2	159.9	200.3	149.6
Thailand	17.9	22.7	23.6	45.3	65.4	57.7
Viet Nam	...	...	16.6	51.8	70.7	89.0
The Pacific						
Cook Islands	...	...	...	...	...	...
Fiji	48.0	42.4	39.5	58.8	68.3	62.8 (2014)
Kiribati	...	35.7	42.0	92.4	90.9	...
Marshall Islands	...	...	...	...	88.9	102.8 (2013)
Micronesia, Fed. States of	...	...	84.3 (1983)	...	...	...
Nauru	...	...	...	...	...	...
Palau	...	...	...	66.9	76.5	...
Papua New Guinea	40.1	40.8	51.4	48.4	58.9 (2004)	...
Samoa	...	...	...	50.4	52.6	...
Solomon Islands	...	79.3	74.9	55.8	55.9	66.2 (2014)
Timor-Leste	...	...	...	...	26.1	57.4 (2014)
Tonga	...	56.6	69.9	58.4	51.2	56.5 (2014)
Tuvalu	...	...	...	...	...	...
Vanuatu	...	...	64.8	53.1	48.3	51.1 (2014)
Developing Member Economies[b]	9.6	16.7	23.0	36.8	42.0	29.3

continued on next page

Table A1.6 *continued*

Regional Member	1966	1976	1986	1996	2006	2015
Developed Member Economies[b]	...	13.0	8.4	10.3	16.2	19.4
Australia	15.1	13.4	18.1	19.3	21.4	21.2
Japan	9.0	12.6	7.2	9.2	14.9	18.9
New Zealand	21.7 (1971)	29.3	26.1	26.8	30.0	27.5
Regional Members[b]	...	14.4	12.9	19.9	30.4	27.0
World	11.8	18.1	17.5	21.1	28.6	28.1

... = data not available, GDP = gross domestic product, Lao PDR = Lao People's Democratic Republic.

[a] Where no data are available for the specific year headings, available data for the earliest and/or nearest years are reflected.

[b] Regional and subregional aggregates are calculated using data available for the respective year headings and no imputations are made for missing values. Moreover, aggregates are provided for subregions/regions where at least two-thirds of the countries are represented.

Sources: Asian Development Bank. Statistical Database System. sdbs.adb.org (accessed 12 January 2017); World Bank. World Development Indicators Database. http://data.worldbank.org (accessed 12 January 2017); ADB estimates.

Table A1.7: Poverty and Inequality[a]

	Proportion of Population below $1.90 a Day (2011 PPP)		Proportion of Population below $3.10 a Day (2011 PPP)		Gini Coefficient	
	1996[b]	Latest Year	1996[b]	Latest Year	1996[b]	Latest Year
Developing Member Economies						
Central Asia						
Afghanistan	...	...	...	...	...	...
Armenia	17.9	2.3 (2014)	40.4	14.6 (2014)	0.444	0.315 (2014)
Azerbaijan	7.3 (1995)	0.5 (2008)	24.8 (1995)	2.5 (2008)	0.347 (1995)	0.318 (2008)
Georgia	6.0	9.8 (2014)	17.2	25.3 (2014)	0.371	0.401 (2014)
Kazakhstan	6.3	0.0 (2013)	22.9	0.3 (2013)	0.354	0.263 (2013)
Kyrgyz Republic	30.6 (1998)	1.3 (2014)	51.5 (1998)	17.5 (2014)	0.464 (1998)	0.268 (2014)
Pakistan	15.9	6.1 (2013)	60.5	36.9 (2013)	0.287	0.307 (2013)
Tajikistan	54.4 (1999)	19.5 (2014)	86.1 (1999)	56.7 (2014)	0.295 (1999)	0.308 (2014)
Turkmenistan	42.3 (1998)	...	69.1 (1998)	...	0.408 (1998)	...
Uzbekistan	45.5 (1998)	66.8 (2003)	69.2 (1998)	87.8 (2003)	0.447 (1998)	0.353 (2003)
East Asia						
China, People's Rep. of	42.1	1.9 (2013)	71.5	11.1 (2013)	0.428 (2008)	0.422 (2012)
Hong Kong, China	...	...	...	...	...	...
Korea, Rep. of	...	...	...	...	0.307 (2012)	0.302 (2014)

continued on next page

Table A1.7 continued

	Proportion of Population below $1.90 a Day (2011 PPP)		Proportion of Population below $3.10 a Day (2011 PPP)		Gini Coefficient	
	1996[b]	Latest Year	1996[b]	Latest Year	1996[b]	Latest Year
Mongolia	13.9 (1995)	0.2 (2014)	36.9 (1995)	2.7 (2014)	0.332 (1995)	0.320 (2014)
Taipei,China	...	...	...	...	0.336 (1995)	0.337 (2015)
South Asia						
Bangladesh	35.1 (1995)	18.5 (2010)	73.2 (1995)	56.8 (2010)	0.329 (1995)	0.321 (2010)
Bhutan	35.2 (2003)	2.2 (2012)	60.9 (2003)	13.3 (2012)	0.468 (2003)	0.388 (2012)
India	45.9 (1993)	21.2 (2011)	79.6 (1993)	58.0 (2011)	...	0.352 (2011)
Maldives	10.0 (2002)	7.3 (2009)	36.5 (2002)	23.3 (2009)	0.413 (2002)	0.384 (2009)
Nepal	61.9 (1995)	15.0 (2010)	85.5 (1995)	48.4 (2010)	0.352 (1995)	0.328 (2010)
Sri Lanka	8.9 (1995)	1.9 (2012)	38.9 (1995)	14.6 (2012)	0.354 (1995)	0.392 (2012)
Southeast Asia						
Brunei Darussalam	...	...	...	...	...	...
Cambodia	30.1 (1994)	2.2 (2012)	67.0 (1994)	21.6 (2012)	0.382 (1994)	0.308 (2012)
Indonesia	45.9	8.3 (2014)	77.6	36.4 (2014)	...	0.395 (2013)
Lao PDR	30.7 (1997)	16.7 (2012)	67.9 (1997)	46.9 (2012)	0.349 (1997)	0.379 (2012)
Malaysia	1.8 (1995)	0.3 (2009)	10.7 (1995)	2.7 (2009)	0.485 (1995)	0.463 (2009)
Myanmar	...	...	...	...	...	...
Philippines	17.7 (1997)	13.1 (2012)	41.7 (1997)	37.6 (2012)	0.460 (1997)	0.430 (2012)

continued on next page

Table A1.7 continued

	Proportion of Population below $1.90 a Day (2011 PPP)		Proportion of Population below $3.10 a Day (2011 PPP)		Gini Coefficient	
	1996[b]	Latest Year	1996[b]	Latest Year	1996[b]	Latest Year
Singapore	...	...	...	...	...	...
Thailand	2.3	0.0 (2013)	13.9	0.9 (2013)	0.429	0.379 (2013)
Viet Nam	34.8 (1998)	3.1 (2014)	69.1 (1998)	12.0 (2014)	0.354 (1998)	0.376 (2014)
The Pacific						
Cook Islands	...	...	...	...	...	...
Fiji	5.5 (2002)	4.1 (2008)	21.9 (2002)	18.5 (2008)	0.396 (2002)	0.428 (2008)
Kiribati	...	14.1 (2006)	...	34.7 (2006)	...	0.376 (2006)
Marshall Islands	...	...	...	...	...	...
Micronesia, Fed. States of	11.4 (2005)	17.4 (2013)	28.5 (2005)	39.4 (2013)	0.431 (2005)	0.425 (2013)
Nauru	...	...	...	...	...	...
Palau	...	...	...	...	...	...
Papua New Guinea	53.2	39.3 (2009)	70.2	64.7 (2009)	0.554	0.439 (2009)
Samoa	...	0.8 (2008)	...	8.4 (2008)	...	0.427 (2008)
Solomon Islands	45.6 (2005)	...	69.3 (2005)	...	0.461 (2005)	...
Timor-Leste	44.2 (2001)	46.8 (2007)	72.8 (2001)	80.0 (2007)	0.376 (2001)	0.316 (2007)
Tonga	2.8 (2001)	1.1 (2009)	7.6 (2001)	8.2 (2009)	0.378 (2001)	0.381 (2009)
Tuvalu	...	2.7 (2010)	...	16.3 (2010)	...	0.411 (2010)
Vanuatu	...	15.4 (2010)	...	38.8 (2010)	...	0.372 (2010)

continued on next page

Table A1.7 continued

	Proportion of Population below $1.90 a Day (2011 PPP)		Proportion of Population below $3.10 a Day (2011 PPP)		Gini Coefficient	
	1996[b]	Latest Year	1996[b]	Latest Year	1996[b]	Latest Year
Developed Member Economies						
Australia	...	...	...	...	0.337 (1995)	0.349 (2010)
Japan	...	...	...	...	...	0.321 (2008)
New Zealand	...	...	...	...	0.323 (2011)	0.333 (2012)

... = data not available, 0.0 = magnitude is less than half of unit employed, Lao PDR = Lao People's Democratic Republic.

[a] Poverty estimates are consumption-based except for Armenia (1996) and Malaysia which are income-based. Inequality estimates are also consumption-based except for Armenia (1996); the Republic of Korea; Malaysia; New Zealand; and Taipei,China which are income-based. For the Republic of Korea and New Zealand, the gini coefficients are based on disposable income post taxes and transfers. For Taipei,China, the gini coefficients are based on disposable income.

[b] Data nearest to 1996 were used if data for 1996 were not available.

Sources: ADB. 2016. *Key Indicators for Asia and the Pacific 2016*; Directorate-General of Budget, Accounting and Statistics.http://eng.dgbas. gov.tw/mp.asp?mp=2 (accessed 8 November 2016); OECD Database on Income Distribution and Poverty. http://www.oecd.org/social/ inequality-and-poverty.htm (accessed 8 November 2016); World Bank. World Development Indicators Online. http://databank.worldbank. org/data/reports.aspx?source=world-development-indicators (accessed 8 November 2016).

Table A1.8: Life Expectancy at Birth
(number of years)

Regional Member	1966	1976	1986	1996	2006	2014
Developing Member Economies						
Central and West Asia[a]	53	57	61	62	64	67
Afghanistan	35	40	46	54	57	60
Armenia	68	71	69	69	74	75
Azerbaijan	63	65	66	65	69	71
Georgia	66	69	70	70	73	75
Kazakhstan	61	64	69	64	66	72
Kyrgyz Republic	59	62	65	67	68	70
Pakistan	50	56	59	62	64	66
Tajikistan	59	61	63	63	67	70
Turkmenistan	57	60	62	63	65	66
Uzbekistan	61	64	67	66	67	68
East Asia[a]	52	64	68	70	74	76
China, People's Rep. of	51	64	68	70	74	76
Hong Kong, China	70	73	77	80	82	84
Korea, Rep. of	58	64	69	74	79	82
Mongolia	53	57	59	61	66	69
Taipei,China	...	...	74 (1992)	75	78	80 (2013)
South Asia[a]	46	52	56	61	65	69
Bangladesh	49	50	56	63	68	72
Bhutan	35	42	49	57	66	69
India	45	52	56	61	65	68
Maldives	41	49	58	66	75	77
Nepal	38	44	51	59	66	70
Sri Lanka	62	67	69	69	74	75
Southeast Asia[a]	55	59	64	67	69	70
Brunei Darussalam	65	69	72	74	76	79
Cambodia	42	21	52	56	64	68

continued on next page

Table A1.8 *continued*

Regional Member	1966	1976	1986	1996	2006	2014
Indonesia	52	58	62	65	67	69
Lao PDR	45	48	52	57	62	66
Malaysia	63	67	70	72	74	75
Myanmar	48	53	57	61	64	66
Philippines	60	62	64	66	67	68
Singapore	67	71	74	77	80	83
Thailand	58	63	69	70	73	74
Viet Nam	62	63	69	72	74	76
The Pacific[a]	46	50	56	59	63	65
Cook Islands	...	...	70 (1992)	71	74	75
Fiji	58	62	65	67	69	70
Kiribati	52	56	58	63	65	66
Marshall Islands	...	...	63 (1998)	67	70	73
Micronesia, Fed. States of	60	64	66	67	68	69
Nauru	...	...	58 (1992)	59	64	66
Palau	...	...	67 (1990)	67	70	73
Papua New Guinea	43	50	55	58	61	63
Samoa	53	58	63	68	71	74
Solomon Islands	52	58	57	60	66	68
Timor-Leste	37	34	45	55	65	68
Tonga	64	67	69	70	72	73
Tuvalu	...	...	61	62	63	66
Vanuatu	50	56	62	66	70	72
Developing Member Economies[a]	50	59	63	66	69	71
Developed Member Economies[a]	71	75	78	80	82	83
Australia	71	73	76	78	81	82
Japan	71	75	78	80	82	84
New Zealand	71	72	74	77	80	81

continued on next page

Table A1.8 *continued*

Regional Member	1966	1976	1986	1996	2006	2014
Regional Members[a]	51	60	64	67	70	72
World	56	61	65	67	69	71

... = data not available, Lao PDR = Lao People's Democratic Republic.

[a] Regional aggregates are population-weighted averages estimated using data available for the respective year headings given in the table. Aggregates are provided for subregions/region where at least two-thirds of the countries and 80% of the total population are represented.

Sources: ADB. 2016. *Key Indicators for Asia and the Pacific 2016;* Directorate-General of Budget, Accounting and Statistics.http://eng.dgbas.gov.tw/mp.asp?mp=2 (accessed 8 November 2016); World Bank. World Development Indicators Online. http://databank.worldbank.org/data/reports.aspx?source=world-development-indicators (accessed 8 November 2016); ADB estimates.

Table A1.9: Mortality Rate, Aged 5 Years and Below[a]
(per 1,000 births)

Regional Member	1966		1976		1986	1996	2006	2015
Developing Member Economies								
Central and West Asia[b]	...		...		132.6	114.5	90.5	70.8
Afghanistan	328.7		273.6		209.2	148.6	116.3	91.1
Armenia	...		88.1		59.1	36.8	22.2	14.1
Azerbaijan	...		108.2	(1982)	99.0	92.1	48.6	31.7
Georgia	68.6	(1975)	66.3		49.8	43.0	22.7	11.9
Kazakhstan	84.5	(1971)	76.4		57.5	51.8	30.3	14.1
Kyrgyz Republic	112.6	(1975)	110.0		75.0	58.9	37.9	21.3
Pakistan	209.8		169.6		148.7	123.0	99.3	81.1
Tajikistan	152.8	(1972)	136.0		118.3	116.2	61.5	44.8
Turkmenistan	...		138.8	(1977)	100.0	88.7	68.0	51.4
Uzbekistan	...		126.7	(1979)	80.8	68.7	52.5	39.1
East Asia[b]	...		...		52.6	43.8	21.5	10.6
China, People's Rep. of	119.1	(1969)	79.8		53.7	45.6	21.9	10.7
Hong Kong, China	...		...		...	...	...	...
Korea, Rep. of	77.8		23.5		9.3	5.3	5.2	3.4
Mongolia	...		179.9	(1978)	130.0	80.3	40.3	22.4
Taipei,China	...		...		...	...	...	...
South Asia[b]	...		...		143.5	104.6	69.6	46.0
Bangladesh	232.3		214.5		167.7	108.6	63.0	37.6
Bhutan	278.6	(1969)	228.4		158.8	99.8	54.8	32.9
India	226.3		188.6		141.2	105.3	71.5	47.7
Maldives	297.9		193.4		114.5	65.8	20.1	8.6
Nepal	293.1		234.2		169.5	101.8	56.6	35.8
Sri Lanka	78.9		61.4		26.9	19.5	13.2	9.8

continued on next page

Table A1.9 continued

Regional Member	1966		1976		1986		1996	2006	2015
Southeast Asia[b]	...		...		84.2		56.3	38.1	27.1
Brunei Darussalam	...		16.8	(1982)	14.1		10.3	9.0	10.2
Cambodia	310.0	(1975)	285.6		119.6		122.6	60.4	28.7
Indonesia	188.2		136.5		99.5		63.6	39.6	27.2
Lao PDR	...		208.3	(1978)	178.1		135.5	93.5	66.7
Malaysia	67.3		39.9		20.5		12.9	8.1	7.0
Myanmar	187.5	(1968)	155.3		121.3		92.7	68.1	50.0
Philippines	90.4		82.0		71.6		44.0	34.9	28.0
Singapore	33.6		16.0		10.4		5.0	2.9	2.7
Thailand	118.6		73.7		46.0		27.0	17.0	12.3
Viet Nam	91.8		75.9		58.5		39.5	27.7	21.7
The Pacific[b]	...		...		99.1		78.8	64.6	51.1
Cook Islands	71.0		36.8		26.5		20.9	12.2	8.1
Fiji	58.5		51.6		34.1		25.8	23.8	22.4
Kiribati	160.7		124.8		111.9		79.4	64.8	55.9
Marshall Islands	101.1		76.0		58.7		41.9	39.9	36.0
Micronesia, Fed. States of	...		57.2	(1981)	58.6		55.9	45.9	34.7
Nauru	...		...		56.9	(1990)	46.4	39.0	35.4
Palau	...		41.8	(1984)	39.9		30.4	22.1	16.4
Papua New Guinea	165.0		119.9		95.5		82.0	72.9	57.3
Samoa	...		39.0	(1984)	35.8		24.9	19.1	17.5
Solomon Islands	141.4		68.4		43.3		34.8	33.4	28.1
Timor-Leste	...		...		210.0		134.0	78.5	52.6
Tonga	66.7		35.3		24.8		18.6	16.7	16.7
Tuvalu	83.9	(1975)	80.3		59.3		49.7	35.6	27.1
Vanuatu	128.1		84.8		44.6		29.9	28.0	27.5
Developing Member Economies[b]	201.9		135.2		101.3		82.2	54.0	36.5

continued on next page

Table A1.9 continued

Regional Member	1966	1976	1986	1996	2006	2015
Developed Member Economies[b]	22.5	13.0	7.9	5.8	4.1	3.1
Australia	22.1	16.2	11.0	6.8	5.6	3.8
Japan	22.6	12.5	7.1	5.5	3.6	2.7
New Zealand	22.5	17.7	13.4	8.4	6.5	5.7
Regional Members[b]	191.9	131.1	99.2	80.5	53.0	35.8
World	171.2	126.6	98.6	84.0	60.1	42.5

... = data not available, Lao PDR = Lao People's Democratic Republic.

[a] Where no data are available for the specific year headings, available data for the earliest and/or nearest years are reflected.

[b] Weighted averages estimated using annual live births for the respective year headings.

Sources: United Nations Inter-agency Group for Child Mortality Estimation. http://www.childmortality.org (accessed 28 December 2016); World Bank. World Development Indicators Database. http://data.worldbank.org (accessed 28 December 2016); ADB estimates.

Table A1.10: Adjusted Net Enrollment Rate,[a] Primary Education, Both Sexes (% of relevant age group)

Regional Member	1966	1976	1986	1996	2006	2014	2015
Developing Member Economies							
Central and West Asia	...	...	...	...	71	74	...
Afghanistan	...	27 (1974)	...	29 (1993)	...	...	...
Armenia	...	...	...	87 (2002)	90	...	96
Azerbaijan	...	...	92 (1991)	93	84	95	94
Georgia	...	...	...	84	95	99 (2011)	...
Kazakhstan	...	...	...	94 (2000)	98	99	100
Kyrgyz Republic	...	...	...	92	96	98	...
Pakistan	...	...	...	59 (2002)	66	73	74
Tajikistan	...	...	...	94 (2000)	97	97	98
Turkmenistan	...	...	...	...	...	...	...
Uzbekistan	...	...	...	...	97 (2007)	97	97
East Asia	...	...	91	91	96	97	...
China, People's Rep. of	...	...	94 (1987)	91	...	...	...
Hong Kong, China	...	...	...	...	...	...	...
Korea, Rep. of	97 (1971)	97	99	99	100 (2007)	96 (2013)	...
Mongolia	...	...	...	85	97	96	97
Taipei,China	...	...	...	...	...	...	...
South Asia	...	67	73	82	95	98	...
Bangladesh	51 (1970)	76	60	72 (1990)	96	95 (2010)	...
Bhutan	...	23 (1978)	...	55 (1998)	77	89	...
India	61 (1971)	...	77 (1990)	84 (2000)	97 (2007)	95	...
Maldives	...	...	...	93 (1997)	98	97 (2009)	...
Nepal	...	59 (1983)	67 (1988)	66 (1999)	81 (2004)	95	97
Sri Lanka	...	78 (1977)	98	100 (2001)	97	97	...

continued on next page

Table A1.10 continued

Regional Member	1966		1976		1986		1996		2006		2014		2015
Southeast Asia	...		80		93		93		92		95		...
Brunei Darussalam	...		90	(1977)	80		99	(1995)	...		...		...
Cambodia	...		...		...		83	(1997)	94		95		89
Indonesia	70	(1971)	76		97		93		94		93		...
Lao PDR	...		...		65	(1988)	69		82		95		93
Malaysia	84	(1970)	85	(1972)	...		96	(1994)	98		98		98
Myanmar	61	(1971)	65	(1978)	...		90	(2000)	89		95		...
Philippines	...		97		94		96		87		97	(2013)	...
Singapore	94	(1970)	100		98	(1984)	89	(1995)	80	(2007)	79	(2009)	...
Thailand	76	(1973)	76	(1974)	...		...		94		92		91
Viet Nam	...		97	(1977)	91	(1985)	99	(1998)	92		98	(2013)	...
The Pacific	...		...		...		74		59		89		...
Cook Islands	...		...		...		91	(1998)	98	(2010)	98		97
Fiji	...		...		97	(1992)	93		99		97	(2013)	98
Kiribati	...		99	(1979)	97		98		...		98		97
Marshall Islands	...		...		...		...		98	(2002)	100	(2011)	78
Micronesia, Fed. States of	...		...		...		...		...		87		84
Nauru	...		...		...		...		77	(2012)	87		...
Palau	...		...		...		...		...		99		80 (2016)
Papua New Guinea	...		...		...		...		...		87	(2012)	...
Samoa	...		...		...		93	(1994)	98	(2007)	97		97
Solomon Islands	...		...		...		...		81		...		...
Timor-Leste	...		...		...		...		77	(2008)	98		97
Tonga	88	(1970)	97	(1975)	97		95	(1998)	99		99		...
Tuvalu	...		...		...		...		...		96		98
Vanuatu	...		85	(1981)	75	(1989)	98	(1998)	99	(2005)	...		...

continued on next page

Table A1.10 continued

Regional Member	1966		1976	1986	1996		2006	2014	2015
Developed Member Economies	...		100	100	99		99	99	...
Australia	96	(1971)	98	96	95		96	97	...
Japan	100	(1971)	100	100	100	(1995)	100	100	...
New Zealand	100	(1970)	100	100	99		99	98	...
World	72	(1970)	78	81	82		89	91	...

... = data not available, Lao PDR = Lao People's Democratic Republic.

[a] Where no data are available for the specific year headings, available data for the earliest and/or nearest years are reflected. Subregional aggregates are figures generated by the UNESCO Institute of Statistics and pertain to the year headings only.

Source: United Nations Educational, Scientific and Cultural Organization (UNESCO) Institute for Statistics. http://data.uis.unesco.org/Index.aspx (accessed 17 February 2017).

2. ADB: Institutional, Operational, and Financial Highlights Tables

Table A2.1: Regional and Nonregional Members, Years of Membership
(as of 31 December 2016)

Regional Member	Year of Membership
Afghanistan	1966
Australia	1966
Cambodia	1966
India	1966
Indonesia	1966
Japan	1966
Korea, Rep. of	1966
Lao PDR	1966
Malaysia	1966
Nepal	1966
New Zealand	1966
Pakistan	1966
Philippines	1966
Samoa	1966
Singapore	1966
Sri Lanka	1966
Taipei,China	1966
Thailand	1966
Viet Nam	1966
Hong Kong, China	1969
Fiji	1970
Papua New Guinea	1971
Tonga	1972
Bangladesh	1973

Regional Member	Year of Membership
Myanmar	1973
Solomon Islands	1973
Kiribati	1974
Cook Islands	1976
Maldives	1978
Vanuatu	1981
Bhutan	1982
China, People's Rep. of	1986
Marshall Islands	1990
Micronesia, Fed. States of	1990
Mongolia	1991
Nauru	1991
Tuvalu	1993
Kazakhstan	1994
Kyrgyz Republic	1994
Uzbekistan	1995
Tajikistan	1998
Azerbaijan	1999
Turkmenistan	2000
Timor-Leste	2002
Palau	2003
Armenia	2005
Brunei Darussalam	2006
Georgia	2007

Nonregional Member	Year of Membership
Austria	1966
Belgium	1966
Canada	1966
Denmark	1966
Finland	1966
Germany	1966
Italy	1966
Netherlands	1966
Norway	1966
Sweden	1966

Nonregional Member	Year of Membership
United Kingdom	1966
United States	1966
Switzerland	1967
France	1970
Spain	1986
Turkey	1991
Portugal	2002
Luxembourg	2003
Ireland	2006

Lao PDR = Lao People's Democratic Republic.

Source: ADB. 2016. About ADB – Members. https://www.adb.org/about/members (accessed 12 December 2016).

Table A2.2: Share of Subscribed Capital and Voting Power
(as of 31 December 2016)

	Year of Membership	Subscribed Capital[a] (% of total)	Voting Power[b] (% of total)
Regional			
Afghanistan	1966	0.034	0.326
Armenia	2005	0.298	0.537
Australia	1966	5.786	4.928
Azerbaijan	1999	0.445	0.654
Bangladesh	1973	1.021	1.115
Bhutan	1982	0.006	0.303
Brunei Darussalam	2006	0.352	0.580
Cambodia	1966	0.049	0.338
China, People's Rep. of	1986	6.444	5.454
Cook Islands	1976	0.003	0.301
Fiji	1970	0.068	0.353
Georgia	2007	0.341	0.572
Hong Kong, China	1969	0.545	0.734
India	1966	6.331	5.363
Indonesia	1966	5.446	4.655
Japan	1966	15.607	12.784
Kazakhstan	1994	0.806	0.944
Kiribati	1974	0.004	0.302
Korea, Republic of	1966	5.038	4.329
Kyrgyz Republic	1994	0.299	0.538
Lao PDR	1966	0.014	0.310
Malaysia	1966	2.723	2.477
Maldives	1978	0.004	0.302
Marshall Islands	1990	0.003	0.301
Micronesia, Fed. States of	1990	0.004	0.302
Mongolia	1991	0.015	0.311
Myanmar	1973	0.545	0.734
Nauru	1991	0.004	0.302
Nepal	1966	0.147	0.416
New Zealand	1966	1.536	1.527
Pakistan	1966	2.178	2.041
Palau	2003	0.003	0.301
Papua New Guinea	1971	0.094	0.374
Philippines	1966	2.383	2.205
Samoa	1966	0.003	0.301
Singapore	1966	0.340	0.571
Solomon Islands	1973	0.007	0.304
Sri Lanka	1966	0.580	0.762
Taipei,China	1966	1.089	1.170
Tajikistan	1998	0.286	0.528
Thailand	1966	1.362	1.388

continued on next page

Table A2.2 continued

	Year of Membership	Subscribed Capital[a] (% of total)	Voting Power[b] (% of total)
Timor-Leste	2002	0.010	0.306
Tonga	1972	0.004	0.302
Turkmenistan	2000	0.253	0.501
Tuvalu	1993	0.001	0.300
Uzbekistan	1995	0.674	0.837
Vanuatu	1981	0.007	0.304
Viet Nam	1966	0.341	0.572
Subtotal		**63.533**	**65.155**

	Year of Membership	Subscribed Capital[a] (% of total)	Voting Power[b] (% of total)
Nonregional			
Austria	1966	0.340	0.571
Belgium	1966	0.340	0.571
Canada	1966	5.231	4.483
Denmark	1966	0.340	0.571
Finland	1966	0.340	0.571
France	1970	2.328	2.161
Germany	1966	4.326	3.759
Ireland	2006	0.340	0.571
Italy	1966	1.807	1.744
Luxembourg	2003	0.340	0.571
Netherlands	1966	1.026	1.119
Norway	1966	0.340	0.571
Portugal	2002	0.113	0.389
Spain	1986	0.340	0.571
Sweden	1966	0.340	0.571
Switzerland	1967	0.584	0.765
Turkey	1991	0.340	0.571
United Kingdom	1966	2.042	1.932
United States	1966	15.607	12.784
Subtotal		**36.467**	**34.845**
Total		**100.000**	**100.000**

Lao PDR = Lao People's Democratic Republic.

Notes: Numbers may not sum precisely because of rounding. For other details, see table on Statement of Subscriptions to Capital Stock and Voting Power (OCR-8) in the Financial Statements of the *2016 ADB Annual Report*.

[a] Subscribed capital refers to a member's subscription to shares of the capital stock of ADB.

[b] The total voting power of each member consists of the sum of its basic votes and proportional votes. The basic votes of each member consist of such number of votes as results from the equal distribution among all members of 20% of the aggregate sum of the basic votes and proportional votes of all members. The number of proportional votes of each member is equal to the number of shares the capital stock of ADB held by that member.

Source: ADB Controller's Department.

Table A2.3: Board Constituencies through the Years

1966	1971	1987	2016
REGIONAL			
Republic of Korea; Taipei,China; Viet Nam	Republic of Korea; Taipei,China; Viet Nam	Republic of Korea; Papua New Guinea; Sri Lanka; Taipei,China; **Vanuatu**	Republic of Korea; Papua New Guinea; Sri Lanka; Taipei,China; **Uzbekistan**; Vanuatu; Viet Nam
Philippines, Pakistan	Philippines, Pakistan	Philippines, **Maldives**, Pakistan	Philippines, **Kazakhstan**, Maldives, **Marshall Islands, Mongolia, Timor-Leste,** Pakistan
Australia	Australia; **Hong Kong, China; Papua New Guinea**	Australia; Hong Kong, China; **Kiribati; Solomon Islands**	Australia; **Azerbaijan**; Cambodia; **Georgia**; Hong Kong, China; Kiribati; **Federated States of Micronesia; Nauru; Palau;** Solomon Islands; Tuvalu
Indonesia, Afghanistan, Cambodia, Sri Lanka, Lao PDR, Nepal	Indonesia, **Fiji**, New Zealand, Samoa	Indonesia, **Cook Islands**, Fiji, New Zealand, Tonga, Samoa	Indonesia, **Armenia**, Cook Islands, Fiji, **Kyrgyz Republic**, New Zealand, Tonga, Samoa
New Zealand, Malaysia, Thailand, Singapore, Samoa	Malaysia, Nepal, Singapore, Thailand	Malaysia, **Myanmar**, Nepal, Singapore, Thailand	Malaysia, **Brunei Darussalam**, Myanmar, Nepal, Singapore, Thailand
India	India	India, **Bangladesh, Bhutan**, Lao PDR, Viet Nam	India, Afghanistan, Bangladesh, Bhutan, Lao PDR, **Tajikistan, Turkmenistan**
Japan	Japan	Japan	Japan

continued on next page

Table A2.3 continued

1966	1971	1987	2016
		People's Republic of China	People's Republic of China
	Sri Lanka, Afghanistan, Cambodia, Lao PDR		
NON-REGIONAL			
Canada, Denmark, Finland, Norway, Sweden, United Kingdom	Canada, Denmark, Finland, Netherlands, Norway, Sweden	Canada, Denmark, Finland, Netherlands, Norway, Sweden	Canada, Denmark, Finland, **Ireland,** Netherlands, Norway, Sweden
United States	United States	United States	United States
Germany, Italy, Netherlands, Austria, Belgium	Germany, Austria, United Kingdom	Germany, Austria, United Kingdom	Germany, Austria, **Luxembourg, Turkey,** United Kingdom
	France, Belgium, Italy, **Switzerland**	France, Belgium, Italy, **Spain,** Switzerland	France, Belgium, Italy, **Portugal,** Spain, Switzerland

Lao PDR = Lao People's Democratic Republic.

Notes: ADB members in bold font are new members. Cambodia was not represented in the Board of Directors from 1975 to 1993 and Afghanistan was not represented in the Board of Directors from 1987 to 1994.

Source: ADB Office of the Secretary.

Table A2.4: Board of Directors and Constituencies
(as of 31 December 2016)

Director	Alternate Director	Members Represented
Won-Mok Choi (KOR)	M P D U K Mapa Pathirana (SRI) *(end of service was 30 Jun 2016)*	Republic of Korea; Papua New Guinea; Sri Lanka; Taipei,China; Uzbekistan; Vanuatu; Viet Nam
Paul Dominguez (PHI)	Muhammad Sami Saeed (PAK)	Kazakhstan, Maldives, Marshall Islands, Mongolia, Pakistan, Philippines, Timor-Leste
Mathew Fox (AUS)	Scott Dawson (AUS)	Australia; Azerbaijan; Cambodia; Georgia; Hong Kong, China; Kiribati; Federated States of Micronesia; Nauru; Palau; Solomon Islands; Tuvalu
Bhimantara Widyajala (INO)	Mario Di Maio (NZL)	Armenia, Cook Islands, Fiji, Indonesia, Kyrgyz Republic, New Zealand, Samoa, Tonga
Zhongjing Wang (PRC)	Wenxing Pan (PRC)	People's Republic of China
Philaslak Yukkasemwong (THA)	Rokiah Hj Badar (BRU)	Brunei Darussalam, Malaysia, Myanmar, Nepal, Singapore, Thailand
Kshatrapati Shivaji (IND)	Sherafjon Sheraliev (TAJ)	Afghanistan, Bangladesh, Bhutan, India, Lao People's Democratic Republic, Tajikistan, Turkmenistan
Koichi Hasegawa (JPN)	Masashi Tanabe (JPN)	Japan
David Murchison (CAN)	Joar Strand (NOR)	Canada, Denmark, Finland, Ireland, Netherlands, Norway, Sweden
Swati Dandekar (USA)	Michael Strauss (USA)	United States
Maurizio Ghirga (ITA)	Johannes Schneider (SWI)	Belgium, France, Italy, Portugal, Spain, Switzerland
Mario Sander (GER)	Philip Rose (UKG)	Austria, Germany, Luxembourg, Turkey, United Kingdom

AUS = Australia, BRU = Brunei Darussalam, CAN = Canada, GER = Germany, IND = India, INO = Indonesia, ITA = Italy, JPN = Japan, KOR = Republic of Korea, NOR = Norway, NZL = New Zealand, PAK = Pakistan, PHI = Philippines, PRC = People's Republic of China, SRI = Sri Lanka, SWI = Switzerland, THA = Thailand, UKG = United Kingdom.

Source: ADB Office of Secretary.

Table A2.5: List of Presidents

	Name	Date	Period Covered
1	Takeshi Watanabe	24 November 1966–23 November 1971	6 years
		24 November 1971–24 November 1972	
2	Shiro Inoue	25 November 1972–23 November 1976	4 years
3	Taroichi Yoshida	24 November 1976–23 November 1981	5 years
4	Masao Fujioka	24 November 1981–23 November 1986	8 years
		24 November 1986–23 November 1989	
5	Kimimasa Tarumizu	24 November 1989–23 November 1991	4 years
		24 November 1991–23 November 1993	
6	Mitsuo Sato	24 November 1993–23 November 1996	5 years and 2 months
		24 November 1996–15 January 1999	
7	Tadao Chino	16 January 1999–23 November 2001	6 years
		24 November 2001–31 January 2005	
8	Haruhiko Kuroda	1 February 2005–23 November 2006	8 years and 2 months
		24 November 2006–23 November 2011	
		24 November 2011–18 March 2013	
9	Takehiko Nakao	28 April 2013–23 November 2016	
		24 November 2016–present	

Source: ADB. About ADB. https://www.adb.org/about (accessed 10 October 2016).

Table A2.6: Annual Meeting Venues and Dates

Year	Event	Date	Venue/Country
1966	Inaugural	24–26 November	Tokyo, Japan
1968	1st	4–6 April	Manila, Philippines
1969	2nd	10–12 April	Sydney, Australia
1970	3rd	9–11 April	Seoul, Republic of Korea
1971	4th	15–17 April	Singapore, Singapore
1972	5th	20–22 April	Vienna, Austria
1973	6th	26–28 April	Manila, Philippines
1974	7th	25–27 April	Kuala Lumpur, Malaysia
1975	8th	24–26 April	Manila, Philippines
1976	9th	22–24 April	Jakarta, Indonesia
1977	10th	21–23 April	Manila, Philippines
1978	11th	24–26 April	Vienna, Austria
1979	12th	2–4 May	Manila, Philippines
1980	13th	30 April–2 May	Manila, Philippines
1981	14th	30 April–2 May	Honolulu, United States
1982	15th	28–30 April	Manila, Philippines
1983	16th	4–6 May	Manila, Philippines
1984	17th	25–27 April	Amsterdam, Netherlands
1985	18th	30 April–2 May	Bangkok, Thailand
1986	19th	30 April–2 May	Manila, Philippines
1987	20th	27–29 April	Osaka, Japan
1988	21st	28–30 April	Manila, Philippines
1989	22nd	4–6 May	Beijing, People's Republic of China
1990	23rd	2–4 May	New Delhi, India
1991	24th	24–26 April	Vancouver, Canada
1992	25th	4–6 May	Hong Kong, China
1993	26th	4–6 May	Manila, Philippines
1994	27th	3–5 May	Nice, France

continued on next page

Table A2.6 *continued*

Year	Event	Date	Venue/Country
1995	28th	3–5 May	Auckland, New Zealand
1996	29th	30 April–2 May	Manila, Philippines
1997	30th	11–13 May	Fukuoka, Japan
1998	31st	29 April–1 May	Geneva, Switzerland
1999	32nd	30 April–2 May	Manila, Philippines
2000	33rd	6–8 May	Chiang Mai, Thailand
2001	34th	9–11 May	Honolulu, United States
2002	35th	10–12 May	Shanghai, People's Republic of China
2003	36th	30 June	Manila, Philippines
2004	37th	15–17 May	Jeju, Republic of Korea
2005	38th	4–6 May	Istanbul, Turkey
2006	39th	4–6 May	Hyderabad, India
2007	40th	6–7 May	Kyoto, Japan
2008	41st	5–6 May	Madrid, Spain
2009	42nd	4–5 May	Bali, Indonesia
2010	43rd	3–4 May	Tashkent, Uzbekistan
2011	44th	5–6 May	Ha Noi, Viet Nam
2012	45th	4–5 May	Manila, Philippines
2013	46th	4–5 May	Delhi, India
2014	47th	4–5 May	Astana, Kazakhstan
2015	48th	4–5 May	Baku, Azerbaijan
2016	49th	3–5 May	Frankfurt, Germany
2017	50th	4–7 May	Yokohama, Japan

Source: ADB. All Annual Meetings. https://www.adb.org/about/all-annual-meetings (accessed 6 October 2016).

Table A2.7: Staff Members (end of year)

	1966	1976	1986	1996	2006	2016
Total Staff	40	760	1,604	1,961	2,405	3,092
Category						
Management	2	2	4	4	5	7
International staff	11	288	599	669	856	1,103
National and administrative staff	27	470	1,001	1,288	1,544	1,982
Location						
Headquarters						
Management	2	2	4	4	5	7
International staff	11	288	591	639	756	949
National and administrative staff	27	470	986	1,174	1,170	1,383
Field Offices						
International staff	0	0	8	30	100	154
National and administrative staff	0	0	15	114	374	599
Gender						
Women	15	308	740	1,023	1,358	1,804
International staff	*1*	*5*	*25*	*100*	*249*	*375*
Men	25	452	864	938	1,047	1,288
International staff	*10*	*283*	*566*	*539*	*507*	*574*
Nationality, by Region						
Asia and the Pacific	39	669	1,383	1,707	2,056	2,665
Developing members	*33*	*614*	*1,268*	*1,567*	*1,872*	*2,413*
Nonregional	1	91	221	254	349	427
ADB Members Represented	6	33	37	43	54	60

Notes: Staff information include Management, international staff, and national and administrative staff. They include Director's advisors and assistants, staff on special leave without pay, and on secondment status. Staff data are sourced from the Budget, Personnel, and Management Systems Department and may not tally with the numbers from ADB's annual reports which used different cuts of staff data. Management includes the President and Vice-Presidents.

Source: ADB Budget, Personnel, and Management Systems Department.

Table A2.8: Annual Number of Staff (end of year)[a] and Internal Administrative Expenses Budget

Year	Staff				Budget
	Management	International	National and Administrative	Total	Internal Administrative Expenses ($'000)
1966	2	11	27	40	
1967	2	56	132	190	3,040
1968	2	94	204	300	5,215
1969	2	143	289	434	6,484
1970	2	159	328	489	7,363
1971	2	191	358	551	8,562
1972	2	207	379	588	10,142
1973	2	222	400	624	10,664
1974	2	231	412	645	13,472
1975	2	254	437	693	17,332
1976	2	288	470	760	19,694
1977	2	304	499	805	22,628
1978	3	333	540	876	25,957
1979	3	359	647	1,009	32,604
1980	3	416	731	1,150	42,372
1981	3	467	798	1,268	58,746
1982	3	517	864	1,384	68,585
1983	3	552	941	1,496	77,524
1984	4	573	954	1,531	82,639
1985	4	586	985	1,575	87,918
1986	4	599	1,001	1,604	89,265
1987	4	601	1,025	1,630	94,242
1988	4	606	1,053	1,663	98,446
1989	4	600	1,061	1,665	109,405
1990	4	604	1,063	1,671	120,052
1991	4	613	1,106	1,723	135,280
1992	4	632	1,149	1,785	145,612
1993	4	645	1,253	1,902	161,930

continued on next page

Table A2.8 continued

Year	Staff				Budget
	Management	International	National and Administrative	Total	Internal Administrative Expenses ($'000)
1994	4	660	1,281	1,945	168,259
1995	4	656	1,278	1,938	188,266
1996	4	669	1,288	1,961	189,881
1997	4	666	1,302	1,972	199,497
1998	4	682	1,293	1,979	204,817
1999	4	681	1,288	1,973	206,969
2000	4	728	1,325	2,057	215,363
2001	4	759	1,400	2,163	226,905
2002	4	790	1,424	2,218	239,992
2003	5	831	1,475	2,311	258,740
2004	5	855	1,534	2,394	279,539
2005	4	883	1,569	2,456	296,770
2006	5	856	1,544	2,405	312,897
2007	5	847	1,591	2,443	332,864
2008	5	874	1,626	2,505	357,150
2009	5	927	1,670	2,602	388,868
2010	6	1,024	1,803	2,833	439,488
2011	6	1,055	1,897	2,958	496,352
2012	6	1,076	1,969	3,051	544,797
2013	7	1,083	1,886	2,976	576,604
2014	7	1,074	1,916	2,997	598,388
2015	7	1,104	1,994	3,105	617,701
2016	7	1,103	1,982	3,092	635,624

[a] Values are planned internal administrative expenses and not actual amounts.

Source: ADB Budget, Personnel, and Management Systems Department.

Table A2.9: Establishment of Field Offices

Year	Field Office
1982	Bangladesh Resident Mission
1984	South Pacific Regional Mission[a]
1987	Indonesia Resident Mission
1989	Nepal Resident Mission
1989	Pakistan Resident Mission
1992	India Resident Mission
1995	North American Representative Office
1996	European Representative Office
1996	Cambodia Resident Mission
1996	Japanese Representative Office
1996	Viet Nam Resident Mission
1997	Kazakhstan Resident Mission
1997	Sri Lanka Resident Mission
1997	Uzbekistan Resident Mission
1999	Kyrgyz Republic Resident Mission
2000	Lao PDR Resident Mission
2000	Philippines Country Office
2000	People's Republic of China Resident Mission
2000	Special Liaison Office in Timor-Leste[b]
2000	Mongolia Resident Mission
2002	Afghanistan Resident Mission
2002	Papua New Guinea Resident Mission
2003	Azerbaijan Resident Mission
2003	Tajikistan Resident Mission
2004	Pacific Subregional Office
2004	Thailand Resident Mission
2005	Pacific Liaison and Coordination Office
2008	Armenia Resident Mission
2008	Georgia Resident Mission
2008	Turkmenistan Resident Mission
2013	Bhutan Resident Mission
2014	Myanmar Resident Mission

Lao PDR = Lao People's Democratic Republic.

Note: Establishment dates indicated above are dates of the host country agreements but if these are not available, establishment dates based on R-papers circulated/approved by the Board of Directors were used.

[a] The South Pacific Regional Mission in Vanuatu was closed in 2005 when the Pacific Subregional Office was opened in the Fiji Islands and the Pacific Liaison and Coordination Office (PLCO) began operations in Sydney.

[b] The Special Liaison Office in Timor-Leste (SOTL) was established under the Pacific Regional Department in July 2000 and functioned as a regional mission when Timor-Leste joined ADB in 2002. ADB and Timor-Leste entered into a Host Country Agreement on 9 January 2003 pursuant to which ADB is entitled to establish a "Representative Office" that includes a resident mission. In October 2013, the Board approved the establishment of a resident mission in Timor-Leste through the renaming of SOTL to Timor-Leste Resident Mission.

Source: ADB. 2016. Establishment of Field Offices. *The ADB Archives Gallery.* https://www.adb.org/sites/default/files/publication/176469/adb-archives-gallery.pdf

Table A2.10: Selected Financial Highlights, 2012–2016

($ million)	Approvals				
	2012[a]	2013[a]	2014[a]	2015[a]	2016[a]
Loans, Grants, and Others					
By Source					
Ordinary Capital Resources	10,136	10,363	10,438	13,413	14,389
Loans	9,602	10,186	10,233	12,938	13,797
Guarantees	403	35	20	341	515
Equity Investments	131	142	185	134	77
Asian Development Fund	3,005	3,850	3,091	2,867	3,073
Loans	2,312	3,008	2,686	2,514	2,556
Grants	693	843	405	353	518
Special Funds[b]	4	7	0	7	9
Grants	4	7	0	7	9
Subtotal	13,145	14,219	13,529	16,287	17,471
By Operations					
Sovereign	11,300	12,611	11,610	13,655	14,970
Loans	10,607	11,768	11,205	13,301	13,943
Guarantees	–	–	–	–	500
Grants	693	843	405	353	527
Nonsovereign	1,841	1,602	1,919	2,626	2,502
Loans	1,307	1,425	1,714	2,150	2,410
Equity Investments	131	142	185	134	77
Guarantees	403	35	20	341	15
Subtotal	13,141	14,213	13,529	16,280	17,471
Technical Assistance					
Technical Assistance Special Fund	142	148	152	139	162
Special Funds[c]	9	7	7	3	7
Subtotal	151	155	158	141	169

continued on next page

Table A2.10 continued

($ million)	Approvals				
	2012[a]	2013[a]	2014[a]	2015[a]	2016[a]
Cofinancing Including Trust Funds					
Sovereign	**2,155**	**3,714**	**4,216**	**6,142**	**8,225**
Trust Funds Administered by ADB	206	299	147	205	402
Bilateral	944	1,753	902	2,232	3,263
Multilateral	939	1,655	2,733	3,492	4,250
Others[d]	65	6	434	213	311
Nonsovereign[e]	**6,117**	**2,933**	**5,006**	**4,593**	**5,836**
Subtotal	**8,272**	**6,647**	**9,222**	**10,735**	**14,061**
TOTAL	**21,568**	**21,021**	**22,909**	**27,163**	**31,701**

– = nil, 0 = less than $500,000.

Note: Numbers may not sum precisely because of rounding.

[a] Operational approvals (loans, grants, equity investments, and guarantees) are based on gross approvals.

[b] Special funds other than ADF such as Asia Pacific Disaster Response Fund and Climate Change Fund.

[c] Special funds other than Technical Assistance Special Fund include Climate Change Fund, Financial Sector Development Partnership Special Fund, and Regional Cooperation and Integration Fund.

[d] "Others" includes private sector cofinancing through foundations and corporate social responsibility programs, and any public source, such as national development banks, that do not fall under official cofinancing.

[e] Nonsovereign cofinancing includes commercial cofinancing such as Trade Finance Program cofinancing, B loans and parallel loans, among others.

Table A2.11: Operational Approvals by Member and by Decade, 1967–2016
($ million)

Developing Member Economy	1967–1976	1977–1986	1987–1996	1997–2006	2007–2016	Total	% of Total
India	–	250	6,338	10,478	25,032	42,097	15.8
China, People's Rep. of	–	–	6,346	11,969	18,076	36,390	13.6
Indonesia	377	3,398	9,313	8,462	11,622	33,172	12.4
Pakistan	431	2,800	5,769	7,673	13,074	29,746	11.1
Bangladesh	190	1,737	2,999	3,468	9,998	18,392	6.9
Philippines	464	1,964	3,695	3,430	7,959	17,512	6.6
Viet Nam	45	–	967	3,138	12,019	16,170	6.1
Sri Lanka	76	493	1,260	2,130	4,259	8,217	3.1
Thailand	313	1,417	2,100	1,634	1,396	6,861	2.6
Korea, Rep. of	552	1,518	262	4,015	–	6,347	2.4
Uzbekistan	–	–	50	925	5,370	6,345	2.4
Kazakhstan	–	–	230	555	4,560	5,344	2.0
Nepal	102	448	954	885	2,519	4,907	1.8
Azerbaijan	–	–	–	119	4,241	4,360	1.6
Afghanistan	59	36	–	1,026	2,873	3,995	1.5
Regional	–	–	241	669	2,542	3,452	1.3
Lao PDR	12	60	574	654	1,513	2,813	1.1
Cambodia	2	–	246	714	1,501	2,463	0.9
Papua New Guinea	36	237	273	397	1,368	2,311	0.9
Myanmar	113	418	–	–	1,733	2,264	0.8

continued on next page

Table A2.11 continued

Developing Member Economy	1967–1976	1977–1986	1987–1996	1997–2006	2007–2016	Total	% of Total
Georgia	–	–	–	–	2,153	2,153	0.8
Malaysia	294	989	667	–	10	1,960	0.7
Mongolia	–	–	315	353	1,155	1,823	0.7
Kyrgyz Republic	–	–	160	469	1,076	1,705	0.6
Tajikistan	–	–	–	308	1,112	1,420	0.5
Armenia	–	–	–	–	1,186	1,186	0.4
Bhutan	–	25	27	125	536	713	0.3
Fiji	7	54	61	129	269	519	0.2
Timor-Leste	–	–	–	10	303	313	0.1
Samoa	14	37	40	40	147	277	0.1
Maldives	–	3	31	98	124	255	0.1
Solomon Islands	4	25	15	36	132	212	0.1
Singapore	128	53	–	–	–	181	0.1
Turkmenistan	–	–	–	–	125	125	0.0
Tonga	1	10	37	10	61	118	0.0
Hong Kong, China	42	60	–	–	–	102	0.0
Taipei,China	100	–	–	–	–	100	0.0
Vanuatu	–	5	24	22	48	99	0.0
Marshall Islands	–	–	31	47	20	98	0.0
Cook Islands	–	3	21	6	57	87	0.0
Micronesia, Fed. States of	–	–	17	58	9	84	0.0
Palau	–	–	–	–	70	70	0.0

continued on next page

Table A2.11 continued

Developing Member Economy	1967–1976	1977–1986	1987–1996	1997–2006	2007–2016	Total	% of Total
Kiribati	2	1	2	10	37	52	0.0
Tuvalu	–	–	–	8	19	27	0.0
Nauru	–	–	–	5	11	16	0.0
Grand Total	**3,361**	**16,041**	**43,063**	**64,075**	**140,311**	**266,851**	**100**

– = nil, Lao PDR = Lao People's Democratic Republic.

Notes: Figures from 1997 to 2016 are based on gross approvals of loans, grants, equity investments, and guarantees. Data from 1968 to 1996 are net of terminations (they exclude operations approved by the ADB Board of Directors but terminated before they were deemed effective).

Sources: For 1967 to 1996: ADB loan, technical assistance, grant, and equity approvals database; for 1997 to 2016: ADB's eOperations Dashboard, Cognos database and ADB, Strategy and Policy Department.

Table A2.12: Operational Approvals by Fund Source and Type, 1967–2016
($ million)

Year	Ordinary Capital Resources			Asian Development Fund			Total ADB
	Sovereign	Nonsovereign	Total	Loans	Grants	Total	
1968	42	-	42	-	-	-	42
1969	76	-	76	22	-	22	98
1970	212	-	212	34	-	34	246
1971	203	-	203	52	-	52	254
1972	222	-	222	94	-	94	316
1973	303	-	303	118	-	118	421
1974	375	-	375	173	-	173	548
1975	494	-	494	166	-	166	660
1976	540	-	540	236	-	236	776
1977	615	-	615	272	-	272	886
1978	778	-	778	381	-	381	1,159
1979	835	-	835	416	-	416	1,252
1980	958	-	958	477	-	477	1,436
1981	1,147	-	1,147	531	-	531	1,678
1982	1,138	-	1,138	546	-	546	1,684
1983	1,190	3	1,193	703	-	703	1,896
1984	1,551	0	1,551	684	-	684	2,235
1985	1,171	3	1,175	637	-	637	1,811
1986	1,357	12	1,369	636	-	636	2,005
1987	1,463	46	1,509	958	-	958	2,466
1988	1,958	94	2,051	1,083	-	1,083	3,135
1989	2,171	157	2,328	1,363	-	1,363	3,691
1990	2,419	109	2,528	1,480	-	1,480	4,008
1991	3,247	177	3,424	1,347	-	1,347	4,771
1992	3,904	55	3,960	1,154	-	1,154	5,114
1993	3,730	203	3,933	1,298	-	1,298	5,230
1994	2,502	49	2,551	1,177	-	1,177	3,728
1995	3,963	167	4,130	1,455	-	1,455	5,585
1996	3,490	179	3,669	1,666	-	1,666	5,335
1997	7,749	169	7,919	1,620	-	1,620	9,538
1998	4,859	264	5,123	987	-	987	6,110

continued on next page

Table A2.12 *continued*

Year	Ordinary Capital Resources			Asian Development Fund			Total ADB
	Sovereign	Nonsovereign	Total	Loans	Grants	Total	
1999	3,762	154	3,916	1,070	–	1,070	4,986
2000	4,102	356	4,458	1,592	–	1,592	6,051
2001	3,940	68	4,008	1,362	–	1,362	5,369
2002	3,898	241	4,138	1,633	–	1,633	5,771
2003	4,539	393	4,931	1,379	–	1,379	6,310
2004	3,705	607	4,312	1,242	–	1,242	5,554
2005	3,885	822	4,707	1,376	247	1,622	6,329
2006	5,542	960	6,502	1,279	275	1,554	8,057
2007	7,347	1,321	8,669	1,893	519	2,412	11,081
2008	6,924	1,913	8,838	1,790	707	2,497	11,335
2009	10,902	1,735	12,637	2,210	911	3,122	15,758
2010	8,629	1,846	10,475	2,213	967	3,180	13,655
2011	9,201	2,106	11,306	1,955	597	2,552	13,858
2012	8,295	1,841	10,136	2,312	693	3,005	13,141
2013	8,761	1,602	10,363	3,008	843	3,850	14,213
2014	8,519	1,918	10,438	2,686	405	3,091	13,528
2015	10,788	2,626	13,413	2,514	353	2,867	16,280
2016	11,887	2,502	14,389	2,556	518	3,073	17,462
Total	179,286	24,697	203,983	55,833	7,035	62,868	266,851

– = nil.

Notes:

1. Figures from 1997 to 2016 are based on gross approvals of loans, grants, equity investments, and guarantees. Data from 1968 to 1996 are net of terminations (they exclude operations approved by the ADB Board of Directors but terminated before they were deemed effective).

2. Data for the Asian Development Fund (ADF) include loan approvals from the Agricultural Special Fund (ASF) and the Multi-Purpose Special Fund (MPSF) which were both established in 1968 as two of ADB's special funds. The ASF was formally terminated in 1973 and its resources were consolidated with those of MPSF. In the same year, the ADB Board of Governors adopted a resolution authorizing the establishment of ADF. In 1975, the Board of Governors adopted a resolution arranging the transfer of MPSF resources to the ADF.

Sources: For 1967–1996: ADB's loan, technical assistance, grant, and equity approvals database; for 1997–2016: ADB's eOperations Dashboard, Cognos database and ADB Operations Planning and Coordination Division, Strategy and Policy Department.

Table A2.13: Outstanding Portfolio and Loan and Grant Disbursements
($ million)

Year	Disbursements				Outstanding Balances		
	OCR Loans	ADF Loans	ADF Grants	Combined Total	OCR Loans	ADF Loans	Combined Total
1968	2	–	–	2	1	–	1
1969	7	0	–	8	8	0	8
1970	16	2	–	17	23	2	25
1971	44	5	–	49	64	7	71
1972	50	11	–	61	118	19	137
1973	120	26	–	147	235	46	281
1974	160	27	–	188	380	72	451
1975	285	77	–	362	626	133	759
1976	263	63	–	327	881	198	1,079
1977	273	84	–	356	1,203	325	1,528
1978	295	167	–	462	1,605	554	2,159
1979	361	125	–	486	1,799	606	2,405
1980	429	150	–	579	2,099	799	2,897
1981	518	149	–	667	2,334	872	3,206
1982	620	175	–	795	2,685	986	3,670
1983	715	222	–	937	3,106	1,176	4,282
1984	702	298	–	1,001	3,287	1,366	4,653
1985	620	390	–	1,010	4,539	2,000	6,539

continued on next page

Appendixes 439

Table A2.13 continued

Year	Disbursements				Outstanding Balances		
	OCR Loans	ADF Loans	ADF Grants	Combined Total	OCR Loans	ADF Loans	Combined Total
1986	612	413	–	1,024	5,998	2,751	8,749
1987	693	539	–	1,232	7,678	3,913	11,591
1988	957	692	–	1,649	7,524	4,476	12,000
1989	1,347	888	–	2,235	7,521	4,999	12,520
1990	1,689	1,063	–	2,752	9,391	6,371	15,762
1991	2,066	1,037	–	3,104	11,043	7,612	18,654
1992	1,880	888	–	2,767	12,023	8,183	20,206
1993	2,016	925	–	2,941	13,718	9,376	23,094
1994	2,501	1,186	–	3,688	16,499	11,357	27,856
1995	2,442	1,145	–	3,587	17,530	12,310	29,840
1996	2,563	1,234	–	3,797	16,109	12,468	28,577
1997	5,304	1,154	–	6,458	18,839	12,266	31,105
1998	5,623	1,144	–	6,766	24,760	14,324	39,084
1999	3,710	1,114	–	4,824	28,344	15,960	44,304
2000	2,884	1,135	–	4,019	28,231	15,532	43,762
2001	2,850	1,024	–	3,874	28,739	14,832	43,571
2002	3,067	1,136	–	4,202	29,234	17,233	46,467
2003	2,688	1,128	–	3,816	25,506	20,047	45,552
2004	2,508	1,055	–	3,563	24,309	21,627	45,936
2005	3,498	1,247	1	4,747	23,569	20,238	43,807
2006	4,420	1,338	34	5,793	26,192	21,522	47,714

continued on next page

Table A2.13 continued

Year	Disbursements				Outstanding Balances		
	OCR Loans	ADF Loans	ADF Grants	Combined Total	OCR Loans	ADF Loans	Combined Total
2007	5,234	1,618	63	6,914	30,256	24,018	54,274
2008	6,472	2,043	177	8,692	35,851	26,427	62,278
2009	7,898	2,201	347	10,446	41,732	27,959	69,691
2010	5,944	1,571	358	7,873	45,933	28,977	74,910
2011	6,337	1,385	510	8,232	49,729	29,515	79,244
2012	6,764	1,286	532	8,583	52,814	29,165	81,979
2013	5,985	1,975	576	8,536	53,051	28,680	81,731
2014	7,368	2,203	429	10,000	55,845	27,604	83,449
2015	9,667	2,048	503	12,217	61,889	27,270	89,159
2016	9,763	2,027	463	12,253	67,547	27,367	94,914
Cumulative	132,230	41,812	3,993	178,035	67,547	27,367	94,914

ADF = Asian Development Fund, OCR = ordinary capital resources.

Notes: Loan disbursements indicated above include both sovereign and nonsovereign operations. Numbers may not sum precisely due to rounding off.

Source: ADB Controller's Department.

Table A2.14: General Capital Increases and Capital Composition
(Authorized Capital Stock)

	Initial Subscription	GCI I	GCI II	GCI III	GCI IV	GCI V
Resolution Date by Board of Governors	22 Aug 1966	30 Nov 1971	29 Oct 1976	25 Apr 1983	22 May 1994	29 Apr 2009
Capital Increase						
% Increase	0	150	135	105	100	200
Number of new shares	110,000	165,000	414,800	754,750	1,770,497	7,092,622
Composition of Capital (%)						
Callable	50%	80%	90%	95%	98%	96%
Paid-in	50%	20%	10%	5%	2%	4%
Components of Capital						
Convertible Currency	50%	40%	40%	40%	40%	40%
National Currency	50%	60%	60%	60%	60%	60%
Composition of Capital, Increase						
in SDR million	1,100	1,650	4,148	7,547	17,705	70,926
Callable	550	1,320	3,733	7,170	17,351	68,089
Paid-in	550	330	415	377	354	2,837
in USD million	1,100[a]	1,650[b]	4,790[c]	8,163[d]	25,043[e]	106,272[f]
Callable	550	1,320	4,311	7,755	24,542	102,021
Paid-in	550	330	479	408	501	4,251

continued on next page

Table A2.14 continued

	Initial Subscription	GCI I	GCI II	GCI III	GCI IV	GCI V
Composition of Capital, Cumulative[g]						
in SDR million	1,100	2,750	7,221	14,768	34,910	106,389
Callable	550	1,870	5,823	12,993	32,480	101,084
Paid-in	550	880	1,398	1,775	2,430	5,306
in USD million	1,100[a]	2,750[b]	8,338[c]	15,974[d]	49,378[e]	159,408[f]
Callable	550	1,870	6,724	14,054	45,941	151,459
Paid-in	550	880	1,614	1,920	3,437	7,950

GCI = general capital increase, SDR = special drawing right.

Note: Numbers may not sum precisely because of rounding.

[a] Translated at the exchange rate of $1 per SDR as of 22 August 1966. At the time of ADB's inception, the original authorized capital of ADB was $1 billion. Of this amount, $500 million was paid-in shares and another $500 million was callable. In November 1966, the Board of Governors approved an increase of $100 million of authorized capital.

[b] Translated at the exchange rate of $1 per SDR as of 30 November 1971.

[c] Translated at the exchange rate of $1.15471 per SDR as of 29 October 1976.

[d] Translated at the exchange rate of $1.08163 per SDR as of 29 April 1983. There are no daily rates in Bloomberg for 1983, only month-end rates.

[e] Translated at the exchange rate of $1.41445 per SDR as of 20 May 1994.

[f] Translated at the exchange rate of $1.49835 per SDR as of 29 April 2009.

[g] Includes special capital increases of new and existing members.

Sources: ADB Controller's Department and annual reports.

Table A2.15: Donor Contributions on Asian Development Fund by Replenishments
($ million)

	ADF I[a] 1973–1975	ADF II 1976–1978	ADF III 1979–1982	ADF IV 1983–1986	ADF V 1987–1990	ADF VI 1992–1995	ADF VII 1997–2000	ADF VIII 2001–2004	ADF IX 2005–2008	ADF X 2009–2012	ADF XI 2013–2016	ADF 12[b] 2017–2020	Total	%
Regional	364	320	907	1,458	1,631	1,901	1,325	1,387	1,633	2,201	3,041	1,743	17,909	50.61
Japan	320	273	792	1,212	1,321	1,583	1,019	1,061	1,178	1,612	2,035	1,125	13,532	38.24
Australia	37	42	111	230	287	272	175	185	218	299	640	337	2,834	8.01
Korea, Rep. of	–	–	–	4	5	15	54	81	122	154	168	89	692	1.96
China, People's Rep. of	–	–	–	–	–	–	–	–	30	35	45	100	210	0.59
New Zealand	7	5	4	6	14	11	23	20	25	32	33	8	190	0.54
Taipei,China	–	–	–	2	–	15	15	15	18	22	23	12	122	0.34
Hong Kong, China	–	–	–	1	1	3	15	16	19	26	33	–[c]	115	0.33
India	–	–	–	–	–	–	–	–	–	–	30	42	72	0.20
Malaysia	–	–	–	–	–	–	10	–	5	6	10	5	36	0.10
Indonesia	–	–	–	3	2	–	10	–	–	–	–	14	29	0.08
Singapore	–	–	–	–	–	–	–	4	4	6	9	5	27	0.08
Brunei Darussalam	–	–	–	–	–	–	–	–	10	6	6	1	22	0.06

continued on next page

Table A2.15 continued

	ADF I[a] 1973–1975	ADF II 1976–1978	ADF III 1979–1982	ADF IV 1983–1986	ADF V 1987–1990	ADF VI 1992–1995	ADF VII 1997–2000	ADF VIII 2001–2004	ADF IX 2005–2008	ADF X 2009–2012	ADF XI 2013–2016	ADF 12[b] 2017–2020	Total	%
Thailand	–	–	–	–	–	–	4	3	3	4	5	3	21	0.06
Kazakhstan	–	–	–	–	–	–	–	–	–	–	6	3	9	0.02
Nauru	–	–	–	–	–	0.4	–	–	–	–	–	–	0.4	0.00
Nonregional	**346**	**441**	**1,234**	**1,802**	**2,011**	**2,312**	**1,363**	**1,540**	**1,777**	**2,029**	**1,788**	**838**	**17,479**	**49.39**
United States	150	180	445	520	584	680	400	412	461	461	360	190	4,842	13.68
Canada	35	76	171	283	299	307	126	133	179	207	193	102	2,111	5.96
Germany	53	53	141	211	236	276	177	165	195	222	194	87	2,009	5.68
United Kingdom	42	42	113	133	137	165	103	137	202	233	315	166	1,787	5.05
France	–	–	105	188	194	216	140	126	148	160	129	57	1,463	4.13
Italy	22	31	76	135	159	186	108	111	131	138	92	48	1,238	3.50
Netherlands	16	13	50	78	90	106	66	83	98	108	81	16	804	2.27
Sweden	–	11	26	44	49	84	40	39	53	63	80	24	513	1.45
Spain	–	–	–	29	28	34	14	129	67	129	65	–[d]	495	1.40
Switzerland	7	8	26	42	44	55	36	35	41	48	53	28	423	1.20
Norway	4	6	15	25	28	38	24	27	37	45	50	26	326	0.92
Austria	–	7	18	30	31	37	23	25	29	42	43	23	309	0.87
Denmark	6	7	16	29	32	42	24	25	34	21	25	13	275	0.78
Belgium	7	7	18	29	29	31	19	21	24	33	35	18	271	0.77
Finland	4	–	14	26	29	11	18	14	19	33	29	13	210	0.59

continued on next page

Table A2.15 continued

	ADF I[a] 1973–1975	ADF II 1976–1978	ADF III 1979–1982	ADF IV 1983–1986	ADF V 1987–1990	ADF VI 1992–1995	ADF VII 1997–2000	ADF VIII 2001–2004	ADF IX 2005–2008	ADF X 2009–2012	ADF XI 2013–2016	ADF 12[b] 2017–2020	Total	%
Turkey	–	–	–	–	40	47	16	5	6	6	6	2	128	0.36
Ireland	–	–	–	–	–	–	–	–	28	45	27	15	115	0.33
Portugal	–	–	–	–	–	–	30	17	20	28	1	0.3	96	0.27
Luxembourg	–	–	–	–	–	–	–	35	4	5	11	9	64	0.18
Total Contributions	710	761	2,141	3,260	3,642	4,212	2,688	2,926	3,410	4,229	4,829	2,580	35,389	100.00

– = nil, 0.00 = 0.001, ADF = Asian Development Fund.

Notes:
1. Actual donor contributions are based on contributions indicated in instruments of contribution except for ADF 12, which mostly represent pledged amounts as of 30 March 2017. Contributions for certain replenishments include the allocations to the Technical Assistance Special Fund.
2. Donor contributions in US dollar equivalent were calculated using the relevant Board of Governors' resolution exchange rates.
3. Actual donor contributions include additional contributions from new ADF donors provided after the conclusion of the respective replenishments.
4. Numbers may not sum precisely because of rounding.

[a] ADF I includes the transfer of the Multi-Purpose Special Fund contributions of $223 million equivalent.
[b] This was the first ADF replenishment after the ADB Board of Governors' approval to combine the ADF lending operations with OCR. To differentiate it from earlier replenishments, the numeral suffix was changed from Roman to Arabic.
[c] Hong Kong, China has indicated its desire or intention to contribute to ADF 12, subject to obtaining the authorization of its legislature, with the amount to be confirmed.
[d] For ADF 12, Spain will not be able to take a decision on its pledge until a new government is formed and all necessary approvals are obtained.

Source: ADB.

Table A2.16: Asian Development Fund Replenishments by Funding Sources ($ million)

Item	ADF I[a] 1973–1975	ADF II 1976–1978	ADF III 1979–1982	ADF IV 1983–1986	ADF V 1987–1990	ADF VI 1992–1995	ADF VII 1997–2000	ADF VIII 2001–2004	ADF IX 2005–2008	ADF X 2009–2012	ADF XI 2013–2016	ADF 12[b] 2017–2020
1. Donor contributions (a + b)	710	761	2,141	3,260	3,642	4,212	2,688	2,926	3,410	4,229	4,829	2,580
a. ADF allocation	710	761	2,141	3,260	3,569	4,072	2,688	2,926	3,189	3,890	4,453	2,119
b. TASF allocation					73	140			221	339	376	461
2. ADF internal resources[c]	3	61	141	153	462	1,101	2,231	3,695	4,821	8,355	8,594	180[d]
3. OCR net income transfer							230	350	160	480	480	1,038[e]
4. Set-aside resources[f]	57											
Total replenishment (1 + 2 + 3 + 4)	**770**	**822**	**2,282**	**3,413**	**4,104**	**5,313**	**5,149**	**6,971**	**8,391**	**13,064**	**13,903**	**3,798**

ADF = Asian Development Fund, OCR = ordinary capital resources, SDR = special drawing right, TASF = Technical Assistance Special Fund.

Notes:
1. Actual donor contributions are based on contributions indicated in instruments of contribution except for ADF 12, which mostly represent pledged amounts as of 30 March 2017. Contributions for certain replenishments include the allocations to the Technical Assistance Special Fund.
2. Donor contributions in US dollar equivalent were calculated using the relevant Board of Governors' resolution exchange rates.
3. Actual donor contributions include additional contributions from new ADF donors provided after the conclusion of the respective replenishments.
4. Numbers may not sum precisely because of rounding.

[a] ADF I includes the transfer of the Multi-Purpose Special Fund contributions of $223 million and $3 million income from loan and investment.
[b] This was the first ADF replenishment after the ADB Board of Governors' approval to combine the ADF lending operations with OCR. To differentiate it from earlier replenishments, the numeral suffix was changed from Roman to Arabic.
[c] ADF internal resources include loan service payments (principal and interest) from borrowers, income from liquidity investment, and drawdown of ADF liquidity.
[d] For ADF 12 (grant–only operations), $180 million includes only income from liquidity investment, as loan reflows are part of concessional OCR operations after the merger of ADF lending operations with OCR on 1 January 2017.
[e] Subject to the approval of the Asian Development Bank's Board of Governors.
[f] Represents the transfer from OCR paid–in capital of SDR47.6 million.

Source: Asian Development Bank.

Table A2.17: History of Asian Development Fund Replenishments

Replenishment Period	Key Highlights
1973–1975	**Establishment of the Asian Development Fund (ADF) and Initial Mobilization (ADF I)** Main issues: Technical matters such as amount to be mobilized, levels of individual contributions, and procedures to establish the Fund. Agreed at Donors' Meeting: $525 million, of which donor contribution: $525 million Actual replenishment: $770 million (including the ordinary capital resources [OCR] set–aside resources of $57 million equivalent), of which actual donor contribution: $710 million (including the transfer of the Multi-Purpose Special Fund contributions of $223 million equivalent) **ADF formally established** Contributions to the initial mobilization reached $260 million, triggering conditions required for the Fund to be legally effective.
1976–1978	**First ADF Replenishment (ADF II)** Main issues: Eligibility of countries for soft loans, consensus that concessional loans should go to countries in special difficulties, and drop in United States (US) share from 29% to 22%. Agreed at Donors' Meeting: $830 million, of which donor contribution: $830 million Actual replenishment: $822 million, of which actual donor contribution: $761 million
1979–1982	**Second ADF Replenishment (ADF III)** Main issues: One-year lag on US contribution to ADF II and its inability to give unqualified commitments for its ADF III contribution. Agreed at Donors' Meeting: $2,150 million, of which donor contribution: $2,150 million Actual replenishment: $2,282 million, of which actual donor contribution: $2,141 million
1983–1986	**Third ADF Replenishment (ADF IV)** Main issues: Difficulties of donors in maintaining previous shares (developing member countries participated in the ADF replenishment for the first time). Agreed at Donors' Meeting: $3,205 million, of which donor contribution: $3,205 million Actual replenishment: $3,413 million, of which actual donor contribution: $3,260 million

continued on next page

Table A2.17 *continued*

Replenishment Period	Key Highlights
1987–1990	**Fourth ADF Replenishment (ADF V)** Main issues: Possible hardening of ADF loan terms; and ADB assistance to the private sector, country strategies and policy dialogue, technical assistance operations, project quality, and personnel policies. Agreed at Donors' Meeting: $3,600 million, of which donor contribution: $3,600 million Actual replenishment: $4,104 million, of which actual donor contribution: $3,642 million
1992–1995	**Fifth ADF Replenishment (ADF VI)** Main issues: Poverty and social sector issues (e.g., environment, population, and women in development); policy reforms in developing countries; and ADB's strategic planning, organizational structure, and country programming process. Agreed at Donors' Meeting: $4,200 million, of which donor contribution: $4,200 million Actual replenishment: $5,313 million, of which actual donor contribution: $4,212 million
1997–2000	**Sixth ADF Replenishment (ADF VII)** Main issues: A new planning framework for ADF resources (to make it more self-financing) and a review of ADF-related and other financial policies. Agreed at Donors' Meeting: $6,300 million, of which donor contribution: $2,610 million Actual replenishment: $5,149 million, of which actual donor contribution: $2,688 million **ADF VII Midterm Review** The first formal ADF midterm review discussed implementation progress of ADF VII commitments; adverse impact of the Asian financial crisis on ADF VII; and the plans and time frame for ADF VII.
2001–2004	**Seventh ADF Replenishment (ADF VIII)** Main issues: In alignment with its Poverty Reduction Strategy, ADB was urged to provide more support to social development, good governance, private sector development, gender, environment, and regional cooperation, and to exert more efforts toward stronger partnerships. Agreed at Donors' Meeting: $5,645 million, of which donor contribution: $2,905 million Actual replenishment: $6,971 million, of which actual donor contribution: $2,926 million

continued on next page

Table A2.17 continued

Replenishment Period	Key Highlights
2005–2008	**Eighth ADF Replenishment (ADF IX)** Main issues: Development effectiveness and progress toward the Millennium Development Goals; meeting special needs of countries (e.g., transition from conflict, debt challenges); strengthening regional cooperation; and commitment to a new strategic reform program. Agreed at Donors' Meeting: $7,035 million, of which donor contribution: $3,347 million Actual replenishment: $8,391 million, of which actual donor contribution: $3,410 million **ADF IX Midterm Review** Review of development effectiveness through change and in weakly-performing countries, implementation of performance- based policy, the new human resources policy, independence of the Independent Evaluation Department, and cooperation with development partners.
2009–2012	**Ninth ADF Replenishment (ADF X)** Main issues: Effectiveness of ADF operations, implementation of the Paris Declaration in ADF countries, and ADB's reform agenda. ADF X negotiations were in parallel with the review of ADB's Long–Term Strategic Framework. Agreed at Donors' Meeting: $11,283 million, of which donor contribution: $4,191 million Actual replenishment: $13,064 million, of which actual donor contribution: $4,229 million **ADF X Midterm Review** The review took stock of the ADB's reform agenda and proposed refinements to the ADF results framework. Development effectiveness was reviewed in the context of climate change mitigation and adaptation, fragile and conflict- affected situations (FCAS), and regional cooperation and integration (RCI).
2013–2016	**Tenth ADF Replenishment (ADF XI)** Main issues: ADB's work in ensuring food security, FCAS, preparing for and responding to crisis, and operations for climate change adaptation and mitigation. Agreed at Donors' Meeting: $12,395 million, of which donor contribution: $4,646 million Actual replenishment: $13,903 million, actual donor contribution: $4,829 million **ADF XI Midterm Review** The review covered stocktaking of the reform agenda, refinements to the ADF results framework, strategic directions of ADF operations for promoting climate change mitigation and adaptation, ADB's work in FCAS and RCI, and update on the status of debt relief, among others.

continued on next page

Table A2.17 continued

Replenishment Period	Key Highlights
2017–2020	**Eleventh ADF Replenishment (ADF 12[a])** First replenishment after the ADF–OCR combination was approved. ADF is a grant-only operation. Main issues: Inclusive and sustainable development in concessional assistance-only countries with a focus on FCAS and other key priorities, mainstreaming gender in operations, promoting food security, supporting private sector development, improving governance and capacities, strengthening preparedness and response to climate change and disasters, and promoting regional public goods. Agreed at Donors' Meeting: $3,764 million (resources for the ADF grant operations), of which donor contribution: $2,546 million (the lower amount than ADF XI reflects lessened burden on donors following the combination of ADF and OCR), of which donor contribution: $2,546 million Actual replenishment (as of 30 March 2017): $3,798 million, of which donor pledged contribution: $2,580 million

Notes:

1. Actual donor contributions are based on contributions indicated in instruments of contribution except for ADF 12, which mostly represent pledged amounts as of 30 March 2017. Contributions for certain replenishments include the allocations to the Technical Assistance Special Fund.

2. Donor contributions in US dollar equivalent were calculated using the relevant Board of Governors' resolution exchange rates.

3. Actual donor contributions include additional contributions from new ADF donors provided after the conclusion of the respective replenishments.

[a] This was the first ADF replenishment after the ADB Board of Governors' approval to combine the ADF lending operations with OCR. To differentiate it from earlier replenishments, the numeral suffix was changed from Roman to Arabic.

Source: ADB.

Table A2.18a: Official Cofinancing from Bilateral Partners, 1967–2016 ($ million)

Financing Partner	Contributions to Trust Funds[a]	Contributions to Project-Specific Cofinancing		
		Loans[b]	Grants	TAs
Australia	181		621	206
Austria	9			12
Belgium	64			0.2
Canada	115		187	32
China, People's Republic of	40	695		0.04
Denmark	15	200	55	10
Finland	70		47	33
France	31	2,788	1	8
Germany	0.1	2,546	40	1
India		59		1
Indonesia	0.5			
Ireland	2			
Italy	3			
Japan	2,831[c]	10,956	33	1
Korea, Republic of	94	1,344	4	1
Kuwait		17	15	
Luxembourg	33			1
Netherlands	69		346	44
New Zealand	0.5		100	13
Norway	87		218	36
Portugal	15			
Saudi Arabia		20		
Singapore				5
Spain	59			1
Sweden	108	158[d]	142	68
Switzerland	37		36	22
Taipei,China		7		1
United Arab Emirates		60		
United Kingdom	593	94[e]	905	115

continued on next page

Table A2.18a *continued*

Financing Partner	Contributions to Trust Funds[a]	Contributions to Project-Specific Cofinancing		
		Loans[b]	Grants	TAs
United States	156		12	7
Uzbekistan		340		
Total – Bilaterals	**4,611**	**19,283**	**2,760**	**618**

TA = technical assistance.

Note: Totals may not add up because of rounding.

[a] Refer to committed contributions to single and multi-partner trust funds and to special funds administered by ADB, except the Asian Development Fund and the Technical Assistance Special Fund.

[b] Concessional loan cofinancing from official development assistance, national development banks, and sovereign wealth funds.

[c] Includes $1,125 million contributions to the Japan Special Fund and $172 million to the Japan Scholarship Program.

[d] Includes risk transfer arrangements for a sovereign portfolio.

[e] This refers to equity participation in a nonsovereign portfolio.

Source: ADB Office of Cofinancing Operations.

Table A2.18b: Official Cofinancing from Multilaterals, 1967–2016 ($ million)

Financing Partner	Contributions to Trust Funds[a]	Contributions to Project-Specific Cofinancing			Total
		Loans	Grants	TAs	
World Bank		10,879	174	1	11,054
Islamic Development Bank		1,735			1,735
European Investment Bank		1,711	7	1	1,719
OPEC Fund for International Development		1,038			1,038
Clean Technology Fund		804	5	14	823
European Union			606	93	699
International Fund for Agricultural Development		478	28	1	507
Eurasian Development Bank		435			435
Strategic Climate Fund		91	231	43	365
ASEAN Infrastructure Fund		320			320
European Bank for Reconstruction and Development		216	11	0.01	227
Global Environment Facility			145	78	223
Global Partnership for Education			197	0.4	197
Asian Infrastructure Investment Bank		160			160
North Atlantic Treaty Organization through its Afghan National Army Trust Fund	140				140
United Nations Development Programme				116	116
Nordic Development Fund	8	11	18	36	73
Global Agriculture and Food Security Program			39		39

continued on next page

Table A2.18b continued

Financing Partner	Contributions to Trust Funds[a]	Contributions to Project-Specific Cofinancing			Total
		Loans	Grants	TAs	
Asian Investment Facility			36		36
Green Climate Fund			31		31
Trust Fund for Forests			8	8	16
Pacific Region Infrastructure Facility			12		12
Neighbourhood Investment Facility			8		8
United Nations Children's Fund			4	0.2	4
International Federation of Red Cross and Red Crescent Societies			2		2
Public-Private Infrastructure Advisory Facility				1	1
Islamic Financial Services Board				1	1
Cities Alliance				1	1
World Health Organization			0.5		0.5
Partnership for Market Readiness Fund				0.3	0.3
Global Mechanism				0.3	0.3
Global Road Safety Partnership				0.2	0.2
United Nations Population Fund				0.1	0.1
Commonwealth Secretariat				0.1	0.1
Total – Multilaterals	**148**	**17,877**	**1,562**	**394**	**19,981**

ASEAN = Association of Southeast Asian Nations, OPEC = Organization of the Petroleum Exporting Countries, TA = technical assistance.

[a] Refer to committed contributions to single and multi-partner trust funds.

Sources: ADB Office of Cofinancing Operations and Controller's Department.

Table A2.18c: Official Cofinancing from Private Foundations, 1967–2016 ($ million)

Financing Partner	Contributions to Trust Funds[a]	Contributions to Project-Specific Cofinancing		Total
		Grants	TAs	
Climate Cent Foundation	26			26
POSCO	20			20
Bill & Melinda Gates Foundation	15		3	18
Eneco Energy Trade B.V.	15			15
Phu Bia Mining Limited		6		6
The Rockefeller Foundation	5			5
Others			1	1
Chevron USA		1		1
Credit Suisse AG			0.1	0.1
Total – Private Foundations	**81**	**7**	**4.1**	**92**

TA = technical assistance.

[a] Refer to committed contributions to single and multi-partner trust funds.

Source: ADB Office of Cofinancing Operations.

Table A2.19: List of Active and Closed Trust Funds and Special Funds
as of 31 December 2016

Active Trust Funds and Special Funds

Fund Name	Partner	Cumulative Contribution Committed ($ million)	Year of Establishment
Single Partner Trust Funds			
Japan Scholarship Program	Japan	172.5	1988
Technical Assistance Grant Fund (France)	France	25.8	1989
Technical Assistance Grant Fund (Finland)	Finland	12.5	1990
Technical Assistance Grant Fund (Norway)	Norway	4.2	1991
Australian Technical Assistance Grant	Australia	62.4	1993
Technical Assistance Grant Fund (Belgium)	Belgium	2.4	1996
Swiss Cooperation Fund for Consulting Services	Switzerland	2.3	1998
Denmark Cooperation Fund for Technical Assistance	Denmark	5.0	2000
Japan Fund for Poverty Reduction	Japan	742.0	2000
Spanish Cooperation Fund for Technical Assistance	Spain	9.6	2000
Canadian Cooperation Fund on Climate Change	Canada	3.4	2001
Denmark Cooperation Fund for Renewable Energy and Energy Efficiency in Rural Areas	Denmark	7.1	2001
Japan Fund for Information and Communication Technology	Japan	10.7	2001
Cooperation Fund for Project Preparation in the Greater Mekong Subregion and in Other Specific Asian Countries	France	5.1	2004
Japan Fund for Public Policy Training	Japan	22.0	2004
People's Republic of China Regional Cooperation and Poverty Reduction Fund	People's Republic of China	40.0	2005
e-Asia and Knowledge Partnership Fund	Republic of Korea	72.2	2006

continued on next page

Table A2.19 continued

Fund Name	Partner	Cumulative Contribution Committed ($ million)	Year of Establishment
Netherlands Trust Fund under Water Financing Partnership Facility	Netherlands	34.8	2006
Asian Clean Energy Fund under Clean Energy Financing Partnership Facility	Japan	55.7	2008
Investment Climate Facilitation Fund under Regional Cooperation and Integration Financing Partnership Facility	Japan	31.5	2008
Integrated Disaster Risk Management Fund	Canada	9.7	2013
Sanitation Financing Partnership Trust Fund under Water Financing Partnership Facility	Bill & Melinda Gates Foundation	15.0	2013
Japan Fund for the Joint Crediting Mechanism	Japan	43.8	2014
Leading Asia's Private Sector Infrastructure Fund	Japan	220.0	2016
Total - Single Partner Trust Funds (Active)	**25**	**1,609.7**	
Multi-Partner Trust Funds			
Governance Cooperation Fund	Canada, Denmark, Ireland, Norway	7.2	2001
Gender and Development Cooperation Fund	Australia, Canada, Denmark, Ireland, Norway	12.0	2003
Cooperation Fund for Regional Trade and Financial Security Initiative	Australia, Japan, United States	3.0	2004
Cooperation Fund in Support of Managing for Development Results	Canada, Netherlands, Norway	2.9	2004
Financial Sector Development Partnership Fund	Luxembourg	6.4	2006
Multi-Donor Trust Fund under Water Financing Partnership Facility	Australia, Austria, Norway, Spain, Switzerland	52.7	2006
Clean Energy Fund under Clean Energy Financing Partnership Facility	Australia, Norway, Spain, Sweden, United Kingdom	103.0	2007

continued on next page

Table A2.19 continued

Fund Name	Partner	Cumulative Contribution Committed ($ million)	Year of Establishment
Carbon Capture and Storage Fund under Clean Energy Financing Partnership Facility	Australia, United Kingdom	73.5	2009
Urban Environmental Infrastructure Fund under Urban Financing Partnership Facility	Sweden	21.5	2009
Afghanistan Infrastructure Trust Fund	North Atlantic Treaty Organization through its Afghan National Army Trust Fund, Japan, United Kingdom, United States	694.0	2010
Canadian Climate Fund for the Private Sector in Asia under Clean Energy Financing Partnership Facility	Canada	80.7	2013
Regional Malaria and other Communicable Disease Threats Trust Fund under Health Financing Partnership Facility	Australia, Canada, United Kingdom	29.6	2013
Urban Climate Change Resilience Trust Fund under Urban Financing Partnership Facility	Rockefeller Foundation, Switzerland, United Kingdom, United States	150.7	2013
Asia Pacific Project Preparation Facility	Australia, Canada, Japan	63.1	2014
Pacific Business Investment Trust Fund	Australia	7.6	2014
Typhoon Yolanda Multidonor Trust Fund	Finland, United Kingdom	8.5	2014
Project Readiness Improvement Trust Fund	Nordic Development Fund	7.8	2016
Future Carbon Fund	Belgium, ENECO Energy Trade, Finland, Republic of Korea, POSCO, Sweden	115.0	2008
Total Multi-Partner Trust Funds (Active)	18	1,439.2	

continued on next page

Table A2.19 continued

Fund Name	Partner	Cumulative Contribution Committed ($ million)	Year of Establishment
Special Funds[a]			
Japan Special Fund	Japan	1,124.7	1988
ADB Institute	ADB, Australia, Indonesia, Japan, Republic of Korea	239.7	1996
Regional Cooperation and Integration Fund	ADB, Japan	59.6	2007
Financial Sector Development Partnership Special Fund	ADB, Luxembourg	13.5	2013
Total Special Funds (Active)	**4**	**1,437.5**	

Closed Trust Funds and Special Funds

Fund Name	Partner	Cumulative Contribution Committed ($ million)	Year of Establishment	Year of Closure
Single Partner Trust Funds				
Technical Assistance Grant Fund (Switzerland)	Switzerland	19.4	1980	2001
Technical Assistance Grant Fund (Netherlands)	Netherlands	1.6	1991	2004
Technical Assistance Grant Fund (Sweden)	Sweden	1.9	1992	1998
Italian Cooperation Fund for Consulting Services	Italy	2.7	1999	2011
Technical Assistance Grant Fund (New Zealand)	New Zealand	0.5	1999	2016
Netherlands Cooperation Fund for Promotion of Renewable Energy and Energy Efficiency	Netherlands	6.0	2000	2011
Technical Assistance Grant Fund (United Kingdom)	United Kingdom	37.2	2001	2012
Australia-ADB South Asia Development Partnership Facility	Australia	11.3	2006	2016
Total - Single Partner Trust Funds (Closed)	**8**	**80.6**		

continued on next page

Table A2.19 continued

Fund Name	Partner	Cumulative Contribution Committed ($ million)	Year of Establishment	Year of Closure
Multi-Partner Trust Funds[b]				
Cooperation Fund for the Water Sector	Netherlands, Norway	21.5	2001	2010
Cooperation Fund in Support of the Formulation and Implementation of National Poverty Reduction Strategies	Netherlands	6.0	2001	2009
Poverty Reduction Cooperation Fund	United Kingdom	55.8	2002	2010
Poverty and Environment Fund	Norway, Sweden	8.7	2003	2014
Cooperation Fund for Fighting the Human Immunodeficiency Virus/Acquired Immunodeficiency Syndrome (HIV/AIDS) in Asia and the Pacific	Sweden	19.2	2005	2015
Fourth High Level Forum on Aid Effectiveness Trust Fund	9 bilaterals, 3 multilaterals	1.3	2011	2015
Asia Pacific Carbon Fund	Belgium, Climate Cent Foundation, Finland, Luxembourg, Portugal, Spain, Sweden	152.8	2006	2015
Total - Multi-Partner Trust Funds (Closed)	7	265.3		
Special Funds[a]				
Asian Tsunami Fund	ADB, Australia, Luxembourg	514.8	2005	2011
Pakistan Earthquake Fund	ADB, Australia, Belgium, Finland, Norway	141.6	2005	2014
Total - Special Funds (Closed)[c]	2	656.4		

[a] Special funds (except the Japan Special Fund) get contributions from ADB through transfers from ordinary capital resources; excludes the Asian Development Fund, Technical Assistance Special Fund, Climate Change Fund, and Asia Pacific Disaster Response Fund.

[b] Refers to trust funds established to receive contributions from multiple financing partners.

[c] Excluding the Agricultural Special Fund and the Multi-Purpose Special Fund, established in 1968 and terminated in the 1970s with nearly all the resources transferred to the Asian Development Fund.

Sources: ADB Office of Cofinancing Operations and Controller's Department.

Table A2.20: Annual New Borrowings
($ million)[a]

Year	Long-Term	Short-Term[b]	Total	Cumulative
1969	16	-	16	16
1970	22	-	22	38
1971	122	-	122	160
1972	59	-	59	218
1973	31	-	31	249
1974	42	-	42	291
1975	313	-	313	604
1976	529	-	529	1,133
1977	117	-	117	1,250
1978	390	-	390	1,640
1979	348	-	348	1,987
1980	458	-	458	2,445
1981	668	-	668	3,113
1982	882	-	882	3,995
1983	979	-	979	4,975
1984	972	-	972	5,946
1985	792	-	792	6,738
1986	813	-	813	7,551
1987	537	-	537	8,088
1988	435	-	435	8,523
1989	645	-	645	9,167
1990	849	-	849	10,016
1991	1,298	-	1,298	11,314
1992	3,050	-	3,050	14,364
1993	1,720	-	1,720	16,084
1994	1,335	-	1,335	17,419
1995	1,715	-	1,715	19,134
1996	584	-	584	19,717
1997	2,263	3,325	5,588	25,305
1998	7,819	1,798	9,617	34,922
1999	4,816	370	5,186	40,108
2000	1,693	-	1,693	41,801
2001	1,207	400	1,607	43,408

continued on next page

Table A2.20 *continued*

Year	Long-Term	Short-Term[b]	Total	Cumulative
2002	5,945	200	6,145	49,553
2003	4,141	-	4,141	53,694
2004	1,629	-	1,629	55,323
2005	3,966	264	4,230	59,553
2006	5,397	179	5,576	65,129
2007	8,854	-	8,854	73,984
2008	9,372	-	9,372	83,356
2009	10,359	-	10,359	93,714
2010	14,940	-	14,940	108,655
2011	14,009	438	14,446	123,101
2012	13,217	1,850	15,067	138,168
2013	11,975	750	12,725	150,892
2014	14,249	475	14,724	165,616
2015	18,948	1,317	20,265	185,881
2016	20,602	2,330	22,932	208,814
Total	**195,119**	**13,695**	**208,814**	

Note: Numbers may not sum precisely because of rounding.

[a] Borrowings up to 1980 were translated at exchange rates adopted by the Bank at the end of each year of borrowing. Borrowings up to 1992 were translated at ADB exchange rates effective at the date of Board approval of each borrowing except for 7.375% Swiss Franc bonds of 1990/2000, which were translated at ADB exchange rate as of 14 October 1990. Borrowings thereafter were translated at exchange rates effective on the date the terms of the borrowing were determined by the President. Effective 1 January 2007, borrowings were translated at exchange rates as of trade date.

[b] Outstanding euro commercial papers at the end of the year.

Source: ADB Treasury Department.

Table A2.21: First Organizational Structure, 1966

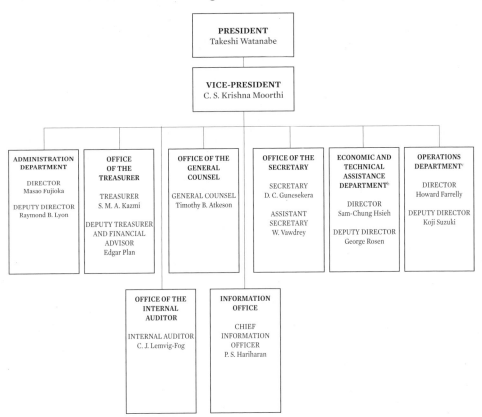

a First ADB President Takeshi Watanabe set up the above tentative organization structure and made initial appointment of officers and staff on 24 November 1966 in preparation for the opening of the Bank. This organization structure remained in place throughout 1967. The first heads of departments joined ADB between 1966 and 1967.

b The Economic and Technical Assistance (TA) Department had functions related to TA and economic studies regarding the developmental problems of member countries. It had two divisions: an Economic Division and a TA Division. In 1969, the Economic and TA Department was dissolved. A new Projects Department was formed which absorbed a substantial portion of the TA Division of the Economic and Technical Assistance (TA) Department. The Projects Department also assumed the technical appraisal of projects, which had been the main responsibility of the Operations Department. At the same time, a new Economic Office was established to conduct economic research.

c The Operations Department had functions related to the Bank's lending operations. It had three divisions: East and West Divisions and a Project Division in charge of technical appraisal and supervision of projects. In 1969, the Project Division was absorbed by the newly formed Projects Department. The restructured Operations Department assumed some of the functions of the TA Division of the Economic and Technical Assistance Department, particularly those relating to country coordination.

Table A2.22: Organization Chart, 2016[1]
(as of 31 December 2016)

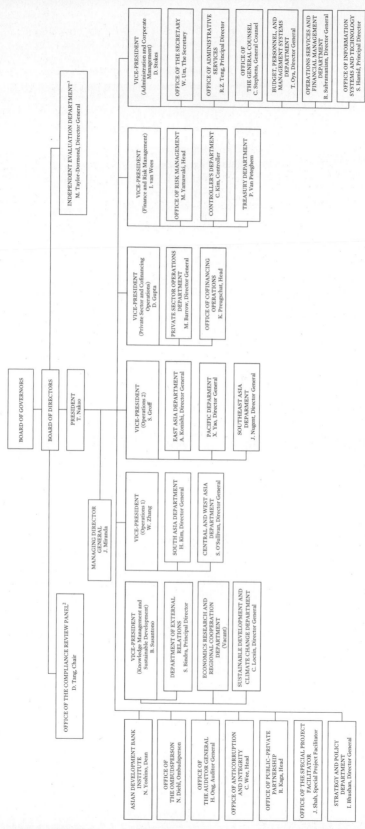

[1] To contact management and senior staff, go to http://www.adb.org/contacts/management-senior-staff

[2] The Compliance Review Panel reports to the Board of Directors.

[3] The Independent Evaluation Department reports to the Board of Directors through the Development Effectiveness Committee.

Table A2.23: ADB Sector and Thematic Group
(as of 31 December 2016)

Sector Groups			Thematic Groups		
Sector	Committee Chair	Technical Advisor	Theme	Technical Advisor/Committee Chair[a]	Co-Chair[a]
Education	Sungsup Ra (Director, Human and Social Development Division, SARD)	Brajesh Panth	Climate Change and Disaster Risk Management	Preety Bhandari (Director, Climate Change and Disaster Risk Management Division, SDCC)	Amy Leung (Deputy Director General concurrently Chief Thematic Officer, Thematic Advisory Service Cluster, SDCC)
Energy	Ashok Bhargava (Director, Energy Division, EARD)	Yongping Zhai	Environment	Daniele Ponzi	Jiangfeng Zhang, (Director, Environment, Natural Resources and Agriculture Division, SERD)
Finance	Bruno Carrasco, (Director, Public Management, Financial Sector, and Trade Division, SARD)	Anna Lotte Schou-Zibell	Gender Equity	Sonomi Tanaka	
Health	Ayako Inagaki (Director, Human and Social Development Division, SERD)	Soonman Kwon	Governance	Gambhir Bhatta	Kelly Bird (Director, Public Management, Financial Sector, and Trade Division, SERD)
Transport	Xiaohong Yang (Director, Transport and Communications Division, CWRD)	Tyrrell Duncan	Public–Private Partnership	Takeo Koike (Director, Office of Public–Private Partnership)[b]	

continued on next page

Table A2.23 continued

Sector	Sector Groups			Thematic Groups		
	Committee Chair	Technical Advisor	Theme	Technical Advisor/Committee Chair[a]		Co-Chair[a]
Urban	Sangay Penjor (Director, Urban and Social Sector Division, EARD)	Vijay Padmanabhan	Regional Cooperation and Integration	Arjun Goswami		Ying Qian (Director, Public Management, Financial Sector and Regional Cooperation, EARD)
Water	Qingfeng Zhang (Director, Environment, Natural Resources, and Agriculture Division, EARD)	Gil-Hong Kim (Senior Director concurrently Chief Sector Officer, Sector Advisory Service Cluster, SDCC)	Rural Development and Food Security (Agriculture)	AKM Mahfuzuddin Ahmed (Advisor, Agriculture, Rural Development and Food Security Unit, SDCC)		Akmal Siddig (Director, Environment, Natural Resources and Agriculture Division, CWRD)
			Social Development	Amy Leung (Deputy Director General concurrently Chief Thematic Officer, Thematic Advisory Service Cluster, SDCC)		

CWRD = Central and West Asia Department, EARD = East Asia Department, OIC = officer in charge, SARD = South Asia Department, SERD = Southeast Asia Department, SDCC = Sustainable Development and Climate Change Department.

[a] The Thematic Group (TG) Committee is Chaired by the Technical Advisor. A member of the Committee may be selected by the TG Chair to act as Co-Chair except for the Public–Private Partnership (PPP) Thematic Group.

[b] The PPP Thematic Group adopts separate operating guidelines reflecting its responsibilities and operational structure. The PPP is led by the Technical Advisor and does not have a designated Chair and Co-Chair.

Source: ADB Sustainable Development and Climate Change Department.

3. ADB: Impact of the ADF–OCR Merger and ADB's Financial Statements

Combination of ADF and OCR Resources

In 2014, ADB introduced a proposal to enhance ADB's financial capacity in a sustainable manner through more efficient and effective management of its capital resources. The proposal entailed combining ADF lending operations with the OCR and retaining the ADF as a grant-only operation. ADB would continue concessional lending on the same terms and conditions as currently provided to ADF countries through the OCR window, while the ADF would continue to provide grant assistance.

In April 2015, the Board of Governors adopted a resolution authorizing the termination of ADF's loan operations and the transfer of ADF's loans and other assets to OCR effective 1 January 2017 (the 2015 Resolution). This resolution was further amended in June 2016. Accordingly, on 1 January 2017, ADB transferred ADF loans and other assets totaling $30,812 million from ADF to OCR. The transferred ADF assets composed of loans including accrued interest totaling $27,088 million and liquid assets totaling $3,724 million. The source of funding for ADF came from donor contributions, OCR net income transfer and set-aside resources.

The transfer of these assets was treated as a contribution from ADF to OCR and a return of the set-aside resources from ADF to OCR. This resulted in the recognition of one-time income of $30,748 million in OCR and a return of the set-aside resources of $64 million. The corresponding income recognized in OCR has been allocated to ordinary reserves as from 1 January 2017 following the adoption of Board of Governors Resolution No. 387.

Appendix Tables 3.1 and 3.2 show the summary effects of the transfer of certain ADF assets on 1 January 2017.

The proportionate interest of ADF donors in the transferred assets as of 1 January 2017, taking into account the value of paid-in donor contributions that have been made available for operational commitments which are deemed by ADB to be applied for the transferred assets, was determined in accordance with Article V of the Regulations of the Asian Development Fund. The value of each donor's paid-in contributions was fixed in US$ based on the SDR value of each donor contribution as of 1 January 2017. This was then used to determine the sources of funds in the transferred assets on 1 January 2017, the date of the termination of the ADF loan operations and transfer of assets to OCR. Under the 2015 Resolution, the proportionate interest of an ADF donor will be taken into account in the event of the withdrawal of that donor from ADB and ADB's repurchase of its shares, and in the theoretical termination of ADB operations and liquidation of its assets. Appendix Table 3.3 shows the funding sources of the transferred assets.

Table A3.1: Asian Development Bank—Ordinary Capital Resources Summary Statement of Effect of Asset Transfer from ADF
($ million)

	Balance as of 31 December 2016	Asset Transfer from ADF 1 January 2017	Balance as of 1 January 2017
Due from banks	661	0	661
Investments for liquidity purposes	26,025	3,696	29,721
Securities purchased under resale arrangements	102	12	114
Loans outstanding — Operations[a]			
Sovereign			
Regular	62,413	–	62,413
Concessional	–	27,025	27,025
	62,413	27,025	89,438
Nonsovereign	5,186	–	5,186
	67,599	27,025	94,624
Equity investments — Operations	814	–	814
Other debt securities — Operations	150	–	150
Accrued interest receivable	387	79	466
Derivative assets	29,143	–	29,143
Other assets	973	–	973
TOTAL ASSETS	125,854	30,812	156,666

continued on next page

Table A3.1 continued

	Balance as of 31 December 2016	Asset Transfer from ADF 1 January 2017	Balance as of 1 January 2017
TOTAL LIABILITIES	108,640	–	108,640
EQUITY			
Capital Stock			
Subscription installments matured	7,154	–	7,154
Less – capital transferred to ADF and discounts	79	(64)	15
	7,075	64	7,139
Nonnegotiable, noninterest-bearing demand obligations on account of subscribed capital	(676)	–	(676)
	6,399	64	6,463
Net notional maintenance of value receivable	(1,474)	–	(1,474)
Ordinary reserve			
From ADF assets transfer	–	30,748	30,748
From retained earnings	12,211	–	12,211
Subtotal	12,211	30,748	42,959
Special reserve	340	–	340
Loan loss reserve	172	–	172
Surplus	1,065	–	1,065
Cumulative revaluation adjustments account	88	–	88
Net income after appropriation – 2016	(11)	–	(11)
Accumulated other comprehensive loss	(1,576)	–	(1,576)
TOTAL EQUITY	17,214	30,812	48,026
TOTAL LIABILITIES AND EQUITY	125,854	30,812	156,666

– = nil, 0 = amount less than $0.5 million, ADF = Asian Development Fund.

Note: The undisbursed ADF loan balance as of 31 December 2016 of $8,444 million was assumed by ordinary capital resources on 1 January 2017.

[a] Including net unamortized loan origination cost, allowance for loan losses and Heavily Indebted Poor Countries debt relief, and fair value adjustment.

Source: ADB Controller's Department.

Table A3.2: Asian Development Bank—Asian Development Fund Summary Statement of Effect of Asset Transfer to OCR
($ million)

	Balance as of 31 December 2016	Asset Transfer to OCR 1 January 2017	Balance as of 1 January 2017
Due from banks	281	(0)	281
Investments for liquidity purposes	5,726	(3,696)	2,030
Securities purchased under resale arrangements	13	(12)	1
Loans outstanding — Operations[a]	27,306	(27,306)	–
Accrued interest receivable	87	(79)	8
Other Assets	172		172
TOTAL ASSETS	**33,585**	**(31,093)**	**2,492**
TOTAL LIABILITIES	**2,637**	**–**	**2,637**
FUND BALANCES			
Contributions received			
Contributed resources – net of unamortized discount	32,667	–	32,667
Set-aside resources	64	(64)	–
Transfers from OCR and TASF	1,703	–	1,703
	34,434	(64)	34,370
Nonnegotiable, noninterest-bearing demand obligations on account of contributions	(1,633)	–	(1,633)
Accumulated deficit			
From operations	(361)		(361)
From asset transfer to OCR		(31,029)	(31,029)
Subtotal	(361)	(31,029)	(31,390)
Accumulated other comprehensive loss	(1,492)	–	(1,492)
TOTAL FUND BALANCES	**30,948**	**(31,093)**	**(145)**
TOTAL LIABILITIES AND FUND BALANCES	**33,585**	**(31,093)**	**2,492**

– = nil, 0 = amount less than $0.5 million, OCR = ordinary capital resources, TASF = Technical Assistance Special Fund.

[a] Net of allowance for Heavily Indebted Poor Countries debt relief.

Source: ADB Controller's Department.

Table A3.3: Proportionate Share of Funding Sources of the ADF Assets Transferred to OCR

Source of Funds in ADF	$ million	%[a]	Source of Funds in ADF	$ million	%[a]
Donor Contributions					
Australia	$ 2,213	7.18	Malaysia	24	0.08
Austria	257	0.83	Nauru	0	0.00
Belgium	231	0.75	Netherlands	716	2.32
Brunei Darussalam	17	0.06	New Zealand	157	0.51
Canada	1,889	6.13	Norway	266	0.86
China, People's Republic of	84	0.27	Portugal	79	0.26
			Singapore	18	0.06
Denmark	242	0.79	Spain	432	1.40
Finland	180	0.58	Sweden	436	1.42
France	1,270	4.12	Switzerland	359	1.17
Germany	1,679	5.45	Taipei,China	90	0.29
Hong Kong, China	93	0.30	Thailand	15	0.05
India	24	0.08	Turkey	114	0.37
Indonesia	14	0.05	United Kingdom	1,440	4.67
Ireland	79	0.26	United States	4,060	13.18
Italy	1,099	3.57	**Subtotal**	29,309	95.13
Japan	11,197	36.34			
Kazakhstan	4	0.01	OCR Net Income Transfers	1,439	4.67
Korea, Republic of	484	1.57	Set-Aside Resources[b]	64	0.20
Luxembourg	47	0.15	**Total**	**$ 30,812**	**100.00**

ADF = Asian Development Fund, OCR = ordinary capital resources.

Note: 0 = $0.3 million and 0.00 = 0.001%.

[a] Determined from the special drawing right value of all contributions received, excluding unpaid installments and amounts withheld from pro pata exercise as of 31 December 2016 based on the exchange rates set forth in the relevant authorizing Resolution of the Board of Governors, in accordance with Article V of the Regulations of the Asian Development Fund.

[b] Based on Article 19.1 (i) of the Agreement Establishing the Asian Development Fund.

Source: ADB Treasury Department.

4. ADB: Time Line of Key ADB Milestones, 1950s to 2016

	Inception Years and First Decade, 1950s to 1976
Late 1950s to early 1960s	• Discussions begin on the establishment of a possible Asian development bank.
1963	• A private plan for the establishment of the Asian Development Bank (ADB) is unofficially issued.
	• The first Ministerial Conference on Asian Economic Cooperation is held in Manila under the auspices of the United Nations Economic Commission for Asia and the Far East (ECAFE) and a resolution is passed endorsing a proposal to establish a regional bank for Asia.
1964	• An ECAFE Working Group of Experts is established to work on the idea of an Asian development bank and completed its report in October.
1965	• Japan (in February) and the United States (US) (in April) announce support for the establishment of ADB.
	• A draft agreement establishing ADB is adopted at the second ECAFE ministerial conference (November–December, ECAFE resolution 62XXI) after both Japan and the US express support.
	• Members decide on Manila as the head office of ADB, and 22 governments sign the ADB Charter (with another nine countries signing before the prescribed deadline of 31 January 1966).
1966	• The Agreement Establishing the Asian Development Bank is ratified (22 August) by 31 founding members—ADB Charter comes into effect.
	• The Inaugural Meeting of ADB's Board of Governors is held on 24–26 November in Tokyo, Japan; Takeshi Watanabe is elected as ADB's first President.
	• Ten Directors are appointed (seven regional and three nonregional).
	• The first Board of Directors meeting is held (17 December); C. S. Krishna Moorthi from India is appointed Vice-President.
	• ADB formally opens for business on 19 December 1966 at its temporary premises on Ayala Avenue in Makati, Philippines.

1967	- The first technical assistance (TA) project to Indonesia on food grain production is approved.
- The first regional TA for the Asian Agricultural Survey is launched to guide ADB operations in agriculture and rural development.
- Switzerland joins ADB as a nonregional member.
- ADB begins processing 12 loan applications, mainly covering food production and rural development.
1968	- ADB approves its first ordinary capital resources (OCR) loan, a finance sector loan to Thailand's Industrial Finance Corporation for onlending to private industries.
- A total of seven OCR loans are approved.
- ADB formulates policies on procurement and employment of consultants.
- ADB adopts the Special Funds Rules and Regulations, which provide for an Agricultural Special Fund, a Multi-Purpose Special Fund, a Technical Assistance Special Fund (TASF), and other funds deemed necessary.
- The first Annual Meeting is held in Manila.
1969	- Hong Kong, China joins ADB.
- The Board's composition increases from 10 to 12 (8 regional and 4 nonregional).
- ADB approves its first loan on concessional terms for an irrigation project in Indonesia.
- ADB approves its first energy sector loan for an electricity supply project in Malaysia.
- ADB issues its first bond, a Deutsche mark (DM) bond issue for DM60 million ($16 million) in West Germany, to augment OCR for lending to developing members.
- A Southeast Asia regional transport survey is undertaken to study the needs of transport development in Indonesia, Laos, Malaysia, the Philippines, Singapore, Thailand, and Viet Nam.
- A study on Southeast Asia's economy is commissioned and completed in 1970 by 12 experts; this fed into Hla Myint's study of industrialization policies and development strategies in Southeast Asia (published in 1972).
1970	- Fiji and France join ADB.
- The first cofinancing agreement for a fertilizer plant in Indonesia is approved, with funding from Japan, the US, and the International Development Association of the World Bank.

	• The first ADB bond is issued in Asia (Japan), marking the first time that yen bonds are sold to the public in Japan by a foreign entity.
	• ADB approves its first education sector loan for a college expansion project in Singapore.
1971	• Papua New Guinea joins ADB.
	• Takeshi Watanabe is reelected as ADB President at the Fourth Annual Meeting held in Singapore.
	• The Board approves the first general capital increase, authorizing a 150% increase from the initial $1 billion capitalization.
	• The Asian Industrial Survey is prepared jointly with the United Nations Economic and Social Commission for Asia and the Pacific (completed in 1973) to consider long-term perspectives for industrialization and regional cooperation.
1972	• Shiro Inoue becomes ADB's second President.
	• Tonga joins ADB.
	• The Board adopts policies on extending loans on concessional terms from Special Funds resources; concessional loans rise sharply.
	• With changes in foreign exchange value experienced by several member countries, ADB adopts the US dollar with gold content as a unit of account.
	• The Liquidity Policy is approved, allowing ADB to maintain liquid assets at no less than two-thirds of 3 years' projected loan disbursements.
	• The first ADB headquarters on Roxas Boulevard is inaugurated.
	• Formulation of the Strategy for Bank Operations in Less Developed Regional is started (and completed in 1973).
1973	• Bangladesh, Myanmar, and Solomon Islands join ADB.
1974	• The Asian Development Fund (ADF) is formally established to provide concessional lending to ADB's poorest members.
	• Kiribati and Tuvalu (formerly Gilbert and Ellice Islands) join ADB.
	• The Study on Bank Operations in South Pacific Developing Member Countries is undertaken.
1975	• Negotiations begin for the first ADF replenishment (effective 1976 and covering up to the end of 1978).

	- The Second Asian Agricultural Survey is launched (completed in 1977) to reassess ADB's strategy in supporting agriculture and rural development; published in 1978 as Rural Asia: Challenges and Opportunities. - ADB lending to industry through development finance institutions (DFIs) begins, as a detailed review of ADB lending to DFIs is conducted. - Cofinancing with multilateral and bilateral sources assumes greater prominence, allowing ADB to participate in larger projects.
1976	- Taroichi Yoshida becomes ADB's third President. - The Cook Islands joins ADB. - Negotiations for the second general capital increase starts (effective 1977). - The review of methodologies for economic and financial appraisal of Bank-assisted projects is completed. - The review of Bank loans and procedures is completed. - Domestic procurement for ADB-financed projects is modified.

Second Decade, 1977–1986

1977	- The Board approves the establishment of the Audit Committee. - ADB conducts a comprehensive review of financial policies, disbursements, and other loan administration matters; pursues simplification of procedures; and issues revised guidelines on the use of consultants and procurement. - The criteria for ADF lending are reviewed. - ADB explores engagement in guarantee operations. - TA operations are reviewed.
1978	- ADB's annual lending reaches the $1 billion mark. - The Maldives joins ADB. - Negotiations for the second ADF replenishment start (effective 1979). - ADB's first loan in the health sector is approved for Hong Kong, China. - ADB introduces program lending to support importation of production inputs in high-priority sectors; ADB approves its program loan for a low-lift pump maintenance program in Bangladesh.

- The Review of ADB's Operations in the Agriculture Sector in the South Pacific introduces multiproject loans for packages of public sector projects; the first multiproject loan is extended in 1979 in Tonga.
- Developing member countries (DMCs) are grouped into three categories (A, B, and C) to determine access to concessional lending from the ADF.
- ADB reviews domestic procurement and local currency financing.
- ADB evaluates the role of forestry and forest industries in the socioeconomic development of the region.
- Operational guidelines for mineral development projects are issued.
- An additional post for Vice-President is approved, taking over responsibilities for financial, administrative, and other services functions.
- The Development Policy Office is created to strengthen ADB's capability in policy formulation and review and to identify new directions and approaches to Bank activities.
- The Post-Evaluation Unit is detached from the Economics Office and established as an independent office reporting directly to the President.

1979
- ADB reviews several policies and strategies, including its role in agriculture and rural development, operations in the fisheries sector, environmental considerations in operations, and its role in population activities.

1980
- The Regional Energy Survey is initiated (completed in 1981) to determine country priorities and plan ADB's lending and TA for energy development.
- ADB issues its policy on Streamlining of Loan and TA Processing.
- Sector lending is introduced, and ADB approves its first two sector loans (water supply in Indonesia, highway sector in Thailand).

1981
- Masao Fujioka is elected ADB's fourth President, assuming office on 24 November.
- Vanuatu joins ADB.
- The Study of Bank Operational Priorities and Plans is undertaken (completed in 1982) to review the entire range

	of policies and procedures that affect operational programs and to develop strategies and guidelines for operations in the medium term up to the end of 1987.
1982	• Bhutan joins ADB.
	• Negotiations for the third replenishment of the ADF start (effective 1983).
	• The third general capital increase (GCI III) negotiations start (completed in 1983).
	• ADB's first resident mission is established in Dhaka, Bangladesh.[1]
	• A study on streamlining loan administration is conducted.
1983	• GCI III is approved.
	• The Board approves proposal for construction of a new headquarters in Mandaluyong City, Philippines.
	• ADB makes its first direct equity investment in a private sector project to a development investment corporation in the Republic of Korea and a second one in Pakistan.
	• ADB conducts a comprehensive review of its financial policies.
	• ADB's role in agriculture and rural development is reviewed.
	• A study of capital markets in selected DMCs is conducted.
	• A study of the Bank's role in the South Pacific DMCs in the 1980s is conducted.
	• ADB's third Vice-President is appointed.
1984	• ADB's first regional office is established in the Pacific, in Port Vila, Vanuatu.
	• The Board's Budget Committee is established.
1985	• Masao Fujioka is unanimously elected President for a second 5-year term.
	• ADB approves the Policy on the Role of Women in Development to ensure that specific consideration is given to the role and needs of women in all relevant aspects of Bank lending and TA operations.
	• ADB reviews its assistance to the private sector to provide an operational approach and broaden support and lending; the review leads to the establishment of ADB's Private Sector Division in 1986.
1986	• The People's Republic of China and Spain join ADB.
	• India begins borrowing.

- The fourth replenishment of the ADF and TASF starts (effective 1987).
- ADB starts direct lending to private enterprises and financial institutions without government guarantees.
- A pool-based variable lending rate system is introduced in response to increasing globalization and deregulation.
- ADB reviews the investment needs of the power subsector for 1986–1990.
- ADB conducts a review of its environmental policies and procedures focusing on safeguards aspects.

Third Decade, 1987–1996

1987
- ADB establishes an external panel led by Japan's former foreign minister, Saburo Okita, to conduct an in-depth study of the Bank's role in the 1990s (completed in 1989).
- A framework of cooperation between ADB and nongovernment organizations is approved.
- A revised policy on program lending (in support of sector policies and adjustment programs) is issued.
- A disaster and emergency assistance policy with focus on Pacific countries is adopted.
- ADB reorganizes its organizational structure, creating an environment unit.
- The Indonesia Resident Mission is established in Jakarta.
- ADB reviews its income and liquidity policies along with loan charges.

1988
- The Task Force on Poverty Alleviation convenes to formulate guidelines for ADB action and recommend directed and specific poverty-oriented projects.
- A policy on education focusing on primary, nonformal, and environmental education is adopted.
- ADB intensifies project administration efforts and introduces innovative and streamlined project administration procedures, e.g., delegation of more authority to executing agencies, earlier procurement, and recruitment of consultants.
- A new policy framework for guarantee operations that allows ADB to guarantee loans by private financial institutions to DMCs is approved.

1989	- A comprehensive review of private sector operations is undertaken.
- A policy on streamlining of TA is issued.
- The Japan Special Fund and Japan Scholarship Program are established by the Government of Japan.
- Kimimasa Tarumizu becomes ADB's fifth President.
- ADB launches the Asian Development Outlook, an annual publication series on the economic performance and prospects of the Bank's DMCs.
- The Panel Report on the Role of ADB in the 1990s is issued, highlighting social infrastructure, living standards of the poorest groups, and protection of the environment as new priorities.
- Private sector activities are reorganized within the new Private Sector Department.
- A policy framework for speedy rehabilitation assistance to DMCs after natural disasters is designed.
- The Environment Unit is upgraded to a division.
- A primary education (girls) sector loan to Pakistan is approved, the first loan in which women are targeted exclusively as beneficiaries.
- Resident missions are established in Pakistan and Nepal.
1990	- The Marshall Islands and the Federated States of Micronesia join ADB.
- A task force on strategic planning is established to examine ADB's strategic planning processes and institutional arrangements.
- The Environment Division is upgraded to the Office of the Environment.
1991	- Mongolia, Nauru, and Turkey join ADB.
- The Strategic Planning Unit is established under the Office of the President to develop and coordinate ADB's strategic planning.
- A high-level task force is appointed to recommend ADB's private sector operational activities.
- ADB moves to its new headquarters in Mandaluyong City, Philippines.
- An administrative tribunal comprising three judges is established as an independent external and impartial appeal mechanism for the resolution of employment disputes.

	• The fifth replenishment negotiations of the ADF and TASF start.
1992	• The first Medium-Term Strategic Framework, 1992–1995 is approved.
	• ADB establishes the Greater Mekong Subregion Economic Cooperation Program.
	• ADB resumes operations in Cambodia.
	• The Social Dimensions Unit is established to integrate cross-cutting social issues in Bank operations.
	• The India Resident Mission is established.
	• ADB approves its first information technology strategy.
1993	• Mitsuo Sato becomes ADB's sixth President.
	• Tuvalu joins ADB.
	• The Medium-Term Strategic Framework, 1993–1996 is formulated to establish a strategic planning process in ADB and sharpen country focus.
	• The Three-Year Rolling Work Program and Budget Framework is introduced.
	• At the country level, country operational strategy studies are formulated.
	• The Guidelines for Incorporation of Social Dimensions in Bank Operations are issued.
	• ADB resumes lending in Viet Nam.
	• ADB reviews its major financial policies and currency management practices.
	• The Human Resources Development and Management Operational Study is completed.
1994	• Kazakhstan and the Kyrgyz Republic join as members.
	• The fourth general capital increase (GCI IV) is approved.
	• The Medium-Term Strategic Framework, 1994–1997 is formulated to highlight the expanded role and operational agenda for ADB.
	• A policy on population is adopted, highlighting the relations between population growth and economic development.
	• The policy on the role of women in development is updated.
	• The Report of the Task Force on Improving Project Quality recommends (i) further strengthening of project preparation, (ii) adopting stronger country focus, (iii) undertaking internal

	reorganization of ADB, (iv) emphasizing capacity building in DMCs, and (v) increasing beneficiary participation.
	• The Confidentiality and Disclosure of Information as well as the Information Policy of ADB endorse the presumption in favor of disclosure for a more open, accessible, and transparent organization—the first among multilateral development banks.
	• The Bank structure is reorganized based on geographic (East and West) and functional (programs and projects) specializations to pursue better country focus.
	• A new market-based window is established.
1995	• The sixth replenishment of the ADF is started (effective 1997).
	• Uzbekistan joins ADB.
	• ADB becomes the first multilateral organization to have a Board-approved governance policy that introduces the concept of sound development management.
	• ADB establishes an inspection function.
	• The policy on involuntary resettlement, which is designed to protect the rights of people affected by a project, is approved.
	• The policy on forestry is adopted, balancing production and conservation and encouraging participatory approaches.
	• The Strategy for the Bank's Assistance to Private Sector Development is approved, highlighting sustainable investment in infrastructure and the finance sectors.
	• The new energy sector policy is approved.
	• The new policy on agriculture and natural resources research is approved.
	• The Cofinancing Strategy and Review of Guarantee Operations is approved.
	• ADB establishes its first representative office in North America.
	• ADB creates its website (www.adb.org).
1996	• Mitsuo Sato is reelected for a second term as President.
	• ADB reviews its program lending policy, whereby sector analysis becomes a precondition for the modality, and poverty, social, environmental, and mitigation measures are emphasized.
	• A new sector development program is introduced.
	• ADB revises its human resources strategy.

- The ADB Institute is established.
- The European Representative Office and the Japanese Representative Office are established.
- Resident missions are established in Cambodia and Viet Nam.

Fourth Decade, 1997–2006

1997
- ADB approves its largest single loan—a $4 billion emergency loan to the Republic of Korea in the wake of the Asian financial crisis.
- The ADB Institute is inaugurated.
- First formal midterm review of the Asian Development Fund (ADF VII) is undertaken.
- ADB formulates its Policy on Fisheries.
- Resident missions are established in Kazakhstan, Uzbekistan, and Sri Lanka.

1998
- Tajikistan joins ADB.
- ADB adopts a formal graduation policy.
- Anticorruption policy is adopted.
- The policy on cooperation with nongovernment organizations is updated.
- The policy on the role of women in development is replaced by a gender and development policy that adopts mainstreaming as a key strategy.
- The policy on indigenous peoples is approved to ensure that indigenous peoples participate and benefit equally from ADB operations.
- The third Asian Agricultural Survey is launched.
- ADF loan terms are reviewed.

1999
- Tadao Chino becomes ADB's seventh President.
- ADB declares poverty reduction as its overarching goal and adopts a poverty reduction strategy.
- Negotiations for the seventh ADF replenishment start (effective 2000).
- Azerbaijan joins ADB.
- ADB adopts a health policy.
- ADB formulates an urban sector strategy.

	• A review of program lending policy introduces a special program loan to allow ADB to provide large-scale support to crisis-affected OCR countries and a cluster approach to enhance flexibility and extend the time frame for program implementation.
	• ADB reviews its policy on guarantee operations.
	• ADB establishes the Asian Currency Crisis Support Facility.
	• The Regional Economic Monitoring Unit is established in the Strategy and Policy Office.
	• The Anticorruption Unit is established within the Office of the General Auditor.
	• The Kyrgyz Republic Resident Mission is established.
2000	• Turkmenistan joins ADB.
	• ADB initiates work on its new Long-Term Strategic Framework, 2001–2015.
	• A microfinance development strategy is approved.
	• The Review of the 1995 Energy Policy is completed.
	• A private sector development strategy is developed.
	• A medium-term agenda and action plan to promote good governance is approved.
	• The Resident Mission Policy is approved.
	• Resident Missions are established in the Lao People's Democratic Republic, Mongolia, and the People's Republic of China.
	• The Philippine Country Office is established.
	• The Development Effectiveness Committee is established.
	• ADB and the Government of Japan establish the Japan Fund for Poverty Reduction.
	• The Strategy and Policy Office is upgraded to the Strategy and Policy Department.
2001	• Tadao Chino is reelected as President for a new 5-year term.
	• ADB's Long-Term Strategic Framework, 2001–2015 is launched, focusing on sustainable economic growth, inclusive social development, and governance as core areas of intervention.
	• The accompanying Medium-Term Strategic Framework, 2001–2005 is launched, defining the operational priorities and organizational changes required to enhance development impact.

	- The Social Protection Strategy is approved. - The Water Policy is formulated. - ADB reviews its strategic directions for its private sector operations. - A strategic approach for information and communication technology is developed. - A performance-based allocation policy for ADF resources is adopted. - ADB introduces London interbank offered rate-based products. - The Operations Evaluation Office is upgraded to a department. - The NGO Center is established in the Office of Environment and Social Development.
2002	- Portugal and Timor-Leste join ADB. - The Education Policy is updated. - The Environment Policy is approved. - New business processes are put in place for programming; for economic, thematic, and sector work; and for project processing and implementation. - ADB resumes operations in Afghanistan (after 23 years), and in the newly independent Timor-Leste. - ADB approves its new Liquidity Policy. - A new thematic poverty-focused multidonor channel financing agreement is established. - Major reorganization is undertaken to strengthen the country focus in ADB operations; five regional departments are created (East and Central Asia, Mekong, Pacific, South Asia, and Southeast Asia); and the Regional and Sustainable Development Department is created. - The Economics and Development Resource Center is renamed Economics and Research Department to be ADB's major knowledge department, reporting directly to the President. - Resident missions are established in Afghanistan and Papua New Guinea.
2003	- Luxembourg and Palau join ADB. - ADB initiates a comprehensive review of its Poverty Reduction Strategy. - The new Evaluation Policy is issued and the Operations Evaluation Department is made to report directly to the Board through the Development Effectiveness Committee.

- The Inspection Function is reviewed and replaced by a new Accountability Mechanism Policy; the Compliance Review Panel and Office of Special Project Facilitator are established.
- A policy on ADB's role in combating money laundering and the financing of terrorism is issued.
- ADB provides support to respond to HIV/AIDS and avian influenza.
- A comprehensive review and revision of ADB's Operation Manual is completed.
- A comprehensive review of financial management policies is undertaken.
- ADB prepares its new Human Resources Strategy and Gender Action Plan.
- A fourth Vice-President is appointed to oversee knowledge management and sustainable development.
- ADB creates a new Managing Director General post to facilitate the coordination of the work of senior management.
- Resident missions are established in Azerbaijan and Tajikistan. The Timor-Leste Resident Mission is established, replacing the Special Liaison Office in Timor-Leste.
- Negotiations for the eighth replenishment of the ADF start.

2004
- The ADB reform agenda is adopted to include 19 Bank-wide initiatives, chief among them, Managing for Development Results.
- ADB enhances its Poverty Reduction Strategy.
- The Disaster and Emergency Assistance Policy is approved.
- The Knowledge Management Framework is formulated.
- The Information System and Technology Strategy for 2005–2009 (ISTS II) is approved.
- A new human resources strategy is approved.
- A new sector and thematic classification is introduced; capacity development is added as a new theme.
- Business processes are streamlined, focusing on client orientation and responsiveness, efficiency, and product quality.
- ADB's first female Vice-President (Khempheng Pholsena) is appointed.
- The resident mission is established in Thailand; a regional office is established in Suva, Fiji, to replace the South Pacific Regional Mission in Vanuatu.

	- The Results Management Unit is established in the Strategy and Policy Department, and the results-based country strategies and programs are introduced.
- ADB launches local currency bond issues in Hong Kong, China; India; Malaysia; and Singapore.
2005	- Haruhiko Kuroda becomes ADB's eighth President.
- Armenia joins ADB.
- ADB endorses the Paris Declaration on Aid Effectiveness.
- The Asian Tsunami Fund is established; ADB commits more than $850 million for recovery in the tsunami-hit areas of India, Indonesia, the Maldives, and Sri Lanka.
- ADB pledges support for the rehabilitation of earthquake-devastated Pakistan, starting with the establishment of the Pakistan Emergency Fund.
- A HIV/AIDS strategic directions paper is approved.
- ADB adopts its new Public Communications Policy, which makes information about ADB operations publicly available.
- ADB introduces, on a pilot basis, an array of financing instruments (including multitranche financing facilities) under the Innovation and Efficiency Initiative to provide DMCs with greater flexibility in meeting their investment needs.
- ADB reviews its Supplementary Financing Policy.
- The new performance-based allocation policy for ADF becomes effective.
- ADB adopts a centralized risk management structure, and the Risk Management Unit is established.
- The Anticorruption Unit in the Office of the Auditor General is upgraded to an Integrity Division.
- The Office of Regional Economic Integration is established to replace the Regional Economic Monitoring Unit to provide a strategic focus on regional cooperation and integration initiatives.
- The Pacific Liaison and Coordination Office is established in Sydney, Australia.
2006	- Haruhiko Kuroda is reelected for a second term as President.
- Brunei Darussalam and Ireland join ADB.
- ADB's second medium-term strategy (MTS II) is adopted.
- ADB commissions a panel of eminent persons (led by United Nations Conference on Trade and Development Secretary

	General Supachai Panitchpakdi) to refine ADB's long-term goals and advise on key trends and development challenges in ADB. • The Regional Cooperation and Integration Strategy is approved. • The Private Sector Development Strategy is reviewed. • ADB establishes the Water Financing Partnership Facility to support investments, reforms, and capacity development in the water sector. • The Second Governance and Anticorruption Plan is approved. • The new Financing Partnership Strategy is approved. • The Ethics Committee is established by the Board. • Country groupings across ADB's regional departments are realigned. • ADB launches its $10 billion Asian currency note program.
Fifth Decade, 2007–2016	
2007	• Georgia joins ADB. • Extensive consultations are launched during the 40th Annual Meeting for ADB's new Long-Term Strategic Framework (LTSF) based on the Eminent Persons Group report. • ADB approves a new approach to achieve development effectiveness in weakly performing countries.
2008	• The Board approves the new LTSF for 2008–2020 called Strategy 2020, reaffirming ADB's focus on poverty. • ADB becomes the first multilateral development bank to adopt a corporate results framework. • The first Development Effectiveness Report released in November. • The ninth replenishment of the ADF starts (effective 2009). • A review of the graduation policy is completed. • A review of TA operations is completed. • The Operations Evaluation Department is renamed Independent Evaluation Department; ADB approves a new evaluation policy to further strengthen the department's independence. • ADB reviews the operations of its resident missions to assess the achievement of their objectives and expectations.

	- The strategy on human resources is reviewed.
	- Responding to rising demand from member countries, ADB mainstreams the multitranche financing facility, one of the instruments implemented on a pilot basis since 2005.
	- The Regional and Sustainable Development Department is reorganized to create a climate change unit; the Agriculture, Rural Development and Food Security team is formalized.
	- Resident missions are established in Armenia, Georgia, and Turkmenistan.
	- Around $4 billion additional resources are allocated to address food, commodity, oil price, and global financial crises in the region.
2009	- ADB approves a 200% general capital increase, a critical step in securing the funds needed to implement Strategy 2020—an increase that was the largest to date and the first since a 100% increase in 1994.
	- In response to the global financial crisis, ADB creates the Countercyclical Support Facility and expands its Trade Finance Facilitation Program.
	- A new energy policy is approved.
	- A new operational plan for sustainable food security and an action plan for implementing disaster and emergency assistance policy are approved.
	- ADB approves its New Safeguard Policy Update, unifying three safeguard policies on the environment, involuntary resettlement, and indigenous peoples into a single document.
	- A new Managing for Development Results (MfDR) action plan is adopted to guide the MfDR process across ADB.
	- The approach to mainstreaming gender in operations is updated.
	- ADB's new exposure management policy for nonsovereign operations is established, which sets the limits for nonsovereign exposure.
	- The Human Resources Committee of the Board is established.
	- The Risk Management Unit is upgraded to the Office of Risk Management.
	- The Unit for Institutional Coordination is created in the Budget, Personnel, and Management Systems Department.
2010	- ADB creates the new post of Vice-President for Private Sector and Cofinancing Operations.

	- New operational plans are completed for climate change, sustainable transport, and education.
- To improve service delivery and increase internal efficiency, ADB introduces new streamlined business processes for country partnership strategies and loan delivery.
- ADB's supplementary financing policy is reviewed and renamed "Additional Financing."
- Our People Strategy, a comprehensive plan to recruit, retain, and develop ADB staff, is approved.
- ADB establishes a credit guarantee and investment facility to guarantee bonds in the region.
- ADB signs the cross-debarment agreement with participating multilateral development banks.
- ADB issues thematic bonds (water and clean energy) for the first time.
- Results-based work plans are introduced to align department, division, and staff work plans with Strategy 2020 priorities.
2011	- Haruhiko Kuroda is reelected for a third term as President.
- New operational and action plans (2011–2020) are completed for the water sector and finance sector.
- A new public communications policy is approved to help expand and speed up access to ADB information.
- The Project Design Facility is established.
- ADB undertakes a review of its policy-based lending.
- ADB mainstreams nonsovereign public sector financing.
- ADB consolidates commercially related operations by transferring commercial cofinancing from the Office of Cofinancing to the Private Sector Operations Department.
2012	- The tenth ADF replenishment starts (effective 2013).
- New operational and action plans are completed: for public–private partnership (2012–2020), the Environment Operational Directions (2013–2020), and the Urban Operational Plan.
- A review of the ADB Results Framework is completed.
- The Accountability Mechanism Policy is reviewed and updated.
- ADB pilots the Disaster Response Facility.
- ADB introduces results-based lending.
- Normal operations in Myanmar are resumed (last loan project was approved in 1986).

2013	- The Knowledge Sharing and Services Center is established in the Regional and Sustainable Development Department.
- Takehiko Nakao is elected as ADB's ninth President and assumes office in April.
- The Midterm Review of Strategy 2020 is initiated.
- The following operational and action plans are completed: Gender Equality and Women's Empowerment Operational Plan (2013–2020), Knowledge Management Directions and Action Plan (2013–2015), Finance++ at ADB, Social Protection Operational Plan (2014–2020), Operational Plan for Enhancing ADB's Effectiveness in Fragile and Conflict-Affected Situations, and Implementation Review of Second Governance and Anticorruption Action Plan.
- ADB approves a revised results framework.
- ADB completes a procurement governance review and implements a 10-point procurement reform plan.
- The establishment of a resident mission in Timor-Leste is approved after being upgraded from a special office. The Bhutan Resident Mission is established.
- The Office of the Vice-President (Finance and Risk Management) is established to oversee the Treasury Department, Office of Risk Management, and Controllers.
- The Office of the Vice-President (Administration and Corporate Management) is established.
2014	- The Midterm Review of Strategy 2020 is completed (April) and the Midterm Review Action Plan is developed (July).
- ADB holds discussions on the proposal combining ADF lending operations with OCR ("Project Galaxy").
- The Office of Public–Private Partnerships is established to enhance ADB's public–private partnership operational approach and strengthen efforts to implement the Public–Private Partnerships Operational Plan 2012–2020.
- The Operational Plan for Integrated Risk Management, 2014–2020 is approved.
- ADB establishes a resident mission in Myanmar.
- The Third Atrium of ADB headquarters is officially opened to allow for ADB's expansion.
2015	- ADB's 67 Board of Governors unanimously approves the proposal to combine ADB's ADF lending operations with its

- OCR balance sheet (ADF–OCR merger). With this, ADB's financing capacity dramatically increases by up to 50% (effective January 2017).
- ADB scales up support to help DMCs deliver on internationally agreed commitments under the new Sustainable Development Goals and new climate deal (COP21).
- ADB joins other multilateral development banks for the Third International Conference on Financing for Development in Addis Ababa.
- Consultations on developing ADB's new corporate strategy, Strategy 2030, commence.
- ADB announces that it will double annual climate financing to $6 billion by 2020, the first multilateral development bank to commit to a sizable climate finance target.
- ADB is the first among multilateral development banks to be accredited by the Green Climate Fund.
- ADB starts negotiations on the 11th replenishment of the ADF and TASF (completed in 2016 and effective 2017).
- Operational plans for agriculture and natural resources (2015–2020) and health (2015–2020) are approved.
- ADB reorganizes the Regional and Sustainable Development Department and strengthens its sector and thematic groups with full-time secretariats to better build and share expertise across the Bank.
- ADB establishes the Economic Research and Regional Cooperation Department (bringing together the Office of Regional Economic Cooperation and the Economics and Research Department).

2016
- Takehiko Nakao is reelected as President for a further 5 years beginning on 24 November.
- To support the ADF–OCR merger, ADB approves a new concessional policy and reviews its financial policies, capital adequacy framework, and accounting approach.
- Revisions to ADB's anticorruption policy are made to include tax integrity and due diligence.
- ADB approves the first contingent disaster risk financing in the Cook Islands, the first privately financed solar project in Cambodia, and results-based lending for an elderly care project in the People's Republic of China.

- ADB successfully closes the transaction advisory mandate for the Turkmenistan–Afghanistan–Pakistan–India (TAPI) natural gas pipeline project.
- The Asia Pacific Project Preparation Facility officially launches operations, assisted by several donor countries.
- ADB approves the first two projects cofinanced with the Asian Infrastructure Investment Bank in Pakistan and Bangladesh.
- An innovative guarantee agreement with the Swedish International Development Cooperation Agency (Sida) is signed to allow ADB to increase financing by $500 million over the next 10 years.
- A landmark agreement with the Japan International Cooperation Agency is signed to finance private sector infrastructure projects for $6 billion.
- The first operational plan on regional cooperation and integration (2016–2020) is approved.
- The Board approves a paper on organizational resilience to strengthen ADB's ability to respond to disruptions, adversity, and change.
- ADB establishes a Respectful Workplace Unit in the Office of Anticorruption and Integrity (to be operational in 2017).

[a] Resident mission establishment dates indicated in this time line are dates of the host country agreements. If these are not available, establishment dates based on R-papers circulated/approved by the Board of Directors were used.

Sources: ADB Annual Reports; ADB.2016. ADB Through the Decades. Volumes 1-5; ADB website (www.adb.org).

INDEX

Boxes, figures, notes, and tables are indicated by b, f, n, and t following the page number. Photographs are indicated by italicized page numbers.

A
Abe, Shinzo, 15, 322
Abramowski, Helmut, 52
accountability, 195, 197, 264–67, 276, 319–21
ADB. *See* Asian Development Bank
ADB Institute (ADBI), 197–99, 224–25, 310, 314
ADF. *See* Asian Development Fund
Afghanistan
   ADF grants to, 269
   CAREC and, 279*b*
   field office in, 197, 198*f*, 283
   as fragile state, 261
   HIPC debt relief for, 247*n*21, 318
   lending to, 82, 101, 201
   life expectancy in, 4
   regional cooperation and, 27
   resident mission in, 259*n*12
   technical assistance to, 101
   Turkmenistan–Afghanistan–Pakistan–India Pipeline (TAPI), 311*b*
Afghanistan Infrastructure Trust Fund (AITF), 341
AFIC (Asian Finance and Investment Corporation), 139
African Development Bank, 29
Agricultural Special Fund (ASF), 88, 96–98
agriculture
   in Decade 1 (1967–1976), 53–58, 69, 75–76, 79–80, 93, 100–101
   in Decade 2 (1977–1986), 113, 115, 117, 123, 126, 128–30, 133, 136, 147–48
   in Decade 3 (1987–1996), 169–70, 191, 194, 201–3
   in Decade 4 (1997–2006), 213, 237, 256, 258, 279*b*, 284–85
   in Decade 5 (2007–2016), 309, 312, 341, 345–46
   food security and, 24–26
   infrastructure, 78–79
Ahluwalia, Isher Judge, 282
Ahluwalia, Montek K., 161
aid effectiveness, 162, 244–46, 264–67, 266*b*, 307
Aid for Trade program, 242
AIDS/HIV, 127*b*
AIF (ASEAN Infrastructure Fund), 319
AIIB (Asian Infrastructure Investment Bank), 303, 343
AITF (Afghanistan Infrastructure Trust Fund), 341
Akamatsu, Kaname, 18
Akihito (Emperor of Japan), 243
AMF (Asian Monetary Fund), 229–30
APEC (Asia-Pacific Economic Cooperation), 160, 230
Aquino, Benigno S., III, 328*b*
Aquino, Corazon, 182, *248*
ARIC (Asia Recovery Information Center), 223, 277

Armenia, lending to, 313
ASEAN. *See* Association of Southeast Asian Nations
ASEAN Infrastructure Fund (AIF), 319
ASF (Agricultural Special Fund), 88, 96–98
Asia Disaster Response Fund, 341
Asian Agricultural Survey, 6, 122
Asian Bond Markets Initiative, 224, 239, 319
Asian Development Bank (ADB)
first decade (1967–1976), 53–105. *See also* Decade 1
second decade (1977–1986), 107–55. *See also* Decade 2
third decade (1987–1996), 157–206. *See also* Decade 3
fourth decade (1997–2006), 207–87. *See also* Decade 4
fifth decade (2007–2016), 289–355. *See also* Decade 5
ADF–OCR merger, 467–72
ADF replenishments, 443–50
annual meeting venues and dates, 425–26
annual new gross borrowings, 461–62
bilateral partners, cofinancing from, 451–52
board of directors and constituencies, 421–23
capital composition, 441–42
cofinancing, 451–55
as development organization, 3–6, 4*f*
establishment of, 31–52
field offices, establishment of, 430
financial highlights, 431–32
as financing institution, 6–11, 9*f*
general capital increases, 441–42
headquarters, 48–50, *68*, *154*, *354*
leadership succession, 11–15
as multilateral agency, 2–3
multilaterals, cofinancing from, 453–54
operational approvals by fund source and type, 436–37
operational approvals by member and decade, 433–35
organizational structure, 463–64
outstanding portfolio loans and grant disbursements, 438–40
presidents, list of, 424
private foundations, cofinancing from, 455
regional and nonregional members, 418
sector groups, 465–66
share of subscribed capital, 419–20
special funds, list of active and closed, 456–60
staff, 139–40, 321–22, 427–29
thematic groups, 465–66
time line of milestones, 473–93
trust funds, list of active and closed, 456–60
voting power, 419–20
Asian Development Fund (ADF)
Decade 1 (1967–1976), 104
Decade 2 (1977–1986), 124, 129, 132, 137, 142, 147, 150–51
Decade 3 (1987–1996), 181–82, 199–200, 205
Decade 4 (1997–2006), 222–23, 256, 261, 267–70, 281, 286–87
Decade 5 (2007–2016), 312, 318–19, 322, 332–41, 347–49
establishment of, 7, 69, 95–99, 96–98*b*

Asian Development Review, 143, 161
Asian Economic Cooperation,
  35–37
Asian Energy Survey, 6
Asian Finance and Investment
  Corporation (AFIC), 139
Asian financial crisis, 207–33
  ADB response, 14, 190, 213–15,
    214–15*t*, 219–21
  AFIC and, 139
  causes of, 172, 225–28
  criticism of international rescue
    operations, 228–29
  currency stabilization support
    programs, 209, 210*t*
  development agenda influenced
    by, 253–54, 277, 307–8
  Indonesia, 211–12, 217–19, 227*f*
  Korea, Republic of, 209–11, 216–17,
    227*f*
  lessons learned, 10, 232–33,
    271–72
  Malaysia, 227*f*
  newly industrialized economies
    (NIEs), 222–23
  Philippines, 227*f*
  policy reforms, 223–25
  regional impact, 3, 212–13, 236–40
  regional initiatives, 229–32
  research programs, 223–25
  Thailand, 168, 208–9, 215–16, 227*f*
Asian Infrastructure Investment
  Bank (AIIB), 303, 343
Asian Monetary Fund (AMF),
  229–30
Asian Transport Survey, 6
Asia-Pacific Economic Cooperation
  (APEC), 160, 230
Asia Pacific Project Preparation
  Facility (AP3F), 331

Asia Recovery Information Center
  (ARIC), 223, 277
Asia Regional Integration Center,
  238
Association of Southeast Asian
  Nations (ASEAN)
  ADB cooperation with, 295, 319
  Asian financial crisis response, 239
  Chiang Mai Initiative and, 231–32
  expansion of, 160, 172
  Infrastructure Fund, 319
  regional cooperation model of,
    60, 277, 278*b*, 280
  REMU and, 223–24, 277, 278*b*
Aung San Suu Kyi, 298, 323, *354*
Australia
  aid to Pacific Island countries, 171
  Asian financial crisis and, 209–10,
    223
  Asia Pacific Project Preparation
    Facility (AP3F) and, 331
  ECAFE and, 47
  funding from, 32, 92*n*32, 98*b*, 197,
    339
  health sector projects in, 127*b*
  Regional Malaria and Other
    Communicable Diseases Threats
    Trust Fund and, 341
  voting share of, 85
  Water Financing Partnership
    Facility and, 271
Austria, 271, 326*b*
Azerbaijan
  CAREC and, 279*b*
  Countercyclical Support Facility
    and, 313
  field office in, 197, 198*f*
  macroeconomic stabilization in,
    237
  resident mission in, 259*n*12

B
Badar, Rokiah Hj, *355*
Balmaceda, Cornelio, 43, *62*, *67*, 133–34
Bambawale, A. T., 125–26
Bandaranaike, Solomon, 32
Bangladesh
  AIIB projects in, 303, 343
  economic growth in, 169, 237–38, 290, 305
  education sector projects in, 179*b*
  field office in, 197, 198*f*
  health sector projects in, 127*b*
  independence of, 23, 82
  lending to, 93–94, 100–101, 147, 203, 313, 345
  poverty in, 297
  remittances to, 294–95
  resident mission in, 139
  South Asia Subregional Economic Cooperation and, 279*b*
  technical assistance to, 101, 147
  urban sector projects in, 326*b*
Bank for International Settlements (BIS), 33
Bank Indonesia, 211, 226
basic human needs paradigm, 109–10
Belgium, 50*t*
Bengal Initiative for Multi-Sectoral Technical and Economic Cooperation (BIMSTEC), 278–79*b*
Bergsten, Fred, 110
Betham, Gustav, 81
Bhutan
  economic growth in, 170, 305
  field office in, 197, 198*f*
  life expectancy in, 4
  Rural Electricians Training Program, *350*
  scholarship program, 196
  subregional cooperation programs, 279*b*
Bhutto, Benazir, *155*
Bill & Melinda Gates Foundation, 244
BIMP-EAGA (Brunei Darussalam–Indonesia–Malaysia– Philippines East ASEAN Growth Area), 278*b*
BIMSTEC (Bengal Initiative for Multi-Sectoral Technical and Economic Cooperation), 278–79*b*
BIS (Bank for International Settlements), 33
Black, Eugene, 41, 103
board of directors
  in 1966, 52, 52*t*
  list of, 421–23
Boret, Long, *65*
Brandt Commission, 109
Brundtland Commission, 161, 178
Brunei Darussalam
  as ADB member, 280, 284*n*51, 344
  ECAFE and, 27*n*18
  economic shocks in, 60
  subregional cooperation programs, 278*b*
Brunei Darussalam–Indonesia–Malaysia– Philippines East ASEAN Growth Area (BIMP-EAGA), 278*b*
Burki, Shahid Javed, 161
Busan Fourth High Level Forum on Aid Effectiveness, 246
Buu, Hoan, 72, 90

C
callable capital, 7, 84*n*21, 180, 183, 315, 332

Index 499

Cambodia
  ASEAN and, 160
  Disaster Response Facility and, 338
  ECAFE and, 27n18
  economic growth in, 168–69, 185–86, 237
  field office in, 197, 198f
  health sector projects in, 127b
  instability in, 21, 114
  lending to, 201
  life expectancy in, 114
  subregional cooperation programs, 278b
  Tonle Sap Poverty Reduction and Smallholder Development Project, 250
Camdessus, Michel, 218
Cameron, David, 301
Canada, 32, 50t, 88, 92n, 96–98b, 109, 331, 341
capital flight, 211, 226
capital flows
  Decade 1 (1967–1976), 59
  Decade 3 (1987–1996), 158–59, 163
  Decade 4 (1997–2006), 228, 238–39
  Decade 5 (2007–2016), 293–94
capital markets
  ADB borrowing program in, 7
  Decade 1 (1967–1976), 69, 73, 86–87, 99
  Decade 3 (1987–1996), 159, 172, 184
  Decade 4 (1997–2006), 215, 225, 231, 255
capital subscriptions, 43, 45, 48, 83–84
CAREC. *See* Central Asia Regional Economic Cooperation
Carroll, Lewis, 66

Castro, Amada, 38
Center for Global Development (CGD), 334
Central Asia. *See also specific countries*
  Decade 1 (1967–1976), 100
  Decade 2 (1977–1986), 147
  Decade 3 (1987–1996), 170, 185, 187
  Decade 4 (1997–2006), 235, 237, 254, 259, 280
  Decade 5 (2007–2016), 290, 293, 305
Central Asia Regional Economic Cooperation (CAREC), 172, 249, 278–79b
Chadwick, John, 96, 98
Chalker, Lynda, 185
charter of ADB, 44–47, 46b
Chen Muhua, 154
Cherat Cement Company, 138b
Chiang Mai Initiative (CMI), 231–32, 239, 295
Chiang Mai Initiative Multilateralization (CMIM), 295, 319
China, People's Republic of
  Cultural Revolution, 24
  Decade 1 (1967–1976), 53, 56–58, 78, 81, 101, 103
  Decade 2 (1977–1986), 107, 110, 112, 115–19, 121, 137, 144–46, 147, 149
  Decade 3 (1987–1996), 158–59, 162–67, 169, 172, 174–76, 180, 182–84, 186–89, 192, 197, 200–204
  Decade 4 (1997–2006), 210, 223, 229–30, 235–39, 242, 255, 268, 277, 282–84
  Decade 5 (2007–2016), 290–300, 303, 305, 313, 319, 325, 327, 331, 342, 344–45

economic growth in, 3–4, 4f, 17,
  18–20, 22–27
establishment of ADB and, 33, 34,
  47, 50
field office in, 197, 198f
Great Leap Forward, 24
health sector projects in, 127b
isolation of, 23–24
Nanpu Bridge project (PRC), 248
resident mission in, 259n12
subregional cooperation
  programs, 278–79b
China Investment Bank, 175
Chino, Tadao, 62, 250–51
  accountability mechanisms and,
    320
  ADF replenishments and, 318
  Asian financial crisis and, 233, 235
  establishment of ADB and, 43
  Gender Action Plans and, 331
  leadership of, 14, 253–58, 260–62,
    265, 269–70, 272, 274, 285, 314
Choi, Won-Mok, 355
civil society
  accountability mechanisms and,
    321
  ADB collaboration with, 347, 359
  development agenda and, 255
  finance architecture and, 245–46
  globalization and, 241
  JFPR partnerships with, 342
  sustainable development and,
    263–66, 276
climate change, 271, 297–301, 309,
  324–27, 329, 341
Clinton, Bill, 160
CMI (Chiang Mai Initiative),
  231–32, 239, 295
CMIM (Chiang Mai Initiative
  Multilateralization), 295, 319

cofinancing
  from bilateral partners, 7, 10,
    451–52
  Decade 1 (1967–1976), 99–100, 105
  Decade 2 (1977–1986), 124, 133,
    142, 151
  Decade 3 (1987–1996), 183, 192,
    206
  Decade 4 (1997–2006), 215, 223,
    271, 287
  Decade 5 (2007–2016), 312–13,
    327, 339–43, 340t, 349
  from multilaterals, 10, 453–54
  from private foundations, 10, 455
Cold War, 157, 160, 162, 172, 185, 204
Colombo Plan, 28
Commission on Growth and
  Development, 117
Communicable Diseases Threats
  Trust Fund, 341
concessional lending, 335
Conferences of the Parties (COPs),
  15, 299, 300
Cook Islands, 24, 101, 171
Copenhagen Accord, 299–300
COPs (Conferences of the Parties),
  15, 299, 300
Countercyclical Support Facility
  (CSF), 313, 322
Credit Guarantee and Investment
  Facility (CGIF), 319
Crisis Management Committee, 182
CSF (Countercyclical Support
  Facility), 313, 322
Cultural Revolution (PRC), 24, 33,
  117
Cyclone Evan, 338
Cyclone Ian, 338
Cyclone Ita, 338

D

DAC (Development Assistance Committee), 245
Dae-jung, Kim, 209
Dandekar, Swati, 355
Dawson, Scott, 355
Decade 1 (1967–1976), 53–105
    ADB bonds, 85–87
    ADF establishment, 95–99, 96–98b
    agriculture, 54–56
    capital market borrowing, 99–100
    character of ADB, 69–105
    cofinancing, 99–100
    crisis-related programs, 93–95
    economic shocks, 60–61
    finance sources, 83–84
    financing operations, 78, 79b, 81–83
    general capital increases, 84–85, 95–99
    industrialization, 56–60, 57t
    Inoue's leadership, 91–93
    leadership transition, 89–90
    oil money recycling, 99–100
    operational summary, 100–102, 101–2f, 104–5t
    priorities, 79–81
    research activities, 74–78
    Special Funds, 87–89
    technical assistance, 78, 79b
    vision for ADB, 70–73, 72b
Decade 2 (1977–1986), 107–55
    basic human needs paradigm, 109–10
    China, People's Republic of, 116–19, 117t, 144–46
    country strategies, 140–41
    development agenda, 123–26
    financing operations, 126–29, 127–29b, 136–39, 137f, 138b, 140–41
    flexible lending arrangements, 140–41
    Four Tigers economies, 110–12
    Fujioka's leadership, 132–34
    general capital increases, 131–32, 141–42
    India as borrower, 146–47
    operational summary, 147–50, 149f, 150–51t
    Pacific island countries, 116
    priorities, 134–36
    private sector operations, 136–39, 138b
    resident missions, 139–40
    South Asia, 115–16
    Southeast Asia, 112–15
    staff, 139–40
    stagflation, 108–9
    structural adjustment, 109–10
    surveys and reviews, 130–31
    Yoshida's leadership, 121–23
Decade 3 (1987–1996), 157–206
    ADB Institute, 197–99
    capital flows, 158–59
    Central Asia, 170–71
    China, People's Republic of, 166–67, 187–89
    development agenda, 160–62, 177–80, 179b
    field offices, 197–99, 198f
    financing operations, 190–91, 196
    Fujioka's leadership, 174–77
    general capital increases, 182–84
    globalization, 163–65
    India, 187–89
    newly industrialized economies (NIEs), 165–66
    operational summary, 199–205, 201–2f, 205–6t
    Pacific island countries, 171

policy reforms, 192–95, 193–94*b*
regional developments, 157–72
resource mobilization, 191
Sato's leadership, 189–90
scholarships, 196
South Asia, 169–70
Southeast Asia, 167–69
states and markets, 162–63
strategic planning, 184–86
structural adjustment, 162, 166, 170
Tarumizu's leadership, 180–82
trade arrangements, 159–60
transition economies, 185–87
Decade 4 (1997–2006), 207–87
   accountability, 264–67
   ADB operations, 253–87
   ADF replenishments, 267–70
   aid effectiveness, 264–67, 266*b*
   Asian financial crisis, 207–33. *See also* Asian financial crisis
   capital flows, 238–39
   Chino's leadership, 253–55
   development agenda, 242–44, 245–46*t*
   finance architecture reforms, 244–47
   financing operations, 280–82, 281*f*
   fragile states, 260–62
   globalization, 239–42
   governance, 262–64
   Indonesia, 211–12, 217–19, 227*f*
   Korea, Republic of, 209–11, 216–17, 227*f*
   Kuroda's leadership, 272–73
   Millennium Development Goals, 242–44
   newly industrialized economies (NIEs), 222–23
   operational summary, 283–86, 284–85*f*, 286–87*t*

   ordinary capital resources operations, 270–72
   organizational reforms, 258–60
   policy reforms, 223–25
   recovery from crisis, 236–38
   regional cooperation, 277–80, 278–79*b*
   research programs, 223–25
   strategic planning, 256–58
   structural adjustment, 229
   sustainable development, 262–64
   Thailand, 208–9, 215–16, 227*f*
   trade arrangements, 238–39
Decade 5 (2007–2016), 289–355
   accountability, 319–21
   ADB operations, 307–55
   ADF replenishments, 318–19, 336–39
   ASEAN Infrastructure Fund, 319
   climate change, 298–301
   cofinancing, 339–43, 340*t*
   Credit Guarantee and Investment Facility (CGIF), 319
   development agenda, 325–31
   development finance sources, 301–3
   environmental pressures, 296–98
   financing operations, 332–35, 336*f*
   general capital increases, 314–16, 316–17*t*
   global financial crisis, 291–93, 312–14
   globalization, 303–4
   human resources, 321–22
   inequality, 296–98
   Millennium Development Goals, 301, 302*f*
   multilateral development banks, 343
   Nakao's leadership, 322–24
   operational summary, 344–48, 345–46*f*, 348–49*t*

regional growth, 289–91
staff, 321–22
strategic framework, 307–12
Strategy 2020, 324–25
sustainable development, 293–96
Sustainable Development Goals, 301, 302*f*
trust funds, 339–43, 340*t*
Deng, Xiaoping, 166
Denmark, 50*t*, 97*b*
Desai, Morarji, 83
development agenda
    Asian financial crisis and, 253–54, 277, 307–8
    Decade 2 (1977–1986), 123–26
    Decade 3 (1987–1996), 160–62, 177–80, 179*b*
    Decade 4 (1997–2006), 242–44, 245–46*t*
    Decade 5 (2007–2016), 325–31
development finance institutions (DFIs), 79–81, 137
Dhaka Water Supply and Sewage Association, 326
Di Maio, Mario, *355*
Disaster Response Facility, 310, 318, 338–39
Djiwandono, Soedradjad, 211, 226
Doha Round (WTO), 304
Dominguez, Paul, *355*
donor countries. *See also specific countries*
    Decade 1 (1967–1976), 88, 91–92, 95, 99
    Decade 2 (1977–1986), 124, 162
    Decade 3 (1987–1996), 183, 197
    Decade 4 (1997–2006), 222, 247, 258
    Decade 5 (2007–2016), 320, 333–34
    financing from, 7–8

Dulles, John Foster, 31
Durban Platform for Enhanced Action, 300
Durrani, Hamidullah, *251*

E
Earth Summit, 161, 299
East Asia. *See also specific countries*
    Decade 1 (1967–1976), 100, 102
    Decade 2 (1977–1986), 113, 149
    Decade 3 (1987–1996), 158, 164–65, 200–201
    Decade 4 (1997–2006), 222, 283–84
    Decade 5 (2007–2016), 296, 344–45
    field offices in, 197, 198*f*
    lending to, 100, 147
Economic Commission for Asia and the Far East (ECAFE)
    development agenda and, 254
    establishment of ADB and, 31–32, 35–39, 41, 45
    on food security, 24–25
    on regional cooperation, 26–28
education programs
    Decade 1 (1967–1976), 53, 100–101
    Decade 2 (1977–1986), 113, 128, 144, 147–48
    Decade 3 (1987–1996), 161, 178, 179*b*, 192, 194, 202
    Decade 4 (1997–2006), 256, 264, 285
    Decade 5 (2007–2016), 302, 305–6, 309, 324, 329, 346
emerging economies, 13, 225, 294, 303–4. *See also specific countries*
Endogenous Growth Theory, 20
energy issues
    Decade 1 (1967–1976), 61, 69, 79–80, 100–101

Decade 2 (1977–1986), 109, 129–31, 133, 147–48
Decade 3 (1987–1996), 187, 196, 201–3
Decade 4 (1997–2006), 213, 237, 256, 263, 283, 285
Decade 5 (2007–2016), 302, 329, 339, 341, 345–46
subregional cooperation programs, 279*b*
environmental issues
Decade 1 (1967–1976), 72
Decade 2 (1977–1986), 108–9
Decade 3 (1987–1996), 161, 184, 193
Decade 4 (1997–2006), 253, 263, 268, 282
Decade 5 (2007–2016), 296, 298, 309, 321, 324, 329
subregional cooperation programs, 278–79*b*
equity investments, 5, 7, 138–39, 180, 200, 311*b*, 335
Ershad, Hussain Muhammad, 153
establishment of ADB, 31–52
board of directors and voting groups, 52, 52*t*
charter, 44–47, 46*b*
chronology of official meetings, 36–38*t*
earlier proposals, 31–33
ECAFE role in, 35–39
first president, 51–52
headquarters, 48–50, 68
Japan's role in, 41–42
preparations for, 42–44
scope of membership, 40
Tokyo Study Group and, 33–34
US role in, 41–42
Watanabe and, 33–34

Europe. *See also specific countries*
Decade 1 (1967–1976), 69, 86–87
Decade 2 (1977–1986), 119
Decade 3 (1987–1996), 159, 164, 185, 192, 197
Decade 4 (1997–2006), 210
Decade 5 (2007–2016), 292, 303, 305
ADB membership and, 2
capital markets in, 6, 18
establishment of ADB and, 27–28, 38, 40
European Bank for Reconstruction and Development, 185, 279*b*, 303, 342
European Economic Community, 124
exchange rates, 107, 164, 225, 231, 317, 323
Expert Group on Regional Cooperation, 36
Export Financing Facility, 214, 216
Export–Import Bank, 214
exports
Decade 1 (1967–1976), 58–59, 80
Decade 2 (1977–1986), 111–13, 115, 119, 122–23
Decade 3 (1987–1996), 164–65, 168, 172
Decade 4 (1997–2006), 225, 227, 236–37
Decade 5 (2007–2016), 292–93
economic growth and, 19–20

F

famine, 24–25. *See also* food security
Farmanfarmaian, Khodadad, 44–45, 62
FDI. *See* foreign direct investment
Feliciano, Florentino P., 44

field offices, establishment of, 197–99, 198f, 430
Fifth Road Improvement Project, 213
Fiji, 101, 171, 259
finance sector
  Decade 1 (1967–1976), 80
  Decade 2 (1977–1986), 118
  Decade 3 (1987–1996), 167
  Decade 4 (1997–2006), 212–13, 216–17, 221, 240, 283
  Decade 5 (2007–2016), 309
financial crises. *See* Asian financial crisis; global financial crisis
financial markets
  Decade 1 (1967–1976), 86–87, 89
  Decade 2 (1977–1986), 133
  Decade 4 (1997–2006), 208, 210–11, 224, 232
  Decade 5 (2007–2016), 291, 344
  ECAFE and, 38
Financial Sector Program Loan, 187, 217
Financial Supervisory Agency of Japan, 224
financing operations
  Decade 1 (1967–1976), 78, 79b, 81–83, 94, 101–2
  Decade 2 (1977–1986), 126, 127–29b, 136–39, 137, 137f, 138b, 140–41, 148–49
  Decade 3 (1987–1996), 190–91, 196, 199–202
  Decade 4 (1997–2006), 281, 283–85
  Decade 5 (2007–2016), 332–36, 336f, 345–46
Finland, 50t, 250
First World Conference on Natural Disaster Reduction (1994), 243
Fischer, Stanley, 218
flexible lending arrangements, 140–41

flying geese paradigm, 18, 20, 53, 164, 239
food security
  Decade 1 (1967–1976), 54–55, 61
  Decade 2 (1977–1986), 129
  Decade 5 (2007–2016), 302, 309, 318, 329
  economic growth and, 24–26, 25t
foreign direct investment (FDI), 114, 118, 159, 165–66, 305
foreign policy, 28, 32
Four Tigers economies, 18–20, 20t. *See also* newly industrialized economies (NIEs)
Fox, Mathew, 355
fragile states, 260–62
France, 21, 101, 109, 139
Frank, Victor, 173, 181
Fraser, Malcolm, 152
Fujioka, Masao, 153–55
  on ADB mission, 6, 70, 173
  on Balmaceda, 43
  leadership of, 13, 132–41, 143–46, 149–50, 174–75, 177, 180
  on reform needs, 121
Fujiyama, Aiichiro, 49
Fukuda, Takeo, 51

G

Gandhi, Indira, 153
GATT (General Agreement on Tariffs and Trade), 159
GCF (Green Climate Fund), 327, 329
GCI. *See* general capital increases
Geithner, Timothy, 230
gender equality
  Decade 2 (1977–1986), 143–44
  Decade 3 (1987–1996), 160, 179b, 193
  Decade 4 (1997–2006), 242, 256, 262, 264
  Decade 5 (2007–2016), 302, 329, 331

General Agreement on Tariffs and
   Trade (GATT), 159
general capital increases (GCI)
   Decade 1 (1967–1976), 84–85,
      95–99
   Decade 2 (1977–1986), 131–32,
      141–42
   Decade 3 (1987–1996), 182–84,
      190, 193, 200
   Decade 4 (1997–2006), 255, 257,
      270, 273, 280
   Decade 5 (2007–2016), 312,
      314–17, 316–17t, 321
   leadership of ADB and, 13–14
   table of, 441–42
Georgia
   field office in, 197, 198f
   lending to, 313, 344
   urban sector projects in, 326b
Germany
   financial markets in, 133
   funding from, 92n32
   Plaza Accord and, 109
   technical assistance from, 111
   urban sector projects funding
      from, 326b
Ghirga, Maurizio, 355
global financial crisis, 3, 14, 289–95,
   305, 312–15, 322, 342
globalization
   Decade 3 (1987–1996), 159, 163–65
   Decade 4 (1997–2006), 207, 225,
      235, 239–43
   Decade 5 (2007–2016), 294, 298,
      303–4
   regional impact of, 12
GMS. *See* Greater Mekong
   Subregion
governance
   Decade 3 (1987–1996), 160, 194–95

Decade 4 (1997–2006), 215, 226,
   256–57, 262–64, 271
Decade 5 (2007–2016), 306, 308,
   318, 329, 358
establishment of ADB and, 44
health sector projects, 127b
Greater Mekong Subregion (GMS),
   92, 127b, 186, 278b, 296, 337b, 341
Great Leap Forward (PRC), 24
Green Climate Fund (GCF), 327, 329
Green Revolution, 53–56, 61, 77, 80,
   93, 115, 122, 130
Groff, Stephen, 355
Guangxi Zhuang Autonomous
   Region, 186, 278b
Gunesekera, Douglas, 43, 62, 66
Gupta, Diwakar, 355
Gyohten, Toyoo, 32, 33, 225

H

Hach, Nguyen Cao, 62
Hamzah, Tengku Razaleigh, 123, 124
Ha Noi Metro Rail System Project
   (Viet Nam), 353
Harvard University, 77
Hasegawa, Koichi, 355
HCMC (Ho Chi Minh City), 186,
   326b
headquarters of ADB, 48–50, 68,
   154, 354
Health Sector Projects, 127b
Heavily Indebted Poor Countries
   (HIPC), 246, 247nn21–22, 318
Hennessy, John M., 177
High Level Forum on Aid
   Effectiveness, 244
HIPC (Heavily Indebted Poor
   Countries), 246, 247nn21–22, 318
Hirschman, Albert, 77
Hitotsubashi University, 75, 134

HIV/AIDS, 127*b*
Ho Chi Minh City (HCMC), 186, 326*b*
Hong Kong, China
  economic growth in, 18–20, 20*t*
  lending to, 147
  life expectancy in, 4
  Sha Tin Hospital Polyclinic, 126, 152
Hoontrakool, Sommai, *62*
Hsieh, Sam-Chung, 77
Huang, P. W., 28*n*20, 34*n*10
human resources. *See* staff

I

Ichimada, Hisato, 31
IFCT (Industrial Finance Corporation of Thailand), 79*b*
IMF. *See* International Monetary Fund
import substitution industrialization (ISI) strategies, 25–26
inclusive growth, 308–9, 318, 337*b*
India
  Decade 1 (1967–1976), 55, 59–60
  Decade 2 (1977–1986), 116, 121, 125, 144, 146–47, 150
  Decade 3 (1987–1996), 163, 169, 174–75, 177, 180, 182, 187–88, 200–204
  Decade 4 (1997–2006), 235, 238, 277, 282–83
  Decade 5 (2007–2016), 290–91, 293–94, 296–300, 303, 305, 342, 344–45
  development agenda in, 34–35, 38–39
  economic growth in, 3–4, 4*f*, 20, 22–23, 25, 27
  field office in, 197, 198*f*
  independence of, 17–18
  Innovation and Efficiency Initiative and, 275*b*
  lending to, 13, 146–47
  Rajasthan Urban Development Project, *154*
  subregional cooperation programs, 279*b*
  Tsunami Emergency Assistance Project, *350*
  Turkmenistan–Afghanistan–Pakistan–India Pipeline (TAPI), 311b
Indonesia
  Decade 1 (1967–1976), 55, 57, 59, 61, 74, 78–79, 81, 100–101
  Decade 2 (1977–1986), 108, 112–14, 140–41, 147
  Decade 3 (1987–1996), 163–64, 167, 174, 177, 201, 203
  Decade 4 (1997–2006), 207, 210–15, 217–20, 225–27, 229–30, 238, 283–84
  Decade 5 (2007–2016), 290, 293, 297–300, 303, 305, 342, 344
  economic growth in, 3–4, 4*f*, 20–22, 27–28
  education sector projects in, 179*b*
  field office in, 197, 198*f*
  independence, 17–18
  Innovation and Efficiency Initiative, 275*b*
  lending to, 100, 147
  Madrasah Education Development Project, *351*
  subregional cooperation programs, 278–79*b*
  Tajum Irrigation Project, 79*b*
  technical assistance to, 101, 147

Indonesia–Malaysia–Thailand
   Growth Triangle (IMT-GT)
   program, 278–79*b*
Industrial Finance Corporation of
   Thailand (IFCT), 79*b*
industrialization
   Decade 1 (1967–1976), 54, 56–60,
   57*t*, 77
   Decade 2 (1977–1986), 109
   Decade 3 (1987–1996), 164
   economic development and,
   25–27, 35
inequality, 296–98
information and communication
   technology (ICT)
   Decade 1 (1967–1976), 100–101
   Decade 2 (1977–1986), 147–48
   Decade 3 (1987–1996), 202–3
   Decade 4 (1997–2006), 239, 271,
   283, 285
   Decade 5 (2007–2016), 298,
   345–46
   subregional cooperation
   programs, 279*b*
Innovation and Efficiency Initiative,
   275*b*
Inoue, Shiro, 68
   Krishna Moorthi's influence on,
   74
   leadership of, 12, 89–93, 95,
   98–103, 149
   retirement of, 121–22
   on social impact of ADB, 124–25
integrated disaster risk
   management, 310
Inter-American Development Bank,
   29, 39, 51, 86
interest rates, 107–9, 192, 292, 294, 313
International Development
   Association, 100, 247*n*22

International Labour Organization
   World Employment Conference,
   109
International Monetary Fund
   (IMF)
   Decade 2 (1977–1986), 122, 141,
   144
   Decade 3 (1987–1996), 161–62, 187,
   189, 197
   Decade 4 (1997–2006), 208–13,
   217–20, 228–32, 241, 246–47, 272
   Decade 5 (2007–2016), 293, 313,
   318, 323
   subregional cooperation
   programs, 279*b*
International Rice Research
   Institute (IRRI), 27, 54–55
Iran, 27, 39, 44, 48–49, 108
Iraq, 158, 236
Ireland, 284*n*
Islamic Development Bank (IsDB),
   100, 142, 279*b*, 313, 339
Italy, 50*t*, 109

J
Japan
   Decade 1 (1967–1976), 53, 56,
   85–89, 96–97, 100
   Decade 2 (1977–1986), 109–11,
   113–14, 118–19, 122, 124
   Decade 3 (1987–1996), 158,
   163–64, 172–73, 181
   Decade 4 (1997–2006), 209–10,
   223–24, 229–31, 239, 241, 243, 272
   Decade 5 (2007–2016), 290, 293,
   295, 313, 316, 322, 331, 333, 339, 357
   economic growth in, 3, 4*f*, 18, 20*t*,
   27–28
   establishment of ADB and, 31–32,
   35, 37–39, 41–43, 48–51

funding from, 92n32, 197
Myanmar reengagement and, 337*b*
Japan Fund, 272, 328*b*, 341
Japan Fund for Poverty Reduction (JFPR), 272, 328*b*, 341–42
Japan International Cooperation Agency (JICA), 328*b*, 337*b*, 339, 342
Japan–PRC Treaty of Peace and Friendship (1978), 118
Japan Scholarship Program (JSP), 196, 341–42
Japan Special Fund (JSF), 151, 206, 287, 341, 349
JFPR (Japan Fund for Poverty Reduction), 272, 328*b*, 341–42
JICA. *See* Japan International Cooperation Agency
Jin, Liqun, 343
Johnson, Lyndon B., 41–42, 84, 87, 88
Johnson Sirleaf, Ellen, 301
JSF (Japan Special Fund), 151, 206, 287, 341, 349
JSP (Japan Scholarship Program), 196, 341–42

K
Kali Gandaki "A" Hydroelectric Project (Nepal), *249*
Karzai, Hamid, 261
Kashiwagi, Mikio, 332
Katz, Stanley, 125–26, 185
Kazakhstan
　Decade 3 (1987–1996), 170–71, 187, 201, 204
　Decade 4 (1997–2006), 237
　Decade 5 (2007–2016), 313, 344
　field office in, 197, 198*f*
　resident mission in, 259n12

subregional cooperation programs, 279*b*
Kennedy, David M., 74
Khmer Rouge, 114
Kiribati, 101, 171n
Kishi, Nobusuke, 31
Kojima, Kiyoshi, 134
Korea, Republic of
　Decade 1 (1967–1976), 53, 56–58, 78, 81, 100
　Decade 2 (1977–1986), 110–11, 145, 147
　Decade 3 (1987–1996), 163–65
　Decade 4 (1997–2006), 207–11, 213–14, 216–17, 219–20, 222–23, 227, 239, 268, 271, 283
　Decade 5 (2007–2016), 290, 295, 313, 319, 342, 344
　economic growth in, 18–20, 20*t*, 22, 27
　education sector projects in, 179*b*
　funding from, 197
　lending to, 100, 147
　subregional cooperation programs, 278*b*
Korea Development Investment Corporation, 138
Korea Exim Bank, 339
Korea Institute of Science and Technology, 179*b*
Korea Standard Research Institute, 179*b*
Krishna Moorthi, C. S., 43, *62*, 65–66, 73–74, 90, 125
Krishnamurti, R., 36*t*
Kuroda, Haruhiko, *350*
　ADB mission and, 253, 257, 286, 289, 307, 308
　Gender Action Plans and, 331
　global financial crisis and, 312

on inequality, 296–97
leadership of, 14, 262, 271–74, 276–82, 314–16, 320–22
Kuwait, 47, 99
Kyoto Protocol, 263, 299, 310
Kyrgyz Republic
  Decade 3 (1987–1996), 170, 187, 201, 204
  Decade 4 (1997–2006), 254
  Decade 5 (2007–2016), 290, 295, 344
  field office in, 197, 198f
  resident mission in, 259n12
  subregional cooperation programs, 279b

L
Lall, K. B., 35
Lao Bao International Border Gate, 248
Lao People's Democratic Republic
  Decade 3 (1987–1996), 160, 164, 168–69, 185–86
  Decade 4 (1997–2006), 237, 266
  Decade 5 (2007–2016), 296, 319
  economic growth in, 21
  establishment of ADB and, 50
  field office in, 197, 198f
  health sector projects in, 127b
  Lao Bao International Border Gate, 248
  Nam Theun 2 Hydroelectric Project, 251
  resident mission in, 259n12
  scholarship program for, 196
  subregional cooperation programs, 278b
LCL (local currency lending), 10, 275b, 343
Leading Asia's Private Sector Infrastructure Fund (LEAP), 342

Lee, Allan, *351*
Lee, Bong-Suh, 220
Lee, Kuan Yew, 23, 112, 163
Leekpai, Chuan, 207, 209
Lewis, John P., 134
Liberation Tigers of Tamil Eelam (LTTE), 260
Liberia, 301
life expectancy, 4, 114–15
Lin, Justin, 282
liquidity, 219, 231, 292, 295
local currency lending (LCL), 10, 275b, 343
Loganathan, C., 32
Long-Term Strategic Framework (LTSF), 14, 257–59, 262, 286, 307–8
Louvre Accord, 109
low-income countries, 73, 98, 135, 140, 247, 297, 313, 333. *See also specific countries*
Low-Lift Pump Maintenance Program (Bangladesh), 128–29b
LTSF. *See* Long-Term Strategic Framework
LTTE (Liberation Tigers of Tamil Eelam), 260
Luxembourg, 284

M
Maastricht Treaty, 159
Macapagal, Diosdado, 48, *63*
MacArthur, Douglas, II, 32
Madrasah Education Development Project (Indonesia), *351*
Malaysia
  Decade 1 (1967–1976), 53, 57, 59, 61, 78, 81
  Decade 2 (1977–1986), 108, 112–14, 119, 123

Decade 3 (1987–1996), 159, 163–64, 167–68
Decade 4 (1997–2006), 207, 210, 212, 227, 239, 283
Decade 5 (2007–2016), 290, 294
economic growth in, 18–21, 27
education sector projects in, 179*b*
establishment of ADB and, 48
Second Compensatory Forestry Sector Project, *155*
subregional cooperation programs, 278*b*
urban sector projects in, 326*b*
Maldives, 149, 196, 279*b*
Managing for Development Results (MfDR), 265, 320
Manila Framework, 230
manufacturing sector
Decade 1 (1967–1976), 58–59, 69
Decade 2 (1977–1986), 112–14
Decade 3 (1987–1996), 163, 164–65, 167
Decade 4 (1997–2006), 237, 239
economic growth and, 19
Marcos, Ferdinand, *67*, 90
Marshall Islands, 171*n*, 204
Marshall Plan, 28
McMahon, Billy, 83
MDGs. *See* Millennium Development Goals
medium-term strategies (MTSs), 257, 258, 281, 282
Meiji Restoration, 5, 17–18
Mekong River Commission, 278*b*
memorandum of understanding (MOU), 311*b*, 343–44
Mexico, 51, 55, 109, 228–30, 244, 265
MfDR (Managing for Development Results), 265, 320
MFF (multitranche financing facility), 275*b*, 326*b*

Micronesia, Federated States of, 171*n*, 204
middle-income countries. *See also specific countries*
ADB strategy for, 325, 347
economic growth in, 282, 290, 305–6
financing of ADB and, 244
poverty in, 297
Millennium Development Goals (MDGs), 242–47, 253, 256, 260, 289, 301–2, 302*f*, 307, 315, 318, 320
Miranda, Juan, *355*
Mishan, Ezra, 161
Miyazawa, Kiichi, 231
Miyazawa Plan, 158
Mizoguchi, Toshiyuki, 161
Modi, Narendra, 305
Mohamad, Mahathir, 113
monetary policies, 5–6, 108, 190, 228, 292
Mongolia
Decade 3 (1987–1996), 164, 204
Decade 5 (2007–2016), 323, 342, 344
education sector projects in, 179*b*
field office in, 197, 198*f*
lending to, 313
resident mission in, 259*n*12
subregional cooperation programs, 279*b*
Monterrey Consensus, 245–46
Monterrey International Conference on Financing for Development, 245
MOU (Memorandum of Understanding), 311*b*, 343–44
MPSF (Multi-Purpose Special Fund), 88, 96–98
MTSs (medium-term strategies), 257, 258, 281, 282

Mulford, David C., 146
multiproject loans, 126, 128
Multi-Purpose Special Fund
  (MPSF), 88, 96–98
multitranche financing facility
  (MFF), 275*b*, 326*b*
Murchison, David, *355*
Myanmar
  Decade 1 (1967–1976), 57, 77, 101
  Decade 2 (1977–1986), 133
  Decade 3 (1987–1996), 160, 169, 186
  Decade 5 (2007–2016), 290, 295–96, 298, 305, 319, 322–23, 336–38
  economic growth in, 17, 27–28
  field office in, 197, 198*f*
  health sector projects in, 127*b*
  subregional cooperation programs, 278–79*b*
Myint, Hla, 77
Myrdal, Gunnar, 22–23

N

Nachmanoff, Arnold, 124
Nakao, Takehiko
  on ADB headquarters location, 49
  Asian financial crisis and, 230
  civil society and, 265
  on economic growth in region, 305–6
  leadership of, 15, 307, 320, 322–36, 343–44, 347–48, *353–55*
Nam Theun 2 Hydroelectric Project
  (Lao PDR), *251*, 266
Nanpu Bridge (PRC), 176, *248*
National Development Leasing
  Corporation, 10, 138*b*
natural resources, 58–59, 77, 170, 194, 238, 297, 341. *See also* environmental issues
Nauru, 24

Naya, Seiji, 142
NDB (New Development Bank), 303, 343
Nepal
  Decade 1 (1967–1976), 71, 82, 101
  Decade 2 (1977–1986), 147
  Decade 3 (1987–1996), 170
  Decade 5 (2007–2016), 290, 295, 314, 338, 342
  education sector projects in, 179*b*
  field office in, 197, 198*f*
  Kali Gandaki "A" Hydroelectric Project, *249*
  subregional cooperation programs, 279*b*
  technical assistance to, 101, 147
Nergui, Burmaa, *352*
Netherlands
  funding from, 92*n*32, 97*b*
  Southeast Asia instability and, 21
New Development Bank (NDB), 303, 343
newly industrialized economies
  (NIEs). *See also specific economies*
  Decade 1 (1967–1976), 57–59
  Decade 2 (1977–1986), 107, 110–12, 115, 119
  Decade 3 (1987–1996), 158, 163–67, 172
  Decade 4 (1997–2006), 222–23, 239
  Decade 5 (2007–2016), 290, 296, 304–5
  economic growth in, 18–19
New Miyazawa Initiative, 231
New York Stock Exchange, 87
New Zealand
  aid to Pacific island countries, 171
  Cook Islands and, 24
  funding from, 92*n*32

Ngee Ann Technical College, 65, 179b
NGOs. See nongovernment organizations
NIEs. See newly industrialized economies
Nimmanahaeminda, Kraisri, 64
Nixon, Richard, 60, 88
nongovernment organizations (NGOs), 3, 161, 174, 192, 193b, 241, 263, 266b, 303
nonsovereign public sector financing, 275b
North Viet Nam, 42, 91
Norway, 271

O

OCR. See ordinary capital resources
OECD. See Organisation for Economic Co-operation and Development
Office of Public–Private Partnership (OPPP), 331
official development assistance (ODA), 28, 118, 158, 303
Ogata, Sadako, 249
Ohashi, Kaoru, 31, 33–34
Ohkawa, Kazushi, 75
oil shocks
 Decade 1 (1967–1976), 54, 60, 80, 91–93, 98–99
 Decade 2 (1977–1986), 108, 110–11, 113, 115, 121, 124, 129, 131
 Decade 4 (1997–2006), 274
 economic growth and, 12
Okita, Saburo, 35, 39, 77, 177
Okita panel, 181–82, 184
OPEC. See Organization of the Petroleum Exporting Countries
OPEC Fund for International Development, 142

operational summaries
 Decade 1 (1967–1976), 100–102, 101–2f, 104–5t
 Decade 2 (1977–1986), 147–50, 149f, 150–51t
 Decade 3 (1987–1996), 199–205, 201–2f, 205–6t
 Decade 4 (1997–2006), 283–86, 284–85f, 286–87t
 Decade 5 (2007–2016), 344–48, 345–46f, 348–49t
OPPP (Office of Public–Private Partnership), 331
ordinary capital resources (OCR)
 Decade 1 (1967–1976), 78–79, 83, 94, 104–5
 Decade 2 (1977–1986), 137, 150–51
 Decade 3 (1987–1996), 180–81, 183, 200, 205
 Decade 4 (1997–2006), 222–23, 268, 270–72, 273, 281–83, 286–87
 Decade 5 (2007–2016), 312–13, 332, 334–36, 338, 340–41, 347–49
Organisation for Economic Co-operation and Development (OECD)
 bilateral assistance from, 118
 economic growth in, 290
 establishment of ADB and, 35
 Japan as member, 33
 Korea, Republic of, as member, 165, 209
 as model for ADB, 135
 organizational structure of ADB, 463–64
Organization of the Petroleum Exporting Countries (OPEC), 61, 94, 124
Oshima, H. T., 161

P

Pacific island countries. *See also specific countries*
  Decade 2 (1977–1986), 116, 119, 147
  Decade 3 (1987–1996), 171, 196, 204
  Decade 4 (1997–2006), 259
  Decade 5 (2007–2016), 291, 295, 298, 329
  economic growth in, 24
  lending to, 100, 147
Pakistan
  Decade 1 (1967–1976), 57, 78, 81, 94, 100
  Decade 2 (1977–1986), 129, 138, 140, 147
  Decade 3 (1987–1996), 169, 194, 201, 203
  Decade 4 (1997–2006), 237, 243, 283–84
  Decade 5 (2007–2016), 290, 297, 303, 343–45
  economic growth in, 23, 25, 27
  establishment of ADB and, 32, 34, 39
  field office in, 197, 198*f*
  Innovation and Efficiency Initiative, 275*b*
  lending to, 100, 147
  subregional cooperation programs, 279*b*
  Sui–Karachi gas pipeline, 94
  technical assistance to, 147
  Turkmenistan–Afghanistan–Pakistan–India Pipeline (TAPI), 311*b*
Pakistan–India Natural Gas Pipeline, 311*b*
Palau, 24
Pan, Wenxing, *355*
Panitchpakdi, Supachai, 282
Papua New Guinea
  Decade 1 (1967–1976), 101
  Decade 2 (1977–1986), 116
  Decade 3 (1987–1996), 171, 196
  Decade 5 (2007–2016), 291
  field office in, 197, 198*f*
  lending to, 313
  resident mission in, 259*n*12
Paris Declaration, 244–45
Park, Chung-hee, *66*, 111
Payne, Julian, 254
People's Bank of China, 118
Philippines
  Decade 1 (1967–1976), 55, 57–60, 70, 89–90, 100–101
  Decade 2 (1977–1986), 114, 129, 133, 141, 147–48
  Decade 3 (1987–1996), 159, 168, 182, 201, 203
  Decade 4 (1997–2006), 207, 212, 227, 230, 284
  Decade 5 (2007–2016), 290, 293–95, 297–98, 300, 305, 327–29, 331
  economic growth in, 22, 24–25, 27–28
  establishment of ADB and, 38–39, 43, 48–49
  field office in, 197, 198*f*
  Innovation and Efficiency Initiative, 275*b*
  lending to, 100, 147
  subregional cooperation programs, 278*b*
  technical assistance to, 101, 147
Pholsena, Khemphemg, 260
Plaza Accord (1985), 108, 114, 164
Portugal, 284*n*
PovcalNet Database, 297
poverty and poverty reduction programs

Decade 1 (1967–1976), 61
Decade 2 (1977–1986), 109
Decade 3 (1987–1996), 157, 161, 170, 178, 182, 184, 188, 196
Decade 4 (1997–2006), 208, 212, 226, 233, 235, 238, 242–43, 247, 253, 255–57, 263, 271–73, 282
Decade 5 (2007–2016), 297, 301–2, 308–9, 314, 316, 324, 341, 347, 358
economic growth and, 14, 22–23, 25
Poverty Reduction Strategy (PRS), 14, 256–58, 262, 264, 272, 282–83
PRC. *See* China, People's Republic of
Preuss, Wolf, 99
Primary Education Project in Pakistan, 194
private sector
Decade 2 (1977–1986), 133, 136–39, 138*b*, 143
Decade 3 (1987–1996), 162, 172–73, 175, 178, 184, 192–95
Decade 4 (1997–2006), 210, 257, 259, 263, 265, 266, 276
Decade 5 (2007–2016), 305, 322–23, 329–30, 343, 344, 347, 358
economic growth and, 2, 6, 10
Private Sector Operations Department (PSOD), 259, 275*b*, 330, 342
PRS. *See* Poverty Reduction Strategy
public–private partnership (PPP), 202, 330
purchasing power parity, 297, 358

Q
Qureshi, Anwar Iqbal, *62*

R
Rajasthan Urban Development Project (India), *154*
Ramos, Fidel, 168
Rao, P. V. Narasimha, 169
Rao, V. K. R. V., 22
Reagan, Ronald, 109
reconstruction programs, 25, 91, 185, 261–62, 279*b*, 303, 338, 342
reform agenda, 132, 136–37, 139
Regional Economic Monitoring Unit (REMU), 223–24, 277
Regional Malaria and Other Communicable Diseases Threats Trust Fund, 341
regional overview. *See also specific countries*
in 1960s, 17–30
agriculture, 390–92
child mortality, 412–14
exports of goods and services, 399–401
GDP, 384–89
imports of goods and services, 402–4
industry, 393–95
life expectancy, 409–11
population data, 381–83
poverty and inequality, 405–8
primary education, adjusted net enrollment rate, 415–17
services, 396–98
regional resource center, 142–43, 180
REMU (Regional Economic Monitoring Unit), 223–24, 277
renewable energy projects, 263, 303
Republic of Korea. *See* Korea, Republic of

research activities, 74–78, 223–25
resident missions, 139–40
resource mobilization, 93, 96, 192
risk management, 216, 271, 322
Risk Management Unit, 271
Rockefeller Foundation, 54, 326b, 341
Rogers, Joe, 173
Rojas, Sixto K., 77
Rose, Philip, *355*
rural areas, 56–57, 117–18, 124
rural development
    Decade 1 (1967–1976), 53–54, 56, 61, 69
    Decade 2 (1977–1986), 123, 125, 128–30, 144
    Decade 3 (1987–1996), 188; 194
    Decade 4 (1997–2006), 256
    Decade 5 (2007–2016), 309, 329
Rural Electricians Training Program, *350*
Rural Enterprise Credit Program, 216
Russian Federation, 164, 303. *See also* Soviet Union

S

Sadli, Mohammad, 163, 177
Saeed, Muhammad Sami, *355*
Sakakibara, Eisuke, 229
Samoa, 24
Samut Prakarn Wastewater Management Project, 264
Sander, Mario, *355*
SARS (severe acute respiratory syndrome), 244, 262
SASEC. *See* South Asia Subregional Economic Cooperation
Sato, Eisaku, 41, 357
Sato, Mitsuo, *250*

    on ADB mission, 173
    on Asian financial crisis, 215, 226n24
    leadership by, 184, 189–91, 195, 197, 199, 204
    leadership of, 13–14
    retirement of, 253
    Watanabe nominated by, 51
Saudi Arabia, 47, 99
Saudi Arabian Monetary Agency, 99
Schaefer-Preuss, Ursula, *352*
Schneider, Johannes, *355*
scholarships, 196, 341–42
Schultz, T. W., 75
Schulz, Günther, 126, 185
Second Compensatory Forestry Sector Project (Malaysia), *155*
Second Ministerial Conference on Asian Economic Cooperation, 37
Second Nam Ngum Development Fund Agreement, 92
sector groups, 465–66
sector lending, 126, 128, 140
Sen, Amartya, 25, 163, 177
Setaphanichkarn, Luang Thavil, 35
severe acute respiratory syndrome (SARS), 244, 262
Shanghai, 175–76, 188, 303
Shanghai Municipal Engineering Design Institute, 176
Sha Tin Hospital Polyclinic (Hong Kong, China), 126, 127b, *152*
Sheraliev, Sharafjon, *355*
Shivaji, Kshatrapati, *355*
Shultz, George P., 319
Siaosi, Tofa, 82
Singapore
    Decade 1 (1967–1976), 56–58, 81, 85

Decade 2 (1977–1986), 110, 112, 139, 147
Decade 3 (1987–1996), 159, 163, 165, 192
Decade 4 (1997–2006), 210, 223–24, 268, 277
Decade 5 (2007–2016), 290, 295
economic growth in, 18–20, 20*t*, 23, 27
education sector projects in, 179*b*
establishment of ADB and, 48
lending to, 147
Singh, Manmohan, 169, 187
Sithi-Amnuai, Paul, 35
Soeharto, 212, 218
Solomon Islands, 101, 171, 331, 338
South Asia. *See also specific countries*
Decade 1 (1967–1976), 56–59, 81, 100, 102
Decade 2 (1977–1986), 107, 115–16, 119, 149
Decade 3 (1987–1996), 169–70, 201
Decade 4 (1997–2006), 237, 259, 283–84
Decade 5 (2007–2016), 290, 296, 314, 345
economic growth in, 22–24
field offices in, 197, 198*f*
lending to, 100, 147
stagnation in, 22–23
South Asia Subregional Economic Cooperation (SASEC), 172, 278–79*b*
Southeast Asia. *See also specific countries*
Decade 1 (1967–1976), 53, 56, 58–59, 75–78, 81, 100, 102
Decade 2 (1977–1986), 107, 112, 115, 119, 133, 147, 149

Decade 3 (1987–1996), 158, 160, 163, 165, 167–69, 170, 201
Decade 4 (1997–2006), 211, 235, 237, 259, 266, 280, 283–84
Decade 5 (2007–2016), 290, 294, 296, 298, 344–45
economic growth in, 20–22
establishment of ADB and, 31–32, 41–42
field offices in, 197, 198*f*
instability in, 21–22
lending to, 100, 147
Soviet Union, 44, 157, 164, 170, 186, 204, 261, 283. *See also* Russian Federation
Spain, 149, 271
SPD. *See* Strategy and Policy Department
special economic zones, 112, 117–18
Special Funds
Decade 1 (1967–1976), 79*b*, 87–89
list of active and closed, 456–60
Special Project Implementation Assistance, 141
Sri Lanka
Decade 1 (1967–1976), 55, 57, 59, 94, 100
Decade 2 (1977–1986), 116, 139–40
Decade 3 (1987–1996), 170
Decade 4 (1997–2006), 237
Decade 5 (2007–2016), 296, 305, 314, 331
economic growth in, 17, 23, 27
establishment of ADB and, 32
field office in, 197, 198*f*
resident mission in, 259*n*12
subregional cooperation programs, 279*b*
staff, 139–40, 321–22, 427–29
stagflation, 108–9

Stephens, Christopher, 334
Stokes, Deborah, *355*
Strand, Joar, *355*
Strategy 2020, 308–310, 312, 318, 324–25
Strategy and Policy Department (SPD), 184, 280–81, 336, 345–46
Strategy and Policy Office (SPO), 184
Strauss, Michael, *355*
Streeten, Paul, 77
structural adjustment, 109–10, 162, 166, 170, 229
Sui–Karachi gas pipeline (Pakistan), 94
Sukarno, 21
Sullivan, Peter, 218
Summers, Lawrence, 282
supply-side economics, 109–10
Susantono, Bambang, *355*
sustainable development
  Decade 3 (1987–1996), 160–61, 178
  Decade 4 (1997–2006), 260, 262–64
  Decade 5 (2007–2016), 293–96, 298, 302, 314, 329, 357
  subregional cooperation programs, 278*b*
Sustainable Development Goals (SDGs), 289, 301–2, 302f, 320, 327, 358
Sweden, 50*t*, 98*b*
Switzerland
  as ADB member, 101
  financial markets in, 133
  funding from, 271
  Urban Climate Change Resilience Trust Fund and, 341
  urban sector project funding from, 326*b*

T

Taipei,China
  economic growth in, 18–20, 20*t*, 110, 112, 165–66, 239
  industrialization in, 56–58, 57*t*
  lending to, 78, 81
  People's Republic of China's membership in ADB and, 144–46
  Yangmei freeway project, 67
Tajikistan
  Decade 4 (1997–2006), 261, 284
  Decade 5 (2007–2016), 295, 303
  field office in, 197, 198*f*
  resident mission in, 259*n*12
  subregional cooperation programs, 279*b*
Tajum Irrigation Project (Indonesia), 79*b*
Taliban, 311*b*
Tamil Nadu, 147
Tanabe, Masashi, *355*
Tan An Integrated Agricultural Project (Viet Nam), 95
TAPI (Turkmenistan–Afghanistan–Pakistan–India Pipeline), 310, 311*b*
Tarumizu, Kimimasa, *155, 248*
  on economic development in region, 157
  leadership of, 13, 150, 180, 181–85, 189, 191
Task Force on Improving Project Quality Review, 194
technical assistance
  Decade 1 (1967–1976), 78, 79*b*, 82–83, 91, 94, 101–5
  Decade 2 (1977–1986), 118, 137, 140, 147–51
  Decade 3 (1987–1996), 174, 176, 200–203, 205, 206

Decade 4 (1997–2006), 213,
214–15, 220, 223, 283–85, 286, 287
Decade 5 (2007–2016), 339–43,
348, 349
establishment of ADB and, 46
health sector projects, 127*b*
Myanmar reengagement and,
337*b*
urban sector projects, 326*b*
Technical Assistance Department,
77
Tengku Razaleigh Hamzah, 123, 124
TFP (Trade Finance Program), 314,
322, 342
Thailand
Decade 1 (1967–1976), 57–59,
78–79, 81, 91, 100
Decade 2 (1977–1986), 113–14, 128,
133, 139
Decade 3 (1987–1996), 159,
163–64, 168, 186
Decade 4 (1997–2006), 207–11,
213–15, 219–20, 227, 230, 238–39,
259, 264, 266, 283
Decade 5 (2007–2016), 290, 294
economic growth in, 18, 20, 27
education sector projects in, 179*b*
establishment of ADB and, 35, 38,
48
field office in, 197, 198*f*
Industrial Finance Corporation of
Thailand, 79*b*
lending to, 100
subregional cooperation
programs, 278–79*b*
Theppana Wind Power Project,
353
Thatcher, Margaret, 109
Theppana Wind Power Project
(Thailand), *353*

Timor-Leste
independence movement in, 24
life expectancy in, 4
resident mission in, 259*n*12
Tokyo Imperial University, 33
Tokyo Stock Exchange, 189
Tokyo Study Group, 33–34, 39–40, 44
Tonga, 101, 126, 171*n*, 338
Tonle Sap Poverty Reduction and
Smallholder Development Project
(Cambodia), *250*
tourism, 278–79*b*, 291
trade arrangements and facilitation.
See also exports
Decade 3 (1987–1996), 159–60
Decade 4 (1997–2006), 238–39
subregional cooperation
programs, 279*b*
Trade Finance Program (TFP), 314,
322, 342
transaction advisory services (TAS),
331
Transatlantic Trade and Investment
Partnership, 304
transition economies, 185–87
transport projects
Decade 1 (1967–1976), 55, 69, 76,
79–80, 100–101
Decade 2 (1977–1986), 128, 147–48
Decade 3 (1987–1996), 187, 196,
201–3
Decade 4 (1997–2006), 256, 283,
285
Decade 5 (2007–2016), 329, 339,
341, 345–46
subregional cooperation
programs, 279*b*
Trudeau, Pierre, *153*
trust funds
Decade 1 (1967–1976), 105

Decade 2 (1977–1986), 151
Decade 3 (1987–1996), 206
Decade 4 (1997–2006), 287
Decade 5 (2007–2016), 339–43, 340*t*, 349
list of active and closed, 456–60
Tsunami Emergency Assistance Project (India), *350*
Turkey, 204
Turkmenistan
field office in, 197, 198*f*
subregional cooperation programs, 279*b*
Turkmenistan–Afghanistan–Pakistan–India Pipeline (TAPI), 310, 311*b*
Tuvalu, 171*n*, 204, 339
Typhoon Haiyan, 298, 327, 328*b*, 342
Typhoon Yolanda, 328*b*
Typhoon Yoling, 90

U
U Nyun, 27, 31, 35–36, 48–49, 51, *62*
U Thant, 17
Um, Woochong, *355*
UNDP. *See* United Nations Development Programme
UNFCCC (United Nations Framework Convention on Climate Change), 299, 329
United Kingdom
Asian financial crisis and, 224
development agenda and, 162
establishment of ADB and, 33, 47
funding from, 92*n*32, 261, 339, 341
global financial crisis and, 291
health sector projects and, 127*b*
Plaza Accord and, 109
Southeast Asia instability and, 21
urban sector project funding from, 326*b*
United Nations
ADB charter and, 46
development agenda and, 160
funding from, 2
Millennium Development Goals (MDGs), 242–47, 253, 256, 260, 289, 301–2, 302*f*, 307, 315, 318, 320
on the People's Republic of China, 144, 149
regional cooperation and, 25–27, 91
on South Asia economic development, 115
Sustainable Development Goals (SDGs), 289, 301–2, 302*f*, 320, 327, 358
United Nations Conference on Trade and Development, 282
United Nations Development Programme (UNDP), 160, 279*b*
United Nations Economic and Social Commission for Asia, 20
United Nations Framework Convention on Climate Change (UNFCCC), 299, 329
United States (US)
Asian financial crisis and, 220, 224–25, 230, 232
capital markets in, 6
development agenda and, 123–24, 160–62, 173–74, 195, 243, 316–17
economic growth in, 304
establishment of ADB and, 31–32, 37, 41–42, 43, 47, 51
funding from, 84–85, 92*n*32, 95, 98*b*, 100, 158, 183
general capital increases and, 190–92

global financial crisis and, 291–92, 294–95
imports from Asian countries, 238
monetary policy in, 107–9
Plaza Accord and, 114
Southeast Asia instability and, 21
Special Funds and, 87–88
Urban Climate Change Resilience Trust Fund, 341
Urban Primary Health Care Project, 127*b*
Utomo, Kusno, 65
Uzbekistan
   Decade 3 (1987–1996), 170, 201, 204
   Decade 5 (2007–2016), 300, 321, 344
   education sector projects in, 179*b*
   field office in, 197, 198*f*
   resident mission in, 259*n*12
   subregional cooperation programs, 279*b*

V

van Wees, Ingrid, 355
Vanuatu, 149, 171, 259, 339, 344
Viet Nam
   agricultural reforms in, 114–15
   Decade 1 (1967–1976), 77, 90–92, 95
   Decade 2 (1977–1986), 114–15
   Decade 3 (1987–1996), 160, 164, 168, 185–86, 201
   Decade 4 (1997–2006), 237, 239, 284
   Decade 5 (2007–2016), 290, 305, 313–14, 319, 344–45
   economic growth in, 21, 25, 27, 33
   education sector projects in, 179*b*
   field office in, 197, 198*f*

   Ha Noi Metro Rail System Project, 353
   health sector projects in, 127*b*
   instability in, 12
   Lao Bao International Border Gate, 248
   subregional cooperation programs, 278*b*
   Tan An Integrated Agricultural Project, 95
   urban sector projects in, 326*b*
Vinicchayakul, Serm, 51
Virata, Cesar, 55, 58, 168
vocational education, 126, 179*b*
Volcker, Paul, 108
voting power, 419–20

W

Waldheim, Christa, 68
Waldheim, Elisabeth, 68
Waldheim, Kurt, 68
Wang, Zhongjing, 355
Washington Consensus, 162, 172, 240
Watanabe, Takeshi, 62, 64, 66–67
   on ADB mission, 103
   establishment of ADB and, 31, 33–34, 36, 38, 39–40, 43, 45, 49
   Krishna Moorthi's influence on, 74, 125
   leadership of, 11–12, 51–52, 70–76, 83, 85, 87–91
Water Financing Partnership Facility, 271
Western Samoa, 24, 78, 81–82
West Java Phase II Gas Pipeline Project, 275*b*
Widodo, Joko, 305
Widyajala, Bhimantara, 355
Wolfensohn, James, 177, 250

women
  development agenda and, 143–44, 160–61, 174, 182, 193–95, 264
  health sector projects and, 127*b*
  in senior and professional positions in ADB, 14, 139, 203, 260, 321
World Bank
  concessional financing support to IDA countries, 247*n*22
  Decade 1 (1967–1976), 54, 70, 74, 86–87, 91–92, 100
  Decade 2 (1977–1986), 110, 117–18, 125, 132, 141, 144, 146
  Decade 3 (1987–1996), 161–64, 177, 187–88, 196, 199
  Decade 4 (1997–2006), 210, 212–13, 217–18, 220, 227, 232, 241, 243, 246–47, 266, 272
  Decade 5 (2007–2016), 297, 303, 308, 313, 318, 327, 339
  establishment of ADB and, 33–35, 40, 44, 51
  Myanmar reengagement and, 337*b*
  regional cooperation and, 28
  subregional cooperation programs, 279*b*
  Typhoon Haiyan response, 328*b*
World Trade Organization (WTO), 157, 159, 166, 236–38, 304
World War II, 60, 157

Y

Yangmei freeway project (Taipei,China), 67
Yangpu Bridge, 176
Yao, Xianbin, *352*
Yeoh, Michelle, *352*
Yongchaiyudh, Chavalit, 209
Yoshida, Taroichi, *152–53*
  address to annual meeting (1980), 107
  Krishna Moorthi's influence on, 74
  leadership of, 12, 103, 121–25, 129, 131–34, 149
Yossundara, Suparb, 77
Young Professionals Program, 139
Yukkasemwong, Philaslak, *355*

Z

Zhang, Wencai, *355*